BOOKS
TO
DIE FOR

BOOKS
TO
DIE FOR

The World's Greatest Mystery Writers
on the World's Greatest Mystery Novels

EDITED BY

John Connolly and Declan Burke

ASSISTANT EDITOR

Ellen Clair Lamb

EMILY BESTLER BOOKS
—
ATRIA
NEW YORK   LONDON   TORONTO   SYDNEY   NEW DELHI

ATRIA PAPERBACK
An Imprint of Simon & Schuster, Inc.
1230 Avenue of the Americas
New York, NY 10020

First Emily Bestler Books/Atria Paperback edition October 2016

EMILY BESTLER BOOKS / ATRIA PAPERBACK and colophons are trademarks of Simon & Schuster, Inc.

For information about special discounts for bulk purchases, please contact Simon & Schuster Special Sales at 1-866-506-1949 or business@simonandschuster.com.

The Simon & Schuster Speakers Bureau can bring authors to your live event. For more information or to book an event contact the Simon & Schuster Speakers Bureau at 1-866-248-3049 or visit our website at www.simonspeakers.com.

Designed by Kyoko Watanabe

Manufactured in the United States of America

10   9   8   7   6   5   4   3   2   1

The Library of Congress has cataloged the hardcover edition as follows:
   Books to die for : the world's greatest mystery writers on the world's greatest mystery novels / edited by John Connolly and Declan Burke.—1st Emily Bestler Books/Atria Books hardcover ed.
       p.   cm.
Includes bibliographical references and index.
   1. Detective and mystery stories—History and criticism.   I. Connolly, John.
II. Burke, Declan.
   PN3448.D4B64   2012
   809.3'872—dc23   2012029221

ISBN 978-1-4516-9657-8
ISBN 978-1-4767-1036-5 (pbk)
ISBN 978-1-4516-9658-5 (ebook)

CONTENTS

INTRODUCTION

Why does the mystery novel enjoy such enduring appeal? There is no simple answer. It has a distinctive capacity for subtle social commentary, a concern with the disparity between law and justice, and a passion for order, however compromised. Even in the vision of the darkest of mystery writers, it provides us with a glimpse of the world as it might be, a world in which good men and women do not stand idly by and allow the worst aspects of human nature to triumph without opposition. It can touch upon all these facets while still entertaining the reader—and its provision of entertainment is not the least of its many qualities.

But the mystery novel has always prized character over plot, which may come as some surprise to its detractors. True, this is not a universal tenet: there are degrees to which mysteries occupy themselves with the identity of the criminal, as opposed to, say, the complexities of human motivation. Some, such as the classic puzzle mystery, tend toward the former; others are more concerned with the latter. But the mystery form understands that plot comes out of character, and not just that: it believes that the great mystery *is* character.

If we take the view that fiction is an attempt to find the universal in the specific, to take individual human experiences and try to come to some understanding of our common nature through them, then the question at the heart of all novels can be expressed quite simply as: Why? Why do we do the things that we do? It is asked in *Bleak House* just as it is asked in *The Maltese Falcon*. It haunts *The Pledge* as it does *The Chill*. But the mystery novel, perhaps more than any other, not only asks this question; it attempts to suggest an answer to it as well.

But where to start? There are so many books from which to choose, even for the knowledgeable reader who has already taken to swimming in mystery's dark waters, and huge numbers of new titles appear on our bookshelves each week. It is hard enough to keep up with authors who are alive, but those who are deceased are at risk of being forgotten entirely. There are many treasures to be found, and their burial should not be permitted, even if there are some among these authors who might have been surprised to find themselves remembered at all, for they were not writing for the ages.

And so, quite simply, we decided to give mystery writers from around the world the opportunity to enthuse about their favorite novel, and in doing so we hoped to come up with a selection of books that was, if not definitive (which would be a foolish and impossible aim), then heartfelt, and flawless in its inclusions if not its omissions. After all, the creation of any anthology such as this is inevitably accompanied by howls of anguish from those whose first instinct is always to seek out what is absent rather than applaud what is present. (We could probably have given the book the alternative title *But What About . . . ?*)

With that in mind, let's tackle just one such elephant in this particular room. It's Raymond Chandler, as is so often the case when mystery fiction is under discussion. *The Big Sleep* is the Chandler novel frequently cited as the greatest mystery ever written, often by those who haven't read very much at all in the genre. In fact, so ingrained has this idea become that *The Big Sleep* is a novel beloved even of people who have never read it, or who have seen only the 1946 movie based upon it. Fond though we are of *The Big Sleep*—for there is much in it of which to be fond, and much to admire—there's a strong case to be made that not only is it not the greatest mystery ever written, it's not even the greatest mystery Chandler ever wrote.

The Big Sleep is not the subject of an essay in this volume, but if not *The Big Sleep*, then what? Well, two of Chandler's novels are discussed here. The appearance of one, *Farewell, My Lovely*, could probably have been anticipated, but the second, *The Little Sister*, is slightly more unexpected. When we were discussing this project with Joe R. Lansdale, who writes here on *Farewell, My Lovely*, we all agreed, with the misplaced confidence of those who are convinced that they can get the army to Moscow before winter sets in, that Michael Connelly would pick *The Long Goodbye*, as his affection for it was widely known (although that affection, as you'll see when you read his essay, is tied up with Robert Altman's 1973 film adaptation of the novel). While *The Long Goodbye* does get a glowing mention in Connelly's essay, he chose instead to focus on *The Little Sister*, because that book is more personal to him.

Which brings us to the main thinking behind this anthology. This is not a pollster's assembly of novels, compiled with calculators and spreadsheets. Neither is it a potentially exhausting litany of titles that winds back to the dawn of fiction, chiding the reader for his or her presumed ignorance in the manner of a compulsory reading list handed out in a bad school at the start of summer to cast a pall over its students' vacation time. What we sought from each of the contributors to this volume was passionate advocacy: we wanted them to pick one novel, just one, that they would place in the canon. If you found our contributors in a bar some evening, and the talk turned (as it almost inevitably would) to favorite novels, it would be the single book that each writer would press upon you, the book that, if there was time and the stores were still open, they would leave the bar in order to purchase for you, so they could be confident they had done all in their power to make you read it.

If nothing else, that should explain the omission of any title that, even now, might prove to be a source of aggravation to you, the reader— and, in the great scheme of things, we'd hazard there are fewer than might be expected, and certainly few neglected writers, although, inevitably, there are those, too, or else this book would be too heavy to lift. There is greatness in all of the novels under discussion in this volume, but, equally, there is huge affection and respect for them on the part of their advocates.

This brings us to the second purpose of this book. Because of the personal nature of the attachment that the contributors have to their chosen books, you will, in many cases, learn something about the contributor as well as the subject, and not a little about the art and craft of writing along the way. Thus, we have Joseph Wambaugh, as a young cop-turned-writer, finding himself in the extraordinary position of discussing a work in progress with Truman Capote; Linwood Barclay, then only an aspiring novelist, sharing a meal with Ross Macdonald, a meal that arises out of one of the simplest and yet most intimate of reader-writer connections, the fan letter; and Ian Rankin encountering the extraordinary figure of Derek Raymond in a London bookstore. More important, as all writers are the products of those who went before them, those whom we love the most tend to influence us the most, whether stylistically, philosophically, or morally (for, as someone once noted, all mystery writers are secret moralists). If a writer whose work you love is featured in this book as the subject of an essay, then there's a very good chance that you'll also enjoy the work of the essayist, too. Similarly, if one of your favorite writers has chosen to write, in turn, on a beloved writer of his or her own, then you're probably going to learn a great deal about how that contributor's writing came to be formed, as well as being introduced to the novelist at least partly responsible for that act of formation.

While this volume is obviously ideal for dipping into when you have a quiet moment, enabling you to read an essay or two before moving on, there is also a pleasure to be had from the slow accumulation of its details. Reading through the book chronologically, as we have done during the editing process, patterns begin to emerge, some anticipated, some less so. There is, of course, the importance of the great Californian crime writers—Dashiell Hammett, Raymond Chandler, Ross Macdonald, and James M. Cain—to the generations of writers who have followed them and, indeed, to one another: so Macdonald's detective, Lew Archer, takes his name in part from Sam Spade's murdered partner in *The Maltese Falcon*, while Chandler builds on Hammett, and then Macdonald builds on Chandler but also finds himself being disparaged by the older author behind his back, adding a further layer of complication to their relationship. But the writer who had the greatest number of advocates was not any of these men: it was the Scottish author Josephine Tey, who is a figure of huge significance to a high number of the female contributors to this book.

Or one might take the year 1947: it produces both Dorothy B. Hughes's *In a Lonely Place*, in which the seeds of what would later come to be called the serial killer novel begin to germinate, and Mickey Spillane's *I, the Jury*. Both are examinations of male rage—although Spillane is probably more correctly considered as an expression of it—and both come out of the aftermath of the Second World War, when men who had fought in Europe and Asia returned home to find a changed world, a theme that is later touched upon in a British context in Margery Allingham's 1952 novel, *The Tiger in the Smoke*. But 1947 was also the year of the infamous, and still unsolved, Black Dahlia killing, in which the body of a young woman named Elizabeth Short was found, mutilated and sliced in half, in Leimert Park, Los Angeles. It's no coincidence that John Gregory Dunne sets *True Confessions*, his examination of guilt and corruption, in that year, while the Black Dahlia killing subsequently becomes a personal touchstone for the novelist James Ellroy, whose own mother's murder in California in 1958 also remains unsolved. The pulp formula in the United States then adapted itself to these changes in postwar society, which resulted in the best work of writers such as

Jim Thompson, Elliott Chaze, and William McGivern, all of whom are considered in essays in this book.

Finally, it's interesting to see how often different writers, from Ed McBain to Mary Stewart, Newton Thornburg to Leonardo Padura, assert the view that they are, first and foremost, novelists. The mystery genre provides structure for their work—the ideal structure—but it is extremely malleable, and constantly open to adaptation: the sheer range of titles and approaches considered here is testament to that.

To give just one example: there had long been female characters at the heart of hard-boiled novels, most frequently as femmes fatales or adoring secretaries, but even when women were given central roles as detectives, the novels were written, either in whole or in part, by men: Erle Stanley Gardner's Bertha Cool (created under the pseudonym A. A. Fair), who made her first appearance in 1939; Dwight V. Babcock's Hannah Van Doren; Sam Merwin Jr.'s Amy Brewster; Will Oursler and Margaret Scott's Gale Gallagher (all 1940s); and, perhaps most famously, Forrest and Gloria Fickling's Honey West in the 1950s.

But at the end of the 1970s and the beginning of the 1980s, a number of female novelists, among them Marcia Muller, Sue Grafton, and Sara Paretsky, but also Amanda Cross and, in her pair of Cordelia Gray novels, P. D. James, found in the hard-boiled mystery novel a means of addressing issues affecting women, including violence (particularly sexual violence), victimization, power imbalances, and gender conflicts. They did so by questioning, altering, and subverting the established traditions in the genre, and, in the process, they created a new type of female fiction. The mystery genre embraced them without diminishing the seriousness of their aims, or hampering the result, and it did so with ease. It is why so many writers, even those who feel themselves to be working outside the genre, have chosen to introduce elements of it into their writing, and why this anthology can accommodate such a range of novelists, from Dickens to Dürrenmatt, and Capote to Crumley.

But this volume also raises the question of what constitutes a mystery—or, if you prefer, a crime novel. (The terms are often taken as interchangeable, but "mystery" is probably a more flexible, and accurate, description given the variety within the form. Crime may perhaps be considered the catalyst, mystery the consequence.) Genre, like beauty, is often in the eye of the beholder, but one useful formulation may be that, if one can take the crime out of the novel and the novel does not collapse, then it's probably not a crime novel; but if one removes the crime element and the novel falls apart, then it is. It is interesting, though, to note that just as every great fortune is said to hide a great crime, so, too, many great novels, regardless of genre, have a crime at their heart. The line between genre fiction and literary fiction (itself a genre, it could be argued) is not as clear as some might like to believe.

In the end, those who dismiss the genre and its capacity to permit and encourage great writing, and to produce great literature, are guilty not primarily of snobbery—although there may be an element of that—but of a fundamental misunderstanding of the nature of fiction and genre's place in it. There is no need to splice genre into the DNA of fiction, literary or otherwise: it is already present. The mystery novel is both a form and a mechanism. It is an instrument to be used. In the hands of a bad writer, it will produce bad work, but great writers can make magic from it.

JOHN CONNOLLY AND DECLAN BURKE, DUBLIN, 2012

BOOKS
TO
DIE FOR

The Dupin Tales
by Edgar Allan Poe (1841–44)

J. WALLIS MARTIN

Edgar Allan Poe (1809–49) was an American author, poet, editor, and critic best known for his tales of mystery and imagination, many of them decidedly gothic in tone. For mystery readers, though, his fame rests on the three short stories he wrote about the character of Le Chevalier C. Auguste Dupin, which Poe described as his tales of "ratiocination." Intellectual yet imaginative, brilliant but eccentric, Dupin became the template for fictitious detectives to come, among them Sherlock Holmes, who name-checks Dupin in the very first Sherlock Holmes story, A Study in Scarlet, *albeit by describing him as "a very inferior fellow."*

> Residing in Paris during the spring and part of the summer of 18–, I there became acquainted with a Monsieur C. Auguste Dupin.

So begins the story that many consider to be the earliest in which a private detective assists the police by solving a murder mystery. "The Murders in the Rue Morgue" is the first of three stories in which Dupin solves a case that has baffled police, and Poe's importance to, and influence on, subsequent generations of writers of crime, mystery, and tales of the supernatural is significant. Consider the following passage, which might have been drawn from a story in which Sherlock Holmes or Poirot took the place of Dupin:

> "Tell me, for Heaven's sake," I exclaimed, "the method—if method there is—by which you have been enabled to fathom my soul in this matter."

Dupin obliges, and the benefactor of his powers of analysis can only marvel at him.

"The Mystery of Marie Rogêt" was a sequel to "The Murders in the Rue Morgue," and opens with the following observation: "There are few persons, even among the calmest thinkers, who have not occasionally been startled into a vague yet thrilling half credence in the supernatural," whereas in "The Purloined Letter," Dupin is exhorted to help the police retrieve a letter stolen from a woman who is being blackmailed.

These three stories comprise *The Dupin Tales*, but as they have been analyzed elsewhere, I will not deconstruct them here. What interests me about them is what we can learn about Poe's character from his portrayal of his alter ego (many academics agree that Dupin is undoubtedly that), for when introducing Dupin for the first time, the narrator of the story describes him thus:

> This young gentleman was of an excellent—indeed of an illustrious family, but, by a variety of untoward events, had been reduced to such poverty that the energy of his character succumbed beneath it, and he ceased to bestir himself in the world, or care for the retrieval of his fortunes. By courtesy of his creditors, there still remained in his possession a small remnant of his patrimony; and, upon the income arising from this, he managed, by means of a rigorous economy, to procure the necessaries of life, without troubling himself about its superfluities. Books, indeed, were his sole luxuries, and in Paris these are easily obtained.

The description accords with what we know of Poe's personal circumstances when he wrote the story. The narrator goes on to say:

> It was at length arranged that we should live together during my stay in the city; and as my worldly circumstances were somewhat less embarrassed than his own, I was permitted to be at the expense of renting, and furnishing in a style which suited the rather fantastic gloom of our common temper, a time-eaten and grotesque mansion, long deserted through superstitions into which we did not inquire.

The "common temper" of which Poe wrote may have been a reference to the moods of elation and despair that plagued him all his life, and support a posthumous diagnosis of bipolar disorder. Were he alive today, Poe might well agree with the diagnosis, for he was, in fact, aware that his moods were cyclic, and that they alternated in nature. In a letter to the poet James Russell Lowell, whose own temperament was deeply moody, he wrote:

> I can feel for the "constitutional indolence" of which you complain—for it is one of my own besetting sins. I am excessively slothful, and wonderfully industrious—by fits. There are epochs when any kind of mental exercise is torture, and when nothing yields me pleasure but solitary communion with the "mountains & the woods"—the "altars" of Byron. I have thus rambled and dreamed away whole months, and awake, at last, to a sort of mania for composition. Then I scribble all day, and read all night, so long as the disease endures.

As is so often the case for those who suffer from bipolar disorder, Poe's personal life was a disaster. He was reputed to be irresponsible, unstable, and impossible to deal with. The following is an excerpt from Poe's letter to his guardian, John Allan, after the latter refused to pay gambling debts Poe incurred at university:

> Did I, when an infant, solicit your charity and protection, or was it of your own free will, that you volunteered your services in my behalf? It is well known to respectable individuals in Baltimore, and elsewhere, that my Grandfather (my natural protector at the time you interposed) was wealthy, and that I was his favourite grandchild—But the promises of adoption, and liberal education which you held forth to him in a letter which is now in possession of my family, induced him to resign all care of me into your hands. Under such circumstances, can it be said that I have no *right* to expect any thing at your hands?

Poe's accusation was grossly unfair. John Allan had in fact provided for him well, but he eventually lost patience with Poe's appeals for money. As a result, the relationship broke down when Poe was in his early twenties.

Inability to handle money, and a tendency to overspend with scant regard for the consequences, are features of bipolar disorder. (Consider Poe's purchase of three yards of Super Blue Cloth and a set of the best gilt buttons, bought at a time when he was almost two thousand pounds in debt!) So, too, is an ability to focus on a piece of work to the exclusion of all else. However, this was but a small part of what the manic stage of the illness enabled Poe to do. The illness blessed yet cursed him with a clarity of vision, a heightening of the senses which he describes vividly in "The Fall of the House of Usher":

> He entered, at some length, into what he conceived to be the nature of his malady. It was, he said, a constitutional and a family evil, and one for which he despaired to find a remedy—a mere nervous affection, he immediately added, which would undoubtedly soon pass off. It displayed itself in a host of unnatural sensations. Some of these, as he detailed them, interested and bewildered me; although, perhaps, the terms and the general manner of their narration had their weight. He suffered much from a morbid acuteness of the senses; the most insipid food was alone endurable; he could wear only garments of certain texture; the odours of all flowers were oppressive; his eyes were tortured by even a faint light; and there were but peculiar sounds, and these from stringed instruments, which did not inspire him with horror.

And again, in this extract from "The Tell-Tale Heart":

> TRUE!—nervous—very, very dreadfully nervous I had been and am; but why *will* you say that I am mad? The disease had sharpened my senses—not destroyed—not dulled them. Above all was the sense of hearing acute. I heard all things in the heaven and in the earth. I heard many things in hell.

The period during which those who suffer from bipolar disorder experience a heightening of the senses can last for days or months before the decline into a depression that can be mild to severe. Poe's depressions were deep, and following one such period, he wrote:

I went to bed and wept through a long, long, hideous night of despair—When the day broke, I arose & endeavoured to quiet my mind by a rapid walk in the cold, keen air—but all *would* not do—the demon tormented me still. Finally I procured two ounces of laudnum [*sic*] . . . I am so *ill*—so terribly, hopelessly ILL in body and mind, that I feel I CANNOT live . . . until I subdue this fearful agitation, which if continued, will either destroy my life or, drive me hopelessly mad . . .

In the above, Poe refers to having procured two ounces of laudanum with which to self-medicate. Another drug of choice was alcohol. Elevated rates of drug and alcohol abuse are often to be found in bipolar individuals, and premature death is a feature of the illness. It is likely that a combination of the two led to Poe's premature death in 1849. "We know now that what made Poe write was what made him drink," observed one of his biographers: "alcohol and literature were the two safety valves of a mind that eventually tore itself apart."

J. Wallis Martin (PhD St. Andrews) is publishing director of the Edgar Allan Press Ltd. Her novels have been published internationally, and adapted for the screen. She lives in Bristol. Visit her online at www.wallis -martin.co.uk.

Bleak House
by Charles Dickens (1853)

SARA PARETSKY

Charles Dickens (1812–70) was a prolific writer of short stories, plays, novels, nonfiction, and journalism, and also found time to edit magazines, collaborate with fellow authors, perfect the concept of the publicity tour, and father ten children. He was also a crusader for social justice, borne out of his own childhood, which saw his father, John, imprisoned for debt in the Marshalsea Prison, where he was joined by all of his family except Charles, who, at the age of twelve, went to work at Warren's Shoe Blacking Factory, and visited his family on Sundays. His first novel, The Pickwick Papers, *was published serially from 1836–37, and he died leaving his final book,* The Mystery of Edwin Drood, *unfinished.*

Dickens was prolix. His novels often depend on ludicrous coincidences. He also had a great narrative and storytelling gift. He is also the writer who most empowers me. Every time a reader zings off an angry letter, telling me they read to be entertained, not to hear about society's woes, I think, yeah, well, tell that to Dickens.

If every crime novel in the world suddenly disappeared and only *Bleak House* remained, it would be a good place to rebuild the missing library. It contains the germ of John Grisham, Ed McBain, Anne Rice, and Patricia Highsmith, with a whiff of Mr. and Mrs. North, within its sprawling narrative.

Bleak House is a novel of lies and secrets, of crime and immorality. At its center is the famous case of *Jarndyce v. Jarndyce*, which exposes massive abuse by the courts of law to perpetuate legal careers rather than to render justice. Along the way, Dickens also considers the crimes of abusing the poor and the homeless, crimes of keeping a large part of the population illiterate and underfed, and the hypocrisies, if not outright crimes, committed in the name of religion. There is, almost by the way, a murder.

Every form of the crime and horror genres is present here, starting with the vampire novel. The courts are the overreaching vampires, sucking the life out of parties to suits, often quite graphically. One litigant, Gridley, dies of a ruptured heart from the strain of twenty-five years of trying to get a will resolved. Dickens creates a physical vampire in a lawyer named Vholes, who consumes a young litigant, Richard Carstone. Richard, his cousin Ada, and Esther Summerson, the heroine-narrator of *Bleak House,* are three of the central figures of the novel. Esther is desolated by Richard's succumbing to the seduction of the courts. She recoils from the lawyer Vholes, as any healthy, life-loving person would. Esther describes Vholes as

> a sallow man with pinched lips that looked as if they were cold,
> a red eruption here and there upon his face, tall and thin . . .
> Dressed in black, black-gloved, and buttoned to the chin, there
> was nothing so remarkable in him as a lifeless manner . . .

The gothic novel, with ghosts and highborn ladies, shows up in the noble Dedlock family, which has an actual ghost walk at the family estate in Lincolnshire. Lady Dedlock, whose secrets drive the novel's action, is a noted beauty and leader of the fashionable world. She would be at home, up to a point, in a book by Georgette Heyer or Mary Stewart.

Bleak House is also that popular staple, a novel based on law courts and lawyers. And it is a detective novel, with a killer, and a detective. Inspector Bucket, a kind of deus ex machina of the novel, shows up anytime one of the characters needs to find a person or a document.

Bucket is busy everywhere. He knows so many people in London's underworld that he can search its slums without fear of assault. He goes on the road looking for witnesses among people who are "on the tramp," that is, moving from place to place, desperate to find work. He has contacts up and down the tightly clamped strata of the legal world.

Bucket appears in the lodgings and offices of clerks, law writers, stationers to the courts, and their servants and hangers-on. He also knows the powerful solicitor Mr. Tulkinghorn, lawyer to the rich and famous, including the Dedlock family. It is Mr. Tulkinghorn who is murdered.

In a modern crime novel, Tulkinghorn's death would occur near the book's beginning; the murderer would be revealed near the end. We're three-quarters of the way through *Bleak House* before Tulkinghorn dies, and his death is quite unexpected. In a novel where every conversation is reported in complete—some might say, excruciating—detail, we learn about the murder in an offhand, underreported way:

> A very quiet night . . . even [in] this wilderness of London . . . What's that? Who fired a gun or pistol? . . . foot-passengers start, stop and stare about them . . . people come out to look . . . It has aroused all the dogs in the neighborhood, who bark vehemently . . . But it is soon over.

A few paragraphs on, we learn that the cleaning crew discovers Tulkinghorn's body when they arrive the next morning, but even then, there is more description of the Roman mural in the room than of the dead man.

It wasn't that Dickens didn't care about detectives or police work. In fact, he was keenly interested in both. When the Metropolitan Police established the Detective Department in 1842, Dickens and Wilkie Collins followed the cases—quite literally. They traveled around England to where the most sensational crimes had taken place. They made friends of the detectives, were allowed to accompany them on their investigations, and wrote newspaper and magazine articles with their own theories on how to solve high-profile crimes.

Dickens wrote several essays about Charles Field, the head of the Detective Department, for his magazine *Household Words*. Bucket's methods, his disguises, his ability to melt into crowds, the way he spies on the people he's tracking, were all based on Field.

As Judith Flanders points out in *The Invention of Murder*, Bucket resembles Field physically. In *Household Words*, Dickens described him (under the very faint disguise of "Wield"), as having "a large, moist, knowing eye . . . and a habit of emphasizing his conversation by the aid of a corpulent forefinger, which is constantly in juxtaposition with his eyes or nose."*

When Bucket is closing in on Tulkinghorn's killer, Dickens says,

---

*Judith Flanders, *The Invention of Murder* (New York: HarperPress, 2011), p. 178.

Mr Bucket and his fat forefinger are much in consultation . . . When Mr Bucket has a matter of this pressing interest . . . , the fat forefinger . . . seems to rise to the dignity of a familiar demon. He puts it to his ears, and it whispers information; he puts it to his lips, and it enjoins him to secrecy; he rubs it over his nose, and it sharpens his scent . . .

Tulkinghorn's killer is a woman named Hortense, who has been Lady Dedlock's maid. She is a Frenchwoman with such a furious temper that she is described throughout the novel as a wild animal. In Chapter 12 she is "a very neat She-Wolf, imperfectly tamed." In Chapter 54, when she finds out that Bucket's wife has been tailing her, she "pant[s], tigress-like," and says she "would love to tear [Mrs Bucket] limb from limb."

Dickens drew Hortense from life, from the character of a Swiss woman named Maria Roux (Manning) who, in 1849, was convicted, along with her husband, of murdering her lover. The crime Hortense commits in *Bleak House* is completely different in motive and victim from the one that the Mannings carried out. However, when Bucket arrests Hortense, her furious language and her attempt to assault him come directly from the trial transcripts for Maria Manning.*

Two of the original detectives of the Metropolitan Police, Jonathan Whicher and Charles Field, were famous throughout England for their impressive memories. They were famous, too, for their ability to make deductions about the lives and livelihoods of the people they watched. Dickens, who had followed Field and Whicher on a number of occasions into London's bleakest slums, modeled Bucket's analytical skills on theirs.

When Bucket is taking a reluctant witness with him to a slum known as "Tom All-Alone's," he passes some people on the tramp and studies them. From their dress, he can tell that the men are brickmakers and that the women are newly up from the country. Bucket, and Field, made their deductions some thirty years before Sherlock Holmes produced his monographs on such subjects as clay, handwriting, or dress.

Later crime writers, from Conan Doyle to Dorothy Sayers, turned

---

*Ibid., pp. 158 ff.

the professional police into stolid lower-class men who needed constant help from Holmes or Peter Wimsey to solve their cases. It wasn't until the second half of the twentieth century, with the cops of the 87th Precinct, or police like Dalziel and Pascoe, that the skilled police detective came back into vogue. But Dickens admired the Metropolitan Police and gave them their due.

While Esther Summerson is the perfect domestic angel whom Dickens celebrates in all his heroines, the other women in *Bleak House* are brought to life with a passionate and compassionate pen. Lady Dedlock, nursing a guilty secret that sets the novel in motion, is a major masterpiece, as is her maid, Hortense. One of the hangers-on in the courts of law, Miss Flite, is a delicious character, with her caged birds named for the different aspects of helplessness petitioners feel around the courts. Miss Flite flits through the narrative like one of her own birds; she is not just an addict of the courts of Chancery, but can elucidate the addiction for Esther and Ada.

Dickens writes with contempt of religious hypocrisy, and of the punishment religious folk mete out on so-called fallen women, or on the poor. He writes, too, with compassion about violence against women in his sections on Jenny and Liz, the brickmakers' wives. Their husbands—called "their masters"—are always beating. Like battered women everywhere, Jenny and Liz move furtively, anxious to avoid further violence, but desirous as well of alleviating some of the suffering in the other destitute women and children among whom they live.

In *Bleak House* the murder of Tulkinghorn is not the center of the novel, nor is it the most heinous crime Dickens describes. It is for that reason that the murder occurs so late in the novel and with so little fanfare.

Two other crimes rouse Dickens to a tigerlike rage of his own. One is the courts of Chancery. This is the main current of the novel, and he writes scathingly, but wittily, of the courts and the enormous numbers of people the drawn-out legal actions employ.

The other crime that is entwined with the novel is the abominable neglect of the poor in nineteenth-century England. Dickens brings a savage pen to this outrage, partly through the brickmakers and their wives, and partly through the character of Jo, who plays a minor but pivotal role in the novel.

Jo has no last name, no recollection of his birth or his parents, and no life except to rise from his squalid dwelling early each day to sweep a crosswalk for pedestrians; if they tip him for the work he can eat, and pay for another night in the slum where he sleeps.

A stationer, a Mr. Snagsby, occasionally gives the boy half a crown. When Bucket takes the unwilling Snagsby to find Jo in Tom-all-Alone's, they go to

> A black, dilapidated street . . . where the crazy houses were seized upon, when their decay was far advanced, by some bold vagrants, who . . . took to letting them out in lodgings. Now, these tumbling tenements contain, by night, a swarm of misery . . . Twice, lately, there has been a crash and a cloud of dust in Tom-all-Alone's . . . and each time, a house has fallen. These accidents have made a paragraph in the newspapers and have filled several beds in the hospital . . . the proprietress of the house—a drunken face tied up in a black bundle; and flaring out of a heap of rags on the floor of a dog-hutch which is her private apartment—[tells them where to find Jo.]

In one of his comic masterpieces, Dickens has created the character of Mrs. Jellyby, who neglects her family while she focuses on saving Africans in remote Borrioboola-Gha. Her gaze is remote: she is always looking at Africa and can't see the squalor in her own household. She and her unfortunate children and husband dance through the narrative and both lighten and darken it, but Dickens uses her myopia to highlight the neglect of Jo and Jenny and Liz.

> Jo is not softened by distance and unfamiliarity; he is not a foreign-grown savage; he is the ordinary home-made article. Dirty, ugly, disagreeable to all the senses, in body a common creature of the common streets . . . Homely filth begrimes him, homely parasites devour him . . . native ignorance, the growth of English soil . . . sinks his immortal nature lower than the beasts that perish . . . He shrinks from [other people]. He is not of the same order of things . . . He is of no order and no place.*

---

* "Homely" in this passage means "home-grown."

It is Jo's death, not that of the solicitor to the rich and famous, that Dickens describes in detail. It is the crime committed against him by an indifferent society—characterized by Dickens as the "Toodles and Doodles"—that Dickens cares about. It is the author's passion for these crimes that elevates *Bleak House* from a run-of-the-mill detective novel to an enduring masterwork of fiction. And in the bleak house that is contemporary America, Dickens's vision helps keep me going.

Sara Paretsky is a novelist and essayist best known for her private eye V. I. Warshawski, who helped change the treatment of women in crime fiction. Paretsky's awards include the Cartier Diamond Dagger from the British Crime Writers' Association, the Edgar Grand Master from the Mystery Writers of America, and Ms. Magazine's Woman of the Year. Visit her online at www.saraparetsky.com.

A Tale of Two Cities
by Charles Dickens (1859)

RITA MAE BROWN

Charles Dickens (1812–70) was a prolific writer of short stories, plays, novels, nonfiction, and journalism, and also found time to edit magazines, collaborate with fellow authors, perfect the concept of the publicity tour, and father ten children. He was also a crusader for social justice, borne out of his own childhood which saw his father, John, imprisoned for debt in the Marshalsea Prison, where he was joined by all of his family except Charles, who, at the age of twelve, went to work at Warren's Shoe Blacking Factory, and visited his family on Sundays. His first novel, The Pickwick Papers, *was published serially from 1836–37, and he died leaving his final book,* The Mystery of Edwin Drood, *unfinished.*

Help! Murder! Police!

Does this sum up the mystery novel? There should be blood and corpses somewhere, and the killer must be found.

Since Dame Agatha Christie, the mystery novel has focused on a tightly plot-driven work of fiction, wherein the reader's curiosity to know who killed X, and if Y and Z will be victims, too, becomes a burning need. This is why the ideal mystery review often uses the words "page-turner."

Dame Agatha's plots, while ingenious, were inhabited more by stereotypes than by fully fleshed characters. The mystery writers who came in her wake, such as P. D. James, create living, breathing characters, and have moved the mystery novel some way out of the suburbs of genre fiction.

For me a mystery novel is not circumscribed. While I might write within the genre tradition, I can be somewhat suspicious of it. My favorite mystery novel is *A Tale of Two Cities*, published in 1859.

Many of you have read this gripping novel by Charles Dickens. There were people alive when he was a young man who had lived through the

French Revolution. As most of you also know, we are celebrating the two hundredth anniversary of his birth this year. Now there's an excuse for a party every day.

Why would I think that this novel—with the best opening line ever, "It was the best of times, it was the worst of times"—is a mystery? Because it revolves around one of the oldest devices in theater and literature, that of mistaken identity. Solve the question of identity, and you solve the problem.

You have many choices as to where you might like to pinpoint the beginnings of this device. *Oedipus the King,* a tragedy written by Sophocles (496–406 BC), used it to shattering effect. Plautus, the Roman playwright (254–184 BC), used it in his comedies. Shakespeare cribbed from Plautus, and both writers still make us laugh. Solving the question of authentic identity takes as much detective work as solving the mystery of who beheaded five men in exactly the same fashion, leaving their heads on the steps of St. Sebastian's Catholic Church. (There's a plot for an aspiring writer.)

Until the publication of *A Tale of Two Cities,* the play or novel frequently ended with true identity being unmasked to tears or laughter. *A Tale of Two Cities* ends with the main character being believed in his false identity. It is one of the most emotionally affecting endings of any novel that I know. You are rooting for the mystery to remain unsolved.

Dickens is showered with much-deserved praise for his characters, characters that leap off the page into your mind, your memory. Once you meet Uriah Heep you will never forget him, and you hope not to meet him again. The characters to whom you gravitate often reveal something about yourself. We all want David Copperfield and Oliver Twist to survive, no matter who our favorite characters are. We close these two volumes of Dickens hoping that the young men of the titles will flourish.

We close *A Tale of Two Cities* knowing our hero will not flourish. We close that novel saddened, uplifted, and thankful that we didn't live through France's dreadful convulsion.

Many a literary critic would say that *A Tale of Two Cities* is a conservative novel. Well, the mystery is a conservative form. Oh, the subject matter may contain sexual depravity, characters may toss f-bombs like grenades, and the hero or heroine is usually a deeply flawed character, failure ever his or her shadow. Some are even legitimate antiheroes. The form is *still* conservative. The fads of lengthy sex scenes, decayed corpses exhaustingly described, and descriptions of violence that occur about every twelve minutes cannot change the form. (And by the way, do we ever have a hero, antihero, or heroine who is impotent? If so, let me know. That would be something new. No matter how dreadful their past or horrendous their present, their parts work wonderfully well.)

What is a mystery novel, anyway? What is the form? It's simple: an incident occurs that destroys balance. The destruction may be to one individual, a family, a guild or a group, or an entire community. Economically describing how mistrust and violence undo a community was one of Dame Agatha's great gifts. Indeed, as the story unfolds, the reader in a sense becomes part of this community. Who committed or commissioned this misdeed? Initially, the most believable suspects are cleared while other suspects are unearthed, and their secrets unearthed with them, but none of these individuals is usually the culprit. Sometimes the secrets are nasty and sometimes rather thrilling: you know, the vicar has three wives in three different villages—and on a vicar's salary, no less. Slowly, our detective or seeker, no matter how initially unwilling, unravels the tangled mystery.

Here's the rub. Discovery of the truth doesn't mean that the perpetrator always faces the justice of the state but, in finding the truth, balance, or a form of balance, is restored. Existence can again be orderly. That's conservative. You are never left hanging at the end of a mystery.

Real life, on the other hand, tends to be the reverse. No wonder the mystery is such a popular form of fiction.

Back to Dickens. Every "hosanna" shouted at him for his fabulous characters really is deserved, but he also deserves credit for taking a two-thousand-year-old convention and standing it on its head, the convention that truth, identity, and some form of justice is always revealed.

Dickens wrote just the reverse.

That's why *A Tale of Two Cities* is my favorite mystery.

An Emmy-nominated screenwriter and a poet, Rita Mae Brown is the best-selling author of Rubyfruit Jungle, *her memoir* Animal Magnetism, *the* Mrs. Murphy *series, the* Sister Jane *foxhunting series, her canine mystery series featuring Mags Rogers, and her novels* Bingo, Six of One, *and* Loose Lips. *Brown lives in Afton, Virginia, with her cats, hounds, horses, and big red foxes. Visit her online at www.ritamaebrown.com.*

The Dead Letter
by Metta Fuller Victor (1867)

KARIN SLAUGHTER

Metta Fuller Victor (1831–85) was a pioneer not just in the field of "dime novel" fiction, the precursor to the modern mass-market paperback, but also in the development of the mystery novel in the United States. She began contributing stories to newspapers at the age of thirteen, and pub-lished Poems of Sentiment and Imagination, with Dramatic and Descrip-tive Pieces, *written with her sister, Frances, in 1851, quickly followed the same year by her first novel,* The Senator's Son. *Hugely popular in her day, she was also the editor, at various times, of* Home *magazine and the* Cosmopolitan Art Journal.

Many great women writers have been forgotten to history, from Anna Katharine Green, who is credited with creating the first series detec-tive (Ebenezer Gryce of the New York Metropolitan Police Force) to E.D.E.N. Southworth, whose serialized thrillers were widely translated in their day, but none languish in obscurity more than Metta Fuller Victor. With *The Dead Letter* (1867), Victor was the first American writer—male or female—to publish a full-length detective novel in the United States. She was, in fact, at the cusp of a wave of detective fiction that is oft ignored by literary historians, who mostly concentrate on Edgar Allan Poe, credited as the writer of the earliest detective short sto-ries, then skip straight to Dashiell Hammett, as if fifty years of American crime writing had never existed.

Writing as Seeley Regester, Victor built on the two-tiered narrative structure pioneered by Poe in "The Murders in the Rue Morgue." She opens *Letter* in the middle of the investigation to better concentrate not on the fact of murder but on the horrors left in its wake. In the first pages, we find Richard Redfield, gentleman lawyer and amateur detective, reeling with shock over the clue that he's just uncovered in the murder of Henry Moreland. This shows a marked departure from the Poe formula: our detective is not a socially isolated, coldly rational outsider, but a morally invested insider. The crimes that occur in *Letter* resonate throughout the community. The story explores the home and family lives of both victim and perpetrator. The reader feels a connection with the morally driven detective figure and follows his emotional journey as he seeks to understand the complexities of good and evil.

With the massive success of *The Dead Letter*, and that of her next mystery, *The Figure Eight* (1869), Victor helped the firm of Beadle & Adams, the creator of the dime novel, to become one of the most successful publishers of the antebellum period. A Mormon mother of nine, Victor wrote more than a hundred novels in almost every genre, from fantasy to adventure and Westerns. Like her contemporary, Harriet Beecher Stowe, she was a staunch abolitionist who wrote about the scourge of slavery. Unlike Stowe, she explored other issues of the day, from domestic strife to polygamy. *The Dead Letter* is, in fact, an amalgamation of all the genres Victor loved, providing the reader with social commentary as well as murder, intrigue, and a thrilling side trip through the lawless territories of the American West.

There are myriad other ways in which Victor's structural arc stands in stark contrast to Poe's. Victor's novels were not driven to immediate climax, but filled with reversals, twists, and misdirections that both prolonged the denouement and arguably made the climax that much more rewarding. Victor didn't just set out the facts of the crime: she explored social mores, distinguishing between the upper and middle classes with a subtle reference to clothing or manner. She described atmosphere and scenery in careful detail, giving her stories an air of grounded reality. The characters in Victor's books were not cynical about crime. They felt loss and tragedy to their very core. For these reasons and more, it seems that the Victor formula, not Poe's, is the convention to which modern crime fiction more closely hews.

Why, then, is Victor lost to obscurity?

The world of fiction—especially crime fiction—has a tendency to ignore the contributions of women, no matter how popular they become. In fact, popularity has often delegitimized the work of many women writers. Let's not forget that Daphne du Maurier, arguably one of the finest suspense writers of all time, was chided by many critics of her day for being "lightweight." Patricia Highsmith, who exiled herself to France, was excoriated by the American literati for her psychologically dark crimes and ambiguously drawn characters. That both women had their work adapted into hugely successful films ensured their longevity. They are now being rediscovered by a generation of scholars; however, to a certain extent, this disparity between commercial and critical success is an ongoing issue. Today, one seldom reads the phrase "transcending the genre" when a reviewer is describing a crime novel written by a woman. It seems as if it is more acceptable for women to write feisty tales of independent gals than it is for them to write serious crime fiction.

That the name Seeley Regester and not Metta Fuller Victor appears on the original cover of *The Dead Letter* is not an anomaly. Neither is the fact that the price—fifty cents—marked the tome as several steps above a typical dime novel. Throughout history, women have published their work under pseudonyms in hopes of finding a larger, more legitimate readership. Having a gender-neutral or male-identified name was, and to some degree still is, considered a positive marketing position. There was a reason Louisa May Alcott chose to publish her thrillers under the anonymous authorship of "the Children's Friend." Surely, Mary Anne Evans (George Eliot), Isak Dinesen (Karen von Blixen), and Currer Bell (Charlotte Brontë) were precursors to J. K. Rowling, P. D. James, and J. A. Jance.

And with good reason.

A quick perusal of any of the major book review sections shows a staggering disparity between the number of featured books by female versus male authors, not to mention the paucity of women included on the short lists of major literary prizes. Drill it down to just crime fiction authors, and the chasm becomes wider. Even the editors of this collection had a hard time finding authors (both male and female) to talk about female writers. This is not due to willful ignorance on the part of the fine writers who are included here, but because a great deal of our literary history has either been suppressed or lost.

This issue has never been so glaringly illustrated as by Victor. Many early popular works by women have disappeared, or have been dismissed as their era's equivalent of "chick lit," but it's shocking to find that the person who *created an entire genre* has effectively been erased from our consciousness.

One of the problems with bringing this omission to light is that taking a stand for women is often seen as being anti-men. It's a useful device for dismissing an uncomfortable problem, but, of all readers, crime fiction readers—readers who seek out books that discuss the injustices in society—should be able to see beyond this specious charge. It's also worth pointing out that the majority of book buyers, some 80 to 85 percent, are women, so to place the problem squarely at the feet of men is not only lazy but wrong. (And it should probably be added that Anna Katharine Green, who shaped the future of serialized crime fiction, was a staunch opponent of both the feminist movement and women's suffrage.) In this matter, as in many others, women have proven to be our own worst enemy.

It is an indisputable fact that those who love the crime genre have long been invested in celebrating the early masters, from Poe to Chandler to Boucher, and beyond. I submit that we should be actively promoting all of the predecessors on whose shoulders we stand—not just Victor, but Shirley Jackson, Miriam Allen deFord, Helen MacInnes, and countless others. We owe it to ourselves to truly understand the roots of the genre that has given so many of us not just hours of reading pleasure, but a community, a sense of belonging, and a vocation.

Both women and men have long toiled in this oft-ghettoized genre to craft believable stories with well-drawn, compelling characters. Poe's formula called for a masterful detective whose intelligence and cold eye were the only tools needed to catch the killer. Victor believed that exploring the world of the criminal—his or her family, neighbors, and relationships—was the best route to solving the crime. She combined social commentary with good old-fashioned murder. Women are not the only authors who have picked up the mantle of Victor's original narrative structure. While writers such as Mo Hayder, Denise Mina, and Gillian Flynn continue to excel at exploring the psychological aspects of crime, one might posit that the starkly rendered atmosphere, the multilayered relationships, and the strong female characters found in the works of Michael Connelly, Mark Billingham, and Lee Child share a kinship with the crime novels of Metta Fuller Victor.

Karin Slaughter is the author of several number one best sellers. A passionate supporter of libraries, Slaughter spearheaded the Save the Libraries campaign (www.savethelibraries.com) to help raise funds for ailing libraries.

She has donated all income from her e-short story "Thorn in My Side" to both the American and British library systems. For her twelfth novel, Criminal, Slaughter exhaustively researched racial and gender politics in the Atlanta Police Department during the 1970s, resulting in a deeply personal exploration of her hometown and her country during a period of enormous social change. Visit her online at www.karinslaughter.com.

The Moonstone
by Wilkie Collins (1868)

Wilkie Collins (1824–89) was a hugely prolific English writer, producing thirty novels in his lifetime in addition to plays, short stories, and essays, although he remains best known for his novels The Woman in White *(1860) and* The Moonstone *(1868). T. S. Eliot described the latter as "the first, the longest, and the best of modern English detective novels in a genre invented by Collins and not by Poe." Collins was a huge celebrity author in his day, yet still managed to maintain two distinct long-term relationships simultaneously, dividing his time in London between Caroline Graves, whom he claimed was his wife (although they never married), and the younger Martha Rudd, with whom he had three children under the assumed name of William Dawson.*

In the early hours of Saturday, June 30, 1860, somebody cut the throat of three-year-old Saville Kent. This was the start of the Road Hill House case. The tortuous and painful unraveling of this horrific real-life murder gripped the mind and terrified the imagination of Victorian Britain.

Some crimes have a deeper, darker resonance that stretches far beyond the horror of the act and its immediate consequences. Think of Jack the Ripper or the Lizzie Borden case; think of the Boston Strangler or the murder of James Bulger. Such cases are so shocking that they infiltrate our culture; often they trigger changes that ripple through society and wash up in unexpected places.

One of the ripples from Saville Kent's murder led eventually to Wilkie Collins's *The Moonstone* and to the unintended creation of a hugely influential variety of what we now call crime fiction.

As Kate Summerscale showed in *The Suspicions of Mr. Whicher* (2008), her study of the Kent murder, the impact of the case derived from the fact that it was not a matter that could be safely pigeonholed as a crime concerning poor and morally inadequate people living in remote urban slums on the margins of society. This, in terms of the great Victorian reading public, was about People Like Us. It was a middle-class affair set in a substantial country house: it was clear from the start that the little boy's murderer must be one of the family or one of their servants. There was trouble in paradise, and paradise would never be quite the same again.

Wilkie Collins was a commercially astute author, and it's not surprising that he should have decided to capitalize on elements of the Kent murder when he was casting around for the subject of a new novel in the late 1860s. He lived very much in the present, and his novels set out to reflect and comment on the rapidly changing world around him. At the time, he was riding a wave. The decade had begun with the enormous critical and financial success of *The Woman in White* (1860), perhaps his best novel. This was followed by *No Name* (1862) and *Armadale* (1866), a pair of flawed masterpieces that were almost equally lucrative.

The Moonstone was published in 1868. We know a good deal about how Collins planned the book: he set out, quite consciously, to undermine the sensation novel, a genre he had done much to invent, by creating a plot that provided rational solutions to a series of apparently bizarre events. His early books, he said, had set out "to trace the influence of circumstance on character." With *The Moonstone*, it was the other way round.

The Moonstone does not revolve around a murder but, in other respects, the parallels with the Road Hill House case are striking. At the heart of the novel is a country-house mystery with a limited circle of suspects. The story unfolds in a series of narratives supposedly written by different people—a technique that Collins had used very effectively in *The Woman in White* to orchestrate a complex plot and reveal the inner lives of a variety of characters. It is also, in essence, one of the basic techniques of both criminal investigation and the classical detective story: the investigator persuades each suspect to give his or her version of events; the investigator then sifts, sorts, and weighs the different accounts to arrive at the truth. In *The Moonstone,* as in perhaps most detective fiction, a sort of meta-investigation takes place alongside the fictional one, for the reader becomes the detective as well.

Another similarity between the novel and the Road Hill House case is the police response. In real life, the baffled local police called in Inspector Whicher of the newly created detective force at Scotland Yard. Collins mimics this, creating his own Whicher in the shape of Sergeant Cuff.

The dramatic tension of the Saville Kent investigation obsessed contemporary observers and later cast a long, sometimes baleful shadow over British crime fiction. The investigating officer, whom the law empowered to search the most private places and interrogate suspects regardless of their status, was not a gentleman; by definition, a police detective belonged to the lower orders. In Britain's class-ridden society, the detective's freedom to pry into the lives of his social superiors was profoundly disturbing. Yet the real Whicher and the fictional Cuff had reputations as investigators that impressed even their critics. Their methods fascinated the public, and so did the challenge of the puzzle and the thrill of the chase. In the words of Wilkie Collins himself, Victorian Britain had caught "the detective fever."

In the novel, the mystery revolves not around murder but around the theft of a great diamond, known as the Moonstone because it is said to wax and wane with the moon. Rachel Verinder inherits the diamond from her wicked uncle, who had looted it from an Indian temple. On the night of her eighteenth birthday it is stolen. Suspicion falls on the inmates of the house, including the servants. It also falls on some visitors, a party of Indian jugglers.

It's interesting that the novel treats the Indians very sympathetically—and this at the high noon of the British Empire, only a few years after the bloody suppression of the Indian Mutiny. But Wilkie Collins was always a subversive author whose work attacked the hypocrisy and injustice sometimes practiced by his own readers. He instinctively defended the vulnerable of Victorian society: people from other races than his own, the poor, servants, and women. (It has to be admitted that Collins himself was not entirely consistent where women were concerned. He never married, but for many years maintained two mistresses and their families in separate London homes.)

The local police are called to investigate the theft of the diamond, but they prove ineffectual. Scotland Yard arrives in the person of Sergeant Cuff, a man of experience and dogged sagacity with a taste for growing roses. (He is also, according to Peter Ackroyd, the first detective to use a magnifying glass as an essential part of his professional equipment.) Cuff is certainly no cipher, but an amateur, Rachel's cousin Franklin Blake, pursues a parallel investigation to that of the police. Collins lays down the template for the dual investigation, professional and amateur, that characterizes so much crime fiction.

Fear and uncertainty permeate the novel like a fog. Collins creates an illusion of solidity and historicity with the logical processes of the investigation, and with the multinarrative technique. But in truth, the story line doesn't have a great deal to do with gritty realism. The opiated visions of laudanum color *The Moonstone* in more ways than one. Not only does the drug figure significantly in the plot, but Collins was dosing himself with ever-increasing quantities in a largely vain attempt to deal with ill-defined pains that frequently racked his body from early middle age. His work resembles Poe's in its precarious balance between the rational and the logical on the one hand, and the terrors of the unconscious mind on the other.

The result of this combustible set of ingredients is the book that T. S. Eliot famously called "the first and greatest of English detective novels." We can quibble with both these rather sweeping judgments, but not with a great deal of conviction. Wilkie Collins effectively invented the format of the classic Golden Age detective story that was to dominate British crime fiction for so long. It's hard to imagine how Conan Doyle could have created Sherlock Holmes without the example of Edgar Allan Poe's Chevalier Dupin stories. Similarly Christie, Sayers, and their colleagues wrote by the light of the sinister glow from *The Moonstone*.

But the novel is far more than a footnote in literary history. *The Moonstone* has never been out of print since it was published. Radical, challenging, and supremely entertaining, it is a book to read if you haven't already. And if you have, give yourself the pleasure of reading it again.

Andrew Taylor's novels include the best seller The American Boy, *chosen by the* Times *as one of the top ten crime novels of the decade; the Roth Trilogy (filmed for TV as* Fallen Angel*); the Lydmouth Series;* Bleeding Heart Square; *and* The Anatomy of Ghosts. *He has most recently been awarded the CWA Diamond Dagger and Sweden's Martin Beck Award. He has written another novel but can't decide what to call it. He is the* Spectator's *crime fiction reviewer. Visit him online at www.andrew-taylor.co.uk.*

The Adventures of Sherlock Holmes by Sir Arthur Conan Doyle (1892)

LINDA BARNES

Sir Arthur Conan Doyle (1859–1930) was one of the pivotal figures in mystery writing. A physician and writer born in Edinburgh, Scotland, he is best known as the creator of "consulting detective" Sherlock Holmes and his faithful amanuensis, Dr. John Watson, although he also wrote a number of historical novels, and a series of adventure stories featuring the character of Professor Challenger, the best known of which remains The Lost World. *He was friends for a time with the magician Harry Houdini, and became fascinated by Spiritualism in later life, a consequence of a series of bereavements that included the loss of his wife, Louisa, and his son Kingsley, leading Conan Doyle to seek proof of an existence beyond the grave.*

The curtains were the color of midnight, their edges weighted with a white-ball fringe that gleamed in the darkness like the stars that studded the midwestern sky. The room measured ten feet by twelve feet, sheltering narrow twin beds, a tall wooden chest, and a mismatched bureau with drawers that creaked alarmingly. The windows, one at the head of my bed, one off to the side, were awkwardly placed and small, but provided a cross breeze on stiflingly hot summer nights. The bedspreads echoed the midnight curtains, and each lonely pillow was encased in a navy sham.

"Stop playing with the curtains and go to sleep!"

Would that I could. I counted the balls of yarn that edged the curtains: a habit, a ritual, a sort of pagan rosary. There were monsters in the closet, demons under the bed. Across the room, my sister slept peacefully, her face to the wall, her bed a safe haven. She had not read "The Speckled Band."

The door slammed. The silence echoed. As I counted the yarn balls,

I strained to hear the telltale noises: the click of the lock, the metallic clank, the slither and hiss of the snake.

Wait! Was that a low, clear whistle?

Vernon Baker, the next-door neighbor, kept dogs, haughty standard poodles. He could be outdoors summoning his pets, yet what if it were not the innocent neighbor but the mad doctor, Grimesby Roylott, the terror of Stoke Moran, whistling to recall the swamp adder, "the deadliest snake in India," from its nightly predation? In the impenetrable darkness, my heart pounded like a jackhammer.

I believe I was ten years old and in elementary school when I encountered "The Speckled Band," that premier mystery, the eighth of twelve tales collected in *The Adventures of Sherlock Holmes*. I might even have been eleven. An insatiable reader, quick as lightning, my literary needs proved a challenge to the school librarian. As soon as I finished one book, she hurriedly thrust another into my questing hands. Teen romances alternated with biographies of worthy or scandalous women. I read about society weddings, Napoleon's Josephine, elopements, and Florence Nightingale.

Then, in class, unexpectedly, "The Specked Band," isolated from its fellows. After a week of sleepless nights, I petitioned for and received the full *Adventures of Sherlock Holmes,* each story a small revelation, a gift of plot structure, character, and language. From "A Scandal in Bohemia" to "The Copper Beeches" in one long gulp, then back to the beginning to reread, with many a stop along the way.

"My life is spent in one long effort to escape from the commonplaces of existence. These little problems help me to do so." So says Sherlock, according to the faithful Watson, in "The Red-Headed League," the second adventure in the book, and what child raised in a cookie-cutter neighborhood would not echo his desire? "You share my love of all that is bizarre and outside the conventions and humdrum routine of everyday life," the master tells Watson, and I picture my younger self nodding, rapt and enthralled. "Depend upon it, there is nothing so unnatural as the commonplace," Holmes states in "A Case of Identity," adding for good measure, "The little things are infinitely the most important." Sherlock inspired me to view my ordinary surroundings in a different way, to observe rather than see, to listen rather than hear, to take note of the extraordinary in the ordinary.

"A man should possess all knowledge that is likely to be useful to him in his work," Sherlock says in "The Five Orange Pips," and Watson, eager to please, earnestly summarizes what Holmes terms "his limits": "Philosophy, astronomy, and politics were marked at zero, I remember. Botany, variable, geology profound as regards the mud-stains from any region within fifty miles of town, chemistry eccentric, anatomy unsystematic, sensational literature and crime records unique, violin player, boxer, swordsman, lawyer, and self-poisoner by cocaine and tobacco." How Holmes's eccentric knowledge must have intrigued and fascinated a bookish girl tethered to a rote curriculum. When I chose fencing as an elective, Holmes urged me on.

"What a fool a builder must be to open a ventilator into another room, when, with the same trouble, he might have communicated with the outside air." Surely it was extraordinary that the very room in which I slept would possess a small grille—a ventilator, I assumed, rather than a heating duct—that seemed to connect with the next room, the small study recently converted to my baby brother's bedroom. True, there was no false bellpull that dangled down to my pillow, but the vent, the vital and perhaps deadly pathway to the next room, existed in fact. My bed was not bolted to the floor, but I could hardly move it without inciting speculation.

My father would know that I suspected him.

I had a slightly older sister; in my mind we counted as twins, just as Helen and Julia Stoner of "The Speckled Band" were twins. My father, I assumed, had wanted only two children, an unmatched set, one boy and one girl, and now that my mother had finally achieved the boy, I had become the extra child, the surplus girl; that, to my ten-year-old self, seemed a motive for my removal as clear and powerful as Grimesby Roylott's desire to ensure his continued inheritance.

"When a doctor does go wrong he is the first of criminals. He has nerve and he has knowledge." My father was not a medical doctor, but he was a brilliant engineer. Like Roylott, he had nerve and knowledge. Like Roylott, he had served in the army. Like Roylott, he had traveled to distant lands and returned with exotic souvenirs. I listened to the silent and menacing night, to the even sigh of my sister's breath.

"Do not go to sleep; your very life may depend upon it."

What if? those stories said to me. *What if?* they whispered as they invited me into the realm of deductive reasoning, into a universe where I could, by the use of observation and imagination, emulate a hero.

The Adventures of Sherlock Holmes, being a collection of short stories rather than a novel, is, strictly speaking, outside the approved parameters of this collection. I chose it nonetheless, not only because it's fun to break the rules, but because I consider it a shining example of the series mystery in miniature. Single mystery novels delight me. I yield to no one in my admiration of *The Moonstone, Rebecca,* and *The Thin Man,* but to my mind it is the series mystery that offers the ultimate in entertainment. The continuing series promises more than a single tale, more than a glimpse of a moment in time; it offers an ongoing conversation, a relationship with beloved and familiar characters. The impact of the series does not rest on any one particular tale but rather on a cumulative impression derived over a period of time. *The Adventures of Sherlock Holmes* is a microcosm of that which I love best in detective fiction, a series of stories that provides the reader with the opportunity to experience the delineation, development, and flowering of character.

In each story, another facet of Holmes's personality glistens, another fact is learned, another doorway yawns. "A Scandal in Bohemia" gives us, in addition to a portrait of "the late Irene Adler of dubious and questionable memory," Sherlock's pride in his craft, his fallibility, and his continuing admiration of "The Woman" who defeats him. We find that failure does not stop him. "It is better to learn wisdom late than never to learn it at all," he says in "The Man with the Twisted Lip."

In "The Five Orange Pips," Holmes's client, John Openshaw, dies. "It becomes a personal matter with me now," my hero states as he relentlessly hunts down the perpetrators. This is one of the hallmarks of a successful series: the detective, whether an amateur or the coolest of professionals, becomes personally involved. What could more personally involve Holmes than the unexpected visit of Grimesby Roylott to Baker Street, the evil doctor's taunting reference to "Holmes, the meddler; Holmes, the busybody; Holmes, the Scotland Yard Jack-in-Office," followed by his bending-the-iron-poker demonstration of brute strength and impending violence?

Another joy of the series mystery is the cast of recurring characters that surrounds the protagonist. The *Adventures,* alas, does not include any of the Mycroft Holmes tales, but we do meet Sherlock's foil,

Lestrade, the ferret-like champion of the ordinary police force, and we encounter Watson again and again, as narrator, admirer, accomplice, and staunch companion.

"The lowest and vilest alleys in London do not present a more dreadful record of sin than does the smiling and beautiful countryside," Holmes states in "The Copper Beeches," and even as a child I knew that he spoke the truth, for crime was no stranger to my neighborhood. Years earlier, a body had been discovered on my front lawn, a teenaged boy shot to death by a former neighbor, a police officer. To this day, I don't know the true facts of that case ("Data! Data! Data! I can't make bricks without clay."), but I remain convinced that Holmes could have solved it. Sherlock sees beneath the surface. He reads the signs. He recognizes that there is always ample reason to fear.

The detective series conquers fear, and conquers death, with an implicit promise: that the detective will not die. Holmes was, he is, and he will be. He has returned from the Reichenbach Falls, come back from the dead. Immortal, he continues to thrive, portrayed by Basil Rathbone, Nicol Williamson, and many others in the movies, by Jeremy Brett in the beloved British television series, by Benedict Cumberbatch in the contemporary BBC TV series *Sherlock*, and kept vibrantly active in the Mary Russell novels by Laurie R. King. Other characters may have a story, but Holmes has a life so vivid that he endures forever.

For a month, in the darkened bedroom of childhood, I slept with a yardstick concealed at my side, a poor substitute for the long thin cane with which Holmes beat back the deadly reptile. Then the terror broke like a fever and subsided as suddenly as it came.

Born in Detroit, Michigan, Linda Barnes is an award-winning mystery writer. She has written two acclaimed Boston-set series of mystery novels, one featuring the sometime actor and private investigator Michael Spraggue, and the other centering on the six-one redheaded detective Carlotta Carlyle, the most recent of which is Lie Down with the Devil. *She lives in Boston, Massachusetts. Visit her online at www.lindabarnes.com.*

The Hound of the Baskervilles
by Sir Arthur Conan Doyle (1902)

CAROL O'CONNELL

Sir Arthur Conan Doyle (1859–1930) was one of the pivotal figures in mystery writing. A physician and writer born in Edinburgh, Scotland, he is best known as the creator of "consulting detective" Sherlock Holmes and his faithful amanuensis, Dr. John Watson, although he also wrote a number of historical novels, and a series of adventure stories featuring the character of Professor Challenger, the best known of which remains The Lost World. *He was friends for a time with the magician Harry Houdini, and became fascinated by Spiritualism in later life, a consequence of a series of bereavements that included the loss of his wife, Louisa, and his son Kingsley, leading Conan Doyle to seek proof of an existence beyond the grave.*

Would Arthur Conan Doyle agree with even half of what's been written about his iconic character, Sherlock Holmes?

Does it matter?

Not at all. Eye of the beholder holds sway, and you're invited to pile on. There are fifty-six short stories, but I recommend Doyle's finest of four novels, *The Hound of the Baskervilles,* to understand why Holmes's story can never end, but extends from the horse-drawn-carriage era of 1887 into the twenty-first century—with fresh horses.

This novel is rich in atmosphere, like the poisonous air of the detective's Baker Street residence in London. As described by the narrator, Dr. Watson, "the room was so filled with smoke that the lamp upon the table was blurred by it." The cause was "the acrid fumes of strong tobacco which took me by the throat and set me coughing. Through the haze, I had a vague vision of Holmes in his dressing gown, coiled up in an armchair with his black clay pipe between his lips."

The smoking man is jazzed on nicotine chased with pots of caffeine, and the floor is littered with maps of a distant place he has never seen. Yet Holmes is immersed in that atmosphere as a visitor "in spirit," imagining an isolated mansion, the wild landscape of the moors by night, and the family curse of a giant hound whose job it is to kill off generations of aristocrats—the Baskervilles.

In an earlier work of 1893, "The Final Problem," Conan Doyle got rid of Holmes by tossing the detective down the Reichenbach Falls, presumably to his death, and then was surprised to find himself the most hated man in London as a consequence. Public outcry forced him to bring back Sherlock Holmes.*

Now here's where it gets eerie. Holmes would've found his own way back to life without any help from his creator. He's not contained by Doyle's stories: he's alive. Spookier still, he cannot die, not one more time. Modern screenwriters, playwrights, and novelists have continued his saga, and none of them dares to kill him off. They're all afraid of the rabble, the ugly mob that is us—the fans of Sherlock Holmes.

So here we have a shining (blindingly so), original character for the ages, and he has tragic flaws aplenty (though the ancient Greeks mandated only one). And yet, on May 3, 1902, the *New York Times* had to defend this book against the mockery of Mark Twain, who poked fun at Doyle's work in a satire titled "A Double-Barrelled Detective Story." In rebuttal, the *Times* maintained that *The Hound of the Baskervilles* "in construction, movement, and finish, is a fine piece of work." Then G. K. Chesterton, in his review for the *Daily News,* complained of Doyle sneering at Edgar Allan Poe in a previous story, while imitating that more esteemed writer's creation of Monsieur Dupin. (Other critics make distinctions between "imitation" and "influence.") But Chesterton added that Sherlock Holmes "has passed out of the unreality of literature into the glowing reality of legend." In this instance, Holmes got a better review than Doyle.

You think that's strange? Just you wait.

The book's appearance on best-seller lists in America was credited to

---

* *The Hound of the Baskervilles* (1902) is the first work to follow the character's premature death, though it precedes the comeback story of Holmes's resurrection, "The Adventure of the Empty House," in 1903. So presumably we're meant to believe that events in the 1902 novel took place before Holmes's demise in "The Final Problem," a short story of 1893. Do not reread this. Just . . . let it go.

the lack of a sane line between truth and fiction, the myth that Sherlock Holmes was an actual person: corporeal, not fictional. How insane is that? Well, there was an actual Baskerville family (and Sir Arthur was their frequent houseguest).* You might say the hound existed, too, if only in folklore. Show me a moor anywhere in England, and I'll show you a giant, ghostly dog with glowing red eyes.† And twenty-seven years later, T. S. Eliot chimed in on the madness with this quote on Holmes: "The plain fact is, he is more real than his progenitor."

Sherlockians, loyal fans of Sherlock Holmes, took strangeness even further by forbidding members to speak the name of Sir Arthur Conan Doyle at their meetings. Holmes was flesh-and-blood real to them, and any mention of Doyle's authorship was an intolerable contradiction of their faith. So . . . this is a damn fan club, and the poor author is worse than dead to these people; it's as if he had never lived. And that's strange, because T. S. Eliot also said, "I am not sure that Sir Arthur Conan Doyle is not one of the great dramatic writers of his age."

Till the end of his days, the author, merely life-size in a world that wanted giants, could not compete with the fictional man.

Feeling sorry for Doyle?

What about Holmes? His own creator tried to murder him (poor bastard); he was a flaming drug addict (no wonder); and he suffered clinical depressions stemming from the boredom of a beautiful mind with nothing to do between finding brilliant solutions to mysteries that no one else could penetrate.

---

*The Baskerville family's home, Clyro Court, has since been repurposed and renamed the Baskerville Hall Hotel. In a contest of sorts over bragging rights for the story's true setting, it wins for the architectural and landscaping similarities to the estate in the novel, though it is not, as Doyle describes it, a fourteenth-century castle. This gray-stone manor house was built in 1839.

†Bertram Fletcher Robinson takes credit for inspiring the novel by relating a hound-of-hell legend to the author—though British folklore was already crawling with phantom devil dogs. Doyle does acknowledge his friend in the clothbound edition of 1902, but Robinson's own story of this contribution, made on a golfing holiday in March 1901, leaves little time before serialization in the August edition of *The Strand Magazine* that same year. Given the cliffhanger style of this serial format, the novel was well plotted and paced before the first of eight installments, and not written on the fly (though serials do offer time for rewrites). Prolific Doyle dashed off many a short story in this same span, though novels are more widely spaced in the Holmes canon, suggesting they might've been a year or more in the making, but the author wrote his magnum opus in less than six months.

What else might make us sympathetic to Sherlock Holmes? Well, there's his other addiction, to shag tobacco. He's rude, aloof, and untidy. Also, in more recent times, he's been diagnosed with sociopathy, autism, and Asperger's syndrome, but let's put the pop psychology aside. Too facile.

Consider the plight of the genius. It's taxing for him to deal with ordinary intellects, rather like us trying to converse with a household pet, a dog that is willing, even eager, but can't hold up his end of a conversation. High intelligence is Sherlock Holmes's most remarkable disability. (At school, I had a friend with an IQ of 186. He was so preoccupied with his thoughts that he walked into trees and could not be trusted to cross a road on his own.) Holmes is obsessively focused, concentrating on criminal acts to the exclusion of social pursuits. You won't see him out dancing. No ball games. No prayer circles.

And there are holes in his education, perhaps a practical matter of storage space in memory. He has encyclopedic arcane knowledge, but he can't be bothered to learn anything that won't help him solve a puzzle. He doesn't have the recipe for boiling an egg, or instructions for taking out the trash that covers his carpet. Rules of etiquette elude him, and the polite lie would not occur to him.

Holmes may be cold, but not intentionally cruel, and so he has no idea why acquaintances should take offense at being treated as lower life forms. Just try to imagine his having an earnest "relationship talk" with a woman. Now stop that before you hurt yourself. This is why we love him so—he could never love us—but occasionally he will admire a quality in someone, and that is something to shoot for. We aim for grace.

Handicaps galore, Holmes also languishes in bouts of melancholia, periods when he cannot get out of bed to greet a client at the door. Even a brilliant man may need a keeper of sorts.

Enter his companion, Dr. John Watson.

Poor Watson sometimes gets a critic's short shrift as the foil (a hack writer's device to make another character shine by comparison), and Arthur Conan Doyle may actually have intended that. But here's a dirty secret of authors: more can emerge from the writing than was ever intended by the writer.

So instead of getting all stick-to-the-author's-intent-you-filthy-bastard, I say play Holmes's game. See what the evidence reveals about the good doctor, a former soldier. Brave. Honorable. Loyal? Oh, God, yes. And for all of this, he cannot stand out as a literary character unless coupled with Holmes, and Holmes has days when he can't even stand up without Watson. Imagine half a wheel. That's Sherlock Holmes, cerebral, ill-mannered, and cold. But half a wheel goes nowhere. The other half? That's John Watson, the one with all the social graces, compassion, and a gun. Now the wheel is whole, and they can roll. (For support of this idea, look to "The Adventure of the Blanched Soldier" and "The Adventure of the Lion's Mane." I'm not the first or the tenth to note that both stories are failures for the absence of Watson.)

In the early pages of *The Hound of the Baskervilles*, a visitor to Baker Street suggests that Sherlock Holmes might be "the second highest expert in Europe." This does not go over well, and the detective tells him to consult the better man. After much back-stepping apology on the part of the would-be client, the matter of rank is settled: Holmes rules. Does this suggest narcissism? Much of Sherlockian lore will say so, though, in my own view, I doubt it. (Back to the analogy of pets: Might your dog believe that you're conceited? You do think you're smarter than the dog, right?)

A true fop of a narcissist would lose Watson's respect, and Holmes never does. I believe he's simply aware of where he belongs in the pantheon. Does Holmes preen, or chase after compliments? No, and no. So the logic prevails. He's only a stickler for facts. The man is the most brilliant player in the field of deduction—an honest observation, even though it is his own.

When we meet Holmes in this novel, he has a history shaped by previous stories: he's kicked cocaine, defeated his archenemy, and vanquished death itself. He is nuanced to completion, but not quite a man in full. He never becomes a sexual being, but he doesn't need to be. We have Watson for that, the one who chases the ladies and sometimes marries them. Those who are looking for romance can go away and read a lesser novel. The rest of us are in it for love of the game, for love of the man. And the man is fearless. Keep turning the pages to witness his chasing across dark moorland laced with quicksand, in pursuit of a hellhound.

Can we ever get enough of him? Not likely. Fortunately, there is more to come. And to all the future authors of Holmes novels, plays, and films, a few words of caution: it's not a matter of what you should or should not do. Try as you might, you cannot kill him. Try if you like, but he'll survive you and all your descendants as well.

He can never die.

Long live Sherlock Holmes.

Carol O'Connell writes: I was raised to be a painter, earned a degree in fine arts, and then took a wrong turn somewhere. Failing in my ambition to live as a cliché starving artist and die in a Manhattan gutter, I became a novelist and jettisoned the rent-money job after the success of my first book, Mallory's Oracle, *in 1994. I write every day—but never on Facebook. There's no website or Twitter account, either, and my cell has a text blocker. I agreed to write this piece in exchange for a bottle of wine, and that should fill in the blanks on bad habits.*

The Assassin
by Liam O'Flaherty (1928)

DECLAN BURKE

Born on Inishmore on the Aran Islands, Liam O'Flaherty (1896–1984) fought for the Irish Guards on the Western Front during World War I, where he was wounded and may have suffered shell shock. A committed socialist, O'Flaherty is best known as a literary author in both English and Gaelic, and particularly as a distinguished short-story writer, although he won the James Tait Black Memorial Prize for The Informer *(1925), a crime novel filmed by John Ford and released in 1935.*

In a novel it would have been a peaceful Sunday morning, and the assassins' target not only a government minister but a minister for justice. The assassins would have been reactionary revolutionaries and the minister on his way to mass, and all of them former blood brothers who had fought the world's biggest empire to a standstill and then split to become bitter enemies during a Civil War in which the minister had ordered the execution of the assassins' vengeance-seeking comrades, among them the best man at his own wedding.

Apart from a couple of commas, that's pretty much how it really happened. On the Sunday morning of July 10, 1927, the then-Irish minister for justice, Kevin O'Higgins, was assassinated by anti-Treaty IRA volunteers as a reprisal for O'Higgins's role in the execution of more than seventy IRA prisoners during the Civil War of 1922–23, among them Rory O'Connor, who had been best man at O'Higgins's wedding.

Interesting times, as the Chinese might say.

Given all the guns lying around in 1927, and the unsated bloodlust, and the kind of blinkered mentality that believed the execution of a minister for justice was a strategically good idea, who would be mad enough to write a novel about the assassination of a ruthless government minister, from the perspective of the deranged killer, and title it *The Assassin*?

Step forward, Liam O'Flaherty.

Liam O'Flaherty is best known in Ireland today as an important literary writer who occasionally dabbled in genre novels, and it's unlikely that the author himself, given that he was prone to a supercilious tone when discussing his crime titles, would disagree. And yet, *The Assassin* wasn't even O'Flaherty's first crime novel. *The Informer* (1925), described as "a little mastermind of its kind" by the *Sunday Times*, follows the traitorous Gypo Nolan as he scuttles through the rat runs of Dublin's slums, desperately trying to stay one step ahead of his betrayed comrades.

"O'Flaherty," wrote Ruth Dudley Edwards in her essay on the author in *Down These Green Streets* (Liberties Press, 2011),

> had worked out the plan of *The Informer*, "determined that it should be a sort of high-brow detective story and its style based on the technique of the cinema. It should have all the appearance of a realistic novel and yet the material should have hardly any connection with real life. I would treat my readers as a mob orator treats his audience and toy with their emotions, making them finally pity a character whom they began by considering a monster."

That sneering tone wouldn't necessarily endear O'Flaherty to crime fiction readers; the dedication of *The Assassin* ("To my creditors") suggests that his motives for writing the novel were rather less than noble.

And yet. Should O'Flaherty's motives and intentions matter? Should his attitude to the crime novel undermine the impact of what he created?

It's worth noting, before we go any further, that the publications of both *The Informer* and *The Assassin* predate the publication of Dashiell Hammett's *Red Harvest* (1929). Hammett is rightfully lauded for his achievements, for the quality of grim truth he brought to the crime novel, and for portraying a particular reality in, as Raymond Chandler said, "a spare, frugal, hardboiled" way, and for taking murder out of the Venetian vase and dropping it back in the alleyway.

(Of course, Hammett and Carroll John Daly and their fellow Black Maskers had been publishing short stories since the early 1920s that featured the staccato, brutal style. O'Flaherty, during his wanderings of the world, had spent two years in America, working at a succession of menial jobs, and even at one point as an activist for the Wobblies; it would be fascinating to learn if he had picked up the embryonic hard-boiled style during his stay in the States.)

The story of *The Assassin* follows Michael McDara as he returns to Ireland, a merchant seaman shell-shocked by war but now determined to rally his former comrades, the anti-Treaty dissidents with left-leaning politics, with a monumental "holy act": the killing of the government's symbol of power, referred to only as "Him."

It's a revenge fantasy and a paranoid thriller, and an exploration of the psychology of a self-loathing killer, and there are times when it feels like reading Patricia Highsmith's take on *Crime and Punishment*—that lurid, yes, that poisonously cold, and at times that ludicrously overwritten. But if Hammett is to be credited with kick-starting the hard-boiled crime novel in 1929, Liam O'Flaherty is entitled to his portion, and perhaps as a bridge of sorts between the nineteenth- and twentieth-century crime novel. This, delivered in the pared-down style, could have been lifted from the socially conscious crime narratives of Charles Dickens:

> He entered Capel Street and turned northwards. Now he was in the heart of a slum district. The smells, of which his senses were peculiarly conscious, became more violent and nauseous. But to him they were as sweet and intoxicating as they were unpleasant to the normal citizen. They whetted his appetite for the act he was going to perform. Everything here excited a savage hatred of society in him: barefooted children with a hectic flush on their pale, starved faces, tottering old people with all manner of disease scarring their wasted features, offal in the streets, houses without doors and with broken windows, a horrifying and monotonous spectacle of degrading poverty and misery everywhere. The foetid air reeked with disease.

Later, the character of Kitty, something of an early femme fatale and the unfortunate subject of religion-hating McDara's twisted interpretation of the whore-Madonna dichotomy, finds herself in the Shelbourne Hotel, which was then, as now, a haven for the prosperous from the madding crowds of Dublin's streets:

She looked back into the lounge. She saw an enormously fat woman, with bare neck and shoulders, reclining in an arm-chair. The woman had jewels on her fat neck and on her flabby hands. Her feet were propped up on a cushion. She had a heavy jowl. She looked unhappy, suffering either from sore feet or indigestion; goodness knows from what she suffered. But Kitty did not pity her suffering face. To Kitty she was symbolical of the degradation of the people, sin and gluttony and acceptance of tyranny. A parasite! Something to be torn limb from limb, to be wiped out, to be burned alive.

A picture of the starving people came before Kitty's mind and she saw them pouring into this hotel, after the act, with axes and sledgehammers . . .

A half-hour passed.

Few novels, crime or otherwise, possess *The Assassin*'s quality of prolonged, sublimated rage, of its disgust at the way the world is. It is not a novel that is particularly interested in asking questions of its time and culture, or proposing solutions to problems. It is a barbaric yawp, a howl of frustration, and a call to arms, and it is not great art; very much of its time, it has not worn the years well.

Nonetheless, I would urge you to read it: for its vividness, its whiff of cordite, its utterly compelling psychotic blend of compassion and rage; for the way it not only worms beneath the skin of its time and place, but burrows in under the knuckle, too.

Read it once. You will not need to read it again.

Declan Burke is the author of Eightball Boogie *(2003),* The Big O *(2007), and* Absolute Zero Cool *(2011). He is the editor of* Down These Green Streets: Irish Crime Writing in the 21st Century *(Liberties Press, 2011), and hosts a website dedicated to Irish crime fiction called* Crime Always Pays. *His latest novel is* Slaughter's Hound *(2012). He lives in Wicklow with his wife and daughter, where he is not allowed to own a cat, or be owned by one. Visit him online at www.crimealwayspays.blogspot.com.*

The Bastard
by Erskine Caldwell (1929)

ALLAN GUTHRIE

The author of twenty novels, more than 150 short stories, and twelve nonfiction titles, Erskine Caldwell (1903–87) is best known for his novels Tobacco Road *(1932) and* God's Little Acre *(1933). A Southern writer committed to writing about the dispossessed and marginalized in society, both black and white, Caldwell was ostracized by his peers for betraying his class and culture. On its publication in 1929, his debut novella,* The Bastard, *suffered problems with censorship, and was banned in Portland, Maine, the city in which Caldwell operated a bookstore.*

In the 1990s, while I was working for a bookshop chain, I had the good fortune to have a line manager who persuaded me to read some crime fiction. Up to that point, I'd read mainly literary fiction, and wasn't aware of what I was missing—luckily, he was. The novel that he recommended to me was Philip Kerr's *A Philosophical Investigation,* a near-future thriller about a violent sociopath code-named Wittgenstein. Well, I blew through the book in no time at all. Immediately, I picked up another crime novel. And then another. And from there, crime fiction quickly became my staple literary diet.

The more I read, the more I found myself drawn toward novels that dealt with abnormal psychology, and to this day I remain a huge fan of fiction that unsettles the reader. I admire writers who don't play safe, who allow "unsympathetic" characters to have a voice—often the hugely disturbing voice of a damaged psyche, but that's the point: violent psychopaths should be disturbing.

It was a good few years after my introduction to crime fiction that I stumbled across Erskine Caldwell's 1929 novella, *The Bastard.* Caldwell (most famous for the best-selling Southern novels *Tobacco Road* and

God's Little Acre) isn't known as a crime writer, although there are plenty of criminal types peppered throughout his work. But for his debut, Caldwell decided to write about Gene Morgan, one of the most thoroughly unpleasant protagonists in the whole of crime fiction.

Caldwell's book is a character-driven tale about the nomadic Mr. Morgan, the bastard son of a prostitute. He drifts into a new town and we follow him as he gets work, gets laid, meets the love of his life, gets married, and finally we're by his side when he resolves a difficult situation with one of the most terrifying acts of casual violence that you're ever likely to encounter.

Gene Morgan stakes a convincing claim to be the first example of an antihero in noir fiction.

It's hard to define noir fiction—many have tried, and most have failed. I associate noir fiction with crime stories that often feature criminals as protagonists (of course detective protagonists do exist in noir— Ken Bruen's Jack Taylor and Ray Banks's Cal Innes are two of the most oft-cited, although Cal Innes is actually an ex-con). Those protagonists are often doomed. They're rarely heroic (unlike the often chivalrous detectives of hard-boiled fiction, with which noir is often confused). And they live in a world that's rotten to the core with corruption.

Gene Morgan fits that definition perfectly: he's a multiple murderer, a rapist, a thief; he's doomed by his own psychopathology; he couldn't be less heroic—a damsel in distress is a potential target rather than someone to be rescued; and corruption runs through every level of society. (When he spends the night in the can for being drunk, his jailer turns out to be more of a criminal than the unfortunates he locks up.)

The fact that *The Bastard* might be the first work of noir fiction ought to make it a key text, and yet it has never received much recognition. It was first published by Heron Press (a tiny New York publisher) and suffered problems with censorship soon after publication, including a ban by the county attorney in Portland, Maine—where Caldwell was living—as a result of which the publisher refused to pay him, leaving Caldwell raging. In later years, the author seemed to be dismissive of the book. In his preface to a mid-1950s reprint edition, he describes the work as "storytelling in a time of youth," which suggests he thought of it as immature.

Which it may well be. Debut titles often are, and writers rarely enjoy reading their early work. Writers take time to hone their skills, to find their voices, to mature. You can certainly quite easily pick holes in the book: the main character is over the top; there are too many coincidences; the violence is random and overdone; he falls in love with his wife-to-be, Myra, far too quickly; some of the dialogue reads like it came from a manual of hard-boiled lingo. But what we do see in *The Bastard* is an early study of a casual psychopath, long before Jim Thompson presented us with Lou Ford in *The Killer Inside Me*, or Horace McCoy with his depiction of Ralph Cotter in *Kiss Tomorrow Goodbye*. Caldwell goes further—the world Gene Morgan inhabits is a godless one, and Gene is far from alone in his appalling callousness and cruelty.

At one point Gene is in jail overnight when a young girl is brought in. The guard rapes her, and then lets Gene into her cell to do the same. Which he does. He also steals her gold ring. And then he's let out at midday and goes "home to dinner, whistling all the way."

At another point, Gene's friend, John, kills a worker at a sawmill. The man dies after becoming entangled with the machinery. Their response is to prop his mouth open and pour water down his throat so they can enjoy watching it trickle from the mass of intestine protruding from where a rip saw has bisected his stomach.

In another incident, a work colleague, Froggy, asks Gene to impregnate his wife (they want children, and Froggy isn't able to oblige 'cause he's "broke down . . . with the clap"), then changes his mind as Gene and his wife are about to get down to business. Gene's none too pleased by the interruption, so he shoots him. When Froggy's wife asks what Gene did with her husband's body, Gene replies that he "kicked it downstairs" and that he'll "dig a hole for it in the morning . . ." She doesn't seem too bothered. All she has to say is, "Oh!" and Gene turns out the light so they can get back to business as if nothing has happened.

The one decent person in Gene's world is Myra, the woman with whom he falls in love, marries, and has a child. In another book, falling in love with Myra would change Gene for the better. Not in this story. It so happens that the girl of Gene's dreams is a Morgan, too, and although it's never spelled out, the suggestion is that they're related—possibly cousins. Their child, Leon, is born with long-term medical problems that initially present as physical deformities, then manifest themselves as mental health issues. Eventually, Gene concludes that "Leon would never get well . . . If he lived to be twenty or thirty years old he would still be without enough sense to sit in a chair without being tied there." The doctors agree.

Myra loves Leon and thinks the doctors will take him away and kill him. It's her great fear, because "I love him more than anything else in the world, next to you, Gene." But Myra's looking in the wrong place. It's not the doctors she should fear. A true bastard to the end, Gene takes his son out to the park, finds a quiet spot by the river, and drowns him.

He knows Myra will suffer, and feels sorry for her, repeatedly saying "poor kid" to himself as he watches her shadow in the window from the street outside their house before he leaves for good. Gene thinks of his final act of infanticide as one of kindness. He knows Myra won't cope on her own with Leon, and he's definitely going to leave her, so in his twisted mind, Gene's making life easier for her. "Now she won't have to bother all the time about the kid. Hell, the poor kid'd died if she'd stayed up in that damn flat much longer—never going to no more movies or nothing. Hell, I guess I done right."

There's a hint of self-doubt in that last sentence, and there's the fleeting possibility of redemption as he circles the block where Myra lives one more time. But it's never realized and Gene remains true to character, the quintessential antihero, a bastard to the end.

Allan Guthrie is an award-winning Scottish crime writer. His debut novel, Two-Way Split, *was short-listed for the CWA Debut Dagger Award and went on to win the Theakstons Crime Novel of the Year. He is the author of four other novels,* Kiss Her Goodbye *(nominated for an Edgar),* Hard Man, Savage Night, *and* Slammer, *and three novellas,* Kill Clock, Killing Mum, *and* Bye Bye Baby, *a Top Ten Kindle best seller. He's also cofounder of a digital publishing company, Blasted Heath, and a literary agent with Jenny Brown Associates. Visit him online at www.allanguthrie.co.uk.*

The Maltese Falcon
by Dashiell Hammett (1930)

MARK BILLINGHAM

Dashiell Hammett (1894–1961) was an American novelist, short-story writer, and political activist. Born in Maryland, he worked at various jobs before taking up a role as an operative at the Pinkerton National Detective Agency, which provided the inspiration for much of his writing. He is widely regarded as the father of the modern American mystery, and his five novels, published in the space of five years between 1929 and 1934, are classics of the genre. For the final thirty years of his life he was involved in a relationship with the playwright Lillian Hellman. He died of lung cancer following a lifetime of heavy smoking and drinking, his body further weakened by tuberculosis and the aftereffects of imprisonment for his political beliefs.

"Let's talk about the black bird . . ."

I had read Sherlock Holmes at school, and also discovered popular fiction in the form of *The Godfather* and *Jaws*, but when I saw John Huston's film of *The Maltese Falcon*, and found a Picador edition of Hammett's *Four Great Novels*, everything came together.

Though not even Hammett's favorite of his novels, *The Maltese Falcon* has been routinely described as the greatest mystery novel ever written. Eighty-two years on from its first publication, its importance as the novel that kick-started the hard-boiled movement—and its influence on Chandler, Macdonald, and the rest—is hard to dispute. I would suggest, however, that its reputation rests on far more than the place it rightly holds in the history of the genre.

Simply put, it is a great novel, as well as being a significant one.

I have always had issues with the phrase "mystery fiction"—the term routinely used in the United States to describe what we in the U.K.

would call "crime fiction." It certainly seems inadequate when taking into consideration much that has been written in that genre from the second half of the twentieth century onward, when a good many of the greatest "mystery" novels would stake no claim to being mysteries at all. That is to say, the "mysterious" element, where there is one—typically the "whodunit," of course—is far from being the most important aspect of the book.

The Maltese Falcon, however, is the book that for me most perfectly fits the mold of the mystery novel. Indeed, with his third novel, and most especially with its protagonist, Sam Spade, Hammett could be said to have created the mold in the first place, and—if I might be allowed to stretch the analogy to breaking point—to have smashed the damn thing to pieces once it was finished.

The central mystery lies not in the novel's byzantine plot. The falcon itself is the most famous MacGuffin in literature, and Spade's involvement with those searching for it is no more than a means to an end. He falls in with Brigid O'Shaughnessy, Casper Gutman, and Joel Cairo, feigning an interest in the falcon and playing these three off against one another for no reason other than to apprehend his partner's killer.

Doesn't he?

There is, of course, at least one other interpretation of Spade's actions, and it is the way in which Hammett leaves readers to schematize the character's consciousness, to decide for themselves his true motivations, that creates a mystery far more complex and absorbing than a killer's identity or the whereabouts of an ancient artifact.

The reader can only guess what Spade is thinking as he walks the streets after visiting the scene of the murder of his partner, Miles Archer, or beds Brigid O'Shaughnessy. The reader has only Spade's words and his seemingly calm, precise actions on which to base any theory. In his earlier advertising days, Hammett had written about this technique, which he called meiosis.

> It is a rhetorical trick, the employment of understatement, not to deceive, but to increase the impression made . . .

Hammett had learned early on that "less is more," and uses that knowledge to supreme effect throughout the novel. The characterization is as pared down as the prose, revealed solely through dialogue alone.

The action is used sparingly and is all the more effective for it, and of the three murders that take place in the course of the narrative, only one death—that of Captain Jacoby—is shown. Though guns are brandished often enough, the conflict is created for the most part through the machinations of the novel's major characters, each of whom seems willing to do almost anything to lay a hand on the elusive falcon; a prize that—like those in pursuit of it—turns out to be far from what it seems.

The cast of murderers and manipulators has never been bettered. Gutman, Cairo, O'Shaughnessy, and Wilmer, the boy gunman, were all based on individuals with whom Hammett had come into contact during his time as a Pinkerton agent. O'Shaughnessy was a former client, Wilmer a criminal christened the "midget bandit," Cairo a forger, and Gutman a suspected German agent (though many have suggested he was based largely on Fatty Arbuckle, whose rape case Hammett had worked on). Only Spade himself came solely from Hammett's imagination:

> Spade has no original. He is a dream man in the sense that he is what most of the private detectives I worked with would like to have been and in their cockier moments thought they approached.

Though fixed in many people's minds as the archetypal hard-boiled detective, Hammett's "dream man" is no Chandlerian knight-errant, and neither is he Humphrey Bogart. Iconic as that performance certainly was, it is significant that, for his 1941 film adaptation, John Huston wanted George Raft for the role. Raft, known primarily for his portrayal of killers, was certainly closer to Hammett's description of a "blond Satan" than Bogart, and it is arguable that, had Huston got his first choice, Spade's motivations might have remained every bit as shifting and shadowy to moviegoers as they had been to readers.

"Your private detective," Hammett said, "wants to be a hard and shifty fellow, able . . . to get the best of anybody he comes into contact with, whether criminal, innocent by-stander or client."

Though no slouch plot-wise, Hammett was always more interested in exploring moral ambiguities, and nowhere does he do it better than through the character of Sam Spade. Hammett's trick is to allow the reader to believe that Spade *is* morally corrupt—the casually lit cigarette at the news of Archer's murder, the removal of Archer's name from the door, the affair with Archer's wife—only to reveal much later that he may not be quite as bad as he would like people (and Hammett would like us) to believe.

"Don't be too sure I'm as crooked as I'm supposed to be . . ."

Hammett's use of misdirection in this cause is masterfully done. For the vast majority of the book, the murder of Miles Archer is never mentioned, and Spade appears to focus on the pursuit of the falcon while actually searching for his partner's killer. To this end, he is willing to do whatever is necessary. This includes falling into bed with archetypal femme fatale Brigid O'Shaughnessy (though this is not to say that he does not enjoy it). As far as any doubts about O'Shaughnessy's character are concerned, Hammett uses Effie Perrine—arguably the only wholly decent character in the book—to offer what appears to be the definitive judgment. When Spade asks Effie her opinion of Brigid, Effie tells him, "I'm for her," and, from that point on, the reader is for her, too, trusting completely in Effie's judgment.

In the same way, the reader falls for the picture presented of Spade, largely by himself. We are encouraged to see Spade as unlikable at the very least, thanks to his affair with Iva Archer, his partner's wife, but even taking the period into consideration, this is hardly symptomatic of moral bankruptcy. Though keen to preserve his own somewhat dubious image, Spade goes so far as to hand over the thousand dollars he took from Gutman, which, bearing in mind the drugging and beatings he has taken, he might well have considered reasonable recompense for his pains. There are clues, of course, as to the character that Spade does his best to mask, notably when he waltzes Gutman's daughter around a hotel room in an effort to keep her alive. She is a character who really serves no other purpose in the novel than to give us a glimpse of Spade's honorable side.

Much has been said about—and perhaps too much read into—the so-called Flitcraft Parable, the digression in which Spade tells Brigid the story of a missing Tacoma real estate agent. There seems little point in adding to the weight of this analysis, save to say that for me it simply and skillfully illustrates Spade's pragmatic worldview. In a world in which chance plays an important part, he is a man who will do whatever is necessary to get the job done, however tempting it might be to "play the sap." When he finally hands Miles Archer's killer over to the authorities, he has no regrets, no second thoughts. Instead, Spade reels off seven—*seven*—good reasons why it makes sense to send the culprit to what will certainly be the death chamber.

The simplest reason of all is also the most revealing: "When a man's partner is killed, he's supposed to do something about it."

Dorothy Parker "mooned" over Spade for days after reading the novel, and while later on she would be even more love-struck by Philip Marlowe—fickle, that Algonquin mob—it was clear that his new type of detective in a new kind of novel had become instantly iconic. It is interesting to speculate as to whether, had he continued to write, Hammett would have brought back Spade in further novels. I like to believe that he would have resisted the temptation. The character had served its purpose, and Hammett was surely savvy enough to recognize—even back then—the inherent law of diminishing returns within which series characters operate. Marlowe was certainly a lot less interesting in *The Long Goodbye* than he was in *The Big Sleep*, and though Hammett's poor health robbed us of some wonderful work, we should be grateful that we were never given the chance to get inside the head of his most famous character.

Any discussion of Hammett's work would be incomplete without sufficient tribute to the prose itself. Chandler is usually held up as the more accomplished stylist, but I'm not convinced. Eighty-something years on and I think *The Maltese Falcon* holds up far better than many of the Marlowe novels, not least because the "comedy" is far blacker and more restrained. Though Spade is not the wisecracker that Marlowe would be, the fizzing, fat-free exchanges with Brigid and, most particularly, with Gutman, are beautifully structured master classes in rhythm and economy. In places, the dialogue is not a million miles away from the sort of comedy of manners being acted out across the Atlantic on West End stages, and it is tempting to wonder whether Hammett had ever read Noël Coward, whose play *Private Lives* was first performed the same year that *The Maltese Falcon* was published. Take out the guns, throw in a tennis racket and a pair of French doors . . .

Reading Hammett now, it is hard to separate the work from what we know about the man. His left-wing views and passionate devotion to the cause of civil rights are clear as day in much of his writing. Sam Spade remains unafraid and unbowed, and though physically a lot more fragile than his creation, Hammett spent much of his life showing the same refusal to yield in the face of persecution from the State Department, the IRS, and Joe McCarthy.

It is this principle, this allegiance to the underdog, hand in hand with unequaled style and the creation of a new kind of popular novel, that makes Hammett so unique and enduring.

A very different kind of radical storyteller—the Clash's Joe Strummer—chose to read *The Maltese Falcon* as he lay in the hospital recovering from hepatitis in 1978.

Hammett is also uniquely cool . . .

Raymond Chandler may have given hard-boiled detective fiction a style, but it was Hammett's ball he was running with.

Mark Billingham is one of the U.K.'s tallest and most acclaimed crime writers. His series of novels featuring DI Tom Thorne has twice won him the Theakstons Crime Novel of the Year Award, and the books have been nominated for seven CWA Daggers. His debut novel, Sleepyhead, *was chosen by the* Sunday Times *as one of the one hundred books that had shaped the decade. A television series based on the Thorne novels starred David Morrissey as Tom Thorne, and a series based on his stand-alone novel* In the Dark *is in development with the BBC. Mark Billingham's latest novels are* Rush of Blood *(U.K.) and* The Demands *(U.S.). Visit him online at www.mark billingham.com.*

The Glass Key
by Dashiell Hammett (1931)

DAVID PEACE

Dashiell Hammett (1894–1961) was an American novelist, short-story writer, and political activist. Born in Maryland, he worked at various jobs before taking up a role as an operative at the Pinkerton National Detective Agency, which provided the inspiration for much of his writing. He is widely regarded as the father of the modern American mystery, and his five novels, published in the space of five years between 1929 and 1934, are classics of the genre. For the final thirty years of his life, he was involved in a relationship with the playwright Lillian Hellman. He died of lung cancer following a lifetime of heavy smoking and drinking, his body further weakened by tuberculosis and the aftereffects of his imprisonment for his political beliefs.

In February 1931, in New York City, Dashiell Hammett was thirty-six years old and had published three novels. *The Maltese Falcon*, his third novel, had been described as "the best American detective story yet written" and had been reprinted seven times in 1930. In February 1931, in New York City, Dashiell Hammett was a success. And he had waited a long time to be a success. He had practiced for it. He had prepared for it. Dashiell Hammett had left his wife and two daughters in California. He had moved to New York City. He had checked into a hotel. He had hit the city. He had painted the town red. A few shades of red. Dashiell Hammett was the Toast of the Town.

In February 1931, in New York City, Dashiell Hammett was trying to finish his fourth novel. Held back by laziness. Held back by drunkenness. Held back by illness. In February 1931, in New York City, Dashiell Hammett stopped being lazy. He stopped being drunk. He stopped being ill. In February 1931, in New York City, in one thirty-hour writing session, Dashiell Hammett finished his fourth novel. Dashiell Hammett believed his fourth novel was the best novel he had written. Dashiell Hammett believed his fourth novel was the best novel he could write. His fourth novel was *The Glass Key.*

The book begins with the roll of dice. Green dice across a green table. The narrator, in a third person, subjective voice—and that, if you care about reading, if you care about writing, matters because it is rare, because it is both objective and subjective, because it is the mark of a genius—is Ned Beaumont. Ned Beaumont drinks. Ned Beaumont gambles. Ned Beaumont fixes things—people and situations—for Paul Madvig. Paul Madvig is a politician. And like all politicians, without any exceptions, Paul Madvig is corrupt—and that, if you care about the world, is not a glib statement, that is a true statement—and the whole point of the story of the novel. That politicians are corrupt. That politics is corruption. That politicians are criminals. That politics is crime. Robbery and murder. Democracy and capitalism. Man fucks man. Man kills man. Man eats man. Because capitalism makes people greedy, because capitalism makes people selfish. Cruel and vain. In America, in anywhere. Then and now. After the Crash of 1929, before the Crash of 2008. In 1931, in 2012. In another election year. A man is murdered. The murdered man is the son of a senator. Paul Madvig is the main suspect. Ned Beaumont can either help Paul Madvig or hinder Paul Madvig. Paul Madvig wants the senator's daughter. For his ambition, for his career. Ned Beaumont wants the senator's daughter, too. Not for ambition, not for career. He has no ambition, he has no career. And the book ends with one man staring at an open door.

But *The Glass Key* is also a book about friendship. *The Glass Key* is also a book about loyalty. Friendship and loyalty. In the face of corruption, in the midst of crime. Friendship and loyalty borne from experience and trial, from witness and testimony. In *Dashiell Hammett: A Life,* Diane Johnson wrote, "In Ned Beaumont—principled, forlorn, afflicted with an uneasy worldliness and the ability to understand the meaner motives and ambitions of his friends, and tubercular—Hammett produced his nearest self-portrait." And Raymond Chandler agreed. In *The Simple Art of Murder,* Chandler wrote that *The Glass Key* was "the record of a man's devotion to a friend" and swooned that Hammett "was spare, frugal, hard-boiled, but he did over and over again what only the best writers can ever do at all. He wrote scenes that seemed never to have been written before."

But by 1944, André Gide was searching in vain for a copy of *The Glass Key*. André Malraux had especially recommended *The Glass Key* to André Gide. André Gide was desperate to read *The Glass Key*. André Gide regarded Dashiell Hammett's first novel, *Red Harvest*, as "a remarkable achievement, the last word in atrocity, cynicism and horror. Dashiell Hammett's dialogues, in which every character is trying to deceive all the others and in which the truth slowly becomes visible through the haze of deception, can be compared only with the best of Hemingway. But if I speak of Hammett, it is because I seldom hear his name mentioned . . ."

After February 1931, after New York City, Dashiell Hammett would write another book. *The Thin Man*. But after *The Thin Man*, there were no more books. No more novels. There was laziness. There was drunkenness. There was illness. And there was war. Hammett served as a sergeant in the U.S. Army. And there was politics. Hammett joined the Communist Party United States of America. Hammett became president of the Civil Rights Congress. And there was persecution. The Civil Rights Congress was designated a Communist front group. Hammett was asked for the names of contributors to a CRC bail fund. Hammett was asked for the whereabouts of CRC fugitives. But Hammett was very loyal. Hammett was a good friend. Hammett refused to rat. Hammett refused to give the names of people. Hammett took the Fifth. Hammett was found guilty of contempt of court. And so there was prison. Hammett cleaned toilets in a West Virginia penitentiary for six months. And after his release, there was still persecution. Hammett refused to cooperate with the so-called McCarthy hearings. Hammett, who had fought for the U.S. Army in two world wars, was deemed an Un-American. Hammett was blacklisted. Hammett could not work. More persecution and now poverty. The IRS hounded Hammett for back taxes. The IRS took Hammett's royalties. And then there was despair. Despair at his writing, at the failure of his writing. And despair at the world, at the failure of the world. Despair and failure. Retreat and withdrawal. Until Dashiell disappeared. Until Hammett vanished . . .

I have been asked many times over the years why he did not write another novel after *The Thin Man*. I do not know. I think, but I only think, I know a few of the reasons: he wanted to do a new kind of work; he was sick for many of those years and getting sicker. But he kept his work, and his plans for work, in angry privacy and even I would not have been answered if I had ever asked, and maybe because I never asked is why I was with him until the last day of his life . . .

—Lillian Hellman

In angry privacy, Dashiell hated the world. In angry privacy, Dashiell loved the world. And so Dashiell drank. In angry privacy. To destroy the world. And he drank. In angry privacy. To save the world. And he drank. In angry privacy. And he drank. Until there was no more world, no more world to hate or to love, to destroy or to save. In angry privacy. Until there was no more Dashiell. Only his books. But what books. And the best of those books, the very best of any books, the book every person should read at least once, and every writer at least once a month, is *The Glass Key.*

David Peace was declared one of the Best Young British Novelists by Granta in 2003. The four novels of his Red Riding Quartet were condensed into a three-part TV series broadcast by Channel 4 in 2009. He followed the quartet with GB84 *(2004), a fictional account of the miners' strikes of 1984–85, which won the James Tait Black Memorial Prize in 2005. Peace subsequently published* The Damned Utd *(2006), about Brian Clough's ill-fated tenure at Leeds United.* Tokyo: Year Zero *(2007) and* Occupied City *(2009) are the first two books of a proposed Tokyo Trilogy. David Peace currently lives in Japan.*

Have His Carcase
by Dorothy L. Sayers (1932)

REBECCA CHANCE

Dorothy Leigh Sayers (1893–1957) was born in Oxford, England, where her father was headmaster of Christ Church Cathedral School. She took modern languages and medieval literature at Somerville College, Oxford, and in 1923 published her first novel, Whose Body?, *which introduced her most enduring creation, the anxious, flawed amateur sleuth Lord Peter Wimsey. Sayers is one of the most important writers of the Golden Age of mystery writing. She tested and stretched the boundaries of the genre, touching on issues of morality and justice (both human and divine) and the nature of the academic and literary lives, and experimenting with parody and social commentary, most often through the character of Harriet Vane, Lord Peter's love interest, who is, like her creator, an Oxford scholar and a wealthy author. Her ambitions for the genre drew harsh criticism, most memorably from the American critic Edmund Wilson, who castigated her in the course of a 1945* New Yorker *essay titled "Who Cares Who Killed Roger Ackroyd?" Wilson commented of Sayers that "she does not write very well: it is simply that she is more consciously literary than most of the other detective-story writers and that she thus attracts attention in a field which is mostly on a sub-literary level," a stance that probably made Wilson few friends in the genre. Later in life, Sayers, a devout Anglican, turned her attention to a translation of Dante's* Divine Comedy, *a project on which she was still working when she died.*

Intrepidly hiking the British coast on a "solitary walking tour . . . dressed sensibly in a short skirt and thin sweater" and carrying "a pocket edition of *Tristram Shandy,* a vest-pocket camera, a small first-aid outfit and a sandwich lunch," Harriet Vane stumbles (as one does) across the corpse

of a young man whose throat has very recently been slit, blood still drip-
ping from the gaping wound. On hearing this news from his old contact,
Salcombe Hardy of the *Morning Star* (as befits a journalist, Hardy is an
old soak with "drowned-violet eyes"), Lord Peter Wimsey jumps in his
Daimler, Mrs. Merdle, and speeds off to investigate. The younger son
of a duke, extremely rich in his own right, Lord Peter is a very talented
amateur detective, and has already saved Harriet from being found guilty
of murder once in the novel *Strong Poison,* falling in love with her in the
process; now he's riding to her rescue again, realizing that she's bound to
be suspected of this crime as well.

In *Strong Poison,* Harriet was behind bars for the entire novel. Now
she's free to help in the investigation, and one of the great pleasures
of the book is the fast-witted, Nick-and-Nora-style flirtation between
her and Lord Peter. Watch them go as Harriet is tasked with becoming
acquainted, for detective purposes, with the "professional dancers" at
the Hotel Resplendent in Wilvercombe, the seaside town where she is
staying:

> "I'll have to get a decent frock, if there is such a thing in Wil-
> vercombe."
>
> "Well, get a wine-coloured one then. I've always wanted to
> see you in wine colour. It suits people with honey-coloured skin.
> (What an ugly word 'skin' is.) 'Blossoms of the honey-sweet
> and honey-coloured menuphar'—I always have a quotation for
> everything—it saves original thinking."
>
> "Blast the man!" said Harriet, left abruptly alone in the blue-
> plush lounge. Then she suddenly ran out down the steps and
> leapt upon the Daimler's running board.
>
> "Port or sherry?" she demanded.
>
> "What?" said Wimsey, taken aback.
>
> "The frock—port or sherry?"
>
> "Claret," said Wimsey. "Château Margaux 1893 or there-
> abouts. I'm not particular to a year or two."
>
> He raised his hat and slipped in the clutch.

I always wonder, on reading this passage, what kind of sherry could
conceivably be considered "wine-coloured": but, that question apart,

this kind of high-flown banter is much harder to pull off than it seems. Many writers in the 1930s and 1940s were attempting arch, apparently effortless repartee, larded with quotations and metaphors, but only Sayers's novels met the challenge successfully. She can move effortlessly between high comedy—the locals Harriet meets while trying desperately to report the murder, or the nervous hiker keen to hide behind her skirts—delicious social observation, and moments of great poignancy. Mrs. Weldon, the widow whose considerable fortune is at the center of the plot, is first considered by Harriet a "predatory hag," but this harsh, misogynistic judgment softens into a sympathetic portrait of the lonely rich women and impoverished gigolos who meet on the dance floor of the grand ballroom at the Hotel Resplendent. The professional dancer Antoine—"rather surprisingly, neither Jew nor South American dago, nor Central European mongrel, but French"—is the character with whom Harriet feels most at ease, and poor Mrs. Weldon, vulnerable and fragile, easily exploited, turns out to be prey rather than predator.

As well as the considerable pleasures of its writing and characters, *Have His Carcase* is also an excellent example of the enjoyment readers derive from the sight of an author working her way through meticulous research, and presenting the results to us so entertainingly that we become utterly absorbed in the most minute of details. In *The Nine Tailors*, for instance, Sayers presents us with campanology; in *Five Red Herrings*, with train timetables and ticketing; while *Have His Carcase* requires her detectives to decipher both tide tables and a fiendishly complicated secret code.

And it is a more well-rounded novel, in my opinion, than either *The Nine Tailors* or *Five Red Herrings*. There's a reason that the detective novels in which Harriet Vane appears are generally the readers' favorites in Sayers's canon: her presence humanizes Lord Peter, makes him vulnerable, and, mercifully, balances out Sayers's compulsion to continually demonstrate how very much better-educated and sportingly superior he is to absolutely everyone else around him. There is a heroic act of derring-do in this novel, as he canters, bareback, across the sands of the beach on which the body was discovered, only for the mare he's riding to come close to throwing him quite unexpectedly. Of course, Lord Peter, who can steer his Daimler around curves like a racing driver, dive off the top of fountains without breaking his neck, and disable opponents with cunning jujitsu holds, is more than a match for a startled, bucking mare: but not even this dashing feat can persuade Harriet to accept his proposal.

> "REFUSE RESEMBLE THRILLER HERO WHO HANGS ROUND HEROINE TO NEGLECT OF DUTY BUT WILL YOU MARRY ME," he telegrams to Harriet, who answers:
> "GOOD HUNTING CERTAINLY NOT SOME DEVELOPMENTS HERE."

It's a salutary reminder that there is something that the powerful combination of Lord Peter's money, education, charm, aristocratic manners, and oenophilic skills can't buy. His quest to win Harriet is reminiscent of that of his friend Freddy Arbuthnot, in love with Rachel Levy, whose mother disapproves of the match between Christian and Jew; Freddy finally wins round Lady Levy by quoting from Genesis, saying that, like Jacob, he'd "served seven years for Rachel." We don't know with certainty how long Lord Peter has to wait for Harriet, but by the time she finally agrees to marry him, he has proved to her that she'll be entering into an equal partnership, and one of the delights of *Have His Carcase* is watching that partnership begin to take shape.

However, the detection, in this novel, is still paramount. The Lord Peter/Harriet books that follow this one, including *Gaudy Night* and *Busman's Honeymoon,* focus increasingly on their relationship and, in due course, their marriage; I, for one, would have liked a few more Sayers novels set in this halcyon period—halcyon for the reader, if not for Lord Peter—where the solving of a crime has more weight than the sexual tension between the two main characters. They are, after all, detective novels first and foremost, and Sayers was at her sharpest when she constructed the plot of *Have His Carcase:* it turns on a superbly simple medical twist that, as in all the best crime fiction, is signaled all the way through but that the reader fails to see.

The solution is revealed on page 440 (in my edition), and a mere four more pages afterward, the book has ended. As Lord Peter would say, once you know "how," you know "who." As is customary with Sayers, the murderer and the motive have been clear for at least half the book; her novels aren't whodunits, but howdunits. And, as is also customary with

Sayers, the novel ends with Lord Peter promptly and bitterly regretting his crucial part in bringing a murderer to justice. The words on which he closes the book are:

> "Well, isn't that a damned awful, bitter, bloody farce? . . . God, what a jape! King Death has asses' ears with a vengeance . . . Let's clear out of this. Get your things packed and leave your address with the police and come on up to town. I'm fed to the back teeth . . . We'll go home. We'll dine in Piccadilly. Damn it! . . . I always did hate watering places!"

Readers may well roll their eyes at this display of Lord Peter's highly refined sensitivities, especially when combined with a side comment on his plans for dinner; but Harriet—less patrician, more practical—has already pointed out that the murderer, if not convicted, will kill again, and she's perfectly right. Though one applauds Sayers's wish to demonstrate that catching killers is not simply an intellectual flexing of wits, but has real, brutal consequences when the death penalty awaits convicted murderers, the hypersensitivity with which she endowed Lord Peter can be wearying. His heightened nerves are partially attributed to shell shock, but his valet Bunter, who, after all, was Lord Peter's batman, enduring the same war as his master, has no similar symptoms—aristocratic nerves being presumably more delicate than working-class ones.

Lord Peter is such a powerful creation that the later variations on this sensitive, cerebral, privileged archetype—Roderick "Handsome" Alleyn, baronet's son and art appreciator; Adam Dalgleish, dark, brooding poet; Thomas Lynley, the eighth Earl of Asherton—all owe a great debt to Sayers, as do the stolid, loyal, working-class sidekicks who usually accompany the heroes. Imitation may be the highest form of flattery, but it rarely outdoes the original, and certainly not in Sayers's case; she was the mistress of her genre, and her writing is unparalleled, clever, sharp, strewn with literary allusions, and endlessly rereadable.

"There is something about virgin sand which arouses all the worst instincts of the detective-story writer," she observes at the start of *Have His Carcase*. "One feels an irresistible impulse to go and make footprints all over it."

But even when her books are no longer virgin sand, when we know exactly where the footprints are leading, the pleasure we derive from reading them is almost as acute as on first reading; more so, perhaps. As with all the great crime novels, you come for the plot but you stay for the writing and the characters, and Sayers provides both in rich abundance.

———

Rebecca Chance is a pen name of Lauren Henderson, who, under her own name, writes elsewhere in this volume on Agatha Christie's Endless Night. *As Rebecca Chance, Lauren has written the racy, crime-themed bonkbusters* Divas, Bad Girls, Bad Sisters, *and* Killer Heels, *to be followed by* Bad Angels *before the end of 2012. They are published by Simon & Schuster. Visit her online at www.rebeccachance.co.uk.*

The Holy Terror
(aka *The Saint v. Scotland Yard*)
by Leslie Charteris (1932)

DAVID DOWNING

Before becoming a full-time writer, the Singapore-born Leslie Charles Bowyer-Yin (1907–93) held a variety of jobs: tin miner, pearl diver, gold prospector, and carny. His first novel, X Esquire, *was published in 1927, while Charteris was still at Kings College in Cambridge; his third, and the first Saint novel,* Meet the Tiger, *appeared in 1928. Charteris wrote short stories, novellas, and novels featuring the Saint for the next thirty-five years, with ghostwriters subsequently penning Saint stories under his editorial supervision. During the 1940s, Charteris also wrote for the Sherlock Holmes radio series starring Basil Rathbone. The TV series* The Saint, *starring Roger Moore, ran from 1962 to 1969; the series was revived, with Ian Ogilvy in the lead role, in the late 1970s.*

Those readers encountering the early Saint books after watching the 1960s TV series must have had rather a shock. They were probably few in number, because Roger Moore's portrayal of Simon Templar, and the story lines the studio gave him, effectively gutted the character of everything that made him special. The written Saint was lithe and volcanic, with an absurdist sense of humor, not beefy, impassive, and given to dry quips. The written Saint was first and foremost a rebel, yet the TV series served up in the rebellious 1960s was somehow drained of all subversive content.

The Holy Terror (1932) was the eighth of thirty-four Saint books that Charteris wrote between 1928 and 1963 (there were another sixteen "collaborative efforts" over the next twenty years, of uneven but inferior quality). Eleven were full-length novels, twelve contained two or three novellas, and the remaining eleven—including the last nine—were collections of short stories. *The Holy Terror* comprises three novellas: *The Inland Revenue*, *The Million Pound Day*, and *The Melancholy Journey of Mr. Teal.*

The Inland Revenue entwines two story lines. The Saint has received a tax bill after writing a successful adventure novel, and as the story begins he discovers that his reason for refusing payment—that he's beneficial to the community, and should therefore qualify for tax-free status as a charitable institution—has been rejected. Someone will have to pay, he concedes, impaling the demand on his mantelpiece. The chosen donor is a blackmailer called The Scorpion, whom he's recently encountered while shaking down a dope-dealing club owner.

The story contains several of Charteris's imaginative set pieces: the unexpected arrival of a real scorpion in the post, an attempted live burial, an armchair that gases anyone who sits in it. The Scorpion, one Wilfred Garniman from suburban Harrow, is a classic Charteris villain—methodical, dispassionate, utterly cold. Even without the penchant for gas, he reads like a stark premonition of Himmler and Co., and, almost needless to say, turns out to be the Inland Revenue inspector responsible for the original tax demand. After throwing Garniman's office desk at him, the Saint turns him over to Chief Inspector Teal, the rotund and usually hapless policeman who features in most of the U.K.-set books.

Teal has a harder time in the other two stories. There's no doubting which side of the law the Saint inhabits in either of these, and the detective suffers accordingly. Nor is there any mistaking what makes the Saint tick: a personal sense of justice that only sporadically chimes with legality, and an endless yearning for excitement. If he also gets richer in the process, so much the nicer, but the money's more a measure of success than an end in itself.

The Million Pound Day opens with another wonderful set piece. Having spent most of the night driving up from Cornwall, the Saint is dozing in a lay-by outside Basingstoke when a terrible scream pierces the dawn. A few seconds later a running man bursts out of the early-morning mist and collapses in our hero's arms. He is swiftly followed by a gigantic negro in bare feet, wearing only a loincloth, "the gleaming surfaces of his tremendous chest" shifting "rhythmically to the mighty movements of his breathing." A dreadful stereotype, of course, but by the standards of the time, not a vicious one. Charteris had seen a lot of the (white-ruled) world before taking up his pen, and always seemed less inclined to prejudice than most of his literary contemporaries. In *The Inland Revenue* he gives the Saint's own novel a South American hero named Mario, and then sends him a letter from a spluttering bigot, accusing him of "Dago" ancestry.

The Million Pound Day has the usual extravagant plot—in postwar years they grew cleverer but less memorable—and the usual quota of splendid one-liners. The villain Kuzela meets his end in typical Charteris fashion. Early in the story, he tries to kill the Saint by sending him a glove containing a sliver of wood coated in nerve poison, and the Saint eventually returns the compliment, enticing the villain into opening a spring-loaded matchbox containing the sliver. There is no question of self-defense. This is an execution, one of many that the Saint happily carries out in his prewar career. In *The Last Hero* (aka *The Saint Closes the Case*) he shoots a scientist who refuses to suppress a weapon he has invented; in "The Death Penalty" he frames one drug dealer for the murder of another, and sends him to the gallows. In *The Saint in New York*, he stands in front of gangster Morrie Ualino, calmly tells him he's there to kill him, and rips him open from stomach to breastbone—hardly the behavior of the usual Hollywood hero.

In this and other respects, the Saint's 1930s persona actually feels much more contemporary than the 1960s TV version, like a cross between Che Guevara and the Clint Eastwood characters of that time. In one story, "The Wonderful War," he even succeeds where Guevara later failed, overthrowing a Latin American government almost single-handedly.

The Million Pound Day ends with Teal frustrated, and the detective's hunger for revenge underpins the third novella. *The Melancholy Journey of Mr. Teal* is a semicomic tale of stolen diamonds, which the Saint wants to steal from the original thieves, and features a more-nuanced-than-usual look at the hero. Halfway through the story, the Saint tells Teal that he has been paying money into the detective's bank account, and will destroy his career with accusations of corruption if denied a free pass. Now, there's nothing nasty about Teal, and even Patricia Holm, the Saint's long-term girlfriend, is disgusted by this maneuver.

The couple made a joint debut in the very first novel, and she appears in a good proportion of the next twenty-five. They obviously share a bed, although this is never spelled out. She's not an artistic foil like Wimsey's

Harriet Vane, Alleyn's Agatha Troy, or Grant's Marta Hallard, but a highly effective partner in crime. And she's not the only one. Women like Audrey Perowne in "The Lawless Lady," Loretta Page in *Saint Overboard*, and Jill Trelawney in *She Was a Lady* are fully capable of living by their strength, nerve, and wits—the last book was even retitled *The Saint Meets His Match*. Neurotic or empty-headed females are, by contrast, in surprisingly short supply. When, at the end of *Melancholy Journey*, the Saint offers Pat his vision of their future—"racketing around the world, doing everything that's utterly and gloriously mad—swaggering, swashbuckling, singing—showing all these dreary dogs what can be done with life"—she simply cries back: "I'm ready for it all!"

He has already redeemed himself by handing Teal a notebook with enough detailed intelligence on criminal operations to guarantee a promotion. *Melancholy Journey* ends in characteristic fashion; the Saint catches up with the first thief, obtains and puts on the trousers with the sewn-in diamonds, and locks the man in the trunk of a fellow passenger—a prudish spinster named Lovedew. Having labeled the trunk with Teal's name, he introduces the detective to Miss Lovedew— "Mr Claud Eustace Teal, who is going to tell us about his wanderings in Northern Euthanasia . . ."—before slipping away with the boodle.

In most respects, *The Holy Terror* is a typical Saint book, but in one— the nature of his enemies—it is not. The Saint spent a lot of time fighting and fleecing traditional criminals, but a large part of his appeal lay in his willingness to take on those whom the law could not, and mention should be made of one such story. "The Sleepless Knight" was included in *Boodle* (aka *The Saint Intervenes*), which was published in 1934, two years after *The Holy Terror* and smack in the middle of the Great Depression. It begins, as several Saint stories do, with the hero reading a newspaper article. This one concerns the charging of a lorry driver with manslaughter after he's run down and killed a cyclist; his defense is that he was ordered—on pain of dismissal and unemployment—to drive more hours than anyone could safely manage. The judge acquits the driver and notes in passing that it should have been the company's owner, Sir Melvin Flager, standing there in the dock. But the fat cat, having done nothing illegal, is beyond punishment.

The Saint decides otherwise. He kidnaps Sir Melvin, straps him to the wheel of a driving simulator for two days and nights, and flogs him each time his imaginary vehicle slips off the imaginary road.

It's now eighty years since the first Saint book was published, and of course they're showing their age. But beautifully constructed plots are always that, and the Saint's trademark blend of murderous idealism still seems remarkably relevant to the world in which we live. Neither toffs nor criminals have grown any less venal, and a contemporary Holy Terror would certainly be spoiled for choice when it came to potential adversaries. A modern-day Saint would no doubt cross swords with al-Qaeda and the Russian mafia, but he would also find time for the odd merchant banker.

———————

*David Downing is the author of the Station series set in Berlin before, during, and after World War II. He has also written other novels (*The Red Eagles*), two works of "faction" (*The Moscow Option *and* Russian Revolution 1985), and many books on military history, rock music, cinema, and the history of football. A Londoner, he has also lived in the United States, and traveled extensively in Europe, Asia, and Latin America. He is currently developing a new series of novels set before, during, and after World War I.*

Fast One
by Paul Cain (1933)

CHUCK HOGAN

Paul Cain was the pseudonym of George Carol Sims (1902–66), the son of a police detective, who wrote seventeen short stories for Black Mask *magazine and one novel, the seminal title* Fast One, *which was published in 1933. Sims had some success in Hollywood as a screenwriter during the 1930s, writing under the pseudonym Peter Ruric. A collection of Paul Cain's short stories,* Seven Slayers, *was published in 1950.*

Raymond Chandler famously called *Fast One* "some kind of high point in the ultra hard-boiled manner."

Chandler's first detective story appeared in *Black Mask* magazine in December 1933, the same year that *Fast One*—originally serialized over five issues the previous year—was published. His quote is always cited as praise, but one can just as easily envision this failed-oil-executive-turned-aspiring-pulp-writer reading Cain's breakneck tale and wondering, "What is left for me?"

Black Mask editor Joseph "Cap" Shaw paid his top authors three cents a word, while demanding they squeeze a nickel's worth out of each one. By 1932, Dashiell Hammett's naturalistic detective fiction had defined and elevated the *Black Mask* style well beyond its crude beginnings, and Shaw wisely made the magazine conform to the ex–Pinkerton operative's image. Later, Chandler would take hard-boiled prose on a long left turn into booze-soaked romanticism, before dropping it off at the cul-de-sac of parody.

Paul Cain (never to be confused with *The Postman Always Rings Twice* author James M. Cain) is the missing link between these two genre godfathers. He represents not a transitional phase, but a hard stop between two distinct styles. Cain took the Hammett ethos and, with the zeal of a mad disciple, followed it all the way to the end. Whereas Hammett was in the practice of giving readers a little more than they wanted (pathos, depth), Cain gave his Depression-era readers *exactly* what they wanted, times a factor of ten.

On October 29, 1933, the *New York Times* reviewed the novel under the headline "Gangsters Gone Mad": "It is in truth a ceaseless welter of bloodshed and frenzy, a sustained bedlam of killing and fiendishness." Also: sadism, malaise, anarchy.

If pulp fiction is the id of literature, then *Fast One* is the id of the id.

> Kells walked north on Spring. At Fifth he turned west, walked two blocks, turned into a small cigar store. He nodded to the squat bald man behind the counter and went through the ground-glass-paneled door into a large and bare back room.

To sum up the first paragraph: a guy runs errands through a creative lack of punctuation and omitted words. The least enticing opening in history? Perhaps in terms of content.

But what this opening paragraph does achieve is an immediate sense of urgency. Perpetual motion is the hallmark of *Fast One,* and one of its many pleasures. Notice that Cain makes no effort to engage the reader. There is no pretense of seduction, of meeting the book buyer halfway. The story and its main character are in midstride before your eyes hit the page. You hop on board *Fast One* like a passing streetcar, only to have it blow through stop after stop, speeding toward the inevitable crash at the end of the line.

The plot—the tale of a man caught between two warring gangs, who is framed for murder—shares elements with Hammett's *Red Harvest.* Gerry Kells is a neutral gambler who wants to be left alone, but he soon realizes that true freedom can be won only through the destruction of these two oppressive forces. So he plays "the middle against both ends," finding that his only chance for survival lies in taking over the rackets himself.

The story is oneiric and surreal, full of betrayals, double crosses, and ambushes. The violence is unrelenting, a tour de force veering into madness. To modern eyes, *Fast One*'s existentialism is inescapable. Like his characters, Cain breaks rules, cutting words for effect and often setting off dialogue lines with colons rather than commas. To wit:

> Kells said: "Uh huh."

The colon makes you stop. It gives the line an extra pause, a kick. You adjust to it quickly, and these bumps become part of the tempo, part of the cadence. The staccato rhythm gulls you into a trance, and things happen in the story that are beyond logic, but by then you are dreaming and the dream is a free fall toward death.

Fast One, Paul Cain's only novel, stands high above the rest of the so-called two-fisted tales of the era because Cain takes the form that Hammett and Shaw established and does something with it: he drives it straight off a cliff.

> She jerked the wheel suddenly, hard, screamed between clenched teeth.
> Kells felt the beginning of the skid; he looked outward, forward into blackness. They were in space, falling sidewise into blackness; there was grinding, tearing, crashing sound. Falling. Black.

Fast One embraces this distinctly American genre so completely that it obliterates it. No one else ever wrote a book like this.

Chuck Hogan is the New York Times *best-selling author of several acclaimed novels, including* Devils in Exile *and* Prince of Thieves, *which was awarded the Hammett Prize for "literary excellence in the field of crime writing," and was adapted into the film* The Town, *directed by and starring Ben Affleck, Jeremy Renner, and Jon Hamm. He is also the coauthor, with Oscar-winning filmmaker Guillermo del Toro (*Pan's Labyrinth*), of the international best-selling* Strain Trilogy, *published in twenty-nine languages. His nonfiction has appeared in the* New York Times *and* ESPN The Magazine, *and his short fiction has twice been anthologized in* The Best American Mystery Stories *annual.*

The Postman Always Rings Twice
by James M. Cain (1934)

JOSEPH FINDER

One of a trio of writers, alongside Dashiell Hammett and Raymond Chandler, credited with creating the hard-boiled novel, James M. Cain (1892–1977) first worked as a journalist before establishing his reputation as an author. Early novels such as The Postman Always Rings Twice *(1934),* Mildred Pierce *(1941), and* Double Indemnity *(1943, but originally published in serial form in* Liberty Magazine *in 1936) were notable for their spare prose, authentic dialogue, and dubious morality—the latter, presumably, prompting Raymond Chandler to dismiss Cain as "a Proust in greasy overalls, a dirty little boy with a piece of chalk and a board fence and nobody looking." A long-lost manuscript of Cain's,* The Cocktail Waitress, *was published in 2012 by Hard Case Crime.*

James M. Cain never understood why he was so often labeled a hard-boiled writer. "I don't know what they're talking about," he said. "I tried to write as people talk." He wasn't referring to his dialogue but his style, his narrative voice. When his first novel, *The Postman Always Rings Twice,* came out in 1934, that very style—plainspoken, colloquial, vernacular, whatever you want to call it—was so arrestingly different that it changed the course of crime fiction.

If you haven't yet read it, or haven't read it in a while, you'll be surprised at how well it holds up. The prose is lean and spare, completely stripped of ornamentation or affectation. It reads like the confession that it reveals itself to be. Cain, the son of a college president and professor who always corrected his grammar, claimed that his biggest literary influence was a bricklayer named Ike with whom he spent a lot of time as a kid. Cain had a good ear, and was captivated by the way that regular guys talked. At the age of forty, having been a reasonably successful journalist and editor, he moved to California, where he became an unsuccessful screenwriter. But there he had a lucky break: he discovered an entirely different kind of regular-guy speech, that of the "Western roughneck" who "has been to high school, completes his sentences, and uses reasonably good grammar." Suddenly, Cain had found his voice, or at least the voice he wanted to use to tell his stories. There was never anything arch or artsy or self-consciously clever about it. It was oral, not floral. No one in Cain's fiction is "as inconspicuous as a tarantula on a slice of angel food" (to quote Raymond Chandler's memorable description of Moose Malloy from *Farewell, My Lovely*).

Then there was the "ragged right margin" he loved so much, another of his innovations. Long stretches of *Postman* are made up of nothing but dialogue, without the *he said* and *she said*. Cain got rid of most of the tedious, repetitive identifiers, figuring that if he did his job right, the reader would know who was talking. If it weren't for Cain, we wouldn't have had Elmore Leonard or Robert B. Parker.

Postman is the story of an unemployed drifter in southern California named Frank Chambers, who falls in love, or at least in lust, with Cora Papadakis, a ruthlessly ambitious Iowa girl married to the Greek American owner of a gas station/roadside diner. The two of them conspire to kill her husband and make it look like an accident.

The story launches you out of the silo from its famous opening line: "They threw me off the hay truck about noon."

And then it accelerates from there.

The novel is barely a hundred pages long. Cain worked hard to distill it to its essence, pruning eighty thousand words until he ended up with a lean, taut manuscript of thirty-five thousand words. His publisher, Alfred A. Knopf, initially rejected it on the grounds that it was too short, pointing out that Cain's contract stipulated a novel of at least forty thousand words. But that was only a pretext. The truth was that Mr. Knopf disliked what he called its "rough, impromptu style" and published it only after considerable arm-twisting by his wife, Blanche, and Cain's mentor and friend, the journalist Walter Lippmann.

Cain was a flop in Hollywood, but his indentured servitude to the movie studios wasn't wasted. It taught him pacing, momentum, and what he liked to call the "algebra" of story construction. ("Suspense comes from making sure your algebra is right," he once said. "Time is your only critic. If your algebra is right, if the progression is logical, but still surprising, it keeps.")

A fellow screenwriter told him about a narrative technique called the "love rack." This has never been satisfactorily defined, but it seems to refer to the dramatic situation in which a couple find themselves when they fall in love. One day Cain had a brainstorm: why not make the *entire plot* a "love rack"? What would happen if "a couple of jerks" discovered that a murder could be a love story, too, only to realize that two people can't live with such a secret?

Inspired by the famous 1920s trial of a woman who convinced her corset-salesman boyfriend to murder her rich husband for the insurance money by making it look like the consequence of a burglary—and who then tried to kill the boyfriend—*Postman* was a huge, immediate best seller. It was also banned in Boston and in Canada, and was notorious for its steaminess, its kinky mixture of sex and violence. Even today, eight decades later, it's strong stuff. When Frank first sees Cora, he observes that "she really wasn't any ravaging beauty, but she had a sulky look to her, and her lips stuck out in a way that made me want to mash them in for her." They kiss, and then "I sank my teeth into her lips so deep I could feel the blood spurt into my mouth." When the two of them are staging the scene to make it look like a car accident, Cora tells him to tear her blouse. "Rip me! Rip me!" she says.

> I ripped her. I shoved my hand in her blouse and jerked. She was wide open, from her throat to her belly . . . I hauled off and hit her in the eye as hard as I could. She went down. She was right down there at my feet, her eyes shining, her breasts trembling, drawn up in tight points, and pointing right up at me.

We're in the head of an amoral, homicidal loser, and we find ourselves actually rooting for him to succeed. There are no sympathetic characters here. Everything rides on the propulsion, the momentum of the narrative, the elegant ironies of the ending.

The Postman Always Rings Twice inspired Albert Camus's existential novel *The Stranger*. It gave birth to an entire genre: noir, both in fiction and in cinema, and inspired countless imitators. It's one of only two crime thrillers on the Modern Library's list of the 100 Best Novels

(Dashiell Hammett's *The Maltese Falcon* is the other). But what's most impressive is how, some eighty years later, James Cain's lean, mean first novel still works. It still thrills; it still enthralls. He got the algebra right.

Joseph Finder is the New York Times *best-selling author of ten novels, including* Buried Secrets, *the second novel to feature "private spy" Nick Heller;* Killer Instinct, *winner of the Thriller for Best Novel; and* Paranoia, *now in development as a major motion picture. His first novel,* The Moscow Club, *was named by* Publishers Weekly *as one of the ten best spy novels of all time. A summa cum laude graduate of Yale, Joe did graduate work at Harvard's Russian Research Center. He lives in Boston with his wife, their teenaged daughter, and a neurotic golden retriever. Visit him online at www.joseph finder.com.*

Murder on the Orient Express
(aka *Murder on the Calais Coach*)
by Agatha Christie (1934)

KELLI STANLEY

The peerless doyenne of the mystery novel's Golden Age, the hugely pro-lific Dame Agatha Christie (1890–1976) wrote eighty mystery novels and short-story collections and nineteen plays, and is heralded as the best-selling novelist of all time by the Guinness Book of Records, *her sales ranking third behind those of the Bible and William Shakespeare. Her best-known creations include Hercule Poirot and Miss Marple, while her play* The Mousetrap, *which first opened in 1952, is still running in 2012 after more than twenty-four thousand performances. She also wrote under the pen name Mary Westmacott. Agatha Christie was the first recipient of the Mystery Writers of America Grand Master Award, and she was made a Dame Commander of the Most Excellent Order of the British Empire in 1971.*

Agatha Christie is not only the best-selling mystery writer of all time, but also one of the most successful writers in any genre. Her career spanned the greater part of the twentieth century, and she is still as popular in the twenty-first. Her most famous protagonists, the Belgian ex–police detective Hercule Poirot and the elderly spinster Jane Marple, are as entrenched in popular culture as Christie herself, the author who argu-ably crystallized the image of the traditional mystery and the traditional (female) mystery writer.

Yet Christie—the undisputed Queen of Crime—is often critically dismissed and pigeonholed by her own phenomenal success. She's too often overlooked as an innovator and too often taken for granted as a "cozy" author, as if murder were nothing more than a pair of fuzzy slippers and a crossword puzzle.

Let me set the record straight, at least as I see it. I write a tough-as-nails female private investigator modeled on the classic hard-boiled and noir traditions of Chandler, Hammett, and Cain, with a good dose of film noir influence thrown in for good measure. Yet Christie has also provided surprisingly strong inspiration for my work.

I've read everything: from her novels and short stories and romances (written as Mary Westmacott) to her autobiography. Nancy Drew may have been my initiation into the crime-fiction genre, and Sherlock Holmes nursed me along, but it was Agatha Christie—not Raymond Chandler or Dashiell Hammett—who first showed me the dark side.

Far from the feel-good Christie image, the books and stories reveal a woman who, early in the development of psychiatry, wrote compelling and disturbing profiles of criminality; who could write from the point of view of the killer before it became the fashion for thrillers du jour; and who could write about evil and call it evil, and knew that it lurked not just on the mean streets of London but along the cobblestones of St. Mary Mead.

Christie's grasp of psychology enthralled me. Her best novels are examples of superb psychological suspense mixed with the baroque ingenuity of the drawing room mystery. Hercule Poirot's "little gray cells" are as adept at therapy as they are at deduction . . . and Miss Jane Marple, the delightful, white-haired, and eternally knitting spinster, evinces a vast knowledge of human behavior based on profiling the population of her tiny, timeless village. She blinks at nothing.

Move over, Clarice Starling.

Dame Agatha, a properly brought-up middle-class Victorian, mingled her interest in psychology with daring, push-the-envelope twists no one had ever before attempted. Her plots can be audacious—so much so, in fact, that they seem to revel in their own meta-textuality, a ballsy sort of acknowledgment and challenge to the reader that this is one puzzle and puzzle maker they will never outwit.

Granted, her reliance on the surprise ending, and the sheer improbability of some of the solutions, earned Christie the ire of my favorite crime-fiction writer and strongest personal influence, Raymond Chandler. In his essay "The Simple Art of Murder," Chandler takes the English traditional mystery in general to task, and Christie and *Murder on the Orient Express* in particular.

Chandler describes the ending of *Murder on the Orient Express* as one that "only a halfwit" could guess. He goes on to suggest that Christie and other writers of the school produced better plots than this one, before finally damning them all by concluding: "There may be one somewhere that would really stand up under close scrutiny. It would be fun to read it, even if I did have to go back to page 47 and refresh my memory about exactly what time the second gardener potted the prize-winning tea-rose begonia . . ."

He does, of course, have a point. Though there are as many tropes and contrivances in hard-boiled fiction as there are in traditional mysteries (and Chandler himself was notoriously weak on plot structure), his real bête noire is setting. For him, murder properly took place in the back alley. For Christie, it took place in estate libraries, in art deco apartments, on luxury liners, and in first-class train compartments. Chandler, who himself had been raised in England, preferred the realistic school of Hammett and Hemingway, though, ironically, the essence of his own enormous contribution to the genre was the insertion of a cynical, world-weary romanticism in the private eye. Romanticism also runs through the stories of his best English compatriots in crime, Christie included.

In 1934, when *Murder on the Orient Express* first saw print, "The Simple Art of Murder" was still sixteen years ahead. Hammett published his last novel that year; Chandler's first, *The Big Sleep,* wouldn't line discriminating bookshelves until five years later.

So why *Murder on the Orient Express*? Why did Chandler single it out for attack and why do I consider it one of Christie's very best?

To begin with, literature needs to be examined within its own time and context. Chandler and Christie have both been slavishly imitated, over and beyond the point of parody. But just as Chandler was the first detective writer to lyrically fuse the private eye to the Romantic knight-errant, Christie was often the first to come up with solutions and puzzles that pushed past the typical plot twists.

By the time Chandler penned his famous essay, Christie's penchant for surprise endings had become as entrenched and imitated as a PI in a dingy office, and Chandler chose *Murder on the Orient Express* as the most egregious offender, offering, as it does, an exotic, upper-class setting with a large cast of characters trapped on a snowbound train, and a tour-de-force solution to the murder. The ending—and I won't spoil it for those who haven't enjoyed the book or the spectacular 1974 film adaptation—is one that the reader never even considers. As she did with *The Murder of Roger Ackroyd* (1926), Dame Agatha spins a yarn that seems to violate the "rules."

But *Murder on the Orient Express* is far more than a logic problem, a cryptogram to be worked out to the tenth degree like an exercise in calculus. I first read the novel when I was about twelve and have reread it many times since. As a child I was able to completely enjoy the surprise. On subsequent rereadings, however, what lingered more than the intellectual and literary delight of such a neat solution was the notion of justice and law and criminality that Christie evoked.

Published in the same year as James M. Cain's seminal *The Postman Always Rings Twice, Murder on the Orient Express* allows us a glimpse of a darker world, one in which the moral integrity of a private detective—even Hercule Poirot—can be compromised.

As in some of her best work—*And Then There Were None* (1939), for example—she draws compelling psychological portraits of guilt and innocence, self-righteousness and self-doubt. If you read these two novels back to back, you'll see how she tackles a similar situation as in *Murder on the Orient Express* and arrives at an even darker, noir-ish conclusion. Of course, by 1939 the winds of war were blowing across the Devon moors, and the idea of guilt, crime, judgment, and punishment raised in the earlier novel sparks a rather different response, with Monsieur Poirot nowhere to be found.

One of my favorite motifs in Christie is her love of masks and masquerades. Her use of this theme could be quite complex, even in her early work (the odd little short stories featuring Mr. Harley Quinn, for example), and she exploits it brilliantly in *Murder on the Orient Express*.

Perhaps the deepest mask of all is the one that this brilliant writer wears in critical circles; she is far too commercially successful to be taken seriously, and the darkness that permeates her best books—the darkness that allowed her to write of the evil in everyone, from children to apple-cheeked old murderesses, the darkness of real pain and real crime and real death—has been covered up in the popular imagination with a thick woolen blanket and drowned by a weak cup of tea.

The "cozy" disguise does Christie a great disservice. Make no mistake. Agatha Christie, like many a Victorian before her, was one hard-boiled Dame.

Kelli Stanley lives in Hammett's San Francisco, where she writes the Miranda Corbie series, the first of which, City of Dragons, *won the Macavity Award for Best Historical Mystery and was short-listed for the* Los Angeles Times Book Prize, *the Shamus Award, the Bruce Alexander Award, and the Reviewer's Choice Award.* City of Secrets *is the sequel;* City of Ghosts *is forthcoming. Her Miranda Corbie short story "Children's Day" was published in the ITW best seller* First Thrills, *while "Memory Book" is available as an e-story from Macmillan. Kelli writes a second series set in ancient Rome, the latest of which is* The Curse-Maker. Nox Dormienda, *her debut novel, won the Bruce Alexander Award. Visit her online at www.kellistanley.com.*

Rebecca
by Daphne du Maurier (1938)

MINETTE WALTERS

Dame Daphne du Maurier (1907–89) was a British author and play-wright. A native of Cornwall, she made the county the setting for many of her books, including probably the best known, Rebecca. *A reclusive woman who was born into a famously theatrical and artistic family, her work has provided the inspiration for a number of films, including Nicolas Roeg's* Don't Look Now *and Alfred Hitchcock's* The Birds.

First published in 1938, *Rebecca* is Daphne du Maurier's most enduring and best-known novel. It's never been out of print, has had numerous adaptations in television, radio, and theater, and was turned into a memorable Oscar-winning film noir (1940), directed by Alfred Hitchcock and starring Laurence Olivier and Joan Fontaine.

Rebecca tells the story of a shy young woman (unnamed throughout the book) who becomes the second wife of widowed Maxim de Winter. Their marriage is a hurried, rather furtive affair, and the new bride learns very quickly that her husband is still obsessed with her predecessor. When she finally arrives at Manderley, his estate in Cornwall, she discovers the house unchanged since Rebecca's death. Memories of the woman are everywhere, pointing up painful comparisons with her timid replacement. Rebecca was everything that her successor is not—beautiful, witty, sophisticated, adored, and admired—and the second Mrs. de Winter develops as much of a fixation on her as Maxim has.

At the time of its publication, *Rebecca* was promoted as a gothic romance—"an exquisite love story . . . with an atmosphere of suspense"—with no hint of the sordid little murder at the heart of the story. Indeed the murder was considered so shocking by Hollywood that it was removed entirely from the film adaptation. The rigid Motion Picture Production Code, which sought to apply moral censorship to movies from 1930–68, meant that Hitchcock had to make Rebecca's death an accident. It was acceptable in dramatic terms for a husband to dislike his wife, but quite unacceptable for him to shoot her through the heart and walk away scot-free.

In view of the anodyne phrases that the publishers used to promote the novel, they, too, may have had reservations about du Maurier's plot. To describe *Rebecca* as "an exquisite love story" is to ignore the fact that Maxim's unexpected attraction to his second wife is subsumed and eaten up by his loathing of his first. Rebecca haunts every page of the novel. Her presence is more strongly felt than anyone else's—including the narrator's—and it's only when the reader learns how she died that Maxim's guilty obsession is explained.

Feminist interpretations of this story look to unearth the dual sides of du Maurier's nature in her depiction of the two Mrs. de Winters— confident extrovert against self-questioning introvert—but I suspect that the character who most closely resembles her is Maxim. He is a reserved man of simple tastes who dislikes the pretense and artifice of high society; he is deeply attached to his house, Manderley, and the beautiful landscape of Cornwall that surrounds it; he is proud of his family name, and he does what he does to protect its honor.

The same traits were apparent in du Maurier. Many of her novels are set against the backdrop of Cornwall, where she lived, and she was fiercely proud of both her maiden name and her married name of Browning—her husband was Lieutenant General Sir Frederick "Boy" Browning, commander of the 1st Airborne Division. I don't doubt that she had great affection for Rebecca—most authors prefer to write flawed and twisted characters—and indeed for her unnamed narrator, the second Mrs. de Winter—who sets out with cold deliberation to help her husband escape the consequences of what he's done—but I see more of du Maurier's wit and humor in Maxim. She would have taken a mischievous enjoyment, I think, from writing herself as a successful murderer.

The cleverness of the story lies in the narrator's naïveté. The second Mrs. de Winter's perceptions of her predecessor are skewed because she lacks the one detail that would explain why Maxim is haunted by memories of Rebecca. Until the murder is revealed, it makes sense to her, and to the reader, that he adored her. Why would he not? Rebecca was the perfect wife, and the perfect mistress of Manderley.

The narrator is also cursed with an overactive imagination, causing her to embroider compelling fantasies around Rebecca from the mementos she left behind. For the majority of the book she lives in Rebecca's shadow, unable to compete on any level with her vibrant rival; and it is only when she understands the reality of the dead woman—explained to her by Maxim in the hours before Rebecca's body is discovered—that she begins to assert herself.

As a novel, *Rebecca* can be read on any level. Du Maurier's prose and mastery of plot confirm it as one of the great classics, but the page-turning suspense, which made it a runaway best seller when it was first published, also confirms its status as a consummate psychological thriller. For those who see Daphne du Maurier as a romantic author, the book ticks every box in the developing *Jane Eyre*-love between the older Maxim and his younger second wife. For crime buffs, it is one of the few murder stories where the voice of the victim resonates loudly on every page, playing not only with the minds of the other characters but also with the reader's.

My own views of Rebecca—just as du Maurier intended—are thoroughly ambivalent. She is the quintessential psychopath—cruel, manipulative, sexually demanding, egotistic, uncaring of anyone else's feelings—but I admire the courage she shows in the moments before her death, and the loyalty she inspired in the handful of people she loved. The most notable of these is Mrs. Danvers, the Manderley housekeeper, who protects Rebecca's memory with all the jealousy of a lover.

Du Maurier's handling of her three main characters shows an extraordinary grasp of psychology at a time when the science was still young. Her artistry lies in her slow revealing of Rebecca's nature, and her unnamed narrator's stumbling journey from ignorance to knowledge. Du Maurier seemed to have a natural understanding of human frailties, and a natural ability to write those frailties into her characters, creating a set of people with distinct and rounded personalities who are as true and valid today as they were in 1938.

Rebecca is a rare and brilliant murder story. It stands alone as an example of how a psychological thriller can, and should, be written.

Minette Walters has published twelve full-length novels since 1992. Specializing in psychological thrillers, and eschewing recurring series characters, she has won every major mystery award, including the Edgar and CWA Gold Dagger, and her work has been translated into more than thirty-five languages. Many of her novels are set in her adopted county of Dorset, and several have been adapted for television. Visit her online at www.minette walters.co.uk.

Brighton Rock
by Graham Greene (1938)

PETER JAMES

Graham Greene (1904–91) famously, or infamously, described his novels of suspense and mystery as "entertainments," a categorization he abandoned in the latter stages of his career. First published with The Man Within *(1929), Greene's reputation as one of Britain's finest writers of the twentieth century rests on novels such as* Brighton Rock *(1938),* The Power and the Glory *(1940),* The Heart of the Matter *(1948),* The Third Man *(1949), and* Our Man in Havana *(1958). Greene was awarded the James Tait Black Memorial Prize in 1948 for* The Heart of the Matter. *In 1986 he was awarded the Order of the British Empire.*

Graham Greene's *Brighton Rock* is, very simply, the book that changed my life. When I first read it at the age of fourteen, as a kid growing up in Brighton, I knew the moment I put it down that I wanted to be a writer, too. I promised myself that, one day, I, too, would try to write a novel set in Brighton, and hoped that it would be even 10 percent as good as *Brighton Rock* . . . As a gentle homage, I created a villain called Spicer in my Roy Grace novel *Dead Like You.*

I'd been addicted to crime novels from a very early age, especially Conan Doyle and Agatha Christie, yet until *Brighton Rock* it seemed to me that the British crime novel was all about the ingenious solving of a complex puzzle, but little more. A body would be discovered early on, frequently in the first chapter, and the rest of the narrative was about the detective hero finding, and ultimately confronting and arresting, the perpetrator. Graham Greene threw the rulebook out of the window. This was the first crime thriller I read that dealt with the inner lives of the villains, and made them the central characters. It truly broke new ground, and is a big influence on the way that I write my Roy Grace crime novels today.

I was hooked by the first line, surely one of the most attention-grabbing opening sentences ever: "Hale knew, before he had been in Brighton three hours, that they meant to murder him." I defy anyone, having read that, to put the book down! It made me realize just how important the first sentence of a book is. I think of that line every time I start a new book, and try to come up with one that is as grabbing. And it is not just that first sentence, either: *Brighton Rock* has an equally strong last line, devastatingly clever and extremely dark. It makes you put the book down with your spine tingling, your imagination soaring.

Greene captures so vividly the dark side of Brighton and Hove, and in many ways his writing is as relevant now as when the book was first written. As a teenager growing up there, I was scarily aware of the criminal undertow that permeated every street and every passageway. There were certain crime families whose names brought a shiver. Historically, they had terrorized the place with their protection rackets, their nascent violence, their weapons, their sheer impunity. In the 1930s the police, it seemed, were powerless and irrelevant to Greene's chilling wise guys.

And yet, far more than being just an incredibly tense thriller, Greene uses this novel to explore big themes of religious faith, love, and honor. As a bonus, it is also unique for being one of the few novels where the original film adaptation, with Richard Attenborough playing Pinkie, is so good that it complements rather than reduces the book.

The characters are wonderfully human, deeply flawed, and tragic. The story is told almost entirely through the eyes of the villains and two women, the garrulous tart with a heart Ida and the dim, fervent Rose: "She . . . was about to mutter her quick 'Our Fathers' and 'Hail Marys' while she dressed, when she remembered again . . . What was the good of praying now? She'd finished with all that: she had chosen her side: if they damned him they'd got to damn her, too."

Pinkie is a masterly creation who, in my view, rates alongside the great villains of fiction, a teenaged gangster who sees his chance to seize control of the gang of much older, more experienced men. A cunning, nasty, ruthless killer he may be, yet one thing haunts him: the fear of eternal damnation from the Catholic faith he cannot shake off. You loathe him but you are mesmerized by him, and at times you even feel sympathy toward him.

What I have always loved about Graham Greene's writing, in all his books, is that he has a way of describing characters, in just a few sentences, that makes you feel you know them inside out and have probably met them. The one thing that makes any novel compelling is the characters created by the author; if they are people about whom you care enough, you would stay with them while they read three hundred pages of the phone directory out aloud. Graham Greene is one of the grand masters of this. Within a few brushstroke lines he makes you feel you would recognize a character walking down the street. Look at flawed but vivid Ida: "Life was sunlight on brass bedposts, Ruby port, the leap of the heart when the outsider you have backed passes the post . . . Death shocked her, life was so important."

The big bonus for me is the palpable sense of place conveyed by Greene, who was not a native of Brighton. I strive for this in my Roy Grace novels. The city of Brighton and Hove is as much a character as are Roy Grace and his team. I have a theory that the common denominator between all the most vibrant cities of the world is a dark undertow of criminal activity. In the U.K. we have plenty of pleasant seaside resorts, but only one has global iconic status: Brighton, for seventy years blessed—or cursed—with the unwelcome soubriquet of "Crime Capital of the UK." Graham Greene put it on the criminal map. I guess I'm doing my best to keep it there . . .

Peter James is best known for his series of Roy Grace police procedurals, which are set in Brighton on England's south coast. The first, Dead Simple, *was published in 2005; the most recent is* Not Dead Yet *(2012). James made his debut in 1981 with the stand-alone title* Dead Letter Drop. *In total, he has published twenty-six titles, with a collection of short stories to be published in 2013. Peter James won the Krimi-Blitz Award for Best Crime Writer in Germany in 2005, and the Prix Polar in 2006. He won the Crime Novel of the Year Award in the ITV3 Crime Thriller Awards 2011. Visit him online at www.peterjames.com.*

Too Many Cooks
by Rex Stout (1938)

ARLENE HUNT

Rex Stout (1886–1975) wrote serials for various magazines for more than fifteen years before publishing his first novel, How Like a God, *in 1929. After writing a political thriller called* The President Vanishes *(1934), he published* Fer-de-Lance *(1934), his first novel in the Nero Wolfe series, all of which are narrated by Wolfe's assistant, Archie Goodwin. Stout's prodigious output included novels, novellas, and nonseries novels, with forty-seven titles in the Nero Wolfe series. Stout was awarded the Silver Dagger by the Crime Writers' Association for* The Father Hunt *in 1959, while the Nero Wolfe corpus was declared Best Mystery Series of the Century at Bouchercon in 2000. In 1959, Rex Stout received the Mystery Writers of America Grand Master Award.*

Over the course of his career, Rex Stout wrote more than forty stories based around the character of Nero Wolfe, world-class detective, and his sidekick, Archie Goodwin. *Too Many Cooks* is the fifth novel in the series and was first published in 1938.

Nero Wolfe is fifty-six. He has brown wavy hair and weighs, according to Archie, one seventh of a ton (although that rises to well over three hundred pounds in some books). Mercurial, verbose, usually unflappable—unless hungry, or a woman threatens tears—Nero Wolfe is a highly sought-after detective, gourmand, orchard fancier, and virtual shut-in. He is a man who guards his privacy and his daily routine with remarkable audacity, so much so that it's something of a marvel the great detective ever gets a lick of work done. Had he no need for the vast sums of money required to run his household, it is doubtful that he would ever task himself with the whims of the hoi polloi. Even when he has accepted a commission, he generally treats his clients with barely contained contempt. Nero is difficult and peevish at times, but he is loyal and steadfast when committed. He is also a genius—a lazy genius, but a genius nonetheless.

Archie Goodwin, Nero's assistant and foil, lives with Nero at his New York brownstone on West Thirty-fifth Street, New York. Archie is in his early thirties. He's handsome, debonair, witty, an excellent dancer, and an all-round good egg—as long as you stay polite around him. All Nero Wolfe stories are told from Archie's perspective, and I feel that it is he and not Nero who is the true heart of the novels as he races round doing his better's bidding, usually in a quite clueless manner, breaking hearts and the occasional jaw in the process.

I think it is fair to say that the relationship between Nero Wolfe and Archie Goodwin is complicated. Indeed, Nero explains this to Archie in one of the books: "You are headstrong and I am *magisterial.* Our tolerance of each other is a constantly recurring miracle." But this yin and yang of detection is central to the novels for, without Archie, Nero could not function, and without Nero, Archie would be all at sea, redundant. Their bickering and verbal swordplay do not detract from their mutual respect, and dare I say it, their mutual affection.

Though I am incredibly fond of all the Nero Wolfe novels, I chose *Too Many Cooks* for two reasons. Firstly, the great Nero, siderodromophobic and loath to travel, is forced, due to circumstance, to leave his brownstone and travel by train to West Virginia. Secondly, Nero, peevish and stubborn as ever, needs to be shot and wounded in order to engage his prodigious brain.

Too Many Cooks opens with a twitchy, nervous Archie Goodwin, pacing a railway station platform, smoking. He says:

> I lit a cigarette with the feeling that after it had calmed my nerves a little I would be prepared to move the Pyramid of Cheops from Egypt to the top of the Empire State Building with my bare hands, in a swimming-suit; after what I had just gone through.

Thus, we learn Nero has accepted an invitation to deliver the keynote address at the gathering of *Les Quinze Maîtres* (the Fifteen Masters, a group of renowned chefs), being held at the Kanawha Spa in West Virginia.

Attending the gathering are Marko Vukcic, Nero's longtime friend and a fellow Montenegrin, and Jerome Berin, a man who has long with-held a recipe for sausage that Nero desperately wants. Archie is along for the ride and spends a great deal of his time making googly eyes at Miss Berin, Jerome's very young and very beautiful daughter.

Phillip Laszio, a much-reviled man of questionable standing in the group, now married to Marko's ex-wife, is also at Kanawha, and it is he who initiates a "friendly" competition whereby the collected gourmands must guess the ingredients of various sauces. Unfortunately, between these courses of haute cuisine, Laszio is found murdered, with a serving knife wedged deep in his back. The police are called: everyone is a suspect.

Nero himself shows little interest in the dead man, and longs only to return to New York; or at least he feels that way right up until the moment someone tries to shoot him through a window. After that, rancor and pride set in motion what cold-blooded murder could not, and with relish Nero turns his formidable attention to uncovering the culprit.

I should say something about the language of *Too Many Cooks*. The novel is written in 1938, a time of great upheaval in American history, and some of the attitudes found in its pages might jar heavily with the modern reader. The servants of the spa are mostly African American men, and are spoken to and treated in a highly racist manner by the local police and some of the characters. They are referred to as *boys, niggers,* and *shines.* One of the guests has a Chinese wife, and she, too, is given short shrift.

Happily, though Stout does not shy away from displaying many of the prevalent attitudes of the time, Nero has other ideas on how to talk to the assembled servants, some of whom are openly hostile to his intrusion:

> That's what I mean when I say I've had limited experience in dealing with black men. I mean black Americans. Many years ago I handled some affairs with dark-skinned people in Egypt and Arabia and Algiers, but of course that has nothing to do with you. You gentlemen are Americans, much more completely than I am, for I wasn't born here. This is your native country. It was you and your brothers, black and white, who let me come here to live, and I am grateful to you for it.

By treating the men with dignity and respect he opens the door for a frank discussion, and through this unearths a vital clue that ultimately leads him to uncover the killer.

Too Many Cooks is an excellent whodunit, rich in language, absorbingly detailed, yet never lacking pace. Nero's circuitous route to the truth is seldom obvious and never dull.

Finally, a word of warning: do not read *Too Many Cooks* while hungry. As Nero is a gourmand, many of Stout's novels are filled with luscious descriptions of food, and *Too Many Cooks* is no exception. Trust me on this: a rumbling stomach will only distract you from the entertainment.

Arlene Hunt is the author of seven crime-fiction novels, five of which feature the popular QuicK Investigation duo, John Quigley and Sarah Kenny. She is also the co-owner of Portnoy Publishing. She lived in Barcelona for five years and now resides in Dublin. Her books have been translated into three languages, and her current novel, The Chosen, *a stand-alone set in the United States, was voted TV3's Book of the Month for November 2011. An earlier novel,* Undertow (2008), *was short-listed for best crime novel at the Irish Book Awards. Arlene has also contributed to many anthologies, including* Down These Green Streets, Requiems for the Departed, *and* Console. *Visit her online at www.arlenehunt.com.*

Rogue Male
by Geoffrey Household (1939)

CHARLAINE HARRIS

The author of almost thirty novels and seven collections of short stories, Geoffrey Household (1900–88) graduated from Oxford with a BA in English literature and served with British Intelligence during World War II. The author of novels for adults and young adults, he is best known for the thriller Rogue Male *(1939), which was filmed twice, first as* Manhunt *(1941) and later as* Rogue Male, *starring Peter O'Toole, in 1976.*

I could have picked any one of three books by Geoffrey Household as the novel I think everyone should read. He's that good, and his books are still fresh despite the passage of time and the passing of the social structure about which he wrote. *Dance of the Dwarves* and *Watcher in the Shadows* would have been equally good choices—both of them are suspenseful, even terrifying—but *Rogue Male* is an essential novel for any serious reader in the mystery and thriller genres.

In 1939, Geoffrey Household published a book that became the template for many, many books to follow. Household's unnamed protagonist is a well-known and definitely upper-class Englishman. His name is recognizable. He's a notable hunter and a fine shot. And he makes an abysmal mistake.

In his short, spare narrative, Household hits the ground running, almost literally. The protagonist is caught by security forces as he's aiming a rifle at a dictator (not named, but clearly Hitler) while the dictator is standing on the terrace of his country home. Our Englishman underestimates the guard's sharp instincts, and this error in judgment leads to his capture.

During his interrogation, the Englishman maintains that he was simply motivated by the sport of seeing if he could get close enough to the dictator to make the shot, and he sticks to his story. Our hero is tortured, but he manages to escape, and despite his grievous wounds and lack of transportation, he makes his way back to England. There he slowly realizes that he cannot surface and resume his life. His own government cannot accept him, either, since that would imply approval of his act. And the dictator's agents are baying at his heels.

The Englishman concludes that he must hide from everyone, not just his pursuers. So he makes his painful way to an area of the country that he knows and loves, though we don't learn the true reason for this until later. There he establishes a burrow—literally, a hole in the ground—to live in until the pursuit dies down. He's had to kill one man in London, and he doesn't want to kill more.

But he's still being tracked, and by someone who's as good a hunter as he is—the fake Englishman who calls himself Major Quive-Smith.

There are so many interesting points to consider in *Rogue Male* that it's hard to know where to start. First, the character of the protagonist—he's a man's man. He's not much of a talker, he's matter-of-fact about the seamier sides of life, and he has a hard time admitting his true motives and emotions, even to himself, despite his evident intelligence. He loves the outdoors, he loves shooting, and he has a thorough knowledge of the English countryside and the English character. He's a detailed observer, which makes his decisions more informed. He has a strong sense of right and wrong and of the obligations of class. He's a strategist.

If I were to mention every spy, secret agent, or action hero who exhibited these same characteristics, it would be a long, long, list: Quiller, Jason Bourne, and a strange combination of Claude Lebel and the Jackal from Frederick Forsyth's justly famous novel *The Day of the Jackal*. I could make a case for the nameless stranger in the Clint Eastwood spaghetti Westerns as being a brother under the skin to Household's rogue male.

It's obvious that the laconic but thoughtful hero hit a powerful nerve in the mind of readers everywhere. And why not? He's dangerous, brave, resourceful, informed, and fit. He has huge reserves of physical endurance and a practical fund of knowledge that never seems to be exhausted.

Emotionally, however, he isn't so educated. The most interesting part of *Rogue Male* comes close to the end of the book when the protagonist, through the journal he's been keeping, admits to himself that he would have pulled the trigger on the dictator. He may have pretended to himself that he was stalking the dictator simply to see if he could get close enough to make the shot, and he may have pretended to his captors that he had no intention of going through with the assassination, but neither of those things is true.

Why? As we learn when he's running for shelter from his pursuers in England, he's lost the woman he loved. Furthermore, as he reveals to us bit by bit, she has been shot as a direct result of the dictator's policies. When he first mentions the woman, he denies he was truly in love. As he comes closer to the truth of himself and his own motivations, he admits that he's been deceiving himself in a massive way. In the terrible confinement of his self-built burrow under the ground, now sealed by enemies waiting outside, this forces our hero to turn inward.

Yet with all these revelations, the shocker that propels the final action of the book is not the death of the hero's fiancée, but the shooting of Asmodeus, a feral cat befriended by the hero over the course of his sojourn in the burrow. The murder of Asmodeus, and the careless tossing of the cat's body down into the burrow, has a galvanic effect on the suffering hero. It's through Asmodeus's death that the hero reclaims his life. Asmodeus's body provides the materials to effect revenge for his murder, and the rage and guilt the hero feels provide the impetus to devise a plan to confound his enemy, the bogus Major Quive-Smith.

It's the hero's own personal code of honor that is triggered by the shooting of the animal. The cat was befriended by him, and tamed (to some extent) by him. It's his fault that the cat approached Major Quive-Smith, our hero reasons, since the hero has taught him that men who keep still are men who have food. It's interesting to speculate what kind of turn *Rogue Male* might have taken if Asmodeus had lived.

This remarkable book, written so long ago, has clearly provided a blueprint for the action hero ever since its great success when it was originally published. If elements seem familiar to the modern reader, it's because Household's tight, tense narrative showed subsequent writers how the job should be done.

Charlaine Harris, New York Times best-selling author, is a voracious reader. She had a hard time picking which book to write about for this collection.

Her most recent novel is the twelfth in the Sookie Stackhouse series, Dead-locked, *and she's edited five anthologies with her buddy Toni L. P. Kelner. This year's anthology is* An Apple for the Creature. *In 2013, the first install-ment of the graphic novel she's writing with Christopher Golden,* Cemetery Girl, *will be on the shelves. Visit her online at www.charlaineharris.com.*

Farewell, My Lovely
by Raymond Chandler (1940)

JOE R. LANSDALE

Raymond Chandler (1888–1959) turned to writing crime fiction at the relatively advanced age of forty-four, publishing short stories with "pulp" magazines such as Black Mask. *His first novel,* The Big Sleep, *was published in 1939 and featured the private detective Philip Marlowe. In total, Chandler published seven novels, all of which featured Marlowe. He also worked as a screenwriter in Hollywood, adapting James M. Cain's* Double Indemnity *(1944) with director Billy Wilder, and adapting Patricia Highsmith's* Strangers on a Train *(1951) for Alfred Hitchcock.* The Blue Dahlia *(1946) was Chandler's only original screenplay; it was nominated for an Academy Award, as was* Double Indemnity. *Chandler's final novel,* Playback, *was published in 1958. His essay "The Simple Art of Murder," first published in the* Atlantic Monthly *in 1944, is regarded as a seminal piece of criticism on crime fiction.*

Interestingly enough, I came to detective fiction seriously, and to Raymond Chandler, and finally to *Farewell, My Lovely*, by the route of science fiction.

I'll come back to that.

I grew up on comic books and superheroes, and by the end of the 1950s, even though I was young, I was beginning to read widely in adult books. I read some crime and detective stuff—Poe, Sherlock Holmes, that kind of thing—and loved it, but the stuff I wanted was stories like *The Maltese Falcon, Double Indemnity, The Postman Always Rings Twice, The Big Sleep*, and their likes, only I didn't know it yet. At that point that kind of story was known to me only through films on the upstart medium of television, not books, and man did I like those films. Shadows and tough guys, squealing tires, gunfire and cigarette smoke, blond babes so sexy they could make a eunuch weep.

When I was young, I wasn't checking to see who wrote what. That came a little later. But I loved those films, and I loved science fiction, and in the early 1970s I fell in love with the first-person novels of a science-fiction writer named Keith Laumer. Most of his third-person material left me cold. I have always preferred first-person narration to any other kind. Hadn't I been weaned on Edgar Rice Burroughs's first-person tales about John Carter of Mars? Burroughs, and Twain's *Huckleberry Finn,* had left a unique and profound impression on me, almost like a wound, and the blade that cut me deepest was first-person narration because I could more easily get into the mind of the main characters, and learn and experience events as they did. Later, *To Kill a Mockingbird* did the same for me, and so on and so on.

I read third-person narration, and liked it plenty, but there was always for me a kind of magic in that "I'm telling the story as it happened" approach, or its close cousin "This is the story that was told to me."

Keith Laumer wrote beautifully in the first person. His books, like *A Trace of Memory* and *A Plague of Demons,* had this snappy style that reminded me of those old films I'd loved. I had come to realize, by this time, that those films were often based on books, but I had never read any of them, so I didn't quite realize that Keith Laumer's favorite writer was Raymond Chandler, and his style was heavily influenced by Chandler's.

And then Laumer wrote a crime novel. I found it in paperback. It was called *Fat Chance.* It had been made into a movie. I don't think the movie was called the same thing. It starred Michael Caine, and I saw it years later and didn't think much of it. But the book, it knocked me dead. The people in it spoke like people I knew, right down to the marvelous similes and metaphors. My father, who couldn't read or write until late in life, and then only enough to kind of dope out the newspaper, comics, and maybe a simple story, talked like that when he talked. He was full of witty sayings and turns of phrase. I think this may have been passed down by generations of storytellers, handed from him to me.

So it was familiar. The characters seemed more like real people. *Fat Chance* was a bit of a parody, though I didn't know it at the time, but the most important thing about that book, with its private detective,

Joe Shaw (obviously named after the famous *Black Mask* editor), was its dedication.

It was dedicated to Raymond Chandler.

The name rang a distant bell, but though I was uncertain where I had seen the name, I knew this: if *Fat Chance* was dedicated to the memory of a long-gone writer and I had enjoyed it, then there was a good chance that I should check out Raymond Chandler, see what he was all about.

There must have been something in the air, because then, like magic, looking through a spin rack at a college bookstore, a paperback jumped out at me: *The Big Sleep* by Raymond Chandler. I thought, Wow, that's the guy in Laumer's dedication. I took it home and read it and was hooked.

Those days were different from now. You couldn't hop on the Internet and find all the books that you wanted by an author. You had to hunt for them. But in this case, it wasn't hard. Chandler's books started to pop up all over; a renaissance was going on, and I didn't even know it.

Suffice it to say I found *Farewell, My Lovely,* and later the rest of his books, but when I read *Farewell,* I went from being a fanatic for his writing to being a superfanatic. For several years I slavishly imitated him, and his work led me to read other prominent detective and mystery writers. I found a number of them whom I loved. Dashiell Hammett, and James M. Cain, all the old Gold Medal crime writers, but Chandler, oh my goodness, he was high wonderful. It wasn't just the story and the characters, it was the language, all oiled up and sassy like a sports car with a naked model in it, one long, feminine leg propped on the dashboard as she drove, the other flat down solid on the gas. I felt such kinship to his writing, and in many ways to Marlowe himself, that it was eerie. I liked that Marlowe was a knight in a savage land, as the old *Have Gun—Will Travel* song went.

Meanwhile I was sending out the Chandler imitations I was writing. I remember one called "Set Up" that went to *Mike Shayne Mystery Magazine.* I tried to get that sense of mystery Chandler had about everything. He has been criticized for not writing clockwork mysteries, but it was just this element that appealed to me. Chandler once suggested that he wanted to write the kind of mysteries that someone would read even if they knew the last page was torn out. He did just that. It wasn't just the mystery that pulled you along. It was the characters and the language.

But my story, "Set Up," was more of an unintentional parody of

Chandler, and the editor told me as much, but he thought it was good enough that I should send him something else. I revised the story and sent it to him, and he wrote back saying it was better, and then I punished him with it again and again until he said, "I hate this story more each time I see it."

In time I did sell to Sam—several stories—but I did it by a constant rereading of Chandler, trying to understand his method, which seemed to be: write the best scene and dialogue possible between people and keep about your work an air of mystery and suspense, and it won't matter if all the gears click together at the end. It's the scenes that matter, and if you have enough good ones, the reader will forgive you anything.

If there is one novel of Chandler's that does it all, it's *Farewell, My Lovely*. The mystery is in some ways a little far-fetched, but the delight of Chandler's prose, his tremendous set pieces, powerful and witty dialogue, and magnificent descriptions raise it above thousands of stories about dead people in the parlor where it's all solved in the end as if it were a crossword puzzle. *Farewell* takes Chandler's hero, Marlowe, through a dark world of murder and corruption, of fine-looking women of low circumstances seeking a grip on the good life. There's a crime and a lie rooted in the past as well, something that would later become a staple for hard-boiled writers, Ross Macdonald being one of the most obvious of that group.

Farewell, My Lovely literally changed my life. I never ceased to love science fiction, but this wonderful crime stuff led me out of the more primitive kinds of science fiction that I had been reading into a world where real people did real things and for real reasons, and not just to satisfy plot motivations. It was, as Chandler suggested in his great essay "The Simple Art of Murder," about giving crime back to those who really commit it. His work is poetic grit: magic sweated up in a rumpled suit, a poorly creased fedora, and a gravy-stained tie. It is about people who seem like people I know or knew, even if my people were rural and Chandler's were not. But they had the same motivations, needs and desires, strengths and weaknesses, savagely driven by their dreams beyond all reason; heading for what seemed like a beautiful sunset, instead they were driving pedal to the metal toward an alluring flame licking up from a wide and deep trash pit into which they would tumble, a cheap little hell of disappointment and misplaced ambitions.

All of Chandler's books moved me in one way or another, but I believe *Farewell, My Lovely* was Chandler at his peak. Not even his more lauded *The Long Goodbye* could capture the delight this book gave me in feeling that, by reading it, I had somehow touched some great truth that I could nearly hold in my hand, but not quite. That's because it is myth, and myth is truth felt but not understood. Myth is the locked house that holds our hopes and dreams.

And Chandler gave me the key.

Joe R. Lansdale is the author of more than forty novels in a variety of genres, including mystery/crime, adventure, Western, and horror. Among the many prizes he has won are an Edgar Award (in 2000, for The Bottoms*), a Booklist Editor's Award, the American Mystery Award, the Horror Critics Award, the "Shot in the Dark" International Crime Writers' Award, and the Critics' Choice Award. He has also won eight Bram Stoker Awards. He is best known, in mystery/crime terms, for his "Hap and Leonard" series of novels, of which there have been ten to date. Joe R. Lansdale is also a member of the Martial Arts Hall of Fame. Visit him online at www.joerlansdale.com.*

Hangover Square
by Patrick Hamilton (1941)

LAURA WILSON

Patrick Hamilton (1904–62) was an English novelist and playwright with an instinctive empathy for the poor and the underprivileged, due in no small part to the difficulty of his own upbringing. (Although his father and mother were both published authors, his father squandered his inheritance, and Hamilton was forced to leave formal education at fifteen.) He worked as an actor and stage manager, and then as a stenographer, before publishing his first novel, Monday Morning, *in 1925. He fell in love with alcohol at an early age—he was a man "who needed whiskey like a car needed petrol"—and died of drink-related organ failure.*

Patrick Hamilton was described by J. B. Priestley as "uniquely individual . . . the novelist of innocence, appallingly vulnerable, and of malevolence, coming out of some mysterious darkness of evil." Despite enormous popularity during his lifetime—his plays *Rope* (1929, filmed in 1948 by Alfred Hitchcock) and *Gaslight* (1938, filmed by Thorold Dickinson in 1940, and by George Cukor in 1944) were spectacularly successful—Hamilton, largely forgotten in the years after his death, has been curiously absent from modern British literary history, and it is only now that his work is beginning to get the recognition it deserves.

At the end of his life, Hamilton said of his novels: "What I was trying to present was a 'black' social history of my times. There were so many 'white' portraits of the twenties and thirties that I wanted to show the other side of the picture." The world he writes about may be narrow—although no narrower than the one portrayed by, say, Raymond Chandler—but, unlike Chandler, it was the world that, for most of his life, he inhabited: his observations are meticulous and vivid, his ability to create atmosphere and tension is second to none, and his novels range from masterpieces of painfully dark comedy (*Mr. Stimpson and Mr. Gorse, The Slaves of Solitude*) to the classic murder story that is *Hangover Square*.

In 1929, Hamilton published *The Midnight Bell*, the first book in the trilogy Twenty Thousand Streets Under the Sky. The other titles, *The Siege of Pleasure* and *The Plains of Cement*, were published in 1932 and 1934. In these books, Hamilton portrays a world of superficially bonhomous boozing in which the characters are lonely and adrift, plagued by unrequited feelings, self-deception, and schemes that invariably come to nothing. Much of Hamilton's fiction takes place either in pubs, dreary hotels, or boardinghouses, all types of no-man's-lands in which people are thrown together by chance rather than inclination. Priestley notes, in his introduction to *Hangover Square* (1941), that "no English novelist of my time has a better ear for the complacent platitudes, the banalities, the sheer idiocy of pub talk, than Hamilton."

Hamilton's fictional milieu reflected his own life: time spent in pubs (his addiction to alcohol led to his death at the age of just fifty-eight) and an obsession with prostitutes. One Lily Connolly is the real-life template for the capricious tart Jenny Maple in Twenty Thousand Streets Under the Sky, object of the unrequited adoration of Bob the barman. In many ways *Hangover Square*, Hamilton's most intense and powerful work, is a retelling of *The Midnight Bell*. Praised by critic James Agate as "a masterpiece of frowst" (the word "frowst" meaning a stale, stuffy atmosphere), it is an extraordinary study of infatuation as well as a preapocalyptic vision of a country on the brink of war. Aimless, dopey George Harvey Bone, living off a rapidly diminishing inheritance in a "large glorified boarding house" in Earl's Court, is obsessed with beautiful, callous Netta Longdon. He hangs about outside Netta's flat for the "miserable pleasure of mere proximity," agonizes over the best time to telephone her, analyzes her every word for a sign of encouragement, and allows himself to be repeatedly humiliated by her friends. His only real source of comfort is the hotel's cat, who comes to his room in search of a warm place to sleep.

Netta is not a prostitute but a failed actress, and Hamilton really goes to town on her, describing her as "like something seen floating in a tank, brooding, self-absorbed, frigid, moving solemnly forward to its object or veering sideways without fully conscious motivation." Impervious to everything—even the weather and the fact that a member of her clique, Peter, routinely forces himself upon her when she is drunk—she harbors a secret ambition to become the mistress of a theater impresario (the

1930s equivalent of a WAG, the term used by the British tabloid press to describe the high-profile wives and girlfriends of male celebrities) and strings Bone along, cadging money while reviling him at every turn.

The novel begins on Boxing Day 1938, two months after the Munich Agreement, and the sense of impending catastrophe as the country heads inexorably toward war is mirrored by the reader's knowledge, right from the start, that the characters are also heading toward a violent climax. Bone is subject—when not drunk or inhabiting the realm of compounded depression, shame, and remorse that is *Hangover Square*—to periods of amnesia, during which his unconscious mind is fixated on killing Netta as a means of freeing himself from his conscious mind's infatuation. It's a fairly clumsy device—Hamilton biographer Sean French describes it as a "literary mechanism rather than a medical condition"—but an effective one, illustrating the self-hypnotizing nature of obsession.

Bone sees Munich as "a phoney business" but Netta and Peter have fascist sympathies and are admirers of Prime Minister Neville Chamberlain's policy of appeasement. This strikes me as writing with the benefit of hindsight (the novel was finished in March 1941), as public opinion was generally in favor of Chamberlain in 1938, although I can't imagine many British citizens went so far as Netta who, "without admitting it to herself," finds Hitler sexually alluring. She is also attracted by the fact that Peter has twice been jailed, once for violence at a political meeting and once for a drunken driving incident that resulted in the death of a pedestrian. Characters connected with cars in Hamilton novels are always suspect: he had been knocked down and critically injured in 1932, and—surely not coincidentally—Netta's flat is located on the stretch of Earl's Court Road where the real accident took place.

Hamilton spent most of his childhood in Hove on the south coast of England, and frequently used its more famous neighbor Brighton as a setting. In fact, the first novel of his Gorse Trilogy, *The West Pier* (1951), was described by Graham Greene as "the best book ever written about Brighton." For Hamilton, it's a place of escape, extending—but never actually keeping—the promise of emotional and sexual fulfillment. In *The Midnight Bell*, Bob's trip to Brighton is aborted when Jenny Maple fails to meet him at the station, and in *Hangover Square*, Netta ruins Bone's chances by turning up drunk with two male hangers-on. Ejected from the hotel for their appalling behavior, they return to London, leaving Bone with the bill. It is this that finally rouses his conscious mind to anger—"he felt he would like to beat [Netta] up, do her some physical damage"—and, although he tries to compartmentalize his life in order to achieve some distance from her, his ego and id come together to lethal effect at the end of the book.

I first read *Hangover Square* in my early teens, with a teenager's black-and-white view of the world, turning the pages with fascinated disbelief. Where was the hero? How was it that I could be both massively irritated with and hugely sympathetic to George Harvey Bone at the same time? How could Netta and Peter be so monstrously, eye-poppingly horrible, and why did I care so much about what was going to happen to them? Why did everyone keep on getting drunk when it had such disastrous consequences? How could an author be so contemptuous of his characters, and yet, at the same time, so engaged and compassionate?

I came back to the book twenty years later with a feeling of trepidation, having discovered that much of what enthralled me as a teenager (books, music, art, people) had proved, on adult inspection, to be embarrassingly disappointing. *Hangover Square* was one of the few exceptions: quite simply, a magnificent piece of British noir.

Laura Wilson's acclaimed and award-winning crime novels have won her many fans. The first novel in her DI Stratton series, Stratton's War, *won the CWA Ellis Peters Award for Best Historical Mystery. Her fifth novel,* The Lover, *won the Prix du Polar European, and two of her books have been short-listed for the CWA Gold Dagger. Her most recent novel,* A Willing Victim, *is published by Quercus, and she is the* Guardian's *crime-fiction reviewer. Visit her online at www.laura-wilson.co.uk.*

Love's Lovely Counterfeit
by James M. Cain (1942)

LAURA LIPPMAN

One of a trio of writers, alongside Dashiell Hammett and Raymond Chandler, credited with creating the hard-boiled novel, James M. Cain (1892–1977) first worked as a journalist before establishing his reputation as an author. Early novels such as The Postman Always Rings Twice *(1934),* Mildred Pierce *(1941), and* Double Indemnity *(1943, but originally published in serial form in* Liberty Magazine *in 1936) were notable for their spare prose, authentic dialogue, and dubious morality—the latter, presumably, prompting Raymond Chandler to dismiss Cain as "a Proust in greasy overalls, a dirty little boy with a piece of chalk and a board fence and nobody looking." A long-lost manuscript of Cain's,* The Cocktail Waitress, *was published in 2012 by Hard Case Crime.*

All journalists know that some stories are just too good to check out. A reliable source recently told me that the film *Miller's Crossing* drew its character names from the criminally obscure James M. Cain novel *Love's Lovely Counterfeit*. I had always heard that this atypical gangster film, made by Joel and Ethan Coen, was based on Dashiell Hammett's *The Glass Key* and *Red Harvest*, but I was happy to run with this new information. Eventually, I ran back to the book, a longtime favorite, and checked it out.

Alas, my informant was wrong, although *Love's* plot and setting do seem to be an influence on the Coens. There is a Caspar in both works, but the roles don't quite align. And where the film had the Dane, the book has the Swede. But the Dane is a sadistic closeted homosexual, while the Swede is a naïve and emotionally cuckolded politician. Like I said, too good to check out. But I'm glad I did because it reminded me to check in with the book I consider one of Cain's best.

Not that I've read them all. Who has? I'd venture to guess that only Cain's biographer, Roy Hoopes, and a few hard cases have made their way through the entire body of work—eighteen books by one publisher's count, with a previously unpublished novel appearing in 2012. (The number is hard to pin down because of the multiple omnibuses of Cain novels and short stories.) Even well-read sorts would be pressed to list more than six of Cain's titles. Of those, *The Postman Always Rings Twice* is the undisputed masterpiece. But, as Cain's first book, it had the advantage of the shock of the new, the shock of the shock. (Two words: Rip me.) *Love* is more interesting to me because the action is not driven by a ruinously passionate affair. It begins with a small beef, one man's betrayal of another. The femme fatale doesn't arrive until the final act and she's not calculatingly fatale, just a kleptomaniac who scrapes a curb at an inopportune moment.

Set in a no-name town somewhere in the American Midwest, *Love* is a book written by someone who knows how things work—pinball machine concessions, bookie joints, political campaigns, the human heart. Cain was a reporter for a couple of Baltimore newspapers, a legacy we share, and he believed in getting the details right, whether it was the insurance business, the look of a first-rate hotel in a second-rate town, or the temperament of the coloratura soprano. *Love's Lovely Counterfeit*, among its other virtues, could be used as a guide to setting up your own illegal video poker enterprise.

Cain, like his female characters, had a weakness for weak men. Ben Grace, the protagonist of *Love*, is "full of grievances, some of them, such as his resentment [of the nickname] Benny, trivial, some of them, such as his dislike for gunfire, vital." He wants to displace the boss, but when he succeeds, he's not much better than the guy he disdained. He thinks he's the smartest guy in the room. He's so clever that he tricks his adversaries into letting him die. His death echoes one earlier in the book, the murder of a boy who got in over his head, and brings the book quietly full circle. I reread a handful of Cain titles—*Postman, Double Indemnity, Mildred Pierce*—but *Love's Lovely Counterfeit* is the one that continues to surprise me.

Laura Lippman, like James M. Cain, is a registered Democrat. She drinks. Visit her online at www.lauralippman.com.

120, *Rue de la Gare*
by Léo Malet (1943)

CARA BLACK

Léo Malet (1909–96) was a French mystery novelist and poet who was involved with the Surrealist movement in the 1930s, and counted among his friends the artist René Magritte and the writer and poet André Breton. He is best known for his series of novels featuring the pipe-smoking Parisian detective Nestor Burma.

In the 1990s, while attending a writing conference at the Book Passage bookstore in Corte Madera (I was trying to figure out a story, and to decide if it was worth telling), my eyes were riveted by a small paperback lodged on the rack of English editions. It showed a cover with an arresting black-and-white photo, a night scene of a damp and glistening cobbled street. The title read *120, Rue de la Gare* by Léo Malet. Like a magnet, the title and photo drew me. Every town, make it every village, in France has a rue de la Gare before the train station, so what could this mean? It had to be in Paris, I thought, intrigued . . .

Those Pan British editions are long out of print, and I've had to hunt on AbeBooks and in the bookstalls on the quai in Paris for the rest, but I now have almost a complete set of Léo Malet. I blame him for starting me on my life of crime. I've since made pilgrimages to the "real" 120, rue de la Gare, and have, with my young son, traveled to the park at Montsouris, where Malet set a famous climax in the reservoir. Over the years, I've checked out the dark underpasses near Gare d'Austerlitz, and looked for the old streets of the 1940s. I've visited the fun fair at Place de la Nation, also used as a crime scene by Malet, and have walked the same narrow streets that Nestor Burma, Malet's detective, walked.

Malet's first novel, *120, Rue de la Gare*, introduced me, and the world, to Nestor Burma; to his smart secretary, la Belle Hélène; to Florimond, the often helpful head inspector of the then Suréte; and to Nestor's famous Fiat Lux detective office near Place des Victoires.

Nestor Burma, like his creator, is released from a German POW camp in the 1940s, but before Liberation. Nestor returns to an Occupied Paris instead of the one that he left behind in 1939. The German forces are everywhere, and so is crime: petty and grand larceny, acts of revenge, and affairs of the heart gone wrong.

That's the setting and milieu in which Nestor is destined to find himself, but on the way to Paris—on a train carrying former prisoners of war—he stretches his legs on the platform at the Lyon train station. *120, Rue de la Gare* starts: "We'd arrived in Lyon—Lyon-Perrache to be precise. It was two o'clock by my watch and I had a nasty taste in my mouth." Nestor Burma has seen a lot of men die in his time, so when a soldier without a name dies on the platform, uttering the final words "120, rue de la Gare," he's only mildly interested. If Nestor doesn't reboard the train, he won't get back to Paris for several days. His *laissez-passez* transit papers will expire in a few hours. Faced with a dilemma, Nestor hesitates. Finally, unwilling to be drawn into the murder and lose his chance to return to Paris, he jumps back on the train. It's only when a colleague meets his death gasping the same phrase that Burma's interest—and fury—are fully aroused. It's time to take out his pipe, discover the secret of this morbid address, and nail the murderer in one fell swoop. Vowing to find out more when he gets to Paris, we're off!

I was hooked from the first page. I felt the touch of the cracked leather train seats, and saw the weary POWs returning home sharing *mégots*, or cigarette butts. I heard the blaring of the train whistle, the clacking of the wheels on the tracks, and felt the quiet undercurrent of desperation of an Occupied France.

To me, *120, Rue de la Gare* reads contemporarily in a way that I've tried to analyze and have now given up on. Perhaps it's the way Malet paints a time of hardship with universal relevance from the perspective of a wisecracking detective. The pace moves quickly, and the hunt is on from the first page of the novel, but it is suffused with a psychological depth and Burma's wry, ironic take on human nature: the frailty of people, the nature of loss, and the road to redemption all passed off with a Gallic shrug.

• • •

Léo Malet, creator of the Nestor Burma series—*le détective de choc*—wrote *120, Rue de la Gare* in the 1940s. Formerly an anarchist, a sometime cabaret singer in Montmartre, part of the Surrealist movement in the 1930s in Paris, a poet and a smoker, his books live on in France today and are almost more popular than those of Georges Simenon, the creator of Inspector Maigret. (As with Maigret, several TV versions of the Burma mysteries emerged over the years.) While Nestor Burma might not be as well known in the rest of the world as Maigret, in France Malet continues to reach new generations of readers through the *band dessinée* graphic novels of his work. Jacques Tardi, the well-known French artist, has illustrated more than twenty-eight of Malet's novels, and every French bookstore, large or small, carries Tardi's versions. Throughout, Nestor leads us through the arrondissements of Paris in his investigations, so that they become characters in the novels—as does Paris itself, but a Paris from another time, a lost era.

Sadly, Malet never completed his planned great cycle of detective stories, *Les Nouveaux Mystères de Paris* ("The New Mysteries of Paris," a deliberate echo of Eugene Sue's nineteenth-century *Mysteries of Paris*), which was to include a novel set in each of the twenty arrondissements of Paris. He managed fifteen, but then gave up. After all, he said, Paris had changed . . .

The Paris through which Malet takes us has a real sense of place, and the truculence of his detective mouthpiece asserts an aggressively French identity. French crime fiction had come under the sway of the American hard-boiled school, but Malet gave it an ironic energy and a distinctly French voice. Burma is caustic, outspoken, and derisive, but behind the murder, mystery, and corruption we sense a real heart in the *détective de choc*.

PS: Thank you, Léo Malet, and to Nestor, for my life of crime.

Born in Chicago, Illinois, Cara Black is the acclaimed author of the Aimée Leduc series of mystery novels, of which the most recent is Murder at the Lanterne Rouge. *Her next book,* Murder Below Montparnasse, *will be published in March 2013. She lives in San Francisco. Visit her online at www .carablack.com.*

The Moving Toyshop
by Edmund Crispin (1946)

RUTH DUDLEY EDWARDS

Edmund Crispin was the nom de plume of Robert Bruce Montgomery (1921–78), an Oxford graduate who first came to the public's attention as a composer, most notably with An Oxford Requiem *(first performed in 1951) and a number of scores for Carry On films, including the original Carry On theme. Montgomery took the pseudonym Edmund Crispin from a Michael Innes novel, writing nine novels that featured Gervase Fen, a professor of English at a fictional Oxford college. He published eight novels from 1944 to 1952, but personal circumstances meant that he would publish only one more novel,* The Glimpses of the Moon *(1977), and a collection of short stories before his death in 1978. A further collection of stories,* Fen Country, *was published posthumously in 1979.*

There are innumerable serious crime novels that I admire enormously, but I hate the snobbery of those who think a book is somehow diminished if it makes you laugh. So here's my small tribute to Bruce Montgomery, who wrote as Edmund Crispin. He died too young, but he left us some delicious confections.

I first read Crispin's novels in my early teens as I was cutting my criminal teeth on Golden Age detectives. I devoured them all: Margery Allingham, John Dickson Carr, G. K. Chesterton, Agatha Christie, Ronald Knox, Ngaio Marsh, Josephine Tey, and lots more. I even developed an affection for the stolid Freeman Wills Crofts, although taking an interest in railway timetables did not come easily to me. But while I enjoyed and admired all these authors, I fell completely in love first with Michael Innes, and then with Edmund Crispin, because they wrote beautifully and made me laugh.

As a part of my reading diet, my mother had fed me all sorts of literate nonsense. I could not get enough of the likes of Stephen Leacock, James Thurber, and P. G. Wodehouse. And having been brought up in an academic world, I adored learning that was lightly worn, and the ridiculing of universities and pompous dons. Michael Innes offered me the magic combination of crime and fun, but there was a mad *joie d'esprit* about Crispin that enchanted me: truly, nothing was sacred. Much later I would write the biography of Victor Gollancz, the left-wing activist and publisher who took his politics deadly seriously. Crispin could not resist poking fun at him in *The Moving Toyshop*, his third novel and the one that, with difficulty, I've selected as my favorite. Which fork in the road should the driver take? "Let's go left," Cadogan suggests, in the course of the novel. "After all, Gollancz is publishing this book."

The Moving Toyshop is convoluted, preposterous, and ingenious, and a worthy tribute to Dickson Carr, whose locked-room mysteries Crispin admired. But it is not for his plots that I love Crispin, but for the wit, intelligence, gaiety, and decency that informed his writing. The novel is dedicated to his friend Philip Larkin, possibly because Crispin makes fun of poets throughout. While—as always—the sleuth is Professor Gervais Fen, an Oxford professor of English, on this occasion the central character is a poet, Richard Cadogan.

Explaining to a young woman why poets do not "look like anything in particular," Cadogan gives some examples. "Wordsworth resembled a horse with powerful convictions; Chesterton was wholly Falstaffian; Whitman was as strong and hairy as a gold rush prospector." Any sort of man could be a poet, he assured her: "You can be as conceited as Wordsworth or as modest as Hardy; as rich as Byron or as poor as Francis Thompson; as religious as Cowper or as pagan as Carew. It doesn't matter what you believe; Shelley believed every lunatic idea under the sun. Keats was certain of nothing but the holiness of the heart's affections."

There's a wonderful pithiness about Crispin's descriptions. Cadogan, for instance, "was lean, with sharp features, supercilious eyebrows, and hard dark eyes. This Calvinistic appearance belied him, for he was as a matter-of-fact a friendly, unexacting, romantic person." The police "were just horribly kind, the way you are to people who haven't got long to live."

I love the choice of words that no one else would think to use. Fen had "an extraordinary hat" and drove a red "extremely small, vociferous, and battered sports car." On entering Fen's college, St. Christopher's,

Cadogan saw "undergraduates staring at the cluttered notice-boards, which gave evidence of much disordered cultural activity. On the right was the porter's lodge, with a sort of open window where the porter leaned, like a princess enchanted within some medieval fortalice."

And which of us has not come across something as frightful as the Mace and Sceptre?—"a large and quite hideous hotel which stands in the very center of Oxford and which embodies, without apparent shame, almost every architectural style devised since the times of primitive man. Against this initial disadvantage it struggles nobly to create an atmosphere of homeliness and comfort. The bar is a fine example of Strawberry Hill Gothic."

In church, "The President of the college, isolated like a germ in his private pew, was feeling disgruntled." The girl Cadogan and Fen were pursuing was "among the altos, hooting morosely like ships in a channel fog—which is the way of altos the world over."

Michael Innes's characters occasionally played games of such learning and obscurity as to make the reader feel small. But there is no cultural snobbery with Crispin's characters. I was much taken by Fen's game, "Detestable Characters in Fiction." Each has five seconds to think of a character, both players must agree on the selection, if you miss your turn three times you lose, and the characters must have been intended to be sympathetic.

> "Ready, steady, go," said Fen.
> "Those awful gabblers, Beatrice and Benedick."
> "Yes. Lady Chatterley and that gamekeeper fellow."
> "Yes. Britomart in *The Faerie Queene*."
> "Yes. Almost everyone in Dostoevsky."
> "Yes. Er—er—"
> "Got you!" said Fen triumphantly. "You miss your turn."
> Those vulgar little man-hunting minxes in *Pride and Prejudice*."

Locked in a cupboard, they play "Unreadable Books," and, to my joy, include *Ulysses*.

Along with the comedy and the adventure, there is great humanity. Cadogan is outraged that some unpleasant people regard a particular death as "euthanasia . . . and not as wilful slaughter, not as the violent cutting-off of an irreplaceable compact of passion and desire and affection and will; not as a thrust into unimagined and illimitable darkness." When a bad guy fires a shot, "that wanton useless act roused in Fen something which was neither heroism, nor sentimentality, nor righteous indignation, nor even instinctive revulsion . . . it was a kind of passionless sense of justice and of proportion, a deeply rooted objection to waste."

Crispin wrote eight novels between 1944 and 1952 as well as making a living as a musician, mainly composing for the cinema. Alcoholism derailed him: the next, last, and disappointing novel did not appear until 1977, and he died at fifty-six the following year. But what he wrote in his prime was a joy. "One of the undiscovered treasures of British crime fiction," says A. L. Kennedy of *The Moving Toyshop*. "Crispin's storytelling is intelligent, humane, surprising and rattling good fun." She's dead right.

Ruth Dudley Edwards has been a teacher, marketing executive, and civil servant, and she is a prizewinning biographer as well as an historian, journalist, and broadcaster. The targets of her satirical crime novels (which have been described as "marvellously entertaining and iconoclastic") include the civil service, gentlemen's clubs, a Cambridge college, the House of Lords, the Church of England, publishing, literary prizes, and politically correct Americans. In 2008 she won the CrimeFest Last Laugh Award for Murdering Americans. Killing the Emperors *is about conceptual art and will be published in the autumn of 2012. Visit her online at www.ruth dudleyedwards.com.*

In a Lonely Place
by Dorothy B. Hughes (1947)

MEGAN ABBOTT

Dorothy B. Hughes (1904–93) was first published as a poet with the collection Dark Certainty *(1933). Her first mystery novel,* The So Blue Marble, *was published in 1940. A poet, critic, and novelist, Hughes is today best known for a trio of novels that appeared in the mid-1940s:* Ride the Pink Horse *(1946),* The Scarlet Imperial *(aka* Kiss for a Killer, *1946), and* In a Lonely Place *(1947). From 1940 onward, Hughes reviewed crime/mystery novels for a variety of newspapers, including the* Los Angeles Times *and the* New York Herald-Tribune, *receiving an Edgar Award in 1951 for Outstanding Mystery Criticism. In 1978, she published a biography of Erle Stanley Gardner. In the same year she was given the Mystery Writers of America Grand Master Award.*

Dorothy B. Hughes's *In a Lonely Place* (1947) may be the most influential novel you've never read. A troubling, razor-sharp exemplar of mid-century noir, it predates the long line of serial killer tales to follow, but, for me, none of the rest comes close. Perhaps its greatest strength is how remarkably clear-eyed it is. It has nary a whiff of the rancid sensationalism of Bret Easton Ellis's *American Psycho* or the nihilism of Jim Thompson's ugly and spellbinding *The Killer Inside Me*, two writers who enjoy or identify with their killers too much to see them with the piercing acuity of Hughes. (Nor is that their aim.) Hughes, however, is less interested in dropping the "ripe red veil" over the reader's eyes than in penetrating it.

I don't use the word "penetrating" lightly. Hughes hoists her killer on the autopsy table, still breathing, and shows us everything he doesn't want us to see about himself: the twin arteries of masculine neurosis and sexual panic that drive his crimes. It turns out that Hughes is up to much more than telling a killer's tale. Through her dissection, *In a Lonely*

Place says more about gender trouble and sexual paranoia in post–World War II America than perhaps any other American novel. And she signals it from the start, naming her killer with a knowing wink: Dix Steele.

We learn almost from the first pages that the handsome, well-groomed Steele is a killer. We also learn that he is a World War II veteran who served as a fighter pilot, the most glamorous of all military positions. Now, however, he is aimless, jobless, but living well, for the moment, in Los Angeles on questionable family funds and a skill at the hustle. Gone are the glory days of the war and Dix has "found nothing yet to take the place of flying wild." He longs for anything to approach "that feeling of power and exhilaration and freedom." During the war, Dix reflects, "you wore well-tailored uniforms, high polish on your shoes. You didn't need a car, you had something better: sleek, powerful fighter planes. You were the Mister." Most of all: "You could have any woman you wanted in Africa or India or England or Australia or the United States, or any place in the world. The world was yours." The loss of power is crushing. As an attempt fleetingly to recuperate—but much more so as a revenge for this loss—he satisfies himself by preying on the youngest and most innocent of girls: at bus stops, on darkened streets, alone in the loneliest of places.

Tellingly, though he is the stalker of prey, Dix's primary fear and rage come from the idea that he is being watched, "seen through" and fatally understood by penetrating women. Time and again he refers to them as "meddler(s)" and "damn snooping dames," calling one woman's eyes "disturbing, they were so wise. As if she could see under the covering of a man." His crimes, while acts of literal penetration, still cannot match the hard gaze of a smart woman. And Hughes offers us two very smart women: Laurel, the beautiful neighbor with whom Dix imagines he's in love, and Sylvia, the wife of Dix's air force buddy, Brub, now a Los Angeles police detective whose investigatory skills pale beside those of his wife.

In another noir novel both Laurel and Sylvia would be presented as femmes fatales, seeking to emasculate and entrap Dix. Sylvia in particular seems to be a powerful threat to Dix, who feels her "burrowing beneath his surface." He tells us, "she had no business trying to find an under self in him; she should have taken him as he was taken, an average young fellow, pleasant company." Long before Sylvia starts to feel truly suspicious of him—or at least as far as we can tell—Dix feels it. She knows what he is, and what he is not. He's an imposter in every way, from the suits he wears to the car he drives. If it weren't for these "snooping dames," Dix could pull off the deception, ward off the larger disillusionment. He is a man who feels under siege, even at the very moment that he is laying siege to unsuspecting women across the city. The more he seeks to show his power over women, the more powerless he feels—and vice versa.

A pervasive—and ultimately convincing—theory of 1940s noir, especially the proliferation of femmes fatales, is that it arises from gender instability and the challenge of returning soldiers. The result is a dark current of books and films about men, alone, facing a world over which they have no control, and in which the greatest threat is emasculation at the hands of women. The male fears that he will be a patsy, a sap, unless he contains their threat (Chandler, Hammett), or reasserts his power, with a vengeance, as we see in Spillane, whose detective Mike Hammer, another World War II vet, kills women with admitted ease. Of course, the women are only the symptom of a larger feeling of disempowerment, and Hammer is more of a folktale figure than a man, a comic book avenger single-handedly taking down the New York City mob, the Red Menace, and any other enemies in his midst. Tellingly, his fevered mind works remarkably similarly to that of Dix Steele or countless other serial killer protagonists. Witness Hammer sitting on his sofa, "dreaming of the things I'd like to do and how maybe if nobody was there to see me I'd do anyway." He tells us that he won't stop until he is "splashing [his enemies'] guts around the room," until he has them "on the dirty end of a stick." He dreams of "fresh corpses."

What we see in *In a Lonely Place*, then, is a cunning, remarkably prescient analysis of a postwar sexual panic that was still under way. Perhaps no year more than 1947, the year of the novel's publication, reflects that panic: it was the year of the Black Dahlia murder, which tore the roof off a Los Angeles thick with sexual violence, missing women, unsolved crimes, and general mayhem. And, of course, *In a Lonely Place* must be set in Los Angeles: the end of the continent, with no place else to go. You've run as far as you can.

Hughes is quite clear that the war did not turn Dix into a killer. Instead, the war offered him all the things that his life at home does not: status, potency, power. But Dix reflects in extremis the worst fear of the returning veterans: that the world they left behind is no longer there. The economic opportunity, the glory, the innocence of their own youth—all gone.

And perhaps most of all, there is the sense that the place of their women has changed: out of the kitchen and into the workforce, potentially in the jobs once occupied by men. And who knew what else they had been up to while their men were gone, whom they allowed into their beds? Once Dix begins to fall for the beautiful and cool Laurel, he feels he's put himself at terrible risk. "They were all alike, cheats, liars, whores," he asserts. "Even the pious ones were only waiting for a chance to cheat and lie and whore. He'd proved it over and over again. There wasn't a decent one among them." Each act of penetration is proof.

Brimming over with just this post–WWII malignancy and sexual panic, *In a Lonely Place* uses the conceit of a serial killer (although hardly a conceit yet) to highlight aspects of the culture that have little to do with serial pathology and everything to do with the gender and sexual tensions of postwar America, and the hard-boiled genre that reflects those tensions. While other noir novels of the day embody, demonstrate, or explore this phenomenon, mostly unconsciously, Hughes anatomizes it, and does so mercilessly. After reading her, one finds oneself looking, with a newly gimlet eye, at every purported femme fatale, every claim of female malignancy and the burning need of noir heroes to snuff that malignancy out. The stunning film version of *In a Lonely Place,* starring Humphrey Bogart and Gloria Grahame, unfolds quite differently. While in many ways it embraces Hughes's complex critique, director Nicholas Ray can't resist putting a luminous romantic sheen on Dix and Laurel's doomed romance. In Hughes's novel, however, there is not a drop of romanticism, nor any opportunity for transgressive thrills. It is a dark, cold gem of a book, a gem without a flicker of heat or light, and one that cuts to the touch.

Megan Abbott is the Edgar Award–winning author of the novels Queenpin, The Song Is You, Die a Little, Bury Me Deep, The End of Everything, *and her latest,* Dare Me, *published in 2012. Her writing has appeared in the* New York Times, *Salon,* Los Angeles Times Magazine, Detroit Noir, Los Angeles Review of Books, L.A. Noire, Best Crime and Mystery Stories of the Year, *and* The Speed Chronicles. *She is also the author of a nonfiction book,* The Street Was Mine: White Masculinity in Hardboiled Fiction and Film Noir, *and the editor of* A Hell of a Woman, *an anthology of female crime fiction. Visit her online at www.meganabbott.com.*

Act of Passion (*Lettre à mon juge*)
by Georges Simenon (1947)

JOHN BANVILLE

One of the most prolific writers of all time, Belgian author Georges Sime-
non (1903–89) published hundreds of novels and 150 novellas, along with
dozens of pulp novels written under a variety of pseudonyms. A former
journalist who drew on his experience of Liège's seedy nightlife for his early
inspiration, he is best known for his series of detective novels featuring
Inspector Maigret, the first of which appeared in 1931, the last in 1972.
Simenon is also highly regarded for his psychological mysteries, or romans
durs. *He was presented with the Grand Master Award by the Mystery*
Writers of America in 1966.

Georges Simenon was one of the master writers of the twentieth century. Some may find this a startling claim. It is true that he is generally
regarded as a "mere" crime writer, author of pulp novels and the inventor
of a much-loved fictional detective. He was also a great drinker—three or
four bottles of red wine a day—and a classic case of satyriasis, who told
his friend, the film director Federico Fellini, that he had slept with ten
thousand women, although his wife dismissed this as boastful exaggeration, saying the real number was only about twelve hundred.

The number of books he wrote, under his own name and numerous
pseudonyms, is also disputed, though it is probably close to eight hundred.
He wrote at what seems impossible speed, dashing off completed novels
in the space of a week or ten days. Among these many books are a score of
masterpieces that can stand beside, or look down on, the work of Camus,
Sartre, or André Gide, to mention only his French contemporaries.

Simenon made a distinction between his crime stories featuring the
phlegmatic and uxorious Inspector Maigret, and what he called his *ro-*
mans durs, literally "hard novels," such as *Dirty Snow, Monsieur Monde*

Vanishes, The Strangers in the House, The Man Who Watched Trains Go By, and *Act of Passion.* These and a handful of other titles have been reissued in handsome paperbacks by New York Review Books over the past few years. For a reader coming fresh to this darker side of Simenon, *Act of Passion* is as good a place to start as any, although no one should miss *Dirty Snow* and *The Strangers in the House.*

So far as I know, *Act of Passion* is unique among Simenon's novels in that it has a first-person narrator, although given the bleakness of the tale it might be better to follow Beckett and say *last*-person narrator. As so very often in Simenon, the protagonist is a middle-aged man who hitherto has lived a blameless life and who suddenly makes a desperate and inevitably disastrous break for freedom and fulfillment. Charles Alavoine is a doctor, a moderately successful general practitioner in the dull little city of La Roche-sur-Yon in the Vendée region of western France. His first wife, the unassuming Jeanne, having died in childbirth, he allows himself to marry a widow, Armande, whom he meets at a bridge party. She is handsome, capable, glacially composed, and she moves in on Alavoine with smooth and irresistible determination, taking over the house in which he has been living in unthinking contentedness with his devoted mother, and reordering his life along invisible though rigid lines that she wastes no time in setting down—"I yielded because she willed me to," says the hapless Charles.

The book takes the form of a letter—the French title is *Lettre à mon juge*—addressed by Alavoine to the examining magistrate who has gathered testimony from him in preparation for his trial for murder. Of Armande, Charles writes: "What I am trying to make you understand, your Honour, is that she came into our house in the most natural way in the world and that, also in the most natural way in the world, she remained." It is the classic predicament of the Simenon protagonist—who is, of course, always male. He does not love his wife, yet is ruled over by her, and he longs for escape.

It is another Simenon trope that nearly every one of his heroes, if we may call them that, trammeled though they are, has at some point in the past been given a glimpse of what life might be like outside the bijou steel cage of married life. For Charles, it was a chance encounter one rainy night in a railway café in Caen with a girl called Sylvia. "For twenty years," he muses ruefully, "I had been looking for a Sylvia without knowing it."

Now, bound by hoops of steel to Armande, he is on the lookout again, and again his need is answered. Caen once more, another railway station, another wet night, and this time her name is Martine. Simenon, with his accustomed masterly spareness, sets the scene: "Martine wanted to dance and I danced with her. That was when I noticed the nape of her neck, very close and very white, with skin so fine that the blue veins showed, and little tendrils of wet hair." This time he does not walk out on the girl, but on the contrary brings her back to La Roche-sur-Yon and into his very home, persuading Armande that he is in need of an assistant in his medical practice. The results are, as we expect, calamitous.

Lolita was published in 1955, eight years after *Act of Passion,* and there are striking similarities between the two books. Both have first-person narrators awaiting trial for murder; Martine is hardly more than the child that Lolita is, and like Lolita she had a beloved precursor in the narrator's lost past; blond Armande is only a slightly more controlled and controlling widow than Lolita's doomed mother, Charlotte Haze, described by Humbert Humbert as "a weak solution of Marlene Dietrich"; and there are direct and uncanny echoes between the two narrating voices—for instance, here is Humbert: "You may jeer at me, and threaten to clear the court, but until I am gagged and half-throttled, I will shout my poor truth. I insist the world know how much I loved my Lolita . . . ," and here is Alavoine: "I loved her, your Honour, I'd like to shout that word till I'm hoarse."

Like Nabokov in *Lolita,* Simenon, in his account of a decidedly un-Wagnerian *Liebestod,* is writing a story not of love but of obsession, whether he is fully aware of it or not. For Alavoine, the poor child Martine hardly exists in her own right, outside his crazed need of her, and she has to die in order that her past be obliterated, since that past is beyond his control. Simenon, himself a driven and violent man, sees deep into the human, and especially the male, heart and does not flinch from the dim, appalling forms he sees heaving and thrashing in that darkness. *Act of Passion* is a report from the lower depths, couched in the most limpid terms, and is one of Simenon's greatest novels.

John Banville's novels have variously won the Man Booker Prize, the James Tait Black Memorial Prize, and the Guardian Fiction Prize. He has also won the Franz Kafka Prize. He has published six crime novels under the pen name Benjamin Black, including the latest, Vengeance. *Visit him online at www.benjaminblackbooks.com.*

I, the Jury
by Mickey Spillane (1947)

MAX ALLAN COLLINS

Mickey Spillane (1918–2006) was the Brookyn-born child of an Irish father and a Scottish mother who grew up to be one of the most commercially successful but critically misunderstood of mystery authors. He served in the U.S. Air Force during World War II, and began his career in comic books before moving to novels. It is said that he wrote his first novel, I, the Jury, in only nineteen days. The comparatively high sex and violence content of his work (for its day), along with the relatively simple structure of his plots, invited the opprobrium of critics, but gained him massive sales. "I have no fans," he told one interviewer. "You know what I got? Customers. And customers are your friends."

I suppose it will come as no surprise to anyone familiar with me and my work that I've signed on to recommend Mickey Spillane's novel *I, the Jury*. Just the same, I had trouble deciding which of Spillane's Mike Hammer novels to recommend, and finally I took the easy way out and just went with the first book.

Mickey Spillane is perhaps the most popular, famous, and influential writer in any genre ever to receive so widespread, and even hysterical, a critical pummeling. Yet his first novel, *I, the Jury*, has been turning up regularly on lists of the best mystery novels of the twentieth century for some time now—perhaps grudgingly, but there the book is.

A small irony is that *I, the Jury*—apart from its shocking striptease conclusion—is perhaps the least typical of the writer's first half dozen Hammer novels, a group of mysteries that (along with Spillane's non-Hammer thriller, *The Long Wait*, 1951) sat for many years at the top of the list of all-time best-selling novels. Not best-selling *mystery* novels, but novels. Period. And as late as the 1980s.

It's difficult to explain to anyone born after 1970 how huge Spillane was. How the sexual content of the books opened doors for writers both genre and mainstream. How the allowable level of violence similarly increased throughout popular fiction and even films and television shows due to Spillane's impact. That James Bond and Shaft wouldn't have happened without Spillane and Hammer, or Dirty Harry and Jack Bauer and every tough-guy hero since with vigilante DNA in his blood.

Spillane and Hammer, more than any other writer and character in any genre of the twentieth century—more than any mainstream author and his work, either—changed popular culture.

So it comes as something of a surprise, all these years later, to discover that *I, the Jury* feels like a fairly standard private-eye mystery, with a complicated plot that descends more from Agatha Christie than Dashiell Hammett. What still separates it from a standard such yarn is Hammer's emotional ranting and raving, the extreme violence of the action scenes, and the still titillating (the perfect word to describe it) sexual content of the novel.

Yet *I, the Jury* pales next to the follow-up novels—*My Gun Is Quick* (1950), *Vengeance Is Mine!* (1950), *One Lonely Night* (1951), *The Big Kill* (1951), and *Kiss Me, Deadly* (1952). All of those key elements—emotion, sex, violence—escalate as Hammer becomes ever more volatile and even mentally ill.

By *One Lonely Night,* the attacks on Spillane had taken a toll on the writer. Though politically conservative, Spillane suffered the same kind of witch-hunt tactics that McCarthy served up to liberals, except Spillane was being attacked by the leftist likes of Dr. Frederic Wertham—we forget that the hysteria of that era was not exclusive to the Right. *One Lonely Night,* probably Spillane's masterpiece, has Mike Hammer taking on the establishment that condemned him in open court as a kill-crazy maniac. It's an overt and audacious response to the literary and social criticism his creator had received. For the record, Hammer decides that God has sent him to earth to destroy evil. Not exactly a standard PI yarn, but wonderful, crazy stuff.

Spillane was a born storyteller, and a gifted natural noir poet, but he was also a blue-collar guy who never dreamed he'd be attacked in such a fashion. He had become a full-time professional writer in the comic-book field before the war, writing such features as *Captain America, Sub-Mariner,* and *The Human Torch.* He created a very tough comic-book private eye, inspired by his boyhood idol Carroll John Daly's Race Williams (star of the famous pulp *Black Mask*), initially calling the character Mike Lancer and later Mike Danger. He tried to peddle the *Danger* feature right after the war but had no success, and in 1945 he wrote a novel about the character instead, renaming him Hammer. That novel was *I, the Jury.*

In *I, the Jury*, Hammer swears over the corpse of his murdered pal Jack Williams (a reference to Race) that he will find the killer and kill that killer, whoever he might turn out to be. Williams, you see, had lost an arm protecting Hammer in a Pacific jungle. Spillane's success is usually linked to sex and violence, but at least as important is the way he linked Hammer to war veterans. Hammer is a combat veteran himself, and his first case is driven by the loyalty one GI in a foxhole feels for another. That loyalty will outstrip even a man's love for a woman.

Hammer is a randy character, although for a while he keeps his hands off his lovely secretary Velda, who, over the course of the series, becomes the love of his life. He is a romantic who falls rather easily in love, which gives *I, the Jury* a heart of tragedy in the midst of all that melodrama. His cop pal is Captain Pat Chambers of Homicide (Spillane was kiddingly invoking the "Pat and Mike" jokes of his childhood). Hammer quickly discovers that his likely suspect list are the guests at a party of Jack's that took place shortly before the murder. This very Christie-like setup leads Hammer to wealthy homes but also down some dark alleys. Shorter than other Hammer novels, *I, the Jury* rockets along, thanks to Hammer's speedy tough-guy first-person, a technique that looks easy but has been mastered by few.

Fires begin with a spark, and *I, the Jury* is the spark that ignited not only Spillane's career but a shift in popular culture that included a sea change in publishing. When *I, the Jury* was initially published in hardcover, it did not set the world on fire, and the reviews were often contemptuous. But when the paperback edition came out, with an evocative cover showing Hammer pointing his trademark .45 at a disrobing blonde, *I, the Jury* exploded. Spillane, whose second novel had been rejected by his publisher, Dutton, due to disappointing hardcover sales, was suddenly asked for more, and right away.

So popular were Spillane's novels in paperback reprint editions that Gold Medal Books initiated the first major line of paperback originals to publish similarly sexy, violent crime novels. Virtually all of Gold

Medal's early output—and that of other paperback publishers following the Spillane trend—were private-eye yarns imitating Mike Hammer, or steamy sexual-triangle novels imitating James M. Cain's *The Postman Always Rings Twice* and *Double Indemnity.*

For all the talk of Hammett and Chandler as the founders of the hard-boiled feast—and I revere them as much as the next guy or gal—it's Spillane and Cain who were the most influential.

Mickey didn't care for James M. Cain, though. He said, "I don't like books written by guys in prison cells."

That's okay. I'm sure Cain didn't like Mickey's books, either. It didn't matter, because readers loved them both.

In the millions.

If you've never read Mike Hammer, or if it's been years since you have, *I, the Jury* is a good place to start. I would strongly suggest reading all six of that first wild round of Hammer mysteries, in order of publication. If you do, you will likely move on to Mickey's later Hammers, written mostly in the 1960s with a couple more toward the end of his life. There are also some posthumous works, unfinished yet substantial manuscripts that some guy named Collins has been working on.

Hammer remains the quintessential tough private eye. In 1947, when *I, the Jury* was published, the private-eye novel had pretty much run its course, although Chandler and Stout were still publishing. Radio in particular had turned the genre into self-parody. Like Robert B. Parker, Mickey Spillane reinvigorated the PI genre in a way that meant scores of other writers could get into the game. For example, the fad for private eyes on television in the late 1950s and early 1960s flowed entirely from Spillane/Hammer. *Peter Gunn,* that cool Brooks Brothers imitation of the hotheaded off-the-rack Hammer, leads us directly to James Bond.

So. See where it started, in a little book called *I, the Jury.* You'll probably like it. If you don't, you'll at least have witnessed the spark that lit the fire.

Max Allan Collins is a novelist, graphic novelist, essayist, songwriter, critic, and filmmaker. He has been honored for both his fiction and nonfiction work, and his graphic novel Road to Perdition *was the basis for the acclaimed Sam Mendes movie starring Tom Hanks. Visit him online at www.maxallancollins.com.*

The Ghost of Blackwood Hall
by Carolyn Keene (1948)

LIZA MARKLUND

Carolyn Keene is the pseudonym that has been used by the authors of the Nancy Drew series of mystery stories since 1930. The books originated with the Stratemeyer Syndicate, a U.S. book-packaging company that specialized in producing works for children, among them the adventures of the Hardy Boys and the Bobbsey Twins. Mildred Wirt Benson (1905–2002) is generally credited with having done much of the writing work on the earliest Nancy Drew mysteries, including The Ghost of Blackwood Hall.

I might have read a few thousand books in my lifetime, but none as important as this one. *The Ghost of Blackwood Hall* by Carolyn Keene, number 25 in the Nancy Drew series, taught me how to read. I spelled my way through it, letter by letter, word by word, and magic happened. At that point, I had seen nothing but the forests of the Arctic Circle in my native northern Sweden, but with this book a whole new world opened up to me. I wanted to go to River Heights. I wanted to drive a blue sports car. I wanted to be an American.

Nancy (or Kitty, as she was called in Sweden, for reasons that nobody can recall) also strengthened me in my belief that all of my boundaries were solely geographical. Nancy could do anything, from catching thieves to changing flat tires, so why couldn't I? She and her friends Bess and George didn't need guys to get things done. They depended on themselves and solved mysteries on their own terms. Numerous powerful women have described Nancy as a role model, a feminist icon, and I couldn't agree more. Annika Bengtzon, the protagonist in my own novels, shares quite a few of her characteristics.

In many ways, these children's mysteries have many similarities to their adult equivalent of modern crime fiction, one of the most significant being their geographical spread. The Nancy Drew books have been translated into about twenty-five languages (the numbers vary). They were an instant success in Scandinavia and parts of Western Europe, and have only recently been published in Estonia. The releases in Latin America and Asia, by contrast, never made much of an impact.

This has also been my experience with the violent entertainment novels of today. You can find extensive reading and writing of crime fiction only in very old and stable democracies. I once asked a bookstore owner in Buenos Aires where the crime section was, and he answered: "There is none. We don't read such things." The Argentinian best-seller lists confirm his statement. You can find just about every kind of genre on it—romance, political biographies, supernatural novels, horror, even porn—but no crime novels.

I spend quite a lot of time in Africa, and when I tell my friends in Kenya that I write fictional books about crimes being committed, they look at me strangely and ask: "Why?" You need freedom of speech, law and order, hope, and prosperity to be able to enjoy fictitious crimes and violence. Many Argentinians still bear the memory of the military banging on the door in the middle of the night: no need for cozy crime there. The Kenyans are living next door to Somalia: any imaginary misconduct is bound to be bleak and tedious in comparison. If you're living too close to the real thing, the urge to indulge in the killing of individuals for the purposes of entertainment seems to be limited.

I personally experienced this a number of years ago. Our foreign minister Anna Lindh was murdered in a department store in Stockholm on September 11, 2003. She was a very good friend of mine. I can still hear myself screaming when I got the call that said she had died.

For the next three years I did not write about mystery or murders. Instead, I was totally focused on the topic of women being haunted and hurt. I wrote a nonfiction book about a woman who was granted asylum in the United States because of domestic violence in Sweden. I did a series of TV documentaries on murdered women. I wrote chronicles, and newspaper articles, and a book about gender issues.

It was only much later that I saw the connection: Anna's death had made it impossible for me even to consider writing crime fiction, and it remained that way for a long time.

In order for a crime novel to work, the killing of a human being has to create chaos and mayhem—otherwise, why bother? The whiter and brighter the society, the darker and blacker the crime appears: the drama is all in the contrast. I think this is why crime fiction from the United States, Great Britain, and Scandinavia seems to be the most popular and successful in our time. Where can you find better, older, more stable democracies on earth? The United States, the Land of the Free and the Home of the Brave; the United Kingdom, with its legacy of empire; and Scandinavia, where the welfare system takes care of you from the cradle to the grave. In what other nations could the contrast between society and criminal behavior possibly be sharper, the betrayal greater, the failure more forceful?

Today, I'm back writing my fierce stories. I'm keeping the memory of Anna Lindh alive as a member of the board of her memorial fund. And when I think about it, I continue to visit River Heights quite often, as a place where imagined things happen.

I never did become an American, but I have a daughter who is.

And I actually do drive a blue sports car.

Liza Marklund was born in 1962 in the small village of Pålmark, close to the Arctic Circle in Sweden. She is an author, journalist, columnist, publisher, and goodwill ambassador for UNICEF. Since her debut in 1995, Liza Marklund has written eleven novels and two nonfiction books. She cowrote the international best seller The Postcard Killers *with James Patterson, making her the second Swedish author ever to reach number one on the* New York Times *best-seller list. Her crime novels featuring the gutsy reporter Annika Bengtzon, the latest of which is* Last Will, *have sold more than 13 million copies in thirty languages to date. Visit her online at www.lizamarklund.com.*

The Franchise Affair
by Josephine Tey (1948)

LOUISE PENNY

---

*Josephine Tey was one of the pseudonyms of Elizabeth Mackintosh (1896–
1952), a Scottish novelist and playwright who found fame with a series of
novels featuring Inspector Alan Grant of Scotland Yard. The most famous
of these is probably* The Daughter of Time *(1951), which combined Mackintosh's twin fascinations with history and crime by having a bedridden
Grant investigate the question of whether or not Richard III was responsible for the murders of his nephews, the sons of Edward IV, commonly
known as the "Princes in the Tower," at the end of the fifteenth century.
Grant also makes a brief appearance in* The Franchise Affair.

It took me an unconscionable length of time finally to read the book that
would become my favorite detective novel of all time, and the reason is
deeply embarrassing.

I'd read all of Josephine Tey's books, save one, and adored them all—
with the exception of *The Daughter of Time*, which I not only adored but
revered for its marriage of tension, history, crime, and curiosity. It was
clearly a masterpiece. (Indeed, the Crime Writers' Association in Britain
named it the best crime novel ever, and rightly so.) But there was one Tey
book I wasn't at all interested in reading. It was in my personal library,
unopened. I had never even read the synopsis on the back.

And my reason for shunning this work?

The title. Dear God, it's true. The title.

It's called *The Franchise Affair.*

Now, I knew it couldn't possibly be a mystery set in a McDonald's
or a Dairy Queen, but I couldn't shake the suspicion that it just might
be . . .

I couldn't tell you what finally made me pick up the book with the green Penguin spine and the bold, no-nonsense type: perhaps boredom, or curiosity, or a higher power weary of my pettiness.

Like all of Josephine Tey's works, *The Franchise Affair* is a slim volume, really more of a novella by today's standards. And like all of Tey's books, each word is a gem, perfectly placed. Her prose is clear, crystalline even; sharp, multifaceted, like prisms on the page, and with those clear words she creates equally multifaceted characters. But what I adore most about her works is, I think, the ambivalence. As a reader I'm never sure who is telling the truth, who is the good guy and who isn't. I want to believe in certain characters, but there is always a shard of doubt.

It's unsettling.

And that's what struck me first, and stayed with me throughout my increasingly enchanting and terrifying reading of *The Franchise Affair.*

Now, I say terrifying, but I don't mean knife-wielding psychopaths, or serial killers torturing their victims. There are no ghouls or vampires, no demented murderers behind the closed doors.

But there are ghosts. The past gets up, takes form, and walks the pages of *The Franchise Affair:* memory, perception, and the fears they feed.

Let me tell you a little about the book. Not much—I don't want to spoil it for you.

It's set in a Kentucky Fried Chicken . . . no, just kidding. The setting is a village in Britain shortly after World War II. We follow a country solicitor named Robert Blair: staid, comfortable, middle-aged. He receives a call one day from a woman he's never met. Marion Sharpe needs his help. She and her elderly mother are new to the village, having moved into the house called The Franchise a few months earlier.

It's a bleak time in the lives of the community, and of these women. The inhabitants of this English village have closed in on themselves and aren't interested in strangers, and especially not the equally reclusive mother and middle-aged daughter.

Then Blair receives a call to tell him something extraordinary and baffling: the Sharpe women have been accused of kidnapping a schoolgirl. The police, including a man from "the Yard," are at The Franchise, investigating. The women claim never to have seen the girl before. The girl claims to have been held by them for days, and barely managed to escape. The schoolgirl offers to prove it by describing the entire interior of The Franchise, including the room in which she was held.

And every detail is correct.

It falls to Robert Blair, the unlikely chevalier, to find the truth and exonerate the austere and unfriendly women who are doing almost nothing to help their cause. But as he digs, his own doubts grow.

I'll say no more, except to beg you not to wait as long as I did before reading this masterpiece of detective fiction and human nature. Like the best crime novels, it's not so much about the crime as the people involved. And, as with *The Daughter of Time*, *The Franchise Affair* is based on an actual event: the eighteenth-century case of Elizabeth Canning.

Josephine Tey was the pen name of the Scottish writer Elizabeth Mackintosh. She also wrote under the name Gordon Daviot. Sadly for us (and certainly for her), Ms. Mackintosh died in 1952 at the relatively young age of fifty-six, having written eight mystery novels under the name Josephine Tey: eight glorious works that have inspired me, and prove less is more—and a suggestion of horror is far more powerful than any demonstration.

Louise Penny writes the Armand Gamache crime novels, set in Quebec. Her books have made international best-seller lists including the New York Times *and London* Times. *She's won the British Dagger and the Canadian Arthur Ellis as well as the American Anthony, Barry, Macavity, and Nero awards. She's the only writer in history to win the coveted Agatha Award four years in a row. Her books are translated in twenty-five languages. Louise lives in Quebec with her husband, Michael, and their dogs. Visit her online at www.louisepenny.com.*

The Little Sister
by Raymond Chandler (1949)

MICHAEL CONNELLY

Raymond Chandler (1888–1959) turned to writing crime fiction at the relatively advanced age of forty-four, publishing short stories with "pulp" magazines such as Black Mask. *His first novel,* The Big Sleep, *was published in 1939 and featured the private detective Philip Marlowe. In total, Chandler published seven novels, all of which featured Marlowe. He also worked as a screenwriter in Hollywood, adapting James M. Cain's* Double Indemnity *(1944) with director Billy Wilder, and adapting Patricia Highsmith's* Strangers on a Train *(1951) for Alfred Hitchcock. The* Blue Dahlia *(1946) was Chandler's only original screenplay; it was nominated for an Academy Award, as was* Double Indemnity. *Chandler's final novel,* Playback, *was published in 1958. His essay "The Simple Art of Murder," first published in the* Atlantic Monthly *in 1944, is regarded as a seminal piece of critical writing on crime fiction.*

There I was in the darkened theater when the movie ended and the lights came up. I was sitting by myself in the student union. It was a Monday night—dollar movie night, to be precise. I was nineteen years old, and I had just seen *The Long Goodbye*, the 1973 Robert Altman–directed film adaptation of the Raymond Chandler novel. The Monday-night movies were usually followed by a discussion led by a student or graduate assistant from the film school. The discussion that followed this showing was spirited because some of those who had watched the film hated it and some loved it. I counted myself in the latter group. I was blown away by its depiction of contemporary Los Angeles and most of all by Elliott Gould's sardonic, sarcastic portrayal of private eye Philip Marlowe.

Listening to the discussion, it didn't take me long to determine that the reason the haters were upset with the movie was because they had read the book on which it was based and objected to the liberties taken with the classic novel. The film took the character of Marlowe—a tarnished knight with an unbreakable code of honor in the book—and made him into a man with a code that allowed for vengeance and murder.

At the time I was a consummate consumer of crime fiction in books, in films, and on television. But I had not read a single book by Raymond Chandler. I was interested only in contemporary stories. I wanted to learn about the world as it was, not read old stories about a bygone world that didn't exist anymore. Chandler was the 1940s and the 1950s. I wasn't interested in those times.

Until I saw that movie. The film, and the discussion that followed it, sent me to the bookstore on Tuesday morning. There I found the movie tie-in, the paperback of *The Long Goodbye* with Elliott Gould as Marlowe on the cover along with his cat (the cat that appeared in the movie but was not in the book!).

I hustled back to the room I shared with two other students and started reading. Thus began the forty-eight hours that changed my life. From movie to book and then to the other books: I finished *The Long Goodbye* in a day and went back to the store Wednesday morning to buy all the Chandlers that they had.

From there I stopped going to classes and simply read and reread.

From there I changed my mind about a lot of things, including the direction of my life.

From there I decided that I wanted to be a writer. Not just a novelist but specifically a novelist who wrote hard-boiled stories about crime and the people on both sides, and in the middle, of the law.

Chandler had proved me wrong with his words. I learned that stories can transcend time. A story from and about the 1940s can mean something in the 1970s or the 1990s or even at the start of a new century. Chandler holds up, and in that alone is the meaning of art.

This essay is to discuss a favorite book. Well, the favorite writer is now obviously on record. Were I to choose one book by Raymond Chandler, I would have to go with *The Little Sister*. Of course, *The Long Goodbye* is the nostalgic favorite because it was what brought me to the table. But the desert island book has got to be *The Little Sister*. That's the one I would like always to carry in my back pocket wherever I go.

As I write this it has been several years since I have read the book in its entirety, while at the same time not a year goes by that I don't read from the book in short refresher segments. Therefore, I am hard-pressed to describe the book's plot in detail. It is simply a "Quest" story in more ways than one. Orfamay Quest, from Manhattan, Kansas, hires Philip Marlowe to find her missing brother Orrin. Marlowe takes it from there and proceeds across a southern California terrain of movie stars, murders, and mostly untrustworthy cops. The plot is serviceable if not overly convoluted.

But the plot is not why this book is my favorite and why it so fittingly deserves mention in this book of favorites. This book is Raymond Chandler at his best, at his most cynical and sarcastic. It is where he captures the essence of character and place in the diamond-sharp bravura of Chapter 13.

Yes, I'm talking about one chapter. Really only four pages—at least in the Vintage Crime/Black Lizard trade edition I keep in my writing room. I know what you're thinking: in your writing room? You just mentioned above that you haven't read the book in years. Yes, that's true. But you see, Chapter 13 I read often. I read it to be awed. I read it to be inspired. I read it because it is my favorite passage of my favorite book by my favorite writer. In four pages Chandler teaches reader and writer what it is to write for the ages. What it is to create art.

> I drove east on Sunset but I didn't go home . . .

So begins Chapter 13. The entire chapter has little to do with the plot or the case that has Marlowe ill at ease and "not human," to use his own words. It's about a drive in and around Los Angeles. Not feeling human, frustrated by his actions and the case at hand, Marlowe takes a drive around his city and he takes us with him. Along the way he describes the Los Angeles of 1949, but it might as well be the Los Angeles of today, or any city any time, when the chips are down and we feel powerless and taken advantage of:

> All I know is that something isn't what it seems and the old tired but always reliable hunch tells me that if the hand is played the way it is dealt the wrong person is going to lose the pot. Is that my business? Well, what is my business? Do I know? Did I ever know? Let's not go into that. You're not human tonight,

Marlowe. Maybe I never was or ever will be. Maybe I'm an ec-
toplasm with a private license. Maybe we all get like this in the
cold half-lit world where always the wrong thing happens and
never the right.

The writer's job is to connect, to tap into the dark folds of the heart
and soul, to make the reader nod—yes, I get it—without even realizing
it. Shared experience. Doesn't matter if you have never been a cop, a
private detective, or a movie star. If you are human, the connections are
there. The great writer can find it in you and bring it out with his words.

Chandler does this. Cynical and hopeful at the same time. He does
it in spades and in such a way that his words jump through time. They
mean just as much now as they did when he typed them three-quarters
of a century ago:

> I smelled Los Angeles before I got to it. It smelled stale and old
> like a living room that had been closed too long. But the colored
> lights fooled you. The lights were wonderful. There ought to be a
> monument to the man who invented neon lights. Fifteen stories
> high, solid marble. There's a boy who really made something out
> of nothing.

I am a disciple of Raymond Chandler. I am a student of Chapter 13.
I read it before I start every book I write. It's a pep talk from the master.
It reminds me of the higher game that is afoot. You can write about detectives working on cases or cases working on detectives. You can use a
crime story to frame a greater story about the world we live in. And if you
are lucky, and can learn well the lesson of the master, you can have them
nodding their heads as they read, even if they don't know it.

---

*Michael Connelly has written twenty-five novels in twenty years, including his
latest,* The Black Box *(2012). He is the author behind the long-running Harry
Bosch detective series, as well as the more recent Lincoln Lawyer series featuring defense attorney Mickey Haller. Connelly is a former journalist who covered courts and crime for newspapers in South Florida, where he grew up, and
Los Angeles, where he lived for fifteen years and sets his novels. He currently
resides in Tampa, Florida. Visit him online at www.michaelconnelly.com.*

Brat Farrar
by Josephine Tey (1949)

MARGARET MARON

Josephine Tey was one of the pseudonyms of Elizabeth Mackintosh (1896–1952), a Scottish novelist and playwright who found fame with a series of novels featuring Inspector Alan Grant of Scotland Yard. The most famous of these is probably The Daughter of Time *(1951), which combined Mackintosh's twin fascinations with history and crime by having a bedridden Grant investigate the question of whether or not Richard III was responsible for the murders of his nephews, the sons of Edward IV, commonly known as the "Princes in the Tower," at the end of the fifteenth century. Grant also made a brief appearance in* The Franchise Affair.

"Prose books are the show dogs I breed and sell to support my cats." So said Robert Graves, whose heart belonged to poetry.

Elizabeth Mackintosh (1896–1951), a Scotswoman who wrote historical plays under the name Gordon Daviot, seems to have had similar feelings about the crime novels she wrote as Josephine Tey. They were her show dogs, inferior to her feline dramas. The plays were moderately successful at the time, but if any are still being performed, I am unaware of it. Indeed, the only reason they are remembered today may be because Sir John Gielgud had his first popular success in one, and it has become part of his biography.

All of her crime novels, however, are still in print. Ask any group of middle-aged female mystery writers to name those eight titles and, nine out of ten times, you will get the complete list: *The Man in the Queue, A Shilling for Candles, Miss Pym Disposes, The Franchise Affair, Brat Farrar, To Love and Be Wise, The Daughter of Time,* and *The Singing Sands.*

If Dorothy L. Sayers and Agatha Christie were role models for the generation preceding mine, Josephine Tey was the role model for ours.

She was never as self-consciously learned as Sayers (*The Daughter of Time* comes closest to academia), and her plots were never as convoluted and far-fetched as Christie's, but they are as deeply satisfying as anything those two icons ever wrote. Her prose style was simple and straightforward— "Nothing up my sleeves, folks"—yet her characters rise from the page as living, breathing, fully rounded humans. Although each of her books has its champions, my personal favorites are *The Franchise Affair* (which Louise Penny discusses elsewhere in this volume) and *Brat Farrar.* Both are my comfort reads when nothing else suits.

A brief synopsis: Brat Farrar, an English orphan in his early teens, runs away to America where he stumbles onto a ranch and falls in love with horses. A few years later, after oil is discovered on the ranch, he takes his severance pay and returns to England at a loose end. There he is accosted on the street by Alec Loding, a down-at-the-heels actor who mistakes him for Simon Ashby, a young man on the verge of inheriting the family fortune and the stud farm that goes with it. Eight years earlier, Patrick Ashby, Simon's thirteen-year-old twin, died. He is presumed drowned, a victim of suicide from grief over the death of his parents. The body was never found.

Loding, who grew up next door to the Ashby farm and knows the family intimately, seizes on the chance to cut himself in on Simon's inheritance. He wants to groom Brat Farrar to pretend to be the older twin, now returned from the dead and back to claim his rightful place. Brat is a decent young man and reluctant to become involved, but once he realizes that horses are a major part of the deal, he agrees. Loding is a born teacher, and Brat is such a quick learner that he is able to fool everyone except Simon.

The family consists of Simon, a calculating charmer who initially insists that the real Patrick is dead; Eleanor, a slightly younger sister who welcomes "Patrick" back with conflicting emotions; the ten-year-old twins, Ruth and Jane; and Aunt Bee, a superb horsewoman who has raised her brother's children and kept the stud farm going. Each is quickly sketched, but so expertly that we see them in the round. We soon know their strengths and weaknesses, their likes and dislikes.

And not just the humans: even Tey's animals have personalities.

Take the horses, the equine counterparts to their owners. There's Simon's Timber: conceited, vain, and an opportunistic killer. There's Jane's Fourposter, an old white pony with "no mouth and an insatiable curiosity"; Regina, who has dropped valuable foals for twenty years; and Bee's Chevron, who "loved jumping and was taking her fences with an off-handed confidence. One could almost hear her humming."

Brat himself is so decent, so likable, so hungry for a real family and a "belonging place," that we find ourselves rooting for him at every close call even though he's a liar and a usurper who uses the good memories everyone has of Patrick to insinuate himself into the fabric of the community. Only gradually do we come to realize that he's in mortal danger and stands a very good chance of following Patrick to an early death.

Part of the pleasure of a Tey novel is the way in which she plays fair all the way. We see everything that her protagonists see, hear every conversation, and are even privy to their thoughts. Surprise endings and ironic twists are not what she aims for. Instead, we get a slow unfolding of plot until all is revealed in a thoroughly satisfying manner.

Tey has been my role model from the start. She is the one writer I still study each time I reread one of her books in an effort to learn precisely how she makes her people and places so vivid that one wants to keep reading about them even after the mystery is solved. As a slow writer, I despaired when I read that she tossed some of them off in six weeks or less. She called them her "annual knitting," something to keep her hand in between the plays.

I will never stop wishing she had stuck with her knitting and forgotten about those plays.

———————————

Margaret Maron has served as national president of Sisters in Crime, the American Crime Writers League, and Mystery Writers of America. Winners of several major mystery awards, her Judge Deborah Knott novels are on the reading lists of various courses in contemporary Southern literature. In 2008, she received the North Carolina Award for Literature, the state's highest civilian honor. Her first series, set against the New York City art world and now available as e-books, featured Lt. Sigrid Harald, NYPD. Visit her online at www.MargaretMaron.com.

Strangers on a Train
by Patricia Highsmith (1950)

ADRIAN MCKINTY

Patricia Highsmith (1921–95) was the troubled author of more than twenty novels and numerous short stories. Born Mary Patricia Plangman, she took her surname from her stepfather, Stanley Highsmith, and had complicated relationships with both Stanley and her mother, Mary, who predeceased her daughter by only a few years, and was accused by Patricia of trying to abort her. Her first novel was Strangers on a Train, *but she is probably best known as the creator of the amoral con man and murderer, Tom Ripley, who featured in five of her novels. Her great gift was the ability to make readers empathize with the most appalling of characters, forcing them to confront the darker corners of their own psyches.*

I first got to know Patricia Highsmith's fiction in the Belfast Central Library during the apocalyptic Northern Irish summer of 1981. It was the time of the hunger strikes: bombs were going off daily, and riots ravaged the city every night, but somehow the library stayed open. The helpful librarians were keen to push this thirteen-year-old boy who was mad about crime writing in the direction of a novelist that they considered to be at the classy end of a rather disreputable genre.

After making my way through the taut, excellent Ripley books, and the short stories, I was steered toward Highsmith's back catalog. For some reason Highsmith's second novel, the lesbian classic *The Price of Salt,* was only to be had on the Special Reserve Shelf, but her debut novel, *Strangers on a Train,* was available in a handsome first edition from the Cresset Press. I was instantly gripped by the plausibility of the story and its neat dissection of the poisonous nature of lies and guilt. I have been a fan of the novel ever since.

Although she was born in Texas in 1921, Patricia Highsmith lived most of her early life in Manhattan with her mother and stepfather, the artist Stanley Highsmith. She grew up in a low-rent bohemian atmosphere on the outer fringes of New York's art scene. A precocious child, she was a voracious reader of fiction, science, art history, and psychology. She had always known that she was going to be a writer, and at Barnard she took literature and English composition.

Her first job in publishing was as one of the bullpen scripters producing comic strips for the publisher Ned Pines, eventually moving up the chain of Fawcett Comics to work on early iconic characters such as Golden Arrow and Captain Midnight.

At a suggestion from Truman Capote she began *Strangers on a Train* at the Yaddo Writers Colony in Saratoga Springs, New York. Determined to make a splash with her debut, Highsmith saw *Strangers* as an attempt at an American *Crime and Punishment*. She admired and envied Dostoyevsky, but read him somewhat cynically through the prism of Albert Camus and Jean-Paul Sartre. Where Dostoyevsky felt that a fallen man could be redeemed through God's infinite love, Highsmith saw no such possibility. Like Camus's Meursault in *L'Etranger,* Highsmith's oeuvre is filled with outsiders attempting to overcome the mores of a tedious, bourgeois society.

Strangers on a Train begins with architect Guy Haines and spoiled scion Charles Bruno meeting in the Pullman car of a train going to the fictional town of Metcalf, Texas. Bruno is oily and unpleasant from the get-go, and perhaps a less weary Guy would have had sufficient will to resist Bruno's demand that they dine together.

Bruno discovers that Guy is having trouble getting a divorce from his wife, Miriam, who stands not only in the way of Guy's happiness with his new girlfriend, Anne, but whose vulgarity is holding back Guy's career as a promising architect with a white-shoe New York firm. In another moment of weakness, Guy admits that if Miriam could only be disposed of, many of his problems would disappear. Bruno, too, wants someone dead. He despises his money-grubbing father, whose affairs embarrass his saintly mother. Wouldn't it be interesting, Bruno suggests, if each committed the other's murder while the beneficiary had a watertight alibi? Guy is repulsed by the idea, and forgets it—and Bruno—when he gets off the train.

Unfortunately for Guy, Bruno is a single-minded psychopath who has gotten it into his head that he and Guy have reached a tacit agreement. At the first opportunity he takes the train to Metcalf, follows Miriam to a funfair, waits until she is alone, and strangles her.

Over the following weeks and months, Bruno begins hounding Guy to fulfill his side of the bargain. He turns up at Guy's offices, at various social occasions, and even at his home, passing himself off as a family friend. Bruno begins blackmailing Guy, telling him that, unless he murders Bruno's old man, he will go to the police and implicate Guy.

Never strong to begin with, Guy starts to unravel, seeing Bruno everywhere, hearing voices, and hallucinating. In order to save his sanity he finally kills Bruno's father. For a while things improve, but then detective Arthur Gerard gets on the case and begins to pick apart Bruno's frequent, silly, and unnecessary lies.

There is an elegiac Spenglerian quality to Highsmith's writing: the Long Islanders in *Strangers,* like Western man in general, have become spoiled, decayed, and corrupt. Bruno kills not because he hates his father, but because this act (or any violent act) is a way of staving off the fatal ennui that comes with twentieth-century life. He is without scruples or regret.

Guy, however, is crippled by guilt and shame. On the verge of madness, he travels to Metcalf to find Miriam's boyfriend in order to confess his role in her death. The diffident hick boyfriend, Owen, is not interested in Guy's story, and tells him to let bygones be bygones. He, too, was glad that Miriam had been killed because she had become a nuisance. Aghast, Guy realizes that he is not going to get beaten up by Owen; in fact, he is not going to get any kind of absolution or penance at all.

Patricia Highsmith tells this deceptively simple story in a prose style that is economical and quietly muscular. She avoids hysteria and hyperbole and builds Guy's prison of remorse brick by toxic brick. The story is a brilliant and entirely believable character study of two flawed men brought low by their fragility and aimlessness. Guy and Bruno are different sides of the same coin, and the novel itself is prophetic of much contemporary fiction: in a postironic, disenchanted world, there are no great causes or faiths to believe in; there is no God watching over us, and if we can get away with murder, there are no consequences in this world or any other.

Neglected as a child, Patricia Highsmith became a somewhat mean-spirited, standoffish young adult, and in middle age her misanthropy morphed into full-blown anti-Semitism and paranoia. She became, in effect, a less charming version of her Nietzschean alter ego Tom Ripley. Ripley has none of the qualms about killing his fellow human beings that so haunt Guy, or even Bruno, and this is one of the reasons why I feel that *Strangers on a Train* is Highsmith's best novel. As she grew more successful and confident, the humanity began to drain from her books. Most of us would not act like the unruffled, aloof Tom Ripley, but every one of us could see himself falling into the abyss of cowardice and mendacity that finally drives poor Guy Haines to kill.

Adrian McKinty was born and grew up in Carrickfergus, Northern Ireland. He moved to New York in the early 1990s where he worked in bars, road gangs, and construction crews. In 2001 he moved to Denver, Colorado, where he taught high school English. His debut crime novel, Dead I Well May Be, *was short-listed for the 2004 Ian Fleming Steel Dagger Award. His 2010 novel,* Fifty Grand, *won the Spinetingler Award and was long-listed for the Theakstons Old Peculier Crime Novel of the Year Award. His most recent book is* The Cold Cold Ground. *Visit him online at www.adrianmckinty .blogspot.com.*

The Tiger in the Smoke
by Margery Allingham (1952)

PHIL RICKMAN

Margery Allingham (1904–66) described mystery writing as "both a prison and a refuge," the form providing her with the discipline and framework that she required to house her stories. She was the creator of Albert Campion, an aristocratic yet modest detective who, over the course of forty years, developed from the "silly ass" of Mystery Mile *into a man of formidable intelligence, aided and abetted by his sidekicks, the former criminal Magersfontein Lugg; the solid, dependable policeman Stanislaus Oates; and Lady Amanda Fitton, who subsequently becomes his wife. Allingham's formula for the mystery novel was deceptively simple—"a Killing, a Mystery, an Enquiry and a Conclusion with an element of satisfaction in it"—but her execution was consummate, and nowhere more so than in* Tiger in the Smoke.

The rebirth of British crime fiction came with the glint of a blade in the fog—Jack Havoc, psychotic knife artist, springing fully formed into the rubble and rationing of a war-weary London.

A man of his time, but also startlingly modern. We can see that now, but not many people did when *The Tiger in the Smoke* came out. A string of savage murders with only one obvious killer—what kind of mystery was that?

It was many years later, long after the now elusive black-and-white movie, when I first discovered *Tiger.* I was about thirteen, and remember bringing it home from the library: a shabby old bottle-green hardback without a dust jacket, the kind of book your mum would rather that you didn't leave on a clean sofa. In fact, I may well have been the last borrower before it wound up in a council skip.

I thought it was the best novel I'd ever read. Atmosphere you could cut with . . . well, a knife.

Born in 1904 into a family of writers and Fleet Street journalists, Margery Allingham was probably the first writer to outgrow the so-called Golden Age of the crime novel.

Her hero was Albert Campion, an upper-class apparent twit with unexpected connections in the worlds of criminal investigation and national security. Mr. Campion was played by Peter Davison in the BBC adaptations of eight Allingham novels broadcast in 1989 and 1990, mainly classic country house–type mysteries with the willowy, bespectacled Campion at the wheel of his Lagonda.

What was noticeable at the time was the one serious omission.

They didn't go near *The Tiger in the Smoke*.

Albert Campion still appears in *Tiger* but, in the aftermath of World War II, it's a sober, middle-aged Campion who, for family reasons, is peripherally involved in the hunt for Jack Havoc, on the run from Wormwood Scrubs and leaving a bloody trail of stab victims across London. Havoc is "that rarity, a genuinely wicked man" who evokes "the ancient smell of evil, acrid and potent as the stench of fever." You know something fundamental has changed in the world of fictional detection when Campion says, "The days when little Albert charged into battle single-handed have gone for good. Havoc is police work."

And Allingham is ready for the new age with a new kind of cop. Gone are the faintly dopey Lestrades and Inspector Japps of yore. Enter DCI Charlie Luke: young, sharp, intelligent, committed, and driven. A hard man of the new school who politely shoulders the diffident Campion clean offstage. Luke is not exactly the mirror image of Jack Havoc, but you get the idea.

The actual force for good in the novel—another departure after decades of wispy vicars—is old Canon Avril, patriarch of a cozy little London community. It's the wisdom of Avril that finally unwraps Havoc's psychology in a late-night church confrontation that has clear hints of an exorcism.

But none of these unforgettable characters has the central role in *Tiger*. The smoke in the title has a double meaning: the famous slang name for London—the Big Smoke—and a description of November fog at its most toxic. The fog is this novel's essential medium, right from its second sentence: "The fog was like a saffron blanket soaked in ice-water."

And Allingham doesn't give up there, oh no. The fog is a "grimy counterpane" and "greasy drapery" with its "smell of ashes grown cold." The fog is Jack Havoc's best friend in his homicidal search for the treasure he believes he deserves, a treasure intended for Meg, the Canon's daughter whose husband was killed in the war—or was he?

It would have been easy to make Havoc just another modern-day Jack the Ripper, but Allingham gives him substance and humanity, of a kind, and a reason to rip, linked to a pervading postwar mood among working-class ex-servicemen—the relief that it was all over giving way to anger and disillusion. What separates Havoc from the tattered band of disabled veterans he hangs out with is a black rage powered by a sense of invulnerability he calls "the Science of Luck." Without exposing the reader to a single image of extreme violence, Allingham has created a killer who makes Hannibal Lecter look like an effete poser.

You can imagine regular readers being slightly aghast to see a posh lady novelist getting down and dirty, but she's clearly loving it, and perhaps a little in love with Charlie Luke. The excitement sets light to her prose. We get the "shriek" of a sash window flying up, and a lovely description of the damage inflicted by a German V2 bomb, "half the street coming down very slowly like a woman fainting."

We get lots of enveloping atmosphere, but never a hint of melodrama. Allingham even backs away from a classic cliffhanger because she feels the need to explain the physical effects of psychological damage and knows that there won't be room for it later.

She uses light and texture like a good film director. After the murk of London, the climax takes place in the blinding clarity of a winter's day on the French coast when, in a scene of tension and strange pathos, Jack Havoc—sapped like a vampire at sunrise—finally discovers his treasure.

As you might expect, *Tiger* shows its age now and then. Detectives are routinely described as "dicks"; someone says, "I ain't chatty but I'm not funky"; and a character's real name is revealed as Johnny Cash. But its teeth aren't blunted and its grip hasn't loosened; no joyful relief in the last chapter, no formal stitching up of loose ends. Approaching the close of the era of suspects-gathered-in-the-library, the final sentence is laconic, stark, and entirely satisfying.

• • •

In search of a new copy of *Tiger* to reread for this piece, I discovered that there wasn't one. Another masterpiece had been allowed to slip out of print.

Now that's a crime.

English author Phil Rickman published his debut, Candlenight, *in 1991. The critics acclaimed him as the next great British horror writer, a reputation enhanced by his following four titles. In 1998, Rickman published* The Wine of Angels, *the first of a long series of novels that blended crime narratives and the supernatural, and featured Merrily Watkins, a Church of England priest and exorcist. There have been eleven titles in the series to date, the most recent being* The Secrets of Pain *(2011). Rickman also writes under the pseudonyms Will Kingdom and Thom Madley. In 2010 he published the first of a proposed historical series,* The Bones of Avalon. *Visit him online at www.philrickman.co.uk.*

Black Wings Has My Angel
(aka *One for the Money*)
by Elliott Chaze (1953)

BILL PRONZINI

Lewis Elliott Chaze (1915–90) was a Louisiana-born writer and journalist who spent much of his later career in Mississippi as the city editor of the Hattiesburg American. *With tongue set gently in cheek, he attributed his desire to write fiction to a combination of ego and money. This resulted in ten novels, both mysteries and nonmysteries, including* Tiger in the Honeysuckle *(1965), set against the backdrop of the civil rights struggle in the United States, as well as short stories and articles for most of the leading magazines of his day, including* Cosmopolitan *and* The New Yorker.

I grew up reading and admiring the paperback original crime novels of the 1950s and 1960s. What publishers such as Fawcett Gold Medal, Dell, Avon, Lion, and others succeeded in doing with these books was to adapt the tried-and-true pulp formula of the previous three decades to postwar American society, with all its changes in lifestyle, morality, and newfound sophistication. Their "life on the mean streets, anything goes" policy drew into their stables not only such established hardcover writers as W. R. Burnett, Cornell Woolrich, Sax Rohmer, Chester Himes, Thomas B. Dewey, and Wade Miller, but also a host of former pulpsters and talented newcomers who went on to have substantial careers in the field: Evan Hunter (Ed McBain), John D. MacDonald, Jim Thompson, David Goodis, Charles Williams, Day Keene, Bruno Fischer, Harry Whittington, Gil Brewer, Stephen Marlowe, Lawrence Block, and Donald Westlake.

These and others produced a host of minor and cult classics for the softcover market, in particular Jim Thompson's *The Killer Inside Me*, John D. MacDonald's *The Damned*, David Goodis's *Street of the Lost*, Charles Williams's *Hell Hath No Fury* (aka *The Hot Spot*), and Gil Brewer's *A Killer Is Loose*. But for my money, *Black Wings Has My Angel*—a one-shot by career newspaperman and part-time novelist Elliott Chaze, who did not publish another piece of crime fiction for sixteen years—is not only the best of the Gold Medal titles, but ranks second only to *The Killer Inside Me* as the finest of all softcover noir novels.

Black Wings Has My Angel originally appeared in April 1953. It had the usual lurid paperback cover art of the period and a typically provocative teaser line: "She had the face of a Madonna and a heart made of dollar bills." The brief back-cover blurb was equally melodramatic:

> It was my own fault, the way it blew up in my face.
>
> I had planned it so carefully.
>
> Until I ran into Virginia.
>
> Virginia and a hundred grand just couldn't mix.
>
> Maybe if you saw her you'd understand. Face by Michelangelo, clothes they drape on those models in *Vogue*, and a past out of a tabloid front page.
>
> Smart guy, that's me, who dreamed the heist for a year—the armored car, the dead guard, the cool green bills . . . the getaway.
>
> Then Virginia, who came for one paid hour—and stayed for all eternity.

Doesn't sound like much, does it? But that poorly contrived capsule description does no justice whatsoever to the novel itself, giving no hint of its power and intensity, the depth of its dark-side character development, its bleak social commentary, the existential savagery of its final pages. In his brief memoir about Chaze (in a piece published in the *Oxford American* [2000]), Barry Gifford called the book "an astonishingly well written literary novel that just happened to be about (or roundabout) a crime," but not even that praise is sufficient. *Black Wings Has My Angel* is a book that must be experienced, not read quickly for casual entertainment. It makes demands on the reader, as any piece of quality fiction does, and delivers hammer blows where other noir novels provide light raps.

Essentially *Black Wings* is a two-character story. The narrator, escaped convict Tim Sunblade (not his real name, which is never revealed, but an alias adopted after his jailbreak "because it smells of the out of doors"), has been hiding from the law by roughnecking on an oil-drilling rig in the South on the Atchafayala River. While relaxing in a local motel he meets and eventually falls for Virginia, a stunning blond, violet-eyed, high-priced call girl who is also on the run. Both are corrupt, beset by money, lust, and private demons, but believing themselves to be more or less in control of their destinies. When they team up and begin feeding each other's hungers, they become a kind of cyclonic force that demolishes their illusions about themselves and each other and whirls them along a path of mutual destruction.

Sunblade is the more complex of the two. Whereas Virginia is an unrepentant bitch, as blackhearted as any woman in fiction, Sunblade has at times led a respectable life and possesses a conscience that wars against his dark side—an ongoing battle he is doomed to lose. As Max Allan Collins wrote in a review of the novel in *1001 Midnights*, "Chaze's anti-hero is too complex to be described as amoral; his immoral deeds haunt him in a manner an amoral individual would shrug off."

The story moves swiftly from the backwoods of Mississippi to New Orleans, to Sunblade's small hometown, to Denver, and ultimately deep into the Colorado Rockies. Its centerpiece is a daring armored-car robbery meticulously planned by Sunblade and executed by him with Virginia's help, but the primary focus throughout is the corrosive relationship between the pair. Their compulsions lead inevitably to a shattering noir ending, one in which, as Collins says, "they ride out an even deeper, dark compulsion: to look into a certain abandoned mine shaft, to stare into the darkness that is death."

As good as *Black Wings* is, it had little commercial and critical success in 1953. In the early 1950s several Gold Medal novels sold upward of half a million copies each, and a few, such as Gil Brewer's *13 French Street,* exceeded the million mark, but Chaze's novel had modest sales and passed unnoticed by newspaper and magazine reviewers. A second paperback edition was published by Berkley in 1962, under the title *One for My Money,* and in 1985 a British hardcover edition appeared from Robert Hale under the slightly different title of *One for the Money,* but both of these editions had small printings and sold more poorly than the Gold Medal original. It would be nearly half a century before *Black Wings* finally began to achieve some of the widespread attention it deserves through a series of U.S. and U.K. reissues.

A brief overview of Elliott Chaze's life and career:

Chaze (1915–90) was by profession a newspaperman of the old school. He began his journalism career with the New Orleans Bureau of the Associated Press shortly before Pearl Harbor, worked for a time in AP's Denver office after paratrooper service in World War II, then migrated south to Mississippi, where he spent twenty years as a reporter and award-winning columnist for the *Hattiesburg American,* and another ten years as the paper's city editor.

In his spare time he wrote articles and short stories for *The New Yorker, Life, Redbook, Collier's, Cosmopolitan,* and other prominent magazines, and, all too infrequently, novels. In an interview he once stated that his motivation in writing fiction, "if there is any discernible, is probably ego and fear of mathematics, with overtones of money. Primarily I have a simple desire to shine my ass—to show off a bit in print."

His literary mainstream novels include *The Stainless Steel Kimono* (1947), a postwar tale about a group of American paratroopers in Japan that was a modest best seller and avowed favorite of Ernest Hemingway; *The Gold Tag* (1950), which, like much of his fiction, has a newspaper background and contains a good deal of autobiography; and the best of all his noncriminous works, *Tiger in the Honeysuckle* (1965), an adroit, explosive tale of the turbulent civil rights movement in the South, which he witnessed firsthand. He also published a wryly amusing collection of essays about his family life in Hattiesburg, *Two Roofs and a Snake on the Door* (1963).

Chaze's second criminous work, *Wettermark* (1969), is similar to *Black Wings* in that it, too, in Barry Gifford's phrase, is a literary novel that just happens to be about (or roundabout) a crime. In its own quiet, sardonic way *Wettermark* is very nearly as good. Its setting is the small town of Catherine, Mississippi (a thinly disguised Hattiesburg), where the protagonist, the eponymous Wettermark, toils as a reporter for the local paper. Wettermark is a tragicomic figure, accent on the tragic—a weary, financially strapped, ex-alcoholic wage slave whose early novelist ambitions have been long since shattered by rejection and apathy. His arrival on the scene of a successful bank robbery plants a seed in his mind, "a glimpse of the green" that is nurtured by circumstance and his personal demons until it blossoms into a cunning heist scheme of his own. The novel is by turns funny, sad, bitter, mordant, and ultimately as dark and unforgiving as *Black Wings*.

Late in his life, after his retirement from newspapering, Chaze wrote three offbeat, ribald (occasionally downright bawdy), and often darkly funny mysteries, all featuring Kiel St. James, a well-meaning but somewhat bumbling city editor for the *Catherine Call* (Catherine having been mysteriously moved from Mississippi to Alabama for this series); Crystal Bunt, Kiel's highly sexed young photographer girlfriend; and Chief of Detectives Orson Boles, a tenacious cop given to wearing hideous lizard-green polyester suits and speaking alternately in Southern grits-and-gravy dialect and perfect English.

Each of the three St. James adventures, *Goodbye, Goliath* (1983), *Mr. Yesterday* (1984), and *Little David* (1985), drew enthusiastic critical praise, but like *Wettermark* and, until recently, *Black Wings*, they seem to have slid into obscurity soon after publication and undeservedly remain there. The best of the trio is *Mr. Yesterday*, which deals with the murders of two eccentric old spinsters, one by a fall and one by an exceedingly bizarre stabbing. The motive for the two killings and the method employed in the latter are quite literally the weirdest, wildest, most inventive, most audacious (and yet completely plausible) ever devised for a mystery novel.

As *Black Wings Has My Angel* and his other novels attest, Chaze was a fine prose stylist and a consummate storyteller; he was also, especially in his later novels, witty, insightful, nostalgic, and irreverent. *Black Wings* and *Wettermark* are his only true noir novels, but there are strong noir elements in all of his book-length fiction. Like Cornell Woolrich, Jim Thompson, and David Goodis, he understood and unerringly depicted the depths and dark reaches of the human soul and what can and does happen when that darkness is given dominion.

In a career spanning nearly half a century, Bill Pronzini has published seventy-five novels, four nonfiction books, and 350 short stories, articles, and essays. His awards include a Mystery Writers of America Grand Master, the organization's highest honor, presented in 2008; three Shamuses, two for best novel, *and the Lifetime Achievement Award from the Private Eye Writers of America; and France's Grand Prix de la Litterature Policiere for* Snowbound *(1988). Two other suspense novels,* A Wasteland of Strangers *and* The Crimes of Jordan Wise, *were nominated for the Hammett Prize in 1997 and 2006, respectively, by the International Crime Writers' Association. His most recent novel is* Hellbox *(Forge 2012), the thirty-sixth in his well-regarded "Nameless Detective" series.*

The Big Heat
by William P. McGivern (1953)

William P. McGivern (1922–82) published more than twenty novels in his lifetime, including a number under the pseudonym Bill Peters. He worked as a police reporter in Philadelphia before moving to Los Angeles in 1960 to write for television and film, and a number of his books were successfully adapted to film, most notably The Big Heat. *His wife, Maureen Daly, is often credited with writing the first young-adult novel,* Seventeenth Summer, *the story of a seventeen-year-old girl's first romance, which was published in 1942.*

It's one of the most vicious moments in movie history. Sadistic hoodlum Vince Stone (Lee Marvin), fed up with incessant needling from his moll, Debby Marsh, splashes a potful of boiling coffee in her face, scarring her for the rest of her short life.

Everyone who loves old crime movies knows the scene. It's unforgettable, especially as it results in the beguiling Gloria Grahame playing the rest of the film with her head half hidden in bandages. In the fifty-eight years since it was made, no review of *The Big Heat* (1953) has failed to cite that scene—or give full credit for its shocking impact to "auteur" director Fritz Lang.

> "You bitch," Stone shouted again. He glared around wildly, and saw the steaming coffee pot on the table. Without thinking, without willing the action, his hand moved; he scooped it up and hurled the scalding coffee into her face.
>
> Debby screamed and staggered backwards, clawing at her face with both hands. She collided with a chair and fell to the floor, her body jackknifing spasmodically, and her gold-sandaled

feet churning and kicking wildly. She stopped screaming almost immediately; the only sound that came from her was a ghastly choking noise, like that of a child who has sobbed itself to a point beyond exhaustion.

Fritz Lang didn't write those words. They're the work of William P. McGivern, a former Philadelphia crime reporter who'd written reams of short fiction in the 1940s before breaking out in 1953 with *The Big Heat.* The success of the film led to subsequent McGivern novels being snapped up by Hollywood and turned into good, sometimes great, crime movies: *Shield for Murder* (1954), *Rogue Cop* (1954), *Hell on Frisco Bay* (1955), and *Odds Against Tomorrow* (1959). In adapting *The Big Heat* as a screenplay, another one-time crime reporter, Sydney Boehm, barely altered the novel. No need: the book is perfectly structured, its characters vividly and efficiently defined. With all due respect to Fritz Lang, a story this strong (and this smartly cast) could have been helmed by any number of Hollywood directors and turned out just as well.

McGivern himself was more generous, declaring in later years, "I don't think that my book is a classic, but I think Fritz Lang's filmed version is. My story is more a modern fable, a fantasy we all enjoy reflecting on, a man hurt by the system in the most cruel way . . . He fights back and he wins, not only a physical victory, but a sort of intellectual and emotional catharsis."

The Big Heat is the tale of an idealistic, straight-arrow police detective, Dave Bannion, who suspects that a fellow cop's suicide might be murder. When his investigation is hindered by his superiors, Bannion sniffs something rotten in the department. Lucy Carroway, once the dead cop's lover, contacts Bannion and cryptically hints at where the metaphorical bodies are buried. Before Bannion can reach her, Lucy is one of the actual bodies. Defying orders to ease off the hunt, the overworked and underpaid flatfoot traces Lucy's murder to local mob boss Mike Lagana; Bannion vows to bring "the big heat" down on the high-living gangster. In retaliation, Lagana goes old-school, planting a bomb in Bannion's car only to have it kill the cop's beloved wife, Kate.

Here *The Big Heat* rushes headlong into harsh territory for the early 1950s: Bannion becomes a vigilante, determined to avenge his wife's death. He turns in his badge but won't relinquish his .38 service revolver. "This gun belongs to me," he snarls. As I pointed out in my 1998 book,

Dark City: The Lost World of Film Noir, the film version of this cops-and-robbers saga quickly becomes an urban Western:

> Locked and loaded, *The Big Heat* gallops into the concrete frontier: there are showdowns in saloons, rustlers biding time with endless hands of poker, a robber baron devouring territory while tin stars look the other way. And most critically, there's the whore with the heart of gold.

While searching for these cross-genre parallels—and lazily giving all credit for the film's greatness to Sydney Boehm and Fritz Lang—I committed a grievous error: I neglected to read the source novel. If I had, I would have realized that William P. McGivern was entirely responsible for the story's freshness and power. Anyone who calls it "Fritz Lang's *The Big Heat*" is succumbing, stupidly, to the cult of the auteur (mea culpa, mea culpa).

The power of *The Big Heat* comes from McGivern finally writing about a world with which he was well acquainted: big-city crime. During the early 1940s he'd earned his bones as an author churning out cut-rate science fiction for *Amazing Stories,* toiling without distinction under editor Raymond Palmer. From 1943–46 McGivern served in the U.S. Army, attaining the rank of sergeant and earning a medal for rescuing comrades trapped by toxic gas inside a bombed tank. After mustering out, he tried to cram in some higher learning by briefly enrolling in the University of Birmingham in England. College was superfluous: it was the next two years that offered the real education—working the police beat for the *Philadelphia Evening Bulletin.* In fact, *The Big Heat* is dedicated to that paper's city editor, Earl Selby. The novel is based on a case McGivern covered during his first year cityside, tracking the civic corruption revealed in a city official's suicide note. He eventually wrote *The Big Heat* in a three-week burst in 1952, while living in Rome.

McGivern's dispassionate reporter's prose is *The Big Heat*'s greatest asset. His characters sometimes rant and rave and spill their guts in righteous monologues, but McGivern's narration remains steady and swift, with a keen eye for telling details and few wasted words. If you've seen the film, you no doubt recall the stunning scene in which Bannion's wife (played by Jocelyn Brando, Marlon's sister) is killed by the car bomb meant for her husband. Here's how McGivern renders it in the novel:

Bannion's car was before the house, under the shade of a tree. Smoke was pouring from it and the front end looked as if it had been flattened by a blow from a mighty fist. He leaped down the steps, his heart contracting with horror, and ran to the side of the car. The front door wouldn't open; it was jammed tight, buckled and wrinkled. Bannion smashed the glass with his fist, shouting to Kate in a wild voice. He got a hold on the door and jerked it open, pulled it completely away from the body of the car with a mighty, despairing wrench, not caring about, not even feeling the glass cutting into his hands.

That paragraph is rendered *precisely* in the movie. In fact, whole sections of the screenplay are lifted almost verbatim from the novel. Scenarist Sydney Boehm, good as he was, was basically stealing money when he cashed that Columbia Pictures check. Perhaps appropriately, it was McGivern who was given the 1954 Best Motion Picture Edgar Award from the Mystery Writers of America for *The Big Heat*, the last time the MWA honored the author of a source novel rather than the screenwriter. Apparently, there was no bad blood between the novelist and Boehm, who in short order was hired to adapt two more McGivern books: *Rogue Cop* for Metro-Goldwyn-Mayer, and *The Darkest Hour*, which Alan Ladd's Jaguar Productions turned into *Hell on Frisco Bay*.

What made McGivern's novels film-ready was his facility at creating memorable characters minus the need for backstories. In the best Hammett tradition, McGivern's characters emerge entirely within the immediacy of the unfolding action, but never feel one-dimensional. Like *The Maltese Falcon*, *The Big Heat* is completely character-driven, full of pace but surprisingly light on action. Glenn Ford's performance as the vengeful cop is completely true to the novel, although the Bannion in the book is more complex, and McGivern's attitude toward him more ambiguous. While Bannion is depicted onscreen as a loving husband-father hounded by villains, on the page McGivern presents him from the outset as a righteous crusader, a man who turns to the parish priest and dog-eared philosophy books for advice and consolation. (St. John of the Cross, Immanuel Kant, Benedict de Spinoza, and George Santayana are all invoked.) Bannion deeply believes there is an underlying order to the world, and that man's inherent nature is good. After his wife's murder, his hell-bent quest for vengeance is depicted as a torturous moral struggle.

He learns that there *is* an underlying order to the world, and it has nothing to do with inherent goodness.

There's a powerful scene late in the story, played in a more minor key in the film, where Bannion confronts the suicidal cop's calculating widow. He's learned that she's extorting payoffs from both the cops and the crooks, using the suicide note her husband left behind, which reveals Lagana's bribery of police officials. Only in the event of her death will the note be made public. Bannion decides to kill her.

> This was the end of it, Bannion thought, seeing her as only the last obstacle between himself and vengeance. When the shot sounded, when this mute, foolishly gesticulating creature was dead, he could put away his gun and call the police. The job would be done . . . He had only to pull the trigger, let the firing pin snap forward, and the steel-jacketed bullet would take care of the rest, take care of this soft, perfumed, sadistic bitch, and with her Stone, Lagana, the hoodlums who had murdered his wife and held this town in their big, bitter grip.

Of course, Bannion retains his humanity and lets Mrs. Deery live. In the novel, as in the film, it's Debby who ends up killing Mrs. Deery, as a way of settling the score with her abusive boyfriend and helping out the "nice guy" cop. But a significant difference between book and film reveals McGivern's priorities, which are at odds with the typically cathartic Hollywood scenario.

In the movie, Debby calls unexpectedly on the dismissive Mrs. Deery, and Boehm's script gives her a terrific line—"We're sisters under the mink"—before she pulls a .38 from her fur-coat pocket and blasts away. It's a great scene, perfectly played by Gloria Grahame and Jeanette Nolan. The shiver of excitement it provides is immensely satisfying.

But McGivern takes a different tack in his novel. He plays it off-screen, in a phone call:

> He knew the voice. "Yes. Where are you?"
>
> "I decided to get out of your hair," she said. "You were a good egg about it, but I was a nuisance." She laughed then, an odd little laugh. "You weren't so tough after all. But that's okay. You're better off being a little soft."

"Are you all right?" he said.

"Sure, I'm fine."

"Where are you?"

"Did I forget that? I'm at Mrs. Deery's, Bannion."

Bannion sat up abruptly. "Are you crazy? What in hell are you doing there?"

"I'm proving something, I guess." She laughed again, softly. "I'm proving I'm a tough guy.'

"Get the hell out of there, Debby."

"No, I'm staying."

Bannion hesitated, feeling a sudden coldness in his stomach. "Where's Mrs. Deery, Debby?"

"She's dead, Bannion."

McGivern withholds the vicarious thrill of retribution. All we get is Bannion's sickening realization that his crusade has turned this otherwise innocent woman into a murderer, a tool of his bitter vengeance.

In the film, Debby pays Vince Stone back with a hot java facial of his own before she dies in the crossfire of a climactic gunfight between Bannion and her ex-boyfriend. In the novel, however, her tough-girl act crumbles; knowing her days are numbered, she shoots herself. Although Bannion achieves his goal, killing Stone and exposing Lagana's corruption of the police department, the victory feels Pyrrhic as he leaves the hospital after Debby has died.

He stood for a moment or two, savoring the early-day sights and sounds of the city, and then he lit a cigarette and waved to a cruising cab. Something had ended this morning, he knew. Now he was starting over, not with hatred but only sadness.

That wasn't too bad, he thought.

It's fitting that McGivern's breakthrough book ends with its morally upright hero victorious, but suffering a precipitous fall from grace. Fallen heroes would be the author's specialty. Barney Nolan, protagonist of 1951's *Shield for Murder,* is a self-righteous cop who kills a bookie and steals the $25,000 in cash the guy is carrying to fund his puny dreams of suburban leisure. He's eventually brought down (not surprisingly) by a tenacious newspaper reporter and a ballsy B-girl. In *Rogue Cop,* corrupt police detective Mike Carmody spends the first half of the novel protecting his naïve younger brother Eddie, also a cop, from the gangsters whose payoffs fund Carmody's lavish lifestyle. He spends the rest of the book seeking vengeance on those gangsters after honest Eddie is murdered. Steve Retnick is the disgraced cop in *The Darkest Hour* (reissued as *Waterfront Cop*), released from prison after serving time for manslaughter and seeking to square up with the mobster who framed him. In *Odds Against Tomorrow* the disgraced cop is Dave Burke, so embittered by his paltry retirement pension that he masterminds—with fatal results for all—the robbery of a small-town bank.

McGivern described this thread running through his work as "tempting indulgence," saying in one of the few interviews he gave that "the frustration of our society forms a powerful thrust for people to take the law into their own hands and, while this is a tempting indulgence, I have tried to make it plain in my books that it never really works."

The only temptation McGivern indulged was writing for television, which he did a lot of in the 1960s and 1970s, for such series as *The Virginian, Ben Casey, O'Hara: U.S. Treasury,* and *Kojak.* In 1975 he wrote the original screenplay (with Dalton Trumbo's son, Christopher) for *Brannigan,* a John Wayne vehicle in which the actor played an Irish American cop dispatched to England to haul a mobster back for trial. It was one of a score of violent 1970s vigilante-cop movies spawned by the huge success of Clint Eastwood's *Dirty Harry.* McGivern had officially come full circle, since Harry Callahan was a direct descendant of *The Big Heat*'s Dave Bannion, the first cop in American crime fiction to throw away his badge and go hell-bent for vigilante justice.

It's a shame William P. McGivern hasn't achieved a legacy like that of his 1950s colleagues such as David Goodis, Jim Thompson, Charles Willeford, and Lionel White. He may not have been in their class as a prose stylist, but his stories were always rock-solid and totally satisfying. *The Big Heat,* as well as all of McGivern's other hard-hitting novels, deserves to be remembered just as much as the film it spawned.

Eddie Muller's 2002 fiction debut, The Distance, *earned the Best First Novel Shamus Award from the Private Eye Writers of America. His books on film noir, including* Dark City: The Lost World of Film Noir, *as well as dozens of*

DVD commentaries, have earned him the mantle "The Czar of Noir." Muller produces and hosts Noir City: The San Francisco Film Noir Festival, the largest noir retrospective in the United States, and he is the founder and president of the Film Noir Foundation, which raises funds to restore and preserve films representative of "America's noir heritage." Visit him online at www .eddiemuller.com.

The Executioners (aka *Cape Fear*) by John D. MacDonald (1958)

JEFFERY DEAVER

A Harvard graduate, John D. MacDonald (1916–86) served with the OSS (the Office of Strategic Services, forerunner to the CIA) during World War II, rising to the rank of lieutenant colonel. The author of more than five hundred short stories, MacDonald published his full-length debut The Brass Cupcake *in 1950. MacDonald also published sci-fi novels, but it was titles such as* The Executioners *(1958) and* One Monday We Killed Them All *(1961) that established his credentials as a superior crime novelist. His first Travis McGee novel,* The Deep Blue Good-by, *appeared in 1964; the last in the twenty-one-book series,* The Lonely Silver Rain, *was published in 1985. MacDonald received the Grand Master Award from the Mystery Writers of America in 1972.*

Colors.

In the 1960s my passion for hard-boiled crime fiction was in full swing. And like many readers, I was particularly enamored of books with continuing characters.

One of my absolute favorite series could easily be spotted on the shelves of the book-and-stationery shop where I spent most of my allowance and lawn-mowing income; you couldn't miss them, thanks to the colors, both on the jackets themselves and in the titles.

The Turquoise Lament, Nightmare in Pink, Bright Orange for the Shroud, The Deep Blue Good-by . . . more than twenty in total.

I'm speaking, of course, of the Travis McGee novels by John D. Mac-Donald.

Set largely in a Florida made both appealing and creepy more by the author's skill than by the reality of the Hanging Chad State, the McGee novels were a pure pleasure: quirky, exotic, insightful, fast-paced, and filled with those details in genre fiction that win and keep readers from Book 1 (I situated one of my own characters on a houseboat in the Hudson River, no less, as an homage to McGee's own floating home, *The Busted Flush*).

Now, I certainly acknowledge the quality and importance of the McGee novels, but I'm not going to talk about them here (except to urge that you start with blue and go all the way to silver; you won't be disappointed). Nor will I do more than mention, in passing, MacDonald's astonishingly prolific output across many genres: novels and short stories in all types of crime fields, science fiction, and nonfiction.

What I'm going to focus on is one of his nonseries books, which, by the way, outnumbered the Travis McGee series.

I'm an author who has written both series and stand-alones, and, truth be told, I probably prefer the stand-alones, and for this reason: while I'm always true to my premise that I write for my readers, the nonseries books allow me to push the boundaries of writing for my own enjoyment. For instance, I really wanted to write a novel in the first person. I thought it would be a great challenge, keeping that point of view and yet incorporating the twists and turns I so dearly love. Since my Lincoln Rhyme and Kathryn Dance novels have always been written in the third person, I couldn't shift to the first for one of the books featuring them; it had to be a stand-alone.

Among the authors I admire who have done both, I think of Barbara Vine, who has produced some great psychological thrillers in stand-alone form, books that are very different from the Inspector Wexford procedurals written as Ruth Rendell. Or consider Evan Hunter's brilliant *Blackboard Jungle*, a stand-alone that I feel transcends the Ed McBain 87th Precinct series, as delightful as those books are.

My favorite stand-alone of John D. MacDonald's is *The Executioners*, published in 1957, and republished as *Cape Fear*, which was the title of the two screen adaptations of the book. I'll refer to it by the author's title in these comments.

The story is quite straightforward. Some years before the book opens, our protagonist, Sam Bowden, stopped drunken serviceman Max Cady from raping a young woman while on leave. Sam also testified at the trial. Though sentenced to life, Cady was released after fourteen years, and he has come to the small town where the Bowdens live, seeking his revenge. His mission is to kill Bowden, his wife, Carol, and their three children—

any or all of them, in no particular order. No elaborate plots or schemes for him, no sadistic talking mannequins or complicated gadgets. He'll rely on guns, poison, or his bare hands if he needs to. He's utterly amoral, smug, and physically dangerous.

MacDonald gives us one harrowing scene after another, which include both confrontations between Cady, the family, and other characters, and crimes that an unseen Cady has pulled off: a poisoned animal, a sniper's bullet aimed at a child, a tampered-with car . . . The times when we *don't* witness Cady, but know that he's lurking, are perhaps the most nerve-racking.

As their life falls apart under the madman's repeated assaults, Sam, Carol, and the police wrestle with how to prevent looming tragedy. Cady, though, proves brilliantly resourceful, outmaneuvering all efforts to arrest or otherwise stop him. At first the aid of the law and the courts is enlisted, with varying degrees of failure. The Bowdens then try to hide from Cady, and finally—as the assaults become bolder and more outrageous—they explore less legal solutions to ridding themselves of the menace.

The lean book (about 210 pages in paperback) charts the inevitable collision between the family, the police, and Cady.

Now, what's so appealing to me about *The Executioners*?

First, I like the fact that it's a simple, linear story. Sam did something right years ago by stopping a crime. Now his good deed has come back to haunt him, literally with a vengeance, and he has to defend his beloved family. Though I love to fill my thrillers with contrapuntal subplots and unexpected twists, one has to be very careful not to overdo it. There was recently a series of crime novels involving—how should I put this?—a female character adorned with body art in the shape of a mythical, fire-breathing creature. (I won't mention the title.) I cannot argue with the rampant popularity of these novels, but I have to admit that I found the plot of the first book, at least, unnecessarily weighty and complicated.

Not so *The Executioners*. From the first hint of an ominous cloud on the horizon threatening to derail a sympathetic family, we move in a speedy and straightforward fashion to a conclusion that is factually unambiguous (though, to its credit, morally less so).

But simple and linear are not, by themselves, laudable attributes in fiction. In the hands of a lesser writer, this unembellished approach could be superficial, if not boring. But MacDonald knows what he's about. He understands that if you're not going for pyrotechnics— whipsawing twists, duplicity, mistaken identity, interweaving subplots, and the like—you need something else to propel the readers through your story. You have to make them wonder, on virtually every page, What is going to happen next? I continually keep in mind Mickey Spillane's dictum: people don't read books to get to the middle; they read to get to the end. Meaning: our responsibility as authors is to grab the readers by the throat in the first scene and do whatever is necessary to get them to the last page, ideally in one sitting.

There's a distinction between surprises and reversals. A surprise occurs when an author intentionally sets up facts to misdirect the readers and ultimately reveals that the truth is very different from what they'd believed. A reversal is simply an unexpected occurrence or revelation that leads to a change in characters' actions going forward; it can occur without any setup whatsoever.

While *The Executioners* has few, if any, surprises as I define them, MacDonald was enough of a craftsman to propel the story forward using dozens of reversals. We're always on edge, wondering what type of brick wall our characters will run into next.

Next, in considering the novel's appeal, I'd cite MacDonald's skill as a stylist—that rare ability to net an idea and mount it with words that complement perfectly, without self-consciousness or confusion.

I'll give a few examples of his taut, bull's-eye-accurate prose. Here is Sam Bowden after he has just hired somebody to beat up Max Cady.

> After Carol was asleep he got quietly out of bed and moved over to the chair by the bedroom window, pulled the blinds up with silent cautiousness, lighted a cigarette, and looked out toward the silver road and the stone wall. The night was empty. His four incredibly precious hostages to fortune were in deep sleep. The earth turned and the stars were high. All this, he told himself, was reality. Night, earth, stars and the slumber of his family . . . Two thousand years ago he could have sat in council with the elders and explained his peril and gained the support of the village, and the predator would be stoned to death. So this action was a supplement to the law. Thus it was right. Yet when he got back into bed, he still could not accept his rationalization.

Here is the family returning home after Cady has been sentenced to a brief jail term; he'll be released in nineteen days. Notice how the comic description of Bowden's youngest boy waking after a long car drive and walking into the house morphs to a tone of some uneasiness, and then to despair.

> They were home by four. Bucky rose up in stuporous condition and drunk-walked to the house. The sky was dark and low and the clouds that hurried by seemed just above the tops of the elms. The wind was gusty and humid. It rattled the windows of the house. The house had a feeling of emptiness. When, at six, the heavy rains came, Sam backed the wagon out into the drive so the rain would wash the dust of the trip from it.
>
> July had come too quickly. And nineteen days could not be made to last.

I think style is especially revealed in crafting those mundane passages that many authors churn out by rote. MacDonald brings his skills to bear on every page in the book. An example that I particularly enjoyed:

> He threw the empty beer can into the lake and watched it move away, glinting on the ripples, pushed by the wind. He watched Nancy eel up onto the stern of the *Sweet Sioux* and go off in a clean dive as lovely as music.

And:

> One man looked properly violent and comfortably shrewd.

And, as a final example, I can't resist citing this passage, in which Sam joins his wife after he's been practicing with a pistol to protect the family against Cady. The "gleam" in his hand is the reflection off the gun.

> He kissed her and then stood holding her in his arms. He looked down over her shoulder and the dark gleam of the sun in his right hand looked incongruous. He was holding his wrist canted so that the weapon would not touch her pale-blue blouse. And

beyond the gun he could see the white target and the penciled heart and five black holes.

Finally, in listing the book's appeal, I have to say that my ultimate pleasure in *The Executioners* is spending time with the people who populate it. The Everyfamily Bowdens are at its core, of course: the parents and their three children. Max Cady's brilliance and evil captivate like a bad accident. But even the tangential characters are compelling: the myriad police, private eyes, law firm partners, family friends, and the locals—all variously appealing, irritating, and shady—who get our immediate attention because MacDonald not only raises them from the page so skillfully but never lets us forget that any one of them could be the next victim. There isn't a clichéd character in the bunch. These folks change their minds; they do clever things and stupid things; they stumble and get outmaneuvered; they succeed accidentally; and they screw up bad, despite their best intentions.

Whatever their role in the book, MacDonald wants us to know these people, to understand them, to get into their minds and hearts. He takes his time. For instance, he goes to some lengths to describe Carol and Sam's meeting and courtship. There's no dramatic development in the flashback, but it's great to read. And not too long: MacDonald is very aware (as are we) that there's a madman out there. But, damnit, we're even more in love with Mr. and Mrs. Bowden after seeing them way back when, and all the more sweaty-palm uneasy the next time Cady gets close.

It's with these portrayals, however, that we see some false steps. I know of no married couples who banter quite so cleverly and relentlessly as Sam and Carol, thank goodness. The children are perhaps a bit advanced for their years at some points, and overly naïve at others.

And one scene in particular with Carol grates. She collapses emotionally after a car crash engineered by Cady, having what amounts to a nervous breakdown, which the (male) doctor treats with tranquilizers and condescension. True, *The Executioners* came out of a different era, the *Mad Men* days, when misogyny went unchallenged, if not unnoticed. But my problem with this treatment (in both senses) of Carol in *The Executioners* is that MacDonald later reveals he knows better. Indeed, it's she, not Sam, who gives voice to the theme of the book.

In the final scene her husband awkwardly tries to express his feelings in the aftermath of Cady, and settles on the heartfelt but lame "I feel enormously alive." Carol, though, gives us the more articulate and insightful response to the cataclysmic events when she describes how she's been fundamentally changed by what has happened.

> "There are black things loose in the world. Cady was one of them. A patch of ice on a curve can be one of them. A germ can be one of them. So just this little thing is what I learned. That all over the world, right now, this minute, people are dying, or their hearts are breaking, or their bodies are being broken, and while it is happening they have a feeling of complete incredulity. This can't be happening to me. This isn't what was meant to be . . . I think maybe I'm stronger and braver. I know I am. Because I know that everything we have is balanced on such a delicate web of incidence and coincidence."

You got it, Carol.

I mean, John.

Finally, I'd like to say a word about the film adaptations of the novel, because they illustrate something about MacDonald's book itself. The first movie was released in 1962 (directed by J. Lee Thompson), the second in 1991 (with Martin Scorsese at the helm). Both movies feature superlative portrayals of the villain: Robert Mitchum in the 1962 version, followed by Robert De Niro in 1991. Gregory Peck and Nick Nolte, respectively, played Sam Bowden. Both films are suspenseful, well acted, and technically accomplished. They also feature certain variations you'd expect in adapting a book for the cinema (in the novel, for instance, the Bowdens have three children; in both films there's only one daughter, to streamline the story).

The 1962 version largely tracked the plotting of the book: Sam Bowden physically stopped Cady from rape under circumstances that were both ethically unchallenging and practically unremarkable. Cady was caught in the act while drunk and nearly unconscious. Sam testified at his trial and off the criminal went to jail.

However, in the Scorsese film, the backstory is this: Public Defender Sam Bowden, representing Cady for the rape, intentionally misplaced evidence to ensure his conviction. Cady has learned what Bowden did and returned for vengeance. Scorsese also has Bowden, a faithful husband and loving father in the book, cheat on his wife with a woman who becomes one of Cady's victims.

Yes, clever plot twists both, but the result was to diminish my connection with the characters, and therefore with the story itself. Tainted heroes and wronged villains can be valid subjects in themselves, or can add complexity to crime stories, but MacDonald knew that, in this novel at least, readers would be best served by the uncomplicated collision of good and evil.

And he was skilled enough to make sure that simplicity did not mean superficiality. In *The Executioners* we have a rich tale of people unnerved, confused, and unsure about how to cope with this exquisite villain. Max Cady's goal of destroying a family is a simple one. What's far harder is for everyone else—read: the rest of us—to respond within the confines of our carefully circumscribed and sheltered lives. MacDonald makes clear that doing so is probably not possible. The only real answer is to meet evil on its own ground.

A former journalist, folksinger, and attorney, Jeffery Deaver is an international number one best-selling author. His books are sold in 150 countries and translated into twenty-five languages. The author of twenty-nine novels, two collections of short stories and a nonfiction law book, he's received or been short-listed for a number of awards around the world. His book The Bodies Left Behind *was named Novel of the Year by the International Thriller Writers Association, and his Lincoln Rhyme thriller* The Broken Window *was also nominated for that prize. He has been awarded the Steel Dagger and the Short Story Dagger from the British Crime Writers' Association and the Nero Wolfe Award, and he is a three-time recipient of the Ellery Queen Readers Award for Best Short Story of the Year. Deaver has been nominated for seven Edgar Awards from the Mystery Writers of America, an Anthony Award, and a Gumshoe Award. He was recently short-listed for the ITV3 Crime Thriller Award for Best International Author.*

His latest novels are Carte Blanche, *the latest James Bond continuation thriller;* Edge; *and* The Burning Wire. *His book* A Maiden's Grave *was made into a movie by HBO starring James Garner and Marlee Matlin, and his novel* The Bone Collector *was a feature release from Universal Pictures, starring Denzel Washington and Angelina Jolie. And yes, the rumors are true, he did appear as a corrupt reporter on his favorite soap opera,* As the World Turns.

He was born outside Chicago and has a bachelor of journalism degree from the University of Missouri and a law degree from Fordham University. Visit him online at www.jefferydeaver.com.

The Pledge
by Friedrich Dürrenmatt (1958)

ELISABETTA BUCCIARELLI

A highly regarded dramatist and essayist, Friedrich Dürrenmatt (1921– 90) also wrote crime novels. While his plays are generally acknowledged to be influenced by the theater of the absurd, Dürrenmatt's detective novels offer an unflinching realism that interrogates the reader as to his or her relationship with the genre. Das Versprechen *(1958), subtitled* Requiem for the Detective Novel, *is the first-person account of a retiring homicide detective and his promise to a mother to find the killer of her eight-year- old girl. The novel was adapted for the film* The Pledge *(2001), directed by Sean Penn and starring Jack Nicholson. Dürrenmatt is also known for his deeply cynical police inspector, Bärlach, who first appeared in 1950 in the novella* Der Richter und sein Henker *(*The Judge and His Hangman*).*

Das Versprechen (*The Pledge*) was first published in Switzerland in 1958. Written by Swiss dramatist, painter, and author Friedrich Dürrenmatt, it is the novel that, above all others, inspired me to weave my first noir crime plots. The main character is Police Inspector Matthäi, who, with a cold temperament and deep commitment to his work, finds himself investigating an incredibly complex case. An abhorrent crime has been committed against a seven-year-old blond girl who is found murdered in a forest just outside the Swiss village of Magendorf, near Zurich. The loathsome peddler who found her body is accused of being the perpetra- tor. He has traces of the girl's blood on his clothes, and, like the victim, he is covered in chocolate. He also has a number of razor blades in his possession, which are deemed to be compatible with the murder weapon.

Following his confession, the man ends up hanging himself. To all intents and purposes, and, according to everyone involved, the case is closed. To everyone, that is, except to Matthäi, a guardian of law and order with those antihero traits commonly associated with noir mysteries rather than detective stories. He is cold and calculating, full of self-assuredness and with no apparent vices. He is stubborn, restless, tormented, and, even worse, his pursuit of a spasmodic trace of truth becomes his greatest inadequacy rather than his most enviable quality.

Profoundly struck by the drama that the girl's family is going through, and by their composed yet excruciated reaction to their pain, Matthäi vows to find the murderer. Ultimately, it is this promise that will radically change his life. It is a promise to his soul, as the victim's mother describes it. It goes beyond his simple duty as police inspector and becomes, at first, a rational and calculated challenge before degenerating into a battle with all the legitimate doubts and impediments that life places between an objective and the path that leads to it. One at a time, his colleagues withdraw their support from his investigation to the point that Matthäi gives up his job at the police station, determined to do things his way. He is convinced that the only possibility of finding the murderer is to lay a trap.

What motivates this decision? One could say "the folly of childhood," an unusual sense of unrest that anyone who has daily contact with children will be familiar with. A drawing done by the victim depicts a giant man wearing a black hat as he holds out tiny hedgehogs to a young girl. A big dark car is drawn on the edge of the sheet of paper. Matthäi is absolutely convinced that it is a drawing of the murderer. In order to capture him, Matthäi will need the endurance of a fisherman: endless patience and the ability to choose both the right location and the correct bait. The ex–police inspector thus ends up identifying a petrol station between Zurich and the canton of Grisons in which to expose a similar-looking young girl to the maniac's temptation, and there he lies in wait as if it were his only reason for living. The wait proves to be excruciating and nerve-racking, until the final denouement, when the cruelty of this case (or the cruelty of chaos) ironically deprives him of his ultimate objective: the capture of the culprit.

The Pledge is a grave and unsettling novel. It is claustrophobic and violent, laden with satire and denunciation. Its pages tangibly radiate the author's critique of the society in which he lives, but it is not limited to Cold War Switzerland, then in search of economic and social reaffirmation. Dürrenmatt is also critical of an entire universe of rationalist certainties that are so rarely capable of reaching satisfactory solutions. As

Dürrenmatt himself states, "the more meticulously man plans, the more likely he is to be subjected to chance."

But *The Pledge* is also a novel about the nature of literary fiction, about the weakness of a plot created solely by clues, a plot that the author repeatedly challenges, stating, without any possibility of contradiction, that facts are never as they appear because they do not abide by mathematical rules. Quite the contrary, they respond better to the chaos of existence dominated by a kind of spectacle of the absurd.

The greatness of this book, always considered crime fiction yet at the same time defined as a true "requiem to the detective story" (as the Italian edition is subtitled), lies in the author's determination to break away from clichés. Dürrenmatt demonstrates how the Truth (with a capital "T") can be revealed through investigation: it is chaos that governs human destiny, not rationality. There is also a deep critique of an imperfect judicial system, satisfied simply to have a culprit while uncovering little of the underlying verity.

Crime writing, in Dürrenmatt's hands, becomes an efficient instrument with which to meditate on life, on the human mind, and on the nature of plot. Skillfully regulated by the intuitions and clues of a thriller, *The Pledge* helps explain how, more often than not, man is in fact ruled by events despite his illusory conviction of dominating them.

According to Dürrenmatt, a story always serves (or should serve) a secondary purpose. It is not just about entertainment, or providing the opportunity for voyeurism that often hides behind the vast popularity of this type of narrative, one that also expects a false and eternal happy ending aimed at restoring the status quo. No, above all the story should insist on exposing evil: that absolutely banal evil that torments man and is made up of wretchedness, cynicism, indifference, and nasty, everyday small-mindedness.

After reading this book I asked a number of friends and acquaintances if they had ever made a promise and, if so, what was it, and what was the outcome? This obsession with the importance of making a promise led me to discover its true essence: the necessity of being faithful and coherent even at the cost of sacrificing one's life, of feeling responsible for one's actions, of getting to the bottom of things despite everyone and everything.

Keeping a promise is perhaps anachronistic in this historical moment, where nothing counts and retracting has become an art. And that is why Dürrenmatt's "little" story must legitimately be considered a classic, providing a basis for ongoing meditation and thoughtful analysis.

The Pledge is a harrowing, emotional, passionate, and desperate novel that does not offer a consolatory or resolved ending, but keeps alive the awareness that a good read (in any genre) is an antidote to the torpor of the mind. Ultimately, it asks the right questions, as opposed to providing the right answers.

Elisabetta Bucciarelli was born in Milan, Italy. She has written for theater, film, and television. As a mystery/crime writer, she is best known for her critically acclaimed series of novels that are set in Milan and feature Inspector Maria Dolores Vergani, the first of which, Happy Hour, *was published in 2005. It was followed by* Dalla parte del torto *in 2007,* Femmina de luxe *(2008),* Io ti perdono *(2009),* Ti voglio credere *(2010) and* Corpi di scarto *(2011). Bucciarelli's screenplay for the short film* Amati Matti *(Beloved Matti, 1996) received a Special Mention at the 53rd Venice Film Festival. Visit her online at www.elisabettabucciarelli.it.*

The Scene
by Clarence Cooper Jr. (1960)

GARY PHILLIPS

Clarence Cooper Jr. (1934–78) led a short and tragic life. His first novel,
The Scene, *was published when he was only twenty-six, and won acclaim for its narrative audacity and its depiction of the lifestyles of the heroin-addicted in the titular Scene, the place in any city where everything is for sale. Unfortunately, Cooper, who was himself a heroin addict, was already in jail by the time the reviews appeared, and his lifestyle meant that mainstream publishers ran scared of him, relegating his subsequent novels to cheap pulp editions. He made one great, final effort for* The Farm *(1967), a daring, experimental love story between addicts set in the infamous Lexington Narcotics Farm, but the novel was judged less by its bravery and quality than by its author's personal failings. Cooper died, penniless and homeless, at the Twenty-third Street YMCA in New York.*

In brooding crime films like *The Killers, Detour,* and *Double Indemnity,* the stories begin with the sense of the foreboding that is the undercurrent to the story about to unfold in flashback. In *Double Indemnity* the antihero Walter Neff is dying from a gunshot wound. In *The Killers,* the Swede awaits, Zen-like, his inevitable demise. In *Detour,* Al Roberts sits quietly in a diner listening to a song on the juke that used to be the song for him and his gal before it all went wrong.

I don't know if the late Clarence Cooper Jr. was a fan of crime films, but in his novel *The Scene* he puts the story in motion with murder and a flashback, and there is certainly foreboding.

In *The Scene,* we are initially introduced to Rudy Black. He is young, ambitious, and ruthless, and all about fattening his pockets. In his dog-eat-dog arena, these are the strengths that he needs to survive. The Scene is an area of an unnamed town, though it could be modeled on parts of Cooper's native Detroit. Cooper describes it this way:

> All the elements of the Scene—the lights, the whores, the tricks in their cars, the razzle of jazz music from the record shop on the corner of Seventy-seventh and Maple—repelled Rudy, the pimp and pusher, made him feel alien, a person without stable ground or purpose, although he knew no other atmosphere but this.

The Scene was originally published in 1960 by Crown, a division of Random House. The *New York Herald-Tribune* noted, "Not even Nelson Algren's *The Man with the Golden Arm* burned with the ferocious intensity you'll find here." Like the two erstwhile godfathers of ghetto lit who would come down the line a little later in the 1960s, Donald Goines and Robert Beck, aka Iceberg Slim (a pimp whose life and fiction would inspire gangsta rapper Tracy Marrow, aka Ice-T, to adopt his swagger and moniker), Cooper wrote from hard-earned experience.

Goines, like Rudy Black, had been a hophead and a third-rate pimp. Reading Iceberg Slim's fictionalized biography *Pimp: The Story of My Life* while in the joint, Goines was still behind bars when he wrote his first two books. Cooper had also served two years at Iona Penitentiary, among others jolts, and by the time *The Scene* and *The Syndicate* came out in 1960, he would be back inside.

Cooper was also, like Goines and Beck, a heroin addict, and although he managed to get clean at times, he would, like his doomed characters, find its pull inescapable. Yet he could also be coldly detached, writing passages in *The Scene* that are harrowing in their authenticity as he shows us the allure and the curse of H. There are various other characters in the book, and Cooper shifts points of view among them: booster girls, first-timers, single mother Black Bertha who pushes junk but doesn't use, a couple of black cops—the growling, cynical veteran Mance Davis and college-educated, idealistic Virgil Patterson. Rollers, the junkies call the cops, out to flip the weak addicts and make the big bust of the Man and the man above the Man, Big Boy. Cooper effortlessly switches in and out of their perspectives. In a cinematic way, he'd cut from a scene before it unfolded fully, keeping his pace fast, sometimes jittery like one of his junkies in search of his "stuff."

Cooper's book came along at a time when the civil rights movement was burgeoning. The Montgomery bus boycott of 1955–56,* a few years before *The Scene* appeared, had been successful, further energizing the fight for equal rights. This aspiration by America's black citizenry was foreshadowed in Ralph Ellison's 1952 novel *Invisible Man* and crystallized in Lorraine Hansberry's play *A Raisin in the Sun,* which ran on Broadway in 1959. Sure, the corrosive effects of racism had been chronicled in books like Richard Wright's novel *Native Son,* a kind of sociopolitical crime novel. But what was the black intelligentsia of the day to make of *The Scene,* with its unapologetic descent into a dark underworld where junkies betrayed one another for a bottle cap of "stuff"? This was not literature that uplifted the race. Cooper wasn't profiled in the pages of *Ebony* or, I imagine, discussed much, if at all, among the self-identified arts and literature crowd. The Urban League wouldn't be inviting him to speak at their annual dinner.

It didn't help that Cooper was imprisoned again as *The Scene* garnered attention. According to the intro to the Old School Books edition, published by W. W. Norton, Cooper played bass in a prison band during this period of imprisonment, and pounded out more novels such as *Weed* and *The Dark Messenger.* These books didn't get mainstream treatment like *The Scene,* and were instead published by Regency, a second-tier outfit of the day.

Yakuza-like—that is, with a perverse honor at being among the lowest—it's noteworthy that Beck and Goines were also published by an outsider press, Holloway House. This was an L.A.-based publisher whose white owners came out of the soft-core girlie market, publishing magazines like *Knight* and *Adam.* One of their first books was *The Trial of Adolf Eichmann,* but they hit their stride as the "publishers of the black experience" with titles like *Daddy Cool* by Goines and *Airtight Willie & Me* by Beck. *Daddy Cool* was also republished by Old School Books, and *Airtight* has recently been returned to print by Cash Money Content, the publishing offshoot from the Cash Money rap record label.

Back then you didn't find Holloway House paperbacks in most bookstores. As a teenager, I bought them at the Thrifty's drugstore in

---

* The bus boycott in Montgomery, Alabama, was sparked by the arrest of a black woman, Rosa Parks, for refusing to surrender her seat on a bus to a white passenger. It eventually led to a U.S. Supreme Court decision that declared unconstitutional the Alabama laws requiring segregated buses.

my South Central, Los Angeles, neighborhood. These days, those first-edition Regency and Holloway House paperbacks fetch a nice price.

When, in 1996, Old School Books republished *The Scene,* it was on the cusp of the explosion of ghetto lit: novels—initially self-published—that reflected a gangsta-rap sensibility of slanging dope big-time and getting over. Cooper, and other forgotten black writers of an under-world aesthetic such as Herbert Simmons and Ronald Deane Pharr, also revived by Old School, didn't really fit into that category; nor did they quite fit among the new wave of black crime and mystery writers whose books had started to drop in the late 1980s.

Cooper died in 1978 from an overdose while rooming at the Twenty-third Street YMCA in Manhattan. His last book, *The Farm,* had been published in 1967, once again by Crown. Apparently, that was the last thing he completed. Tony O'Neill, in his piece on Cooper in the *Guardian* newspaper book blog, said about this last novel, "Cooper wrote an institutional novel as ambitious and complex as *One Flew Over the Cuckoo's Nest.*" He also noted in his piece that Cooper's *The Scene* had been favorably compared to William Burroughs in a *New Yorker* review.

So if you're feeling bogue, need to fix your crime jones, read *The Scene.* To paraphrase Rudy Black, it'll be like mainlining an ounce of stuff for Christmas.

The son of a mechanic and a librarian, Gary Phillips draws on his experiences as an inner-city activist, union organizer, state director of a political action committee, and deliverer of dog cages in writing his tales of chicanery and malfeasance. He has won the Chester Himes Award for his fiction and laments that, even after all these years, his poker playing hasn't improved. He will enjoy his payment of whiskey for his essay in Books to Die For *while smoking a few semi-expensive cigars and contemplating the universe. Visit him online at www.gdphillips.com.*

A Stranger in My Grave
by Margaret Millar (1960)

DECLAN HUGHES

Margaret Millar, née Sturm (1915–94), was born in Ontario, Canada, later moving to Santa Barbara, California, following her marriage to fellow writer Kenneth Millar, who wrote under the pseudonym Ross Macdonald. While, posthumously, his reputation has perhaps overshadowed her own, the situation was reversed earlier in their careers, with Margaret winning the Edgar Award for Best Novel in 1956 for her book Beast in View, *an honor that eluded her husband throughout his career. Her novels were sociologically ambitious and psychologically acute, particularly in their unflinching yet empathetic analysis of the interior lives of women.*

She was the greatest female crime writer of the twentieth century. She had the psychological acuity of Patricia Highsmith without the disfiguring misanthropy. Her spellbinding plots were a match for any of the Golden Age Queens of Crime in terms of technical construction, but the depth and subtlety of her characterization and her meticulous delineation of class, race, and sexual manners in postwar California left those illustrious ladies for dust. She wasn't hard-boiled, but the scene in *A Stranger in My Grave* where Juanita Garcia shatters a door panel with a crucifix while her children weep in fear still chills the blood. She wasn't cozy, but her prose was consistently elegant and her storytelling deft, confident, and reassuring. She wrote with wit and salt and wry amusement about rich and poor alike, and she never made a dull or an indifferent sentence. She had a particular insight into women on the edge of nervous collapse, and her writing drew a disconcerting shadow line between sanity and its alleged obverse. She had a way with yearning, romantic men, and a bracing, astringent attitude toward the vanities and self-deceptions of her own sex. She generally avoided the use of a series detective, foregrounding instead characters who may themselves be more implicated in the action than they realize, or are prepared to concede. In so doing she was, at the very least, one of the parents of the subgenre we now call domestic suspense. She was a profound influence on the work of Ruth Rendell, Minette Walters, Laura Lippman, Sophie Hannah, and many others who toil in that darkened glade of the forest, whether they know it or not. If Jane Austen had landed in Southern California in the 1940s, reacquainted herself with the gothic conventions she had pastiched in *Northanger Abbey*, read some Freud, and tried her hand at crime fiction, she might have written like Margaret Millar. And how she could write!

Of a switchboard operator, from *Beast in View:*

> She was an emaciated blonde with trembling hands and a strained, white face, as if the black leech of the earphones had already drawn too much blood.

Of a vain older woman in the same book:

> The second drink had brought color to her face and made her eyes look like blue glass beads in a doll's head.

Of the same woman as a young mother:

> . . . the conversation was conducted by Verna Clarvoe, who would chatter endlessly on the I-me-my level. Neither of the children had much to say, or if they had, they had been instructed not to say it. They were like model prisoners at the warden's table . . .

And of course there is her famous line from *How Like an Angel*, which, with its sly allusion to a climactic scene of confession and revelation, could form the epigraph to any detective novel:

> Most conversations are simply monologues delivered in the presence of a witness.

A Stranger in My Grave (1960) seems to me her masterpiece, but it emerges from an extraordinarily rich seam of form, including *Beast in*

View, An Air That Kills, The Listening Walls, and *How Like an Angel,* the finest works of her mature period.

> The times of terror began, not in the middle of the night when the quiet and the darkness made terror seem a natural thing, but on a bright and noisy morning during the first week of February.

The tension established at the outset of the novel is characteristic of Millar's work: an atmosphere of gothic dread is invoked and promptly domesticated at the breakfast table of Daisy, "a pretty dark-haired young woman wearing a bright blue robe that matched her eyes, and the faintest trace of a smile. That smile meant nothing. It was one of habit. She put it on in the morning with her lipstick and removed it at night when she washed her face." Daisy sits with her husband, Jim, who is reading items from the newspaper to her as if she is an invalid or a child. When the previous night's dream suddenly convulses her with terror, Jim offers her milk, and warns her to take better care of her health.

> No, it's too late for that, she thought. All the milk and vitamins and exercise and fresh air and sleep in the world don't make an antidote for death.

Millar later revealed the one-sentence idea that had originally set the book in motion: a woman dreams of visiting a cemetery and seeing, engraved on a granite tombstone, her name, the date of her birth, and the date of her death four years previously. Write your way out of that one, kiddo.

Any notion of the diminishing returns that often follow what we would now call such a high-concept pitch are happily absent: the working through of the story is organic and natural, if every bit as complex as one of her husband's novels. The traumatic effect of an event Daisy has confused with her death is gradually confronted, and a tightly wound blood knot of sex, race, and the fight for survival unravels, breathtakingly, on the very last page, in a manner that is electrifying and unbelievably moving.

I mentioned her husband. She was married, of course, to Kenneth Millar, better known as Ross Macdonald, who, of course, just happens to be the greatest male crime writer of the twentieth century: two Canadians (one by birth, the other by upbringing) who saw California plain, two titans of the genre. No wonder the house was said occasionally to have echoed to the sound of slamming doors. Their success as writers and their evident happiness, for the most part, in each other's company was challenged by the arrival of their daughter, Linda, a lost girl whose short and often unhappy life is a disarming presence in their books and often appears to have been foreseen in their pages.

At the time of this writing, none of Margaret Millar's books are in print in the United States. It is more than time to rescue the reputation of this great American novelist. She deserves the kind of reissue program that Richard Yates and Dawn Powell have received in recent years. Yes, she is that good.

Declan Hughes is the author of the Ed Loy PI series: The Wrong Kind of Blood, The Color of Blood, The Price of Blood, All the Dead Voices, *and* City of Lost Girls. *His books have been nominated for the Edgar, Shamus, Macavity, Theakstons Old Peculier, and CWA Dagger awards.* The Wrong Kind of Blood *won the Shamus for Best First PI Novel, and, in France, the Le Point Prize for Best European Crime Novel. Declan is also an award-winning playwright, and the cofounder and former artistic director of Rough Magic Theatre Company. His plays include* Digging for Fire, Twenty Grand, *and* Shiver. *Visit him online at www.declanhughesbooks.com.*

A Night for Screaming
by Harry Whittington (1960)

The word "prolific" may have been invented for Harry Whittington (1915–89), who published more than 170 novels under a variety of pseudonyms, at one point publishing eighty-five titles in one twelve-year period. He was called the "King of the Pulps," and the titles of his novels possess an admirable frankness: Desire in the Dust *(1956),* Backwoods Tramp *(1959),* Strip the Town Naked *(1960),* God's Back Was Turned *(1961), and* Cora Is a Nympho *(1963). Highly regarded for the pace and plotting of what his publisher Stark House describes as "lurid and brisk noir," Whittington adopted the pen name Ashley Carter late in his career, and wrote a series of Southern historical novels.*

The decade of the 1950s saw the death of the pulp magazines. They had a good run, but by 1960 only a handful of titles remained. What took their place? Digest magazines for one thing. Men's adventure magazines for another. But the main replacement for the pulps was the original paperback novel. Beginning with Gold Medal Books in 1950, the market for original paperback fiction exploded. Gold Medal's first print run for most titles was into the hundreds of thousands, and any number of paperback writers sold millions of books. Some, like John D. MacDonald, Lawrence Block, and Donald Westlake, went on to hardback success, but the majority of the writers who specialized in that field saw most of their work published only in paperback and never attained hardcover fame, even though they were equally deserving of it. Jim Thompson and David Goodis, pretty much ignored during their lifetimes, have come to the fore recently, while others remain mostly unknown. One of the best of them, and my particular enthusiasm for nearly fifty years, is Harry Whittington, and one of my favorites of his novels is *A Night for Screaming*.

Whittington did many things well, but what he did best was to take his protagonist and put him (or her, in some cases) in a really bad situation, one from which escape seems impossible. But as bad as things might appear for the protagonist in the beginning, they get even worse. And worse. And then worse still. There's nothing new in piling trouble on trouble, I know. Writers have been doing it since Homer wrote *The Odyssey.* But Whittington is a real expert, and he carries it off in book after book, though nowhere better than in *A Night for Screaming.*

The first-person narrator of the novel is Mitch Walker. Walker's an ex-cop, so he's been around, but there are some things that give problems to even the toughest of men. Walker's been accused of murder, though he's not guilty. Unfortunately for him, he's the only one who believes in his innocence, so he has to go on the run. When the book opens he's in a small town in Kansas, the last place in the world where anybody might expect him to be. Or so he thinks, until Fred Palmer shows up and almost spots him. Palmer is Walker's former partner, and he's a very good detective. He's also someone who'll be quite happy to shoot Walker on sight. In fact, Walker suspects that Palmer would be glad to see him dead.

To escape Palmer, Walker signs up to work at Great Plains Empire Farms, a huge operation where a man can hide out in safety, where the hired hands get a dollar a day, and where nobody asks any questions. Not everyone there is a hired hand, however. A good many of the workers are prisoners from the local jail. They work for free.

The farm might be a good place to hide, but it's far from being a paradise. The overseers are brutal, and the work and living conditions are no better than those on a prison chain gang. Walker can take it, however, as long as he knows that he's safe from Palmer.

The owner of the farm is Bart Cassel, and he's the big man in the county. He likes Walker and lets him know that there's plenty of opportunity for Walker to move into a much better job at the farm. There are other opportunities, too, as Cassel has a plan to help Mitch make a lot of money. Besides the plan, Cassel also has a beautiful wife of whom he's murderously jealous. The wife, Eve, appears to like Walker as much as her husband does, though in quite a different way. She has plenty of problems of her own, and she also has some interesting proposals for Walker.

At this point you might be thinking, Haven't I been on this ride before? No, you haven't. Maybe you've been on similar rides if you've read

James M. Cain or many of the paperbacks from the 1950s, but I can promise you that you've never been on one quite like this. Whittington takes familiar elements and makes them seem fresh and new even now, more than fifty years after the book's original publication.

Part of it is in the plotting. Whittington once wrote an essay based on a talk he'd given. The title was "Baby, I Could Plot," and he wasn't bragging at all. He was just stating the facts, and he proves it again and again in books like *A Night for Screaming*. The setup might not be anything out of the ordinary, but before you get to the end of the novel, at least in this case, you'll have survived several neck-snapping twists, three or four of which come in the last sixty pages or so. When you do get to the end, you'll be wrung out like an old washcloth.

And let me tell you, you'll get to the end in a hurry. Starting this book is like stepping on a jet plane but without the hassle at the airport. Once you start, there's no getting off until you reach the end of the journey.

Another Whittington virtue is characterization. He doesn't write about supermen. Nothing comes easy for his characters. Mitch Walker might be a former cop, but he's as likely to make mistakes as anyone, and he makes more than one in the course of *A Night for Screaming*. And when you cut him, he bleeds. He might figure things out eventually, but as with most of us, it takes him a while. The minor characters are vivid, too. The waitress in the first chapter has only a walk-on, but she practically steps off the page, as do several others.

Finally, there's the emotion. Whittington gets under the skin of his characters so well that their sweat drips on the page. Their fear and pain blaze right through the covers of the book, and for the time you're reading about them, you're right there with them.

Harry Whittington didn't pretend to be the Great American Novelist. He was happy to be the King of the Paperbackers, to give readers a few hours of rousing entertainment, to make them feel and suffer and triumph along with his characters, to give them a book that practically comes alive in their hands. Few could do it as well, and *A Night for Screaming* is the living proof.

Bill Crider is the author of more than fifty published novels and numerous short stories. He won the Anthony Award for Best First Mystery Novel in 1987 for Too Late to Die. *He and his wife, Judy, won the Best Short Story Anthony in 2002 for their story "Chocolate Moose." His story "Cranked" from* Damn Near Dead *(Busted Flush Press) was nominated for the Edgar Award. His latest novel is* Murder of a Beauty Shop Queen *(St. Martin's). Visit him online at www.billcrider.com.*

The Woman Chaser
by Charles Willeford (1960)

SCOTT PHILLIPS

Charles Willeford (1919–88) was a prolific writer of poetry, prose, and criticism, although he is best known among mystery readers for his four novels featuring Detective-Sergeant Hoke Moseley of the Miami Police Department, one of which, Miami Blues *(1984), became a successful film directed by George Armitage. Written at the end of his life, they provided Willeford with his first real taste of public acclaim, but he died of a heart attack shortly after writing the final Moseley book. Willeford's principal strength was his characterization, and he was particularly astute about men and male sexuality. His credo was: "Just tell the truth, and they'll accuse you of writing black humor . . ."*

i. A Self-Made Man

Orphaned as a small child, Charles Willeford ran away from his grandmother as a young teenager when he realized that she couldn't afford to take care of him anymore. After spending a good chunk of the Great Depression jumping freights, he joined the army, eventually serving as a tank commander in the Battle of the Bulge. After the war he served in the U.S. Air Force and taught himself to write. (Two of his best books are memoirs—*I Was Looking for a Street* and *Something About a Soldier*—and neither one contains a molecule of self-pity, just sharp-eyed, sardonic self-observation.)

He was as self-made as any great writer ever was, and the self-made man is a staple cliché of the American mythos. Yet Willeford was as undeluded about the true nature of the American dream as any writer since Twain, Mencken, or Bierce. His antiheroes cheat, brawl, lie, and seduce their way, unencumbered by notions of fair play, through a postwar

American landscape Norman Rockwell never painted, a savage bear-baiting pit that would have made Frank Capra wet his pants in horror. Willeford thought it was funny.

ii. Richard Hudson, Self-Made Artiste

Years after its publication, Willeford dismissed *The Woman Chaser* as a quickie, written for money, but I have to believe that this was an offhand remark, carelessly made. It bears all the hallmarks of his best books, and it's an exhilarating read. More significantly, it harkens back to an earlier work that must have had some serious significance for the author. *The Woman Chaser* features a narrator who bears such a startling resemblance to Russell Haxby, the protagonist of his first published novel, *High Priest of California*,* that it's been suggested the later novel could be considered a sequel. Both characters are callous cynics accomplished at the art of heartless seduction, both car salesmen whose profession has informed and confirmed a bleak view of human nature. They even share a set of initials. And then there's the matter of artistic ambitions and talents.

Any number of Willeford protagonists have a secret artistic skill that's completely self-taught and inexplicable: Frank Mansfield, the voluntarily mute narrator of *Cockfighter*, plays the guitar brilliantly onstage without ever having received a minute's worth of instruction. In *The Burnt Orange Heresy*, art critic Jacques Figueras discovers to his own amazement that he can paint. In *High Priest*, Haxby takes it upon himself to rewrite *Ulysses*, just for laughs. In *The Woman Chaser*, Richard Hudson dances an impromptu and virtuosic pas de deux with his ballerina mother—a scene whose queasily incestuous overtones became even more cringe-inducing when committed to celluloid by Robinson Devor in his very faithful

---

* *High Priest* wasn't the first novel he wrote. That was *Deliver Me from Dallas*, written in collaboration with a writer by the name of W. Franklin Sanders. Sanders had the book published in 1961 in altered form under the title *Whip Hand* without Willeford's knowledge or sanction and, most damningly, without his name on the cover. Dennis McMillan published the original version in 2001, and what's most remarkable about it is what it lacks: the assured, sardonic, insouciance of Willeford's voice, which debuts fully formed and full of confident swagger in *High Priest*.

1999 adaptation. (Taking this creepy vibe several steps further, Hudson deflowers his stepfather's sexually aggressive teenaged daughter Becky. As he sees it, he's doing the kid a favor.)

But *la danse* runs a poor second to Hudson's consuming passion. Having grown tired of the used-car racket, he comes to the realization that he has a desperate need to create a great work of art. But in what form? It doesn't take him long to narrow it down to the only medium he can imagine: "Painting, sculpture, music, architecture, the writing of a novel—all of these art forms take years of apprenticeship . . . *But I knew I could write and direct a movie!*"

iii. The Man Who Got Away

Willeford's original title for the novel was *The Director*, and though Hudson does get his share of casual sex in the book, the publisher's title is a pure bait and switch. Richard Hudson doesn't chase women because he doesn't have to. His stepsister keeps coming back to him until he cuts her off, for fear that her father, Leo, a washed-up director who's Hudson's connection to the studio, will find out about it. When the film gets set up, he screws the actress playing the wife of the lead, and he sets about seducing his pretty and virginal secretary Laura, just for the challenge of it.

So as the car lot he's supposed to be managing goes straight to hell (in an act of casual assholery, he orders his salesmen to dress in Santa suits in the midst of a sweltering L.A. July), Richard makes his movie, a devastatingly bleak film noir about a truck driver who kills a child and leads the cops on a cross-country chase. The trucker finally manages to escape the suburban life he so despises by being beaten to death by an angry mob.

To hear Hudson describe it, the movie sounds like a small masterpiece, wherein lies the problem. It's too short for feature distribution, only sixty-three minutes long, and the studio demands that he add another twenty. It's perfect, he protests, but the money men have no sympathy for the artist's predicament and yank the film away from him. Hudson's revenge is disproportionate and wonderful, and you'll have to read the book to find out what it is.

The irony here—and it's of the cheaper variety—is that Devor's excellent film version, shot in color but printed in beautiful, high-contrast black and white, played briefly in coastal art houses before being submitted to cable TV. The network insisted on running it in color, and with several key cuts, including the moment where Hudson slugs pretty Laura in the belly after she announces that she's pregnant.* I have heard, and perhaps he will correct me if my impression is incorrect, that Mr. Devor objected strenuously to these changes and, like Richard Hudson before him, was informed that his services were no longer required on the film. The cuts were made, the film showed in color, and it has never been released on DVD. Which is a shame.

iv. A Heavyhanded Discussion of Art and Commerce that Willeford Would Have Loathed

Like Philip K. Dick, Willeford died at the height of his creative powers, at a time when his books were finally getting some attention from the larger reading public. As stated, the man did a lot of things in his life, and to those of us who are fanatical admirers of his work it may seem absurd that he spent any energy doing anything else other than writing. But he went through long periods without publishing, and it may be that *The Woman Chaser* is the result of a decade of frustration in dealing with fly-by-night paperback houses, title-changing editors, and troublesome agents. It's commonplace that the novelist has complete control over his or her work, but in fact there are always forces reminding you that your movie has to be longer than sixty-three minutes, or that you can't have the star of your movie punch his pregnant girlfriend, or that it can't be in black and white anymore because these kids today, by God, they want color. I can't speak for him, and wouldn't dare, but I like to think that this book is a lovely middle finger extended at the moneychangers in the literary and artistic temples.

Go read it.

---

*Watching a video of the uncut, black-and-white version supplied by a friend close to the production, I turned to my wife at this particular juncture and said, "He's lost you, hasn't he?" "No," she said with some vehemence. "I'm with him." Such is the power of the Willefordian protagonist.

Scott Phillips lives in St. Louis, Missouri, for reasons he can no longer articulate but that once must have made sense to him. He is the author of any number of depraved books, including The Ice Harvest, *made into a film of the same name by Harold Ramis, and most recently the novel* The Adjustment, *as well as a collection of short stories,* Rum, Sodomy, and False Eyelashes. *Visit him online at www.scottphillipsauthor.com.*

The Light of Day (aka *Topkapi*)
by Eric Ambler (1962)

First published with The Dark Frontier *(1936), Eric Ambler (1909–98) is credited with investing the spy novel with a radical dash of gritty realism. He is best known for* The Mask of Dimitrios *(1939),* Journey into Fear *(1940), and* The Light of Day *(1962), the last of which won the Edgar Award for Best Novel. Ambler also won two Gold Daggers, for* Passage of Arms *(1959) and* The Levanter *(1972), was named a Grand Master by the Mystery Writers Association of America, and was made an Officer of the Order of the British Empire by Queen Elizabeth. An accomplished screenwriter, Ambler wrote the screenplays for* A Night to Remember *(1958),* The October Man *(1947), and* The Cruel Sea *(1953). His autobiography, published in 1985, was titled* Here Lies. *The arrangement of the cover typography allowed it to read* Here Lies Eric Ambler.

"It came down to this: if I had not been arrested by the Turkish police, I would have been arrested by the Greek police."

So begin the adventures of pimp, pornographer, and thief Arthur Abdel Simpson, told in the first person. He is the product of an Egyptian mother and a British sergeant father. Arthur is fond of quoting the wisdom of his father's sayings, such as "Bullshit beats brains." He is probably one of the most fascinating antiheroes of all time. The miracle of Ambler's writing is that the reader somehow wants this decidedly unlovely character to succeed.

The story opens at Athens airport where Arthur spots a likely mark in a Mr. Harper. Arthur gives him his card, with the message "Car waiting outside for Mr. Harper." On the road to the Grande Bretagne Hotel, Arthur offers his services as a guide. That evening, after a visit to a restaurant and club, Arthur leaves him at a brothel and nips back to the hotel, lets himself into Harper's room with a forged passkey, and is in the process of collecting several traveler's check number slips that people keep in case they lose the checks. He plans to use the numbers to collect the replacement checks himself.

He is caught by Harper, who threatens to turn him over to the Greek police unless Arthur does a job for him. The job is to drive a limousine to Istanbul, but at the frontier the Turks take off the doors of the car and find they are full of arms. Arthur's only way out is to spy for the Turkish police by finding out Harper's plans for the weapons.

Ambler is credited with being the inspiration for John le Carré and Graham Greene. He took the spy story away from the gentleman sleuth. The book was made into a film, *Topkapi,* with Peter Ustinov playing Arthur.

Arthur craves a British passport, having only an Egyptian one, which has run out. Although his father was British and he went to school in Britain, he cannot get a British passport because he has a criminal record in Britain. Amusing though the book is, and a real page-turner, Ambler does highlight the dilemma of the stateless person.

Ambler obviously loves Istanbul and has fond memories of the old Park Hotel, which burned down, the one hotel in the world in which, as it was built on the side of a cliff, you entered the reception area and took a lift *down* to your room.

The Light of Day was written in 1962 but is still as fresh as ever.

M. C. Beaton writes: I have two detectives featured in my books—Agatha Raisin and Hamish Macbeth. The new Hamish Macbeth just out is Death of a Kingfisher. *I started my career as a fiction buyer for John Smith & Sons in Glasgow and wrote theater reviews for the* Daily Mail. *I then became fashion editor of* Scottish Field *and moved on to the* Scottish Daily Express *as crime reporter, then moving to Fleet Street to be chief woman reporter of the* Daily Express. *After marriage to journalist and writer Harry Scott Gibbons, and a move to New York and brief spell working for Rupert Murdoch's* Star, *I started to write historical novels, but after more than a hundred of those, I changed to writing detective fiction. The new Agatha Raisin, out in October, is called* Hiss & Hers. *Visit her online at www.mcbeaton.com and www.agatharaisin.com.*

Cover Her Face
by P. D. James (1962)

DEBORAH CROMBIE

Phyllis Dorothy James White (b. 1920) is the award-winning, British-born author of more than twenty books, among them the Adam Dalgliesh and Cordelia Gray mysteries; the dystopian novel The Children of Men *(1992); and a number of works of nonfiction, including* Talking About Detective Fiction *(2009), her study of the genre. She is a Conservative life peer in the House of Lords, with the title Baroness James of Holland Park.*

Cover Her Face was P. D. James's first detective novel, published in 1962, and I initially came across it perhaps ten years later, in the 1970s. Having developed an early preference for English detective fiction, I'd read my way through many of what we now refer to as the Golden Age writers—Christie, Allingham, Marsh, Tey, and particularly Dorothy L. Sayers.

I'm sure I reread *Cover Her Face* at least once while James continued to publish successive novels featuring Metropolitan Police detective Adam Dalgliesh, as well as the two books featuring private detective Cordelia Gray. I do know that I reread it carefully in the late 1980s, when I was just beginning to dip my own toes into the waters of detective fiction, so it was with much anticipation that I looked forward to reading it once more in preparation for this essay, after a gap of more than twenty years.

Now a writer of British detective novels myself, I chose *Cover Her Face* because, in my recollection, it had seemed a watershed novel in the British canon, a leap into modernity from the by then slightly crusty conventions of the British detective novel as it had developed between the wars.

The book begins, as do most of the later James novels, not with the discovery of a body, but with a careful building up of the setting and the characters, with particular attention paid to the victim.

In a medieval manor house in the fictional Essex village of Chadfleet, the Maxie family has taken on a new maid, an unwed mother named Sally Jupp. She is employed to help with the housework and with the nursing of the terminally ill Mr. Simon Maxie. The other members of the household are Mrs. Eleanor Maxie; her son, Stephen, a doctor at a London hospital; her daughter, Deborah Riscoe, a widow; a domestic servant, Martha Bulitaft; Felix Hearne, a decorated war hero and friend of Deborah Riscoe; and Catherine Bowers, a nurse who is a family friend but who has had a relationship with Stephen Maxie.

On the evening of the annual church fête, Sally Jupp announces to the family that Stephen Maxie has proposed to her. The next morning, Sally is found dead in her room, strangled, with the door locked from the inside.

Only then are we introduced to our policeman. Detective Chief Inspector Adam Dalgliesh is a professional detective rather than an amateur dilettante. While a few of the Golden Age detectives were policemen, perhaps most notably Ngaio Marsh's Roderick Alleyn, they were also aristocrats and, in a sense, glorified amateurs who played at solving crimes.

But while Adam Dalgliesh is highly intelligent, educated, and articulate (as well as tall, dark, and handsome, perhaps in tribute to Jane Austen's Mr. Darcy), he is not a "gent." Nor is murder taken lightly in this first James novel, an attitude that marks a departure from most Golden Age whodunits, as does the fact that the victim is not merely a catalyst for the puzzle. Sally Jupp is never likable, but she is real, a complex young woman whose actions, as we see over the course of the novel, set in motion the circumstances that lead to her death. And when the murderer is finally revealed, it is someone with whom we can feel empathy, even if we don't condone the crime.

All these things I remembered, and all, I think, contributed to my sense that this book was in some ways groundbreakingly modern.

But there were other things that surprised me in rereading it. I'd forgotten just how strongly the book draws on its predecessors. It is a country house mystery in every sense. Its cast of characters includes not only the family of the manor house, but the village doctor, the vicar, the woman who runs a local charitable organization (in this case, a home for unmarried mothers), and, of course, the maid, who is the victim.

Class distinctions are drawn quickly and brutally. But if the characters are unaware of their bias, the author is not, and it is at least in part the maid's refusal to stay in her proper place that leads to her undoing. And it is here, in James's finely and sometimes scathingly drawn portraits of her characters, that we see the already sure hand of the novelist.

I found it much more difficult than I'd expected to view this first novel out of the context of those that followed. It surprised me to find that the setting was so amorphous. We know that the story takes place in a village in Essex, and the manor house itself has a strong presence, but the book lacks the detailed sense of place that we have come to expect in James's later novels.

And then there is Dalgliesh, the prototype of the modern fictional British policeman. How little we learn of the man in this first novel! We know, because he is already a chief inspector, that he is both experienced and good at his job. We are told that, many years previously, he lost his wife and unborn child. We have yet to learn that he is a poet, or just how solitary a man he really is. Throughout the course of the novel, he is seen most often through the eyes of the other characters—relentless in his pursuit of the truth, compassionate when it suits his purpose, comfortable with his own authority. And yet, because he does not confide his thought processes to his sergeant, George Martin, and the reader is not otherwise granted access to his deductions, his arrival at the solution to the mystery (the denouement is played out in the business room of the manor house, which might as well be the library) seems almost omniscient. It is only at the very end of the novel, in a beautifully written coda, that we get our first glimpse of Dalgliesh as fallible, human, and vulnerable. But make no mistake: James plays fair with the reader. All the clues are there, and it's a credit to the solution that I remembered it in almost every detail even after such a long gap between readings.

And then there is the prose itself, which then, as now, sets James apart. It is often simple, as in this description of Martingale House as Adam Dalgliesh sees it at the very close of the book, but always moving in its descriptive power:

> The beeches were golden now but the twilight was draining them of colour. The first fallen leaves crackled into dust beneath the tyres. The house came into view as he had first seen it, but greyer now and slightly sinister in the fading light.

It is P. D. James's skilled use of language, I think, combined with her unflinching depth of characterization, that firmly marks *Cover Her Face* as a bridge between the enjoyable but workmanlike whodunits (with the exception of the Peter Wimsey novels of Dorothy L. Sayers) of the years between the wars, and the evolution of the British detective story into its modern incarnation, the detective *novel*, which can take its place with the best of today's literature.

New York Times *best-selling author Deborah Crombie is a native Texan who writes crime novels set in Britain, featuring Detective Superintendent Duncan Kincaid and Detective Inspector Gemma James. The series has received numerous awards, including Edgar, Macavity, and Agatha nominations, and has been published in more than a dozen countries to international acclaim. Crombie lives in north Texas with her husband, German shepherds, and cats, and divides her time between Texas and Great Britain. Her latest novel,* No Mark Upon Her, *was published by William Morrow in February 2012. She is currently working on her fifteenth Kincaid/James novel. Visit her online at www.deborahcrombie.com.*

The Damned and the Destroyed
by Kenneth Orvis (1962)

LEE CHILD

A pseudonym for Kenneth Lemieux, Kenneth Orvis (b. 1923) is one of the very few professional hockey players to turn his hands to crime writing. His novels included The Damned and the Destroyed *(1962),* Night Without Darkness *(1965), and* The Doomsday List *(1974). In 1985, Orvis published the nonfiction title* Over and Under the Table: The Anatomy of an Alcoholic.

I bought this as a sixty-cent Belmont paperback in the spring of 1969, along with another pulp item about a fictional rock trio called the Kavaliers. (You think it's weird to remember what books you bought on a particular day forty-three years ago? Then you're not a writer.)

I didn't pay sixty cents for it, though, because I bought it in Birmingham, England, where I lived. I probably paid less than three shillings for it. What I can't remember is where. Birmingham had a couple of big, stuffy bookstores, and neither of them would have carried a direct import from the States—especially not one like this. I probably got it at a record store. This was pre-Virgin (which started as a small chain of record stores), but there were hip precursors springing up all over, carrying direct imports of American vinyl, and head shop stuff—and this book matched that kind of inventory very well.

The cover was a lurid triumph. The title was in white, in lowercase, over a dark red dried-blood color, and at the top was an oil or pastel picture. On the left was a young woman's face—heavy lidded, messy hair, red parted lips—and behind it and to the right was an orgy: a topless woman (her back turned to us) and couples kissing. The young woman was clearly spaced out. Which went with the first of two strap lines, above the title: "She was beautiful, young, blonde, and a junkie . . . I had to help her!" The second strap line was below the title: "A relentless story of the hell of drug addiction."

My kind of thing, back in 1969.

But you can't judge a book by its cover, and what lay inside was not quite as advertised—although by no means a disappointment. Quite the reverse, actually. This was a solid, high-quality thriller. (But badly put together. I remember a typo on the second page: "actaully" for "actually.")

First surprise: it was Canadian, not American, set in Montreal at the turn of the 1960s. (Copyright date was 1962, I remember.) The opening was a very short expository info dump, via dialogue. The city government had just changed, and an anticrime crusade was starting, aiming "without delay to put vice on ice in Montreal." Then we meet the hero, a private investigator named Maxwell Dent. Like most of his generation, Dent is ex-services, and pretty solid—a bit of a stiff, basically. Then the rich guy with the daughter problem calls him—very Raymond Chandler. The daughter is a heroin addict, and to feed her habit she's stolen a family ring—not only valuable, but recognizable.

And we're off to the races.

What follows is Dent's mission to rescue the lovely Helen Ashton, and to bed Helen's equally lovely big sister Thorn, and to get the ring back, and finally to bust the Back Man, thereby saving future Helen Ashtons from the relentless hell of drug addiction. I guess the mechanics of the narcotics trade are a little dated, but nothing else is, really. This is where thrillers were in about 1960, and not much has changed.

Lee Child turned to writing thrillers after being made redundant by Granada Television in 1995. His debut novel, Killing Floor, *appeared in 1997, featuring his series hero, the peripatetic ex-military policeman Jack Reacher. It won the Macavity and Anthony awards. There are seventeen Jack Reacher novels in total, the most recent being* A Wanted Man *(2012). In 2011, Child won the Theakstons Old Peculier Crime Novel of the Year Award for* 61 Hours *(2010). He was elected president of the Mystery Writers of America in 2009. A film of his novel* One Shot *(2005) will be released in 2013, directed by Christopher McQuarrie and starring Tom Cruise.*

The Hunter
(aka *Point Blank* and *Payback*)
by Richard Stark (1962)

F. PAUL WILSON

Richard Stark was one of the many pen names of Donald Westlake (1933–2008), a hugely prolific writer of novels and short stories, most of them in the mystery genre, who operated under more pseudonyms than most convicted fraudsters. He was a committed writer from his youth, and began writing soft-porn novels under the pen name Alan Marshall at the end of the 1950s before finally publishing The Mercenaries, *his first novel as Donald Westlake, in 1960. He won Edgar Awards in three different categories, and many of his works were adapted for film, most famously his 1962 novel* The Hunter, *which became the basis for John Boorman's 1967 film* Point Blank, *starring Lee Marvin, as well as Ringo Lam's* Full Contact *(1992), and the Mel Gibson vehicle* Payback *(1999).*

As a Lee Marvin fan, I couldn't miss the movie *Point Blank*. And being an aspiring writer at the time (we're talking 1967), I always kept an eye on the credits for the name of the screenwriter. This film had three but was "based on the novel *The Hunter* by Richard Stark."

Who the hell was Richard Stark and how did he get *The Hunter* made into a film?

I went on the hunt myself and found a movie tie-in edition. I didn't know that Richard Stark was a pseudonym for Donald Westlake and wouldn't have cared if I had—Westlake was a relative newbie then. I plunked down fifty cents and started reading.

Whoa! I'd thought the movie gritty and violent, but that was kindergarten fare compared to the novel. The protagonist, Parker, capitalizes the "anti" in "antihero". Parker who? Who Parker? We never know. He has aliases, but most of his cronies, his wife included, know him only as Parker. He even thinks of himself simply as "Parker."

Set in the early 1960s (published in 1962), *The Hunter* opens with:

> When a fresh-faced guy in a Chevy offered him a lift, Parker told
> him to go to hell.

He's in the process of walking across the George Washington Bridge toward Manhattan—a penniless, raw-boned man in ill-fitting clothes, a man with a major chip on his shoulder, a man with a purpose, but we don't know what. By the end of the day he's scammed his way into a new suit, a hotel room, and eight hundred bucks in cash. Along the way, he skates a subway turnstile, bums a dime from "a latent fag with big hips," is needlessly cruel to a diner waitress, forges a license, and empties some poor SOB's bank account. And that's just Chapter 1.

All right . . . this is the bad guy, right? When do we meet the *good* guy? Don't hold your breath.

Chapter 2 opens with Parker looking down at a beautiful blonde whom he's just slugged and knocked to the floor.

As shocking as the scene was, this neophyte writer was struck by the economy of the transition. A page later, intervening events are backfilled in a couple of sentences, but Stark spares us the trip from Parker's hotel to the apartment house, as well as entering the apartment and (most important) delivering the punch. Instead, he plops us in medias res.

The woman is Lynn, Parker's wife. We learn that she betrayed him after a heist and left him for dead to run off with Mal Resnick, one of the heist crew.

> "I was never a whore, Parker," she said. "You know that."
> "No. You sold my body instead."

We learn Parker's mission: to get his hands around Mal Resnick's throat and squeeze the life out of him.

The next morning he finds Lynn dead of an overdose, and his only emotion is anger that he now has to dispose of her body. He spends the day with the corpse, drinking and watching TV. The whole while, his wife is never "Lynn," but simply "her" or "she." He's severed *all* connection. Once night comes, he dumps her body in Central Park. He doesn't want Mal spotting a photo of her in the paper, so he slashes her dead face until it's unrecognizable.

Whew.

In the course of his search for Mal, we learn that Parker and Mal and a crew massacred a dozen or more South American revolutionaries who'd come north with ninety thousand dollars to buy guns. We also learn that Parker was planning (surprise!) to kill Mal and take his share, but Mal got to Lynn and forced her to shoot her husband. They left Parker's body and set the house on fire.

Parker wasn't dead, of course. He pulled himself from the burning building, but before he could start his pursuit he was jailed on a vagrancy charge. Finally, he killed a guard, escaped, and headed for New York.

The story switches to Mal's side. He now has a managerial position in the Outfit (read: organized crime). He'd bungled an assignment a while back, resulting in a big loss to the Outfit, but he used the proceeds from the gunrunner heist to pay off the debt. Now he's sitting pretty . . . until he hears that some tough guy is asking questions, looking for him. Who? When he learns Lynn has disappeared, he knows it has to be Parker, back from the supposedly dead.

After some cat and mouse, Parker tracks him down, gets his hands around Mal's throat . . . but eases back. Where's the money? When he learns Mal gave it to the Outfit, Parker gets a list of names from him, *then* strangles Mal.

End of story? No. Parker decides that killing Mal isn't enough. Half of that ninety thousand was rightfully his, and he wants it back. To do so, he's going to have to take on the Outfit. Well, why not?

Now things get a bit surreal, but *really* interesting. Everything that's happened so far has been about settling debts. Lynn and Mal owed him. Other people who died simply got in the way. Now, the way he sees it, the Outfit owes him. And what is owed must be paid. Simple as that, as he explains to one of the Outfit's bigwigs:

> "The funnies call it the syndicate. The goons and hustlers call it the Outfit. You call it the organization. I hope you people have fun with your words. But I don't care if you call yourselves the Red Cross, you owe me forty-five thousand dollars and you'll pay me back whether you like it or not."

Throughout the novel, Parker reveals only what's necessary about himself. But as he makes his moves against the mob, we sneak a peek inside him. His lifestyle until now has involved living in luxury resort hotels, financed by one or two juicy heists a year. That pattern was changed by Lynn's betrayal and he's now caught in a new pattern of collecting on debts. The forty-five thousand will allow him to return to his old pattern. This is his true mission: to restore the old lifestyle.

I don't want to spoil the resolution for those who haven't read it, but I will tell you that it doesn't end like any of the film adaptations. In fact, the final chapter has a tacked-on feel.

Only years later did I learn that *The Hunter* was intended as a one-off, but Westlake/Stark's editor suggested he change the ending to allow for more Parker novels. Was Parker killed in the original? Jailed? Sadly, Donald Westlake is no longer around to answer.

But what is it about Parker that created an audience for twenty-four novels and eight films? (Three based on *The Hunter* alone: *Point Blank, Full Contact, Payback.* None of the films has the real Parker—Hollywood can't resist infusing him with empathy—but Brian Helgeland's *Payback: Straight Up: The Director's Cut* comes the closest, and he was fired from the film because of that.) Parker has no respect for life, liberty, or the pursuit of happiness except his own. He's a sociopath who steals and kills without remorse. He has no code, no honor, even among his fellow thieves, as witnessed by his plan to kill Mal and take his share of the heist.

Yet clearly in *The Hunter* he is the wronged party (just marginally so), and we wind up rooting for him. Perhaps it's Parker's single-mindedness and relentless efficiency that draw us.

I remember tearing through *The Hunter* and wanting more more more, and going out to find it. During the reread to write this essay, the 1962 period setting offered a few smiles: ten cents for a cup of coffee; eighty-five cents considered extravagant for a roast beef sandwich; Mal "splurging" thirty-two bucks on a Midtown hotel suite.

I hit some speed bumps that I hadn't noticed before. Stylistically, the writing is crisp and terse enough to overcome a surplus of passive voice. Try as I might to suspend disbelief, Lynn's betrayal of Parker, despite Mal's threats, doesn't wash. Also, the novel seems padded in spots, most blatantly in Mal's dalliance with the prostitute, and in Parker's surreptitious invasion of the Outfit's hotel only to discover what the reader has known for quite a while: Mal has moved out. Knowing Parker's elaborate

B&E will not lead to a confrontation robs the sequence of all sense of anticipation.

These are quibbles against the big picture of a writer taking a major risk in creating a murderous sociopathic protagonist with a supporting cast that includes not a single decent, trustworthy human being. And making it *work*.

The Hunter: a violent, twisty, oft-imitated tour de force crime novel that was sui generis in its time.

F. Paul Wilson is a New York Times *best-selling author who has won the Stoker, Inkpot, Porgie, and Prometheus awards. His forty-five books span science fiction, horror, adventure, medical thrillers, and virtually everything between. He has written for the stage, screen, and interactive media as well, and his work has been translated into twenty-four languages. His latest thrillers,* Nightworld *and* Cold City, *star his urban mercenary, Repairman Jack.* Jack: Secret Vengeance *is the last of a young-adult trilogy starring a fourteen-year-old Jack. Paul resides at the Jersey Shore. Visit him online at www.repairmanjack.com.*

Gun Before Butter
(aka *Question of Loyalty*)
by Nicolas Freeling (1963)

JASON GOODWIN

Nicholas Freeling (1927–2003) first conceived of his series hero Inspector Van der Valk while under arrest in Amsterdam. Formerly a chef, the author wrote eleven Van der Valk titles, the first, Love in Amsterdam, *appearing in 1962. The inspector's widow, Arlette, appeared in a further two novels after Freeling killed off Van der Valk in 1972. The Henri Castang series of novels followed, the first of which,* A Dressing of Diamonds, *was published in 1974. Freeling also published a number of cookery-related titles, which functioned as semiautobiographical works. The winner of the Edgar Award for* The King of the Rainy Country *(1966), Freeling was also the recipient of a Grand Prix de Littérature Policière and a CWA Gold Dagger.*

Nicolas Freeling suffered a career setback in 1972 when he casually topped his detective, Van der Valk, halfway through his eleventh book. Fans were furious, and his French and Swedish publishers dropped the series, but Freeling refused to resurrect him. Arlette, the detective's wife, took over for a spell, and there were stand-alone thrillers both before and after Freeling went on to create Henri Castang, who never had quite the same persuasive power. Perhaps he was too close to Simenon territory—territory that may have informed, but never overshadowed, the original Van der Valk series.

    Gun Before Butter—the title is quirky and brilliant—was the third of them, published in 1963 along with *Because of the Cats*, set in a Euroland that stretched from Amsterdam to Brussels, with Van der Valk as the unconventional policeman in a conventionally Dutch force. Driven by a dispassionate curiosity about human nature, overstepping the mark a tiny bit each time, Van der Valk edges his way into a case, teasing out its details like a man pulling on woolen threads. He cares about the men and women he investigates, sometimes—as in *Gun Before Butter*—to the point of letting the wrongdoer go free.

But then Freeling himself was a pretty unconventional writer. Born in London, and raised in Southampton and the Irish Free State during the war, he slouched around Europe and became a chef. In Amsterdam he went to jail for stealing food from the kitchen; fascinated by the policeman who interviewed him, he began writing his first novel, *Love in Amsterdam,* on prison soap wrappers.

He belonged to a generation that spat out Agatha Christie and her fellows, and admired Chandler. Writers respond to other writers more than they respond to real life, and Freeling was like Chandler in that he rebelled against the type of crime story in which plot is everything. Who cares, Freeling asked despairingly, who killed Roger Ackroyd? Much later he wrote that

> of all those dreadful "rules" invented for the detective story, the most inescapable was that the personages should be cardboard, jiggled about to follow the Plot. The capitals are deliberate, for character was thought indecent, like taking off one's trousers in church, and the Christie juggernaut was there to make the message felt.

In *Gun Before Butter,* instead of the country house, we have the slew of northern Europe, Holland, French Flanders, Benelux, Dusseldorf. Freeling was not an Englishman abroad: he was a European who happened to write in English. Both in their settings, and in their focus on character and slow-burning drama, Freeling's novels belong to a tradition established by Erskine Childers in his 1912 thriller, *The Riddle of the Sands;* Childers, as it happens, was a cousin of Freeling's.

The other obvious comparison is with Georges Simenon, but Freeling (like Childers) was more interested in contemporary issues. Simenon doesn't talk much about the war—he was practically a collaborator—but in Freeling's books memories, compromise, and loss lurk in the background. Van der Valk probes old wounds concealed under the veneer of polite Dutch society, and looks with wry amusement at the arrangements being made to prevent a new outbreak of hostilities. His stories are absolutely of their time, and, like all the best stories, timeless.

In spite of Freeling's avowed disdain for plot, *Gun Before Butter* has plenty of it: not scaffolding, but delicate filigree work that almost invisibly supports the unfolding of the characters and places with which the story deals. There's a fight between Dutch layabouts and some Italian boys with whom Lucienne Englebert, the object of Van der Valk's affections in the book, is associating. Van der Valk remembers the first time that he saw her, at the scene of a car crash that killed her father, a noted conductor. With Van der Valk she's initially frosty, but unbends a little at his musical knowledge. (Her father's womanizing, Van der Valk thinks, had "lent Englebert's music a tiny touch of the spurious, a hint of insincerity.")

Out of disaffection Lucienne commits a pointless misdemeanor, short-changing customers in a shop. She refuses to take a warning and, when Van der Valk reluctantly books her, she does jail time. She then blows her inheritance traveling round Europe and goes to France, where she can get a proper job. She's a rich girl who doesn't want money; what she wants is something real. She's out of Van der Valk's life for the moment, as his attention shifts to the murder of an unknown man in a small house in Amsterdam. There are no suspects, just a few oddities—a car left parked at a rakish angle in the burgerlich Dutch street, a painting in the house that seems too good for it, a link to a country shooting lodge . . .

Police procedural takes over from what is, really, a whispered love story, as Van der Valk patiently sets to work establishing the identity of the dead man. Freeling's tone throughout is confidential, precise, and immediate. The political police are involved: Van der Valk sidesteps them neatly. When the dead man is revealed to be Stam, a butter smuggler, his superiors seem happy to leave it there: Stam murdered by a rival in a dodgy business, with no surprises. Van der Valk, however, knows too much—and so do we—to let it lie; he carries on with the investigation.

Later, he recognizes Lucienne as a pump attendant and mechanic at a roadside garage. Finally, she agrees to tell her story:

> "I was very happy, you know. I should like someone to know about that. I don't think there is anyone but you I can possibly tell."

She doesn't actually tell us her story: Freeling does. He goes back through Lucienne's life: the details of landing her job, meeting a man, falling in love, losing her virginity. The slow and psychologically acute buildup to the murder is what Freeling is interested in: the crime itself—like Van der Valk's own death, many books later—rushes by so quickly that you have to read it twice to catch it. Lucienne is both impeccable and real, a masterpiece of characterization: as autonomous as the Girl with the Dragon Tattoo but much more believable. Freeling, incidentally, writes sex better than almost anyone, but not much in this book.

> There was bouillabaisse for supper, Arlette's economical one of cod and conger-eel, but she had a good hand with the sauce; it was one of her best dishes. He ate tremendously, and afterwards he put *Fidelio* on the gramophone.
> "I do so love this," said Arlette when it got to the sinister rumtytum of Pizarro's entrance.

I wish I'd eaten a soufflé made by Freeling: he must have cooked, as he writes, with a light hand.

Jason Goodwin has published four crime novels set in nineteenth-century Istanbul and featuring the eunuch investigator Yashim. The first, The Janissary Tree *(2006), won the Edgar Award for Best Novel in 2007.* The Snake Stone *(2007),* The Bellini Card *(2008), and* An Evil Eye *(2011) followed. Goodwin has also published nonfiction titles.* On Foot to the Golden Horn, *his account of walking from Poland to Turkey, won the John Llewellyn Rhys/Mail on Sunday Prize in 1993. Goodwin has also published a history of the Ottoman Empire,* Lords of the Horizons *(1999). Visit him online at www.jasongoodwin.info.*

The Spy Who Came in from the Cold
by John le Carré (1963)

(essay translated from the Spanish by Ellen Clair Lamb)

John le Carré is the nom de plume of David Cornwell (b. 1931), who worked for British Intelligence during the 1950s and 1960s. In 1961 he published his first novel, Call for the Dead; *two years later,* The Spy Who Came in from the Cold *(1963) won the Edgar Award for Best Novel. In all, le Carré has published twenty-two novels, including the Quest for Karla Trilogy, which is composed of* Tinker, Tailor, Soldier, Spy *(1974),* The Honourable Schoolboy *(1977), and* Smiley's People *(1979). Other novels include* The Looking-Glass War *(1965),* The Tailor of Panama *(1996), and* The Constant Gardener *(2001). His most recent novel is* Our Kind of Traitor *(2010).*

My name is Alec Leamas, and I don't give a fuck that it doesn't matter. I am that sad bastard, a broken puzzle dedicated to the noble profession of espionage. Since 1963 I've lived on both sides of the Iron Curtain, with enough kisses from Liz to make a hot breakfast and dinner. I'm strictly resolved to keep her out of my business, but the heart is a ruthless hunter, and I do not know whether it's mine, hers, or both that change the orbit of the earth. Life is full of impossible moments, and in the end, love shows up to screw it all up. Coffee and cognac.

I'm actually Élmer, although I'm also Leamas, and at times Smiley, and at other times John le Carré, most of all when I think about the layers of an onion, when I smoke unfiltered cigarettes or when I drink one whiskey too many.

In 1969, there were nineteen things that forced me to consider the kind of life that awaited me: Neil Armstrong set foot on the rugged moon; *Midnight Cowboy* was voted best film at the Academy Awards (and I saw it seven times); I used acid for the last time; I moved to

Mexico City; I was expelled from a communist cell because I read only novels; I loved Janis Joplin; the famous *Abbey Road* album came out; the Woodstock Festival happened; the Doors were heard in a Mexico City bar; the Metro mass transit opened; a robust Czech with short hair tried to hook me up with a scholarship a month after a CIA agent told him not to and I panicked; and at the end of November I tore through *The Spy Who Came in from the Cold*, the brilliant novel by John le Carré, published in Spanish in 1964.

Taking to the streets to demand the release of the political prisoners of 1968 and the president's resignation, I let my imagination run wild: I saw Karl Riemeck with his bicycle, shot down in front of Alec Leamas. I dreamed of an action-packed life of espionage and the turbulence of the Cold War, with its Iron Curtain and its secretive men. I spent hours suffering along with Alec's journey of self-destruction, which even Control's fatherly ministrations could not reduce—through his isolation, his poverty, his work in the library, Liz Gold (so lacking in charm), his illness, and the row with the shopkeeper. Fucking shopkeepers, they're all the same, well deserving the occasional back of one's hand. Why send the guy up the river for such a minor offense? I imagined Leamas as strong, confident, intelligent, tough enough not to care about anyone—except for Liz, who must have been a skinny old skank, pestering him with the Ronettes and their bitching song: "Be My Baby."

Leamas again: What, you didn't like it? Well, fuck you, you fucking faggots scared of your first time. Quiet, Alec, try this elixir of the Aztec gods. Gods? Save it for your grandmother. It's tequila. Pfft, don't give me any more of that crap, the Americans must like it, they'll drink anything; why do you say that about Liz, maybe you've met her? What do you think? I like a little meat on the bones, some curves, and I stay away from whiners. You want to shut up? I won't let anyone talk about her that way, not you, not anyone. You saw what I did to the shopkeeper's face. Ford was an idiot. Yes, and you killed that guard at the hunting lodge, too. Life has its things that set me afire. What is the essential characteristic of a spy? Being a nonentity. Do you think you got this offer for being handsome or smart? I thought about it. No, a spy is someone who doesn't exist, who has neither memories nor friends nor home, not even a thin woman who gets excited about the queer music you hear nowadays. Hey, a little more respect for the Beatles. Pfft, pour me another scotch and leave me alone, I have to do something with my life. If you want to be happy, don't cross the wall. What, and stay here forever? You're crazy. And if you make it to the future? I don't give a damn. Another drink, please.

My best friend and I were living in a military boarding school where one night we ran into some hooligans eager to bust some heads—"What's up, fuckers?" We went to eat our greasy dinner and had to retreat, harassed by troublemakers who wanted the few pesos our parents had sent us. That was when I turned to find Alec Leamas in a state of anger that made him want to quit. I watched him evade his trackers and be hateful to Ashe and defy the angel of death. Something's driving that bastard, I speculated, and it didn't surprise me when Kiever showed up to arrange for Alec's defection. Of course: if the British did not want him and he could earn a few bucks with his history, fine. It was a dazzling world of false passports, name changes, public telephones, and impersonations. I liked what he did with Peters in the Netherlands and his attitude when he crossed into East Germany. I also liked that they were always eating.

I distrusted Fiedler from the beginning. During Peters's interrogation, it becomes clear that this is part of an operation, and Fiedler makes Leamas repeat each item he's confessed. That subtlety seemed queer; what does he have against Leamas? Why fuck with him like that? And the case against Mundt coming together bit by bit, as perhaps Fiedler hates him even more than Alec. The excitement was killing me, but I had to put the book down at that point to get some sleep before rising at six the next morning, as required where I lived.

In my dreams, Leamas walked through the door, mortally wounded. *What the hell, it's Fiedler, right? Fucking asshole. Forget it, have you seen Liz? Alec, leave that skank—no butt, no boobs, what kind of woman is that? I need to go to the library, there's a key I need. Okay, but first I'll take you to the Red Cross, you're in really bad shape. Better come with me to the English hospital, they're more reliable. We went, we took a taxi. We could still see a black car clearly behind us. Absentmindedly, I ordered the cabdriver to turn around, and he showed me a cold smile and a shining gold tooth.* I woke up. I managed to read three pages before six o'clock.

There is one part, during the full confrontation before the Tribunal, where Alec says that this is the most twisted intrigue of his career. What dogs. The struggle between Fiedler and Mundt is resolved: good and evil have fought again, and Leamas has been only a piece of the vast puzzle, just like Liz, Peters, Kiever, Karden, and all the others. At this point, I am Leamas, but not John le Carré. The denouement is so brilliant that I could not imagine it, much less foresee it. At this moment, le Carré sets himself apart; he is the orchestrator, the demiurge, the genius who kept us watching the balls in motion, but also a protective shadow, compassionate and demanding, an iconic writer. Writing a masterpiece is a revelation that happens only one time among many, in rooms so narrow that they can hold no one else.

What panties was Liz wearing, Leamas? Because the Brazilians just invented the bikini. I'm going to rip your guts out, Élmer Mendoza. How dare you, you fucking alcoholic drunk piece of shit. Like a fuckup, I told you, I'm not staying on this side of the Brandenburg Gate. If you stay you'll register at the Humboldt University, where you'll be a lousy student, and you can kill time looking at the pictures of all the Nobel Prize winners (all twenty of them), or walking along the Unter den Linden. You know what? I've had enough. I don't have to put up with your nonsense, I'm no idiot. Aren't you? It doesn't matter to me. Did you know that this year the American Neil Armstrong landed on the moon? I don't believe it, but it would have to be one of them, they're completely insane. The Beatles are breaking up, but a hard-rock band's emerged that will make history: Led Zeppelin. That's it, I'm going to smash your face in for lying. It's 1969. Hallucinate, and I don't have to listen to your rubbish. What's special is that you're going to be here forever, into the next century and longer, Alec Leamas, The Spy Who Came in from the Cold. *I'll make you pay, you mangy dog, with my own hands. You want a fight? Cross the wall, bastard, and bring your old skank with you. I'll be waiting.*

Élmer Mendoza is a professor of literature at the Universidad Autonoma de Sinaloa in Mexico and a member of the Colegio de Sinaloa and the Mexican Academy of the Spanish Language. Between 1978 and 1995 he published five books of short stories, and two volumes of essays, and his first novel, A Solitary Murderer, *was published in 1999. He has since published six more novels, including two featuring the character of policeman Edgar "Lefty" Mendieta, and won the Tusquets International Prize in 2007 for his novel* Silver Bullets. *He is regarded as the patriarch of north Mexican crime literature, one of the most skilled users of the slang language of Mexican criminality as a literary language, and a specialist in the subgenre of narcocultura, which examines the impact of the drug trade on Mexican society.*

Ten Plus One
by Ed McBain (1963)

DEON MEYER

Ed McBain (1926–2005) was an American novelist and screenwriter. He was born Salvatore Lombino in New York, and served in the navy in World War II. In 1952 he legally changed his name to Evan Hunter, and it was under this name that he gained fame for his novel The Blackboard Jungle *(1954), as well as his adaptation of Daphne du Maurier's short story "The Birds" for the Alfred Hitchcock film of the same title. Although he wrote science fiction and, like many genre writers of his time, pornography under a variety of pseudonyms, it is as Ed McBain that he is most fondly remembered by mystery readers. He began using the McBain identity in 1956 for* Cop Hater, *the first novel in the 87th Precinct series, largely in order to distinguish his mystery fiction from any literary work that he might produce under his own name. The series, which focuses on a team of detectives in the city of Isola, a fictionalized version of New York, virtually invented the modern police procedural, although McBain disdained the term. "Never procedurals," a character comments in McBain's 1995 novel* Romance. *"And not mysteries, either. They were simply novels about cops. The men and women in blue and in mufti, their wives, girlfriends, boyfriends, lovers, children, their head colds, stomachaches, menstrual cycles. Novels."*

I bought it at Don's Book Exchange for seventy cents in 1976, when I was eighteen years old—a Pan paperback, now falling apart. There is a sniper rifle tied to a chair on the cover photograph. And the legend: "An 87th Precinct Mystery."

It is my favorite crime novel of all time.

I love every one of McBain's books, which have sold more than 100 million copies since their first publication. Born Salvatore Albert Lombino, he wrote fifty-five 87th Precinct narratives, in addition to thirteen

Matthew Hope novels, a slew of stand-alones—many under his legally adopted name of Evan Hunter—and several screenplays, of which the Alfred Hitchcock film *The Birds* is perhaps the most famous.

I had never really tried to figure out why I admire *Ten Plus One* so much until I began writing this piece. I wasn't even sure that beloved books should be dissected and analyzed: would it not spoil the absolute pleasure, that immersive, enthralling, captivating reading experience where you just get lost in the book?

I needn't have worried.

First off, there's the matter of "Hail, Hail the Gang's All Here" (to paraphrase another of McBain's always charming titles), his so very human, flawed, and fascinating characters: Detectives Steven Louis Carella, Meyer Meyer ("Jew on Fire"), and Bert Kling. Miscolo from the clerical office, Lieutenant Byrnes, and the Tweedledum and Tweedledee of Homicide Division, the wiseass pair of Monoghan and Monroe.

Then there's McBain's voice—the wry, ironic, witty third-person omniscient narrator that makes his books so totally unique. (This is where my biggest admiration for him as an author lies. I attempted a similar style early in my career, only to discover that I was not nearly smart and talented enough.) "Nothing is allowed to die in the spring," he writes. "There's a law that says so—Penal Law 5006, DEATH IN THE SPRING."

And there is his postmodern self-reflection, self-parody, and self-reference, long before such tools were fashionable, like naming a character "Salvatore Palumbo," and describing him as "a wiry little man," or injecting comments by characters on the nature of crime stories.

All of which adds up to a certain exuberance, as if he really enjoyed writing and was happily fascinated by human beings and this wonderful world, particularly his fictitious city of "Isola" ("island" in Italian, but really New York, where he was born and lived for almost all his life). I think he loved the whole concept of the city as melting pot, always reflected in the variety of his lesser characters and their vocations, among them David Arthur Cohen, the gag writer, with whom he has so much fun in this novel—and for whom he wrote several original gags in the process.

But above all there is the perfect plotting of this novel, the deepening of the mystery (why is the sniper shooting people who participated in a college play twenty-three years ago?), the ever-rising suspense as the pressure mounts on the detectives. All of the crime fiction elements are there as waypoints in the superlative structure—the red herring, the certain suspect, and the sting in the tail.

———————————

South African crime author Deon Meyer is a former journalist, advertising copywriter, Internet manager, and brand strategist. He has published nine novels and two short-story collections in Afrikaans. His books have been translated into twenty-five languages worldwide. Accolades include Le Grand Prix International de Littérature Policière, the Deutsche Krimi Preis, the Swedish Martin Beck Award, and a Barry Award in the United States. Deon lives near Cape Town with his wife, Anita, and their four children. He is passionate about South Africa, Mozart, motorcycles, cooking, and Free State Cheetahs and Springbok rugby. Visit him online at www.deonmeyer.com.

The Chill
by Ross Macdonald (1964)

Ross Macdonald is the pseudonym of the American mystery writer Kenneth Millar (1915–83), whose reputation rests on the series of novels that he wrote between 1949 and 1976 featuring private investigator Lew Archer, named, in part, after Sam Spade's partner, Miles Archer, in The Maltese Falcon *by Dashiell Hammett. Set in and around Santa Teresa, a fictionalized version of Santa Barbara in Southern California, the books combine elements of the psychological thriller and the whodunit to create what screenwriter William Goldman described as "the finest series of detective novels ever written by an American."*

Writers are products of accumulation: we are the children of those writers whom we ourselves have read and loved. Sometimes, their shadows are so great that it takes us years to escape from under them, if we ever truly escape them at all.

Thus it is that, if I were to come up with a list of the writers who have influenced and formed me, it would include two American mystery novelists without whom I would not be writing at all, so significant was their impact upon me. One of those is James Lee Burke, who remains, I believe, the greatest living prose writer in the genre. The other, now deceased, is Ross Macdonald. (I fully accept that, if Macdonald were alive, he might not see his influence upon me as something to trumpet very loudly. Similarly, if Jim Burke ever decides to nod politely in my direction before hurrying on his way, a faintly distressed look upon his face, then I will take the hint, and there will be no hard feelings on my part.)

Burke taught me that the language of mystery fiction can aspire to the language of the finest literature, that there really should be no distinction between the two. A genre novel is not a poor relative of literature because

212

it is a genre piece: it is poor only if its writing is poor and its reach is so modest as to count as the barest flexing of a muscle. There is only good writing and bad writing.

Macdonald, meanwhile, is the genre's first great poet of empathy and compassion, the creator, in private detective Lew Archer, of a man so attuned to the pain of others, so unable to turn his face from suffering that, by the final novel in the Archer sequence (*The Blue Hammer*, 1976), he has become almost a Christ figure, his existence defined by his capacity to take on the burdens of humanity and, in doing so, achieve some release for those in agony and a form of redemption for himself.

Macdonald, or Kenneth Millar to give him his true name, was an interesting, conflicted man. He was born in California but raised in Canada. In the wake of his father's abandonment of the family, he lived an itinerant, almost Dickensian existence with his mother. He became a tearaway in his youth and was lucky not to spend his postteen years in prison. His background gave him an insight into the problems faced by the young in their formative years, and his books are strewn with troubled children, often seeking, or haunted by, parental figures who have failed them or, as with Macdonald himself, who have abandoned them entirely.

He married Margaret Sturm in 1938 (she herself, as Margaret Millar, was a fine mystery novelist in her own right, and is dealt with by Declan Hughes elsewhere in this volume). In the course of a sometimes difficult, thorny marriage they had one daughter, Linda. In 1956, Linda Millar killed a young Mexican in a drunk-driving incident, striking him so hard that she drove him through the windshield of a parked car. On the advice of counsel, both Macdonald and his daughter (who was heavily sedated for the trial) refused to testify. It may have been the response of a panicked parent, but it was also an act of moral cowardice on Macdonald's part. I'm speculating here, but given the nature of Macdonald's writing, and its intense compassion for children, I can't help but feel that Macdonald must have looked back with a degree of shame on his behavior during the trial. He might well have been trying to protect his own child, but in the course of doing so he forgot about the other child in the case, the dead child. I wonder how often the image of that boy came back to haunt him.

Three years later, Linda disappeared from her college dorm, setting off a massive police hunt and leading Macdonald to court the media in an effort to ensure her safe return. She was finally found in Reno,

Nevada, and was admitted to psychiatric care. Eventually, Linda married and gave birth to a son, James. She died of a "cerebral incident" in 1970, and her son James subsequently died of a drug overdose, although Macdonald himself was in the grave by then.

All of this is important because it is hard to separate Macdonald's work from his life. The books allowed him a certain psychological distance from his own difficulties, but there is always the sense that he was using Archer as a means of refracting his personal experiences. (When I talk to writing groups—which is rarely, as I'm not sure that I understand very much about the process of writing at all, at least where it concerns my own work—I tend to tell them that fiction is not reflective but refractive by nature: it takes human experience and allows us to see its constituent parts broken down and examined in new and unfamiliar ways. If that's true, then central characters like Lew Archer or, indeed, my own Charlie Parker, function as prisms.)

And Macdonald practiced much of what he preached: he engaged in environmental activism—the relationship between man and his environment being a significant theme in his later books, including *The Underground Man* (1971) and *Sleeping Beauty* (1973)—long before it was fashionable to do so, and when the singer-songwriter Warren Zevon, a big mystery fan who adored Macdonald's work but had met his idol only once, was in danger of killing himself through drug abuse, it was Macdonald who appeared on his doorstep to intervene. In acknowledgment of Macdonald's solicitude, the dedication on Zevon's 1980 album *Bad Luck Streak in Dancing School* reads "For Kenneth Millar, *mi migliore fabbro.*" Zevon apparently quoted one of Archer's own lines from *The Doomsters* back to Macdonald when he arrived: "It was one of those times when you have to decide between your own inconvenience and the unknown quality of another man's troubles." Years later, Zevon commented of Macdonald that "he meant that stuff. Obviously. He was that guy."

The first full-length Lew Archer novel, *The Moving Target*, was published in 1949, but it would be fair to say that Macdonald initially viewed his mystery novels as a way to earn money and be in print while he prepared to write a more literary novel about familial strife. It was probably only with the publication of *The Galton Case* in 1959 that Macdonald realized the Archer novels would enable him to pursue the themes of familial conflict that interested him the most, and were thus destined to be the body of work upon which his reputation would rest.

Opinions differ on which of Macdonald's novels is the greatest. *The Galton Case* is frequently named, but it's a difficult, overcomplicated book, I think. Although a crucial turning point in Macdonald's writing, it lacks the elegance of his most accomplished work. For me, *The Chill* (1963) is Macdonald's crowning glory, a novel that represents the quintessence of his thematic concerns while also functioning as a sleek, near-perfect thriller with one of the genre's greatest endings.

Macdonald described *The Chill* as having "my most horrible plot yet." It is, in many ways, an angry, uncanny, profoundly gothic book into which he channeled his unhappiness at the time: disappointment at his best friend's divorce, his inability to get his book on Coleridge published, his dissatisfaction with academia, and his hurt at comments made about him by Raymond Chandler. In fact, on one level the book can be read as a sly, extended dig at Chandler.

Chandler's presence has obscured Macdonald's posthumous reputation in much the same way that it did while he was alive. Chandler, the older writer, clearly saw Macdonald as a rival, and did his very best to belittle the younger novelist whenever possible, not recognizing that Macdonald was part of a progression, drawing on Chandler to create something new and move the genre forward, just as Chandler had earlier drawn on Hammett. After Chandler's death, Macdonald became aware of letters against him that Chandler had written, including one to James Sandoe, published as part of *Raymond Chandler Speaking*, which described Macdonald as a "literary eunuch" and criticized the "pretentiousness" of his phrasing. This has tended to be the default mode of criticism where Macdonald is concerned, a reaction, perhaps, to a certain reticence and poise in his writing, a distrust of the kind of excessive literary or stylistic distractions that inferior writers in the genre sometimes use to disguise the emptiness of their work.

It's unlikely that Chandler would have been quite so vituperative had he not felt threatened both by Macdonald's writing and the critical acclaim that he was receiving. Macdonald, in turn, landed a couple of good punches of his own, remarking that Chandler lacked "tragic unity" and believed "a good plot was one that made for good scenes, as if the parts were greater than the whole."

In the end, I would argue that Macdonald was the better novelist of the two, and certainly the better plotter. Chandler's rather haphazard approach to plotting is generally excused on the basis that he was more interested in character than plot, but this is to ignore the fact that it is not an either/or relationship between the two elements. If they are both handled properly, then plot should come out of character. Or, as Macdonald once said: "I see plot as a vehicle for meaning."

Originally entitled *A Mess of Shadows,* from a line in the W. B. Yeats poem "Among School Children," *The Chill* takes some of its structure and imagery from Coleridge's "The Rime of the Ancient Mariner": a sad story told by a character seeking release and deliverance; a mist-shrouded environment; and the death of a bird, in this case a pigeon rather than an albatross, although the latter gets a nod when a photographer's camera is described as hanging from his neck "like an albatross."

Like all of Macdonald's work, it is a novel obsessed with the impact of the past upon the present. As Archer tells Mrs. Hoffman, "History is always connected to the present." Again and again, we are reminded of the resonance of old acts. Dr. Godwin's voice is "like the whispering ghost of the past." In catching a glimpse of himself, Archer thinks that he looks like "a ghost from the present haunting a bloody moment in the past." And, in a wonderful image, Archer describes the questions raised by Mrs. Delaney as sticking "in my mind like fishhooks which trailed their broken lines into the past."

Earlier, I described *The Chill* as "near-perfect," although it implies that Macdonald erred in some way in the book's creation, and I don't think that's true. Its imperfections—no, better to call them "complications," the word used in the clockmaker's art to refer to features beyond the basic requirements of display—are deliberate, a testament to Macdonald's courage as a writer and his absolute refusal to fall back on sentimentality. While Alex Kincaid, the man whose missing bride sparks the story, is another of Macdonald's troubled youths, tainted by the actions of an earlier generation, he is also something of a jerk, and it's difficult to feel a great deal of sympathy for him. By contrast, Macdonald kills off one of the book's most attractive characters disturbingly early, and in doing so accentuates the horror of the murderous, semimythic female figure that stalks the novel and gives it the power of nightmare.

Arguably, Macdonald is the first great psychological novelist that the genre produced. While Chandler tends to look for sociological explanations, Macdonald instead looks inward at the dynamics of families, and in particular the wrongs done to children, the sins of the fathers (or mothers) that are visited on the sons (or daughters). In this sense, *The*

Chill falls into a group of Macdonald's books that touch upon Oedipal dread. Macdonald described his first experience of therapy as a defining moment for him, and on one level his novels can be viewed as a series of extended Freudian meditations.

And then there is Lew Archer himself. He remains one of the most enigmatic of detectives. Throughout the series we learn almost nothing about his past, apart from the fact that he was once married, which gives him a sense of loneliness and dislocation. We are offered few, if any, of the little day-to-day details of his existence that have become the stock-in-trade of the modern detective hero: no cute sidekicks, no dogs, no quirky tastes in opera or fast cars. For Macdonald, such elements would have served only as a distraction from the central fact of Archer's existence: he is a profoundly moral being, with an almost limitless capacity for pity and empathy. He is neither as tough, nor as cynical, as Chandler's Philip Marlowe. In *The Barbarous Coast* (1956), Archer notes: "The problem was to love people, to serve them, without wanting anything from them." It is an extraordinary statement of intent, perhaps even more so now than it was over fifty years ago. In many ways, the society that he inhabits is unworthy of Archer, although he never sees himself in those terms. He is not self-interested. Instead, his interest is directed at the lives of others in an attempt both to understand their actions and undo the harm that has been done to them. His innate goodness may explain some of the hostility that has been directed toward him by critics and writers who mistake cynicism for realism, and confuse sentimentality with genuine emotion.

Macdonald died of Alzheimer's disease in 1983. One of the most moving moments in Tom Nolan's excellent biography of the writer sees Macdonald, his mind failing, struggling to use his typewriter, and being able to type only the word "broken" over and over again. Read *The Chill*, then read the rest of Macdonald's books. We will not see the likes of him again.

John Connolly was born in Dublin in 1968. He is the author of sixteen books, including The Book of Lost Things, Nocturnes, *the Samuel Johnson books for younger readers, and the Charlie Parker series of mystery novels, the latest of which is* The Wrath of Angels. *Like most writers, he is waiting to be found out. Visit him online at www.johnconnollybooks.com.*

Pop. 1280
by Jim Thompson (1964)

JO NESBØ

(essay translated from the Norwegian by Kari Dickson)

Dubbed the "Dimestore Dostoevsky" by novelist Geoffrey O'Brien, Jim Thompson (1906–77) published more than thirty novels during his career. Despite early critical praise, and particularly positive reviews from Anthony Boucher in the New York Times, *Thompson's talent went largely unrecognized during his lifetime. He made his debut in 1942 with* Now and On Earth, *and is best known for novels such as* The Killer Inside Me *(1952),* Savage Night *(1953),* A Hell of a Woman *(1954),* The Getaway *(1958), and* The Grifters *(1963), all of which were characteristic of an oeuvre that unflinchingly explored the darkest and nastiest recesses of the human psyche. "He let himself see everything, he let himself write it down, then he let himself publish it," declared Stephen King. Well served by film adaptations, and particularly French filmmakers, Thompson's* The Killer Inside Me *was remade in 2010, directed by Michael Winterbottom and starring Casey Affleck.*

There's a clip in the Sylvester Stallone film *Cop Land*. The clip only lasts about one or two seconds, and doesn't have much to do with the rest of the film. It's a brief flash of a sign showing the number of inhabitants in the town. The sign says, "Pop. 1280."

I looked around the cinema when it came on the screen, and listened. No reaction. Obviously. Because it was 1997 and this was a coded message for the initiated few, a bonus for those who had dived into the deepest depths of pulp literature and found Jim Thompson, the genius who portrayed the American psychopath in the first person some forty years before Brett Easton Ellis did the same in *American Psycho*.

I personally hadn't had to dive so deep myself. I was served Jim

Thompson on a silver platter by a friend, Espen, who told me it was "old, but good stuff." The book had the very promising title of *Pop. 1280* and a not-quite-so-promising sheriff on the cover. And maybe that was the only way to discover Jim Thompson: you had to be guided to him by someone like Espen, someone who moved freely beyond the main highways and narrow paths of literary snobbery.

Because Jim Thompson is not to be found in any best-seller list or serious literary publication; he was neither the talk of the town nor a cult phenomenon. Jim Thompson died in 1977, but by then, in a way, he had already been dead a long time. Written off, labeled as a mediocre crime writer who, by the end of his seventy-year life, had destroyed any credibility he might still have enjoyed by writing bad books with one aim in mind: to give the readers what he thought they wanted, so that he could earn enough money to cover his rent, medical expenses, and alcohol consumption. He had betrayed his own talent and his real fans, and undermined any possibility of ever being taken seriously again. There weren't many who saw a reason to go to Jim Thompson's funeral. Fewer still actually turned up, due to a printing error in his death notice. It was like the final chapter of a Jim Thompson novel.

Then in 1984, Black Lizard Press started to print Jim Thompson again. And it was one of these paperbacks that Espen gave me.

I read. Opened my eyes. And understood.

I then proceeded to read the rest of Thompson's work—not every single line and page, but the best and most important books, because I quickly learned that it was necessary to separate the wheat from the chaff. At his best, Jim Thompson was fantastic. At his worst, he was therefore all the more remarkably bad. How could the author who had written *Savage Night, Hell of a Woman*, and *The Grifters* also write *The Rip-Off*? (Given the limited attention that Jim Thompson has received in Norway, it is unbelievable that this particular book has been translated into Norwegian [*Bløffen*, published by Cappelen], but read it and compare it to the rest if you want to see just how much an author's production can vary, in terms of quality!)

The answer lies possibly in Jim Thompson's desperate consumption of alcohol and the associated deterioration in his health. For here was a candle that burned at both ends, and—I'm taking a chance here as Jim Thompson never denied himself a dodgy metaphor—that is precisely why it burned so bright. So brightly, in fact, that between 1952 and

1954, in the space of just eighteen months, he wrote twelve novels, including some of his very best. Following this eruption of creativity, the gaps between each book, and between the high points in his writing, got longer, whereas the periods between his excessive drinking and his stints in the hospital grew shorter. *Pop. 1280*, which he wrote in 1964, was his last great work. He returned to the figure of the bad sheriff (Nick Corey), the same figure with which he started out in 1952 when he introduced Lou Ford in *The Killer Inside Me*.

And after that, it was over: the decline had started, before he ever managed to become the Raymond Chandler or Dashiell Hammett that he could have been. And yet, on his deathbed, he said to his wife: "Just wait, I'll be famous within ten years of my death." I think we can answer that statement with Sheriff Nick Corey's mantra: "I wouldn't say you was wrong, but I sure wouldn't say you was right, either."

But in my book, Jim Thompson is still the greatest crime writer. And so I can only say to you what Espen said to me back then when he handed me that copy of *Pop. 1280*: "I envy you, because you still haven't read this."

Jo Nesbø is a Norwegian author best known for his police procedurals featuring Detective Harry Hole. He made his debut in 1997 with Flaggermusmannen *(The Bat), although the first of his novels to be translated into English was* Marekors *(2003), published in translation as* The Devil's Star *(2005). In total there are nine Harry Hole novels, the most recent of which is* Phantom *(2012). A film adapted from his stand-alone novel* Hodejegerne *(2008), aka* Headhunters *(2011), was released in 2012. Nesbø has won a slew of literary prizes in Scandinavia, including Best Norwegian Crime Novel Ever Written for* The Redbreast *in 2004.*

Roseanna
by Maj Sjöwall and Per Wahlöö (1965)

QIU XIAOLONG

Maj Sjöwall (b. 1935) and Per Wahlöö (1926–75) were a Swedish writing couple—lovers as well as coauthors. They are widely regarded as the godparents of modern Scandinavian crime fiction, but their sequence of ten novels featuring Detective (later Inspector) Martin Beck of Stockholm's National Homicide Department has influenced generations of mystery writers worldwide. Sometimes slow moving, often witty and tender, always engrossing, the Beck novels are unabashed socialist critiques of Swedish society contained within the framework of the mystery genre. "We realised that people read crime and through the stories we could show the reader that under the official image of welfare-state Sweden there was another layer of poverty, criminality and brutality," Sjöwall said in a 2009 interview with the Guardian *newspaper in Britain, a statement of intent that might equally have been echoed by the late Stieg Larsson, creator of the Millennium Trilogy. "We wanted to show where Sweden was heading: towards a capitalistic, cold and inhuman society, where the rich got richer, the poor got poorer." They planned ten books, and ten books only, taking turns to write alternate chapters. Wahlöö died shortly before the publication of the final Beck book,* The Terrorists.

I first came across *Roseanna* by Maj Sjöwall and Per Wahlöö in a St. Louis city library book sale: old and worn out, retailing for twenty-five cents, along with several other books by the same authors. It was in the mid-1990s, I remember, when I was a student from China, working hard on my PhD dissertation in comparative literature. I had never heard of the two Swedish authors before, though I had enjoyed detective stories; first, like forbidden fruit, in China, and then like supermarket product in the United States. *Roseanna* might give me a much-needed break, I

supposed, from all those befuddling new historicist and deconstruction-
ist terms in the dissertation.

But the book gave me an almost mind-boggling shock, although
not so much in terms of the story line. The naked, raped body of a
young woman is dredged up from the bottom of a Swedish lake; with
her identity as well as her nationality unknown to the police, and with
no one reported missing in the area and no matches to her description
found in the records, Inspector Martin Beck of the Stockholm Homicide
Squad and his colleagues begin a long and studious search. This involves
interviewing a lot of people, and following a number of false leads and
directions, before a portrait of the dead woman, and of her psychopathic
killer, slowly emerges out of the painstaking, meticulous investigation.
With the evidence of the case long vanished, however, the police then
have to risk a great deal to trap the murderer into a confession.

It was in the way the crime story was told that *Roseanna* came as a
shock to me. In contrast to other heroes in the genre I had encountered
years earlier, such as Sherlock Holmes or Hercule Poirot, Inspector Martin Beck reads almost like an antihero. He is hardworking and consci-
entious, and finally solves the case through his persistence, yet through
luck as well—at least to some extent. He is by no means as brilliant or
as full of incredible deductive power as those "great masters," and the
police work of which he is a part can be slow, sometimes even boring,
with repeated missteps.

Roseanna nonetheless held me spellbound—not just because of the
investigation, but more because of a realistic, panoramic representation
of the social, political, and cultural circumstances in which the human
tragedy takes place. The characters are rounded, real, fully developed, not
convenient stage props designed simply for the presentation of a mystery.
Roseanna, even though a victim at the beginning of the story, comes to
life in the course of the investigation with chilling detail and psychological depth. And then there is the unhappy yet unyielding Inspector Martin Beck, moping about the problems in his police work and his family
life, and his colleagues who plod through the intrigues and struggles of
the case while dramas unfold in their personal lives.

To me, *Roseanna* served as an eye-opener. It more than subverted my
ideas about the genre formed earlier in China, with translation at the
time limited to a handful of authors like Conan Doyle or Agatha Chris-

tie. It greatly enlarged the horizon of crime fiction for me and opened up a world of new possibilities.

I went on, of course, to devour the remaining books in the series, and no longer the twenty-five-cent copies from the library book sales. What a great series it proves to be, again and again, with each of the books engaging, readable as a fascinating stand-alone, and character- as well as plot-driven. But for me, perhaps more than anything else, they are excellently written novels with a sociological approach full of penetrating insight and vivid details, as well as brilliantly executed police procedurals.

Naturally, I researched Maj Sjöwall and Per Wahlöö. They started writing the Martin Beck police mysteries with the intention of using "the crime novel as a scalpel, cutting open the belly of the ideologically pauperised and morally debatable so-called welfare sate of the bourgeois type." From their clearly defined socialist viewpoint, they set out to expose the inequality, injustice, and crime of capitalist society, a dynamic critique of social evils through the form of the police procedural.

A few years later, when I first tried to write a novel about contemporary Chinese society in transition, I met with some structural problems. It was *Roseanna* and the Martin Beck series that came to the rescue. Under the influence of the two Swedish authors, I, too, decided to adopt the form of the crime novel, one in which Inspector Chen looks into the problems unfolding in China today, struggling through one investigation after another in an ongoing series. It's something of which I could never have dreamed when I first picked up *Roseanna* in that St. Louis city library.

Chinese author Qiu Xiaolong first visited the United States in 1988 to research a book on T. S. Eliot. Accused of previously fund-raising for subversive students in the wake of the Tiananmen Square protests, he found himself unable to return home for fear of persecution by the Chinese Communist Party. Now domiciled in St. Louis, Missouri, Qiu Xiaolong has written six crime/mystery novels, all of them featuring the poetry-quoting Chief Inspector Chen Cao. His first novel, Death of a Red Heroine, *was published in 2000, and won the Anthony Award for Best First Novel. The most recent novel is* Don't Cry, Tai Lake *(2012). He has also published a collection of poetry,* Lines Around China *(2003).*

In Cold Blood
by Truman Capote (1966)

JOSEPH WAMBAUGH

Truman Capote (1924–84) was born Truman Streckfus Persons in New Orleans, Louisiana. He led an unsettled early life, raised by relatives following his parents' divorce. He was reunited with his mother following her marriage to the Cuban-born Joseph Capote, who adopted the young Truman and gave him his surname. Capote began writing when he was eleven, and by his early twenties had already gained a reputation as a writer of short stories, as well as publishing his first novel, Other Voices, Other Rooms, *in 1948.* In Cold Blood, *his most famous work, was inspired by a short article in the* New York Times *of November 16, 1959, describing the murder of the Clutter family in Kansas. Assisted by his friend and fellow writer Harper Lee, Capote began a lengthy process of investigation of the crime and its aftermath. Originally serialized in 1965, it was published in book form early the following year. Capote described* In Cold Blood *as a "nonfiction novel," and stood over the veracity of all that he had written, even in the face of accusations of distortion and fabrication.*

It is difficult for me to get beyond Truman Capote's *In Cold Blood* when I'm asked to name my favorite crime novel. Of course I know that the groundbreaking book was not precisely a novel, but, to quote Capote, a "nonfiction novel." However, in recent years much has been written, and two feature films have been made, suggesting that the great book was more of a novel than any of us realized when we read it in 1966. Now we know that Truman Capote had become so caught up in re-creating the story's characters, particularly with the killer Perry Smith, that the line between fact and fiction was blurred. But whether it is a novel, or reportage written in the style of a novel, it is a superb and unforgettable book about a crime and its consequences.

The crime itself was terrible. In November 1959, two young, small-time criminals staged a home invasion in the rural community of Holcomb, Kansas, intending to steal money from a farmer, Herb Clutter. Before they left the Clutter home, Perry Smith and Dick Hickock had shotgunned to death Herb Clutter's wife and their two teenagers. Mr. Clutter, bound and helpless, died from a slashed throat, followed by a shotgun round to the face. Five years later the two killers were hanged for the murders.

The book is less interested in the bogeyman terror of the event or the whodunit aspect of the investigation than in the psychological exploration of the criminal mind and motive, which had not been done in such depth since Dostoyevsky's *Crime and Punishment*. But Capote went much further in bringing vividly to life the Clutters and all others in the story, and by making that quiet midwestern community almost a character in itself so that readers could better appreciate the horror that this crime represented in such an unlikely place.

I was an LAPD cop at the time of the book's publication, taking graduate English classes at Cal State, Los Angeles. I saw that there was much to learn from Capote's method if ever I hoped to fulfill a secret ambition to write about the things that I was experiencing on the streets of Los Angeles. I watched Capote's television appearances where he claimed to have a "photographic memory" with no need for note-taking during his many interviews of the people of Holcomb, Kansas. This troubled me because I was in the business of interviewing people who'd been victims, witnesses, or perpetrators of crime, and the notebook and pen that I carried were far more important to me than the handgun on my hip. I had never met a detective or anyone else with a "photographic memory" sufficient to replace pen and paper.

Cut to 1971 when I had become "the writing cop," having penned a runaway best-selling novel, *The New Centurions*, which was soon to be made into a movie. I was determined to remain with the LAPD for twenty years, despite the media attention that was making my job as a detective sergeant almost impossible. That was when *The Tonight Show*, still in New York at the time, booked me for a show they were planning with a crime theme. Of course, my publisher was excited, and I agreed to do it.

The show featured author Truman Capote along with Alvin Dewey, the investigator from the Kansas Bureau of Investigation who had worked the Clutter murder inquiry. Capote and Dewey were friends, and Truman called the older man "Pappy." I was too nervous to now remember anything I said to Johnny Carson, but one thing I will never forget is that, during a commercial break, the old lawman turned to the young lawman, and whispered to me, sotto voce, "Truman fell in love with Perry Smith, but I didn't. Truman portrayed me as feeling pity for Smith at the end, but the truth is, if I'd been asked to stand in for the hangman, I could've dropped that killer without batting an eye."

That was my first personal indicator that *In Cold Blood* might be more of a novel than I had realized, but there had been several who'd questioned Capote's depiction of people and events from the date of publication. It has even been maintained that, in order to transform his book's main character from a conscienceless sociopath into a sinner capable of remorse and redemption, Capote had invented the book's poignant apology spoken by Perry Smith by the scaffold. Other witnesses that day have said that Smith said nothing before he mounted the steps.

My wife, Dee, had a great time in the green room that evening chatting with Truman Capote while I was out in front of the cameras, and he invited us for drinks at "21" following the show and to his Palm Springs home after we returned to California. That desert visit was momentous in my life as a writer.

It was a blister of a summer day in Palm Springs, with the temperature hovering around 115 degrees. Truman's housekeeper was a charming older black woman who had been a dancer at the Cotton Club in New York back in the day. I had expected to find Jack Dunphy there, Truman's longtime partner whose name, along with that of Truman's lifelong friend author Harper Lee, is on the dedication page of *In Cold Blood*. But Capote's Palm Springs houseguest was a hunky bartender from a New York gay nightclub.

We were all immediately served screwdrivers made with fresh-squeezed orange juice and one-hundred-proof vodka as we sat by the pool and chatted. Rather, I sat by the pool because, after sipping her second screwdriver, Dee excused herself and asked for directions to the bathroom. She later told me that, while in the bathroom, the ceiling started to spin wildly and she felt as though she might faint. She actually got down on the floor and pressed her cheek to the cool tiles hoping to revive. After several minutes she pulled herself up and staggered through the nearest doorway, which happened to lead to the master bedroom, where she collapsed onto the bed.

Ten minutes passed before Truman stood and said to me, "I'd better look for Dee."

What happened next, according to Dee, was that Truman entered the bedroom and in his memorable, squeaky little lisp said, "You go ahead and take a nice nap, Dee, honey."

Which she did. Truman returned to the pool and explained to me that booze and scorching desert days often produce similar results.

During the time that my wife was indisposed and the housekeeper had gone home, I had just enough grain alcohol in me to seize the opportunity to tell Truman Capote of a crime that had haunted me for several years. It was the story of a March 1963 kidnapping of two LAPD officers from the streets of Hollywood, culminating in the murder of Officer Ian Campbell in a remote onion field ninety minutes north of L.A. I told Truman that, just as in his book, one of the two small-time young criminals was named Smith, and the aftermath of the killing was more interesting to me as a writer than the event itself.

I told him how the surviving officer, Karl Hettinger, was callously subjected to roll call appearances where he had to tell rooms full of cops about how he had surrendered his weapon while his partner had a gun in his back, and how that decision had led directly to murder. Karl Hettinger, a scrupulously honest man, soon began engaging in a baffling series of shoplifting episodes that became ever more reckless until he was finally caught and resigned from the LAPD as a common thief.

I had seen Karl Hettinger around the Police Administration Building from time to time and thought that perhaps overwhelming guilt over his partner's murder had been crying out for punishment, because after Hettinger suffered dismissal and disgrace his shoplifting compulsion vanished as mysteriously as it had come. It seemed to me that his was a classic case of post-traumatic stress disorder, even though the Vietnam War had not as yet made the condition well known and understood by the general public, nor by the world of law enforcement.

Finally, I told Truman I had learned from reading *In Cold Blood* that if I were ever to write this story as a nonfiction novel, I must remember never to let the murder victim be forgotten. At the end of his book Truman brought back Nancy Clutter's school friend, who had grown into a lovely young woman, in order to remind the reader of what Nancy could have been had she lived. I wished to somehow bring back the murdered cop, a physician's son of Scottish parentage, who had been an avid bagpiper. I hoped to do it in a scene with Ian Campbell's widowed mother, Chrissie, and Ian's daughter, and Ian's love of the mournful bagpipes.

Suddenly, I was embarrassed when I looked at my watch and realized that I had talked, and Dee had slept, for more than an hour! I apologized for monopolizing Truman's time, but he shook his head and said something that I'll always remember.

He said, "I wish I could write that story."

When I heard those words from the lips of Truman Capote, I knew that the book would be written. During my off-duty hours I interviewed sixty people connected to the case, including both imprisoned killers, read thousands of pages of court transcripts, and examined numerous case exhibits. Then I took a six-month leave of absence from the LAPD to write, but I was so ferociously energized—partly from my day with Truman Capote—that I completed the project in three months and returned to my job as a working detective for another year.

My wife and I saw Truman on a few more occasions, and he was always friendly and kind, but it was obvious that alcohol and prescription drugs were taking a toll on him. When *The Onion Field* was ready for publication, I was thrilled by a generous jacket quote from the master himself.

As for my wife, she has never believed that it was the Palm Springs heat and the screwdrivers that caused her collapse that day. She swears to all that Truman Capote "slipped her a mickey" in order to be alone with her "cute young cop." Then she is quick to add, with not a little pride, "But it was okay, because I think I may be the only woman ever to have slept in Truman Capote's bed."

Joseph Wambaugh is the author of twenty-one books, both fiction and nonfiction, since 1971 when he was a detective sergeant with the Los Angeles Police Department. Visit him online at www.josephwambaugh.net.

Endless Night
by Agatha Christie (1967)

LAUREN HENDERSON

The peerless doyenne of the mystery novel's Golden Age, the hugely pro-lific Dame Agatha Christie (1890–1976) wrote eighty mystery novels and short-story collections and nineteen plays, and is heralded as the best-selling novelist of all time by the Guinness Book of Records, *her sales ranking third behind those of the Bible and William Shakespeare. Her best-known creations include Hercule Poirot and Miss Marple, while her play* The Mousetrap, *which first opened in 1952, is still running in 2012 after more than twenty-four thousand performances. She also wrote under the pen name Mary Westmacott. Agatha Christie was the first recipient of the Mystery Writers of America Grand Master Award, and she was made a Dame Commander of the Most Excellent Order of the British Empire in 1971.*

It's one of Christie's less famous novels: no Poirot or Marple, no exotic Egyptian locations or idyllic-seeming English country villages, just a poor young man, Michael Rogers, who meets an American heiress and tells her of his dream to commission a famously eccentric architect to build a house for him on a plot of land called Gipsy's Acre. The couple elope, settle down in the new house, and find themselves persecuted by an increasingly unpleasant series of events that leads, of course, to trag-edy. It's narrated by Michael, which makes it one of the rare Christies written in the first person: but does Michael have more in common with Dr. Sheppard from *The Murder of Roger Ackroyd*, or Jerry Burton from *The Moving Finger* and Mark Easterbrook from *The Pale Horse*?

Endless Night exemplifies every one of Christie's great strengths: her restraint, her refusal to rely on padding. The book has a small cast and a limited setting. Like Jane Austen, writing on "two inches of ivory,"

Christie's plots are tight, exquisitely oiled mechanisms, a refreshing contrast to the fashion for overblown modern thrillers that push their plots and characters to a pitch of insanity, piling twist upon twist until meaning becomes lost, the story turns back on itself, everything is upended, and nothing matters any longer. Christie, however, is skilled enough to limit herself to one dazzling major twist, a perfect sleight of hand that leaves readers gasping as the rug is pulled out from under their feet . . .

Her fairness in the distribution of her clues. As the *Times Literary Supplement* wrote in 1943 of *The Moving Finger*: "Anyone ought to be able to read [the author's] secret with half an eye—if the other one-and-a-half did not get in the way." The plot of *Endless Night* stands up to constant rereading. Christie never cheats. Some of her other plots—*Evil Under the Sun, Death on the Nile*—may depend on the kind of perfectly timed, overelaborate choreography that would be impossible to achieve with any certainty in real life, but *Endless Night*'s deceptive simplicity doesn't allow for any dashing across islands, any trips on dahabiyahs, or any lightning-fast costume changes. Consequently, disbelief never has to be suspended. There's no Hitchcock "icebox" moment when you think: but would that really have worked? Wasn't it impossible to pull off?

Her concision. *Endless Night* is a mere two hundred pages. Incredibly, four people die in the span of the novel, and the murders of two others are recounted: it sounds like a ridiculous amount of drama to pack into what can scarcely be seventy thousand words, but Christie could achieve in two hundred pages what other writers can't in double that number. Other writers, telling the same story, would pile on paragraphs, pages, even chapters of elaborate description, burying the reader under accumulations of words like wool being pulled over our eyes; Christie doesn't need to do that. Her sparse, simple language is extraordinarily efficient. "One doesn't realise in one's life the really important moments—not until it's too late," Michael says, watching his wife play the guitar and sing, and even with the benefit of hindsight, even knowing the solution to the mystery, that sentence can be interpreted in at least two different ways.

Her subtlety. Although the book is so short, the pace, nonetheless, is slow and measured as Michael tells us his story: the crescendo builds so gradually that by the time Christie begins to unfold the solution, we have been lulled into submission by the andante of the narrative. The revelation not only takes the reader completely by surprise, but challenges us to believe it. In the space of one and a half short pages, Christie gives two pointers, the second clearer than the first, chords struck with increasing emphasis, and finishes with the third, a paragraph that starts innocuously and concludes with the upending of almost everything that we have taken for granted up till now, and leaves us breathless.

Her ability to chill us to the bone with minimum gore. The moments that the murderers reveal themselves in *Sleeping Murder, Murder Is Easy, Death Comes as the End*, or *Nemesis* are genuinely frightening; they linger in the reader's memory much more deeply than the currently fashionable, gruesomely detailed torture scenes of young nubile women imprisoned in basements by psychotic serial killers. It's no giveaway to say that *Murder Is Easy* also features a serial killer; that is made clear right at the start of the novel. But all that the murderer does, like the killers in the other three books cited, is to reveal intent by reaching out, hands outstretched, for the throat of the next victim. That's all: no blood, no eviscerations, no spiked torture instruments or wicked array of knives. And yet one shivers just remembering the revelation: it's the betrayal that is so frightening, the reality that one is infinitely more likely to be killed not by a stranger but by someone whom one knows and trusts.

Her poignancy. *Endless Night* is "serious—a tragedy really," Christie said in an interview for the *Times* on its publication, and though Michael's voice is cheerful, blithe, positive, we feel dark clouds hovering over the narrative from the very beginning. Our hearts break a little for the main victim, but also for the killer; although she's a writer who is often considered to enforce an old-fashioned, snobbish moral code, Christie is wonderfully good at evoking sympathy for her murderer(s). Look at *Death on the Nile*, for instance, or *Murder at the Vicarage*. And she doesn't neglect the innocents, caught up in crimes that are not of their making. One feels great empathy for Dolly Bantry in *The Body in the Library*, fretting and worrying about her husband's emotional decline as he lives under the suspicion of murder, while *Ordeal by Innocence* hinges almost entirely on the suffering of the Argyle family when a long-past crime is exhumed and they find themselves all suspects once again.

Her flair for the gothic. The fetishizing of Verity's body by the killer in *Nemesis;* the baroque sacrifice planned for the end of *Hallowe'en Party;* the obsession with the gardens in that book, and with the house in *Endless Night*: all excellent examples of the mid-twentieth-century domestic gothic revival, whose most famous incarnation, of course, is *Rebecca*. Like Manderley in *Rebecca*, *Endless Night* revolves around Michael's desire for Gipsy's Acre, his dream house, a desire shared by his wife, Ellie. "I wanted"—he says—"there were the words again, my own particular words—I want, I want—I wanted a wonderful woman and a wonderful house . . . full of wonderful things. Things that belonged to *me*." The William Blake poem from which the title derives, sung by Ellie to Michael, emphasizes the gothic theme:

> Every night and every morn
> Some to Misery are born . . .
> Some are born to Sweet Delight
> Some are born to Endless Night.

And of course, the final hook: that the end of the book sends the reader right back to the start to begin rereading it, to see how cleverly Christie has woven the net in which she's caught you. In that way, *Endless Night* is truly endless, an *ouroboros* whose head eats its tail in perpetuity. But that observation applies to almost all of Christie's books. You read them first for the denouement and then you return to them over and over again, for the pure pleasure of watching her lead you down the garden path. To quote the words with which Michael starts and ends the novel:

> In my end is my beginning—that's what people are always saying. But just what does it *mean*? And just where does my story begin? I must try and think . . ."

Lauren Henderson was born in London and educated at Cambridge, where she studied English literature. A journalist for newspapers and magazines before she turned her hand to fiction, she published her debut novel, Dead White Female, *the first of her Sam Jones mysteries, in 1995. Alongside the Sam Jones novels, Lauren has also written crime titles for young adults, romantic comedies, and a nonfiction title,* Jane Austen's Guide to Dating. *Lauren has been described as both the Dorothy Parker and Betty Boop of British crime fiction. Visit her online at www.laurenhenderson.net.*

Skin Deep
(aka *The Glass-Sided Ants' Nest*)
by Peter Dickinson (1968)

LAURIE R. KING

Peter Malcolm de Brissac Dickinson (b. 1927), author and poet, was born in Livingston, northern Rhodesia (now Zambia), and educated at Eton and Cambridge. He was an editor and reviewer for Punch *magazine for seventeen years, and has written extensively for both adults and young adults alike. He has twice won the Crime Writers' Association's Gold Dagger, as well as Guardian and Whitbread awards for his young-adult fiction.*

The trouble with recommending a writer like Peter Dickinson is: Where to begin? With his anthropological investigation of chimpanzee language, Marsh Arabs, terrorism, and the making of a hero (*The Poison Oracle*)? His delightfully quirky and all too believable alternative history of the British royal family (*King and Joker*)? A tense and thoughtful historical novel of politics, class, and romance (*A Summer in the Twenties*)? Another view of history and politics: the rich and the not rich, the innocent and the corrupt, the past and its present, a clock and its cessation (*The Last Houseparty*)? What about the "baroque spoof" (the author's words) of *The Old English Peep Show* (*A Pride of Heroes*) with its crumbling country manor house held up by lions, both feline and hominid? Or his story of Africa and the gender war, another weave of now and then, this time seen through the eyes of an aging journalist who appears to have some power, and his fresh young mother, who appears to have none (*Tefuga*)? And what of the delicious *Perfect Gallows*, a famous actor's slow and unwilling exploration of guilt, an acknowledgment of the dangers in letting a sacrifice go unacknowledged?

Pick up any one of this extraordinarily gifted writer's adult novels and you'll find a gem, an alternate universe with larger-than-life characters, a vivid sense of place, and a startling view of how the world actually does work, told in language one can taste on the tongue, and wrapped up in a satisfying and tightly constructed mystery—mystery as *intellectual puzzle,* and as *mysterium,* an exploration of the depths of human nature. (He writes brilliant young-adult novels as well, which tend toward fantasy rather than crime.)

This body of diverse and unforgettable work started with a bang—Dickinson's first two novels both won the CWA Gold Dagger Award. (The only person other than Ruth Rendell/Barbara Vine to win two years running.) His books tend to be short in word count, if long on impact, and his devout insistence on writing what he wants means that many of them are now out of print, since best-seller lists are more often inhabited by stories that resemble those we have heard before.

As a reader, I adore Peter Dickinson: for the unexpectedness of his plots and language, the richness of his internal monologues, the gorgeous peppering of humor and tragedy and absurdity in a crime novel—just what one might expect from a former *Punch* editor. As a writer, however, I find Dickinson a source of sheer despair, even as I play the How Does He *Do* That? game and try to pull his books to pieces, mapping out the rhythm of those quick sparks of humor, studying the pace of his writing and how his pagelong paragraphs merge seamlessly with rapid-fire dialogue, noting how he occasionally—only occasionally—gives himself permission to use a sharply unexpected, even deliberately awkward word, for effect:

> The air was soggy with burned herbs, through whose haze the homemade candles shone yellowly.

(Yellowly? I would have to battle my editor for that word. And she would be right to remove it, just as Dickinson was right to put it in. Hence the despair.)

As I say: even as I pick his books to pieces, I am filled as much with wonder as frustration. I will never be able to do this, and yet it can be done.

Still, the point of this essay is not to speak of technical matters. My goal is to praise Peter, not to bury him in analyses, so I shall say merely that, in crime fiction, we look for the same qualities as in other fiction: character, story, ideas that resonate, and the compelling language in which the story is told.

Let us begin with Dickinson's characters. The opening scene of *The Glass-Sided Ants' Nest* (also known as *Skin Deep*) finds Superintendent James Pibble of Scotland Yard on his way through the streets of London to a homicide. He tells his constable driver to slow down, then immediately lapses into a fret about what the man thinks of him, a relatively big fish in the waters of Scotland Yard:

> What did the current generation of sprats make of Superintendent Pibble, aging, unglamorous, graying toward retirement? Did they know how much luck had gone into his reputation for having a knack with kooky cases? Probably . . .
> Wandering unwary through the jungle of self, Pibble fell into the pit.

First of all, has there ever been such a gloriously perfect name for the antihero of a crime series as *Pibble*? It cannot be an accident that the mind hears an echo of Lear's "Pobble who has no toes," a person (or creature?) who has lost said toes to the fishes (or to mermaids?). James Pibble, Scotland Yard genius of the quirky, has indeed been touched by some daft bit of magic, rendering him a cross between Sherlock Holmes and Buster Keaton: even as a villain trips him down the stairs, his mind is coldly noting the clues.

However Pibble is no buffoon, despite the pratfalls and the serial absurdities of his life. If heroism is defined not as fearlessness, but as soldiering on despite one's fear, then Pibble is a mighty hero indeed. Mild of temper and apologetic in manner, he has no choice but to trudge implacably toward a solution—even a solution he knows will be ethically wrong and potentially catastrophic. For James Pibble, terror is his common state, if not from actual threat (a bash, a needle, a man-eating lion) then from one of his plentiful debilitating neuroses. Yet on he goes, hunkered down against the psychic onslaught from the kind of assured male who reduces him to a shivering five-year-old; confused and blushing in the presence of an unapproachable female; meekly telephoning home to his comfortable harridan of a wife for talk of chops and curtains and the fickleness of fame.

The appearance in the story of that self-assured male—kryptonite to Pibble's superpowers—is inevitable:

> Without apology, [Caine] laid himself full length in the only chair, a vanquished object with a torn cover . . . He looked as though he and a few friends owned the world. Pibble decided that he would feel less abject perching on the edge of the desk than standing subservient before this arrogant layabout.

The greatest assertion of dignity that Pibble can manage is to perch with his rump on the desk instead of standing, hat in hand, before this latest manifestation of his life's nemeses.

Equally complex is the scene where Pibble is interviewing the wife of this dread enemy in her kitchen, and drops an unexpected question. In a few lines, Dickinson draws a clear portrait both of Mrs. Caine's nature and of Pibble's own marriage, while slipping in a clue or two as well:

> "Sit in the armchair and I shan't fall over you."
>   Small chance of that, thought Pibble, watching her do her cooking trick; she hardly moved a step to get kettle and milk onto the gas, then mugs, spoons, tea, Nescafé, milk, sugar, teapot, and biscuits onto the table. Accustomed to Mrs. Pibble's flurried dashes to unrelated cupboards, he found the process fascinating. Often she did not have to look before reaching the right container off a shelf.

> The effect [of Pibble's question] was like hail at a garden fête, prattle and parasols one moment and a scurry for shelter the next. Mrs. Caine's small features, animated so far like those of a little girl in her granny's feather hat, became pinched and suspicious.

As for compelling language ("prattle and parasols"), Dickinson's compact, note-perfect style packs an entire graduate course into these 186 pages. His use of language is distinctive, a rich texture of sound and precision rarely achieved by the most highbrow of fiction, delivered here in a self-deprecating manner so appropriate for a story about an inspector named Pibble. Throwaway genius abounds:

> Supper was a misery, stale fish in an ectoplasm sauce, and a lonely silence.

Or when Pibble comes across some paintings, done in a New Guinean style that is "naïve but not childlike":

> There was a heron with a fish in its stomach. There was a European businessman with bowler, brolly, and blue pin-stripe; you could see both his wallet and his esophagus. Pibble nearly laughed aloud with pleasure.

In a discussion of rock climbing and the vast, high face of a grand Victorian house:

> Pibble tried to imagine himself spread-eagled and hurrying across that ornate façade. A chill center of nerves twitched to life in his palms.

Or in describing the wooden owl that has been used as the murder weapon:

> There was a little dried blood and a few white hairs behind its right ear. Almost as though some enemy had waited for it in the dark and coshed it savagely with a human.

Some of us writers would give parts of our anatomy to be able to summon a wooden owl coshed savagely with a human.

The third element of Dickinson's fiction—the plot—may on occasion sound as unlikely as a news headline (fiction being in general required to be more realistic than life), but in structure, his plots are tight enough to satisfy the most attentive of readers. He has a knack (How does he *do* that?) for appearing to lose control of his story, allowing the plotline to sag, then meander, only to give a tiny twitch to the controls and have the whole thing snap into place, taut as a sail under wind.

Complex character, satisfying language, well-built plot: yes, all those. But if I had one thing to point to that sets a Dickinson novel apart, it would be that ineffable sense of "otherness" at their core.

The Glass-Sided Ants' Nest (written in the 1960s) concerns a Stone Age (and possibly cannibalistic) New Guinean tribe, the Ku. These middle-aged men and women, survivors of a Japanese attack during the closing years of World War II, now live in a huge old boardinghouse in London, which they have remade into a slice of their native land. For years they have gone their way, aging in their urban backwater, preserving much of their way of life thanks to one of their number, an anthropologist who has been a member of the tribe since the days of the attack.

Odd? Yes. But there is more. The anthropologist is Dr. Eve Ku, a British woman who, when forced to flee into the jungle with the others nearly two decades before, assumed the symbolic identity of a man. Symbol became reality, however, so that now even her husband, born to that tribe, refers to her as male: "Eve has gone for a walk. He is upset."

And yes, in the eyes of the tribe, theirs is a gay marriage.

But this gay/heterosexual man/woman anthropologist/tribal (wo) man is just one character in the cast, and his/her status is only one of the minor human puzzles in the story. There is the youngest member of the tribe, who decides that being a shamanic drummer is the same as being Ringo. There is an apparent sidetrack (one of those nonmeandering story lines) involving a local criminal syndicate; there is a lover from the past; there are key architectural oddities in the Victorian building that shelters a New Guinean village ("Neither taste nor wealth could assail its inherent dreadfulness."); there is . . .

There is more, much more than the sum of the book's parts.

Superintendent Pibble and his creator both go their own way, their quick brilliance aimed slightly off-kilter, suffering the slings and arrows of outraged storytelling. One gets the clear impression that had either man focused on the prize valued by the rest of the world (for the fictional character, his next promotion; for the flesh-and-blood man, best-seller lists), each would now have large buildings named after him. Instead, the patient reader is gifted with an indelible impression of having met someone extraordinary, and that, having met him, some integral part of the mind has been forever reshaped.

That one has been made a permanent citizen of the world of Peter Dickinson.

Laurie R. King has been a published and prizewinning author for more than twenty years, and has written more than twenty novels, including her immensely popular and well-loved series of novels featuring Mary Russell, onetime apprentice and now wife to Sherlock Holmes, the latest of which is Pirate King. *She lives in the San Francisco Bay Area. Visit her online at* www.laurierking.com.

The Goodbye Look
by Ross Macdonald (1969)

LINWOOD BARCLAY

Ross Macdonald is the pseudonym of the American mystery writer Kenneth Millar (1915–83), whose reputation rests on the series of novels that he wrote between 1949 and 1976 featuring private investigator Lew Archer, named, in part, after Sam Spade's partner, Miles Archer, in The Maltese Falcon *by Dashiell Hammett. Set in and around Santa Teresa, a fictionalized version of Santa Barbara in Southern California, the books combine elements of the psychological thriller and the whodunit to create what screenwriter William Goldman described as "the finest series of detective novels ever written by an American."*

If it weren't for the font used on the covers of the Bantam paperback editions of Ross Macdonald's novels, I might never have discovered him. And had that been the case, what would turn out to be one of the most important events in my life would never have happened.

In the summer of 1970, I was fifteen years old. I was at my local bookstore, which was the twirling metal paperback display stand at the IGA grocery store in Bobcaygeon, Ontario. Bobcaygeon, a resort town in the heart of the Kawartha Lakes district with a population of about twelve hundred permanent residents, did not at that time have an actual bookstore. So it was here that I would find the latest Fawcett edition of Donald Hamilton's Matt Helm novels, or a new Nero Wolfe, or a reissue of some Hercule Poirot or Miss Marple mystery.

On this particular visit, my eyes were drawn to *The Goodbye Look*. It was, the cover informed me, the newest Lew Archer novel, and it must have been a damn good series because there was a blurb from the *New York Times Book Review* that read: "The finest series of detective novels ever written by an American." (The quote, by the way, was from William Goldman's front-page review.)

The title and the author's name were presented in a bold, three-dimensional font. The block letters appeared to lift off the page in a style that was almost identical to the one used in the title sequences for a television spy show, *The Man from U.N.C.L.E.*, that had gone off the air two years earlier. I had been, not to put too fine a point on it, obsessed with that program to the point of writing my own seventy-page novellas—seven or eight of them—based on the show's characters. I would spend hours, when I was twelve and thirteen years old, drawing that exact typeface for my novellas' title pages.

So, I figured, with a font like that, it had to be a good book, right? Right.

I devoured *The Goodbye Look*. Having finished it, I hunted up all the Archer novels I could find: *The Instant Enemy, Find a Victim, The Galton Case, The Wycherly Woman.*

There was something different about these books. There was something going *on.* As good as Christie and Stout and Hamilton were—and look, they were very good—their characters' efforts to expose the guilty were parlor games, the literary equivalent of pulling an ace of spades from the deck and proclaiming: "And that's your card!"

Yes! Wow! Great trick!

And then you tossed the book aside, instantly forgot it, and picked up another one. But when Lew Archer exposed a killer, it *meant* something, because violent deaths in a Macdonald novel were presented in a larger context. Murder was a product of environment. Violence grew from family dysfunction, the corruption of wealth and power. Alienated youths, searching for meaning in an increasingly materialistic and meaningless world, drifted with tragic results.

These people were seriously screwed up. Maybe, at some level, I was subconsciously identifying. I'd lost my father when I was sixteen; my domineering mother wanted to control every aspect of my life; my brother was hearing voices. Here, in a Lew Archer novel, were people who had more problems than I did.

What's not to love?

At the heart of *The Goodbye Look*, and all of the Archer novels, are buried family secrets, secrets that, like weeds, inevitably break through and expose themselves to the light. And it's Archer who, through his investigations, shines this purifying light.

Before I started writing this essay, I reread *The Zebra-Striped Hearse*, which was first published in 1962. I'd not read it since the mid-1970s, but it holds up beautifully, and Archer sums up the most recurring Macdonald theme in eight words: "The past is the key to the present." And then there is this: "People start out young on the road to being murderers. They start out equally young on the road to becoming victims. When the two roads intersect, you have a violent crime."

Ross Macdonald—the pseudonym under which Kenneth Millar wrote his books—was, without question, throughout my late teens and early twenties, my favorite writer on the planet. So, in my final year at Peterborough's Trent University, where I was pursuing an English degree during those lulls when I was not having a good time, it seemed appropriate to write a thesis on the evolution of the private eye as an iconic character in literature. I started with Dupin, worked through Holmes, Spade, Marlowe, all building to what I considered the supreme example: Archer.

As I started doing my research, I thought, Why not write the author himself, care of Alfred A. Knopf, his hardcover publisher, and ask him a few questions. Several weeks later, to my surprise, I received a reply, written in Millar's small, almost illegible hand. He pointed me to some pieces that had been written about him, including a *Newsweek* cover story, and was pleased to hear from someone in Ontario, where Millar had spent his formative years.

Then I did a terrible thing.

I had written a detective novel and asked if I could send it to him. I realize, today, what a tremendous imposition this was. What the hell was I thinking? This was a man who hit the *New York Times* best-seller list, whose novel *The Moving Target* had been made into the hit movie *Harper* starring Paul Newman. This was a man who was contracted to crank out a book a year. Like he was going to agree to read a book by some twenty-year-old kid from Canada.

But that's what Kenneth Millar did.

So I mailed him my manuscript. And he wrote back. His letter began: "I was delighted to get your novel, and more delighted when I read it. It shows great promise and something more than promise. It has distinction."

There were criticisms. The book needed a subplot. It was "too fast, too spare." Okay, all true. I could definitely improve the manuscript. The important thing was, Kenneth Millar had read my book.

We began a correspondence that went on for a couple of years. One day, this: "I expect to be in Peterborough about May 2 and hope to be able to spend a little time with you." I was running our family business—a cottage resort and trailer park—and had just finished taking the garbage to the dump when the phone rang. It was Millar. Could I join him and his wife, the mystery writer Margaret Millar, for dinner? They were staying with a relative in a beautiful old house along the Otonabee River, about a mile south of Trent University.

I was available.

I wish I could tell you everything that happened that night, everything Kenneth Millar and I talked about. The excitement of the moment had a way of obliterating some of the details. But I can tell you I brought him a copy of the skin magazine *Gallery* because it contained an interview with him that he'd never seen. His face flushed slightly, and he excused himself to tuck it away in his luggage where neither his hosts, nor Margaret, would come across it.

I drove him out to Trent University and gave him a tour. We paused on the Faryon Bridge, which spans the Otonabee, connecting one half of the university with the other, and which was named in honor of one of Margaret's relatives.

At dinner, I mentioned how much I loved the opening of *The Underground Man*, in which Archer helps a young boy feed peanuts to the jays. "I'll write another one like that for you," he joked.

I recall how, when it came time for me to leave and Millar was showing me out, he became confused and opened a closet instead of the front door. (He would write only one more novel, and seven years later he would die from Alzheimer's disease.)

I remember thinking it never really happened.

Ross Macdonald, the novelist, demonstrated for me that the conventions of a crime novel could do more than entertain. They could be used to serve the goals of literature: to enlighten, to give us insight into our world, to make us think.

Kenneth Millar, the man, through his kindness and generosity, gave me the confidence to pursue my goal of becoming a writer. He allowed me to believe it was possible that a kid running a trailer park could accomplish things he might otherwise have thought impossible.

No writer has had a greater impact on me professionally, or personally.

There is one detail from that night I don't have to recall, because it sits on my shelf here in my study. It's a hardback copy of Millar's novel *Sleeping Beauty*, which I brought to our dinner in the hope that he would autograph it.

He took a pen from inside his jacket and wrote: "Peterborough, Ontario, May 1 1976. For Linwood, who will, I hope, someday outwrite me. Sincerely, Kenneth Millar (Ross Macdonald)."

Linwood Barclay, a former columnist for the Toronto Star, *is the author of more than a dozen books, including* No Time for Goodbye, *which has been optioned for film, and more recently,* The Accident *and* Trust Your Eyes. *He is married, has two grown children, and lives near Toronto. Visit him online at www.linwoodbarclay.com.*

Fadeout
by Joseph Hansen (1970)

Joseph Hansen (1923–2004) was an American novelist and poet who revo-
lutionized the hard-boiled mystery novel by introducing into the form an
openly gay lead character, the insurance investigator Dave Brandstetter,
who became the protagonist of twelve of Hansen's (many) novels. Hansen,
who disliked the term "gay" and preferred to describe himself as homo-
sexual, was a lifelong activist in the gay rights movement. Brandstetter is
notable for being contented, not tortured, in his sexuality. "My joke," said
Hansen, "was to take the true hard-boiled character in an American fic-
tion tradition and make him homosexual. He was going to be a nice man,
a good man, and he was going to do his job well." It might well have served
as a description of Hansen himself, who was happily married for fifty-one
years to the lesbian artist Jane Bancroft. They had one daughter, Barbara,
who later changed her sex to male and her name to Daniel James Hansen.

In the early 1970s my interest in crime fiction featuring private investigators was sparked by the work of the "big three" authors of the '40s, '50s,
and '60s: Dashiell Hammett, Raymond Chandler, and Ross Macdonald.
Male, tough, uncompromising, and mostly without past histories or
personal lives, their heroes struggled to right wrongs and exact justice in
territories that were strange and dangerous to them. I envied these brave
men going off into those uncharted and dark realms to uncover the truth
and administer justice, but still I found something missing from their
stories. Namely, a personal life and background.

Then, in the early 1970s, I stumbled across *Fadeout,* a Dave Brandstetter novel by Joseph Hansen. The protagonist surprised me: he was an
openly homosexual death claims insurance investigator, and he possessed
a full life apart from his case files and sexual preferences.

Dave has a father, Carl Brandstetter, who owns Medallion Life, the company for which Dave works. Carl wishes his son—already in his forties—would "get out of that [homosexual] life," but he himself is no paragon of normality, seeing as he has had—by his early sixties—nine wives of his own. At the beginning of the series, Dave is mourning Rod Fleming, his partner of twenty years, whom he has lost to cancer only six weeks before; for most of those weeks, he has wanted to die himself, but now has chosen to live. Unfortunately, he is often thwarted in his attempts to build a future by chaotic professional and personal situations.

The Brandstetter series, twelve books that cover a period of twenty years in Dave's life, encompasses many genuine and colorful characters and touches on themes relevant to its day, such as political corruption (*Fadeout*, 1970); bigotry (*The Man Everybody Was Afraid Of*, 1978); pornography (*Skinflick*, 1979); urban decay (*Nightwork*, 1984); AIDS (*Early Graves*, 1987); and the white supremacy movement (*The Boy Who Was Buried This Morning*, 1990).

Theme is important in the Brandstetter novels—in interviews, Hansen admitted using his works to express his rage and pain at the ills of the world—but the primary reason we readers return to them is the characters, especially the character of Dave, a deeply caring and compassionate man, who is sometimes obsessively dedicated to uncovering the truth of the cases that are brought to him.

Some critics claim that the series is flawed because most of Dave's cases involve homosexuals and their problems, and this criticism may have some validity. However, the fact that Dave is gay allows him to become aware of homosexual undertones much more readily than your average investigator. All detectives draw upon their knowledge of the world to reach their conclusions, and a gay man in a largely straight world has more knowledge than most.

The last novel in the series, *A Country of Old Men* (1991), was deliberately intended by Hansen to be the final chapter in Dave Brandstetter's life, and provides an overall view by bringing back old friends and revisiting old haunts. The story begins with Dave being lured out of retirement by one old friend, Madge Dunstan, to piece together the truth behind a wildly improbable tale of kidnapping, violence, and murder told to her by a near-feral young boy whom she finds one morning wandering on the beach near her house.

At nearly seventy, Dave has been lured out of retirement before—

too many times, perhaps, he acknowledges. Now his firm commitments to truth and justice once again overwhelm him and, despite failing health and the pleas of his now life partner, TV newsman Cecil Harris, to stay out of the matter, he plunges into it with the zeal he's brought to all his previous cases. But investigation is not as easy as it used to be; Dave's physical strictures and the accompanying slowness of age hamper him. Still, he moves stolidly and effectively through L.A.'s pop music scene and its assorted eccentric denizens.

The result is a vivid portrait of Los Angeles as it was in the 1990s: corrupt but curiously innocent; uncertainly evolving toward the new century; torn between old stereotypes and new directions. However, Dave has watched and understood past evolutions, and he himself remains the same thoughtful, compassionate, and emotional man we encountered on page one of *Fadeout*.

Hansen did not intend Dave Brandstetter to be a gimmicky character capitalizing upon the then slight emergence of gay literature into the mainstream. Rather, he sought to create a believable individual who happens to be homosexual (Hansen's preferred word, rather than "gay"). Hansen was once quoted as saying that almost everything written about homosexuals is distorted, and that he set out to "right a wrong." This he did admirably, through the intelligent use of atmosphere and character.

For instance, in *A Country of Old Men:* the crackling of mesquite logs in the fireplace of Dave's Laurel Canyon living room; the scent of freshly chopped herbs in his cookshack; the flavors and aromas of Max Romano's restaurant in Hollywood. The actions—and often antics—of recurring characters: Kovaks, the crazy artist; restaurateur Max Romano; Madge Dunstan, the lesbian who can never quite manage to keep a lover; Amanda, Carl Brandstetter's ninth wife, a stepmother young enough to be Dave's grown daughter but old enough to boss him around when it's good for him; Cecil Harris, neophyte black newscaster who becomes Dave's final—and perhaps truest—love. All of these combine to create the world of Dave Brandstetter, which the reader finds himself anxious to enter and far more reluctant to leave.

Joseph Hansen is primarily known for the Brandstetter novels, but beginning in 1952 when he first published a poem in the *New Yorker,* his output was eclectic: in addition to poetry, mainstream and explicitly sexual novels, two gothic novels, and various essays, he also taught numerous workshops and hosted a 1960s radio show, *Homosexuality Today*, as well as helping to found Hollywood's first gay pride parade. Besides Brandstetter, he created a second private investigator, Hack Bohannon, a former deputy sheriff who runs a horse farm.

Hansen was married to the former Jane Bancroft from 1943 until her death in 1994, ten years before his own. Of their mixed lesbian/gay marriage he had this to say: "Here was this remarkable person who I wanted to spend the rest of my life with. So something was right about it, however bizarre it seemed to the rest of the world."

A changing world, yes, and through his writings Joseph Hansen did much to call attention to that change while providing a consistently high level of entertainment for gay and straight readers alike.

Marcia Muller has authored more than thirty-five novels, three of them in collaboration with her husband, Bill Pronzini. Together, the Mulzinis—as their friends call them—have coedited a dozen short-story anthologies and a five-pound nonfiction book on the genre, which can also be used as a doorstop. In 2005 Muller was named a Grand Master, the highest award of the Mystery Writers of America. Pronzini was given the same honor in 2008, making them the only living couple to share the title (Ross Macdonald and Margaret Millar were similarly honored). The Mulzinis live in Sonoma County, California, in a house full of cats and books. Muller's next Sharon McCone novel, Looking for Yesterday, *will be published by Grand Central Publishing in October 2012. Visit her online at www.marciamuller.com.*

The Friends of Eddie Coyle
by George V. Higgins (1970)

ELMORE LEONARD

George V. Higgins (1939–99), sometimes referred to as the "Balzac of Boston"—although he would probably have preferred a comparison to Dickens—was a lawyer, academic, columnist, and author. He was a prosecuting attorney in the Organized Crime Section of the Massachusetts Attorney General's office before turning to private practice, and his pursuit of mobsters and lowlifes lent a particular pungency to his fictional portrayals of their kind. Unfortunately, he was probably cursed by the fact that his first novel, The Friends of Eddie Coyle, *was his best. Despite writing many others, he struggled to escape Eddie's shadow. His 1990 book* On Writing *is honest about the writer's trade to the point of being depressing, and is probably better read after one has become a published writer, rather than before.*

In the winter of 1972, my agent at the time, H. N. Swanson in Hollywood, called to ask if I'd read a recently published novel called *The Friends of Eddie Coyle*. I told him I hadn't heard of it and he said, "This is your kind of stuff, kiddo, run out and get it before you write another word." Swanie was a legend in the movie business, having represented F. Scott Fitzgerald, Raymond Chandler, and James M. Cain. I did what I was told, bought the book, opened to the first page, and read: "Jackie Brown at twenty-six, with no expression on his face, said that he could get some guns." I finished the book in one sitting and felt as if I'd been set free. So this is how you do it.

The reviews were all raves. Joe McGinniss in the *New York Times* said that George Higgins has "given us the most penetrating glimpse yet into what seems the real world of crime—a world of stale beer smells . . . and pale unnourished little men who do what they have to do to get along." Walter Clemons in *Newsweek* said *Eddie Coyle* "isn't a thriller (though it is—stunningly—that) so much as a highly specialized novel of manners." The review in the *New Yorker* nailed it in the opening paragraph by listing these friends of Coyle—the man himself described as "a small fish in the Boston underworld"—the bank robbers Jimmy Scalisi and Artie Valantropo; the gun dealer Jackie Brown; Dillon the bartender, a character to keep your eye on; and a dealing T-man, Dave Foley. They're the book. They reveal themselves not only by what they do, but also by the way they speak, their sounds establishing the attitude or style of the writing.

To me it was a revelation.

I was already writing in scenes, trying to move my plots with dialogue while keeping the voices relatively flat, understated. What I learned from George Higgins was to relax, not be so rigid in trying to make the prose sound like writing, to be more aware of rhythms of coarse speech and the use of obscenities. Most of all, George Higgins showed me how to get into scenes without wasting time, without setting up the scene, where the characters are and what they look like. In other words, hook the reader right away. I also realized that criminals can appear to be ordinary people and have some of the same concerns as the rest of us.

George Higgins learned all this on his own. He majored in English at Boston College, which was my major at the University of Detroit Mercy, another Jesuit school. Higgins went on to Stanford, he said "to learn how to write fiction," which he found out "can't be taught, but I didn't know that then." I left school to write Chevrolet ads and also failed to learn anything about writing. Higgins joined the Associated Press as a rewrite man, a step in the right direction referred to as "like toilet training." He returned to Boston College for a law degree, got a job as an assistant U.S. attorney, and loved it, meeting a parade of characters he would soon be using in his novels.

Still, getting published was tough. Along the way from Stanford to *Eddie Coyle*, Higgins wrote as many as ten books that he either discarded or were rejected by publishers—perhaps for the same reason my first novel with a contemporary setting, *The Big Bounce*, was rejected by publishers and film producers eighty-four times in all, editors calling the book a "downer," void of sympathetic characters—the same ones I'm writing about thirty years later. Higgins's agent at the time of *Eddie Coyle* read the manuscript, told him it was unsalable, and dropped him. Let this be an inspiration to beginning writers discouraged by one rejection after another. If you believe you know what you're doing, you have to give publishers time to catch up and catch on.

In the beginning, both Higgins and I had to put up with labels applied to our work, critics calling us the second coming of Raymond Chandler. At the time we first met, at the Harbourfront Reading in Toronto, George and I agreed that neither of us had come out of the Hammett-Chandler school of crime writing. My take on *The Friends of Eddie Coyle*, for example—which I've listed a number of times as the best crime novel ever written—makes *The Maltese Falcon* read like Nancy Drew. Our method in telling stories has always been grounded in authenticity based on background data, the way it is as well as the way such people speak. We also agreed that it's best not to think too much about plot and begin to stew over where the story is going. Instead, rely on the characters to show you the way.

Five years after *Eddie Coyle*, a *New York Times* review of one of my books said that I "often cannot resist a set piece—a lowbrow aria with a crazy kind of scatological poetry of its own—in the Higgins manner." And that's how you learn, by imitating.

Higgins has been called the Balzac of Boston while I've been labeled the Dickens of Detroit. We didn't discuss it, so I'm not sure what George thought of his alliterative tag. What I wonder is who I'd be if I lived in Chicago.

George V. Higgins died on November 6, 1999, only days short of his sixtieth birthday. During the past twenty years or so his name and mine have appeared together in the press—often in the same sentence—some 178 times. I'm honored.

Addendum:

There's not much I can say about George V. Higgins that I didn't say twelve years ago when I wrote this piece, which was the introduction to the paperback edition of *The Friends of Eddie Coyle* that came out in 2000. I can only say whatever I felt about that work then, I feel about it now with interest. It doesn't get any better than *Eddie Coyle,* which is a blessing and a curse. You know you're reading the best, but you also want to top it. (Elmore Leonard, January 2012)

———————————

Regarded by his peers as a "writer's writer," the best-selling and critically acclaimed Elmore "Dutch" Leonard is the author of forty-six novels. Originally a writer of Westerns, he was first published in 1953 with The Bounty Hunters. *He turned to writing crime novels in 1969, with* The Big Bounce *(*The Moonshine War *was published in the same year), and has continued to write crime novels since. His most recent novel is* Raylan *(2012). He was given his nickname in high school by a classmate, who named him after the Washington Senators' pitcher Emil "Dutch" Leonard. Visit him online at www .elmoreleonard.com.*

The Steam Pig
by James McClure (1971)

MIKE NICOL

James McClure (1939–2006) was a South African–born journalist and novelist best known for his Kramer and Zondi series of mysteries set in the land of McClure's birth, as well as two fine nonfiction studies of police at work in Liverpool and San Diego. Tromp Kramer is an Afrikaner police lieutenant, Mickey Zondi a Zulu detective sergeant, and the novels in which they feature are sly but impassioned studies of the realities of life in apartheid-era South Africa, influenced by McClure's work as a journalist in Natal. McClure, married with a family, and under police surveillance because of his work, left South Africa and moved to England in 1965. He departed journalism in 1974 to write fiction full-time, but his heart was really in the newspaper business. He missed the camaraderie of the newsroom and, following a brief stint as an undertaker, he returned to his former trade, eventually becoming editor of the Oxford Mail, *a post in which he remained until his retirement. Intending to return to fiction, he died with a novel left unfinished.*

When James McClure's *The Steam Pig* appeared in 1971, it came "like a slam to the kidneys," to quote the *New York Times Book Review*. At least that's how it was received outside South Africa. Inside, the reception was less enthusiastic. McClure was not much reviewed, and when he was, the notices were short. There was, however, a small coterie of left-leaning readers who snapped up *The Steam Pig*, but, their attentions aside, McClure remained underappreciated, if not unread.

Yet *The Steam Pig* was unique. Nothing like it had appeared in South African fiction before. Sure, there was a handful of mysteries in the English tradition that had been published in the late 1950s, and a few PI stories had appeared in a magazine called *Drum* during the same decade, but nothing as visceral, as sardonic, as cutting, as ironic as this.

In the early 1970s, South African literature in English was largely the late-bourgeois world of Nadine Gordimer's novels. Crime fiction wasn't on the radar, and it isn't difficult to understand why.

Crime novels featuring cops who solved crimes would be read as reinforcing the dictates of the state: in this instance, the apartheid state. If the state brought order to chaos, what were you saying about a state founded on racial discrimination that enforced its laws by exploitation, division, and abuse, not to mention torture, disappearances, and deaths? No liberal, self-respecting writer was going to side with the police by writing a police procedural. The cops were the enemy. They were an invading army.

McClure might have agreed with this, but he had a different strategy. A South African by birth, he had worked as a reporter in the Durban and Pietermaritzburg area of what is now the province of KwaZulu/Natal, before immigrating to the U.K. in 1965. By then, apartheid was an iron fist. The resistance movements were banned, their leaders either imprisoned on Robben Island or in exile. The security branch was a frightening reality. You could be detained without representation for up to 180 days.

Into this drops *The Steam Pig*, a novel that begins with a beautiful girl on a tray in a funeral parlor being adored by the undertaker.

> Look at her. Like that poet had said: a thing of beauty was a joy for ever.
>
> The perfect figure, and bones good for years yet. The navel, a dainty dish, was especially fine.
>
> His eyes felt none of the chill of the taut white skin. His fingertips rejoiced in the spring of the jet hair. Like the toes, the fingers were exquisitely shaped and well cared for. Not a mark or blemish anywhere.

This scene, this tone of voice, was new in South African literature. But it didn't stop with this unsettling, slightly risqué description. No, next there is a mix-up in the mortuary, and the wrong body goes off to the incinerator. Because of this mistake the young girl, whose death has been signed off as a heart attack, is put on the slab for an autopsy. And lo, she has been murdered with that particularly nasty weapon: a sharpened bicycle spoke inserted under the armpit and into the heart.

The wonder of this instrument, according to the pathologist examining her remains, is that "as you withdraw a thin thing like a bike spoke, it seals off, see? All those layers, muscles, lungs, tissue, close up." If you weren't looking for a wound, you wouldn't find one. So you can't really blame the GP who wrote her off as a "cardiac arrest," especially as she had a history of heart trouble.

It is this discovery of a murder that introduces Lieutenant Tromp Kramer and his assistant, Sergeant Mickey Zondi. A white man and a black man who not only enjoy one another's company but make a formidable team—in itself this was unusual, both literally and figuratively. Indeed, Kramer elects to work with Zondi rather than his white colleagues, something they cannot understand. Why would a white man deliberately choose to partner with a black man? It is unfathomable. The truth is that, as likeable as Kramer is, he is not as smart as Zondi; and although Zondi plays second fiddle throughout the investigation, it is Zondi who puts things together.

Their walk-on scenes are fascinating in their differences. Here's Kramer's entrance:

> A suspect in the next room screamed. Not continuously, but at irregular intervals which made concentration difficult. Then the typewriter unaccountably jammed. The report was not going to be finished on time; Colonel Du Plessis had stipulated four o'clock and it was already 3.55 with at least a page to go.
>
> "So you can bloody well stick it, Colonel, sir," Lieutenant Tromp Kramer declared loudly. He was quite alone in the Murder Squad office.

The horror of the tortured prisoner's scream juxtaposed with the humor of the jammed typewriter and Kramer's irritation are part of McClure's subversive strategy. His intention throughout the book is to lampoon and satirize the apartheid state. So Kramer is introduced in a police station that doubles as a torture chamber, a not uncommon situation in those days.

Zondi, on the other hand, arrives on the scene by surprising his "boss" who has fallen asleep on the couch in the murdered woman's rooms. Interestingly, Zondi always calls Kramer "boss," and never uses the more loaded Afrikaans word "baas," which came to signify subservience but also, according to the inflection, sarcasm.

Zondi, who is a dapper dresser in a "snapbrim hat . . . [and a] zoot suit," immediately begins examining the photographs of the murdered woman.

> Zondi tucked in the corners of a smile and went on with his illicit scrutiny of Miss Le Roux's bromide image. Even dead a white woman had laws to protect her from primitive lust.
>
> "You want to get me into trouble, hey?"
>
> Zondi ignored him. The photographs were sharp and expertly printed, but the lighting had been too oblique and Miss Le Roux seemed to have ended up with a lot of her curves in the wrong places. Nevertheless, Zondi nodded his approval before tossing the envelope across.
>
> "A good woman," he said. "She could have given many sons."
>
> "Is that all you ever think about?" asked Kramer, and they both laughed. Zondi was an incorrigible pelvis man.

Such is the bantering, knockabout relationship between Kramer and Zondi—at the time a seditious idea in itself. However, McClure never accords Zondi the same presence and authority in the story that he does the lieutenant, so Kramer remains the boss.

Many years later, permutations of this duo were to resurface in South African crime fiction when it began to appear in the mid-2000s, having lain dormant (with one exception: Wessel Ebersohn) for almost a quarter of a century. It was as if McClure had set a convention for local crime novels where the crime-fighting protagonists would be drawn from different groups. Or maybe he just hit on a good thing. After all, the wisecracking duo is a stock-in-trade in literature (think Rosencrantz and Guildenstern, think Vladimir and Estragon), and maybe McClure's antecedents saw the same advantages.

But beyond the duo, McClure also left a stylistic legacy of irony and humor, and a fascination with corruption in the public and private sectors. *The Steam Pig*, for instance, is about the lasciviousness of white businessmen and town politicians; it is about blackmail; it is about gang turf wars. It is about a casual viciousness and violence that permeates a society, not only in the state's political system but in the underbelly, too. These elements, too, have been inherited by the South African crime writers currently building a foundation for the genre.

The Steam Pig was not banned by the apartheid government, possibly because the censors felt the references to "kaffirs," "wogs," and "coolies" indicated that the writer supported the status quo. And, as the "cheeky black bastard," as Kramer affectionately calls Zondi, was working for a white boss and the white boss "solved" the crime, all was well in the land of separate development. In fact, the only novel in the eight-book Kramer and Zondi series to be banned was *The Sunday Hangman*, which criticized the prison system. For the rest, the satire went unremarked in South Africa.

It did not go unremarked elsewhere.

Kingsley Amis said of McClure (who died in Oxford, U.K., in June 2006): "[He] provides not only action, pace, excitement and similar old-hat stuff, but more sense, more insight, more feeling, more about what it must be like in South Africa, more wit, more ingenuity, more craftsmanship, more *art* than you could find displayed by the sort of writer you see lengthily and respectfully reviewed in a month of Sundays (and of weeklies and dailies too)." The *Washington Post* reviewer called *The Steam Pig* "a revealing picture of the hate and sickness of the apartheid society." The *New York Times* wrote: "Few first novels make this kind of impact."

Fortunately Soho Press in New York recently republished the novel, and gave it a new lease on life. This is just as well, as no South African publisher will touch it because of the controversial language. Strangely, though, Soho Press used a blurb on the cover that reads as if it might have been lifted from the 1971 edition: "In this award-winning first book of James McClure's mystery series set in apartheid-era South Africa, a beautiful blonde has been murdered by a bicycle spoke through the heart, a Bantu gangster signature. It's up to Lieutenant Kramer, the white detective, and Sergeant Zondi, his Bantu assistant, to figure out who killed her and why." In a country agonizing over the language in

Mark Twain's books and over the use of the word "negro," didn't "Bantu" cause an editor to think twice? Apparently not.*

The Steam Pig, winner of the 1971 CWA Gold Dagger, continues its contentious life. It remains an exhilarating read, despite an ending that verges on farce. And, despite the bad language, it will always be the cornerstone of South African crime fiction.

Mike Nicol is an author, journalist, editor, and online creative writing teacher. His writing life started with the publication of a slim volume of poems, Among the Souvenirs, *in 1979. He has written a number of novels and nonfiction works, including a short biography of Nelson Mandela. In recent years he has turned to crime fiction with the publication of his Re-venge Trilogy:* Payback, Killer Country, *and* Black Heart. *His latest book is* Monkey Business: The Murder of Anni Dewani: The Facts, The Fiction, the Spin. *Visit him online at mikenicol.bookslive.co.za.*

---

* The term "Bantu" as a description of Bantu-speaking South Africans became discredited in the middle of the twentieth century when South Africa's ruling National Party, which was responsible for the introduction of apartheid, began using the term as a racial categorization.

Dance Hall of the Dead
by Tony Hillerman (1973)

WILLIAM KENT KRUEGER

Tony Hillerman (1925–2008) was one of the most admired mystery writers of his generation. A decorated combat veteran of WWII, he worked as a journalist, and subsequently taught the subject at the University of New Mexico at Albuquerque. It was there that he began writing novels, including the series that would make his reputation, the Navajo mysteries featuring Joe Leaphorn and Jim Chee of the Navajo Tribal Police. Dance Hall of the Dead *won the Edgar Award for Best Novel in 1974.*

In any literary genre, the great writer is one who has been the first to open a gate through which others pass. For me, that would be Tony Hillerman.

I write about the state in which I live, Minnesota, and about the Anishinaabeg—or Ojibwe, as they're also known—a culture that had made its home around the Great Lakes since long before white men ever set foot on the North American continent. In large measure, I do this because of Hillerman, because he bucked early criticism of his significant use of the Navajo culture in his first manuscript and, in his three decades as a writer, proceeded to introduce millions of readers to a world about which they knew almost nothing.

Who was Tony Hillerman? A journalist, a university professor, an amateur anthropologist, archaeologist, and ethnologist, and, by the time he passed away in 2008, an author with more than thirty books to his credit. Although some of his work was nonfiction, what Hillerman is best known for are the eighteen novels in the Navajo Tribal Police mystery series, set in the Four Corners region of the American Southwest and featuring two Navajo cops, Joe Leaphorn and, later, Jim Chee.

Before I explain any more about Hillerman, let me explain my own connection with his work.

At the time I'm writing this essay, I've published eleven novels in my own mystery series featuring Cork O'Connor, a man of mixed heritage, part Irish and part Ojibwe. I began the first in this series, a book titled *Iron Lake,* in 1992. I was just over forty years old. And I didn't read mysteries.

I'm the son of a high school English teacher who raised his children on literature with a capital "L." Growing up, I cut my literary teeth on Alexandre Dumas, Robert Louis Stevenson, H. G. Wells, Jack London, and Jules Verne. I read Arthur Conan Doyle, but only because he was considered a classic writer in his way, and I read him as literature, not genre fiction. The Hardy Boys? Nancy Drew? Never touched the stuff. But when I hit forty, after years of trying unsuccessfully to write and publish the Great American Novel, I decided that it was time to get myself into print, whatever it took. When I looked at what people were reading, more often than not, it was a mystery. So I started to read in the genre in order to understand what I was going to write. My great good fortune was to begin that reading with Tony Hillerman.

My first introduction to Hillerman was *Dance Hall of the Dead,* the second book in which his iconic Navajo policeman, Joe Leaphorn, appears. What I discovered, first and foremost, was Hillerman as crafter of fine fiction. Here was a guy who did everything that I thought a writer of classic fiction ought to do. His characters were memorable. His language was powerful. His themes were timeless. His observations of details, physical and psychological, were precise and telling. His setting was profoundly sensual. And on top of all this, he offered readers a deep look into a culture that was exotic and, at the same time, oddly familiar and invitingly human. By the time I finished the book, I was hopelessly hooked on Hillerman and on mystery as a genre.

Lieutenant Joe Leaphorn first appeared as an adjunct character in *The Blessing Way,* Hillerman's debut novel, a story that centered, more or less, on a white protagonist. When Hillerman submitted the manuscript to an agent, she told him frankly that it wasn't very good, and famously advised him to get rid of the Indian stuff. Hillerman wasn't sure that he agreed and sent a note to Joan Kahn, a well-known mystery editor at Harper & Row, asking if she might be willing to read the manuscript.

Her one-sentence reply: send it in. She read it, liked it, and agreed to publish it, pending certain edits. The novel came out to great critical and popular acclaim, and was nominated for the Edgar Award for Best First Novel.

Hillerman published a second novel, *The Fly on the Wall*, which wasn't set in the Southwest, didn't deal at all with the Navajo, and didn't sell nearly as well as *The Blessing Way*. Even as he was working on this manuscript, Hillerman later admitted, he "was yearning to get back to the Navajo Reservation and to the Navajo Tribal Policeman Joe Leaphorn."

In *Dance Hall of the Dead*, Leaphorn steps fully into the spotlight and becomes the character around which the story pivots. To any reader unfamiliar with Hillerman's series, or to any collector looking for one novel by Hillerman to include in his or her collection, this is the book that I would recommend. Why? Although it's not the first novel to feature Leaphorn, it's the first in which the quintessential characteristics of a Hillerman novel come together, in which all the elements that would propel the series to national prominence and to a place in the rarefied air of genre masterpieces fall into place.

Briefly, *Dance Hall of the Dead* deals with the disappearance of two Indian boys, one Zuni and one Navajo. An incredible amount of spilled blood at the spot where the boys were last seen leads officials to suspect that a homicide may have occurred. Leaphorn represents only one of several law enforcement agencies called in to participate in the investigation. From his first appearance on the page, his unique humanity is evident. He's an odd duck: a Navajo, born of The People, but also a man of the world. He's been to college so he understands the larger, more sophisticated picture, but without losing a sense of the Navajo way of life, the importance of *hozho* (harmony), and the necessity, as the Navajo put it, to walk in beauty. He's a man who tries to balance the world as it is with the world as the Navajo sensibility believes it should be. He achieves this balance with a sense of humor, the Navajo's understanding of the importance of patience, and the trained mind of an investigator.

White law enforcement officials and suspects often underestimate Leaphorn, viewing him as a hick lawman, and an Indian to boot. In *Dance Hall of the Dead*, he's written off time and again by the FBI special agent in charge of the homicide. This is fine with Leaphorn. It frees him to do what he does best, which is to investigate the situation with his patient understanding of the many cultures that occupy the barren, beautiful landscape of the Southwest.

Use of the landscape for multiple purposes is one of Hillerman's strongest suits. Here's an example, a passage in which Leaphorn, in his search for the missing Navajo boy, reflects not only on the nature of the land but also on its consequence.

> He saw the beauty, the patterned cloud shadows, the red of the cliffs, and everywhere the blue, gold, and gray of dry country autumn. But soon the north wind would take the last few leaves and one cold night this landscape would change to solid white. And then George Bowlegs, if he was hiding somewhere in it, would be in trouble. He would survive easily enough until the snow came. There were dried berries and edible roots and rabbits, and a Navajo boy would know where to find them. But one day an end would come to the endless sunshine of the mountain autumn. An arctic storm front would bulge down out of western Canada, down the west slope of the Rockies. Here the altitude was almost a mile and a half above sea level and there was already hard frost in the mornings. With the first storm, the mornings would be subzero. There would be no way to find food with the snow blowing. On the first day, George Bowlegs would be hungry. Then he would be weak. And then he would freeze.

What Hillerman accomplishes here, this economy of exposition, he also manages when dealing with characters. For the reader, he often identifies a peripheral character, or one whose true identity is not yet known, through the use of some prominent feature, a kind of character shorthand. A mysterious prowler who leaves only moccasin prints is referred to as the Man Who Wore Moccasins, or sometimes simply Moccasins. The female half of a young Navajo couple who supply information is simply called Young Wife.

All this, any fine writer might do, but one of the talents that sets Hillerman apart is his ability to suffuse the plot with a sensitive examination of Native cultures and to do so without dragging the pace of the story. He generally accomplishes this remarkable feat by making the nuances of the cultures and their spirituality, whether Navajo, Zuni,

Pueblo, or Ute, an integral part of the plot. So it is that as Joe Leaphorn ponders all the mysterious elements surrounding the boy's disappearance, trying to find some pattern, he lapses into a memory of what he'd been taught by his very wise grandfather.

> "When the dung beetle moves," Hosteen Nashibitti had told him, "know that something has moved it. And know that its movement affects the flight of the sparrow, and that the raven deflects the eagle from the sky, and that the eagle's stiff wing bends the will of the Wind People, and know that all of this affects you and me, and the flea on the prairie dog and the leaf on the cottonwood." That had been the point of the lesson. The interdependency of nature. Every cause has its effect. Every action its reaction. A reason for everything. In all things a pattern, and in this pattern, the beauty of harmony. Thus one learned to live with evil, by understanding it, by reading its cause. And thus one learned, gradually and methodically, if one was lucky, to always "go in beauty," to always look for the pattern, and to find it.

Hillerman's plots are not marvels of convolution. They rise naturally, and rather simply, out of the setting and the kinds of people, Indian and white, who inhabit it. Very often, Hillerman weaves a story that suggests involvement of otherworldly forces, only to have Leaphorn discover, in the end, that the true hand behind the crime is most assuredly human. *Dance Hall of the Dead* is no exception, although the novel's final resolution is an unexpected surprise, yet one very much in keeping with the secretive nature of the culture at the novel's heart.

When I'm asked who has most influenced my writing, I point to Hillerman. Asked the same question, Hillerman pointed to an Australian writer, Arthur W. Upfield, who created Inspector Napoleon Bonaparte, a part-Aborigine investigator. "Upfield," Hillerman wrote, "had shown me—and a good many other mystery writers—how both ethnography and geography can be used in a plot and how they can enrich an old literary form."

It may be that there is nothing new under the sun, but a great writer makes this seem absolutely untrue. Hillerman opened a gate for me and for others like me, freeing us to investigate other cultures while we investigate crime. My own belief is that the result is a story compelling in its delivery while remaining respectful of its unique cultural heritage. This is what Hillerman did so well, and what the rest of us strive for.

———————————

William Kent Krueger writes the New York Times *best-selling Cork O'Connor mystery series. After studying briefly at Stanford University, Kent set out to experience the real world. Over the next twenty years, he logged timber, worked construction, tried his hand at freelance journalism, and eventually ended up researching child development at the University of Minnesota. He currently makes his living as a full-time author. He lives in St. Paul, a city he dearly loves, and does all his creative writing in a lovely little coffee shop near his home. The twelfth novel in his series,* Trickster's Point, *will be released in the fall of 2012. Visit him online at www.williamkentkrueger.com.*

Daddy Cool
by Donald Goines (1974)

KEN BRUEN

Donald Goines (1937–74) began his writing career while incarcerated in Michigan's Jackson Penitentiary. Influenced by the work of Iceberg Slim, Goines—who also wrote under the pseudonym Al C. Clark—produced sixteen novels in four years. In novels such as Dopefiend *(1971),* Whoreson *(1972),* Black Gangster *(1972), and* Daddy Cool *(1974), Goines wrote about the ghetto experience of inner-city African Americans. His blend of standard English and urban African American dialect was later hailed as an influence by rap artists such as Ice-T, RZA, and Tupac Shakur.*

Noir has mutated to such a degree that it has almost lost meaning. The most recent addition I've encountered is a form of, I kid you not

Hip-hop Noir.

Why not?

If it gets the kids reading, it gets my vote. As long as the unlikely creator of such a concept gets a mention along the noir highway.

Donald Goines.

A favorite staple of mystery is the hit man. Really hard to miss with the theme. The package comes with instant allure, a ready-made plot, and any twist you can add. But few in this category stand the ultimate test.

Time.

Daddy Cool was first published in 1974, then reissued in 2003, by the ultracool Holloway House. Their books would establish the black urban school of literature and *Daddy Cool* became the bible of rappers. Almost any of the major global rap hits sound like they were lifted wholesale from Goines.

The plot of the novel is straightforward. Larry Jackson is a ruthlessly efficient hit man. His trademark is a knife, to such an extent that he teaches his adored daughter the art of that weapon. He runs a pool hall as cover for his trade.

The seeds of the coming tragedy are sown early, with his stepsons ripping off a numbers racket.

In recent years, studies of black culture and the influence of rap have led academics to enter the fray where Goines is concerned.

Signal for outrageous assertions.

It's truly a stretch to label Goines

"*The black Shakespeare.*"

And it gets worse.

Proving that if you bring academics to the trough, you'll get shite and phew-oh, they've referenced *Hamlet* when discussing *Daddy Cool.*

Joyce would laugh anew.

While serving one of his prison terms, Goines read *The Count of Monte Cristo* and its influence, albeit slanted, is evident. *Daddy Cool* is unique in many ways, not least as one of the rare novels to be reinvented as a graphic novel.

Goines came from a relatively well-off family, yet he would only truly be at ease among the pimps, dope dealers, con artists, and bootleggers, due in no small part to his constant heroin jones. It was during his stretch in the Michigan State Pen that he began to write: firstly Westerns, like that other great master of Detroit dialogue, Elmore Leonard, but it was his discovery of the writer Robert Beck, aka Iceberg Slim, that led Goines to mystery fiction.

He began using a blend of basic English, suffused with the dialect of the black neighborhoods, to create his own style.

On release from prison, he and his common-law wife moved to the Watts district of Los Angeles, believing a geographical change would help alter his lifestyle.

It didn't.

He'd write in the morning, then shoot up in the afternoon. And, in an astonishing five years, he wrote sixteen novels. The mix of ghetto slang filtered with dialectical form continued to refine his art. His pseudonym, Al C. Clark, was soon to be replaced by Donald Goines.

"He was a real storyteller, you read his books and you were . . . there."

So said the rap star DMX, who discovered Goines while serving a term in jail himself. In a nice twist, he would play the lead in the 2004 movie of Goines's novel *Never Die Alone*.

The sheer volume of books written in those four years had Goines finishing novels within a month. The fevered pace of his output should detract from the pace of *Daddy Cool* but instead it adds a tension to the portrait of a stone-cold killer.

Daddy Cool is feared and respected for his lack of any emotion and his trademark is lighting a cigarette before he kills. His absence of haste in his killings, never in a hurry, belies the speed at which the book was composed.

The only love of Daddy Cool's life is his daughter and he attempts to warn her about the pimp she is seeing. The fallout leads to the pimp turning her out and the scene is set for revenge.

". . . his eyes all aglow, wanting to see if we'd be interested in his books."

So said Bentley Morris of the legendary Holloway House, specialist publishers in black literature.

Goines had a twofold dream: a book, then a movie.

Ernest Dickerson, Spike Lee's cinematographer, who would later film *Never Die Alone*, thought initially that they were too dark, too bleak, for the screen.

Goines's major legacy, though, lies with the rappers.

From

AZ

Through

RZA

To Tupac

And even a rapper who calls himself Donny Goines, acknowledging his influence. In his lyrics Tupac Shakur refers to Goines as

"My father figure."

Goines, after his move to Watts, became more politicized and compared the turmoil of the ghetto to a race war.

He and his common-law wife were shot to death by two white men. Arguments continue as to the motive behind the killings. Was it a drug deal gone horribly wrong?

Or

The growing grievance of black gangsters who objected to Goines's depiction of them in his novels, based on a belief that his narrative and characterizations were a map for the Feds to identify them?

Daddy Cool is frequently compared to the novels of Chester Himes, but the broad comedy in Himes's work is not Goines's style, whose aim was far too lethal for such a luxury. The work of the major mystery writers, including Mosley, owes a debt to Goines.

His reputation continues as the rappers create their own bloody scenarios from Goines's life and death. Through writers like Goines, the daily legacy of black urban existence is transformed into bleak art, and a stark indictment of ghetto damnation.

———

Ken Bruen (b. 1951) was born in Galway in the west of Ireland. He earned a PhD in metaphysics at Trinity College, then taught all over the world for twenty-five years. After a short detention in a Brazilian prison, Bruen moved to London, where his early novels are set. He is best known for his series of Jack Taylor private eye novels set in Galway, the first of which was The Guards *(2001); novels in that series have won Bruen the Shamus Award, the Macavity Award, and the Barry Award. The films* London Boulevard *(2010) and* Blitz *(2011) were adapted from his novels of the same name. Bruen's most recent publication is* Headstone *(2011), the ninth in the Jack Taylor series. Visit him online at www.kenbruen.com.*

The Wrong Case
by James Crumley (1975)

DAVID CORBETT

James Crumley (1939–2008) is one of the most influential crime fiction authors of the last half century. Ray Bradbury's series detective Elmo Crumley is named for him, and the opening line of his novel The Last Good Kiss *(1978) is frequently cited as the greatest opening line in crime fiction history. First published in 1969 with* One to Count Cadence, *and best known for creating the series characters Milo Milodragovitch and C. W. Sughrue (who appeared together in 1996's* Bordersnakes), *Crumley won the 1994 Hammett Prize, awarded for best literary crime fiction, for* The Mexican Tree Duck *(1993).*

I came to crime fiction late. Like a lot of the smugly educated, I felt perfectly justified in belittling what I'd never read. But I had the good sense to boot myself out of the ivory tower, abandoning a fellowship in linguistics at Berkeley to get my heart broken and my nose bloodied.

First stop, theater. I reacquainted myself with menace through Harold Pinter, with emotional battle through Arthur Miller and Tennessee Williams and Edward Albee. I was learning, climbing down off the rickety ladder of my arrogance, getting closer to the honest stuff of reckless life.

Then an offer came up through a friend—a job as a private investigator. "If you want to write, you can't beat this place for material." Understatement of my life. Only a nitwit would refuse. A bigger nitwit than me.

I took to the job, did it well. People talked to me, a skill you can't teach. And it fed a competitive hunger to get the infamous lowdown that I didn't know I possessed.

A year or two into dick work I decided, finally, to pick up a crime novel, see what all the bother was about. I selected Chandler's *The Long Goodbye*. I won't say that I was hooked but, at long last, I got it. If this was crime fiction, it spoke of my world, if from a windy perspective. But in the half that it got right there was far more to admire than there was to dismiss in the half it got wrong.

From Chandler I wandered the map awhile, from Cain to Thompson to Charyn to Connelly to Burke, skidding along the mystery aisle aimlessly, utter impulse in control.

I can't even remember how or when I happened upon James Crumley. But I did. And things stopped cold. That odd giddy sense of *This is it* came to me as it has only a handful of times as a reader.

The writing echoed Chandler, sure, with its haunted bravado and tough-guy wit, but also Tom McGuane and William Kittredge, writers who'd expanded my idea of what it meant to live in the West, crafting a language that suited the region's harshness and beauty, the clarity of its light and the savageness of its history, its contempt for enclosure, its equation of sophistication with something to hide.

In his wit, his compassion, his skill, his command of language, Crumley showed me once and for all that there was no such thing as "mere" crime fiction. There was great writing and there wasn't. I knew which one this was.

Unlike many of my crime-writing peers, it wasn't *The Last Good Kiss* I picked up first, but *The Wrong Case*. And so I met Milo Milodragovitch before C. W. Sughrue. I don't know if reversing that order would have changed much, but in Milo I found, almost unwittingly, a kindred spirit.

Crumley got a great deal right, of course—the petty bribes to phone-company insiders, the indifferent lies offered to witnesses to speed things along, and the one thing every PI sooner or later tells his client: "You're not paying me to believe you, you're paying me to find out what happened."

But, like many PI novelists, Crumley also indulged in the macho excesses that in lesser hands so often seem laughable. For example, if a hypothetical private detective blew away the columns to a witness's house so the whole front of the place collapsed, just because said witness was a mouthy punk—in leathers and lavender eye shadow, no less—he wouldn't just spend a few hours in the pokey like Milo. He'd do real time and get his license yanked.

But something in Crumley's handling of that scene and all the others like it, with their rough-and-tumble antics and bullying swagger, made it all seem not just acceptable, but true, even necessary. He set a tone that kept you off-balance, a tone that blended a kind of sly irony with heartsick desperation, an understanding that the battle for the good is fought by ingeniously flawed men doing the ridiculous in the service of some angry, inscrutable truth.

From my own tattered Catholicism I recognized in Crumley's world the warring angels of crippling sin and unearned forgiveness. Shame and guilt haunt every reflection, every exchange, not just because so many drunks populate the pages. The drunks form a chorus, representing an open acceptance of *the weakness of our nature,* as the Roman rites before the grave put it so neatly.

In Crumley's fiction, drunkenness stands for the restless truce each person makes with what he can bear and what, in the end, does him in, and each drunk is broken and mended in his own unique way.

Lee Child has sniffed at the "bullet in the heart hero," the protagonist whose forward momentum suffers the relentless drag of a ghost of pain or loss. Don't cops and lawyers and hit men and, yes, PIs just do what they do because, after all, it's their job?

I'll admit, I've often cringed at the tortured motivations of my fictional avatars. They never seem to find the competitive juice of the adversarial system, the pride in a job well done, or the fear of being thought inadequate—with the threat of not getting paid—more than enough reason to raise their game. Always worked for me.

But Crumley, for my money, got to something wiser than a writerly trick. Milo's bullet in the heart would doom any number of lesser men, and the ghost he carries on his back isn't a burden. It's him.

When he's all of ten years old, his parents crown one more stinking mean fight with the father going for his shotgun, only to accidentally blow off his own face when the trigger catches on the open bolt of his Remington .30-06.

Milo's mother, a hypocritical harpy, eviscerates every drunk she can name—at the risk of too much information, another touch that resonated. She excoriates none of them more than her dear, dead husband, and dumps the departed's clothes off at the Salvation Army. Milo hunts down the derelicts who've bought them, buying every item back so he can burn it in a ritual of grief and mercy. In so doing, he gets a bit more than he bargained for:

I learned that they were men also, that they had lives full of chances too, not all of which had gone begging. And they still had dreams, dreams and lies enough to live with them. Unlike my mother, they were honest drunks, not too often ashamed. In their odd moments, drunk or sober, they knew who and what they were; they had looked at the world for a long steady moment, and found it wanting. As they took on individual faces and histories, I began to see them, both in the bars and at work—many did work, shoveled Meriwether's shit like white niggers—and the more I saw them, the more I preferred them to sober citizens. And I understood the defiance in the pathetic motto: I ain't no alcoholic, Jack, I don't go to no fucking meetings. And they needed no army for their salvation.

Ten years later, when he's off in Korea doing everything imaginable to avoid combat, Milo learns that his mother, after checking herself into a posh rehab facility, has wrapped a nylon stocking around her neck and hanged herself, leaving her son to wonder at the family legacy of pitiless luck.

Crumley reminded me, as no other writer had, that justice, like drink, is a balm for suffering, not a cure, and we never escape it. And so when Helen Duffy enters Milo's office, asking to find her brother, he experiences not just the call to adventure but a rumbling in his crotch. And, ironically, his conscience. She's the most beautifully confused woman he's ever seen, a "woman so strong that she could believe in hope and trust and families and love, a woman who had survived without luck." She might just offer him a chance at something new: a cleansing, a renewal. He thinks this even as he lusts for her and she lies to him, and continues lying until he's left with nothing but the choice to forgive her or not.

This constant battle between guilt and solace, crime and comfort, insight and blindness, threatens to split Milo in two at every turn—and that seesaw pressure propels the action forward as much as any external event. It also renders him capable of appraising human nature with a cold but uncritical eye.

In Amos Swift, the fat, jolly pathologist who smokes illegal Cubans to escape the antiseptic stench of the morgue, Milo recognizes a man who has decided that he'd rather take his chances with the dead than the dying.

In the wife of a professor whose tastes have turned to young men, Milo sees what he thought he'd left behind when his divorce work dried up, one more sign of a dead marriage: "She stood framed in the saffron glow, a tall woman, her long hair growing lank in the damp air, her strong hands strangling her waist with the cord of her ragged robe."

Even the inanimate world speaks of something lost. From the reflections of colored lights in the wind-rippled pools of rainwater dotting a motel parking lot, he imagines a city flickering at the bottom of a black sea.

But the most honest and telling details always zero in on Milo's own broken soul. In the span of two paragraphs we get Milo recounting the shameless routine of divorce work—bribing motel night clerks, bugging rooms where illicit trysts end in a camera flash, "startled faces and scurrying bodies frozen in the explosion." Then we see him waiting in his truck, hoping to follow up on an earlier invitation from a voluptuous bartender, Vonda Kay, "the biggest breasts and the sweetest disposition west of the Big Muddy . . . the most comfortable one-night stand in town, as warm as freshly baked bread, as loving as a puppy." He imagines taking her home where they can "have breakfast, smoke a little dope, and sleep comforted by the creek, the soft brush of the spruce needles, the placid warmth of two old veterans, our nerves ruined in the front lines of love and failure." But she walks out of the bar with another man, and Milo heads home alone.

This all might turn maudlin, of course, or at least too terribly sad, if not for Milo's sneaky, savage, Falstaffian wit. The laughs come like the drinks, as balm and consolation, a wink in the eye of the shit storm.

When I read this book I realized how much of the urgency I felt in myself as I did my job wasn't mere competitive juice and righteous giddyup. It came out of a dark well of shame and bitterness. Like Milo, I felt compelled to get people to talk to me because "they were somehow guilty, and I was somehow the law."

But the opposite was also true: I was guilty, and they were the law.

David Corbett is the author of four novels: The Devil's Redhead, Done for a Dime *(a New York Times* Notable Book*),* Blood of Paradise *(nominated for numerous awards, including the Edgar), and* Do They Know I'm Running

(Spinetingler Award, Best Novel—Rising Star category, 2011). David's short fiction and poetry have appeared in numerous magazines and anthologies, with two stories selected for Best American Mystery Stories *(2009 and 2011). Mysterious Press/Open Road Media reissued his first two novels, plus a story collection, in May 2012, and Penguin will publish his book on the craft of characterization in early 2013. Visit him online at www.david corbett.com.*

Last Bus to Woodstock
by Colin Dexter (1975)

PAUL CHARLES

Colin Dexter (b. 1930) is the creator of Inspector Morse, the Oxford-based police detective with a taste for Wagner, real ale, cryptic crosswords, and bamboozling his faithful sidekick, Detective Sergeant Lewis. Morse first appeared in 1975, in Last Bus to Woodstock, *and went on to feature in twelve subsequent novels, the last of which,* The Remorseful Day, *was published in 1999. Awarded the Order of the British Empire in 2000, Dexter was handsomely decorated by various crime writers' organizations throughout his career, eventually receiving the Crime Writers' Association Cartier Diamond Dagger for lifetime achievement in 1997. The TV series* Inspector Morse, *with John Thaw playing Morse, ran to thirty-three episodes between 1987 and 2000, with Dexter making a cameo appearance in almost every episode, and finally receiving a speaking part in 1993.*

I can remember very clearly how I discovered *Last Bus to Woodstock,* one of my favorite books.

I'd been on a long tour of Italy with one of the songwriters with whom I'm lucky enough to work. As was often the case with these trips, friends from back home would send out stuff to help me pass the time, including videos of U.K. TV shows so I could continue my viewing on the tour bus as I traveled through foreign parts. One such video was an early episode of the TV series *Morse.* When I eventually got round to viewing it, two hours, including adverts, positively flew by.

There was one scene, not too far into the episode, where Morse and his faithful sidekick, DS Lewis, having been to view the scene of the crime and examine the victim, drive back through the Oxfordshire countryside and pull in alongside a cornfield. The scene with all of its colors—the yellow of the corn, the greens of the trees, the blues of the sky, and the maroon Jaguar—was very potent and emotive. Morse and Lewis were just standing with their backs to the camera, staring at the view. It was quite a lengthy scene considering that there was no dialogue, just Barrington Pheloung's hypnotic score. It was calm, relatively quiet, with no movement whatsoever—well, maybe just a gentle breeze idling through the corn and the bushes. The scene was clearly set up to allow Morse, Lewis, and the TV audience to reflect on the loss of life and consider what had been discovered so far. I thought it was extremely brave television and I was intrigued to discover if it was the director of the production or the author of the original work who had been responsible for the innovative approach.

The very next day I found a bookstore in Milan specializing in English-language books. As luck would have it they had two Morse titles, *Last Bus to Woodstock* and *The Dead of Jericho,* and the author of the series was Colin Dexter. I discovered that if the scene in the TV series had come from the director, then the mood created was most definitely the work of the author.

In 1973 Colin Dexter, then in his midforties, an ex–classics master, senior assistant secretary of the Oxford Local Examinations Board, and national crossword champion, took his young family on holiday to Wales. It rained nonstop. To while away the time he read both of the crime novels that he found in the guesthouse. (He has always been too discreet to reveal the titles.) The thought struck him that he could do better, and so he started to write. The first words he put to paper were:

> "Let's wait just a bit longer," said the girl in the dark-blue trousers and the light summer coat. "I'm sure there's one due pretty soon."

Colin Dexter returned to Oxford, completed his story, had it typed up, and sent it off to Collins, which, with its famous Gollancz yellow-jacketed detection series, was one of the top crime publishers of the day. After five months of silence Dexter contacted Gollancz again. He pointed out that they had the only copy of his manuscript, and asked if they could send it back, "please." Gollancz returned the manuscript along with a lengthy critique, pretty much telling him not to give up his day job marking examination papers.

Next Dexter sent his manuscript to Lord Hardinge of Penshurst at Macmillan. Lord Hardinge was just coming down with flu, so he took the manuscript home with him and retired to bed. He read the book overnight, contacted the author the very next day, and told him that he wished to publish *Last Bus to Woodstock* exactly as it was.

In *Last Bus to Woodstock* (which didn't make it to TV until the final episode of the second series in 1988), Sylvia Kaye, the girl in the dark-blue trousers and the light summer coat, ends up dead in the car park of the Black Prince public house, and Morse and Lewis embark on their first investigation.

Sylvia Kaye is trying to catch a bus to Woodstock. She and another girl, whom she may or may not have known, seem to be in a hurry. Each has a rendezvous, one secret and one not. They ask a lady already waiting at the bus stop for the time of the next bus, and subsequently decide to hitch a lift. One ends up dead in the car park, and one doesn't. Morse and Lewis then have to discover the identity of the other girl, and their investigation throws up enough suspects and illicit affairs to make even Lady Chatterley's lover blush.

Let's see now: there's Bernard Crowther, a university lecturer; his wife, Margaret; and Peter Newlove, a friend of both Bernard's and Margaret's. Then there's Jennifer Coleby, who works with Sylvia (they may or may not have known each other); there's Jennifer and Sylvia's boss, Mr. Palmer; and that's before we even consider Sylvia's porn-distracted "boyfriend," John Sanders. Morse and Lewis are further confronted by a couple of suspect letters, which Morse takes great pleasure in dissecting in exacting detail; a genuine suicide; flat tires; flat batteries; flatmates (of Jennifer Coleby, that is; in this case, Sue Widdowson, a nurse); and not one, but two seemingly realistic confessions.

Morse falls hopelessly in love, yet, as is invariably the case for the poor soul, his love is in vain. He and Lewis chase a healthy shoal of red herrings and Morse exclaims a few times, "Lewis, you're a genius!" without Lewis having the slightest clue as to what he may have said to kick-start Morse's labyrinthine imagination.

Morse follows Dexter's lead in his love of crossword puzzles and his passion for the works of Wagner and A. E. Housman. Dexter, through

Morse, makes clear early in his first book how fastidious, and witty, he intends to be in the usage of the English language.

> "Yes, a witness, sir. A Mrs. Mabel Jarman. She saw the murdered girl . . ."
> "You mean," interrupted Morse, "she saw the girl who was later murdered, I suppose."

Morse, while explaining his approach to detective work to Lewis, says, "They tell me you can climb the Eiger in your carpet slippers if you go the easy way."

In the early books Lewis was Welsh, middle-aged, older than Morse by several years, balding, and overweight. For the television adaptation (and the Morse novels that came after the TV series began broadcasting) he became a Geordie, thick-haired, slimmer, and younger than Morse by several years. The Lancia of the pre-TV novels was replaced by the scene-stealing maroon Jaguar XJ6 Mk II (registration number 248 RPA). For the television films, John Thaw (apparently) insisted Morse lose his leanings for seedier locations and lustful dalliances.

The main trio behind the TV films—Colin Dexter, Ted Childs, and John Thaw—all appeared to be simultaneously hitting their creative peaks in their respective fields. We had Dexter's well-drawn characters and clever plotting; executive producer Ted Childs's brave, innovative idea of holding out for the precious two-hour slots on prime-time television, and his insistence on rotating several screenwriters and directors in order to keep the thirty-three TV films fresh; and, finally, John Thaw in the role that it appeared he'd been waiting his entire life to play. I mean, with hindsight it really couldn't have failed, could it? *Morse*—the TV series—was so successful that it brought British detective fiction in general and Colin Dexter in particular into the publishing and media mainstream. So much so, in fact, that the final two Dexter books—*Death Is Now My Neighbour*, where Morse's Christian name is revealed, and *The Remorseful Day*—were covered in depth by all the U.K. national media, including frequent mentions on the TV and radio news bulletins. Both titles ruled the best-seller lists for ages.

As a writer Colin Dexter never suffers from a blank page or screen (although I don't believe that he's ever written using any method other than pen and ink). "You never wait for the Almighty to whisper in your ear," he says. His logic is you just put two people on a page, they start a dialogue, and you have the start of your scene or story. He concedes that the initial result might be terrible but his point is that, when you have something down on the page, you at least have a chance of making it better.

Dexter's books are essentially puzzles. He once said that he was as anxious for the detective to manage without a pathology lab as he was for the crossword puzzler to manage without a dictionary. Dexter is not scared of dropping clues aplenty and of allowing world-weary Morse to be completely in the wrong, or to have his head turned by a beautiful woman. He infuses his work with the happiness and humor, the sadness and misery, of real life. Lewis is never confident and clearly never capable of leading a case, but at the same time he's the perfect foil and sounding board for Morse, even though it's often a one-way conversation.

There are some great writers of crime fiction out there but few seem as capable as Dexter—or Michael Connelly—of catching the kaleidoscope of real life. Dexter's eye for detail, his understanding of human nature, and his ear for dialogue immediately pull you right into the thick of his story. He hooks you in such a way that you don't even know you've been hooked. He is clearly concerned with making his pages easy to read. He loves to break up the physical density of print on the page with dialogue. His chapters are short and snappy and the books are over all too soon. There is just such pleasure to be taken in the actual reading of his work, even before you consider his trademark twists, turns, and red herrings that come together in one almighty wallop at the end of the book.

In the case of an anthology like this one, I suppose that one has to give a balanced view and offer some kind of criticism. So, after very careful consideration, my main criticism would have to be that, unfortunately, Colin Dexter limited us to only a mere thirteen classic Morse mysteries, plus one volume of collected Morse short stories. I do thank the editors for the excuse to read them again. I can happily report that they're standing the test of time perfectly.

Paul Charles was born and raised in the Northern Irish countryside. He is the author of the acclaimed Detective Inspector Christy Kennedy series.

*The most recent title—*A Pleasure to Do Death With You—*is the tenth in the series. He is also the author of a couple of music-related novels, namely* First of the True Believers *(2002), which uses the story of the Beatles as a backdrop, and* The Last Dance *(2012), set in the legendary Irish Showband scene of the late 1950s and the early 1960s. Charles may be unique in that not only was he around in the 1960s, but he also remembers the decade vividly. Visit him online at www.paulcharlesbooks.com.*

3 to Kill
(*Le petit bleu de la côte ouest*)
by Jean-Patrick Manchette (1976)

JAMES SALLIS

Jean-Patrick Manchette (1942–95) was a French writer of short, violent crime novels who translated American crime fiction, including the work of Donald Westlake and Ross Thomas, into French as well as producing crime fiction of his own. Manchette, who was a student activist and a contributor to the newspaper La Voix Communiste, *is credited with the invention of the* néo-polar, *a politically and socially engaged version of the traditional French* polar, *or detective novel. "Just as one must never leave the critique of fascism to democrats," he once remarked in an essay, "the critique of democracy must not be abandoned to cretins."*

Warn your children and the weak of heart. There is meat here. There is gristle. There is bone.

If they're about anything at all beyond mere entertainment, the arts are about amazement and recognition. Certain paintings, poems, books, and music seem somehow to be in our blood, braided into the DNA: from our first encounter they're a part of us. That's precisely how I felt upon initially hearing Mozart's horn concerti and the blues or, years later, Cajun music, or when I fetched up on those first lines of Apollinaire, Cendrars, Queneau.

Asked about my devotion to crime fiction by interviewers or by audience members at speaking engagements, I tell them that's the way crime fiction was for me: a crucial part of my intellectual history, amazingly a *familiar* part, from the moment I first cracked open *The Maltese Falcon.* Then, after blathering on about mysteries being the quintessential urban fiction, quoting Nathanael West to the effect that in America the novelist has no need to *prepare* for violence, or citing D. H. Lawrence's observation that Americans have murdered their way into democracy, like any good hunting dog I come to point.

Quite often these days, the game in the bush tends to be Jean-Patrick Manchette.

Each era, I suspect, fumbles its way to a distinctive popular voice, some form uniquely suited to the time's self-image, its deeper needs and anxieties. Victorian England had its "penny dreadfuls," the United States in the placid 1950s had those subterranean original paperbacks by such writers as Richard Matheson, David Goodis, and Jim Thompson. As Geoffrey O'Brien observed in *Hardboiled America: The Lurid Years of Paperbacks,* "These novels, and the covers that illustrate them, speak of the ignoble corners of life beyond the glow of Jane Powell, *Father Knows Best,* and the healthy, smiling faces in magazines advertising milk or frozen dinners or trips to California."

Increasingly I've come to wonder if the thriller—massive engines set in motion and grinding on far beyond our tiny lives and ken, provisional realities imploding page by page, horizontal rather than vertical thrust—may not best define and serve our time.

France, of course, adopted American crime fiction early on, giving the genre literary cachet and spilling out to the world at large a defining word, "noir," with publication of works by Hammett, Chandler, Himes, and their French-born disciples in Gallimard's *La Série noire.* Writers largely forgotten here, such as Horace McCoy, W. R. Burnett, and others, remain well known there. In France thrillers are referred to as *polars.* And in France the godfather and wizard of *polars* is Jean-Patrick Manchette.

Much about Manchette seems quintessentially French: the stylish glistening surface of his prose, his objectivist method, his adoption of a "low" art form to embody abstract ideas. This may go far toward explaining why he remains virtually unknown in the States, with but three of his books available in translation and those largely, it would seem, unread. In Europe, having salvaged the French crime novel from the bog of police procedurals and colorful tales of Pigalle lowlife into which it had sunk, Manchette is a massive figure.

I have vivid memories of standing with the Mexican writer and novelist Paco Taibo on a veranda at a conference in the Bahamas going on and on about Manchette. Heavyweights of crime writing were there: editors, critics, writers. But each time we were joined, because so few knew his work, Paco and I had to start over.

"The crime novel," Manchette claimed, "is the great moral literature of our time"—and he set about proving it.

For Manchette, and for the generation of writers that followed him, the crime novel is no mere entertainment, but a means to strip bare the failures of society, ripping through veils of appearance, deceit, and manipulation to expose to the air the greed and violence that are society's true engines.

Coming from the extreme left as an advocate of Guy Debord's Situationism, Manchette consistently skewered capitalist society and indicted the media for its emphasis on spectacle. He saw the world as a giant marketplace in which gangs of thugs—be they leftist, terrorist, or socially approved stand-ins such as police and politicians—compete relentlessly, and in which tiny groups of alienated individuals go on trying to cling to the flotsam of their lives. He folds quotations, allusions, and parodies of literary writers like Stendhal and Baudelaire into his work, alludes constantly to music, painting, and philosophy, juxtaposes the vulgar and the precious, jams depictions of quotidian life against scenes of such extreme violence as to call into question the whole of bourgeois—of accepted, apparent, innocent—existence.

"He was like an electroshock to the chloroformed country of literature and the French thriller," Jean-François Gérault wrote. (Take note of that "and.") Elsewhere Gérault suggested that Manchette "had reached a formal perfection that was impossible to surpass."

Effectively Manchette's career ran only some eleven years or so. The ten novels were published by Gallimard from 1971 to 1982. Following this, he worked as a translator (of Ross Thomas, Donald Westlake, and Alan Moore, among others), as a scenarist for film and TV, as an editor, as a reviewer of films, and an essayist on thrillers and crime fiction. After 1989, treatment of, and complications from, a pancreatic tumor made work impossible. He died in 1995 in Paris of lung cancer, aged fifty-three.

From the first page of *3 to Kill*, from virtually any page of Manchette, you know right away that you're in the hands of a master, that the safe, predictable carnival ride for which you've paid has become more like plunging headlong and helpless down rapids.

And sometimes what used to happen was what is happening now: Georges Gerfaut is driving on Paris's outer ring road. He has entered at the Porte d'Ivry. It is two-thirty or maybe three-fifteen in the morning . . . He has had five glasses of Four Roses bourbon. And about three hours ago he took two capsules of a powerful barbiturate. The combined effect on him has not been drowsiness but a tense euphoria that threatens at any moment to change into anger or else into a kind of vaguely Chekhovian and essentially bitter melancholy, not a very valiant or interesting feeling . . .

Georges Gerfaut is a man under forty. His car is a steel-grey Mercedes. The leather upholstery is mahogany brown, matching all the fittings of the vehicle's interior. As for Georges Gerfaut's interior, it is somber and confused . . . Via two speakers, one beneath the dashboard, the other on the back-window deck, a tape player is quietly diffusing West Coast–style jazz . . .

The reason why Georges is barreling along the outer ring road, with diminished reflexes, listening to this particular music, must be sought first and foremost in the position occupied by Georges in the social relations of production. The fact that Georges has killed at least two men in the course of the last year is not germane. What is happening now used to happen from time to time in the past.

One is never on safe ground with Manchette, as here we're immediately off-kilter and off-balance, often unsure just where in the story we find ourselves—in medias res, flashback, reverie, or trapped in some sort of eternal recurrence?

Stopping to aid a severely injured man, Gerfaut attracts the attention of the man's attackers. They then set upon Gerfaut who, at first failing to connect the two incidents, nonetheless steps aside and out of his own life to turn the killing back on them. A standard thriller plot, the pursued becoming pursuer: the amazement is in seeing how much of the world's confusion, savagery, and sideways comedy Manchette effortlessly loops and lassos into his novel.

Here is the opening of *The Prone Gunman:*

> It was winter, and it was dark. Coming down directly from the Arctic, a freezing wind rushed into the Irish Sea, swept through Liverpool, raced across the Cheshire plain (where the cats lowered their trembling ears at the sound of the roaring in the chimneys) and, through the lowered window, struck the eyes of the man sitting in the little Bedford van. The man did not blink.
>
> He was tall but not really massive, with a calm face, blue eyes and brown hair . . . An Ortgies automatic pistol with a Redfield silencer rested on his lap.

Another standard, archetypical plot: the hired killer who wants to give it all up. Again, the pleasure is in seeing how many ways Manchette can twist and turn his story on the spit of that plot, how much weight he manages to pack into scenes that appear on the surface to be purely objective, the gravity of it all. Things move fast, almost at a blur—then excruciatingly slow. Sentences are clipped, breathless. Charged language everywhere, sometimes to the point of the incantatory.

We are there, and flayed. With Manchette we drive the ring road about Paris again and again. We are calm. We have an automatic pistol in our lap. Its weight is the weight of history. Gristle here—and bone, shining beneath the light.

Jean-Patrick Manchette's are lean, muscular books that deserve serious reading. In this age of hyperbole and unremitting puffery, our age, they have the uncommon decency and grace to appear much simpler than they are: to mean much more than they say.

They have grace.

Best known perhaps for the Lew Griffin books and Drive, *James Sallis has published fourteen novels, more than a hundred stories, collections of poetry, a translation of Raymond Queneau's novel* Saint Glinglin, *three books on music, and reams of criticism on literature of every sort. Once editor of the landmark science-fiction magazine* New Worlds *in London ("Way, way back in the day"), Jim contributes a regular books column to the* Magazine of Fantasy & Science Fiction. *Visit him online at www.jamessallis.com.*

Touch Not the Cat
by Mary Stewart (1976)

M. J. ROSE

*Mary Stewart (b. 1916) is an English novelist known for her work in the field of romantic suspense, with gothic undertones, and for her five-book sequence of Arthurian novels, published between 1970 and 1995, that blurred the lines between historical and fantasy fiction. The first three novels in the series—*The Crystal Cave, The Hollow Hills, *and* The Last Enchantment—*are generally referred to as the Merlin Trilogy.*

> My lover came to me on the last night in April, with a message
> and a warning that sent me home to him.

So begins *Touch Not the Cat* by Mary Stewart. The opening quote refers to a message delivered telepathically to Bryony Ashley, aged twenty-two, by an unknown lover whom she has always believed would eventually reveal himself. She receives this communication on the eve of her father's death. He's been killed in a mysterious automobile accident far from home. As a result, ownership of her family home, Ashley Court, has passed via trust to Emory, her cousin.

The ensuing story is true to the mores of the gothic genre. As the jacket copy describes the plot, it all begins with an inheritance:

> At first, Bryony feels relief that she has not inherited the respon-
> sibility of the Court. She knows that she possesses the true Ash-
> ley legacy: the "gift." Three hundred years ago that gift was called
> "The Sight," and had caused an Ashley ancestor to be burned
> at the stake. Today Bryony calls it the gift of telepathy, and she
> is also aware that at least one of the other Ashley [cousins] has
> this gift.

Throughout the years this strange telepathic communication has led Bryony to think of this other Ashley as her "phantom lover." The intimate relationship with this lover is complete in every way but one: the physical.

Alone after her father's death, Bryony resolves to discover who that secret lover is, and decipher a dying message left by her father that mentions a cat. Is it the animal on the family crest in the gazebo that centuries of Ashleys used for illicit assignations? Or was he alluding to the American woman trying to seduce Emory?

As the publisher wrote, "The garden pavilion is in the center of a complicated maze of hedges and shrubbery notoriously difficult to get out of. Bryony knows the maze well, but does not guess the harrowing significance it will come to play in her life as well as that of her phantom lover."

A family estate in disrepair; peril; danger; a suspicious death; theft; and the age-old story of Romeo and Juliet—all play a part in the novel that introduced me to what has become my favorite genre. But why that novel? What was it about Stewart's book that stayed with me more than those by Poe, Christie, Hammett, Highsmith, Chandler, and all of the other fine mystery writers I read?

In her 1976 book *Literary Women*, Ellen Moers coined the term "Female Gothic." She explained that, in gothic writing, "fantasy predominates over reality, the strange over the commonplace, and the supernatural over the natural, with one definite authorial intent: to scare. Not, that is, to reach down into the depths of the soul and purge it with pity and terror (as we say tragedy does), but to get to the body itself, its glands, muscles, epidermis, and circulatory system, quickly arousing and quickly allaying the physiological reactions to fear."

Indeed it was the gothic genre that reached me on that deeper level. Novels such as *Rebecca* by Daphne du Maurier, *Northanger Abbey* by Jane Austen, *Frankenstein* by Mary Shelley, and Charlotte Brontë's *Jane Eyre* were the most dog-eared on my shelves. Certainly the supernatural is evocative and atmospheric. Family curses, wills, inheritances, madness, ghosts, and vampires are frightening. But even more fascinating and often terrifying was the psychology of the characters explored in these novels.

And that was what hooked me.

Since the late 1700s, women gothic writers have symbolically used the heroine's journey through atmospheric buildings and gardens, through pathways and caverns, as a metaphor for the journey from the innocence of childhood to sexual maturity. The castles or estates themselves, with their grand rooms and circular turrets, functioned as metaphors for the rich, sexualized, and complicated interior lives of the main characters.

The mystery of inheritance is indeed the mystery of our own selves. Stories about young women becoming heirs to estates and setting off to claim or save them are, in fact, stories about young women coming into their own and becoming sexually independent beings.

Anne Williams, in her book *Art of Darkness: A Poetics of Gothic,* wrote, "The affinity between the gender and the genre expresses the terror and rage that women experience within patriarchal social arrangements, especially marriage." Fear, apprehension, then resolution and relief: such emotional reactions are strong. When we're finished reading, and if the author has done her job—which Stewart does so well—we're left deeply emotionally satisfied. It's difficult to describe the roller-coaster ride a reader experiences in the pages of a good gothic novel and not associate it with a form of sexual awakening.

It's why so many young women relate to and are drawn to the genre.

The tradition of this genre that takes its name from medieval architecture goes back to the eighteenth century. And, indeed, gothic mysteries usually have strong buildings at their center. Sometimes they are metaphors, at other times mirrors. In *Touch Not the Cat,* Stewart uses them as both.

But I didn't think about any of this when I first read *Touch Not the Cat,* or any of the other fine suspense novels Stewart penned. I didn't even think about whether this book was a gothic novel, or a thriller, or a mystery, or a romance. On her own website, Stewart writes that she has always been hesitant to categorize her novels. "I'd rather just say that I write novels, fast-moving stories that entertain. To my mind there are really only two kinds of novels, badly written and well written. Beyond that, you cannot categorize . . . Can't I say that I just write stories? 'Storyteller' is an old and honorable title, and I'd like to lay claim to it."

I, too, have always bristled at forcing books into categories, as both a reader and a writer. I only care about how good a book is. For me, a book to die for is one that keeps me entertained and enthralled, obsessed with the book while I am reading it and, when it's over, satisfied.

And *Touch Not the Cat* does all that.

M. J. Rose is the internationally best-selling author of twelve novels, including The Book of Lost Fragrances, *and three nonfiction books on marketing. Rose graduated from Syracuse University, spent the '80s in advertising, has a commercial in NYC's MoMA, and in 2005 created the first marketing company for authors—AuthorBuzz.com. The television series* Past Life *was based on her Reincarnationist series. She is one of the founding board members of the International Thriller Writers as well as cofounder of Peroozal.com and BookTrib.com. Rose lives in Connecticut with her husband, the musician and composer Doug Scofield, and their very spoiled and often photographed dog, Winka. Visit her online at www.mjrose.com.*

Cutter and Bone
by Newton Thornburg (1976)

GEORGE PELECANOS

Newton Thornburg (1929–2011) was an American novelist most famous for his 1976 masterpiece, Cutter and Bone, *a book that manages to be simultaneously funny, angry, and despairing. It was filmed as* Cutter's Way *in 1981, although Thornburg later dismissed the movie, unfairly and inaccurately, as "mediocre." In an interview in 2005 with the British journalist Bob Cornwell, Thornburg said that he had never considered himself a "pure" crime writer.* "Cutter and Bone *is a straight novel, no matter how you look at it—strong characterizations, simple plot. I don't like novels with private eyes—you know, formula ones. I like crime stories, but I like them to be about ordinary people, not crime professionals." Thornburg continued to publish for the next two decades, sustained mostly by reprints and movie options, but he was cursed by misfortune: his wife of thirty-three years died in 1986, a son was lost to alcoholism, and in 1998 a stroke paralyzed his left side, leaving him physically unable to write. He ended his days in a Seattle retirement home, and his death went almost entirely unremarked.*

Films have always driven me to the novels on which they were based. As a teenager, I was a movie freak but relatively unenthusiastic about reading. Then an English professor at college flipped my switch and turned me on to crime fiction. So Robert Clouse's *Darker than Amber* sent me to John D. MacDonald's Travis McGee series; *Point Blank* and *The Outfit* led to the Parker novels of Donald Westlake writing as Richard Stark; Ulu Grosbard's *True Confessions* convinced me to read John Gregory Dunne's superb novel of the same name. Such was the case with the film *Cutter and Bone*, directed by Ivan Passer, which I saw in a DC art house in 1981 at the time of its brief theatrical run. The film made such an impression on me that I knew I had to read the book, but that proved difficult. Nine years later I found a used, Blue Murder–edition paperback in a flea market. The time spent searching for it was worth every minute.

The film of *Cutter and Bone* is an extraordinary neo-noir character study, with brilliant performances by Jeff Bridges, in fine playboy/post-hippie mode as Bone, a lacerating John Heard as Cutter, and a shattering turn by Lisa Eichhorn as the doomed Mo. United Artists buried the picture and botched its release after a regime change at the studio, and realized too late what it had when the film began to pick up praise and festival awards. The powers that be renamed it *Cutter's Way*, thinking that audiences would (mis)take something called *Cutter and Bone* to be a comedic buddy film about surgeons. It's a top-drawer movie that is less underrated than it is underviewed, as it soon vanished from theaters and the public consciousness. The novel, written by Newton Thornburg, suffered a similar fate.

Why is it that certain groundbreaking novels often disappear from the radar screen while other, lesser works remain in print? Along with James Crumley's *The Last Good Kiss*, Kem Nunn's *Tapping the Source*, and most anything written by Elmore Leonard in the early to mid 1970s, Newton Thornburg's *Cutter and Bone* seemed to challenge the very foundation of the traditional crime novel when it was first published in 1976.

The *New York Times* did attempt to rescue the book from the genre ghetto in its initial review, calling *Cutter and Bone* "a classy big league act" and "the best novel of its kind in ten years." But the *L.A. Times* review was more typical, predictably describing it as "a superlative novel out of Ross Macdonald country." Well, they got the superlative part right, but the connection to Ross Macdonald's Lew Archer series, apart from the Santa Barbara setting, could not be more wrong. Macdonald and his fictional detective never did seem to "get" the younger generation; it was, famously, a thread of bafflement that continued throughout the Archer books. In *Cutter and Bone*, Thornburg not only got young people, he nailed them to the wall.

When we first meet Richard Bone, onetime ad-exec-turned-gigolo/bum, he is shaving with a Lady Remington razor after his latest trick. Bone has been in love only a couple of times, once in adolescence and once, briefly, with his ex-wife. He's currently in love with Mo, the alcohol-and-pill-freak live-in girlfriend of his best friend, Cutter, quite possibly the most cynical lead character ever to appear in a work of mainstream American fiction. Cutter stepped on a claymore during his tour of Vietnam, and now walks with a cane that complements a reconstructed leg of plastic and steel. What's left of him is best described by Thornburg with the typical, dead-on, economic prose style that hits the right staccato notes throughout the novel:

> What a sight the man made, what a celebration of the grotesque: the thinning Raggedy Ann hair, the wild hawk face glowing with the scar tissue of too many plastic surgeries, the black eyepatch over the missing eye and the perennial Apache dancer's costume of tight black pants and black turtleneck sweater with the left sleeve knotted below the elbow, not pinned up or sewed but knotted, an advertisement, spit in your eye.

Late one night, walking to his temporary home at the Cutter residence, the drunken Bone witnesses a body being dumped in an alley garbage can by the silhouette of a husky older man. The victim is a young runaway hooker, found with a staved-in skull and semen in her mouth and on her face. The next day, glancing at the newspaper photograph, Bone makes the mistake of telling Cutter that he thinks—he *thinks*—the man he sees in the news photo, a major business tycoon, is the killer of the girl.

The remainder of the novel involves Cutter and Bone's attempts to make some sense of the murder and their own wasted lives, but don't expect a tidy resolution. The idea that a murder can be "solved" is the Great Lie of the mystery novel to begin with, and here the author turns that peculiar notion on its soft head. For once, a writer chooses not to patronize us, singing us softly back to sleep as one would a child awakened by a nightmare. Thornburg tells us, very plainly, that the nightmare is real.

So this isn't about a puzzle, and though there is a love story, beautifully rendered, the novel describes the death of love rather than its bloom. What the novel seems to be about, ultimately, is America's festering wound in the wake of Vietnam. Set and written in its time, and remarkably wise without the benefits of hindsight, *Cutter and Bone* describes a crippled country, chronically high or hungover, shell-shocked but looking forward to "the better days" which will soon arrive—careful what you wish for—in the form of Reagan and Thatcher. Thornburg doesn't dwell on Vietnam specifically, but he does give one mind-blowing soliloquy to Cutter, describing to Bone the *Life* magazine photos—My Lai, the napalmed child, *those* pictures: we have all seen them—of the horror and what it really means:

> I studied them all right. I went to school at those pictures. And you know what I found out? I found out that you have three reactions, Rich, only three. The first one is simple—I hate America. But then you study them some more and you move up a notch. There is no God. But you know what you finally say, Rich, after you've studied them all you can? You say—I'm hungry.

That is flat-out brilliant writing, but Thornburg is not done. If anything, the last third of the book, where Cutter and Bone travel to Middle America Ozark country to confront their suspect, is where the author really turns on the juice, hurtling the reader toward a climax that reads like a paranoid's fever dream. Guaranteed, the last few pages of this novel will leave you reeling; the ending is both shocking and right.

There are very few novels, in fact, that have rocked my world to the degree that *Cutter and Bone* did the first time I read it. My original copy, bought in 1990, went through several continents with me more than once, until I put it into the hands of a fellow traveler on a European train. By then its influence had entered my subconscious. In 1994 I published a pulp/noir thriller called *Shoedog*, which, in its alienated, drifter protagonist and its cut-to-black ending, drew inspiration from Thornburg's masterpiece.

Many writers spend their creative lives trying to pen that one book that will put them into the pantheon, but the truth is, few succeed. Newton Thornburg did so, in spades, with *Cutter and Bone*.

George Pelecanos is the author of eighteen novels and served as a writer/producer on HBO's The Wire, The Pacific, *and* Treme. *He has a full head of hair, searing blue eyes, and drives a special-edition Mustang modeled on the car driven by McQueen in* Bullitt. *Also, he's married, with three kids, two dogs, and a house in the suburbs. So much for the myth of the roguish independent author. Visit him online at www.hachettebookgroup.com/features/georgepelecanos/.*

The Main
by Trevanian (1976)

JOHN MCFETRIDGE

Rodney Whitaker (1931–2005), a New York–born film scholar and novelist, chose to write his nonfiction under his own name and his fiction under such a variety of noms de plume that even Contemporary Authors, *the usually comprehensive guide, was forced to concede, somewhat ruefully, that it was "difficult to determine how many works he has published with other names." The pseudonym Trevanian is probably the best known of them, under which he wrote* The Eiger Sanction *(1972),* The Main *(1976), and* Shibumi *(1979), to which the mystery writer Don Winslow recently penned a companion volume,* Satori. *His books sold in the millions, in no small part due to Trevanian's gifts for characterization and description, and his desire to avoid the formulaic.*

The flag of the city of Montreal has upon it symbols of the four founding peoples: a fleur-de-lys for the French, a rose for the English, a thistle for the Scots, and a shamrock for the Irish. (Missing is any symbol for the First Nations people who were already there when the Europeans arrived.)

Over the years, though, Montreal became a city of two solitudes—the French and the English, with no distinctions between English, Scots, and Irish.

The literature of the city reflected this separation, as very little was translated from one language to the other. Many English Montrealers may have read Gabrielle Roy's *The Tin Flute* and Roch Carrier's *The Hockey Sweater,* but that's about it. Most French Montrealers read . . . well, I don't even know. One of the most famous English-Canadian novels is Hugh MacLennan's *Two Solitudes,* published in 1945 and translated the following year into Spanish, Dutch, Swedish, German, and a few other languages, but not into French for another twenty years.

There was also a physical separation in the city, as most French Montrealers lived on the east side of the island and most English Montrealers lived on the west. Down the middle ran St. Lawrence Boulevard/Rue St. Laurent, known as the Main.

Maybe it's not surprising that it took an outsider to try and bring the two solitudes together in a single book—American Rodney Whitaker writing under the pen name Trevanian—and it was a crime novel in which he did so. What better way to get characters from different social groups to interact than by following the leads in a murder investigation?

The Main was written in the 1970s, as the generation that came of age in the postwar years of *Two Solitudes* was giving way to a new generation, and dividing walls were beginning to crumble: between English and French Montreal, between generations, and even between conceptions of right and wrong. It's set in late November during what the characters refer to as "pig weather," a melancholy time: it gets dark early, and it's cold but it hasn't snowed yet, so it isn't even fun. It feels like the end of an era.

And the main character is pretty melancholy, too. Lieutenant LaPointe is a widower still mourning the loss of his beloved wife twenty-five years earlier. He continues to live in the same apartment, and has changed nothing. Although he has been promoted many times, he still acts as a beat cop walking up and down the Main. In the book's first chapter, LaPointe is playing cards with his friends: Moishe, the concentration camp survivor; David, another recent widower; and a priest, Father Martin, who feels that he's lost his flock. Instead of playing cards, Moishe leads them on a long discussion about the difference between a crime and a sin.

Oh, and we find out early on, before we even get to the body (this is a murder mystery, after all), that Lieutenant LaPointe has an inoperable heart condition and won't make it through the winter.

When the body finally does show up, it's that of a truly unlikeable guy: a young man, probably a criminal illegal immigrant just stopping off on his way from Italy to New York, known on the Main for his (too-aggressive) sexual prowess with too-young women. So his murder may not be a sin but it's certainly a crime, and it's on LaPointe's "patch," so the old cop takes over the case from the homicide detective to whom it's been assigned, and gives it a full investigation. He also takes over the other detective's "Joan," the term given to the young English cop that he was training. This device gives LaPointe the chance to expound on his views, and those views are sort of the left-wing version of Dirty Harry. Yes, the politicians and the police brass, with their political correctness and overconcern for the "rights" of criminals, have made being a cop impossible, but for LaPointe the real problem is that it makes it difficult to protect the citizens of the Main who are never far from his thoughts, those citizens who are too poor to be of any concern to the politicians or LaPointe's politically ambitious superiors. The Joan, meanwhile, is a college-educated Anglo named Guttmann who would prefer to do things by the book. Still, LaPointe and Guttmann make a good team.

One character says about himself that he "looks for philosophy where there is only narrative," and that's a good description of *The Main:* there is more philosophy than narrative and that's what makes it such a great book.

That, and its setting. It has become a bit of a cliché to say that setting is a character in mystery fiction but there's no doubt that Montreal, or at least the Rue St. Laurent, is a principal character here, and it is captured extremely well. So, too, is the period in question, the early '70s. As in so many other parts of the world, there had been great upheaval in Montreal in the late '60s and early '70s, and every social structure was being questioned. In Quebec the main issue was, of course, the emergence of French-Canadian nationalism—the Quiet Revolution, as it was called. It may be surprising that a time of such great conflict in Canada produced so little crime fiction, but *The Main* tackles the issues head-on. In fact, the murder mystery in the novel even turns on a language school and the young, bilingual woman who runs it.

Writing as Trevanian, Rodney Whitaker is best known as the author of the spy novels *The Eiger Sanction, The Loo Sanction,* and *Shibumi.* It has been reported that Whitaker intended *The Eiger Sanction* as a parody and was disappointed when critics didn't see it that way. In some ways, *The Main* feels like a parody as well: all the clichés of the mystery novel are present, but they're used with a seriousness of intent.

I have little doubt that if *The Main* were one of a series, Lieutenant LaPointe would be among the very best and most well-known fictional detectives. As it is, this is the only Lieutenant LaPointe mystery, and one well worth reading.

John McFetridge was born, and grew up, in Greenfield Park, on the south shore of Montreal, and spent a lot of time on the Main before moving to Toronto where he now lives and sets his novels: Dirty Sweet, Everybody Knows This Is Nowhere, Swap, *and* Tumblin' Dice. *John's upcoming novel,* Black Rock, *takes place in Montreal in 1970. Visit him online at www.john mcfetridge.blogspot.com.*

The Animal Factory
by Edward Bunker (1977)

JENS LAPIDUS

Edward Bunker (1933–2005) was an American author, screenwriter, actor, and, notably, a criminal for the first half of his life. According to his memoir, Education of a Felon *(2000), he was the youngest-ever inmate to be incarcerated in San Quentin Prison, and was regarded by fellow criminals as being so hard and fearless as to border on the insane. Inspired by an encounter with the death row prisoner, and writer, Caryl Chessman, Bunker began to write his own book while imprisoned. It was almost two decades before it was finally published under the title* No Beast So Fierce *(1973). The money that he earned from writing and, subsequently, acting enabled Bunker to earn a living without resorting to bank robbery or drug dealing. On film, he is most fondly remembered as the doomed Mr. Blue in Quentin Tarantino's* Reservoir Dogs.

The crime novels of today describe crime from an investigative perspective. It's about murder, vicious and cold-blooded, and organized criminal acts. Generally we follow a police detective or a private investigator's search for the truth. Sometimes we even get to see the world through the eyes of the offender, and we are allowed to engage with the cold, and all too often twisted, reasoning of the criminal mind from an insider's perspective. In the mainstream crime novel, the end is usually the same: the murder mystery is solved, and the culprit is revealed and can be arrested.

But what happens after the intrigue has been resolved? What happens when the status quo has been restored? What happens to the victims and what happens to the offenders?

These questions are rarely answered, but in *The Animal Factory* Edward Bunker kicks off where most other crime novels stop. He tries to answer the last question: What happens next to the perpetrators of crime, and how are criminals treated by our society?

Bunker's point of view may not be revolutionary, but he manages to condense his opinions and make them shine through the story without ever imposing them upon the reader.

From that perspective, *The Animal Factory* is without a doubt one of the greatest novels about life in prison. It is also a sharp critique of the Western world, especially of the American prison system.

And finally, by extension, Bunker's ultrarealistic story is about our own vision of man.

The Animal Factory describes Ron Decker's life over a single year, or what is supposed to be one, in the "Bastille by the Bay": San Quentin Prison. Ron has been convicted of a minor marijuana offense but is handed down a disproportionately long sentence. He is of an intelligent and pacifistic nature, and has never before been to prison. Pretty soon he meets gang leader Earl Copen, a scarred "third-timer" with more experience of life behind bars than a tiger at the zoo. In other words, Earl is the opposite of the sweet and protective in *The Shawshank Redemption.* Ron's problem, in addition to being a rookie, is that he's good-looking, something that can lead to serious problems inside San Quentin.

Ron and Earl become friends—and not a second too late. When three other inmates try to trick Ron into a cell to rape him, Earl reveals their plan and talks to them in his own unique way, which quickly makes them lose interest in Ron.

Ron and Earl's friendship grows, and develops into an almost family-like relationship, which surprises them both. Earl teaches Ron how to keep his balance on the narrow line between the prisoners' own code of honor and the rules of the prison administration, two completely opposing systems. If you break the code of honor, it could mean death. If you upset the administration, it could mean additional time behind prison walls, which in San Quentin is just the same as death but in a more extended form. At the same time Ron is constantly ruminating about what might be the ultimate cost to him of Earl's protection.

Bunker describes the conduct of prison life as accurately as Jane Austen treats the English upper class of the 1800s. It's a world in which there are only violent solutions to conflict and prison authorities deliberately encourage structural racism. The background noise is always the clatter and tumult of immediate danger.

Bunker's language is brutal, pragmatic, and credible, which is probably due to the fact that he himself spent a substantial amount of time in juvenile detention centers and jail. However, that does not automatically mean that you can write about such experiences. But Bunker *can* write: even if he chooses a relatively simple way to express himself, the language reflects his experiences and his time. In addition, he masters the historical details of his narrative to perfection.

In recent decades, a series of novels and films have dealt with criminals and the criminal realm. Sometimes, the descriptions tend to romanticize crime and criminality as a lifestyle. Bunker never falls into that trap. The shit almost rises from the pages, and anything more unglamorous than life in San Quentin is hard to imagine. Running parallel to this is often a kind of envy on the part of the prisoners toward the nine-to-five society, toward the middle class, the ordinary citizens. Perhaps it's just that the pain of not being a part of the inner clique of society drives a defense mechanism that expresses itself through hatred.

Finally, Ron and Earl plan to escape from prison by an ingeniously contrived route. I won't reveal if they manage their getaway or not, but I can at least venture to suggest that the system has changed them, an alteration that fundamentally affects their views on the concept of freedom.

Is it possible to compare *The Animal Factory* with *One Day in the Life of Ivan Denisovich,* Aleksandr Solzhenitsyn's epic of the Soviet Gulag? These books reflect two different systems and their concepts of detention, and two different ways to survive. On a purely literary level, the two works are competing in different sports, yet both authors have a phenomenal sense for the details of incarceration, and both depict the struggle of an individual to maintain his dignity in institutions designed to break one as a person.

The Animal Factory was published thirty-five years ago, but I, who work as a defense lawyer in Sweden, feel that its message is still of significance. Prisons in both Sweden and the United States have filled up at an increasing rate over the past decades. The walls have become higher and the climate has hardened. The motivation to care is nonexistent.

Bunker writes that the prospect of rehabilitating those imprisoned in San Quentin is "like trying to make a Moslem by putting someone in a Trappist monastery." Prisons in the Western world (and for all I know in the rest of the world as well) have been, and still are, factories. We have become experts in producing more dangerous criminals at the end of imprisonment from those whom we throw into the system at the start. We have become better at condemning and degrading young men: we do it at a fearsome pace these days. We excel at creating people who are forced to live in their own system, removed from the rest of society.

The Animal Factory should be mandatory reading for most of us, but especially for those who believe that the world becomes a better place by using rough hands.

———————

Jens Lapidus (b. 1974) is a Swedish criminal defense lawyer. He published his debut novel, Snabba cash *(Easy Money), in 2006. He has since published two more titles:* Aldrig fucka upp *(Never Fuck Up, 2008) and* Livet deluxe *(Life Deluxe, 2011). The three novels comprise the "Stockholm Noir Trilogy."* Snabba cash *was published in English as* Easy Money *in 2012. The novel was adapted for film in Sweden in 2010, directed by Daniel Espinosa.*

True Confessions
by John Gregory Dunne (1977)

S. J. ROZAN

John Gregory Dunne (1932–2003) was an American novelist, journalist, and screenwriter whose reputation has been partially eclipsed by The Year of Magical Thinking, *the memoir of mourning that his wife, Joan Didion, wrote about her life in the year following his passing. His most famous novel is* True Confessions, *a study of power, corruption, and Catholicism loosely based around the unsolved Black Dahlia murder in Los Angeles in 1947. It was subsequently filmed with Robert Duvall and Robert De Niro in the starring roles. Dunne and Didion wrote the screenplay, as they did for the movie that gave Al Pacino his first starring role, 1971's* The Panic in Needle Park. *Dunne also wrote an acerbic memoir about his later Hollywood misadventures, entitled* Monster: Living off the Big Screen *(1997).*

In Jewish folklore there is a tale of a rabbi who appeared to die, but was revived. Recovered, he announced that he had, in fact, died, and been granted a brief glimpse of the afterlife. His eager students gathered around him.

> "Tell us, Rabbi: what is the punishment in the afterlife for the sins of youth?"
>> "There is no punishment for the sins of youth," he answered.
>> "Then tell us, what is the punishment for sins of the flesh?"
>> "There is no punishment for sins of the flesh."
>> "The punishment for breaking the Law?"
>> "There is no punishment for breaking the Law. Only one sin is punished in the afterlife."

"Rabbi, please tell us, what is it?"

"False piety."

I hadn't heard that story when I first read John Gregory Dunne's *True Confessions*. I was a college student, living in the Bronx and working a summer job in lower Manhattan. The job was a snore, and worse, I was working for my father. The only good news was that my hour-each-way subway commute gave me a lot of time to read. I did a book a week that summer, but *True Confessions* was the only one that knocked me out, the only one I now remember, and the book that focused my fuzzy aspiration to be a writer into an ambition to write crime.

True Confessions is, more than anything, a book about men and women who've slid into hopelessly compromised lives. Most don't notice how the small concessions they've made over time—some for a greater good, some for convenience, some for venal gain—have corrupted their souls; or they don't admit it to themselves; or they don't think it matters. The book opens and closes in the 1960s, but it's set largely in the Los Angeles of 1947, and a particular Los Angeles it is: the tawdry, cynical L.A. of noir. One of the fascinating things about *True Confessions* is that it has a noir setting but not a noir sensibility. A noir story is the account of a not-so-good man or woman who tries, just once, to touch something good, and, because of all that's come before, fails. *True Confessions* is something else: a tale of people stretching a little less each day, until their moral reach is nearly nonexistent, and the grasp is all.

Nearly: but not, in the end, entirely. Most of the book's characters do go to their deaths as compromised as they've been all their lives. These are all natural deaths, or suicides: no character we meet in this crime novel is gunned down, knifed, or thrown from a bridge; and the murder on which the book centers is a random killing of someone practically no one in the book ever knew. "She wasn't a girl, Tom Spellacy thought. She was a headline. Someone to read about who wasn't your sister. Someone to get your rocks off over."

Two men are at the book's heart: LAPD lieutenant Tom Spellacy, a Homicide detective; and his brother Desmond, a monsignor on the fast track to a bishopric, and the archdiocese's moneyman, working directly for the Cardinal. In the course of the story each has a crucial moment of recognition of what he has become.

For Tom: "He was not certain of many things anymore, but he was sure of one thing: he was a very good cop. Maybe not always honest, but always thorough."

For Des: "He did not have to hear regular confessions, but he liked to help out. It made him feel more like a priest."

Later, at their individual moments of crisis, each makes a choice. One, though he takes a stand, takes it in an unworthy direction; he refuses to rise above the soul-cramped man he has become. The other finds a way back to the man he had planned to be.

Dunne's writing is deceptively gorgeous: simple and straightforward—not in the mannered way of many tough-guy novelists, but convincingly unadorned, and able to make use of the occasional breathtaking turn of phrase without it being out of place. Speaking of two characters who've known and slept with each other for years without ever discussing anything beyond who, in their circle of acquaintance, is banging whom, and for what gain: "It was a slum of a relationship surrounded by acres of indifference." Or, describing the inhabitants of a desert parish: "Old guys whose tattoos are all faded and whose wives wear hairnets and whose children don't call much anymore."

The book opens with first-person narration by Tom Spellacy, a gregarious old man rambling on about what his matter-of-fact tones tell us was a tough but in no way exceptional working-class Irish Catholic life. His opening line is, "None of the merry-go-rounds seem to work anymore." It seems to be just a passing remark, a way to point up the changes wrought by time. He introduces us to most of the book's cast in their present-day guises. Then the story shifts into the past, and to a third-person narrator. So that we make no mistake as to this voice's distance or omniscience, and therefore its reliability, its first words are, "What Tom Spellacy remembered later . . ." In telling the story, this voice is scrupulous in referring to all of the characters by their full names each time it mentions them. In characters' own thoughts and musings they refer to each other however they want, but the narrator keeps us at arm's length from them all, the better to see the emerging patterns.

The story has a locus of evil, a contractor named Jack Amsterdam who is the vague figure behind the soul-rot of both Tom and Des Spellacy; significantly, he barely appears, only stepping twice from the shadows to speak. He's not the real problem. A man willing to sell his soul, Dunne seems to be saying, can always find a buyer.

The merry-go-rounds aren't accidental, either. They're the fantasy, the pretending life; and no, they don't work anymore, for Tom, Des, or any of the other characters. One of the book's crucial moments, the intersection of its two story strands, occurs at an amusement park, when Tom Spellacy meets his brother Des's boss, the Cardinal. The Cardinal observes—to himself—how alike the two men are. This is, in some ways, the point. They are alike. We're all alike in this essential way: we all encounter these choices, reach these moral crossroads. Though as Desmond Spellacy says, "Every priest expected the test at some time or other during his priesthood. Usually in a way where the choice was heroic. Do you still believe in your God? the commandant of the firing squad would say . . . Like a lozenge, that kind of test. Easy to swallow." The tests these characters face are not so lozengelike. Nor so obvious. No firing squads to stand against, no kingpin crime bosses to put away. That would be asking for too much. What they, and we, face every day are the small choices, the easy compromises. The everyone's-doing-it, doesn't-matter-anyway, go-along-to-get-along, it's-for-a-good-cause decisions that, in the end, pile up, take our shape, and define us.

Tom Spellacy, in his homicide investigation, bats aside numerous confessions by people who did not commit the crime but want the glory, or want to be punished, or want whatever it is they hope to gain by confessing, but are lying. Desmond Spellacy hears confessions weekly ("the calibration of sin was the essential element of his trade") but he knows that what he hears doesn't come near the actual sins of which the speakers are guilty. None of these are true confessions. Nor, until right at the end of the book, is any confession by any character, including either of the brothers, whether out loud, or in the heart. It's all false piety, and, in various ways, that sin is punished.

S. J. Rozan, a lifelong New Yorker, is the author of thirteen novels and three dozen short stories. She's an Edgar, Shamus, Anthony, Nero, and Macavity winner, as well as a recipient of the Japanese Falcon Award. S.J. has been guest of honor at a number of fan conventions and in 2003 was an invited speaker at the World Economic Forum in Davos. She's served on the boards of Mystery Writers of America and Sisters in Crime, and as president of Private Eye Writers of America. She leads writing workshops and lectures widely. Her latest book is Ghost Hero. *Visit her online at www.sjrozan.net.*

A Judgement in Stone
by Ruth Rendell (1977)

PETER ROBINSON

Ruth Rendell (b. 1930) is one of the queens of the British mystery novel. Perhaps best known for her series of police procedurals featuring Chief Inspector Wexford, of which there have been over twenty published so far, she has also written over thirty other books, including a number of works of psychological suspense under the pseudonym of Barbara Vine. As Baroness Rendell of Babergh, she is a Labour Party life peer of the House of Lords.

"Eunice Parchman killed the Coverdale family because she could not read or write" is one of the most intriguing opening sentences in crime fiction. Not satisfied with simply naming the killer and the motive, Ruth Rendell then goes on to tell the reader that Eunice gained nothing from her crime but the notoriety she had so painstakingly avoided all her life, and that while Eunice herself was not mad, her partner in crime, Joan Smith, was. Before the first chapter has ended, we also know that there were four members of the Coverdale family living in the house at the time—parents George and Jacqueline, both on their second marriage; George's daughter, Melinda; and Jacqueline's son, Giles—and that all were shot within the space of about fifteen minutes. While *A Judgement in Stone* is not the first crime novel to invert the conventional whodunit structure—*Malice Aforethought* by Francis Iles did something similar in 1931—it is certainly the most chilling.

Over the next few chapters, we get to know the Coverdale family. Rendell is deft in her drawing of character and outlining of relationships, and while on one level it is clear that they are a family of upper-middle-class snobs, we quickly discover other facets of their character; we become privy to their dreams, their secret fears and fantasies. We know that we shouldn't allow ourselves to care for them, if for no other reason than that we know they are going to meet a bloody end in the very near future, but against our better judgment, we do.

The attitudes of the various Coverdales toward Eunice are also interesting. The daughter, Melinda, for example, is a young, idealistic university student who thinks that everyone should be equal and wants Eunice to be part of the family. Giles, the son, doesn't even notice her existence; he is too busy reading the Bhagavad Gita, which he props against the marmalade pot at breakfast time, and harboring incestuous fantasies about Melinda, even though she is not actually a blood relative. George is merely glad that they have found someone to help his wife manage the large house, and Jacqueline herself has no interest in how or what Eunice feels so long as she carries out her duties. As for Eunice, she is puzzled by the lot of them in a blank and blinkered sort of way. Then she meets religious fanatic Joan Smith, who discovers her secret, and so begins the folie à deux that leads to the bloody denouement.

The setting is what W. H. Auden referred to in his essay "The Guilty Vicarage" as "the Great Good Place," a large country house about two miles from the nearest village, with stunning views of the English countryside, views that Constable painted. Into this idyllic setting comes Eunice, who has forged her references, and, we are told early on, has a history of petty blackmail. She also suffocated her own father when caring for him became too great a burden for her. To her, murder was a simple solution to a simple problem, and her greatest problem is keeping her illiteracy secret.

The story is told from the point of view of an omniscient narrator who knows exactly what the future holds for all the characters, and is able to jump in and out of their minds at will, revealing their thoughts, hopes, and dreams, cataloging the decisions that can lead to only one end. There is a sort of matter-of-fact sense of doom and inevitability about it all. The ordinary becomes sinister. After the first lie, the first little innocent act of deception, the course is set by a mixture of chance, destiny, and choice. There is no going back, even as the possible outcomes become more and more limited, and more and more dreadful to contemplate.

A Judgement in Stone is not only about illiteracy, but about the gulf between the classes, between people, and about how little we know even of those whom we put in positions of trust and power. The Coverdales assume that everyone reads books and enjoys some form of culture, whether art or opera, or that they at least aspire to do so; Eunice has never heard a piece of music in her life, except hymns that her father whistled, has never seen a work of art apart from reproductions of *The Laughing Cavalier* and *Mona Lisa,* and has never been able to read a book. Eunice has no imagination, and therefore she has no empathy. Her world revolves around television, domestic work, knitting, and chocolate bars.

And preserving the secret of her illiteracy, of course. That, above all.

For some reason, Ruth Rendell's novels have always fared better in the movies at the hands of continental directors, and *A Judgement in Stone* is no exception. Claude Chabrol made a terrific film version of it in 1995. Called *La Cérémonie,* it stars Isabelle Huppert and Sandrine Bonnaire. Naturally, many things change in the course of a film or TV adaptation of a novel. *La Cérémonie* becomes an attack on that favorite of French institutions, the bourgeoisie, a Marxist comment on the class struggle, but it does so without losing its psychological edge. It keeps the spirit of the novel intact, and Chabrol is just as interested in the dark and malevolent progress of the folie à deux as Rendell is.

Perhaps the most important difference between film and book is that Chabrol doesn't give everything away at the beginning; instead, he unravels the whole series of events as a mystery, as a psychological thriller. We have no idea what is so strange about Eunice (Sophie, in the movie); we find out only bit by bit as the story unfolds, and her illiteracy is finally revealed. We have no idea that she is going to murder anyone, but when she meets up with Joan Smith (Jeanne), that eventuality begins to seem inevitable, too.

Normally, when I'm writing about crime fiction, I worry about spoilers, about giving something important away, but in *A Judgement in Stone,* what happens at the end is exactly what the narrator has already told us will happen. Eunice Parchman and Joan Smith shoot the entire Coverdale family, people we have come to care about, despite their faults, as they are watching *Don Giovanni* on television.

"But," as the narrator tells us at the end of the first chapter, "there was much more to it than that." One of the great strengths of *A Judgement in Stone,* and Ruth Rendell's non-Wexford novels in general, is that they show us the chief interest in a crime novel need not necessarily be the identity, or even the motive, of the killer. Her strength is that she keeps us turning the pages even though we already know what is going to happen, and why.

While it was reading Chandler, Simenon, and Sjöwall and Wahlöö that got me interested in writing crime fiction in the first place, Ruth Rendell was one of the first British crime writers whom I read as an adult, and *A Judgement in Stone* was one of the first books of Rendell's that I read. It sent me in search of others, such as *The Lake of Darkness*, *A Demon in My View*, and *Live Flesh*, and they remain firm favorites to this day.

Peter Robinson was born in Yorkshire, England, which provides the setting for his award-winning and best-selling series of detective novels featuring Detective Chief Inspector Alan Banks. The series has been successfully adapted for television, featuring Stephen Tompkinson as Banks. He divides his time between Yorkshire and Canada. Visit him online at www.inspector banks.com.

The Last Good Kiss
by James Crumley (1978)

DENNIS LEHANE

James Crumley (1939–2008) is one of the most influential crime fiction authors of the last half century. Ray Bradbury's series detective Elmo Crumley is named for him. First published in 1969 with One to Count Cadence, *and best known for creating the series characters Milo Milodragovitch and C. W. Sughrue (who appeared together in 1996's* Bordersnakes), *Crumley won the 1994 Hammett Prize, awarded for best literary crime fiction, for* The Mexican Tree Duck *(1993).*

> Stacy: "Whadda you going to be when you grow up?"
> C.W.: "Older."

C. W. Sughrue, the private investigator at the heart of James Crumley's masterpiece, *The Last Good Kiss,* takes on two cases at the start of the book. The first—to find the writer Abraham Trahearne and return him home from his latest alcoholic bender—is ostensibly accomplished in the first sentence of Chapter 1. Sughrue accepts the second case—to ascertain the fate of Betty Sue Flowers, a woman from Sonoma, California, who vanished ten years earlier in San Francisco—at the end of Chapter 2. From there he sets out on a path that leads him all over the American West, aided at times—if you can call it that—by his new drinking buddy, the novelist Trahearne, and sometimes by a bulldog everyone likes but never enough to hold on to properly.

The Last Good Kiss is about castoffs and a search for belonging. It's also about the thrills of wanderlust, drinking, and the American road. It's about writing and whoring and evil so bland and commonplace that it pulls up the barstool next to you and smiles as it buys you a drink. It begins with arguably the finest sentence to ever open a crime novel—

"When I finally caught up with Abraham Trahearne, he was drinking beer with an alcoholic bulldog named Fireball Roberts in a ramshackle joint just outside of Sonoma, California, drinking the heart right out of a fine spring afternoon." It ends with one of the most original acts of vengeance a hero ever perpetrated on a villain. In between, it reveals itself as an astute examination of America in the 1970s, a trenchant observation of the ways in which men habitually fail to understand women, an homage to both Chandler's *The Long Goodbye* and Kerouac's *On the Road* (and yet just as singularly its own proud beast), and both a hymn to and a condemnation of the artistic temperament. It's a book about loss and the black ash left in the wake of 1960s idealism. But above all else, it's about the hunger for home. Not home as a physical place—though that's in there, too—but as an ideal we reach for but rarely touch.

"Only fools have heroes."

The plot, on the surface, seems as ramshackle as the joint in Sonoma where C.W. catches up with Abraham Trahearne. (*Seems;* trust me, not one line or incident in this book is there by accident.) C.W. is a small-time private investigator in Meriwether, Montana. He's a functioning alcoholic, a hopeless romantic (though it would be news to him), and a brokenhearted casualty of the '60s. Blundering his way through the late '70s, with the "flower children . . . gone sour and commercial or middle-class," C.W. knows "you can't go home again even if you stay there, and now that everyplace is the same, there's no place to run."

But he tries. By the time he tracks down Trahearne, at the request of the novelist's chilly, sexy ex-wife, Catherine, C.W. has cut a swath from Montana to Wyoming to Oregon, northern Utah, southern Idaho, the Nevada desert, Reno, San Francisco, and finally Sonoma. There, his attempts to remove Trahearne lead to a level of bar violence that would be wholly comic if one character didn't get shot in the foot. After that violence, C.W. is hired by Rosie Flowers, the owner of the bar, to find her daughter, Betty Sue, who's been missing for ten years, ever since she stepped out of her boyfriend's car at a red light in San Francisco and never looked back. C.W. agrees to help Rosie, mostly because she gives him no choice, even going so far as to saddle him with a companion for his journey—the redoubtable Fireball Roberts.

"When you go home, take that worthless bulldog with you."

C.W. never sees it, but Fireball Roberts is his doppelgänger—fiercely loyal, plodding yet determined, with a heart as big as the West. One of the ironies of the book is that its best person is a dog that everyone passes off to the next person like a bad penny or a chain letter.

C.W.'s search for Betty Sue—aided at times by Trahearne, his drinking buddy and erstwhile boon companion—leads him into the world of basement pornography, drug addiction, the mafia, and the human detritus flushed down the hills of San Francisco when the bottom dropped out on the peace and love generation and the hopes of Woodstock gave way to the horrors of Manson and the acrid despair of Watergate.

C.W., loyal and bighearted and endlessly hopeful in his own broken way, is passed around as much as Fireball Roberts. As is Trahearne's current wife, Melinda. All the decent souls in the book are too decent to survive the self-serving pragmatists and self-pitying monsters with whom they eventually find themselves swimming. The villains in this book are, for the most part, under the impression that they themselves are largely blameless. Their acts of carnage are collateral and reactionary, not premeditated. They don't *want* to do bad; they'd just prefer it over being inconvenienced. They are, like Fitzgerald's monsters in *The Great Gatsby*, "careless people." When C.W. refuses a bribe, one character warns him, "Everything would be so simple if you could and it will be so awful if you don't." That pretty much sums it up—do what we want or we'll be forced to fill your life to the brim with regret.

> You think you're in love with me, don't you? . . .
> You don't even know me . . . It's very kind of you to care,
> but you don't even know me at all.

Things turn awful in this novel in part because C.W. consistently can't see the women in his life for who they are. Melinda Trahearne, for example, looks different to him every time he sees her; he fails to recognize her on at least two occasions, and late in the novel is surprised to discover that she's beautiful. Betty Sue Flowers, a woman he comes to think he knows through pictures and, unfortunately, pornographic film stock, is constantly changing shape in front of him. Catherine Trahearne morphs in front of his eyes, depending on the light, depending on the day. In a genre known for—hell, quite often *defined by*—its adherence to moth-ball ideals of male virility and female dependency on the same, *The Last Good Kiss* is a ballsy, subversive attack on the male psyche and its fuel tank full of self-aggrandizement and self-pity. The dehumanizing world of pornography that C.W. encounters is but an outgrowth of the male's hopelessly conflicted need to love what he fucks but fuck what he loves. This leads to sentimentalizing, objectifying, and sometimes punishing the woman you feel these things for, or as C.W. puts it, "Like too many men, Trahearne and I didn't know how to deal with a woman like (her), caught as we were between our own random lusts and a desire for faith-ful women so primitive and fierce it must have been innate, atavistic, as uncontrollable as a bodily function . . . As we shared the whiskey, I wondered how long men had been forgiving each other over strong drink for being fools."

The novel wonders as well. By the final pages—as the final two victims are found floating in a nocturnal pool, a scene as ethereal and haunting as any death scene in literature, and most of the characters have realized that their last good kiss was years ago, as the poet lamented, and the careless villains have retreated to their vast carelessness, while the good men and women have been marginalized—there is still room for forgiveness. Because even in the beaten men and women who form the novel's heroic core, the light remains. The hope. The beating heart. The distant promise of home.

Dennis Lehane is the author of a bunch of books, some of which he likes, in-cluding Mystic River, The Given Day, *and* Live by Night, *a gangster novel to be published in October 2012 by William Morrow in the United States and Little, Brown in the U.K. and Ireland. He's wanted to write a gangster novel since he was eight years old; now that the box is checked, he has no idea what to do next to keep people from realizing how completely full of shite he is. Maybe he'll take up origami. While hang gliding. Until then, he lives in Bos-ton and St. Petersburg, Florida, with one wife, two daughters, a vicious beagle, and a sweet but excessively flatulent English bulldog named Marlon Brando. Visit him online at www.dennislehanebooks.com.*

Southern Seas (*Los mares del sur*)
by Manuel Vázquez Montalbán (1979)

LEONARDO PADURA

(essay translated from the Spanish by Ellen Clair Lamb)

Pepe Carvalho, the Barcelona-based gastronome hero of the crime novels of Manuel Vázquez Montalbán (1939–2003), first appeared in Yo maté a Kennedy *(I Killed Kennedy) in 1972. To date nine of Montalbán's novels have been translated into English, the most recent being* The Man of My Life *(2000). Commemorated in his native Catalonia by the Colegio de Periodistas de Cataluña's Manuel Vázquez Montalbán International Journalism Award, Montalbán is also celebrated in the work of Italian writer Andrea Camilleri, whose series hero is called Salvo Montalbano.*

Dear reader, if you are making your first acquaintance with the books of Manuel Vázquez Montalbán, you have the distinct advantage of entering this master of crime's work through the best possible door. I say this from personal knowledge, as my own first encounter with the work of Manuel Vázquez Montalbán was both a shock and a trauma.

It was 1987, and I had just returned to Cuba after an endless one-year stay in Angola, where I had gone to work as an editor for the weekly newspaper of the Cuban expatriate community. During that year—away from my country, almost beyond the boundaries of time, and mostly living in fear—I had to read whatever I could get or was given, haphazardly and with the melancholy of living abroad in a country at war. When I returned to Cuba, it was a pleasure to find that the research and study center for the promotion of the work of Alejo Carpentier and Cuban literature had opened an attractive lending library, stocked entirely with books published outside of Cuba. The new library had been funded (so they said) by Gabriel García Márquez, with contributions from Spanish publishers with whom he had connections.

Since I had lived only in Angola and Cuba, I had read only whatever was published there. Not even books printed in Spain or Mexico were imported, unless you counted the horrible USSR-edited journal *Progress,* which should have been called *Regression.* It was thanks to this one library that I had the chance to encounter authors like Gore Vidal, Kurt Vonnegut, Mailer's work after *The Naked and the Dead,* the latest Vargas Llosa, and many others whose work I devoured. Among them was a Spanish thriller writer called Manuel Vázquez Montalbán.

When I learned of the existence of a Spanish detective novelist, I felt curiosity and suspicion. A Spanish crime writer? My experience of crime fiction—first as a reader, then as a relentless and scathing critic—was rooted, like that of all ordinary Cubans, in the tradition of the classic Anglo-Saxon and French works, moving to the almost always disappointing examples of the "revolutionary Cuban detective novel" (which generally lacked the "novel" part), and stories of espionage from the Soviet Union (Yulian Semyonov, Vladimir Bogomolov). More recently the odd book had slipped through, such as works by the Italian Leonardo Sciascia; the Argentine classic *Operation Massacre* by Rodolfo Walsh (a nonfiction novel in the mold of Truman Capote's *In Cold Blood,* also published in Cuba); Mario Puzo's *The Godfather;* and a few more.

Driven by an interest more anthropological than literary, I borrowed the library's only title by this so-called Spanish crime writer. Its title was *The Spa,* and it had been published in 1986 by the Spanish publisher Planeta. And here followed the traumatic encounter.

The Spa is the eighth of Manuel Vázquez Montalbán's novels to feature the detective Pepe Carvalho, a former Communist Party member, ex–CIA agent, Catalan, and son of Galicia. The novel's plot takes place in the resort of Marbella in southern Spain, where Carvalho comes in pursuit of a detox recommended to him long ago by a certain Isidro Planas, Catalan businessman. During a two-week stay at a medical facility run by German specialists, Carvalho (then unfamiliar to me) is subjected to a strict diet and an endless series of enemas to punish and purify his body, which apparently is given to all imaginable excesses of gastronomy and alcohol. At this resort, so far from Barcelona, where he lives and works as a detective, Carvalho is drawn into an investigation that connects the present with the era of the German Third Reich, and some unregenerate Fascists. And he unravels a mystery.

I cannot say that the reading experience was disappointing. It was a well-written novel, told with assurance, with well-plotted adventures and a command of language above that of the best detective novels. But nothing more. In this novel, Pepe Carvalho does not eat, or drink white wine. He does not fight with his prostitute girlfriend, he does not talk to his friends in Barcelona or run around town, he does not move among the levels of a society marked by its Franco-led past and its recent transition into democracy. He cannot even burn one or more books from his private library in the process of lighting his home fireplace.

The mandatory selection of this particular novel (which was not really a choice, since there was nothing else by that author) gave me an impression of that character and its creator that was totally incomprehensible and, moreover, wrong—or rather, distorted, given my status as a newcomer to this writer's world. Without further ado, I consigned the novelist and his Spanish detective to oblivion, deeming him more than competent as a writer but nothing extraordinary, in my uninformed opinion.

Fortunately, a little over a year later I made my first trip to Spain, invited to participate (as a journalist) in what would be the first Semana Negra in Gijón, Asturias. It was in the days before the meeting, while we were in Madrid, that the Mexican writer Paco Ignacio Taibo stopped at a street bookstall and bought me (for a hundred pesetas) the novel I recommend with every possible accolade: *Southern Seas*, written, of course, by that very Manuel Vázquez Montalbán, considered (as I discovered) the great guru, the master, the jewel of the Spanish crime novel, and—as a bonus—one of the most abrasive and active intellectuals of his time.

During the days of the Semana Negra, always in my role as journalist, I very quickly had the audacity and good fortune to interview Manuel Vázquez Montalbán, who was attending this wonderful meeting for a couple of days. Of course the conversation could not be about his work; it was essentially dedicated to educating me, and through me the ignorant Cuban readers, about the origin and characteristics of the detective novel in that country. On top of that juicy first-hand assessment, I came away from the conversation with something important: the certainty that this Spanish detective novelist was a man of remarkable intellectual powers, and a legendary temper.

It was upon my return to Cuba, in the summer of 1988, that I read *Southern Seas*, a novel that nine years earlier had won the prestigious Premio Planeta (Planet Prize). The shock that I got while reading Vázquez

Montalbán's novel—which I should have read before *The Spa*, to arm myself with the keys to open this literary world and explore it—was so profound that I emerged from it with shortness of breath, a dry mouth, and an alarming conviction: if I were ever to write a detective novel, I would write it the way this Spaniard had written *Southern Seas*, and if I wrote this novel and created an investigator, mine would have to be as vital as Carvalho, skeptical and cynical, who walked freely through the pages of *Southern Seas*, retracing the streets of Barcelona and the routes of his own time in history and humanity.

Encountering this novel was a radical cure for my initial trauma, and also the beginning of a chronic dependency on the works of Vázquez Montalbán, whose novels, detective and otherwise, commanded me to buy them during my trips to Spain, at a time that did not afford me that luxury. It was also the beginning of a quest for even physical closeness with the author, a contact that would become a peculiar friendship— because with Manolo, as I later called him, *everything* was peculiar: even the manner of his death in 2003, in a place as inappropriate as the Bangkok airport, a city he'd used as the setting for one of his novels. Thus, over a period of years, we met several times in Barcelona and Havana, to the point that I asked him to make the presentation of my first novel published in Spain (*Máscaras*, 1997; *Red Havana* in English)—and he asked me to serve as tour guide to the most complicated routes for the purpose of understanding Havana during his research of the Cuban world before Pope John Paul II's visit to the island, for what would become the long essay *And God Entered Havana* (1998).

Having said all this, however, it is time to begin to explain . . . It may already be obvious that, in my opinion, *Southern Seas* is, like everything else here, an excellent novel with a well-plotted and satisfying mystery, as one expects of the best of the genre. But it should also be clear that *Southern Seas* is, above all, an excellent *novel*, and its being a detective novel serves only to double its significance and influence.

Until the arrival of Manuel Vázquez Montalbán and his novel *Tattoo* (1974, the second book to feature Pepe Carvalho), the Spanish detective novel had barely managed to get an identity card. Several writers in the 1920s and later, in the period after 1950 (following the Civil War and the even harder postwar years), had written works in the genre with some success, but without much ability to create a Spanish school of crime fiction or, at a minimum, a unique path that others could find and trace. The arrival of this new novelist, however, fulfilled both these requirements: a national identity for a genre that began to be written in Spanish and an aesthetic route that would quickly place him in the company of other notable authors, such as Andreu Martín, Juan Madrid, and Francisco González Ledesma, among others.

But if the literary qualities of this writer revealed themselves in *Tattoo* and *The Angst-Ridden Executive* (1977), they reached their highest aesthetic and conceptual level in *Southern Seas*. The novel's plot, which begins with the discovery that a wealthy Catalan businessman has died in a place where he'd been hiding for a year, lets Vázquez Montalbán make a grim dissection of Spanish society in the years immediately after the death of dictator Francisco Franco and the establishment of a new democracy, hesitant, threatened, and surprising even to itself.

The gallery of characters through whom Carvalho gets different views of the missing and murdered businessman, Stuart Pedrell, allows the writer to give us the many faces of a vibrant society, a snapshot of a historical moment still in process, with its ideological debates, its opportunism, its political and economic frustrations, its democratic present, and its Franco-era past. The city, meanwhile, shifts from the lowest-class neighborhoods to the brightest bourgeois salons, always passing through Barcelona's historic and charming Las Ramblas, the port, and China-town. It becomes much more than a suitable setting; it serves as the map of a universe changed by new possibilities and marked by the heavy shackles of past dictatorial capitalism. Meanwhile, Carvalho, a hopelessly disenchanted ideologue, uses his personality, his phobias and passions, to open doorways to understanding political frustration and enjoying a feast of the senses through gastronomic and alcoholic delights.

In all these ways and many others—including vibrant language—*Southern Seas* meets the aesthetic standards of a crime novel, but it is intended above all to be a bitter novel of society, with the ability to raise questions and even give some answers. How could it fail to do so, given its author's ideological clarity?

It was no accident that as soon as I finished my immersion in *Southern Seas*, I proceeded in short order to devour *Tattoo*, *The Angst-Ridden Executive*, *Murder in the Central Committee* (1981), *The Birds of Bangkok* (1983), and *Alexandria's Rose* (1984), and needed to revisit *The Spa*. Nor was it luck that a few months after this thrilling discovery of the possibilities of the detective story, brought to me by the work of this author, when I finally had time to start my own novel after six years of hard work with a daily newspaper, one of the compass points that guided me in this adventure was the revelation I'd seen in Manuel Vázquez Montalbán and his irreverent detective, Pepe Carvalho. The other path, of course, bore the stamp of Raymond Chandler and Philip Marlowe. In both cases, the detective novel offered the possibilities I desired: it worked as a highly literary endeavor that could reveal environments, personalities, social traumas, and conflicts among individuals and generations through the simple, intelligent creation of a suspenseful mystery.

As you may have noticed, dear reader, *Southern Seas*, for all this, is far more than a novel. It is, in Spanish, the equivalent of Hammett's *The Glass Key* in English. Except that, instead of the famous Chinese porcelain vase that, according to Chandler, the teacher threw in the street, what the master Manuel Vázquez Montalbán has given us is a compass that points us to Literature (with a capital "L"), which we other writers have tried to use as a guide, for better or worse, as we attempt the difficult task of killing with words: the art of writing the detective novel—in Spanish.

I hope that Manolo, as dissatisfied and lucid as ever, would agree with me, wherever he is—whether in the skies of Bangkok or, as he no doubt would have preferred, in Barcelona's Chinatown, a materialistic heaven, where he might live within reach of the voluptuous odors of his favorite restaurant, Casa Leopoldo.

Cuban author Leonardo Padura Fuentes (b. 1955) is best known for his quartet of Havana-set novels Las cuatro estaciones *(The Four Seasons), which feature Inspector Mario Conde and are also referred to as the* Havana Quartet. *The first in the series,* Pasado perfecto *(aka* Havana Blue*), was published in 1991; the final novel,* Paisaje de otoño *(*Havana Black*) won the 1998 Premio Hammett, awarded by the Asociación Internacional de Escritores Policíacos. Padura is the author of nine novels in total. The most recent,* El hombre que amaba a los perros *(*The Man Who Loved Dogs*), was published in 2009.*

Prótesis (*Prosthesis*)
by Andreu Martín (1980)

CRISTINA FALLARÁS

(essay translated from the Spanish by Ellen Clair Lamb)

Born in Barcelona, Andreu Martín (b. 1949) is the author of more than fifteen crime novels. He made his debut in 1979, publishing three novels that year, and Prótesis *followed in 1980. Martín has also written children's books and comics, and for film, theater, and TV. He has won a number of European literary prizes, including the Premio Çírculo del Crimen, the Deutsche Krimi Preis, and the Alfa 7.*

There is nothing more sinister than the smile of a skull. It is a petrified rictus, cold, expressionless and unchanging. Teeth clenched in a fierce bite. It is a trap that has slammed shut, clapping on its prey and never letting go. It is a laugh that contains no joy, a forced smile, a smile of pain, menace and cruelty. The grin is of an executioner who pretends to be your friend before causing you damage, great damage. Nothing funny is happening now, there's nothing to laugh about, but soon—yes, very soon— just the thought of it . . .

—opening lines of *Prótesis*

With your permission, as I focus on this term "noir," I turn to Wikipedia, not only for a hook but because it has become one of our new minor deities: "The term is associated with a type of detective story in which the resolution of the mystery is not the principal goal, and the conflicts are usually quite violent; the line between good and evil people is blurred, and most of the major characters have lost or failed in their search for truth, or at least a glimpse of it." To that I need to add the stamp of my own dark universe, the essential parts of a genre I'd kill for (don't judge me): a good noir is the insect in the baby's cradle, the rat on a naked woman's sheets, the unlit match that separates claw from meat.

A good noir is one that hurts when you read it.

A good noir describes the space that you, upstanding citizen, share with the psychopath.

A good noir forces you to confront the rotten things within yourself, the things you've buried or learned not to give in to.

A good noir cannot be read without some loss of innocence.

That's *Prótesis*, the masterwork of Andreu Martín: a novel that hurts you, that describes the beast inside you, that destroys your innocence. In *Prótesis* nothing is good—because who or what is truly bad?—and there's nothing to be gained; everyone is born to lose, and is lost. *Prótesis* exposes you completely and nails you with an iron fist of destruction. It is a dissection of amorality and wit in which two characters, policeman and criminal, cling to each other in a macabre dance that leads to death.

Prótesis is also the hardest, most violent novel ever published in Spain, comparable perhaps only to a classic like *The Family of Pascual Duarte* (1942) by Nobel Prize–winner Camilo José Cela. I remember the first time I read it. The awe. In my hands, I held a painful artifact from the grave wherein pulsed Jim Thompson's *Pop. 1280* and Erskine Caldwell's *Tobacco Road.* And it was a Spanish novel, published in 1980.

1980: In Barcelona, Manuel Vázquez Montalbán (b. 1939) had already published the first adventures of his detective, Carvalho: *I Killed Kennedy* (1972), *Tattoo* (1974), and *The Angst-Ridden Executive* (1977). Juan Marsé (b. 1933) had unwittingly joined the ranks of the classics with *If They Tell You I Fell* (1973). And Eduardo Mendoza (b. 1943) had forged his own path in '75 with *The Truth About the Savolta Case.* In less than a decade, these three had created a basis, but Andreu Martín (b. 1949), youngest of them all, would raise the stakes with a work more powerful, more free, more amazing (and perhaps for these reasons, less popular) than any of these: *Prótesis.* The first three painted a city of gray losers, harborside transvestites and women still mending their flesh-colored stockings. This was Barcelona dyed black by a Franco regime that did not allow good police officers or conceive of judges without corruption. The winners were still those who ruled, and the losers were everyone.

"I am a writer because Manuel Vázquez Montalbán wrote *Tattoo*," our author has said (*El País*, February 3, 2011). Maybe so, but Andreu

Martín exploded the boundaries between detective and criminal, winners and losers, innocent and depraved, in order to show us evil: the desire for others' pain and the amorality that comes from forty years of silence, the smell of basements and hunger.

The time: late '70s. In Spain, Franco had just died, the Catholic-Fascist dictator who had been repressing the country for forty years after winning the Civil War. In the broadest terms, a large population of middle-class poor, domesticated and submissive, lived surrounded by: a) a few cells of left-wing radicals; b) a core group of Fascists who had been enriched by the regime; c) a sprinkling of proletarian suburbs, humbled by decades of the military and its reforms; and d) the suburban children of the poorest layers of society, relics of internal emigration, the products of rootlessness and violence. A terrible rage grew in the shadows of these neighborhoods, constructed so badly by industrial development on the outskirts of cities like Barcelona, Madrid, and Bilbao.

Spain is an anomaly in Western Europe. In the suburbs of Barcelona they've built neighborhoods of cheap block where, after their workdays in the factories, immigrants from the poorer regions of Spain share living space with traditionally excluded groups, particularly the Roma.

In this broth bubbles a group of kids who have not yet come of age: El Migue, El Chava, El Marujo, and at the head of the group, El Cachas, followed by a young girl, la Nena, who doesn't wear panties and has known since she stopped sucking her thumb that she'd be a whore (and who cares?).

This is what happens: one night, they grab a couple driving a Renault 12 and take them up Tibidabo, the mountain crowned by Christ, who contemplates the city with open arms from the far side of the harbor. The idea is to rape the woman, beat the man, compete to be the worst, unleash the animal within, steal whatever they can, slake the need for violence that's killing them, and run. But something goes wrong—very wrong—when El Gallego, a bloodthirsty policeman, shows up.

El Gallego: "El Gallego was always a very good cop. He joined the Social [the national police] right out of the military and he had no competition, I tell you. He was a hard man, he was a guy with a lot of balls. Friend to the world, a great companion, but, man, when he threw the gauntlet down on a red, there was no way to prepare yourself. And he shut down many. Many. The anarchists threw a hand grenade and all, and El Gallego, no reaction, hard, hard, hard, he finished them off in the lot of the Carmelite convent, after a shootout with these three scumbags . . . (. . .) and then he walks out of that mess (. . .). Then one day he stops this prick and, seriously, between us, it was like this, this happened to him, he smashed his face in, you get me . . . ! That day the boy was arrested, he would have been about . . . I don't know, fifteen or sixteen . . . 'Leave me alone,' you know?"

After the blow, El Migue gets hold of El Cachas, his friend, his boss, and shows him a face with an eye dangling from a socket whose liquid would be dark red if any light shone through it. But it's black. And everything's already a prison.

El Migue: "Miguel Vargas Reinoso has his skull's smile in a glass, with water and a Corega Tabs tablet. He spends hours and hours watching it, every night, from the time he takes it from his gums until it returns to its place in his mouth. He watches it with his slanted eyes, catlike and unpleasant, while he breathes rhythmically through his nose, perhaps at a rate faster than normal. He spends whole nights staring at it and thinking that it's been a long, long time."

These two are the main protagonists and the cornerstone of *Prótesis,* El Gallego and El Migue. Salvador Gallego and Miguel Vargas Perch Reinoso.

The novel begins eight years after El Gallego destroys Miguel's face and El Migue starts sucking men off in prison. The young man lives only for revenge, delirious with pain beyond measure. El Gallego has simply given up on life after losing his sense of a manhood based on extreme violence. They're compelled to meet again, they need to meet again, they live for and through this reunion. And we, the readers, are absorbed in this story of man as a purely violent creature; the bloody loss of innocence; the twists of a homosexuality impossible to acknowledge or even think of; and the painful recovery of a society, the Spanish society, which must leave these characters of an earlier time behind in order to build a democracy, because they're trouble, and they can't be rehabilitated.

I close with two quotes from the author about his work, which undoubtedly left a mark on his (very successful) later career, to the point of constant references to it becoming a nuisance:

> If we're talking about *Prótesis,* it has an adolescent component of
> rebellion against institutions. When I wrote it, many things had

blown up. Andreu Martín has grown up, and now, at my age, I wouldn't write *Prótesis*. Violence is not heroic, it is not the solution to anything.

—(*El País*, February 3, 2011)

In my teens (an age of solitary pleasures, such as writing, for example), I found the underworld very attractive. The dirty streets, the threat of thugs everywhere, whores on street corners and in barroom doorways, the shell-game operators, the covetous eyes of those men who never seemed to have anything to do. It makes sense that the underworld would fascinate an adolescent: it represents rebellion against the laws imposed by adults (the unknown world, menacing and terrifying), and the rule-breaking represents self-assertion and a sense of discovery distinct from the thoughts and feelings they taught us in childhood. I guess my father (anarchist, sinner and provocateur) also fed the taste for Chinatown.

—(Revisiting *Prótesis*, May 2010)

Cristina Fallarás is a journalist and writer who lives in Barcelona. She has worked as a journalist at different levels for El Mundo, Cadena SER, Radio Nacional de España, El Periódico de Catalunya, Antena3 de Televisión, Cuatro Televisión, COMRàdio, *and* Radiotelevisión del Principado de Asturias. *She has been an editor of street interviews, a reporter, a radio and television writer, an opinion columnist, a writer, a section chief, and a deputy managing editor. She was involved in the design and writing of the daily newspaper* ADN *project, of which she is cofounder and deputy director. She is also cofounder of the online newspaper* Factual. *She currently directs the opinion page and the editing of Sigueleyendo.es, serves as a consultant on communications issues for the publishing sector and the media, and keeps a blog in the* Ellas *section of* El Mundo. *She is the author of five novels, including* Thus Died the Poet Guadeloupe *(2009), a finalist for the international Hammett Prize, and* The Lost Girls *(2011), which won the L'H Confidencial de Novela Negra prize and the Director's Prize at la Semana Negra de Gijón (Gijón Crime Week). She is a frequent contributor to anthologies, and her story "The Story of a Scar" was included in Akashic Books'* Barcelona Noir.

Early Autumn
by Robert B. Parker (1981)

COLIN BATEMAN

Born and raised in Massachusetts, Robert B. Parker (1932–2010) served with the U.S. Army in Korea. His first novel, The Godwulf Manuscript, *featuring PI Spenser and set in Boston, was published in 1973. The author of more than sixty novels, Parker wrote a number of series alongside the Spenser titles, including the Jesse Stone, Sunny Randall, and Cole & Hitch novels. In 1976,* Promised Land *won the Edgar Award for Best Novel. Parker also authored two novels based on Raymond Chandler's character Philip Marlowe,* Poodle Springs *(1989) and* Perchance to Dream *(1991). Parker was presented with the Grand Master Award by the Mystery Writers of America in 2002.*

As a young man you fantasize about becoming a great writer and you study the classics—in my case it was *Catch-22, On the Road, Catcher in the Rye*—and you know you will never be able to write those books, because they are already there.

But you are also torn, because although you crave literary acclaim and you want to write the Great American Novel—despite being from and living in Northern Ireland—what you *really* like reading is pulp fiction. You know that it receives no respect but you love it, and you keep turning the pages; and, as much as the writing, you love the writers. You love the idea of them being paid by the word, and how they pump out thousands and thousands of them. No fannying around taking five years to complete a novel—Jesus, no. Five weeks maximum, with breaks only for sex and whiskey.

In 1990 I was a journalist on a small-town paper with a pile of unpublishable short stories and that same burning desire to write a novel, but not a clue how to write it or what to write it about, even though it was staring me in the face. A girlfriend insisted that I read *The Godwulf Manuscript*, the first Robert B. Parker Spenser mystery, and I devoured it.

The great thing about discovering a writer who has been around for a while is the back catalog—you don't have to wait around for a year for the next book to come out. I sailed through *God Save the Child, Mortal Stakes, Promised Land, Looking for Rachel Wallace,* and all the others. Then later, when I got married—different girl—we got into the habit of holidaying in the United States, and every year, the first thing that I did when I arrived was drive to the nearest bookstore and stock up on Parker, because he had never quite taken off outside of the United States, and there were always new books to be found. He was as prolific as any pulp writer, with three series on the go: Spenser, Sunny Randall, and Jesse Stone. And then there were the Westerns, all written in the same glorious pared-down style.

With Parker there was no fluff. No pages of description, no detailed backstory. There was introspection, but not so deep that you'd drown in it. There were short sentences, smart dialogue, familiar characters and settings. It was as if he'd been given a Chandler novel and told to write one like that, but cut out all the crap, and make it half as long, and a bit warmer, and by God, you're a Boston man, set it there, and you're an academic, so show some smarts, but you were also an infantryman in the Korean War, so make Spenser tough as nails and brilliant with his fists.

Spenser was a private eye, Boston Irish, who should have had all the prejudices that go with the genre and the genes, but whose girl, Susan, was a Jew; whose best friend, Hawk, was black; whose adopted son, Paul, was gay; and who settled arguments with his fists but wasn't above taking in the ballet. Spenser, who knocked back the Bushmills and turned me on to premium-label beer long before it became fashionable in the land of Guinness, but who saved his most lavish descriptions for the clothes that his suspects wore and the meals he cooked for Susan. Spenser had a code and a quest, and he lived by one and was relentlessly on the trail of the other. He was the man we'd all like to be—tough but fair, and funny, and he didn't age, and he had great sex with a beautiful woman on a regular basis but liked his own company, too.

He arrived on the scene *mostly* formed, but Parker and Spenser really hit their stride with two books—*Looking for Rachel Wallace* (1980) and my favorite, *Early Autumn* (1981)—tackling gender politics in the former, and parental strife and the damage it does to children in the latter. In *Early Autumn*, Spenser is hired to protect a boy, Paul Giacomin, who has been kidnapped as part of a custody battle. The book isn't really about solving a case at all, but literally and metaphorically about rescuing a child. Spenser's approach is a mix of old school and liberal arts: realizing that both parents are equally malicious, he more or less kidnaps Paul himself, and brings the poor, wasted, effeminate sloth with him on a camping trip, teaches him to box and lift weights, and literally builds a home with him, while also taking him to galleries and introducing him to the joys of reading: all of this not so much to man him up, but to teach him about life and how to function as an adult in the real world. This wasn't the kind of thing we were used to in crime fiction: yup, Parker was still using the established template, but messing with it, too, and in so doing he changed it for good.

Parker has been described as the bridge between Hammett, Chandler, Macdonald, and the modern crime novel, but he was more than that, because being a bridge suggests that he wasn't a destination in himself. He was. The problem with the PI novel was that it had become a parody of itself: in the same way that the Western was forever ruined by *Blazing Saddles*, so *Play It Again, Sam* and *Dead Men Don't Wear Plaid* were threatening to make it impossible to enjoy the PI genre again.

But somehow Parker took the clichés and filed them down. He gave the PI warmth, and a conscience, and self-awareness while still giving us broads, and lugheads, and fisticuffs, and corpses galore. He also gave us the site-specific PI. Boston is as much a character in the Spenser books as Spenser himself; in his wake, there is not a state in the Union that does not have its own Spenser, and hardly a country in the world.

When I read Spenser it suddenly became clear to me that *my* story was staring me in the face: thirty years of terrorist Troubles that no one had ever treated with a cool, cynical, sarcastic eye, with one-liners and short scenes and shorter sentences.

When I finally started my first novel, *Divorcing Jack*, Spenser was the model, and Parker's was the style; I even named one of my main characters after Parker—though I killed him off pretty soon. Not the style thing, though—it has me yet, and more than twenty novels down the line I still catch myself aping those mannerisms. Back then it was copying; now I prefer to think of it as paying tribute.

Born in Bangor, Northern Ireland, in 1962, Colin Bateman worked as a journalist before publishing Divorcing Jack *in 1995. That novel won the Betty Trask Award, and was subsequently adapted for film. A prolific author, Bateman has written twenty-one novels for adults and an additional eight titles for children and young adults, as well as TV screenplays, a play, and an opera. He was the chief writer on* Murphy's Law, *a TV series that ran from 2001 to 2007.* The Day of the Jack Russell *won the Last Laugh Award for comic crime fiction in 2009. Visit him online at www.colinbateman.com.*

Gorky Park
by Martin Cruz Smith (1981)

JEAN-CHRISTOPHE GRANGÉ

(essay translated from the French by Ellen Clair Lamb)

Martin Cruz Smith (b. 1942), the son of a jazz musician and a nightclub singer who met at the 1939 World's Fair, is a former journalist, and has been a published writer for almost four decades. He is the author, among other works, of an acclaimed series of mystery novels featuring a Russian investigator named Arkady Renko ("a truth-teller," as the author describes him, "an honest man in a dishonest system"), the first of which was Gorky Park. *It has since been followed by six other novels featuring Renko, the latest of which is* Three Stations *(2010).*

Generally speaking, in a detective novel, we engage first with the story. We then notice characters that, if the book is good, show themselves to be moving, amazing, or exciting. If the book is better still, we find ourselves transported into a certain mood, a setting, a way of looking at the world. And, if the novel is a complete success, we further delight in an original style, a unique manner of expression, which provides a genuine aesthetic thrill.

Gorky Park offers all of these pleasures, but in reverse order. We first encounter a breathtaking style, the mark of a great artist. Then, in the mists of an icy Moscow, we discover a series of fascinating characters, men and women who are struggling in the clutches of a terrifying system (we are in the 1980s). Bit by bit, we take the measure of the city and the country as we explore an ecosystem, an environment: the architecture of the streets, the insanity of Soviet tyranny, the depth of Russian tradition . . . until, at last, we realize we are completely spellbound by a story that never disappoints, and holds us to the very last line.

It is at this point that we know we've been handed a masterpiece. As a writer of thrillers, I consider *Gorky Park* the quintessence of the genre, telling the best possible story in the best possible way.

Let me begin with how I discovered this book. I was thirty at the time, and working as a freelance reporter. My wife and I had started a small press agency. Each of us was paired with a photographer, and we sold articles to magazines all over the world. In the winter of 1991–92, Virginia, my wife, embarked on a series of portraits of the world's greatest crime novelists (James Ellroy, Elmore Leonard, Herbert Lieberman, etc.). Included in this list, which we had assembled with the help of publishers, was Martin Cruz Smith. Neither she nor I knew him and, to help, I offered to read some of his books. I began with *Gorky Park*.

As it happened, I started reading it when I myself was heading to an assignment in China at the source of the Mekong River, in the middle of winter. I remember sitting on the plane, and discovering this book that was to determine my future career. I turned the pages, not knowing what excited me most: the plot, the psychology, the style—everything was perfect, everything was sublime.

Ordinarily, you should not divulge too much of a detective novel's story. It would be as if a bride arrived at the church naked. In this case, however, I cannot resist: the plot is too good.

It all starts with the discovery of three mutilated corpses, each wearing ice skates, in Moscow's Gorky Park. They are spotted by a militiaman who has stepped behind a tree to relieve himself. In my memory, it is this guy's urine that melts the ice and reveals the bodies, but I'm not sure of that. What I know for certain is that, throughout the book, there is a deep collusion between the snow, the cold, and the crime—and the pitiless character of the Soviet regime as well. In the end, this conspiracy seems to extend even to trappers lost in an endless forest . . .

This is not an idle connection, because readers will discover that the motive for the murders is an animal. The three victims (two males and one female) had been hoping to go west, taking with them one of the USSR's essential treasures: a pair of sables.

Crime novelists are always looking for an original puzzle, an unusual solution. With his sables, Martin Cruz Smith beats us all: it is at once unique and completely logical. In this vast empire—a superpower, but one in which everyone lives in the blackest misery—exists a treasure: the priceless genes of these little creatures, which would allow the United States to develop a flourishing trade in fur.

We remember Alfred Hitchcock's dictum that for a film to succeed, the villain must succeed. *Gorky Park*'s villain is spectacular: John Osborne, an American businessman, cruel, cynical, omniscient. Almost a supernatural being, he is at once both Russian and American. He has distilled the darkest traits of both countries. He has a sort of instinctive savagery, Siberian tied to an icy capitalism, that is both visceral and totally unscrupulous.

Opposing him is the antihero Arkady Renko, a marginal cop swimming against the currents of the government, his supervisors, his expected career path, and even his family (he is the son of a great Stalinist general). Beneath his listless exterior we find an incorruptible will, and the pugnacity of the lone hero. Another of the novel's brilliant concepts: not only will the guilty not be arrested, but nobody even wants to stop them. In the USSR, crime does not exist, cannot exist. Arkady must fight everyone to conduct his investigation.

I have always thought of the detective novel as a fairy tale for adults, featuring a knight who fights a dragon in a hostile environment. Here, all the necessary elements of the mission are present. Arkady is the hero, a samurai who, like all samurai, has sworn fidelity to his master—in this case, his country. This is one of the book's deepest dimensions: Renko encounters only Russians who dream of moving to the West. Not him: he loves his country. The "hostile environment" is rooted within him, like a disease.

In a good thriller, there are always high points that resemble plateaux on which we may stop and breathe the fresh air of high literature. *Gorky Park* is full of these scenes, such as my favorite, in which Renko interrogates judges and generals in a swimming pool. It's a hot place, steamfilled, where one eats eggs with caviar "as big as marbles" and drinks iced vodka. Or another scene in which he meets his best friend in an abandoned church, rain-soaked, where the angels fade into the walls. It is against this symbolic backdrop that he realizes his companion has betrayed him . . .

Gorky Park uses a multitude of ingenious ideas to advance the investigation. For example, Renko has the idea of bringing the three mutilated heads of his victims to an expert in facial reconstruction (a Russian specialty) for identification. There is no question of a computer, or specialized software. The anthropologist (a dwarf) works only with wax, plaster, and old measuring instruments. The entire book is underscored by the progress on these strange sculptures.

Another outstanding idea: Arkady asks himself where the killer got rid of his gun. He must have thrown it in the river—except for one problem: everything had already been frozen at the time of the triple murder. But Renko knows a place where the water never freezes, because of the boiling discharge from a factory. He searches the area and finds the weapon . . . brilliant!

A final pleasure of *Gorky Park* is the ironic perspective of the author. Martin Cruz Smith does not criticize the Soviet system; he jokes blackly about it, which is much more effective, as when he notes that the "Route of Enthusiasts" is the road that took prisoners to the Gulags, or when he defines vodka as a "liquid tax that never stops rising."

Gorky Park is not a political book: it is much more than that. This is a human book, universal and deeply moving, a tale of hunters that speaks to us about the dark impulses of man when reduced to his innermost solitude. And the novel ends where it begins: in the snow. But this time, the snow is American. It is a way of saying that, on one side or the other, man is always alone, naked.

And he is cold.

Born in Paris, Jean-Christophe Grangé was a journalist before turning to write fiction. The author of nine novels in all, he made his debut in 1994 with Le Vol des cigognes *(*Flight of the Storks*). His most recent offering is* Le passager *(2011), but he is probably best known for 1999's* Les rivières pourpres *(*The Crimson Rivers*), which he adapted with director Mathieu Kassovitz for the film* Les rivières pourpres *(2000), which starred Jean Reno and Vincent Cassel. Visit him online at www.jc-grange.com.*

A Is for Alibi
by Sue Grafton (1982)

MEG GARDINER

Sue Grafton (b. 1940) is the Kentucky-born author of the groundbreaking "Alphabet Series" of detective novels featuring private investigator Kinsey Millhone, some of the inspiration for which she credits to Edward Gorey's illustrated book The Gashlycrumb Tinies, *in which assorted small children meet gruesome ends in strictly alphabetical order. She once threatened to come back from the grave if her children sold the film rights to the series after she was dead. Her decision to fictionalize Santa Barbara, California, as "Santa Teresa" is a tribute to the novelist Ross Macdonald, who was the first to reimagine the city under that name.*

From the moment Kinsey Millhone walks onto the first page of *A Is for Alibi,* she's a presence to be reckoned with. The first novel in Sue Grafton's "Alphabet Series" gets rolling straight out of the gate:

> My name is Kinsey Millhone. I'm a private investigator, licensed by the state of California. I'm thirty-two years old, twice divorced, no kids. The day before yesterday I killed someone and the fact weighs heavily on my mind.

With that hook, Kinsey pulls us into her investigation of a murder case that isn't merely cold, but closed. The cops have already found the killer. The jury convicted her. They sent her to prison and declared justice done.

Then, after eight years, she's paroled. She walks into Kinsey's office, tells her she's innocent, and asks Kinsey to find the real murderer.

The victim, Laurence Fife, was a ruthless divorce lawyer and a relentless philanderer, until somebody poisoned him. His young wife, Nikki, was convicted of the crime. Kinsey takes the case reluctantly; though Nikki insists that she didn't do it, Kinsey has her doubts.

The trail is ash cold. And when Kinsey starts following it, the cops spring bad news: Laurence Fife wasn't the only person murdered eight years earlier. Shortly after his killing, his accountant died in exactly the same way. Nobody had been arrested for that young woman's death, but the cops think Nikki poisoned her, too, for sleeping with Fife.

Laurence Fife died painfully, poisoned by oleander crushed to a powder and substituted for his allergy pills. There were no witnesses, no confession, no forensic proof of the killer's identity. There was only his young wife, the icy blonde who had means, motive, and opportunity.

Still, Kinsey presses the investigation. Her hunt for the truth leads her to a slew of colorful suspects, starting with Fife's ex-wife, Gwen, whom he betrayed, dumped, and reduced to running a dog grooming salon. It leads to Fife's incompetent legal secretary, a woman with "a mouth built for unnatural acts" who now deals blackjack in Las Vegas. It leads to the parents of the murdered young accountant, who have never recovered from their daughter's death. And it leads to Fife's legal partner, Charlie Scorsoni, who's steadfastly loyal to his dead colleague and overwhelmingly attractive to Kinsey. Eventually the trail leads Kinsey into danger, and into a fatal confrontation with a killer.

A Is for Alibi is a classic whodunit freshened up, given depth, and infused with humor. It's humane, warm, and self-aware. And it not only cleared the bar for high-quality mysteries, it raised the standard, permanently.

Deftly plotted, vivid, and convincing, the story has twists, multiple murders, and some well-intentioned B&E by the heroine. It has sex. It has regret, and gunplay. It has a cast of motley neighborhood characters that, over the course of the series, becomes beloved. And in the center of the action it has Kinsey, digging and messing up and saving the day and nearly getting killed because she's after the truth, for the sake of her client and for all those damaged by the crime.

Kinsey doesn't gather the suspects in the library and point at the killer—*aha!*—before wiping her hands clean of the affair and walking away unaffected. Instead, she dives in. For good or ill, she gets involved. Right off the bat, Kinsey tells us that she's in this case up to her ears. And the suspense grows as she realizes that a murderer is on the loose, somebody who's becoming desperate to erase his or her tracks.

The novel has a gritty authenticity that's grounded in the savvy, compelling voice of its protagonist. But the story isn't hard-boiled. At times, it's poignant. Laurence Fife's children from his first marriage have suffered terribly from losing their father. Nikki's imprisonment has essentially orphaned her little boy. Born deaf, he was shunted off to boarding school when Nikki was convicted of killing his dad. Though he gets a second chance to connect with his mother, he has grown up isolated and without a home. As Kinsey comes to believe that Nikki was framed for the murder, the injustice of what has been done to the entire family feels increasingly keen. It drives Kinsey ever harder to discover the truth.

The writing is taut. The book's 214 paperback pages are packed—not only with death, sex, and treachery, but with brightly drawn pictures of Las Vegas, Los Angeles, and the Salton Sea. Plus there's Kinsey's sharp and loving portrayal of Santa Teresa (a fictionalized version of Grafton's hometown, Santa Barbara), the picturesque Southern California city "artfully arranged between the Sierra Madres and the Pacific—a haven for the abject rich."

The story fits solidly in the gumshoe canon. At the same time, it takes the private eye novel into unmarked territory. Kinsey represents the standard PI model, but bent and twisted in original ways. She lives in a tiny one-room apartment because trailers were "getting too elaborate for my taste." She runs three miles a day and hates every minute of it. Her observations are wry and self-deprecating. She's funny, and we love her.

And while the book is a foursquare mystery, it helped break open the crime fiction world to a whole new line of investigators: the women.

Today we read novels and watch movies and television shows with kick-ass heroines, and don't bat an eye. Angelina Jolie in *Salt* is a jacked-up version of a character we know and accept. *Kick-Ass* is *about* a girl superhero. But until recently, this wasn't so. *A Is for Alibi* helped make it possible.

When the novel was published in 1982, Kinsey Millhone—feisty, sharp, resourceful, and vulnerable—was an entirely fresh character. Completely professional, she was also stubborn, human, and artlessly open about her quirks. She cut her own hair with a pair of fingernail scissors. She owned one dress, an indestructible black thing that could be crushed, drenched, possibly even burned, without harm, and that she wore to parties, funerals, and weddings. And she fit so perfectly into the private eye genre that she seemed like she'd always been there.

But for this reader, she was breathtaking. In Kinsey I discovered a young woman doing a job that had previously been restricted to male private investigators, and doing so in a thoroughly grown-up way, inhabiting her life and her story with confidence and uncertainty and charming, flawed honesty. She's a winsome orphan who carries a .22. She's tough and independent, though at some point in the book readers will want to hug her and hand her a cup of cocoa. She holds her own.

Best of all: Kinsey would never think of herself as kick-ass. She'd rather snark than fight. But if forced into a corner, she'll punch her way out.

And the book just swings. It rolls. It barrels down the highway. We're along for the ride, right beside Kinsey, gawping at the drunken, unfaithful socialite who has sharp teeth and a gossip's claws. We ache for Kinsey, motherless, fatherless, living in paradise but alone. We cheer for her because she's an ordinary gal, well trained, smart, one of us.

This is one of those books that slyly, without fanfare, grabs the genre by the heart and carries it off in a new direction. Sue Grafton may not have meant to do so, but she succeeded, wildly. And when I finished it, I thought: *Yes. This is possible. This is what I want to read. This is what I want to write. There's room: Grafton has just created it. Kinsey Millhone is showing us the way. So punch through. Make your own territory.* The mystery novel and our imaginations are big enough to embrace it.

Kinsey is a pioneer, because she has to be. But she's not out there to make a point. She's doing her job, both accepting and battling the world as she finds it. It's 1982, and she's on her own, an American woman facing up to herself and to all the possibilities that people would still deny her. She fights through it for herself and for her clients. For those of us reading her story, she's a friend and a hero.

Meg Gardiner is the author of ten novels, including the Evan Delaney series, the Jo Beckett novels, and the stand-alone thriller Ransom River. *Her novel* China Lake *won the 2009 Edgar Award for Best Paperback Original. The* Dirty Secrets Club *won the RT Reviewers' Choice Award for best procedural novel of the year and was chosen as one of Amazon's top ten thrillers of 2008. Gardiner practiced law in Los Angeles and taught at the University of California, Santa Barbara. She lives near London. Visit her online at www.meg gardiner.com.*

Different Seasons
by Stephen King (1982)

PAUL CLEAVE

Stephen Edwin King (b. 1947) is, quite simply, one of the most success-ful authors in the world. Born in Portland, Maine, he was raised by his mother following his parents' separation while King was still a toddler, and later graduated with a BA in English from the University of Maine at Orono. He sold his first short story in 1967, and published his first novel, Carrie, in 1974. Since then, he has published over seventy books, includ-ing short-story collections and nonfiction, and has been acclaimed across numerous genres, winning mystery, horror, and fantasy awards, as well as a National Book Award for his distinguished contribution to American letters. He still lives in Maine.

The thing about Stephen King is this: he's a horror author. That's every-body's first thought. It used to be my first thought. But the other thing about Stephen King is this: many of his books have a mystery or a crime element to them. You could argue that *Misery* is more a crime novel than a horror story—there's no supernatural component there, just a lady with an ax and a brain that's been wired up all wrong. You could argue that *Needful Things* is a crime novel about a man making a town turn on itself; horror certainly drives the story, but these are actual crimes that the residents of this town are committing. *Bag of Bones, Thinner, Firestarter:* crime and mystery everywhere. Even *The Green Mile*, a fantastic story about an innocent man going to prison, is set around the murders of two young girls. One thing you can't argue is that King's books are full of nice people doing what they can to hide a whole lot of crazy.

I always wanted to be a horror writer. King does that to a lot of people. Yet weirdly, it was Stephen King who introduced me to crime fiction. I just didn't know it at the time. His books were all I read when I was in my late teens. The first was *Pet Sematary*, then *Needful Things*, then

'*Salem's Lot,* then *The Stand.* I had started in a great place. I was maybe seven or eight books into King's work when I bought *Different Seasons.* It's made up of four novellas featuring four different worlds (or seasons), and in each of these seasons you don't really have any idea where King is taking you (though do you ever with his books?).

Different Seasons is certainly not what I was expecting. I went into the bookstore on my lunch break and parted with a small chunk of my hard-earned money like I always did, thinking I was buying a horror novel like I always had, only I ended up buying a mix of stories that weren't horror at all. But I'd parted with my money for a book that has stuck with me for a long time, and I still think about some of the stories inside it nearly twenty years after reading it.

Different Seasons begins with "Rita Hayworth and Shawshank Redemption." Most people know this story—if you go to the Internet Movie Database (IMDB), you'll see that *The Shawshank Redemption* is rated as the #1 movie of all time, alongside *The Godfather.* I think some people keep forgetting this: that the #1 movie voted by the public is a Stephen King story. I read "Shawshank" back in 1993, well before the movie appeared. It's a story about a guy who goes to prison. He's an innocent man found guilty of shooting his wife. Things don't get any better for him, and though bad things happened to land him in prison, even worse things happen once he's inside. And so, over many years, he plans his escape . . .

Halfway through the story I was still waiting for vampires or ghosts to show up. They didn't. They don't show up at all. The story was too good to leave me disappointed by the fact that dead people weren't roaming the streets. I got to the end of "Shawshank" and started the second story, "Apt Pupil." It's the tale of a teenager who learns that his elderly neighbor is a Nazi war criminal. Instead of going to the police, he keeps visiting the old man to learn about his past, and pretty soon the teenager starts going off the rails and doing plenty of dark stuff. Again, no vampires, no ghosts, no aliens—horrible things, sure, but not a horror story.

The third story is "The Body" (which plenty of people will recognize as *Stand by Me,* the movie from 1986), which tells of four kids who, through rumor, hear of the location of the body of a young boy who has gone missing. It's a fairly dark story that shows off King's writing but, once again, there are no werewolves or leprechauns, and the body doesn't come back to life.

"The Breathing Method" is the last novella in the book. I wasn't expecting a horror story by this point, yet that was what I got. A woman is about to give birth, but on the way to the hospital she is involved in an accident, and is decapitated. So focused is she on having the baby, though, that she somehow still manages to stay alive even though her head is a few meters away from her body.

Different Seasons comes with a different effect for each story. "Breathing Method" is quite moving—a woman keeping her body functioning long enough after death to deliver her baby. "The Body" is dark yet tender, a story of four boys growing up, a story of which we all feel we could have been a part. "Apt Pupil" is captivating; it draws you in and makes you wonder just who could be living on your street. And "Rita Hayworth and Shawshank Redemption" is all of these things—tender, captivating, moving—but powerful, too. Very powerful. It's perhaps my favorite story of King's. It's a story that will stay with you forever. It's a story that makes you want to climb into the pages and help this guy out, help him to prove his innocence, help to free him from jail. It's an incredible tale in an incredible book.

So *Different Seasons* ends with horror, yet it's the crime and mystery stories in the collection that I most enjoyed. King had slipped in crime under the radar—and I loved it. He convinced me to widen my reading tastes (okay, so now it's horror *and* crime fiction), and as much as I wanted to be a horror writer, it was the king (no pun intended) of horror writing who steered me off that path and onto the one of writing crime.

Paul Cleave was born in New Zealand, and wanted to be a novelist for as long as he could remember. His first book, The Cleaner, *was published in 2006, a mere six years after it was written, and became one of the biggest-selling books ever to come out of New Zealand. He has since followed it with five more novels, the latest of which is* The Laughterhouse. *He currently lives in London, at least until the immigration people discover that he's there. Visit him online at www.paulcleave.co.nz.*

Indemnity Only
by Sara Paretsky (1982)

Sara Paretsky (b. 1947) is a pioneering figure in modern mystery fiction. She is responsible for taking the traditional male archetype of the hard-boiled novel and transforming and reimagining it to create one of the earliest, and most iconic, of female investigators, V. I. Warshawski, the heroine of most of Paretsky's books. Her novels combine thriller conventions with astute social commentary, and this year marks the thirtieth anniversary of Warshawski's first appearance in print.

I wonder if the great Sara Paretsky realized what a gem and masterpiece she was giving us when she published *Indemnity Only* in 1982? That she was sending, kicking, into our lives one of the most memorable and feisty of private investigators—one hundred and a quarter bucks a day, plus expenses—V. I. Warshawski, Victoria Iphigenia, or just plain "Vic" to her nearest and dearest.

And that's one of the reasons why the first Warshawski novel will always remain one of my favorite crime reads, because at the heart of the story is a "new" woman. There had, of course, been plenty of women in stories about private investigators before, but not like Vic. She touched me because, in many ways, back then she embodied the type of woman I wanted to grow up to be—fresh, youthful, has a mouth on her, couldn't care less about the dishes piling up in the sink, and no way is she playing at being one of the boys. One character mockingly calls her "Philip Marlowe," but they're wrong: this is a woman who is happy in her own skin. Right from the get-go, when a client questions her ability, as a woman, to get the job done, she tells it how it is, speaking for every woman on the planet: *"If things get heavy, I'll figure out a way to handle them—or go down trying.*" Time and again V.I. has to show the lads that she'll tangle with the worst before she gives up on her investigation.

Looking back on the world with our twenty-first-century hindsight, feminist V.I. may seem like no big deal, but back in the early '80s women were still feeling their way toward a different role, and attitude to life, and Sara Paretsky does women with Role and Attitude. This is a woman who can head-butt, kung fu chop, and separate ribs using her open palm. As one character puts it, she's "a wise-ass karate expert." And when it comes to the witty put-downs and sarcasm, V.I. is good at doing that, too:

> "You're no more a detective than I am a ballet dancer."
> "I'd like to see you in tights and a tutu."

Paretsky makes sure, though, that V.I. is not the token tough lady on the block. *Indemnity Only* is full of other like-minded independent women, among them V.I.'s friend Lotty, and redheads punching out guys who just can't take no for an answer.

But V.I. is not one of those superwomen who feel no pain. Every now and again, when she interacts with a character, we get one of those transparent moments when we're able to see the emotion that's right inside of her, such as when she's confronted by bouncy college girl Gail, who oozes a naïve friendliness that makes V.I. feel old and gives her conscience a twist at having to deceive her. She's a woman with daddy issues—her grin turns sour when she thinks of the great things her father had expected from her. In an age when we're all (apparently) size-zero women it is a bit (ahem) "tasty" to read about a character who enjoys her food.

Indemnity Only was the first crime book I ever read where the main character was up front about fighting for the small guy against the big bosses, where politics was laid bare, where social justice wasn't just something sellotaped on to show that the author "cared." Being black, and growing up in a working-class community, these are issues that are not merely close to my heart; they are the very bones that have created the type of adult I am today.

The crime at the heart of *Indemnity Only* is gripping because it took me to places I wasn't expecting to go. The setup is simple: a father wants V.I. to find his son's missing girlfriend. But instead of finding the woman, V.I. discovers a decomposing body slumped at a kitchen table—no, not the girlfriend, but the client's son. And the love interest is still missing . . . and then the plot really starts hotting up. I ended up in a world of unions—the gloriously titled International Brotherhood of Knifegrinders, Shear Edgers, and Blade Sharpeners—insurance companies, and gangsters, where those who should be looking out for the small guy are using him to make a quick buck for themselves.

As well as breaking new ground, *Indemnity Only* draws heavily on the traditions of the classic noir novel. The city is never just a city; it's a place that lives and breathes with the lives of those who have created it. We meet the city of Chicago right on the first page, "moving restlessly, trying to breathe." V.I.'s Polish and Irish heritage paints a cultural mural that adds texture to the city. The use of light, shadow, and dark is exquisite. We move with V.I. through a city where little fires shine here and there, where water is a host of green and red running lights, where one room can go dark in an instant and a single naked bulb illuminates another. I remember the first time I ever read Raymond Chandler, and being struck by the way in which he constructed images of buildings in simple, effective sentences. Sara Paretsky works in this tradition. It would have been so easy for her simply to describe Chicago's murky underbelly, but she doesn't do this; instead, she uses powerful visual images, from drinking holes with mahogany, horse-shaped bars and Tiffany lamps, to stately homes made of dull red brick protected by elegant wrought-iron railings, and on to peep shows and the hidden world of lockups. Throughout, V.I.'s love for, and honesty about, her city shines brightly.

Indemnity Only opened up the writing landscape for female authors like me, making us realize that a woman can be the central character of a book without having to be the stereotype of the aging spinster or the sashaying, high-heeled vamp. One character tells V.I. that she could've been a happy housewife, while another says that she's never going to grace the cover of *Vogue,* but they're so wrong. When it came to opening doors, V.I. and Sara Paretsky were right on the money.

Dreda Say Mitchell is a novelist, broadcaster, journalist, and freelance education consultant who describes herself as a "complete busybody." She is the author of five novels. Her debut, Running Hot, *was awarded the CWA's John Creasey Memorial Dagger for best first crime novel in 2005. She has appeared on BBC television's* Newsnight, The Review Show, *and Canadian television's* Sun News Live, *and has presented* Open Book *on BBC Radio 4. She chaired the Harrogate Crime Writing Festival, Europe's biggest crime festival, in 2011. Her commitment to, and passion for, raising the life chances of working-class children in education has been called inspirational and life changing. Visit her online at www.dredasaymitchell.com.*

LaBrava
by Elmore Leonard (1983)

JAMES W. HALL

Commonly regarded as one of the greatest living American crime novelists, Elmore Leonard (b. 1925) made his publishing debut with The Bounty Hunters *in 1953, and continued to write Westerns until the publication of his first crime title,* The Big Bounce, *in 1969. The author of more than thirty crime novels, Leonard won the Edgar Award for LaBrava (1983). A number of his novels, among them* Get Shorty *(1990),* Rum Punch *(1992), and* Out of Sight *(1996), have been adapted for film; he is currently a co-writer on the TV series* Justified, *which features his series character Raylan Givens. Elmore Leonard was awarded the Grand Master Award by the Mystery Writers of America in 1992, and the F. Scott Fitzgerald Literary Award for Outstanding Achievement in American Literature in 2008.*

A quarter of a century ago, I decided to teach a course in crime fiction at the university where I had worked for most of my adult life. The focus was on crime novels set in Florida. I had plenty to choose from, ranging from John D. MacDonald's smart, tough, and well-known Travis McGee novels to the less celebrated work of Douglas Fairbairn, whose *Street 8,* a thriller set in Miami's newly flourishing Cuban neighborhoods, was an inspiration to me as a young writer whose aim was to write my own realistic Florida crime novel. (One of the wonderful benefits of university teaching is to merge one's vocation with one's avocation.)

LaBrava by Elmore Leonard was one of the books in that long-ago course. Published in 1983, *LaBrava* was set on Miami Beach, more particularly on South Beach in a period before its rise to the internationally celebrated, flashy-neon, art deco, fashionista, late-night-clubbing district it was to become. The year after *LaBrava* was published, that culture-changing TV show *Miami Vice* first hit the airwaves. I use the phrase "culture-changing" in a limited sense, for *Miami Vice* fundamentally changed the landscape of Miami by creating the illusion that a hip, ultra-trendy scene already existed in South Beach. It did not.

But this single TV show was about to change all that.

By focusing its camera on the two or three examples of slightly updated, neon-encrusted art deco hotels, and through the wonders of soundstage mock-ups, the television folk broadcast an imaginary fairy-land of ultracool that began to attract waves of tourists to the area whose sheer numbers caused South Beach to begin its long revitalization.

What truly existed there as *Miami Vice* first appeared was captured with photographic precision and understated realism by *LaBrava*. A ragtag collection of Marielitos, many of them newly released from Castro's prisons, roamed the dilapidated neighborhoods of South Beach and, in a surreal collision of cultures, wound up mingling with (and preying upon) the profusion of Jewish grandmothers who slumped in aluminum lawn chairs on the front porches of run-down, two-story, rent-by-the-hour-day-or-week hotels.

That photographic precision was no accident. Photography drives much of the action in the novel. Joe LaBrava, a former secret service agent, is now reinventing himself as a Diane Arbus–like photographer/artiste. His subjects, like Arbus's, are people of the street: freaks, and hustlers, and hookers, and sad, going-nowhere-fast outcasts. In a kind of quiet postmodernist way, it must be said that Joe's chosen art form is a great deal like Elmore Leonard's. Same subjects, same unadorned style, same parade of ultrarealistic freaks.

LaBrava is a watcher, walking the streets, mingling with the down-and-outers, memorializing them with his snap, snap, snapping. His training as a Secret Service agent serves him well, for he can blend in with the shabby street people and bond with nearly anyone, from the con man who uses a stolen wheelchair as his conveyance, to Jean Shaw, the aging movie star who becomes one of Joe's love interests. The black-and-white images that LaBrava develops in his first-floor hotel room on Ocean Drive are as quaintly old-fashioned and unembellished in technique as the enduring classic black-and-white films that starred Jean Shaw.

In fact, when I taught *LaBrava* long ago I was struck by its use of frequently recurring images of black and white. One of the words, or some permutation of those images, appears on every page. As literature professors like to do, I pointed this out to my students and asked them what they made of it. We considered the obvious associations, such as the tension between white-hatted good guys and black-hatted bad guys. Another interpretation was that black-and-white photos and films were emblematic of an earlier era, a time more simple and minimalist than our current period of gaudy neon and flashy tropical hues and moral ambiguity; a resonance of a kind of nostalgia for a more genuine state of being.

If Elmore Leonard has a favorite theme, then one contender has to be this comparison between the authentic and the artificial. Real heroes go up against false heroes. The laconic, modest cowboy is forced to strap on his gun and outdraw the garish loudmouth armed with badass weaponry. Hemingway is one of Leonard's models. He unabashedly admits this, and surely Leonard learned many lessons from Papa, from his elliptical prose to his spare but snappy dialogue.

And like Hemingway, Leonard is preoccupied with cool, which Hemingway knew as grace under pressure. For both writers one of the ultimate tests of value is authenticity, that no-bullshit genuineness that defines Jake Barnes as well as Joe LaBrava. LaBrava (whose last name has a Hemingway echo that might as easily apply to a bull or a toreador) is a man who has protected presidents, yet now, in his new identity, lives a modest, unassuming existence. A small apartment, cameras instead of guns, skilled at watchfulness. A man whose great gift is his very inconspicuousness.

All this I first noticed in that long-ago literature class in which we put *LaBrava* under an academic microscope. After the course concluded, and in a fit of fan-boy enthusiasm, I wrote Elmore Leonard a letter informing him that I'd found his novel not only first-rate entertainment, but it had "stood up to literary inspection." I advised him about some of the literary techniques that had come to light and how we admired, among other things, his use of "image patterns."

At this time I had not published a novel myself, nor had I met any of the writers, like "Dutch" Leonard, whom I would later be fortunate enough to get to know. I was a nobody; merely a college professor who had been pleased to discover that a book I loved as entertainment also made a profitable object of academic study.

Lo and behold, Mr. Leonard answered my note. He was gracious and succinct. He was pleased to hear that my students had enjoyed his novel and thankful I had let him know about these "image patterns" I had discovered in his work. He went on to say that he didn't think he would make a very good student in my class, however, because he had no idea what an "image pattern" was.

Ah, yes. Leonard's trademark dry wit.

Years later, after I published my own novels and got to know Dutch on a personal level, I discovered that one of the lectures he often gave to libraries and reading groups was something he called his "Funny Letters" speech. And sure enough, my "image pattern" fan letter had made it into that talk. He told me it got a good laugh every time: the pretentious professor finding meanings and techniques that the author never put forth.

One of Leonard's famous admonitions in his *10 Rules for Writing* is to cut away anything that sounds like writing, and surely this is an understandable pose for one who wants to be seen as an unpretentious natural, and not some egghead with a quiverful of literary techniques. So okay, I'll give him that. It is his work, after all, not mine. He knows what he's up to far better than a lowly academic.

But damn it, I just can't help myself. There's a hell of a lot of black-and-white imagery in *LaBrava*. And it sure as hell didn't get there by accident.

———————

James W. Hall is the author of seventeen novels, several collections of poetry, short stories, and essays, and the newly released Hit Lit, *an examination of the biggest best sellers of the twentieth century and a dozen things they have in common. Visit him online at www.jameswhall.com.*

Tapping the Source
by Kem Nunn (1984)

Surfer and novelist Kem Nunn (b. 1948) is credited with inventing the "surf noir" subgenre with his debut offering, Tapping the Source *(1984), a novel nominated in the American National Book Awards' best first fiction category. Nunn subsequently published a further four surf noir titles, the last of which was* Tijuana Straits *(2004), which won an L.A.* Times Book Prize *in the Mystery/Thriller category. He was the cocreator, with David Milch, of HBO's* John from Cincinnati, *a drama set against the backdrop of a Californian surfing community.*

From its earliest days, Southern California was a land of civic boosters who sold America a gorgeous, impossible dream.

With dollar signs in their eyes and subdivision plans in their fists, city fathers and developers hawked the region's glories: dry, healing air, fragrant orange groves, snowcapped mountains, year-round sunshine, and home ownership.

And from all over America they came, desperate to be reborn, to reinvent themselves, to find fame in Hollywood and frolic on the shores of the mighty Pacific where, as Joan Didion once said, we run out of continent.

Here on its golden beaches, the Southern California dream found its apotheosis in the swaying palms, bikini-clad girls, and majestic waves where bronzed surf gods hung ten and made it look so easy. After lolling on the white sands, you'd sip cocktails on the deck of your oceanfront home as the bloodred sun plunged into the waves.

Yes, it was a postcard-perfect paradise. And our Dream Factories spread the Surfin' U.S.A. lifestyle around the globe.

But if boosters exist to perpetuate the myth of endless summer, then thank goodness we have artists to question it, to pull back the veil and illuminate the shadows that the L.A. light casts into such stark relief.

And when it comes to surf noir, no one does it better than Kem Nunn.

Nunn's first book, *Tapping the Source*, was not only a magnificent crime novel, but a finalist for America's National Book Award in 1984. A meditation on lost innocence, *Tapping the Source* explores beach culture, the deceptively alluring face of evil, and a teenaged boy's quest for his missing sister. Nunn's genius was to set his literary noir novel in one of Southern California's most celebrated and hedonistic surf spots—Orange County's Huntington Beach—and then invert the paradise.

In Nunn's book, the stranger who comes to town is Ike Tucker, a naïve seventeen-year-old refugee from the high deserts of eastern California. He arrives in surf city looking for his older sister Ellen, who hitchhiked west two years ago and washed up here, though no one will talk about her except to discourage Ike with vague, ominous warnings. Like most seekers (and private eyes), Ike is a tarnished knight following a mirage that might not be grounded in reality. He never knew his father and his mother disappeared years ago, leaving the siblings stranded in a desert hellhole with a sexually predatory uncle and a religious zealot grandmother. When they were kids, enigmatic, sexy, troubled Ellen was Ike's sole friend and ally. If only he can find her, he can save them both and feel whole once more.

The Huntington Beach depicted in *Tapping the Source* is a sleepy rustic seaside town with a motley population of pensioners, surfers, druggies, bikers, runaways, and layabouts that no longer exists. Even as Nunn wrote his book, the greasy spoons, surf shops, and run-down motels that once lined Beach Boulevard were already being bulldozed as developers bought up the coastal land to build luxury waterfront resorts.

It's a story as old as California itself, one that has played out in beach towns from Santa Barbara all the way to San Diego as blue-collar residents, surf bums, and mom-and-pop shops get squeezed out by rising rents and redevelopment. In many ways, *Tapping the Source* is a coda to an entire postwar era when the laid-back Southern California beach lifestyle seemed not only within reach, but almost an inalienable right.

Yet there is no nostalgia in Nunn's writing, just a steely, hard-boiled sensibility and a stark acceptance of humanity's failings. And the most gorgeous writing about beaches and surfing that you'll ever read. Here's a taste:

> He took great pleasure in the mornings, in walking along the cliffs, close to the edge, the ocean smooth and glassy beneath, the air still and hot against his face and yet laced with the salty dampness of the sea.

At first Ike wipes out spectacularly trying to ride the waves, to the mocking amusement of the locals, a menacing bunch led by a charismatic blond surfer.

> Then one morning something happened that was different. Ike got into a wall of white water from a large outside wave. It grabbed his board, sent it skimming across the surface of the water. Ike got to his feet. He was carrying more speed than he was used to, but he found the speed actually made it easier to stand. The wall slowed slightly, began to reform. Ike leaned into the wave and the board swung easily beneath him. A wall of water rose ahead of him, its face glassy and smooth, streaked with white. He was angling across it . . . he was riding a wave. The wall rose rapidly, began to pitch out, his inside rail caught and over he went . . . he wanted to stop and shout, to raise his arms over his head and shake his fists. He knew now what the hoots and screams he had heard from the surfers beneath the pier were all about. He had gotten into a wave.

But there is a snake in this about-to-be-lost Paradise, and his name is Hound Adams, the good-looking blond surf god who rules the breaks with his cronies. After days spent lounging on the beach and in the water, Hound and his friends throw parties known for booze, drugs, and pretty, pliant girls.

At first Ike is a wistful outsider looking in. And shirking from it, too, because he's heard rumors about the homemade movies that Hound Adams likes to create at his drug-fueled parties. And he senses the surfer knows more about Ellen's disappearance than he lets on.

But the magnetic pull of Adams and his gang is as relentless as the tides. Ike tells himself that he's only infiltrating Hound's world to track down his missing sister. But soon he's seduced by the lifestyle, and agrees to a Faustian bargain of his own.

And with that, all pretense of looking for Ellen evaporates.

> Mornings were still spent with the dawn patrol, in the shadows of the old pier. Then it was home for breakfast and back into bed, only this time the bed was Michelle's. And then it was back to the shop or down to the beach, with a pocketful of Hound Adams's dope and an eye out for the girls, down in the hot sand and maybe a noseful of coke, because he had discovered where Hound Adams found the energy to party all night and surf all day.
>
> [. . .] After that night with the redhead, he had tried not to fuck them, just to recruit them for the parties, sad stupid little girls. And he had laughed at himself for ever thinking there was more to it, something magical, even, and he both wished back the magic and sneered at himself for ever having believed it there.

And with those words, Nunn pierces to the oily heart of darkness that lies beneath the placid beach town. In time, Ike's biker friend Preston will take him up the coast to a famed surf break near Santa Barbara (based on a real place) where they camp out and surf for several days in a pristine, prelapsarian coastal paradise. But even here there are shadows. The best surf spot in all California lies on private land owned by a wealthy recluse who has his own dark connection to Hound Adams. There are menacing security guards, pagan rituals, and debauchery that only great money and privacy can buy. As Ike's girlfriend Michelle is drawn increasingly into Hound Adams's dark orbit, Nunn heightens the stakes for a terrifying climax.

But what will haunt the reader is not the resolution of the mystery itself, but Nunn's achingly beautiful writing about the Southern California coast, one boy's quest for absolution, and the ragged, hard-won acceptance that some secrets refuse to give up their ghosts, no matter how hard we try. But hopefully we learn something along the way.

With *Tapping the Source*, Kem Nunn joins a hallowed group of classic L.A. crime writers who have understood the atavistic pull of the tides and explored the beach's metaphoric possibilities for almost eighty years. For Raymond Chandler, Ross Macdonald, Horace McCoy, Leigh Brackett, and Dorothy B. Hughes, the Southern California coast was far from glamorous. It was a lonely and desperate place where dreams came to die.

By the time Kem Nunn wrote *Tapping the Source,* the beach was already transforming into a fantasy playground for the wealthy and beautiful. But while earlier authors used our golden coast as a backdrop, Kem Nunn was the first to make it a living, breathing central character, the ultimate tanned, blond, and duplicitous femme fatale.

Because in Nunn's world, the Endless Summer doesn't seem so wonderful.

At times, it seems more like a curse.

Denise Hamilton is a Los Angeles native whose crime novels have been short-listed for the Edgar and the Creasey Dagger. She is also editor of the two-volume anthology Los Angeles Noir, *which won the Edgar Award. Visit her online at www.denisehamilton.com.*

Dirk Gently's Holistic Detective Agency by Douglas Adams (1987)

CHRISTOPHER BROOKMYRE

Douglas Adams (1952–2001) is best remembered for his five humorous sci-fi novels collectively known as "the increasingly improbable trilogy" The Hitchhiker's Guide to the Galaxy, which emerged from the BBC radio series of the same name, first broadcast in 1978. Adams also published a pair of detective novels featuring the idiosyncratic private eye Dirk Gently: Dirk Gently's Holistic Detective Agency *(1987) and its sequel,* The Long Dark Tea-Time of the Soul *(1988). Essentially a spoof on the PI subgenre, the first Dirk Gently novel was described by its author as "a kind of ghost-horror-detective-time-travel-romantic-comedy-epic, mainly concerned with mud, music and quantum mechanics."*

It's common enough to have finished reading a novel, particularly a crime novel, and then to thumb back through it, confirming a few details and checking for things that you missed. It is less common to finish a novel and then promptly return to page one in order to reread the thing again in its entirety. In a rarer subgenus still is the phenomenon of being rewarded for your return by the discovery of a kind of shadow book, a different novel specifically intended for those who have already passed this way once and are thus armed with the information required to appreciate the hidden treasures of the parallel book.

Anyone who has read (and inevitably reread) *Dirk Gently's Holistic Detective Agency* will know what I'm talking about. It is not merely a book so intricately plotted and so packed with moments of brilliance that it takes a second pass to appreciate them all: it is a book that reads completely differently the second time around, to the extent that there are jokes and observations clearly intended for the returning visitor. Given that the genre of detective fiction is largely about mystery and revelation, this is an audacious coup, which is not to say that it doesn't excel on that other level, too.

Indeed, the pleasure of any great crime novel lies in the way in which it takes a number of apparently disparate incidents, characters, and clues and asks the reader to ponder how they could possibly be connected. The more disparate, the more apparently random, the greater both the intrigue and the satisfaction as the detective somehow pulls the threads together. In *DGHDA*, it's fair to say that a new bar is set regarding the disparate and random quotients, such that only a detective who aspires to demonstrate "the fundamental inter-connectedness of all things" could possibly find the solution. The apparently motiveless murder of a software entrepreneur, a gravely worried academic with a live horse stuck in his upstairs bathroom, a guilt-ridden computer whizz kid whose new sofa is lodged on a staircase in genuine defiance of the laws of geometry: these would be enough for any mystery story to be getting on with. But add the suggestion that the academic might be several centuries old, that the whizz kid may have been the victim of ghostly possession, and then top it all off with a reference to someone reading "the second, and altogether stranger part" of Samuel Taylor Coleridge's "Kubla Khan"— i.e., the part of the unfinished poem that Coleridge never wrote—and you know you're in territory where Morse would be struggling.

In fact, it's always fun to imagine a couple of the typically hard-bitten and world-weary veteran detectives of conventional crime fiction turning up to the murder scene in Adams's novel, standing over the body of software entrepreneur Gordon Way where he lies slain by a shotgun blast at the rear of his Mercedes on the floor of a gas station forecourt.

"What you reckon, guv?"

"Well, it's obvious, innit. He's been done by an electric monk from another dimension. The monk's been possessed by the ghost of some geezer from a distant galaxy who's been dead for four billion years and is looking for a time machine so that he can go back and prevent the incident that caused life on our planet to begin evolving."

"Yeah, guv. Textbook."

The story had its origins in a *Doctor Who* serial, "Shada," written by Adams but never completed or broadcast due to a strike during the

1979–80 season. Adams reworked the idea but brought to it far more whimsy than the SF/horror hybrid that was called for in its first incarnation. That said, there are some genuinely chilling moments, mostly concerning the possession of spoiled publisher Michael Wenton-Weakes, and Adams's description of this character is one that has served as a warning to me down the years regarding what often lurks beneath the placid exteriors of a number of apparently harmless individuals. "He was one of those dangerous people who are soft, squidgy and cowlike provided they have what they want . . . You would have to push through a lot of squidgy bits in order to find a bit that didn't give when you pushed it. That was the bit that all the soft squidgy bits were there to protect."

However, the most important thing Adams brought to his reworking was its eponymous hero, the indisputable star of the show. Gently carves out his unique place in the detective canon thus: "The whole thing was so obvious that the only thing which prevented me from seeing the solution was the trifling fact that it was completely impossible. Sherlock Holmes observed that once you have eliminated the impossible, then whatever remains, however improbable, must be the answer. I, however, do not like to eliminate the impossible."

He is a magnificent creation: entertainingly infuriating, unflappable to the point of negligence, unfairly damaged yet boundlessly optimistic, and quite unlike any sleuth that has preceded or followed him. Adams was a notoriously reluctant writer, who was once literally shut in a hotel room by his editor in order to make him work, but when he writes about Dirk Gently, you can sense real joy in what he is about. Ideas flow, jokes sparkle, and all of the other characters suddenly become more interesting through sharing a scene with him.

This is a book I've come back to again and again over the years. I won't say that I discover something new every time, as I've read it too often for that. But like many brilliant crime novels, and like many a great comedy routine, it can be savored repeatedly for the genius of its construction and the panache of its execution.

If you've never picked it up and are now planning to do so, then let me just say that I am truly jealous of what you're about to read. Twice.

Christopher Brookmyre was born in Glasgow in 1968 and educated at the University of Glasgow. He worked as a subeditor in London and Edinburgh prior to the publication of his first novel, Quite Ugly One Morning, *which won the First Blood Award in 1996 for the best first crime novel of the year. Fourteen further novels have followed, garnering him two Sherlock Awards and the Bollinger Everyman Wodehouse Prize for Comic Writing in 2006. In 2005 he was named Glasgow University Young Alumnus of the Year and in 2007 he won the Glenfiddich Spirit of Scotland Award for writing. It's not all wine and roses, however, as he is a St. Mirren season ticket holder. Visit him online at www.brookmyre.co.uk.*

The Silence of the Lambs
by Thomas Harris (1988)

KATHY REICHS

Thomas Harris (b. 1940) is an American novelist and screenwriter who is destined to be remembered principally for two things: the refinement of the serial killer novel into a separate subgenre of mystery fiction with two novels, Red Dragon *(1981) and* The Silence of the Lambs *(1988), that are unlikely ever to be equaled; and making cannibalism seem like a sophisticated lifestyle choice for the discerning gourmand. Hannibal Lecter, the cannibalistic psychiatrist who gradually moved from the periphery to the heart of the four novels in which he has featured, arguably with diminishing returns, is one of the great monsters of popular fiction. Harris maintains a low media profile and is reputed to find the process of writing intensely difficult: he has published only five novels in thirty-seven years.*

"How do we begin to covet, Clarice?" We read something good and want to make it our own.

Writing a book is a purge. At the end you're empty, out of ideas, out of inspiration.

Reading a book is a binge. Characters crisscross your mind. You think about them, impressed by the cleverness of some and the stupidity of others. You want to warn of dangers and to point out clues. The experience may leave you trying to draw a border between fiction and reality.

In *The Silence of the Lambs,* Thomas Harris's characters remained in my thoughts long after I closed the cover. His story intrigued and disturbed me. Though years would pass before I'd begin my first novel, the book left impressions that influenced me as a writer.

Lambs opens by introducing Clarice Starling, protégée of Jack Crawford, head of the FBI's Behavioral Science unit. Starling has been chosen to help in the hunt for "Buffalo Bill," a murderer who starves, then skins, his female victims. Hoping for insight into Bill's psyche, Crawford sends Starling to interview Dr. Hannibal Lecter, a cannibalistic serial killer confined to prison. Lecter agrees to meet with Starling, but only if she will answer his questions about her past.

Published in 1988, *Lambs* was both a landmark and a benchmark.

The book was a landmark because Harris painted an honest picture of forensic science in all its tedious, exhausting, unglamorous reality, of professionals with specialized training working at their jobs. When I read *Lambs* I'd been working in forensic labs and at crime scenes for more years than I'll reveal. Harris's depiction of forensic methodology rang true.

There is Crawford, profiling psychopaths in the hope that his efforts will contribute to the apprehension of violent offenders. There is Starling, lifting prints and examining a dead body. There are the Smithsonian entomologists, Pilcher and Roden, identifying a moth pupa extracted from the throat of a corpse.

Harris once worked as a crime reporter. The experience shows in his detailed descriptions of FBI bureaucracy, of police procedure, of the challenges facing an FBI trainee. And Harris did his homework. Buffalo Bill is based on actual predators: Ed Gein paraded before mirrors in the skins of his victims; Gary Michael Heidnik held victims captive in his cellar; Ted Bundy lured victims by wearing a phony cast.

After Crawford, Starling, and Lecter hit the best-seller lists, forensic science became a popular topic, and a fascination with serial killers, largely dormant since Jack the Ripper, was reborn.

Lambs was also a landmark because Harris used a strong woman as the lead character at a time when few were found outside "cozy" or "whodunit" mysteries. Starling is the book's human anchor and the reader's point of entry into a twisted world of murder, insanity, and human depravity. Her character broke ground for future females in novels, women who are tough, smart, tenacious, and not particularly concerned with their hair.

Like forensic anthropologist Dr. Temperance Brennan, the principal character in my own books, Starling is a woman in a man's world. Her FBI training has provided her with G-man tools for professional effectiveness: mental and physical strength, alertness, knowledge of procedural technique. Starling works mainly alongside men, but Harris makes no suggestion that she must sublimate the feminine to succeed.

Starling's female orientation at times helps her to note bits of information that other agents have not. Her examination of one of Buffalo Bill's bloated victims reveals glittery polish on the nails and a bleached upper lip, details that male agents had missed.

When Crawford tells Starling that Lecter triggered a fellow prisoner's suicide, presumably because that prisoner assaulted Starling, she says, "I don't know how to feel about it." Crawford responds, "You don't have to feel any particular way about it." For Crawford, answers lie in the facts of Hannibal's statements. Starling searches for additional meaning in feelings. Following feelings and intuition ultimately leads her to Buffalo Bill.

In blending the masculine and feminine, Harris created a character that appeals to both male and female readers. Women can empathize with Starling's struggle in the man's world of the FBI, where she works alongside male agents as a colleague and not as a sex object. Men can empathize with Starling's methodically professional approach to finding Buffalo Bill, and with her courageous confrontation of him.

By the book's end, Starling has saved a girl, destroyed a villain, and graduated with honors. She has done so by combining her traditionally male-identified FBI skills with her feminine instincts, though I did resolve that my own protagonist would be endowed with a greater sense of humor.

The Silence of the Lambs was a benchmark in the old-fashioned way, with strong characters, an interesting setting, and a gripping plot. Harris's exploration of the workings of the human mind is perceptive and penetrating. His leading players are finely drawn, fascinating, flawed people. The reader is forced to look at things from their perspectives, even though the view is often unsettling.

In their first interview, Lecter regards Starling with her expensive bag and cheap shoes, her concealed West Virginia accent, and her determination to appear confident. Lecter is drawn to her incongruities. Even as she strives to erase the markers of her humble origins, she is proud of her honest, hardworking family. Flash recollections of them, such as her mother washing blood from her father's hat, feed her determination throughout the novel.

Starling's background gives rise to her insecurities. Though smart, educated, and driven, she is haunted by childhood memories of her helplessness to stop the slaughter of lambs on her uncle's farm. Used to keeping people at arm's length, and struggling privately with her doubts, she begins to learn that distance is limiting and isolation does little to bring comfort or alleviate pain.

Starling's adversary, Dr. Hannibal Lecter, is drawn with equal complexity. Lecter is a paradox—a suave, cultured gentleman, but also an unspeakable fiend of depraved self-absorption. He is mannered and monstrous, elegant and evil.

Trained in psychiatry, Lecter has uncanny insight into human nature. He taunts Starling: "Back in your room you have a string of gold add-a-beads and you feel an ugly little thump when you look at how tacky they are now." Yet Lecter is himself devoid of humanity: "I collect church collapses, recreationally. Did you see the recent one in Sicily? Marvelous! The façade fell on sixty-five grandmothers at a special Mass."

First introduced as the antagonist in *Red Dragon* (1981), in *Lambs* Lecter ricochets between protagonist and antagonist. He helps Clarice catch a serial killer, but he also savages innocents in his own escape. Harris's skill is such that at times he actually has us rooting for Lecter, and makes us feel reluctantly pleased by his escape, though we shiver at the thought that there may be a Hannibal Lecter out there somewhere.

Harris is also master of the scene, of "show, don't tell." At a victim's home, Starling observes "everywhere boxes stacked waist-high filling the rooms, passageways among them, cardboard cartons filled with lampshades and canning lids, picnic hampers, back numbers of the *Reader's Digest* and *National Geographic,* thick old tennis rackets, bed linens, a case of dartboards, fiber car-seat covers in a fifties plaid with the intense smell of mouse pee." The owner explains that they are moving, but Starling notes, "The stuff near the windows was bleached by the sun, the boxes stacked for years bellied with age." Though the word is never used, the reader smells and sees the neurosis known as hoarding.

In a book that explores psychological darkness, Harris emphasizes the point by literally placing the reader underground. Starling descends into Lecter's subterranean prison, footsteps echoing past shadowy occupants. Jame Gumb transforms into Buffalo Bill in his basement of horrors, his next victim crying out from the bottom of a well. The penultimate battle scene has Starling flailing blind in the pitch-black.

These physical settings blend with the disturbing psychological portraits drawn by Harris. In 1989, Tempe Brennan didn't exist, though I knew the chill brought on by contact with the violently killed through my forensic work. My experience didn't quite prepare me for the horror of Hannibal the Cannibal. As he drawls, "A census taker tried to quantify me once. I ate his liver with some fava beans and a big Amarone," the reader is slapped with the presence of true evil. Though Starling is physically secure from Lecter, she is not safe. His is a psychic landscape, and in every way Starling is within Lecter's reach. He studies her as a lion studies the gazelle at the watering hole. He could maul her, play with his victim between large psychoanalytic paws, or he could devour her.

The difference between a mystery and a thriller is the element of peril. In *Lambs*, Harris breeds a potent brand of terror. Like the gothic tales of Edgar Allan Poe, the locus of fear is turned inward to that which haunts us. There is no chance of escape, because the horror travels with us, the cries of the lambs burned in our memories. The hunt is for a serial killer, but the larger quest is to silence our inner demons.

Most of all, Harris is a master of plot, and he spins a spellbinding story. A psychopath is kidnapping and murdering young women. The FBI sends a young female agent to interview an imprisoned serial killer. She thinks it's to gather information, but we know it's to gain insight into their quarry. The prisoner, a brilliant and murderous cannibal, will help only if the agent shares intimate details about her own life. She agrees. The twisted relationship between interviewer and interviewee forces the agent to consider her own psychological demons.

That's the surface story. But the real theme is mutual need.

Lecter is driven by his need for freedom. He glimpses an opportunity in Starling, the green FBI trainee, and pursues his goal with cold brutality.

Starling is driven by her need for distinction. Motivated by the memories of her past, she strives to honor her father. Running from her past, she strives to bring honor to herself.

Lecter dangles the hook, a taste of being a real agent. Starling bites. Through iron bars, the mad doctor and the trainee become analyst and patient, teacher and pupil, father and daughter, while always remaining cat and mouse. Their respective quests bind them, for neither can succeed without using the other.

In the end, the characters slake their thirst. The killer is caught, the madman escapes, the trainee is promoted, the story closes. For them, the lambs fall silent. But Harris's masterful characterization, chillingly descriptive prose, and captivating storytelling leave the reader thirsting for more.

For me, Harris's detailed character portrayals and tense plot development were benchmarks of thriller writing, and his Clarice Starling was a landmark example of a new breed of female protagonist. His writing greatly influenced mine.

———————

Kathy Reichs is a professor of anthropology at the University of North Carolina. As a forensic anthropologist, she testified at the UN's International Criminal Tribunal for Rwanda. Her first novel to feature the series heroine Temperance "Tempe" Brennan, also a forensic anthropologist, was Déjà Dead *(1997), which won the 1997 Arthur Ellis Award for Best First Novel. She has subsequently published seventeen novels featuring Tempe Brennan, the most recent being* Bones Are Forever *(2012). Reichs produces a TV series called* Bones, *which is loosely based on Dr. Temperance Brennan, a forensic anthropologist with a sideline in writing novels about a fictional character called Kathy Reichs. Visit her online at www.kathyreichs.com.*

Toxic Shock (aka *Blood Shot*) by Sara Paretsky (1988)

N. J. COOPER

Sara Paretsky (b. 1947) is a pioneering figure in modern mystery fiction. She is responsible for taking the traditional male archetype of the hard-boiled novel and transforming and reimagining it to create one of the earliest, and most iconic, of female investigators, V. I. Warshawski, the heroine of most of Paretsky's books. Her novels combine thriller conventions with astute social commentary, and this year marks the thirtieth anniversary of Warshawski's first appearance in print.

Rage has always driven crime fiction. One of the reasons why women like the genre so much is that for generations we have had so few outlets for fury, and crime fiction offers a splendid one. Traditionally we were allowed to be ill or unhappy, but not angry. Any feelings of violence had to be swallowed or turned against ourselves. We were supposed to be gentle, kind, forgiving, and nurturing, however we actually felt. And we, like Eve, were told over and over again that it was all our fault. Whatever happened, went wrong, or didn't happen was down to women. When I was working in publishing I had a true-crime author who thought it acceptable to write in his introduction that "All murder is women's fault; even little girls can flirt." He was both puzzled and hurt when I told him why the comment had to go.

Educated at a convent school, I had had all this nonsense fed to me so effectively that I barely even knew how angry I was until I discovered Sara Paretsky's work. Reading it, I felt myself not only understood but also vindicated in all kinds of ways. I was so excited by her novels that I read three back to back during one night, never even tempted to sleep. I have not had such a reaction to any other fiction before or since. The three novels were *Killing Orders*, *Bitter Medicine*, and *Toxic Shock*, all led by Paretsky's PI, Victoria Iphigenia Warshawski, who chooses to be known as V.I.

Warshawski rejects almost all personal claims. She cannot bear the idea that families assume the right to their daughters' domestic labor, or that society dares to tell women whom they may sleep with or how they should deal with unwanted pregnancy. She refuses to be tied down by obligations of any kind. She is the embodiment of pure rage. If she's pissed off, she says so, however benevolent the pisser-off may be. If she's threatened, she takes action to defend herself. If she's assaulted physically, she hits back physically. In fact, to be wholly rational about all this, I do not suppose that any human being, male or female, however fit and well trained, could survive everything V.I. suffers, from endless wallops on the head to burnings, drownings, and innumerable fights. But that doesn't matter. What matters is that V.I. Warshawski takes no crap from anyone. I loved her—and still love her—for that.

She has none of the traditional female virtues: she makes love where she wants and with whom she wants and then waves her lovers goodbye. Although she can cook, she only occasionally does so. She leaves her clothes where they fall, rarely cleans her apartment or does the washing-up, and never bothers to moderate her language. Although a lot of the rage is her own, much is also felt on behalf of other people, the clients for whom she goes to extraordinary lengths.

In *Toxic Shock,* the client is Caroline Djiak, eleven years Warshawski's junior, whom she babysat in the old days and who endlessly infuriates her. Caroline wants V.I. to find out who her father was, even though her dying single mother has forbidden any such search. V.I.'s inquiries lead her to a quite different mystery, where she must investigate industrial pollution, corporate fraud, and manipulation of vulnerable workers, but the most involving elements are those that deal with V.I.'s discoveries of the cruelty that was visited on Caroline's mother.

Brought up in an emotionally abusive but physically pristine household, Louisa Djiak and her elder sister were required to scrub the undersides of toilets and sinks among their other pointless household duties, to obey their violent father without question, and to entertain their pedophile uncle. He impregnated Louisa when she was fifteen. Her virtuous parents threw her out of the house to protect the family's honor and to disguise "her shame." They are absolutely certain that it was Louisa's fault her uncle raped and impregnated her, and believe their repudiation of her and their grandchild in some way repairs their moral status, which, in their eyes, she has chosen to damage.

This encapsulates much that has enraged women crime writers for generations, including the appalling doublethink around women and sex: if you won't have sex, you are frigid and mad; if you do, and take pleasure in it, you're a whore. And in many cultures, if you are the victim of rape, as Louisa was, you are to blame. In a more lighthearted vein, Joan Smith dealt with this doublethink in her first crime novel, *A Masculine Ending* (1987). Here academic Loretta Lawson is in Paris for a meeting of a feminist editorial collective and is eating alone in a restaurant. A stranger tries to pick her up. When she declines his proposition, he calls her a whore.

Attitudes to female celibacy also enraged Dorothy L. Sayers, who was writing half a century before Paretsky and Smith. Sayers's *Gaudy Night* (1935) is unfashionable now, and much criticized for pitting the well-off dons of a fictional Shrewsbury College in Oxford against their poorly paid domestic servants as suspects in a nasty case of anonymous abuse, which causes an undergraduate to attempt suicide.

Within the novel it is generally assumed that the author of the poison-pen letters and some accompanying crude, sexually explicit drawings must be one of the academics, driven mad by frustration. Sayers goes to considerable lengths to set up this suspicion, even in the mind of her sleuth, mystery writer Harriet Vane.

Harriet, who is adored and pursued by the absurdly rich and absurdly aristocratic Lord Peter Wimsey, shows him how disturbing she finds her suspicions of the dons. Peter sums up her fears, saying, "Isn't it a fact that, having more or less made up your mind to a spot of celibacy you are eagerly peopling the cloister with bogies? . . . What are you afraid of? The two great dangers of the celibate life are a forced choice and a vacant mind. Energies bombinating in a vacuum breed chimaeras. But *you* are in no danger. If you want to set up your everlasting rest, you are far more likely to find it in the life of the mind than the life of the heart." It is not only Lord Peter's antecedents and enormous wealth that make him a figure of fantasy.

We have all come a long way from Sayers—her fears, her rages, and her ideal of the perfect man—but crime fiction is still being used to explore the doublethink around women and sex, along with the reasons why some men are driven to kill or otherwise punish women they find sexually arousing.

Some women writers of serial killer novels justify their voyeuristic descriptions of violence against women by saying that it is what their female readers want. Others choose to write about murder in a very different style and explore the rage of women who are not—and will not allow themselves to become—victims. For me no one has expressed that rage as thrillingly as Sara Paretsky.

N. J. Cooper worked in publishing before swapping sides to write full-time. Her current series of crime novels features forensic psychologist Dr. Karen Taylor and is set mainly on the Isle of Wight, where she used to holiday as a child. As the sunniest place in the British Isles it is the ideal setting for the darkness and miseries of serious crime. The first four novels in the series are No Escape, Lifeblood, Face of the Devil, *and* Vengeance in Mind, *published in the summer of 2012. Visit her online at www.natashacooper.co.uk.*

Possession
by A. S. Byatt (1990)

ERIN HART

Dame Antonia Susan Duffy (b. 1936), better known as the critically ac-claimed novelist and poet A. S. Byatt, is a native of Sheffield, England. Since her first novel, The Shadow of the Sun *(1964), she has published almost thirty books as writer or editor, including numerous works of fiction and studies of Iris Murdoch, George Eliot, William Wordsworth, and Samuel Taylor Coleridge. She reputedly fell out with her sister, the novelist Margaret Drabble, over a depiction of their mother in one of Drabble's books, as well as Drabble's use of a family tea set as a plot point.*

My love affair with A. S. Byatt's *Possession* started with the title. Byatt herself has said that the title came to her as she caught a glimpse of the famous Coleridge scholar Kathleen Coburn at the British Library. As she watched Coburn circling the card catalog, Byatt began to ponder the relationship between scholar and subject, wondering, Does he possess her, or does she possess him? And that question got her thinking about a novel that conjured the ghostly connections between living and dead minds. One of the beauties of the word "possession" is that it's fraught with meaning—connotations demonic, economic, and sexual that perfectly suit the era in which some of the story is set. The Spiritualism craze was going full-force in the mid-nineteenth century; it was also an era in which women were not independent individuals but mere chattels, possessions belonging to their fathers or husbands. And, of course, the sexual meaning of the word "possession" requires no vulgar explanation. Each of these various, delicious meanings comes to bear as the novel unfolds.

For some reason, I've long harbored a secret penchant for the Victo-rian era; maybe it was cutting my teeth on Dickens, or perhaps it's the richness of the incongruities and contradictions of that period, a prime example being the simultaneous abhorrence of, and fascination with, sex. I'm also interested in the Victorian fascination with fairy tales and folklore, reframing them as one way to contain the primal urges that they fought against within themselves.

Possession certainly contains elements of literary mystery, but does it qualify as a real crime novel? I would argue that it does.

Part of the explanation comes straight from A. S. Byatt herself. As she began writing *Possession,* she says that she thought about the pleasure principle in art: that all art exists not for political indoctrination or moral instruction, but primarily for giving pleasure. Almost more than any other genre, crime novels embody the pleasure principle. Their whole purpose in the great scheme of the universe is to provide readers with page-turning satisfaction.

It's probably no accident that Byatt took some of her inspiration from Umberto Eco, a fellow academic who began writing a murder mystery called *The Name of the Rose* because, as he himself admitted, "I wanted to murder a monk." She also returned to her own reading pleasures as an adolescent, gobbling up Margery Allingham detective stories and Georgette Heyer romances, trying to understand what those forms have in common: a plot, a story, and yes, the pleasure of narrative discovery. With *Possession,* she began writing a story that managed to combine literature high and low, and actually parodied many of the world's most enjoyable literary forms: detective story, epistolary novel, roman à clef, gothic potboiler, romance, fairy tale, and biography.

When I try to express to people what I love about this book, I always explain that it has a bit of everything. The story features two couples, the first being scholars Roland Michell and Maud Bailey, who meet in the present day. While doing research in the London Library, Roland has discovered a slip of paper stuck inside a book that hints at a previously undiscovered acquaintance between Randolph Henry Ash, a supposedly happily married literary lion of the 1850s, and one of his lesser-known contemporaries, the protofeminist (and possibly lesbian) poet Christabel LaMotte. Roland meets up with Maud, an expert on LaMotte, and together they try to discover whether there was a secret relationship between the two poets.

In the course of their amateur investigation, Roland and Maud visit the crumbling LaMotte family demesne, and stop at the same beaches and waterfalls their subjects had visited in secret 150 years before. And, of course, a parallel relationship springs up between the two literary detectives as they forage in the past, looking for evidence of forbidden passion. Hints and clues and hidden meanings abound. There are mementos of illicit meetings, secret letters, and love that is both repressed and requited. So, in addition to rooting around in dusty, mold-ridden libraries (and there is plenty of that, to be sure!), the characters also get to tear around the countryside on mysterious adventures, looking for elusive clues, and end up wielding shovels in a graveyard.

The subplot centers on a wrestling match over who will find Ash's papers (hidden by his wife after the poet's death), and that's where extra layers of intrigue, skullduggery, and even a little grave robbing come in. By incorporating secondary characters Fergus Wolff and Mortimer Cropper, Roland's archrivals for academic glory, Byatt uses her own background as a scholar to celebrate and skewer the dog-eat-dog nature of academia. Here's where she's in roman à clef territory, and I'm not sure anyone has ever approached that task more gleefully.

Some people skip over the poetry contained in *Possession* and read strictly for plot, but I'm here to tell you that doing so is a grave mistake. After deciding that she was not up to the task of writing poems to include in the text, Byatt had almost decided to slip in some early poems by Ezra Pound because they actually sounded an awful lot like Browning, and would therefore fit the period style of her fictional characters. But on the advice of poet D. J. Enright, who said, "Nonsense—write your own," Byatt forged ahead and composed every single Victorian-flavored poem contained in the story. Adding to the intrigue is that Byatt claims to have no memory of writing the poems: she says they seemed to flow from her pen almost as if she were . . . possessed. For any avid solver of puzzles, these poems are far more than just stylistically important to the shape and texture of the novel. The great joy is that they also contain essential clues to the mystery. They're part of what makes *Possession* one of those books that you can read and reread many times, discovering something new with each effort.

Although born and raised in the United States, Erin Hart uses Ireland as the setting for her series of mystery novels featuring pathologist Nora Gavin and archaeologist Cormac Maguire. That choice was inspired by a lifelong fascination with Ireland's history and culture, and by the sad, true tale of a beautiful red-haired girl whose perfectly preserved head was discovered after being hidden for centuries in a desolate Irish bog. Erin and her husband, Irish button accordion master Paddy O'Brien, live in Minnesota, and travel frequently to Ireland. Erin's latest novel is The Book of Killowen. *Visit her online at www.erinhart.com.*

Postmortem
by Patricia Cornwell (1990)

KATHRYN FOX

Patricia Cornwell (b. 1956) was born in Miami, Florida, but started her career as a reporter for The Charlotte Observer *in North Carolina. Specializing in crime reporting, she eventually took a job as a technical writer and, later, a computer analyst with the Office of the Chief Medical Examiner of Virginia, which provided the basis for her most enduring character, the medical examiner Dr. Kay Scarpetta.* Postmortem, *the first in the Scarpetta series, swept the mystery awards in the year following its publication. It is one of the most important early contributions—if not the* most important contribution—*to what is now an established subgenre in mystery fiction: mysteries in which the investigation of a murder is primarily conducted not through the questioning of the living, but by the examination of the dead.*

Great books seem to have a number of things in common. They have to be emotionally charged, informative, and thought-provoking enough to make a profound impact on the reader. Well-developed, multilayered, engaging characters, and a compelling story, are also essential.

More importantly, great books are timely—in the context of the world at large, and in the place we are in our lives when we first open the cover. As with the character arc in a story, I hope to be irrevocably changed by the reading experience.

It is hardly surprising that *To Kill a Mockingbird* and *In Cold Blood* are particular standouts from high school days, but one book that changed my life is undoubtedly Patricia Cornwell's *Postmortem*. First published in 1990, Cornwell's fiction debut was an international best seller that received universal critical acclaim reflected in the host of awards it received, including the Edgar, the John Creasey Dagger, the Anthony and

Macavity Awards, and the French Prix du Roman D'Aventures. With a heavy emphasis on forensic science, it presaged the popularity of what would become a forensic revolution in popular culture.

At the time that *Postmortem* was released, male authors still dominated the crime and thriller lists, and their protagonists were almost all men. Women in crime novels routinely appeared as supporting characters: wives, secretaries, vamps, and victims. *Postmortem* introduces Dr. Kay Scarpetta, arguably the definitive fictional pathologist. Seventeen books later, the Scarpetta series remains one of the most successful in publishing history.

We first meet the chief medical examiner of Richmond, Virginia, on a bleak Richmond night, when her tormented sleep is broken by a police call at 2:33 a.m. On this night, a fourth woman has been brutally raped and murdered by a serial killer. Outside the woman's home, Scarpetta runs the gauntlet of media hounds. Inside, she searches for clues that will steer the investigation in the critical first few hours.

The crime has taken place off the page, ensuring that we are not exposed to gratuitous violence. Through Scarpetta's eyes, we begin to learn about the life and death of the victim, Lori Petersen. As she walks through the modest house, noticing personal details such as the medical journals, violin, and music stand, Lori Petersen becomes a character in her own right. We *see* Lori's life, and Scarpetta accords her the same respect that she would a living patient. Aware that every aspect of Lori's life will be scrutinized by the media, lawyers, and police, Kay Scarpetta is the ultimate victim advocate. Emotion does not cloud her observations, which makes what we learn about murder so much more disturbing. This victim is, in every sense of the word, innocent.

Cornwell cleverly chose to write *Postmortem* in the first-person voice. This is challenging for any author because it restricts how much information can be imparted to the reader. We see and hear what Scarpetta is privy to, and nothing more. On the other hand, first person is the most intimate point of view. It is what helps us understand Scarpetta's motivations, reactions, and challenges.

Evidence suggests the killer entered the house through an unlocked bathroom window. This simple oversight meant the difference between a fulfilling life and an agonizing death. Lori Petersen could have been any one of us, or someone we love. As much as we would like to do so, we cannot detach ourselves from the scene.

For me, the book's introduction is exceptionally chilling. Lori Petersen had alarming similarities to my own life. The same medical journals could be found inside my home, along with a music stand and an instrument. The only difference is that I own a harp, not a violin.

At this point, I had to stop reading and check all the locks in my house. From what reviewers and readers have described, I wasn't the only one. The visceral response Cornwell evokes is powerful in establishing allegiance to Kay Scarpetta.

Those involved in the investigation would sleep easier if Lori Petersen were, in some way, to blame for her own demise. It is here that Sergeant Pete Marino is introduced. There is obvious animosity and a degree of distrust between Scarpetta and the man charged with heading the investigation into the murders. The sergeant immediately focuses on Lori's husband as the most likely suspect, in spite of Scarpetta's reservations.

This is the beginning of a complicated relationship that develops throughout the series. As the chief medical officer, Scarpetta has to work with Marino. In her own words, he was "exactly the sort of detective I avoided when given a choice . . . He was pushing fifty, with a face life had chewed on, and long wisps of graying hair parted low on one side and combed over his balding pate. At least six feet tall, he was bay-windowed from decades of bourbon and beer."

In contrast to Scarpetta's organized, controlled approach to work, Marino is tactless, vulgar, obnoxious, and slovenly. He resents people who are educated, and concludes that Lori Petersen's husband is perverted for writing a dissertation on Tennessee Williams with themes that include sex, violence, and homosexuality. Scarpetta fears the detective's myopia will compromise the investigation.

In a meeting with FBI profiler Benton Wesley, she contemplates Marino's working-class background, and is anything but sympathetic. "The guy's only advantage in life is he's big and white, so he makes himself bigger and whiter by carrying a gun and a badge." The tension between Scarpetta and Marino heightens the drama, but the detective proves he is streetwise and far more competent than the image he projects.

Scarpetta functions in a male-dominated field of medicine, having never experienced the support of female peers. Of four women in her year at medical school, one eventually quit, and another suffered what we are told was a complete nervous breakdown. Now she is embroiled in the testosterone-fueled world of police, lawyers, and politicians. Excluded from the camaraderie and nexus of those with influence, she is professionally vulnerable.

This is a recurring theme for Scarpetta throughout the series. Early in *Postmortem* she reveals, "Isolation is the cruelest of punishments, and it had never occurred to me that I was something less than human because I wasn't a man . . . Survival was my only hope, success my only revenge." We suspect her commitment to work led to the demise of her marriage, and is the reason why she has no children.

One of the most appealing characteristics of Scarpetta is that she is clearly ambitious without signs of ruthlessness. She maintains her humanity and dignity despite being an outsider in her own domain.

She is a true crusader for justice.

In her personal life, Scarpetta struggles with family relationships. In *Postmortem,* her ten-year-old niece, Lucy, is visiting. The only child of Kay's sister, Lucy has suffered a life of rejection and abandonment. Her father died when she was two. Now her self-absorbed mother is marrying again, leaving Scarpetta to break the news to the child. Lucy may have a genius IQ, but she lacks the emotional maturity to cope. Scarpetta struggles with Lucy's erratic behavior and unconditional love.

Over the course of the series, Lucy grows into a woman, becomes an FBI agent, and then a millionaire by the age of twenty-five with a penchant for computers, helicopters, fast cars, and motorcycles. She also has a number of long-term relationships, one with a sociopath that affects those close to her for years. Scarpetta, meanwhile, experiences love and loss throughout the series, but the focus on her work and scientific skills remains. It is her meticulous attention to detail that solves the case.

It's difficult to believe that more than twenty years have passed since Scarpetta first placed a diskette into a computer database and discussed suspects in terms of their blood group as opposed to DNA profile. When Cornwell's debut was written, DNA had been used in only a handful of criminal cases. At the same time, a technological revolution was taking place that would dramatically change policing and criminal trials. Over the next few years crime scene units were developed and specialties like forensic and legal medicine became more recognized.

When I first read *Postmortem,* I had just taken postgraduate medical exams and attained a Fellowship with the Royal Australian College of General Practitioners. I was also attending courses in forensic medicine in order to examine and treat victims of sexual assault. *Postmortem* was the first time that I found a strong female protagonist who never lost sight of the victim. The emphasis on forensic science was compelling, but without a good plot it would have resembled a lecture. The story was well written, suspenseful, and cost me a night's sleep—the ultimate compliment from a sleep-deprived physician!

I had wanted to write a crime novel since high school but was unsure if anyone would want to read a realistic, fictional crime story. *Postmortem* inspired me to write what I was passionate about, and that happened to be forensic medicine and the ripple effect of crime.

Patricia Cornwell's success opened up publishing opportunities for writers like me, and the genre has been rewarded with authors like Kathy Reichs, Linda Fairstein, Jeffery Deaver, and Tess Gerritsen, who continue to bring their unique talents, insights, and experiences to their work. The literary world is richer for it.

Australian novelist Kathryn Fox is a medical practitioner with a specialty in forensic medicine. Her debut novel, Malicious Intent, *was published in 2005, featuring her series heroine, Dr. Anya Crichton. Subsequent novels include* Without Consent *(2006),* Blood Born *(2009), and* Death Mask *(2010). Kathryn has recently set up the "Read For Life" project, which aims to promote literacy by sending children's books to remote communities. Along with Kathy Reichs, Linda Fairstein, and Robin Burcell, she campaigns against domestic violence toward women. Visit her online at www.kathrynfox.com.*

I Was Dora Suarez
by Derek Raymond (1990)

IAN RANKIN

Derek Raymond (1931–1994) was the pen name of the English crime writer Robert Cook, the son of a wealthy textile magnate. Following a period of compulsory National Service, he drifted through Europe and the United States, rejecting his privileged upbringing in favor of an ongoing exploration of the possibilities offered by downward mobility. His lifestyle, which included flirtations with criminality, gave him firsthand experience of the low-life milieu about which he eventually chose to write, and provided the basis for the novel sequence on which much of his reputation still rests: the "Factory" books, regarded by many as the cornerstone of the British noir tradition.

If even half the stories are true . . .

I don't mean the stories he wrote; I mean the life.

To start with, he wasn't even Derek Raymond. He was born Robert Cook, the son of a wealthy businessman. Dropped out of Eton and did his National Service, then sloped off to Paris, mixing with the likes of Burroughs and Ginsberg. Moved to Manhattan and married an heiress. That didn't last, so it was back to Europe and smuggling art, apparently. Even a bit of chokey in Spain; then London, where he became Robin Cook and wrote *The Crust on Its Uppers*. This was the early 1960s and his street smarts went down well. Married again and enjoyed some Soho interludes (vice and gambling, since you ask). Then Italy for a time, before returning to London and yet another marriage, with some taxi driving thrown in. He tried France after that, working on vineyards and as a roofer. London again and wife number four, followed by divorce number four. He went back to the taxis, took on the name Derek Raymond (with a nod to Soho's Raymond Revuebar?), and tried his hand at an-

375

other novel. This was *He Died With His Eyes Open* (1984), the first of the "Factory" series featuring an unnamed London-based detective sergeant as the hero. It went down well in France, where, along with its successor (*The Devil's Home on Leave*), it was turned into a film. Nineteen-eighty-six saw *How the Dead Live* and in 1990 came *I Was Dora Suarez,* the book that, more than any other, blew the bloody doors off. Did Raymond's publisher really throw up after reading the manuscript? It's certainly a visceral and gut-churning piece of prose, one of those stories that never quite leave you in peace once you've finished—if you can finish.

Its author's next marriage ended and he produced the fifth and final "Factory" novel, *Dead Man Upright,* in 1993. A year later he was dead himself at the age of sixty-three.

I'm reminded of the title of a book by Terence Blacker, *You Cannot Live As I Have Lived and Not End Up Like This.* Blacker was writing about another notorious literary figure, William Donaldson. Derek Raymond certainly lived a life worthy of a darkly picaresque novel in its own right. I remember the first time I met him. It was at a party at Maxim Jakubowski's Murder One bookshop on Charing Cross Road. The usual suspects were there: Mike Ripley, Mark Timlin, probably Denise Danks. I don't remember Michael Dibdin and Philip Kerr, though they were part of the gang we all thought of as "Fresh Blood." I was living in France at the time and had seen Raymond (or "Cookie Boy" as Timlin called him) on late-night TV, wearing his trademark beret and discussing anything and everything in fluent French.

In the flesh, he was tall, stick-thin, and had a wineglass welded to one hand. Yes, he wore the beret, and his eyes managed to be milky yet piercing at the same time—reminded me of Keith Richards, actually—eyes that had seen things you hadn't and never would.

Charming, too, though. Signed a book to me with the words "Best of luck" and "love." That book was *Dora Suarez,* a novel the *Times* had already described as having "a metaphysical intensity that recalls the Jacobeans more than any of Raymond's contemporaries. I cannot think of another writer in this field so obsessed with the skull beneath the skin."

A previous "Factory" novel had been reviewed in another paper as "a study in absolute, awful evil," so you get the drift—we are a long way from Poirot and *Dixon of Dock Green*. Raymond's prose is clipped, mordant, angular. His style reminds me of Joseph Conrad, a writer whose second language was English. But this angularity suits the stories, which are full of dread, dislocation, and atomization. The unnamed Detective Sergeant who leads us through these horrors works for the Unexplained Deaths department, based at a cop shop in Poland Street W1, known to everyone as "the Factory." He tells us that he likes his job because "I can get on with it, as a rule, almost entirely on my own, without a load of keen idiots tripping all over my feet." So he works almost as an American-style private eye—even carrying a gun—but with the resources of the police at his disposal should he need them. He operates in a world untroubled by political correctness or form filling. Suspects are leaned on, rules bent and broken.

In *Dora Suarez,* Raymond adds the internal workings of a twisted masochist and hired killer, plus a queasy contemporary version of the Hellfire Club. Then there is the figure of Dora herself, dead at the novel's opening, revealing herself to us slowly and painfully through her diary. This short yet structured novel is English crime fiction's equivalent to Munch's *The Scream*—an eloquent nightmare from which the reader can never completely escape.

Why isn't Raymond better known and more widely read? He became an icon for fans of the *polar* (detective novel) in France, and I've heard writers in the United States and U.K. rave about him. Perhaps his vision was too bleak for the world at large, or perhaps his version of the crime story veered too wildly from the accepted and acceptable norm in the U.K. There are, after all, precious few red herrings, suspects, and twists. Instead, Raymond charts a linear course toward judgment and retribution, while the detective sergeant's soul becomes ever more scarred.

Back in 1997, the *Waterstone's Guide to Crime Fiction* put it well when it said that Derek Raymond was "a disturbing talent" who "deserves to be read by those of a strong disposition and a love of sincerity and savagery." Those milky, piercing eyes had the power of X-ray. They saw horror lurking just below the surface of everyday existence. These books are novels, but also reports from a front line of casual cruelty in a world lacking empathy.

———

Ian Rankin lives in Edinburgh, and is best known for his series featuring DI John Rebus. He has lived in London and France as well as Scotland, and like Derek Raymond once worked on a vineyard. Unlike Derek Raymond, he's only been married once. Visit him online at www.ianrankin.net.

A Dance at the Slaughterhouse
by Lawrence Block (1991)

ALISON GAYLIN

Best known for his Matt Scudder and Bernie Rhodenbarr novels, Lawrence Block (b. 1938) has published more than sixty novels and 100 short stories. In addition, he has written five books for writers, the most recent being The Liar's Bible *(2011). First published in the 1950s under a pseudonym while writing in the paperback porn genre, Block's debut under his own name arrived in 1957 with the short story "You Can't Lose." He has been the recipient of multiple prizes for his novels and short stories, including the Mystery Writers of America's Grand Master Award in 1994 and a Lifetime Achievement award from the Private Eye Writers of America in 2002.*

"I couldn't think how I knew him."
—Matt Scudder, *A Dance at the Slaughterhouse*

A middle-aged man and a teenaged boy watch a boxing match together. They could be father and son, though they don't look very much alike. At one point, the man ruffles the boy's hair—a simple, affectionate gesture. But it's one that sticks in the mind of another spectator, private detective Matt Scudder. He's seen that gesture before, but where?

We've all had experiences like this, those fleeting moments of déjà vu. But rarely do they take us to the obsidian-dark terrain traveled in Lawrence Block's unforgettable, Edgar Award–winning novel. To give you an idea of how not-for-the-faint-of-heart *A Dance at the Slaughterhouse* is: the gesture Scudder recognizes turns out to be one that he'd seen, months earlier, as part of an investigation he'd done for a friend.

He'd seen it in a snuff film.

Talk about a challenge for a writer. Snuff films: the stuff of bad

B-movies and urban legends. In less skillful hands than Block's, such a conceit could have been exploitative, over-the-top, laughable even. But here, it is terrifying. And it is real.

Later, as Scudder re-views the pilfered snuff film with his girlfriend—the clever, good-hearted prostitute Elaine Mardell—she nervously cracks jokes at the start, and then goes completely silent as we hear, in the simplest and barest of terms, what is happening on-screen. It is a scene that will haunt you long after you've finished the book, not just for the horrifying events that the couple witness, but for Elaine's reaction to them. When Scudder stops the film at the halfway point, this very worldly woman seems to be in a pain that's close to physical.

"Her upper arms were pressed against her sides and she was trembling slightly," Scudder informs the reader. "I said, 'I don't think you want to watch the rest of this.' She didn't respond right away, just sat there on the couch, breathing in and out, in and out. Then, she said, 'That was real, wasn't it?'"

It is a true loss of innocence, and we fall along with her. After Elaine heads off to bed, Scudder watches the rest of the film, describing it in the same unflinching way. Unlike Elaine, we cannot leave the room. We cannot look away. And for this awful information, we will never be the same.

Like Scudder, we need to see this thing through to the end, and that we do. Convinced that the stranger at the boxing match is the same masked man he'd seen sexually torturing and killing another young boy on tape, Scudder sets out to find and capture the man and his female accomplice before the new boy—the boy that the stranger seemed so kindly and comfortable with—meets the same fate. In doing so, the inherently moral ex-cop embarks on a labyrinthine path through the darkest corners of New York society, high and low.

In Block's world, evil does not discriminate along class lines. For all the petty thieves, drug dealers, and street hustlers Scudder comes in contact with on his quest to save the unknown boy, they all seem to have aspects to their personality that are admirable, whether it's a good sense of humor, an inbred loyalty, or a strong will to survive. A wealthy, locally famous widower, on the other hand, is a study in cowardice, and he is guaranteed to make the skin crawl.

Scudder's encounter with the widower—and the horrific tale that he tells—is one of the many shocks to the system this book delivers. But it is the characters—all rich and multidimensional—that truly resonate. And none so powerfully as Matt Scudder himself.

A recovering alcoholic who has made some tragic mistakes in his lifetime, Scudder has grown and changed throughout Block's series, and by now he is a man whose every move revolves around self-restraint. Comfortable as he is in his own skin, Scudder often seems at war with his instincts, whether it's the intense desire that justice be served, the intense desire to drink . . . or simply intense desire. Like the rough-edged, pre-Giuliani New York in which the book takes place, Scudder is at once sophisticated and base—anger, passion, excess, and empathy all doing battle beneath that sober, controlled exterior.

Most human beings are a mass of contradictions, and Scudder is, above all, human. Despite his many weaknesses, he is compelled to do good at all costs. One of the most heartbreaking aspects of his character is his frustration with his own limitations, such as the painfully honest moment, late in his investigation, when he raises his hand at an AA meeting. "I've felt like drinking all day," he says. "I'm in a situation I can't do anything about and it feels as though I ought to be able to . . . I'm an alcoholic and I want everything to be perfect and it never is."

Indeed, the world Scudder finds himself in is about as far from perfect as you can get. By the book's chilling climax, he is trapped in a type of nightmare, face-to-face with the worst kind of living, breathing monster. His investigation has led him to the truth, and it is an ugly one. But the question remains: What will he do about it? Will Scudder stand back, stay in control, and let the wheels of justice grind at their own pace—or will he let his anger and hatred overtake him in the same way that he once allowed himself to be consumed by alcohol?

Without giving anything away, I will say that *A Dance at the Slaughterhouse*'s conclusion is possibly the most satisfying I have read, in any book, ever. And the story itself, for all its compassion, and cruelty, and brutal, heartrending contradiction, is one that will stay with me, always.

And to think, it all started with that one, simple gesture.

———

USA TODAY *best-selling author Alison Gaylin began her career with the Edgar-nominated* Hide Your Eyes *and has since been published in the United States, the U.K., France, Germany, Norway, the Netherlands, and*

Japan. Her latest book, And She Was, *is the first in a new series featuring Brenna Spector, a PI blessed—and cursed—with perfect memory. Its sequel,* The Murder Mile, *is due out in the winter of 2013. A graduate of Northwestern University and Columbia University's Graduate School of Journalism, Alison lives in upstate New York with her husband and daughter. Visit her online at www.alisongaylin.com.*

The Black Echo
by Michael Connelly (1992)

JOHN CONNOLLY

Michael Connelly (b. 1956) is one of the most famous, and critically lauded, mystery writers in America. He is the author of twenty-six novels, including the two series of books featuring LAPD detective Harry Bosch, and the "Lincoln Lawyer," Mickey Haller, respectively. Since 2008, these series have been interlinked, as Haller and Bosch have been revealed to be half brothers, and the first of the Haller novels, The Lincoln Lawyer *(2005) was made into a film starring Matthew McConaughey. Connelly is also the author of three novels featuring Jack McEvoy, the most famous of which is probably* The Poet *(1996); three stand-alone books; and* Crime Beat *(2006), a collection of his newspaper journalism. His career received a considerable boost in 1994 when then president Bill Clinton was photographed with a copy of Connelly's fourth novel,* The Concrete Blonde *(1994), under his arm.*

Of the early Californian crime novelists, four may be regarded as indisputably great: they are Dashiell Hammett, Raymond Chandler, James M. Cain, and Ross Macdonald. What links these writers is that none of them, strictly speaking, could be described as lifelong Californians.

Chandler was born in Chicago, Illinois, and spent his early years in Nebraska. He received a classical education at Dulwich College, London (his fellow alumni include the writer P. G. Wodehouse and the explorer Sir Ernest Shackleton), and passed summers in Waterford in Ireland. He eventually reached Los Angeles in 1913, when he was twenty-five, and was actually a British subject for almost half a century. Macdonald, admittedly, was born in Los Gatos, California, in 1915, but was raised in Canada and didn't return to the state until the 1950s. Hammett and

Cain, meanwhile, were both born in Maryland, a state as geographically, culturally, and socially distinct from California as it is possible to imagine.

Yet if we want to explore a fictionalized version of California from the 1920s, when Hammett starts to publish, until the 1970s, when Macdonald's output ceases, then those are the writers to whom we can usefully turn, at least where the mystery genre is concerned. Yes, they are outsiders, but so is every other non–Native American person in the state. California is the place that is sought out when all others have disappointed; it is the end of the line. As Lew Welch put it in "The Song Mt. Tamalpais Sings": *This is the last place. There is nowhere else to go.* But the detective in mystery fiction is also an outsider: by birth, or appearance, or personal eccentricity, or race, or gender, but most especially if the detective is a moral protagonist, an honest being, and perhaps nowhere more so than in the Californian crime novel.

It's no coincidence that the best of the early private eye stories sprang from the state's soil, for California has a long and ignoble history of corruption. In 1899, the founding president of Stanford University, David Starr Jordan, wrote an essay entitled "California and the Californians" in which he bemoaned the political situation in the state. The bosses ruled Los Angeles and San Francisco; land use was uncontrolled; and state government was a puppet of the Southern Pacific Transportation Company, to the extent that the Railroad Commission was described as Southern Pacific's "literary bureau." Jordan saw little hope for change, and the state did not disappoint in this regard. In 2012, a study by the University of Illinois found Greater Los Angeles to be the second most corrupt metro region in the United States, with 1,275 federal convictions since 1976 for extortion, bribery, conflicts of interest, and election crime. (Perhaps embarrassingly for the University of Illinois, the most corrupt region was Chicago, with 1,531 federal convictions, which suggests that there is much to be said for not asking questions to which one doesn't already know the answer.)

If the establishment in a state has been corrupted, if it has been bought and paid for by wealthy and unscrupulous men, then to whom can the poor or the vulnerable turn if they find themselves in a situation of even greater victimhood than the one that they already occupy? Not to the police, because the police function as an arm of the state, and their allegiance is not to justice, or even to the law, but to those who own them.

Even when they are not actively corrupt, they are unable to deal with pervasive evil either because they are hidebound by legalities that are too rigid or insensitive to function properly, or because the system in which they operate is inadequate for dealing with the massive task at hand.

The answer that mystery fiction gives us comes in the form of the private eye, himself a descendant of the Western hero, the gunfighter who cleans up the corrupt town when the law cannot or will not do so. (Hammett's *Red Harvest* [1929] is essentially a Western in which an unnamed operative sets two rival gangs against each other so that they destroy themselves utterly, and is arguably the point at which the Western novel metamorphoses into the private eye novel.) So we have the knight-errant that is Chandler's Philip Marlowe, the empathetic Christ figure that is Macdonald's Lew Archer, and the avenging angel that is Hammett's Continental Op. They are all outsiders, even in this state filled with outsiders, but they are relatively untarnished, and their interests lie in justice, not law.

All of which is a way of putting Michael Connelly into some kind of context. He, too, is an outsider in California: born in Philadelphia, and raised in Florida from the age of twelve, he moved to Los Angeles in 1987, when he was already thirty-one, to take up a position as a crime reporter with the *Los Angeles Times*. In 1992, he published his first novel, *The Black Echo*, featuring the LAPD homicide detective Hieronymus "Harry" Bosch, still Connelly's most iconic creation. Bosch, although a policeman, is himself an outsider. He may carry a detective's badge, but he is at one remove from his own department. When we first encounter him in *The Black Echo*, he has been demoted from the Robbery-Homicide Division to the homicide desk at Hollywood Division because of the shooting of a suspect. Despite being partnered with various detectives over the course of the series, he remains a solitary figure. His relationship with his superiors is confrontational to the point of outright rebellion. At one point, he even temporarily retires from the LAPD to become a private investigator, but something is slightly unsatisfying about the two PI novels in question, *Lost Light* (2003) and *The Narrows* (2004). Bosch's outsider status comes across most powerfully when it is contrasted with the institution of which he is nominally a part: the LAPD. He is at his finest when he is most restricted.

As with all the best detectives, Bosch's personal life is a mess, although he does manage to console himself by bedding a respectable number of women. He is divorced from the former FBI agent and ex-con Eleanor Wish, who first appears in *The Black Echo*, and whose own story is followed in subsequent novels. He has a daughter, Maddie, and a half brother, Mickey Haller, the hero of Connelly's "Lincoln Lawyer" novels.

Reading back over that last paragraph, it strikes me that it's almost a simulacrum of one of Connelly's own. When I first began reading him, I was thrown slightly by his style, or a perceived absence of it. I had been profoundly influenced by the novelist James Lee Burke, whose use of language—lyrical, poetic, and steeped in metaphor—is unparalleled in the genre. Connelly's prose style is closer to the journalistic, which is perhaps unsurprising given his background as a Pulitzer Prize–nominated reporter. It eschews showiness, and reminds me of the editorial edict presented to most news journalists: if you find a particularly lovely turn of phrase in your news story, take it out, because it will distract from the purpose of the piece, which is to communicate and explain. This is not to say that Connelly does not write well: he does (and, like most writers, he can't resist the occasional flourish), but for the most part he favors a style that is studiedly unassuming, which seems rather appropriate if one has met the author under discussion. His prose does not draw attention to itself. It is a tool to be used carefully, sculpting character and action.

I come from a journalistic background myself. Like a lot of journalists, I went into the field because it was a way to be paid to write, but journalism is a discipline, and I found it stifling at times. Writing fiction gave me a freedom that I was denied at the newspaper, and I sloughed off what I considered to be the stylistic shackles of the news desk at the first opportunity. Connelly chose a different path, adapting what he had learned as a journalist to the practice of fiction.

All of these facets of Connelly's craft were already present in *The Black Echo*. As a first published novel, it remains a stunningly accomplished piece of work, and is certainly one of the finest debuts in the genre, unsurprisingly winning the Edgar for Best First Novel. In *The Black Echo*, Bosch, a Vietnam veteran who served as a "tunnel rat," hunting the Vietcong in their underground bases, becomes involved in the investigation into the death of a fellow tunnel rat named Billy Meadows, and discovers that the death may be linked to a bank robbery carried out using tunnels beneath the city. He teams up with the FBI—and the aforementioned Eleanor Wish—to catch the thieves.

The background to the novel was a real-life crime. As Connelly describes it in an interview that I conducted with him in 2002:

> It was weird. I arrived in L.A. for the first time in my life on the day the story broke about the robbery that would inspire my first book. Los Angeles is basically a desert and underneath it are six hundred miles of storm water tunnels in case of flooding. Just like you can drive all over L.A. on the streets, you can also drive under L.A. in tunnels.
>
> A group of burglars—they think it took at least four of them—had these little Honda ATVs, and they drove three miles into one of the tunnels to a point where they were within 150 feet of a bank. They dug their own tunnel underneath the vault, broke in over a weekend, and emptied all the safety-deposit boxes, and then were gone. They were never caught. The closest they ever came to catching them was about a year later when one of the utility guys in L.A. was checking the tunnels and he noticed a piece of plywood on the wall of the tunnel painted to look like concrete. He pulled it away and found another tunnel. They had come back and were in the process of digging another tributary toward a bank so they could hit L.A. again. But this tunnel was going under Wilshire and the police got stuck with this situation of whether they should let them finish the tunnel and ambush them in the vault or, since Wilshire was a major road and might collapse, fill in the tunnel. They went with safety and filled it in, and I guess the guys saw the activity and never went back.

Of such pieces of good fortune are careers made, but a hundred other authors would have botched even such promising material as this. Connelly, though, was gifted from the start. This is more unusual than one might think. James Lee Burke is regarded to have hit his stride with the second Dave Robicheaux novel, *Heaven's Prisoners* (1988), rather than the first, *The Neon Rain* (1987), and Ross Macdonald's early novels are in thrall to Chandler. Meanwhile, Chandler himself—about whom Connelly writes elsewhere in this volume—routinely cannibalized his earlier short stories for plots for his novels: the joins between disparate stories show more obviously in *The Big Sleep* (1939), for example, than in *Farewell, My Lovely* (1940). His sixth novel, *The Long Goodbye* (1953), dispenses with the reworking of old ideas and is, for my money, Chandler's most accomplished work.

But Connelly emerged fully formed with *The Black Echo*, and he has continued to follow Bosch on his mission through a further fifteen books so far, a mission that is at once both professional and personal for the detective: the achievement of a measure of justice in an imperfect, unjust world, and a final understanding of his own place in it. Some of them, including *The Last Coyote* (1995) and *Angels Flight* (1999), may even be regarded as superior outings to *The Black Echo*, but this is not to belittle his achievement with his debut. Instead, it demonstrates just how high Connelly set the bar with that first book, both for himself and for those who followed in his footsteps.

One final comment: it is rare to find an author who is admired by his peers as much for his own personal qualities as for the work he has produced, but Michael Connelly is one of that exceptional breed. He is, as the saying goes, the kind of man who sends the elevator down for others, and a great many of his fellow writers have benefited from his support. The Bosch novels are an adornment to the genre. Their creator is nothing less.

John Connolly was born in Dublin in 1968. He is the author of sixteen books, including The Book of Lost Things, Nocturnes, *the Samuel Johnson books for younger readers, and the Charlie Parker series of mystery novels, the latest of which is* The Wrath of Angels. *Like most writers, he is waiting to be found out. Visit him online at www.johnconnollybooks.com.*

Miss Smilla's Feeling for Snow
(aka *Smilla's Sense of Snow*)
by Peter Høeg (1992)

MICHAEL ROBOTHAM

Peter Høeg (b. 1957) is a Danish writer of fiction who found instant critical and international popularity with his 1992 novel, Miss Smilla's Feeling for Snow, *published in the United States under the more functional title of* Smilla's Sense of Snow. *It is both a thriller, with some elements of science fiction, and an exploration of the individual's place in society, but it can also be regarded as one of the forerunners of the new wave of Scandinavian crime fiction, even if Høeg has since declined to return to the genre.*

Long before Lisbeth Salander, Harry Hole, and Kurt Wallander emerged from the snows of Scandinavia, another giant stepped from the ice. Her name was Smilla Qaavigaaq Jaspersen, but she's best known as Miss Smilla, a heroine with an unforgettable voice and a feeling for snow.

There are some characters in crime fiction that are heart-stopping and others that are heartbreaking, but only occasionally does one emerge that manages to be both of these things, and captures the imagination of writers, critics, and readers as a consequence. Miss Smilla is just such a character—a loner caught between two worlds: the rich, privileged life of her father, a celebrated surgeon in Copenhagen, and the memory of her poverty-stricken yet liberated childhood in Greenland, where she grew up with her Inuit mother, who died when Smilla was a teenager.

> I feel the same way about solitude as some people feel about the blessing of the church. It's the light of grace for me. I never close my door behind me without the awareness that I am carrying out an act of mercy toward myself.

Living in an apartment block in Copenhagen, Smilla befriends a six-year-old boy, Isaiah, another Greenlander, who has an alcoholic, neglectful mother and a need for companionship. They are an odd couple, clinging to the wreckage of their lives, both harboring secrets.

All of this changes, however, when Isaiah leaps to his death from the snow-covered roof of the apartment block. While the boy's body is still warm, the police pronounce his death an accident, but Smilla doesn't agree. She knows that Isaiah was terrified of heights and, more importantly, she can "read" his footprints in the snow. He didn't slip and fall, he ran to his death.

> Isaiah is lying with his legs tucked up under him, with his face in the snow and his hands round his head, as if he were shielding himself from the little spotlight shining on him, as if the snow were a window through which he has caught sight of something deep inside the earth.

Smilla has an almost intuitive understanding of all types of snow, a "feeling" that is visceral and powerful. When the police don't believe her, she launches her own investigation, talking to pathologists and policemen, tax inspectors and retired accountants, piecing together a decades-old conspiracy. The young boy's death gives Smilla's life a sense of purpose and becomes a vehicle for her own self-exploration.

Published in Danish in 1992, *Miss Smilla's Feeling for Snow* was translated into English a year later, leaping out of the crime genre and stunning literary audiences. It won the CWA Silver Dagger in 1992 and spent twenty-six weeks on the *New York Times* best-seller list. Renamed *Smilla's Sense of Snow* in the United States, it was honored as Best Fiction Book of the Year by *Time, People,* and *Entertainment Weekly.* Current world sales are estimated at nearly 40 million copies.

Like all great crime novels, this one is far more than a mystery. Beneath the surface, Peter Høeg is concerned with deeper cultural issues, particularly Denmark's curious postcolonial history and the relationships that exist between individuals and societies. Despite her education and wealthy father, Smilla doesn't feel that she belongs in either Denmark or Greenland. She is stateless, trapped between two fractured worlds—one wealthy and ordered, the other chaotic and beautiful.

Full of action, suspense, contradictions, and mystery, there are undoubted flaws in the novel. Most of the negative comments focus on the conclusion, which drifts into the realm of science fiction and leaves many questions unanswered, but nobody has ever faulted the quality of the writing, which is littered with humor and memorable descriptions.

This is how Smilla describes the mechanic who lives downstairs.

> He is very broad, like a bear, and if he straightened up his head he would be quite imposing. But he keeps his head down, perhaps to apologize for his height, perhaps to avoid the doorframes of this world.
>
> I like him. I have a weakness for losers. Invalids, foreigners, the fat boy of the class, the ones nobody ever wants to dance with. My heart beats for them. Maybe because I've always known that in some way I will forever be one of them.

Smilla meets Isaiah for the first time on the stairs. She's carrying a book and the boy asks her to read him a story.

> One might say that he looks like a forest elf. But since he is filthy, dressed only in underpants and glistening with sweat, one might also say he looks like a seal pup.
> "Piss off," I say.
> "Don't you like kids?"
> "I eat kids."
> He steps aside.

Until the appearance of Lisbeth Salander, I doubt if a more powerful or interesting female character had emerged from Scandinavian fiction. Tough, acerbic, vulnerable, feisty, intelligent, sarcastic, and heartbreaking, Smilla carries the novel from the icy streets of Copenhagen to the edge of the Arctic Circle, on board an icebreaker.

Ice is important for Smilla in a deep, emotional way. Not only does it link her to her Greenlandic roots but it grounds her in the universe and connects her spiritually to the "absolute space." Humankind can understand the mathematical fractals of a snowflake, but we will never control nature, which is beautiful, powerful, brutal, and unforgiving.

This is not a formulaic detective story or a techno-political thriller slowly gathering pace and tension as clues are slowly revealed. Nor is it a

Gorky Park, or a classic whodunit. It straddles all of these, breaking down the borders between genres.

My favorite passages involve Smilla's introspection and her ruminations on love, loss, and displacement. I don't care that the climax of the novel is, well, anticlimactic, unresolved and inconclusive. It doesn't matter. The underlying mystery is my excuse to spend time with Smilla and hear her views on the world.

Peter Høeg is a serious literary novelist in Denmark and the author of four novels, each radically different from the next. I sometimes wonder if the success of *Miss Smilla's Feeling for Snow* almost embarrassed him because he committed a cardinal sin among literary readers and writers—he became popular. I have read his later novels, which are complex and postmodern but lack the same charm as *Miss Smilla's Feeling for Snow,* despite his obvious talent. It doesn't matter. He created Miss Smilla and proved that serious literature can be both entertaining and artful.

Only a handful of books have made me want to be a writer, and this is one of them. I go back to it time and again, searching for secrets and marveling at the language. It's not perfect, it's not conventional, but I'm in love with Miss Smilla and I want us to grow old together.

Michael Robotham is a former journalist and ghostwriter, whose psychological thrillers have been published in twenty-two languages. His career highlights include uncovering Stalin's Hitler files, interviewing Jackie Collins in a bubble bath, and getting into George Michael's shorts. Michael can most often be found on Sydney's northern beaches, where he wrestles with words in a "mezzanine of misery" (room with a view) and funds the extravagant lifestyles of a wife and three teenaged daughters. Visit him online at www .michaelrobotham.com.

A Philosophical Investigation
by Philip Kerr (1992)

PAUL JOHNSTON

Philip Kerr (b. 1956) was an advertising copywriter for Saatchi & Saatchi before publishing his first novel, March Violets, *in 1989. The first of the "Berlin Noir Trilogy," it featured Bernie Gunther, a detective and former police officer working in Germany in 1936. Five Bernie Gunther titles were published after the trilogy was completed, the most recent being* Prague Fatale *(2011). Kerr has also published nine nonseries novels for adults, as well as seven titles for young adults under the pseudonym P. B. Kerr. In 2009, Kerr was awarded the Ellis Peters Historical Award for his Bernie Gunther novel* If the Dead Rise Not.

Spoiler alert—this contribution contains philosophy . . .

Philip Kerr is best known for his Bernie Gunther series, a highly unusual take on the hard-boiled novel, with Gunther starting off as a homicide detective in 1930s Berlin and continuing as a private eye in locations as distant as Argentina and Cuba. To date, there are eight in the series. What's interesting is that Kerr seems only to have envisaged a trilogy (*March Violets, The Pale Criminal,* and *A German Requiem*), published between 1989 and 1991, before returning to Gunther as late as 2006 with *The One from the Other,* to great critical and popular acclaim. But, in the final analysis, our Bernie is just another gumshoe. In 1992, Kerr tried to do something really original with the crime novel.

At this point I should declare an interest. Philip Kerr and I were at school together in Edinburgh, though in typical Calvinist fashion we didn't know each other, despite being only one year apart. I discovered this when I chaired an event with him at the Edinburgh International Book Festival in 2000. At that point in his career he was still writing the high-concept thrillers that made him a lot of money from Hollywood, although no movies were ever made. Onstage he was very critical of crime writers, seeing them as conservative and boring. This almost led my then agent to assault him for demeaning me, but it also offers a clue to this most unusual of crime writers—he knows how to handle the genre with great skill, but is ambivalent about its value. Bear that in mind during my discussion of the novel he wrote immediately after what became known as the Berlin Noir Trilogy.

A Philosophical Investigation is set in 2013, years in the future at the time of writing, which technically makes it a work of science fiction, or rather that awkward creature: a crossover between crime and SF. The society imagined by Kerr is relatively hi-tech, but plagued by what are termed "recreational" or "Hollywood" murders—four thousand sex-killings in the European Community in one year. Serial killers are so common that police officers lay claim to the dead as victims of their favored killer—the Hackney Hammerer, the Lipstick Man, etc. Detective Chief Inspector Isadora "Jake" Jakowicz of London's Metropolitan Police is more thoughtful than her colleagues, with her Cambridge natural sciences degree and service as a forensic psychologist at the European Bureau of Investigation. She also hates men, an inevitable consequence of her job as head of Gynocide, as well as the legacy of an abusive father. But the case that gets under her skin doesn't involve female victims: the Lombroso Killer executes men, and not just random victims.

The first fifty pages of Kerr's book are so replete with intertextual references that the reader struggles to keep up. The opening paragraph refers to Mary Woolnoth and Mylae, both of which appear in the opening section of T. S. Eliot's *The Waste Land*. The second of the novel's two epigraphs is from Eliot's *The Love Song of J. Alfred Prufrock*, establishing the poet as one of three éminences grises. The first epigraph, from Ludwig Wittgenstein's *Philosophical Investigations*, establishes him as another of those éminences. The third is George Orwell, whose writings on murder are discussed, and whose Chestnut Tree Café from *1984* is a key location. So far so confusing, but we haven't even broached the technological side of the novel.

Although Orwell's spectral presence suggests a backward-looking future, one given form by the novel's descriptions of a run-down and dangerous London, there has been scientific progress, even if it doesn't affect the ordinary citizen. Jake's investigation revolves around the complex Lombroso Program, which identifies men without the neural inhibitor that stops them from becoming killers. They are informed of their condition, given code names, and investigated only if they are connected to murders. But, hey, this is a dystopia, and Jake's antagonist, named Wittgenstein, manages to break into the archive and access his fellow sociopaths' details. He then starts executing them.

We know this and much more about Wittgenstein because the narrative is larded with his thoughts, many of which raise significant questions, not just about the ethics of murder—is executing potential serial killers justifiable?—but about life in general, and also about writing. Is the crime novel a tenable proposition when, as the murderer Wittgenstein says, nothing empirical is knowable? He can't resist playing with Descartes, saying "I kill, therefore I am." But crime writers, to delight readers, also commit murder (usually only on paper). Shouldn't we consider why we are so addicted to fictional death? Perhaps we amateur murderers should pay more attention to the real Wittgenstein's dictum (quoted in the novel), "Whereof one cannot speak, thereof one must be silent."

This makes *A Philosophical Investigation* sound like a heavy read. Although it can be so in places, there is also a humorous side. Who could resist a killer named after the weirdest of philosophers doing away with victims such as Dickens, Bertrand Russell, and Socrates? And there is a philosophy professor who—guess what?—writes detective novels in his spare time.

But the real power of the novel derives from the interplay between Jake and the killer. Female cops written by males are common these days, but were much less so in 1992. I think Kerr took a big chance with his main character and, by and large, pulled it off. Jake is mouthy, smart, and tough, but she is also touchingly empathetic, both with the female victims she has to deal with and, ultimately, with Wittgenstein himself. The scenes in which she gets close to him in extremis are very moving, and give this highly cerebral novel a powerful emotional payload. In addition, there is a haunting poetic undertone, partly derived from T. S. Eliot, that embellishes the feelings of longing and loss. Finally, as the use of Orwellian tropes suggests, Philip Kerr has a sharp satirical agenda.

All in all, *A Philosophical Investigation* is a rich feast, and not only for (pseudo)intellectuals. Read it and blow your mind.

Paul Johnston was born in Edinburgh, Scotland, but spends much of his time in Greece. He is the author of three crime series. The first, featuring Quint Dalrymple, is set in a futuristic version of his home city (CWA John Creasey Memorial Dagger for Body Politic*). The second stars half-Greek, half-Scots missing persons specialist Alex Mavros (Sherlock Award for Best Detective Novel for* The Last Red Death*). In the third he lost it completely and turned crime writer Matt Wells into a hard-boiled avenger (* The Death List, *etc.). His latest novel is* The Silver Stain. *Visit him online at www.paul-johnston .co.uk.*

Bootlegger's Daughter
by Margaret Maron (1992)

JULIA SPENCER-FLEMING

Margaret Maron was born on a tobacco farm in North Carolina, and spent time in Italy and New York before returning to that same farm to live with her family. She began her writing career with a series of mysteries set against the backdrop of the art world, and featuring NYPD lieutenant Sigrid Harald, before returning to her native state with the character of District Court Judge Deborah Knott, the titular "bootlegger's daughter" of her first book, and now the heroine of eighteen novels, the latest of which is The Buzzard Table.

Back in 1999 I was on a mission to find out what made a good mystery. I had written half a science-fiction novel (a clichéd, derivative science-fiction novel) and had been sent home from a writing workshop with the strong suggestion that I take what worked (plot, characters) and ditch the half-assed world-building.

I did what I was told, poring over the manuscript for what was salvageable and what was junk. One thing became clear. I hadn't written a space opera; totally unintentionally, I had written a mystery.

My problem? I didn't really read mysteries. I had no clue as to how they worked, what I liked, what was considered *good*. So I took myself off to my local library, and checked out every book I could find that had been nominated for, or had won, the Edgar, the Anthony, or the Agatha Award.

That's how *Bootlegger's Daughter* first came into my hands. Margaret Maron was a veteran author when *Bootlegger's Daughter* was published in 1992. She had an eight-book series built around the lone, socially awkward NYC cop Sigrid Harald. But Maron wanted to write something that reflected the reality of life in her native North Carolina, and she decided to take a new tack, with a new kind of heroine.

Deborah Knott is a lawyer in her early thirties still living in the (fictional) Colleton County, where she was born and raised. The youngest child—and only girl—of twelve, she struggles with sometimes comforting, sometimes smothering familial bonds. Her elderly, larger-than-life father is one of the major landholders in the area, as well as having a racy past as the county's most successful bootlegger. She has to deal with the barely veiled racism and sexism of her legal colleagues, and with the push-pull between her Southern Baptist upbringing and her college-educated cynicism.

She might have been one of dozens of crime-fighting attorneys written before or since, but Deborah Knott has a more interesting destiny before her. As the story begins, she witnesses one of the judges before whom she has to appear throw the book at a black man whose primary crime was being "cocky." Fed up with the "good old boy" system, Deborah marches over to the commissioner's office and registers as a candidate for district court. The rest of the novel follows her as she hits the campaign trail—speaking at fried chicken suppers, shaking hands at the local churches, fending off most of the attempts of her well-meaning family to help her.

In the meantime, Deborah has been asked by a friend's daughter to look into the unexplained death of her mother eighteen years earlier. As happens in the best crime fiction novels, the two parts of the story—1990 and 1972, the old South and the new, the black community and the white—twine together like a tangle of kudzu.

In the decade preceding the publication of *Bootlegger's Daughter*, there had been an explosion of female-centered crime fiction: women cops, women PIs, women investigative reporters. They tended (like Deborah Knott's predecessor, Sigrid Harald) to be quirky loners, professionals, tough gals. Or, conversely, there were the updated descendants of Miss Marple: working girls with traditionally feminine jobs, snooping around candlestick bludgeonings and exotic poisonings.

Deborah Knott was different, and so was the type of story in which she appeared. Neither hard-boiled nor traditionally cozy, *Bootlegger's Daughter* was an early example of what I call the New Traditional. (I just coined that neologism since "medium-boiled" sounds like a bad breakfast.) Violence remains offstage, but the effects of it are harsh, and long lasting. The setting is small-town, but the crimes are caused by real, contemporary social ills. The amateur sleuth appends rather than replaces actual police work. The protagonist's personal life, a vital part of the novel, presents an emotional and psychological sounding board for the action. This is a kind of crime fiction readers are very familiar with today, but in 1992, *Bootlegger's Daughter* was something very new.

Crime fiction centering on a specific location was certainly not new then or now, but *Bootlegger's Daughter* is one of the finest examples of geocentric mystery around. (Yes, I just made up another phrase.) Done badly, scene and setting can be a kind of window dressing: pretty, but irrelevant to the real business of the book. Done well, everything—the nature of the crime, the character of the protagonist, the dangers and motivations and red herrings—flow out of the setting. The history, the economy, the weather, the terrain: as in real life, all of these shape the culture, which in turn shapes the men and women inhabiting the story. In *Bootlegger's Daughter*, you can hear the buzz of insects in the spring air, taste the barbeque and iced tea, smell the baked-brown scent of abandoned tobacco barns. But Maron's real accomplishment isn't evoking eastern North Carolina: it's writing a story that could not take place in any other part of the world. Like the works of Tony Hillerman— arguably the mystery genre's master at evoking a sense of place—nothing in Maron's book can be separated from its setting.

Because the setting is intrinsic to the tale, *Bootlegger's Daughter*—all of the books in the Deborah Knott series, really—highlights the problems and concerns of the New South. Race relations. Homophobia. The tobacco industry. Development. Migrant workers. Government corruption. Environmental depredation. Maron has written about all of these issues, and they give a weight and gravity to her work that is counterbalanced by the lightness of Deborah's family and the spicy amusement of her on-again, off-again love life.

Of course, if I were handing you *Bootlegger's Daughter* and urging you to read it, I wouldn't rattle on about all this. I'd say, "It's a terrific story," and, "Deborah Knott is irresistible," and, "Try it. I guarantee you'll like it." Then I'd serve you up a tall glass of sweet iced tea and show you to the hammock. Let you spend the long afternoon swinging gently, falling in love with Colleton County just like I did, all those years ago.

Although based in the state of Maine, Julia Spencer-Fleming is best known for her series of mystery novels set in the small upstate New York town of Millers Kill, featuring the unusual central character of Clare Fergusson, an Episcopal cleric, alongside the town's chief of police, Russ Van Alstyne. The first novel in the series, In the Bleak Midwinter, *swept most of the major mystery awards when it was published in 2002. Visit her online at www .juliaspencerfleming.com.*

Clockers
by Richard Price (1992)

GAR ANTHONY HAYWOOD

Novelist and screenwriter Richard Price (b. 1949) was born in the Bronx in New York. His first novel, The Wanderers, *was published in 1974, and established his reputation for exploring the reality of the inner-city American experience in an unvarnished style. He has published eight novels in total, the most recent of which is* Lush Life *(2008). A prolific screenwriter, Price was nominated for an Oscar for his screenplay for* The Color of Money *(1986). More recently, Price has written for the groundbreaking TV series* The Wire *(2002–08). In 1999, Richard Price was honored by the American Academy of Arts and Letters.*

In the years just prior to his death in 1996, I used to be my father's chief supplier of his favorite drug: literature. He'd always been a voracious reader of fiction—it was his vast and ever-expanding collection of paperback novels, strewn all over the house in which I grew up, that first drew me to reading, then writing—but in his later years, retired from his architectural practice, reading was just about all the Old Man did.

While his greatest love was science fiction—Asimov, Heinlein, Ellison—I eventually traded that particular genre in for mystery fiction, so when our roles became reversed and he began to look to me for secondhand reading material, he had to settle almost exclusively for the works of such authors as Robert B. Parker, Lawrence Block, Michael Connelly, and the like. For the most part, he enjoyed everything I gave him, but his standards were ridiculously high. Jack Woodward Haywood was a tough critic by nature, and what little crime fiction he'd read to that point had been written only by the most revered names in the field—people like Raymond Chandler and John D. MacDonald. It was a rare book now that got more than a three-and-a-half-star review out of him.

He read hundreds of my hand-me-downs, many by contemporary authors whom I considered—and still do consider—the best of the best: Robert Crais, T. Jefferson Parker, James Lee Burke, Sue Grafton, Elmore Leonard, Ed McBain, Martin Cruz Smith . . .

And only one book blew him completely away: *Clockers* by Richard Price.

"This guy's the real deal," he told me when I asked him what he thought. And coming from my father—a man of few words if ever there was one—this was high praise, indeed.

Curiously, I hadn't yet read *Clockers* myself. I'd started it and put it down, for God only knows what reason. But now, if the Old Man said it was the "real deal"—better than anything I'd given him to read up to that point—it clearly deserved a second look. So I gave it one.

It's a damn good thing that I did.

The story of a black New Jersey drug runner and a disillusioned white cop working a homicide case on the outskirts of the projects where the kid lives and operates, *Clockers* is an urban crime drama of incredible texture and depth, as perfectly pieced together as the proverbial Swiss clock. Reading it from a writer's perspective, you're immediately struck by the vast array of skills Price has on display: plotting that moves at optimum speed, characters that live and breathe, dialogue devoid of a single false note. And this last is no exaggeration: every word of every line Price's people speak in *Clockers* rings true. Every one.

Style is every author's Holy Grail, the identifying mark we seek to place on everything we write in order to establish it as ours and ours alone. But style is a double-edged sword; doled out in the wrong proportions, it becomes a stain instead of a mark, an intrusive impediment to the reader's forward progress.

The style Price exhibits in *Clockers* is a remarkable mixture of authenticity and economy that is only ever apparent in retrospect. While you're reading the book, Price the author is completely invisible, no more a part of the story being told than a fly on the wall. It all looks effortless, so subliminal is the power of his compact prose, but of course, it's anything but.

Strike, the drug-running "clocker" at the center of Price's tale, is a difficult character to like, and Rocco Klein, the burnt-out cop halfheartedly trying to solve just another senseless murder on his and Strike's common turf, even more so. This is because Price has refused to dilute the cold, hard truths both men represent with anything artificial simply to make the reader's task of caring for them easier.

Strike is a teenaged businessman who sees crack no differently than McDonald's sees hamburgers; he even suffers the ulcers typical of legitimate, white-collar enterprise, hence his addiction to Yoo-hoo. Rocco, meanwhile, is an oblivious racist and unrepentant adulterer, a virtual poster boy for the motto "by any means necessary" who has seen too much to be surprised, let alone moved, by anything.

Part of the great pull of *Clockers* is the anxiety a reader is made to feel throughout, waiting for Strike or Rocco to prove himself more compassionate, more alive, than Price would lead us to believe he is. In the hands of a lesser writer, characters this detached and manipulative, wading through daily existences this harsh and seemingly pointless, would tax a reader's patience. Who cares who survives a car wreck if everyone involved is already dead? But Price lends each man just enough humanity, just enough hope for his sorry future, to make writing him off impossible. This is noir without the usual built-in safety net of certain doom; Price makes no promises about how this will all turn out, yet has you hoping for a happy ending his setup would suggest is highly unlikely, at best.

As Strike's struggle to climb the crack trade's corporate ladder and Rocco's homicide investigation inexorably converge, we are introduced to people in their lives no less fascinating than the two men themselves. Strike's employer and mentor Rodney is as schooled and complex as any Wall Street CEO, though to the world at large he looks like little more than the two-bit entrepreneur behind a neighborhood candy store. In any other book, the subordinate clockers under Strike's supervision might have been one-dimensional throw-ins with cute names—Futon, The Word, Peanut—but Price has invested each with distinctive motives and characteristics of his own. Similarly, Rocco's circle of fellow cops and associates—Mazilli, his partner; Sean Touhey, the self-important actor Rocco's coaching up for a possible film role; Rocco's wife, Patty—are all far more than the usual character sketches that populate novels of this kind.

A skeptical reader's initial reaction to a book like this—a tale, for the most part, of black people living and dying in the cesspool of a contemporary American slum, as told by a middle-aged white man—is: What the hell would he know about it? This is a literary trick that's been tried many times before, and usually without much success. But ten pages into *Clockers*, it becomes glaringly obvious that what Price knows about his subject matter is nothing short of everything.

Every goddamn thing.

He knows his characters and the world they inhabit so well, in fact, that one wonders what his research process looked like. Did he take residence in a New Jersey crack house for six months? Spend another six sitting in the bullpen of a Newark police station recording every word he overheard? From the everyday intricacies of the drug trade in which Strike operates to the morass of legal and moral compromises a cop like Rocco must make on an hourly basis just to get by, Price seems to understand it not from second- or thirdhand, but from firsthand experience.

Clockers reads like Pulitzer Prize–worthy journalism, not fiction. It's the novel we are all trying to write: big, sprawling, and unforgettable.

The Old Man was right. Richard Price is the real deal.

Gar Anthony Haywood is the Shamus and Anthony award–winning author of twelve crime novels and numerous short stories. He has written six mysteries featuring African American private investigator Aaron Gunner; two starring amateur sleuths Joe and Dottie Loudermilk; and four stand-alone thrillers. Visit him online at www.garanthonyhaywood.com.

The Long-Legged Fly
by James Sallis (1992)

---

*James Sallis (b. 1944) is perhaps best known for the Lew Griffin mysteries,
set in New Orleans, and the novel* Drive, *which became an acclaimed film
directed by Nicolas Winding Refn. He has published fourteen novels, more
than a hundred stories, a number of collections of poetry, a translation
of Raymond Queneau's novel* Saint Glinglin, *three books on music, and
reams of criticism on literature of every sort. Once editor of the landmark
SF magazine* New Worlds *in London ("Way, way back in the day," as Sallis
puts it himself), he contributes a regular books column to the* Magazine of
Fantasy & Science Fiction.*

James Sallis's *The Long-Legged Fly,* the first of his "Insect" series of detective novels, is a deconstruction of the detective novel in the best sense of
the word. In this series of fables and vignettes from the life of New Orleans PI Lew Griffin, ranging from 1964 to 1990, Sallis reverse-engineers
the detective novel down to its elementary parts, an act of magic and
alchemy that shows both what the detective novel could be in the future,
and what it was all along.

Lew Griffin, Sallis's PI, embodies the hard-boiled dick: he is tough, he
drinks, he is oddly attractive to women; he's clever, he's wise, and he has
a hole in his heart that goes on for days. He is both one with his clients
and the people he investigates, and always, eternally alone. And yet Griffin also deals with the heavy matter of real life.

His father dies. His romantic relationships bloom and then wilt.
Time passes. He is African American in a city, New Orleans, that does
not give us easy answers about race. Griffin is both the archetypal detective and a real, breathing person. Lew's life is complex and rich, full

of mysteries without easy solutions. He both embodies the genre and expands it.

Just as Lew himself is both familiar and new, the mysteries Sallis gives him to solve—or not solve—both fit squarely into the genre and tell us something new about what exactly this genre is. One missing girl case becomes a meditation on personality and identity. The girl is found, but the case is never exactly solved. A middle-of-the-night phone call warns Lew off the case, film noir–style, but Lew admits never knowing who that call came from, or why it was made. Another missing girl case (missing girls being both the great MacGuffin and the great living, breathing, symbolic prize of detective fiction) turns into an inquiry about love.

Sallis knows: we don't turn to mystery fiction to find the girl. You go and find that girl, and another will vanish right before your eyes. There is always another missing girl. We turn to mystery novels not for their answers, but for their questions: Why do people disappear? What do we solve when we solve a mystery? What does the detective know, and why are we so fascinated by it? Sallis has a knack for finding these core mysteries that every book in the genre circles around: "It all seemed so voluntary. But was she really in control? Or driven?" "What was it that started a person sinking? Was that long fall in him (or her) from the start, in us all perhaps; or something he put there himself, creating it over time and unwittingly just as he created his face, his life, the stories he lived by, the ones that let him go on living."

It was this book that made me understand why I love mystery fiction, and why the mystery is such a central metaphor of our time. It isn't because we really want to know whodunit, although, of course, that can be a lot of fun, and Lord knows I like fun. But ultimately, the mystery novel reflects back to us the fundamental state of our own existence: it's a mystery. We don't know what the hell we're doing here (most of us don't, at least), both in the big-picture sense of knowing why we're here, and in the sense of knowing what we're doing on any particular day. Why are we alive? Why do we love people who don't love us back? Why do we sometimes want to be someone else? What do we owe each other, and how do we pay these debts? What's the best way to get from Santa Monica to Silver Lake in rush hour? These are the questions the mystery helps us come to terms with. Not that it gives us answers, of course, but it makes us feel less alone in our state of having so many fucking questions—and gives us hope that, someday, maybe we might have answers of our own.

In a bookstore, Lew reads a poem that says: you must learn to put your distress signals in code. The line comes from the poem "An Interesting Signal / A Very Dull Movie" by David Lunde: *I notice that my spirits are flagging. Metaphor establishes connections between unlike objects. If you would like help, you must put your distress call in code.*

Of course that is what we writers do, every day, and what we have our private eyes do for us. We put our distress signals in a code, in this scenario, the well-known code of detective, client, and case. You would not want our distress if we just handed it to you, and you wouldn't understand our frantic rantings, our tears, our implorations to not make our same mistakes. Why would anyone want a long, uncoded rant on identity and mysteries and time and personality?

Instead, Sallis has put his signals in code—a code that is a joy to read, but at the same time hits our deep receptors for distress signals. And we find ourselves listening, and putting out our own call in return.

Born in Brooklyn in 1971, Sara Gran is the author of the novels Come Closer *(2003) and* Dope *(2006). Before making a living as a writer, Ms. Gran had many jobs, primarily with books, working at Manhattan bookstores like Shakespeare & Co., the Strand, and Housing Works, and selling used and rare books on her own. Her most recent novel,* Claire DeWitt and the City of the Dead *(2011) is set in post-Katrina New Orleans, and features the "strange and brilliant" private eye Claire DeWitt. Visit her online at www .saragran.com.*

The Secret History
by Donna Tartt (1992)

Donna Tartt (b. 1963), a native of Greenwood, Mississippi, is the author of just two novels, The Secret History *(1992) and* The Little Friend *(2002). She published her first poem at thirteen, and attended the University of Mississippi and Bennington College in Vermont, where she went on a blind date with a fellow writing student named Bret Easton Ellis, later to become the author of* American Psycho. *"I can't write quickly," she once admitted. "If I could write a book a year and maintain the same quality, I'd be happy. But I don't think I'd have any fans . . ."*

When *The Secret History* came out, I was nineteen, and halfway through college. I started it on a plane, read straight across the Atlantic, got off the plane dazzled, went home, and read through my jet lag till I'd finished the last page. I can still remember the sense of sheer loss as I realized that I'd never be able to read it for the first time again.

The book is about a tight-knit clique of classics students in a small college in Vermont. Richard Papen—intelligent, arrogant, insecure, new to this rarefied world and entranced by it—is thrilled when he finds himself slowly being let into their group, but gradually he discovers that the intensity and ruthlessness that initially attracted him go much deeper than he thought. The complex web of relationships among the six of them grows and tightens until—and don't worry, this isn't a spoiler—five of them kill the sixth. That act transforms all of their lives.

It wasn't marketed as a mystery novel at all: it was presented as literary fiction, but I think it would be ridiculous to claim that it isn't both. The book itself is one of the best arguments I've ever seen against that tired, lazy distinction.

It's unquestionably literary fiction. It dives deep into enormous themes: the wild human urge toward losing the self, throwing away one's own limitations by dissolving into something limitless; how that urge can turn savagely distorted and destructive when it's trapped by a hyperrational, hyper-individualistic society that doesn't give it room to take its course; the unstoppable march of action and consequence, the immense and unforeseeable chain of events that one small choice can set in motion. The characters drive the plot, rather than the other way around—this story could never have happened to a different set of people—and they're explored down to the subtlest psychological nuances, with such depth that you come out feeling like you're one of that group: a part of their intimacy, elevated by it when it's going right, complicit when it turns dangerous, and bereft when it disintegrates. And the writing is stunning—savage, erudite, utterly beautiful, and so rich you could live on it.

But the book is also a mystery. Not in the conventional sense—this is the farthest thing from a whodunit: on the first page of the first chapter, you find out who killed whom. The first half of the book is spent discovering why; the second half tracks the fallout from the murder, how each of the killers turns into a different person from the one he or she might have been, living in a different world. So there's none of the standard whodunit suspense. But no book has ever had me devouring the pages, desperate for the answer, like this one; no reveal has ever left me breathless, with the hair on the back of my neck standing up, the way this one did.

And that's one of the main reasons I love *The Secret History*: it breaks the rules. There are mystery books that are wonderful because they fit every convention in the most satisfying way. They're perfect examples of the genre taken to its polished peak: Agatha Christie's *Sleeping Murder* or *The Murder of Roger Ackroyd,* for example. And then there are mystery books that are wonderful because they stretch all the genre's boundaries—Josephine Tey's *The Franchise Affair,* Patricia Highsmith's *The Talented Mr. Ripley,* P. D. James's *Innocent Blood.* Those are the ones I love best, and *The Secret History* is one of those. Sure, it's about the mystery surrounding a murder; but it refuses to go along with the convention that says the real mystery is whodunit. For this book, the true mystery is deeper, buried inside the hidden places of the human mind: why the murder happened; what consequences it has for everyone it touches.

You still see people dismissing all genre fiction as cheap, formulaic fluff, or rubbishing all literary fiction as plotless, overwrought navel-gazing. I already knew that was silliness, but *The Secret History* was the book that really brought it home to me that a gripping plot, complex characters, big themes, and beautiful writing aren't mutually exclusive; that writers can offer their readers *and* rather than *or*. It takes the conventions of the two genres, literary and mystery, turns them inside out, and weaves them together to create something recognizable but utterly transformed.

Here's the other reason—well, one of the many other reasons—I love it. *The Secret History* captures something that I'd never seen captured before: the power and the intricacy of those group friendships that you only make when you're around college age. There are maybe six or eight of you, with varying degrees of closeness; you spend hours having passionate conversations about everything from literature to your deepest fears, you stay up all night getting drunk and dancing, you laugh yourselves silly over jokes that make no sense to anyone else, some of you kiss or sleep together or fall for each other or hurt each other. You create a delicate, intricate group balance that sustains all of you through some of the most intense emotions of your lives. My friends and I had boyfriends and girlfriends who came and went along the way; but for sheer power, the flash of adrenaline when I saw the man of the moment never came close to the click of belonging, the rightness, that I felt when I saw my friends.

The characters in *The Secret History* are all those groups of college-aged friends, taken to the extreme. That collective absorption in your private world, to the point where the outside world barely feels real: in the book, that intensifies to the point where the outside world becomes, in very real terms, merely something to be manipulated or destroyed in accordance with the needs of the characters' private world. That sense of belonging to something special coalesces into a concrete form—this is the ultimate in-group, a tiny and almost inaccessible classics department within an exclusive college, an elite within an elite. That "secret language" of catchphrases and shortcuts and in-jokes becomes an actual secret language: when the characters need to talk past an outsider, they do it by speaking ancient Greek. That numinous sense of enchantment, of an unimagined new world slipping into existence and beckoning all around you:

> I don't know what else to say except that life itself seemed very magical in those days: a web of symbol, coincidence, premonition, omen. Everything, somehow, fit together; some sly and benevolent Providence was revealing itself by degrees and I felt myself trembling on the brink of a fabulous discovery, as though any morning it was all going to come together—my future, my past, the whole of my life—and I was going to sit up on my bed like a thunderbolt and say *oh! oh! oh!*

That slowly crystallizes into something real and tangible, with a role of its own to play. For these characters, all the inchoate things that define these friendships are distilled to the point where they take on tangible form.

Those friendships are powerful stuff, and, like all powerful things, they can turn dangerous. For most of us, the worst that happened was the odd broken heart; but for the characters in *The Secret History,* that danger becomes as concrete as everything else. In a lot of ways, that private world is the perfect setting for a murder mystery. The closed-room mystery is a staple of the genre—and it's at its most powerful when the relationships between the suspects and the victim are intense and charged. Plenty of murder mysteries have been set among families, in workplaces, in all the other hothouse worlds where emotions are concentrated. But until *The Secret History,* as far as I know, no one had set one among those friendships.

Since then, plenty of writers have explored what happens when they turn fatal. Lucie Whitehouse did it in *The House at Midnight,* Ian Caldwell and Dustin Thomason did it in *The Rule of Four,* and Erin Kelly did it in *The Poison Tree.* I did it in *The Likeness,* where a group of postgrads believe they're erasing their pasts and creating a shining new life together in a ramshackle old house outside Dublin, until one of them is murdered and turns out not to be who she said she was. But *The Secret History* was first. It was the first book that held up that world and said it was not only important enough, beautiful enough, to be worth writing about—but also mysterious enough, and dangerous enough, to be the setting for murder.

For me, this book redefined the territory that mysteries can claim. When I started writing, more than ten years after I first read it, I was writing within a landscape that *The Secret History* had redrawn for me. I aim to write mysteries that take genre conventions as springboards, not as laws, and never as limitations on quality or scope; books where the real murder mystery isn't whodunit, but whydunit and what it means. If I ever manage that, I—like, I'm willing to bet, a lot of other mystery writers of my generation—owe it to Donna Tartt.

———————

Tana French's first book, In the Woods, *swept all of the main mystery fiction awards, including the Edgar Award for Best First Novel, when it was published in 2007. She has since published three further novels, the latest of which is* Broken Harbour. *Visit her online at www.tanafrench.com.*

Murder... Now and Then
by Jill McGown (1993)

SOPHIE HANNAH

While still at school, Scottish author Jill McGown (1947–2007) was taught Latin by Colin Dexter in his pre–Inspector Morse days. McGown wrote her first novel after being made unemployed by the British Steel Corporation. A Perfect Match *was published in 1983, featuring Chief Inspector Danny Lloyd and Sergeant Judy Hill, and McGown would eventually publish thirteen novels in the series. She also published five nonseries titles, the first,* Record of Sin, *arriving in 1985, the last,* Hostage to Fortune, *published under the pseudonym Elizabeth Chaplin, in 1992. In an obituary written by Val McDermid for the* Guardian, *McGown was described as "one of the generation of crime writers who shifted the genre firmly into the contemporary world."*

Long after I've forgotten the precise details of a book's plot, I remember the feeling I had while reading it. When I first read Jill McGown's *Murder... Now and Then* in 1994, the ending had an effect on me that I will never forget. First, it gave me goose bumps, but these soon gave way to a weird, mind-bending, spine-prickling ripple of recognition as I realized that the threads of the book's denouement were so seamlessly and brilliantly woven into the fabric of the entire novel that the ending of the story was there right from the beginning, unobtrusively all-pervasive. This was not a book that might have concluded in any number of ways, any more than a square can become a triangle at its midpoint.

The structure of *Murder... Now and Then*, with its double time line of past and present, was flawless; none of the ingredients—plot, character, dialogue, narrative choreography—could have been other than it was without bringing down the whole edifice. I believe this is the mark of a true masterpiece: that, reading it, one has a feeling of, "In no possible world could this novel/story/poem/song have been any different." There's an archetypal inevitability about the way such works of art unfold, and there's no doubt that Jill McGown was an artist in the field of crime fiction, one who demanded that her readers focus on every tiny detail of the pictures she painted for them.

All McGown's books are architecturally excellent. Choosing only one to write about was tough. I picked *Murder . . . Now and Then* for a sensible, empirical reason: because it created the farthest-reaching reverberative ripples in me (of the sort described above) on my own personal Ripple Richter Scale. That ripple of recognition is what I still crave when I read detective novels or thrillers. What I'm hoping to recognize, and what all too often is absent even in some pretty good crime fiction, is a shape that cannot be improved upon—a construct that feels so organic and predetermined, but at the same time so irreducible and impossible to confine to any definition, that it makes me question whether it can have been put together by a human being without celestial assistance.

The plot of *Murder . . . Now and Then,* when I describe it, won't sound particularly spectacular: at the opening of a local factory in the town of Stansfield (based on Corby in Northamptonshire, where Jill McGown lived until her death in 2007), Victor Holyoak, the factory's owner, is murdered. One of the guests at the opening is Chief Inspector Lloyd, who recognizes a face from the past, though he can't remember where and when he has seen that face before. Soon Lloyd and his sidekick—and significant other—Detective Sergeant Judy Hill have discovered a connection between Holyoak's murder and another murder from thirteen years ago. The novel follows both story lines, via a parallel narrative structure that works brilliantly, to their unguessable conclusion.

If that blurb makes *Murder . . . Now and Then* sound ordinary, it really isn't. The crimes themselves are not particularly unusual or high-concept in McGown's books; the magic is in the way the stories unfold—and then keep folding and unfolding in surprising directions, creating fascinating and unexpected shapes within shapes, like literary kaleidoscopes. All this is done with quiet efficiency, as if the author and her detectives are slightly embarrassed by their own considerable talents. The plot of *Murder . . . Now and Then* is a brilliantly ambitious and complex maze that expands readers' conceptions of what story can do: how many tentacles it can have and how many convergences there can be between them.

In contrast to the baroque plotting, McGown's series detective protagonists, Chief Inspector Lloyd and Detective Sergeant Judy Hill, are
relatively ordinary. They're warm and likeable, professional and functional. They have their flaws and quirks that prevent them from being
dull, but the best thing about them—particularly when you consider the
egotism of many fictional detectives, who insist on mattering more than
the story they're in—is that Lloyd and Hill consistently demonstrate that
they are at their most interesting when thinking not about their love lives
or promotion prospects, but about the crimes they're trying to unpick.
Their everyday ordinariness is their primary characteristic. They express
themselves and their realities moderately, which is a sign of psychological health, and tend to retain a sense of proportion even when tested by
events.

Stansfield, the town where they live and work, is neither beautiful nor
remarkable. All of these low-key elements leave the spotlight slot free for
the fiendishly puzzling conundrums that they grapple with in each book.
Readers can rely on Lloyd and Hill remaining stable enough to be able to
give their full attention to each tangled mystery they encounter, because
they aren't overloaded with exaggerated character traits, or cumbersome
music or whisky collections that need to be itemized in every chapter. As
a reader, I appreciate detectives who don't try to compete for my attention with the mysteries we are, all three of us, trying to solve.

McGown's is a plot-first approach to characterization, which has the
wonderful effect of making Lloyd and Hill seem modest and unassuming, and demonstrates that so often forgotten truth: that without an
unpredictable plot, character cannot muster the necessary conditions
for revealing itself. McGown cleverly avoided inventing larger-than-life
characters; she understood instinctively that no individual actor in a
drama can ever be as compelling as the situations that arise when lots of
barely connected people brush against each other's needs and priorities
in unexpected ways, creating a cocktail of the unforeseeable. No one in
her books, not even her series detectives, is ever allowed to be the only
pebble on the beach of her creative imagination; she divides her authorial time between the members of her cast with scrupulous fairness and
balance, making sure each gets his or her turn. No one is larger than life,
her novels show us again and again; the infinite plot permutations of the
bizarre everyday render us all vulnerable and insignificant.

It's impossible to convey the flavor of a writer's work in words that aren't written by that writer, so you'll have to take my word for it that Jill McGown was a unique talent. Her stories are as precise and cleverly designed as the best Swiss watches, and, more importantly, they're like no one else's. If, like me, you're a structure freak, if you believe the puzzle aspect of crime fiction matters, read her: she is criminally underrated, out of print now, and the rightful heir to Agatha Christie's plotting throne.

Sophie Hannah is the author of seven best-selling psychological thrillers, the most recent of which is Kind of Cruel. *Her novels are published in twenty-five countries, and two have so far been adapted for ITV1 and broadcast under the series title* Case Sensitive. *Sophie is also an award-winning, best-selling poet, and in 2007 was short-listed for the T. S. Eliot Prize for her collection* Pessimism for Beginners *(Carcanet). Visit her online at www.sophie hannah.com.*

A Simple Plan
by Scott Smith (1993)

MICHAEL KORYTA

Scott Smith (b. 1965) is the American-born writer of two novels, A Simple Plan *(1993) and* The Ruins *(2006), a horror story about young tourists who become trapped on a Mayan ruin in Mexico. Smith has adapted both novels for the screen, and received an Academy Award nomination for his screenplay for* A Simple Plan. *He said that he turned to scriptwriting "to escape a long book that was never going to happen," a reference to a novel he attempted to write between* A Simple Plan *and* The Ruins, *and which was eventually abandoned after one thousand pages.*

Bring up the question of "best debut" with a roomful of crime writers and I'll give you high odds that Scott Smith's *A Simple Plan* is among the first titles mentioned. Simply bringing up the topic of great crime novels will assuredly call it forth as well, but the jaw drops a little more when you read a book like *A Simple Plan* and realize that it is the writer's first published effort.

The initial setup of *A Simple Plan* is in fine keeping with its title. The narrator, Hank Mitchell, and his brother, Jacob, along with Lou (who is Jacob's friend and Hank's nemesis, and one of the most beautifully crafted characters in the book, dumb enough to annoy, sly enough to fear) discover a small, wrecked plane in the snow-covered Ohio woods. There's a bag of cash inside. $4.4 million in cash.

Jacob and Lou want to take it. Hank wants to report it. They argue. It's not stealing, Jacob insists, it's more like discovering a lost treasure.

"There was some sense in what he was saying, I could see that, yet at the same time it seemed like we were overlooking something," Smith notes in one of the all-time great understatements in crime fiction, as crows settle like vultures into the trees, and darkness falls around the three men, the atmosphere a gorgeous gothic promise upon which Smith delivers handsomely.

Simple enough, right? Take the money and run. Only of course they aren't running, that would be foolish. So it is take the money and wait . . . to either do the right thing or to do the just-a-little-bit-wrong thing that won't hurt anyone.

The plotting of *A Simple Plan* is, and should be, widely praised, but I'd argue that the greater genius of the novel is in the way in which Smith renders the voice of Hank, our narrator. In those early pages, Hank is compelling and familiar and reasonable. Oh so reasonable . . .

He's not a typical suspense novel protagonist—no military skills, police background, or heroic traits. No, he's the accountant at a feedstore in a small midwestern town. He has a pregnant wife and a troubled brother and the weight of two lost parents and one lost farm hanging over him, but these are problems we know or can relate to. This man is one of us. He's speaking for us.

And so his first decision—keep the cash for six months, and if no one comes looking for it during that period, the three men will split it up—is so measured, so damned *reasonable* that we can all imagine making it ourselves. "My plan . . . would allow me to postpone a decision until we had more information. I'd be taking a step, but not one that I couldn't undo."

That's all it is! A *postponement* of a potentially damaging decision. What's there to fear? Hank has thought of every angle. He's protected against every possible harm. In his simple plan, there is no threat.

By that night, the first promise has been broken; by the next day, the first murder has been committed. Those dreaded steps that cannot be undone have now been made, quite literally, down a slippery slope, with blood waiting beneath the snow. Hank's character has taken its first ingenious ripple as well. His reasonable façade breaks down in a moment of startling evil—which is then rationalized away. After all, Hank didn't make the mistake that leads to the first killing. He's simply protecting his brother, who made the mistake. We can all understand that, no matter how uncomfortable it makes us. You'd go to special lengths to save your own brother, wouldn't you?

And here Smith really begins his exploration into evil, and the pacing shifts into overdrive. The plot of *A Simple Plan* is a series of brilliantly compounded moral compromises. Hank's good judgment and sound character bend once, and problems ensue, and so they bend again, a little further, to stop the damage, and then . . .

Through it all, we have that voice of measured reason, the alarming one that just might be in each of us.

"Then, of course, there was the other path," Hank observes, looking away from the right choice, the obvious choice, and toward a darker moral ground. "It was already prepared for, already halfway trodden upon. I had the power to save Jacob, save the money. And in the end, I suppose, that was why I did it: because it seemed possible, it seemed like I wouldn't get caught. It was the same reason I took the money, the same reason I did all that follows. By doing one wrong thing, I thought I could make everything right."

I've often thought you could hold that line up to newspaper headlines every day and match it with more stories than not. It is what we wonder so often about so many people: Why on earth would they have done that?

Because it seemed possible, and it seemed like I wouldn't get caught.

The tightening noose of problems related to Hank's decision to keep the money is obviously a critical part of the drama and relentless pacing of *A Simple Plan,* but the grander trick is played out with our narrator on the internal level as the novel progresses. All bad choices aside, we're rooting for Hank, because his choices have been justified and rationalized and explained in a way that—perhaps with a wince or two—we can stomach. And we are worried about him, because his partners in crime are both foolish and dangerous. Jacob and Lou are an alarming duo, lacking Hank's pragmatism, his maturity, his sense of potential danger. His cunning.

It's a shame that he's caught in this mess with them, we think. Until the novel really unfolds, that is, and then you begin to question who is caught with whom.

The echoes of myth, and a near-biblical feel to the story, add a sense of moral weight to *A Simple Plan* that many suspense novels lack. At times the novel seems to draw heavily from the book of Genesis: Jacob dreams of using the money to reclaim the family's lost farm, seeking wisdom in a hopelessly outdated agricultural manual; the brothers who have promised to protect each other ultimately turn upon each other; and from the novel's first selfish choice, the first sin, spins forth a multitude of troubles in which the characters are soon hopelessly mired. Through it all, Smith conjures up one memorable device after another, my all-time favorite being the teddy bear that Jacob brings to Hank's newborn daughter. Turn the key in its belly and a soft nursery rhyme plays. Of course, it's the one toy that Hank's daughter prefers, and, as the relationship between the brothers deteriorates, the key is turned and the tune plays, haunting the pages of the novel.

Later, the carnage having reached its crescendo, Hank the Reasonable having slipped away from us to morph into Hank the Horrifying (a transformation that is all the more chilling to us because we once understood him so well), Hank paces an empty liquor store, walking past a dead clerk while a radio preacher blares forth with the Gospel.

"And is there a difference . . . between a sin of omission and a sin of commission?" the voice asks as Hank proceeds with yet another wrong thing that could, just maybe, make everything right again.

"And then there were hundreds, maybe thousands of people all across the region—Ohio, Michigan, Indiana, Illinois, Kentucky, West Virginia, Pennsylvania—sitting in their homes, driving in their cars, listening," Hank thinks of the radio preacher. "Each of them was connected to the others, and all of them were connected to me, simply by the sound of this man's voice."

He turns the radio off and goes about cleaning up his bloody mess, noting: "Without the preacher's voice, the building had an ominous silence to it. Every noise I made echoed back at me from the shelves of food, sounding furtive, rodent-like."

At this point in the novel, nine people are dead. Hank has gone from a reasonable man with a simple plan to an abhorrent figure, and we wonder what his punishment or reward will be, what will be gained or suffered for all that we've seen, all the blood that has been shed.

Smith gives it to us in a single, beautiful sentence that begins: "It took me four hours to—"

To do what? I leave it for you to find out, but I can remember coming upon that line during my first reading of the book, and it still brings on a dark laugh and a shake of the head. This grand denouement of Smith's blood-soaked tale is the kind of act of smooth confidence that you rarely encounter, the perfect choice perfectly executed, and the fact that it came in his first novel is, I have to admit, a bit maddening. He's so locked into the story that every beat, no matter how jarring, somehow seems natural, and every twist reminds us of the way we once understood Hank, refusing to let us off the hook for our own willingness to go along with it all.

The novel ends with Hank explaining that he often calls upon memories—including a specific image of his brother looking out at the family's lost farm, the windmill creaking, a barn missing—in order to force himself to weep. "And when I weep, I feel—despite everything I've done that might make it seem otherwise—human, exactly like everyone else."

In this is the essential page-turning chill of *A Simple Plan*, the carefully created sense that a man of reprehensible deeds is not that far from you, dear reader, not that far at all.

Smith has published only one more novel in the two decades since his debut. *The Ruins* is a stark, fatalistic horror story, and while this impatient reader hungers for him to return, he need not ever publish again to be assured of a place in the canon of great suspense novelists, a position he achieved upon arrival with *A Simple Plan*.

Michael Koryta (b. 1982) is the author of four novels in the Lincoln Perry series, the first of which, Tonight I Said Goodbye, *was published in 2004 and won the Private Eye Writers of America Best First Novel Award, and the Great Lakes Book Award for Best Mystery. He has also published four non-series novels:* Envy the Night *(2008) won the* Los Angeles Times *Book Prize for Best Mystery/Thriller, while* So Cold the River *(2010),* The Cypress House *(2011), and* The Ridge *(2011) were all* New York Times *Notable Books. His most recent novel is* The Prophet *(2012). Visit him online at www.michaelkoryta.com.*

Dan Leno and the Limehouse Golem
(aka *The Trial of Elizabeth Cree*)
by Peter Ackroyd (1994)

BARBARA NADEL

Peter Ackroyd (b. 1949) is an English novelist, poet, biographer, and critic whose particular passion is the history and culture of the city of London— "its power, its majesty, its darkness, its shadows"—leading him to become its greatest living chronicler. His novels frequently place real historical characters, in whose lives Ackroyd has immersed himself through research, in fictionalized or reimagined settings. These have included the writer Oscar Wilde, the poet Chatterton, the architect Nicholas Hawksmoor, and the English occultist John Dee. "The marvelous thing about research of that nature," Ackroyd has remarked, "is that you can come upon luminous and illuminating details which tend to be neglected by more academic historians, or more professional historians."

I like novels that I want to read again and again. But they also annoy me because they take me away from new literary adventures. As it is, a normal life span is hardly long enough to make even a dent on a fraction of all the good literature in the world. This book, *Dan Leno and the Limehouse Golem*, is a particular offender. Every year it drags me back, tantalizing and teasing me with mysteries that are not only fascinating but are also connected to my own past.

The setting for *Dan Leno and the Limehouse Golem* is London in the 1880s, just before Jack the Ripper began his career. It concerns the rise to fame and then downfall of a music hall artiste called Elizabeth Cree. The book opens with her execution for the murder of her husband, John, and it also ends with a theatrical rendition of the same event. At the same time a serial killer, known as the Golem, is stalking the streets of a London characterized by fog and lamplight, by opium-tinged illusion and the fear of dark-eyed strangers from unknown Eastern Europe. It is a landscape that is both bewitching and very familiar to me.

My paternal grandparents, products of the 1880s themselves, lived in an East End of London that existed beside the one I resided in as a small child in the 1960s. They were an eccentric pair who chose to exist in Edwardian London. They had gas lamps instead of electricity and my grandmother cooked on an old range—that would be enormously fashionable now—and the talk among them was always of a life that had disappeared. I spent a lot of my time in their house and so my early years were colored by tales of green-tinged fog, of funerals like theatrical productions, of murder, of poverty, and I was always surrounded by artifacts such as gas mantles, art pots, and mourning jewelry. In light of that, it is obvious why I'm always drawn to tales of bloody killing in Old London. But this book also appeals to the psychology graduate I grew up to be, too.

Who the killer known as the Golem might be is never revealed, although he speaks to the reader in the first person throughout the novel. Three prominent, and real, people from that era are suspected of being the Golem—Karl Marx, the Father of Socialism; the author George Gissing; and Dan Leno, the music hall star and so-called "funniest man on earth." Leno is also, in the book, instrumental in advancing Elizabeth Cree's theatrical career. Even more intriguing is the fact that all three suspects occasionally see each other, without knowing one another, in the Reading Room at the British Museum. In addition, at various stages during the narrative, they all read something by the famous "opium eater" Thomas De Quincey—significantly (or not) an essay entitled "On Murder, Considered as One of the Fine Arts" (1827). This work, based around the so-called Ratcliffe Highway murders of 1811, charts the bloody killings of the Marr family by a man called John Williams, who subsequently hanged himself and was buried with a stake through his heart. This is very rich and dastardly Victorian fare!

That the serial killer is dubbed "The Golem" is significant inasmuch as it speaks volumes about the prejudices of the day. A Golem is a mythical Jewish creature, originally created in Prague to help protect the community there from Gentile oppression. Now relocated to London, it is a figure of fear and a symbol of the danger inherent in the "otherness" that Judaism represents in a Christian society. Predictably, Marx, a Jew, is suspected of being the killer, as well as two Gentiles, who are nevertheless outsiders, too: Gissing, who lived with an alcoholic prostitute, and Leno, who, as a theatrical, existed outside of mainstream society. With its concentration on the notion of a Jewish villain, *Dan Leno and the Limehouse Golem* acts as a fictional early warning of the madness that engulfed parts of the old East End in the wake of the Jack the Ripper murders. A lot of the early suspects were Jews, and graffiti specifically naming Jews ("The Jewes are not the men to be blamed for nothing.") was found scrawled on a wall and was then scrubbed off by police anxious to prevent unrest between communities. I enjoy these echoes of and from the real historical world as well as the way Ackroyd uses De Quincey's essay as a vehicle for the musings of both the Golem and the other characters on the nature and morality of murder.

Another mystery that haunts this dark and sooty tale is that of Elizabeth Cree, the husband-poisoner whose life is connected to so many of the Golem's victims. A former prostitute, Elizabeth becomes a performer with Dan Leno's company, appearing onstage as both "Little Victor's Daughter," a girl, and the "Older Brother," a man. Hiding her previous profession as well as switching between male and female identities contributes to Elizabeth's feelings of paranoia as the book proceeds. In addition to being an homage to Victorian "bloody murder," *Dan Leno and the Limehouse Golem* is also about identity as a shifting and sometimes tricky concept that can occasionally turn on people and hurt or even kill them.

Observational and speculative jewels are one of the great joys of this novel. I particularly like the hangman who dresses up in Elizabeth Cree's clothes after he has killed her. Who has not speculated on the perversions of executioners? Or is Ackroyd simply playing into a modern audience's assumption that someone who kills, even with the sanction of the State, cannot possibly be "normal"?

Even though it takes me away from pastures new, I will always reread *Dan Leno and the Limehouse Golem* every year because it is a book that gives me so much. I always find something new in it every time I go back to it, and it has become as much a part of me as my memories of my grandparents' gas lamps, their dark pictures of saints and angels, and their terrifying coal cellar where dead bodies, left by Jack the Ripper, lurked, awaiting my childish investigations.

A gray-eyed London rat by birth, Barbara Nadel lives and works in a state of chaos. Oddly, she is married and has a wonderful son. Author of the Istanbul-based Inspector İkmen crime series, her latest book, Dead of Night, *has the nicotine-stained Turkish detective traveling to Detroit. Also out this year is the first book in her new London series entitled* A Private Business. *Based around an Anglo-Bangladeshi private investigation office in East London,* A Private Business *exposes a side of the Olympics site that isn't about sport. Barbara likes cats, green drinks, and wandering around London. Visit her online at www.internationalcrimeauthors.com.*

The Alienist
by Caleb Carr (1994)

REGGIE NADELSON

Caleb Carr (b. 1955) is a novelist, screenwriter, and military historian, with a particular fascination for the late nineteenth century in his fiction, most notably in The Alienist *(1994) and its sequel,* The Angel of Darkness *(1997). Carr grew up on a tough block of the Lower East Side of New York. He has said that the violence of the streets, and of his own home, gave him insights into such behavior. At the age of nineteen his father, the journalist Lucien Carr, stabbed a man to death for making unwanted sexual advances, and was helped by the writer Jack Kerouac to dispose of the body. Carr lives on Misery Mountain in Rensselaer County, New York, his isolation moderated by his admitted preference for dating much younger women. "I have a grim outlook on the world, and in particular on humanity," he told the* New York Times *in 2005. "I spent years denying it, but I am very misanthropic. And I live alone on a mountain for a reason."*

In 1896, New York was at a turning point, a city on the verge. The modern world was being born in New York, where the first movie parlors had opened a few years earlier. The first automobiles had just appeared, and traffic was already in gridlock. In spite of trolleys and cable cars, and the Elevated Railroad—the city's original public transport system—horse-drawn vehicles of every variety careened around town in the thousands.

Vicious newspaper wars were in full swing as readership soared, and every scandal was fodder for what quickly became the tabloid press. Corruption ran deep in the urban fabric: corrupt cops, corrupt politicians, all on the take.

It was also the beginning of an egalitarian age in showbiz, when at the fashionable Delmonico's you could spot Mrs. Vanderbilt as well as

Lillian Russell. Everything was for sale: women and children, sex, and drugs—cocaine, chloral hydrate, benzene. New York's great port, its commerce and stock exchange, and the very rich that profited from it all, made Manhattan the financial capital of the country. Immigrants in their millions—Irish, Italian, Jewish, Chinese, and Caribbean—came looking for work on the docks, in the markets, and in the garment factories, making the city the most densely populated place on earth. All that poverty alongside so much wealth, stirred up with profound political corruption, and plenty of xenophobia, gave it a febrile quality: a city about to explode, a population dancing at the edge of the urban volcano.

All this makes *The Alienist* a brilliant novel that grasps the period by its bulging neck and delivers it, breathing and kicking, onto the page. First published in 1994, Caleb Carr's terrifying thriller turns the island of Manhattan into its greatest character. But this is also the story of a serial killer who is murdering those boy prostitutes who dress, and make themselves up, as girls.

The very graphically described murders are horrible—almost too horrible—each committed with increasing violence; the reader is spared no detail. The police, for the most part, take little interest. What difference if another "foreign" boy is murdered or not? Who will care? But then, this is a police force so corrupt that you can smell the bad flesh.

The book is narrated by John Schuyler Moore on the occasion of Theodore Roosevelt's funeral, more than twenty years after the crimes in question have been committed. As the action begins, we learn that Moore and Roosevelt are great friends, having first met as undergraduates at Harvard, where they were also pals with Dr. Laszlo Kreizler. Roosevelt is now the reform police commissioner of New York, just years before he would become the first American president of the twentieth century. Moore has become a crime reporter on the *New York Times*. And Kreizler is already legendary as an "alienist," called in to assess cases of both the living and the dead.

In the nineteenth century, as Carr points out at the beginning of the book, the mentally ill were "thought to be 'alienated,' not only from the rest of society but from their own true natures. Those who studied mental pathologies were therefore known as alienists." (There is a lot of debate about psychological methods. The pragmatist William James—who taught the Harvard trio—is often discussed, as are the new Freudian notions then much in the wind.)

There is also Sara Howard, a young woman obsessed with the idea of becoming a detective at a time when no well-reared girl—no female at all—would think of such a thing, although it would not be long before the American suffragettes were on the march.

Together with the three men, Howard goes to work on the serial killer case. To avoid the corrupt cops, she and the others, along with a posse of eccentric minor characters, set up an independent headquarters at 808 Broadway, which overlooks Grace Church (the church in which the author Edith Wharton was baptized). When they break for meals, it's often to the old St. Denis Hotel, on Eleventh and Broadway, where there's a pleasant outdoor restaurant. All these buildings remain much as they once were, though 808 Broadway is now a pricey condo, and the St. Denis a building full of shrinks and yoga teachers.

The array of characters—the ex-killers, the prostitutes, the society nobs—reveals plenty about the times. And real people make credible appearances: Lincoln Steffens, the reforming journalist; Jacob Riis, whose photographs of the slums led eventually to better housing and health laws; Charlie Delmonico, who serves the principals (and the rest of society) with oysters and turtle soup.

Dr. Kreizler seems to have an appetite for ordering fabulous feasts for his colleagues in the middle of the task of tracking down the vicious killer. The *aiguillettes* of bass are done in a creamy Mornay sauce, followed by saddle of lamb, canvasback duck with currant *gelée,* some *petits aspics de foie gras;* and later, pears steeped in wine, deep-fried, powdered with sugar, and smothered in apricot sauce—all perfectly paired with the right wines! It seems to be Kreizler's conviction that the best work is done over great meals—or maybe it's just Carr's own appetite writ large. Either way, I love it.

Interestingly, around the time of publication, some critics complained about the torrent of historical detail, the discussion of forensic tools, the pages of local history, even those meals. Carr is a historian as well as a novelist, and it's exactly this, the exquisite evocation of the city, that makes the book so special, so alluring, so much a part of the city landscape it chronicles.

You can smell the fresh peach on which young Moore breakfasts at his aunt's house on Washington Square North, a bastion of genteel comfort. You can smell the stink of the unspeakable slums on the Lower East Side, the tenements where people are literally packed by the dozen into rooms with no windows, no ventilation. My own father was born here in 1903, not long after the time of the book's action.

This was the great age of immigration. Ellis Island had opened in 1892, and millions of people poured in, most of them stopping in New York, where they lived in conditions among the worst on earth.

I can no longer pass Cooper Square, or the Bowery, without thinking of Carr's huge cast of down-and-outs, of criminals and cops. Carr's city, even if it includes opera at the Met, and outings to the theater, is a murderous place. It's not so much the murders themselves that contain the book's true horror; it's the living conditions, the very feel of the seedy rooms where prostitutes took their clients, the stink of the slums.

True, the murders—and the revelation of the killer—are enough to satisfy those readers who go to books for plot. The characters do their job. For me, though, it's the way *The Alienist* tells the story of New York at a moment of tremendous change that enthralls.

People think of New York as a new city, the iconic city of now and the future, of skyscrapers and money, of penthouses and finance houses. It is, in fact, when you take the time to look around a corner, or over the rooftops, a profoundly nineteenth-century town, one that was just coming into its own in the 1890s. The subway was being dug. The Williamsburg Bridge was going up. A cable car ran over the Brooklyn Bridge, joining the two cities. These great engineering feats—the bridges and tunnels, the subways and train stations—were as much a part of the Victorian imagination as London's railway stations.

Many of the killings in *The Alienist* take place near water: on the building site for the new Williamsburg Bridge, at Castle Clinton near the Battery and the river. Manhattan is an island; the city is an archipelago. Carr knows his city.

One of the grand landmarks of the era was the city reservoir, where the terrifying finale of the book takes place. It stood where the Forty-second Street library now stands. It was immense. High walls marked it, with turrets and control towers. People strolled on its ramparts. It has captured the imagination of many writers, among them E. L. Doctorow in his wonderful novel *The Waterworks*.

Having just reread *The Alienist*, I've been thinking a lot about my own neighborhood. The building where I have a loft went up in 1881, in what is now SoHo, where tourists ogle the Louis Vuittons and buy ice cream for four bucks, then walk a few blocks to Mulberry at Bleecker.

This, Carr writes, "marked the heart of a jungle of tenements, brothels, concert halls, saloons, and gambling houses." It also had, he notes, the carnival atmosphere of a brutal Roman circus.

A space as small and dense as Manhattan Island is like an ongoing archaeological dig. You can only go up or down in Manhattan, so you build higher, and look deeper, and uncover these layers or transform them into something else. Everybody complains about change, but there is nothing else in this city. If you fail to embrace it, you end up like the late nineteenth-century Cassandra who announced that—and this seems utterly true in *The Alienist*, where horse-drawn vehicles thrive in their thousands—the city would soon disappear in an environmental disaster made up entirely of the overwhelming quantities of horse manure.

Reggie Nadelson was born, raised, and lives in downtown Manhattan. Once in a while she leaves New York and visits other places, and has lived in London, Paris, and Northern California. A journalist by trade, she has worked for newspapers and magazines in London and New York, and is currently a travel writer for Travel + Leisure. *Her 1991 book,* Comrade Rockstar, *has been sold to Tom Hanks who has plans to turn it into a feature film.* Blood Count, *her ninth mystery in the Artie Cohen series, which takes place in Harlem, was published in 2010. Most of her books are set in New York because she doesn't really know about much else, though she likes the movies a lot, and has worked on a couple of documentaries for the BBC. In* Manhattan '62, *her forthcoming novel, her new hero is Detective Patrick Arthur John Declan Wynne. He is Irish. He likes Irish whiskey a lot. Visit him online at www.reggienadelson.com.*

The Man Who Smiled
by Henning Mankell (1994)

ANN CLEEVES

Henning Mankell (b. 1948) is a Swedish author best known for his Ystad-based police inspector Kurt Wallander, who featured in nine novels in total, along with a collection of novellas, The Pyramid *(2008). The first novel,* Faceless Killers, *appeared in 1991; Mankell's final Wallander mystery,* The Troubled Man, *was published in 2009. A prolific writer, Mankell has also published nonseries crime titles, including* Kennedy's Brain *(2005) and* The Man from Beijing *(2007); a further twelve literary novels, beginning with his debut* Vettvillingen *in 1977; and two series of books for children and young adults. He has also written more than forty plays and a number of screenplay adaptations for TV. Among the many awards Mankell has won are the Glass Key award for* Faceless Killers *in 1992, and the Crime Writers' Association Gold Dagger for* Sidetracked *in 1995.*

Henning Mankell was the first Scandinavian crime writer I read. His books were translated and readily available long before Larsson or Nesbø became best sellers. Of course, Sjöwall and Wahlöö were there before him, but Mankell was mainstream and popular and set the tone for the much-mocked Nordic gloom. His central character, Kurt Wallander, is a classic flawed detective, divorced, troubled, and intuitive. Wallander drinks too much, and rages against the system, but is honorable almost beyond credibility. His team—Ann-Britt Höglund, Svedberg, Martinsson—along with Nyberg the pathologist, Åkeson the prosecutor, and Björk, the team's boss—are well drawn and convincing. I enjoy the books particularly because of the interaction between these colleagues, the tensions and petty professional jealousies. The relationship between Wallander and Ann-Britt, the golden girl just from college, is especially strong. Mankell's stories are set against the flat farmland and dunes of Skåne in southern Sweden. This is small-town territory, populated by farmers and traditional businessmen. Mankell gave me a taste for translated crime fiction and since then it's become my reading passion. The translation of Mankell's work—the majority translated by Laurie Thompson—is clear and unobtrusive.

The Man Who Smiled isn't Mankell's most famous book. That's probably *Sidetracked,* which won the Gold Dagger. *Sidetracked* has an iconic initial scene with a girl running around a field of bright yellow rape and setting fire to herself. That's memorable, and not just because Kenneth Branagh chose it to start his television adaptation of the series, *Wallander.* But I think *The Man Who Smiled* is classic Mankell. If only one of his books were to be remembered, then this would tell you all that you need to know about Kurt Wallander and his creator.

In one sense the plot is preposterous, a crazy conspiracy theory involving big business, a trade in body organs, a gothic castle, and a ruthless rich man. And there is no mystery, no surprise ending. While the rest of the book is told from the point of view of Kurt Wallander, for the first few pages we are inside the head of Gustaf Torstensson, the first murder victim, and he shares his concerns and explains the reasons why he must die. The individuals responsible for the murder have no psychological depth. Really, we have no understanding of their personal backgrounds or their relationships. Yet I found this book compelling. I continued reading it at almost one sitting, not because I needed to understand the shadowy figures of capitalist evil, but because I wanted to spend time with the haunted introvert Wallander, and witness his triumph.

Mankell is brilliant on early visual scenes. In *The Man Who Smiled* it's foggy, and Torstensson, an elderly lawyer, is driving slowly and carefully along a country road. He's just come from a meeting and runs through his problems in his head. A fraud has been committed and he's implicated because he hasn't reported it. It is a sin of omission, not commission. He's anxious about the consequences and worries that he's being followed, but there are no headlights behind him. Then, in the middle of the road ahead of him, he sees a chair, standing like a throne, blocking his way. And sitting on the chair is an effigy. This is a great way to start the novel and to hook the reader.

We first meet Wallander on a beach in Denmark. He's on sick leave. In a previous novel he killed a man in the line of duty and he's had a breakdown fueled by alcohol and self-loathing. The holiday by the seaside is a kind of recuperation. Then, out of the blue, he has a visitor. Sten Torstensson is the son of Gustaf, a lawyer like his father. He and Wallander are not exactly friends, but they've worked together, and he needs Wallander's help. His father's death has been put down as a car accident—an elderly man driving too quickly in the fog—but Sten can't accept that. He wants Wallander to look more closely into the case, but the detective refuses. He has almost decided to leave the police. It is only when he returns to Ystad and reads that Sten has also been killed, apparently murdered during a burglary, that he decides to become involved. He returns to work to head up the murder investigation.

The book was written in the early '90s but its preoccupations seem contemporary. This is a book about the dangers of globalization and corporate greed, the complicated web of finance that makes it almost impossible to pin responsibility for fraud on any individual. We might think of Sweden as almost utopian, compassionate, and organized for the benefit of its citizens, but Mankell often mourns the old ideals, describing a community that has become fractured, self-serving, and intolerant. Wallander's enemy, the eponymous man who smiled, is entirely without compassion or morality. He is Harderberg, the head of a business empire who has set up his headquarters in Farnholm Castle in Skåne. The castle is appropriate—Mankell describes Harderberg as "a man whose power was not unlike that of a medieval prince."

Wallander links Harderberg to the art dealers who bought paintings from his father. Wallander Senior is another recurring character in the novels. He's irascible, unpredictable, and suffering from some form of dementia. In his younger days he churned out kitsch landscape art and the dealers, described by Kurt as "silk knights," would turn up in their silk suits and American cars to buy. As a child Kurt was attracted to these men for their money and their style, but he hated the way his father ingratiated himself with them, while obviously despising them.

The climax to the novel is melodramatic and unlikely. Wallander gains entry to the castle despite its security, overpowers Harderberg's bodyguards, and escapes just in time to prevent Harderberg from flying off in his private jet. But in each of Mankell's novels the plot is the least important element, and we allow ourselves to be carried along by the improbable story because we care about Kurt Wallander, his team, and his ideas about justice.

Wallander appears for the last time in *The Troubled Man*. He'll be missed, but he should not be forgotten.

Ann Cleeves grew up in North Devon and worked as a bird observatory cook, auxiliary coastguard, probation officer, and reader development officer before writing full-time. She has two series of traditional crime stories—one set in Shetland and one in Northumberland. The first Shetland novel, Raven Black, *won the CWA Duncan Lawrie Dagger. The Northumberland books have been adapted for ITV and star Brenda Blethyn as Vera Stanhope. Her latest novel is* The Glass Room. *Visit her online at www.anncleeves.com.*

American Tabloid
by James Ellroy (1995)

STUART NEVILLE

Lee Earle "James" Ellroy (b. 1948) is one of the iconic figures in modern crime fiction, the self-described Demon Dog of the genre. Born in Los Angeles, his life and work have been shadowed by the murder of his mother, Geneva Hilliker Ellroy, in 1958, a case that remains unsolved but was explicitly explored in his nonfiction book My Dark Places *(1996). His novels are densely plotted, bleakly moral, and have latterly been written in a telegraphic prose of short, unadorned sentences, a style that has not proved uncontroversial, with one critic comparing the experience of reading later Ellroy to being hit over the head with a small hammer for six hundred pages.*

"America was never innocent." Thus begins James Ellroy's foreword to *American Tabloid*, and just shy of six hundred pages later, he'll have you convinced.

The first book of the American Underworld Trilogy centers on three men who orbit John F. Kennedy's rise to power, his thousand days of presidency, and, ultimately, his assassination. These bad, bad men are satellites to a world of collusion, conspiracy, and corruption. Kemper Boyd, G-man and scion of a once-wealthy dynasty, is driven by vanity and avarice, hoping to shine in Jack and Bobby Kennedy's reflected glory. Ward Littell, Boyd's fellow FBI agent, is a weak man willing to sell his soul to prove otherwise. Pete Bondurant is a man-mountain, a vicious thug in the employ of Howard Hughes and Jimmy Hoffa, looking for the big money and happy to spill blood to get it.

All three are drawn, like driftwood in a whirlpool, to the epicenter of JFK's presidential campaign. They rally support from the CIA, the mob, and Cuban exiles by aligning them all against a common enemy: Fidel Castro, the Communist leader who has seized power just miles from Miami, the treacherous heel who shafted the Outfit by nationalizing their Havana casinos, the ruthless dictator who tortured and executed his Cuban countrymen. They're all convinced Bad-Back Jack is the man to take the Beard down. And when he doesn't deliver, all roads lead to Dallas.

In *American Tabloid*, James Ellroy shifts his diamond-sharp gaze away from post-WWII Los Angeles and broadens his canvas to cover the entire United States and beyond. It's the hard-as-nails bravura of *The Black Dahlia*, *L.A. Confidential*, and *White Jazz* exploded to sully five years of American history. With an almost tangible glee, Ellroy drags the Kennedy clan through the mud, especially its patriarch, Joseph P. Kennedy. Along the way we meet a mind-boggling cast of historical figures: J. Edgar Hoover, Howard Hughes, Jimmy Hoffa, Jack Ruby, Santo Trafficante, Sam Giancana, Carlos Marcello, and more. Even Ava Gardner, Frank Sinatra, and Marilyn Monroe make appearances. The sheer scale of this story is awe-inspiring, and it's a Herculean feat of plotting and character development.

Like spy novelist John le Carré, keeping up with Ellroy's twists and turns is akin to listening to bebop jazz: if you try to follow every melody, chord, and beat, you'll find yourself dizzy and disoriented. Instead, you must step back and take in the greater arcs, like finding the three-dimensional image in a Magic Eye picture by looking through it. But complexity is not the greatest challenge in reading James Ellroy; the biggest obstacle is your willingness, or otherwise, to follow the author's dark paths.

I first read *American Tabloid* just over a decade ago while I was in the process of deciding that Ellroy was my favorite author. This is the book that sealed the deal. More than that, it's the book that made me realize the depths a skilled writer can plumb while holding on to our empathy for his less than noble characters. Note the choice of word there: "empathy," not "sympathy." Ellroy can bring you to the darkest reaches of the soul, force you to stare unblinkingly at the cruel perversions of which human beings are capable, and send you away with those images seared on your mind—and he has the skill and the courage to make you glad of the journey. That's the key thing I took away from *American Tabloid*: an author's courage can take you places you never wanted to be, with people you never wanted to meet, and in the process teach you something about the nature of mankind.

Here's just one example of that courage in action. In a world whose morals are repugnant to us, most authors will have the protagonist stand apart from the mire. If racism, homophobia, and misogyny are the order of the day, the protagonist will somehow be more enlightened than his fellow man. Not with Ellroy. For the most part, his three protagonists are every bit as bigoted and hate-filled as those around them. Ellroy, the self-proclaimed 'Demon Dog' of crime fiction, has no use for political correctness. His characters' worldviews are as tainted as the money the fictionalized Kennedy dynasty was built on. In a novel where our heroes commit murder, peddle heroin, and plot the assassination of the leader of the free world, why should we expect them to be above such base prejudices? When you open an Ellroy novel, you make a pact with the devil to see how low a character can sink. If you haven't the stomach to go all the way, you'd better just close the book and put it back on the shelf.

It was this utter fearlessness that impacted most upon me, and my writing. The greatest thing I've gained from Ellroy is the will to take my characters farther and deeper into the dark places than I, or the reader, might be comfortable with. When I'm tempted to tone down a scene, throw some artificially sympathetic trait on a character, or generally chicken out, it's *American Tabloid* I remember.

In Ellroy's America, everyone has blood under their nails, from the lowest of street thugs to the holder of the highest office in the land. That bleak and cynical outlook is carried through *American Tabloid*'s sequel, *The Cold Six Thousand*. But it's not until *Blood's a Rover*, the conclusion to the "Underworld USA" trilogy, that the saga's moral core comes into focus: the human and social cost of the lust for power. Taken as a whole, the trilogy must be considered a landmark in American literature, whose political themes seem ever more prescient as time goes by, but *American Tabloid* can simply be appreciated for its most basic nature: a bloody good thriller by a writer at the top of his game.

Northern Ireland author Stuart Neville's debut novel, The Ghosts of Belfast *(aka* The Twelve*), won the* Los Angeles Times *Book Prize for Best Mystery/ Thriller in 2010, the Spinetingler "New Voice" award, also in 2010, Le Prix*

Mystère de la Critique du Meilleur Roman Étranger, and the *Grand Prix du Roman Noir Étranger. The novel was further nominated for the Dilys Award, the Anthony Award, the Barry Award, and the Macavity Award. Neville's second novel,* Collusion *(2010), was also short-listed for the* Los Angeles Times *Book Prize for Best Mystery/Thriller. His current offering is* Stolen Souls *(2011). Visit him online at www.stuartneville.com.*

The Big Blowdown
by George Pelecanos (1996)

DECLAN BURKE

*The novels of George Pelecanos (b. 1957) are for the most part set in Washington DC, spanning a period of time from the 1930s (*The Big Blowdown, *1996) to the present day (*The Cut, *2011). He made his debut with* A Firing Offense *in 1992, the first of the Nick Stefanos trilogy. A second cycle of novels, the DC Quartet, began with* The Big Blowdown *and concluded with* Shame the Devil *(2000). A further series of four novels, featuring private eyes Derek Strange and Terry Quinn, began with* Right as Rain *in 2001; Pelecanos's most recent novel,* What It Was *(2012), is a prequel to that series. Pelecanos has also served as a coproducer and writer on the TV series* The Wire *(2002–08), for which he has won Edgar, Emmy, and Writers Guild of America awards, and is currently coproducing and writing on* Treme *(2010–).*

It was a wandering father job . . .

The Big Blowdown was George Pelecanos's fifth novel. The previous books—the Nick Stefanos trilogy of *A Firing Offense* (1992), *Nick's Trip* (1993), and *Down By the River Where the Dead Men Go* (1995), and the stand-alone *Shoedog* (1994)—had already established Pelecanos as a unique voice, and one of the finest exponents of the modern American crime novel alongside his contemporaries Dennis Lehane, Laura Lippman, and James Sallis.

First-generation Greek American, the son of a Spartan mother and father, Pelecanos invested his work with an outsider's insight into American culture and society, in particular the urban badlands of inner-city Washington DC.

I tell you all this, of course, with the 20/20 clarity of hindsight. When I first stumbled across George Pelecanos, courtesy of a magazine article

I read in the kitchen of a grotty student flat in Galway to distract me from the worst of a hangover, all I knew about the contemporary American crime novel was that, Elmore Leonard and James Ellroy apart, it was a pale and largely pointless imitation of demigods such as Raymond Chandler, James M. Cain, and Jim Thompson.

Anyway, the magazine—I believe it was *Uncut*—claimed that George Pelecanos was the best thing since a very large loaf of thickly sliced bread, and I, as a reader of discerning taste, should get in on the ground floor with his latest offering, *King Suckerman*.

This was 1997, and had I been a reader of discerning taste I wouldn't have needed any magazines to set me up with my next read. I wasn't long out of college, working in a bar and writing part-time for a monthly magazine. I'd written a book-length story by then, a crime novel set in the Greek islands, but when I tell you that the story's single violent death occurs with three short chapters to go, and that the remainder of the story concerns itself with how three guys avoid getting caught up in the consequences of that death, you'll appreciate that I had, putting it gently, yet to develop a feel for the rhythm and pacing of a crime novel.

Anyway, long story short, I read *King Suckerman*.

Boom . . .

Like all the great stuff that has stayed with me over the years—Raymond Chandler, Leonard Cohen, the Pixies, James Ellroy, Rollerskate Skinny, Elmore Leonard—my first reaction was, *I didn't know you were allowed to sound like that.*

Heady stuff. A good old-fashioned tale of revenge and redemption swaggering along with superfly cool, with a retro funk sound track that fairly pounded off the page.

Naturally, I went looking for its predecessor, *The Big Blowdown*.

The Big Blowdown had it *all*. It delivered on everything *King Suckerman* had promised, and more, with the bonus of the period setting of the 1930s and '40s.

Head-melting stuff, especially if you have aspirations to write.

Of course, I missed the whole point. Such things are tough to quantify, but I'll settle now for accepting that I missed it by a country mile. It's fair to say that you read things differently in your midforties than you might have done in your midtwenties.

Because on first reading, Pete Karras, the hero of *The Big Blowdown*, is a cool guy. He's sharp, he's hip, he's dressed to impress. Pete Karras is the smartest guy in any room he walks into. Pete Karras is so cool he joins the Marines and goes off to war in the Pacific and even has the decency to hesitate before killing his first Jap:

> Peter Karras had the first man he ever killed in his sights for ten minutes before he managed to pull the trigger. The man was a sniper who had taken out a Marine in Karras's unit . . .

Pete Karras. What's not to like?

Well, on rereading the same book two decades later, Pete Karras likes himself a little too much. Pete Karras has bought into the myth of Pete Karras, believes he can do his own thing, thumb his nose at people who don't like the nose-thumb schtick. And so Pete Karras winds up in a dark alleyway watching a lead-lined baseball bat swing down out of the night sky, and suddenly Pete Karras isn't anywhere near as cool as he once thought he might be.

Suddenly Pete Karras is a prematurely gray young man with a bad limp and a crappy job and a baby son and a wife with thickening ankles.

He isn't a bad man; he just isn't a particularly good one. Even as he goes about the quasi-tragic business of eking out a tiny measure of dignity and redemption according to the street's unforgiving code, Pete Karras finds himself locked outside what matters most, musing on a fundamental failure of character:

> Karras had a seat in the living room armchair, thinking: *Now what do I do? . . .* I'm just not cut out for this racket. Some guys can sit around with their families and get used to it and even like it, but I'm not built for it. Who the hell am I kidding? It's just not right for me.

What's missing?

A father. Or fathers plural, to be precise.

Right from the start of *The Big Blowdown* we understand that the very young Pete Karras has no relationship with his father, a violent racist who beats Pete's mother and considers his son puny, unmanly. One of the minor characters, Mike Florek, arrives in Washington DC in search of his missing sister, the man of his family despite his tender years. Pete Karras himself grows up to become a bad father, a womanizer estranged from his baby son. In the novel's coda, the father figure toward whom Pete gravitates, the gruff restaurant owner Nick Stefanos, complains that his own son back in Greece has abdicated his responsibilities and foisted his own baby son on the aging Nick.

It's a perverse scenario. The immigrants we meet in *The Big Blowdown*—Greek for the most part, but Italian, Polish, and Irish, too—are fiercely self-defining in terms of their ethnic origins, and yet find themselves stumbling blindly to all points of the moral compass of their new world for the want of a caring, guiding hand on their shoulder.

Pete Karras—and this is why he's cool now, rereading him in my midforties with a child of my own sleeping downstairs in her cot—comes to realize that the best thing that a bad father can do is get out of a child's way, especially if acting on that realization involves the ultimate in self-sacrifice, leaving only a faint, ghostly hand on the shoulder of his growing son.

Life moves on. Two decades after I first read *The Big Blowdown*, I've been lucky enough to have some crime novels of my own published. I'm also very fortunate in that my day job revolves around books and movies, around reviewing novels and interviewing writers.

I interviewed George Pelecanos some months ago, on the publication of his most recent novel, *What It Was*. During the course of the conversation, I asked about a paragraph near the end of the book, when one of the characters speaks of his wartime experience:

> Vaughn lit a cigarette and pushed the lighter in front of Strange so that he could see the Okinawa inlay on the Zippo's face. "First time I killed a man was on that island. I had him in the sights of my M-One for fifteen minutes before I squeezed the trigger. But I did it . . ."

I couldn't help but ask about the significance of a tale so important that it warranted telling twice, in novels over fifteen years apart.

"You know," Pelecanos said, "*The Big Blowdown* was an important book for me. Pete Karras, up until the war, is my father. He lived in a very poor slum in Chinatown [in DC], where all the poorest immigrants lived, and he ended up going to the Pacific and fighting as a Marine. And when he came home, he became a father and husband, and he worked hard for his living, yeah. It's at that point that the characters diverge, but I did want to give my father his due in terms of his early life. Yeah, so that book is very important to me. A lot of people don't know about that book, that it's one of my favorite books."

From the 1930s setting of *The Big Blowdown* right through to *What It Was,* and in his work as a producer and writer on the TV series *The Wire* (2002–2008) and *Treme* (2010–), the best of George Pelecanos's work has been characterized by a clear-eyed and unsentimental compassion for fatherless sons. An immigrant's empathy, perhaps.

I did want to give my father his due . . .

"Just a story," Derek Strange tells Nick Stefanos in the coda to *What It Was.*

"It's just a story," Nick Stefanos tells his friend Costa at the end of *The Big Blowdown.*

Well, yes. But then, all stories are just stories. It's how you tell them that counts, and who you tell them to. What it is you're handing on.

The Big Blowdown, if you read it closely enough, is a crime novel that can make you cry. There aren't enough of those, I think.

———————

Declan Burke is the author of Eightball Boogie *(2003),* The Big O *(2007), and* Absolute Zero Cool *(2011). He is the editor of* Down These Green Streets: Irish Crime Writing in the 21st Century *(Liberties Press, 2011), and hosts a website dedicated to Irish crime fiction called Crime Always Pays. His latest novel is* Slaughter's Hound *(2012). He lives in Wicklow with his wife and daughter, where he is not allowed to own a cat, or be owned by one. Visit him online at www.crimealwayspays.blogspot.com.*

A Crime in the Neighborhood
by Suzanne Berne (1997)

THOMAS H. COOK

Suzanne Berne (b. 1961) won the Orange Prize for her debut novel, A Crime in the Neighborhood *(1997), which concerns itself with the murder of a child against the backdrop of the Watergate scandal, as recounted by a ten-year-old girl. Berne, an associate English professor at Boston College who has taught at Wellesley and Harvard, specializes in psychological narratives in a domestic setting. In addition to* A Crime in the Neighborhood, *Berne has published* A Perfect Arrangement *(2001),* The Ghost at the Table *(2006), and* Missing Lucile *(2010).*

I have always believed that a crime novel, at its best, should simply be a novel in which there is a crime. This casts a very wide net, of course, since there are very few works of fiction that do not involve, at least tangentially, some manner of crime. How much Dostoyevsky would there be without a crime? The same can be said of Thomas Hardy, and certainly of Dickens as well. The larger problem is that many crime writers have pretty much ceased to include those elements of character and atmosphere that add so much to any novel. They have also had a tendency to cast aside any sense of organic development. Nonetheless, I continue to trumpet the so-called literary crime novel and to admire the crime novel that gives readers a full fictional dinner: starter, entrée, and dessert.

Suzanne Berne's *A Crime in the Neighborhood* is not only a novel that happens to be about a crime, but one that beautifully combines the suspense of a crime novel with all the elements that make for a fully rounded reading experience.

There are two crimes in *A Crime in the Neighborhood*. The first is the murder of a little boy. True to the stark and unblinking sense of reality that pervades this novel, the victim is a nasty little bastard, unattractive in every way a child can be unattractive, the sort of kid no one in the neighborhood might actually miss, save for his parents. And yet the murder of Boyd Ellison shakes the lives and rattles the sense of security that has, until now, been the signal reality of the neighborhood. "Mistakes," Berne writes, "are where life really happens," and it is this murder that will mark the grave mistake later to be committed by the novel's thirteen-year-old narrator, the precocious, sensitive, and somewhat dreamy Marsha.

A sense of some great impending wrong pervades *A Crime in the Neighborhood*. Reading it is like sitting on a sunny lawn as a black line of thunderstorms steadily and fearsomely advances along the far horizon. The reader watches helplessly as Marsha is drawn into the investigation, the girl taking note of various details in the way she thinks Sherlock Holmes would have taken note of them. But Marsha, as the reader knows, is no Sherlock Holmes. Rather, she is a young girl on the quivering brink of adulthood, living with her mother and siblings in a home abandoned by her father, who has run off with the "other woman." The loss of the father creates yet another layer of dread in *A Crime in the Neighborhood*. Acts have consequences, often quite unexpected ones, and Marsha's loss of her father has created a perilous imbalance in her life; and, as we learn, a person who loses purchase can grasp for terrible things while attempting to regain it.

It is this Marsha, abandoned by her father, and with her natural inquisitiveness and sense of drama fueled by the murder of a little boy, who first begins to take note of a new neighbor, a bachelor, Mr. Green: "He was a squat man, with a pinkish face, blandly familiar, although he didn't actually resemble anyone I knew. When he bent his head, I saw that he had a bald spot, shaped like a heart."

There is a deadpan accuracy to this description, one that makes it all the more frightening when, to these far from unusual traits, Marsha later adds characteristics of appearance and behavior that are to her mind at first creepy, then sinister, and at last murderous. Helplessly, the reader follows her descent as she becomes just the sort of girl who once conjured up the madness of Salem, but without the outward hysterics; a transformation that is quiet, inward, and for that reason, all the more fraught with terror.

But *A Crime in the Neighborhood* would be no more than a well-done little thriller if it were only about the murder of Boyd Ellison and its impact upon a neighborhood girl. What makes the book memorable is its perfect blending of small story with great theme. Of a burglary, Ms. Berne has a neighbor say: "This break-in stuff is going to turn into a big disaster. Sometimes things like this start small, but then they get out of control. That's what happens. It doesn't take long for a lousy mistake to turn into a crime."

From that simple insight, Ms. Berne builds her novel into a work of genuine and heartbreaking social criticism, and by that means delineates a second, far more sweeping and profound crime in the neighborhood than the murder of Boyd Ellison. She does this without beating a loud philosophical drum. Thus, at one point, when the neighborhood forms a watch group, no one comes to Marsha's house in search of assistance or support: "No one had knocked on our door, probably because they realized my father no longer lived there."

The image of the missing father looms very large indeed in *A Crime in the Neighborhood,* its impact much more disastrous and far-reaching than the occasional missing child. From the Watergate era that is the setting of the novel onward, the rate of divorce and the consequent number of fatherless homes rises continually in the United States.

Ms. Berne connects all this without rubbing our faces in it or for one moment straining Marsha's narrative voice:

> In a confused manner, I think I'd begun to connect my father's leaving us with Boyd Ellison's murder and even with whatever it was that had happened at Watergate. Although I couldn't have explained it then, I believed that my father's departure had deeply jarred the domestic order not just in our house, but in the neighborhood, and by extension the country, since in those days my neighborhood was my country.

As *A Crime in the Neighborhood* so eloquently demonstrates, a book doesn't have to be pretentious or self-conscious in order truly to be about something. Yet even when the book announces its theme, it does so in a way that does not impinge upon the suspense of the narrative or cause it to lose its focus on Marsha as the book's central character. For the social disintegration that is the second crime in the neighborhood is one against which Marsha finally cries out in a quiet, yet devastating passage: "Years later, during one of our infrequent visits, I told my father about that night and how the twins and I had watched from the porch as all the other fathers gathered on the street, talking with their arms folded. 'We were frightened. We needed you . . . And you weren't there.' "

A Crime in the Neighborhood never departs from the crime that generates the book's forward momentum, but neither does it give in to the temptation of many crime writers to toss overboard every aspect of the literary novel—character, atmosphere, a passage so lovely it stops us in our tracks—in order to ensure that the "action" continues at a breakneck pace. For that reason, I think it should be read not only because it is a fine book in its own right, but because it also shows just how fine a "crime novel" can be.

Thomas H. Cook is the author of twenty-six novels and two works of nonfiction. He has been nominated for the Edgar Allan Poe Award seven times in five different categories, and his novel The Chatham School Affair *won the Edgar for Best Novel in 1996. His novel* Red Leaves *won the Barry Award, and various other novels have been nominated for the Strand Award, the Hammett Prize, the Macavity and Anthony awards, the Silver Dagger of the Crime Writers' Association, and France's Grand Prix de Littérature Policière. He has won the Martin Beck Award of the Swedish Academy of Detection twice, the only author ever to have done so.*

Out (Auto)
by Natsuo Kirino (1997)

Natsuo Kirino (b. 1951) is the pen name of the Japanese writer Mariko Hashioka. She has written novels, short stories, and essays, but it was the translation of her 1997 novel Auto (Out) *into English in 2003 that brought her to a larger international audience. Her books frequently deal with the issue of women and power, or their lack thereof. "I feel that this society [Japan] takes advantage of powerless women," she said in an interview conducted shortly after* Out's *English publication. She went on to describe herself as "a sort of 'deviant' that really doesn't fit into an easy category. My debut as an 'author' was as a mystery writer, but in reality, I really don't like mysteries that much. My main motivation to write is to 'observe the fabric of human relationships.' Sometimes the threads that connect people are strong, or warped, or weak, or twisted by the encounters. Isn't that what storytelling is really all about?"*

Out is a story of four women who work night shifts at a boxed-lunch factory in a suburb of Tokyo. Forty-three-year-old Masako likes to keep to herself. Yoshie is a widow with university-aged children. Yayoi is young and beautiful, the mother to two small boys. Kuniko is flashy, overweight, and over her head in debt. They seem to have little in common other than that they work together. But one of them happens to be a murderer, the others her accomplices.

Their story begins on an ordinary night, when the four friends meet to start their usual night shift. From midnight to 5:30 a.m. they work the assembly line at the factory, filling lunch boxes. At dawn they say good-bye to each other and go their separate ways home.

Masako's husband is leaving for work. They hardly speak to each other anymore. Her son, who has dropped out of high school, refuses to talk to her. Yoshie changes and washes her invalid mother-in-law, who scorns her for being late. Yoshie's younger daughter demands yet more money. Yayoi is home in time to get her young children ready for school. Kuniko has a fight with her boyfriend and goes out to look for a better-paid job.

Later in the day, Yayoi's gambling, philandering husband returns home, having been thrown out of the nightclub he frequents. He beats Yayoi, but instead of submitting as usual, Yayoi flies into a rage and strangles him with his tie. Realizing that she has killed her husband, she calls Masako for help. After some convincing, Yayoi's friends agree to cut up the body and dispose of the parts in rubbish bins.

Out, therefore, is not so much a book about "whodunit," but the consequences of crime and punishment, friendship, loyalty, and self-discovery.

Masako is confined in a homelife from which she has been excluded as a person. Yoshie is a slave to other people's problems. Yayoi is a victim of her husband's cruelty and her own weakness. Kuniko cannot resist material goods and the fantasy of a better life. It is life in Tokyo presented without glamour or apology; each of the women is trapped in a place where she does not want to be, and from which she has no way of escaping. As the women navigate the consequences of their actions, and the investigation that follows, they slowly become aware that the murder of Yayoi's husband might be their opportunity for freedom, if they can only get away with it.

Some of the bags containing the body parts of Yayoi's husband are discovered. The police launch a murder investigation. Yayoi is a suspect. The women have to cover their tracks, staying a step ahead of the police. Cracks appear in their fragile solidarity.

The investigation also leads the police to the nightclub where Yayoi's husband was last seen. His missing jacket is recovered. Witnesses report that they have seen the club owner Satake beating up the victim on the night he disappeared. Satake, who has a previous conviction, is arrested, and charged with the murder.

The news brings relief and jubilation to the women. Yayoi collects her husband's life insurance and pays off her friends. Yoshie is happy to buy herself a piece of jewelry as a reward. Kuniko pays off her loan. Masako, who has found the task of cutting up the body thrilling and has not wanted money for her part, takes her share without fully understanding why she is doing so. They go back to work at the factory, gleeful that life is returning to normal.

But they are wrong.

Kuniko's loan shark, Jumonji, becomes suspicious of Kuniko's new income and coerces her into revealing the truth. He decides to blackmail the women, especially Masako, who has a secret of her own.

Satake is released due to lack of evidence. His businesses have collapsed in the time that he has been in police custody. He vows revenge.

Strange things begin to happen around the women. A kind neighbor appears to help Yayoi, looking after her children. Someone is asking questions about Yoshie in her neighborhood. A new security guard starts at the boxed-lunch factory, and moves into the same apartment building as Kuniko.

Masako and Yoshie begin working with Jumonji, cutting up and disposing of bodies for gangsters. Masako asks a coworker at the boxed-lunch factory to keep her earnings safe, and it seems as if Masako is planning something. Yoshie's daughters steal her money and disappear.

Then, one day, Jumonji delivers another body to be dismembered. It is Kuniko . . .

Out is a subtle tale of the psychology of a crime—an unpremeditated murder. As events spiral out of control, the women have to react, exposing who they really are and forcing them to question what they are seeking in life. Masako comes to accept her isolation and the darkness in her own heart. Yoshie no longer wants to be a slave to others. Yayoi is thrilled to be freed of her cruel husband, and feels no remorse for killing him. Kuniko's greed cannot be contained, and eventually consumes her.

When asked why she acted as she did, Masako replies: "Because I want to be alone. Because I want to be free."

Out is brilliant not only for its unrelenting pace, but for its study of the lives of ordinary women in Japan. The society has forced on them duties of family, and demands that they simply accept their fate. It takes an extraordinary event for the women to begin questioning their lives and reexamining their choices. At no point does the book, even in the most page-turning rush of pace, forget to convey the struggles and longings of these women, and how they desperately attempt to escape their burdens. Even though the women are engaged in criminal acts, one cannot help but sympathize with them, and root for them.

There is tenderness in crime, light in darkness.

Diane Wei Liang was born in Beijing. She spent part of her childhood with her parents in a labor camp in a remote region of China. A graduate of Beijing University, Diane took part in the Tiananmen Square protests in 1989. She has an MBA and a PhD in business administration from Carnegie Mellon University. She was an award-winning business professor in the United States and the U.K. Diane is the author of Lake with No Name *(memoir) and three novels:* The Eye of Jade, Paper Butterfly, *and* The House of Golden Spirit. *Her novels have been translated into more than twenty languages. She lives in London. Visit her online at www.dianeweiliang.com.*

Always Outnumbered, Always Outgunned
by Walter Mosley (1997)

Walter Mosley (b. 1952) has published more than thirty books across various genres, including science fiction, literary fiction, short fiction, and non-fiction, but is probably most famous for his mystery novels, in particular his series featuring the black private detective Easy Rawlins, and, latterly, the books featuring ex-convict Socrates Fortlow. These novels function not only as entertaining mysteries in their own right, but as social, political, and cultural histories of Los Angeles and, in particular, of the black experience in that city.

Ten years ago I was in prison. I suppose I should clarify that by saying that I was working in prison, as a writer-in-residence. Actually two prisons, to be precise: a Young Offenders Institution and an adult HMP (Her Majesty's Prison). I loved that job, especially working with the boys in the YOI. I was there for the stories, to show them how to construct them, to see their own, to recognize that the endings they expected weren't necessarily inevitable. It was an honor being able to effect a positive change in their lives, to see them go from angry, uncommunicative youths to pleasant, happy boys. And all through using words and telling stories. Some days were brilliant, but it didn't always work, of course. And when it failed there was no middle ground. Stacking shelves at a Tesco supermarket would have been more rewarding. But those good days, they were worth everything.

The adult HMP was slightly different. Pecking orders had been established, fates accepted. For some, it was hard to tell whether interrupted lives meant being inside or outside the walls.

451

But they all had one thing in common: they wanted escape. Not the physical, going-over-the-barbed-wire kind, but the kind that could take them out of themselves, out of their cells, while they killed time. The library was one of the most popular places in the prison, and horror and crime the most popular genres. They always asked me for recommendations. And the one book I recommended more than any other was Walter Mosley's *Always Outnumbered, Always Outgunned.*

Mosley had been one of my favorite writers ever since I read, along with everyone else it seemed, *Devil in a Blue Dress.* Here was a voice that seemed unique, taking the postwar African American urban experience and filtering it through the prism of private-eye fiction. But not doing it in a way that was worthy, preachy, or dull. Using the crime novel as a form of societal excavation while never forgetting that he had a story to tell, a reader to entertain. Brilliant. My kind of writing.

After that, I snapped up every Easy Rawlins novel as soon as it came out. But Mosley wasn't content just to stay with the one series. (And what a great one it is. While many series start to flag and become repetitive after the first few entries, the Easy Rawlins series just seems to improve. My favorite—so far—is *Little Scarlet,* Mosley's ninth.) Whereas most writers jump genres with all the grace and elegance of a Chinook helicopter airlifting Americans from an embassy roof in Saigon, Mosley deftly and nimbly follows his own muse. Science fiction, comedy, parable, polemic, even erotica, he's done them all, using whichever format best fits the story he wants to tell. And all to an astonishingly successful degree.

Which brings me to *Always Outnumbered, Always Outgunned.* Mosley's eighth novel, it was a shift away from Easy Rawlins. Socrates Fortlow is a murderer and rapist, freed from an Indiana prison, who has moved to Watts in L.A. to try and live as decent a life as he can and make peace with, and atonement for, his violent past. He carries an accumulation of his life's violence and rage within him, and struggles not to resort to using his massive fists, his "rock breakers," to settle arguments.

This short novel comprises fourteen chapters, sequential but not too closely connected, in which Socrates finds himself in various situations that test his hard-won philosophy. He turns a young man away from crime. Runs a killer out of town. Tries to resist the wrong kind of woman. We follow him as he manages to get a menial job, a struggle that becomes an almost Herculean task, as he comports himself with dignity while having only a few cents in his pocket. And in the process, while wrestling with the always present demons of his past, he manages to find his own kind of peace in his own sort of community.

It's no accident that this lead character has been given the name of Socrates, the father of Western philosophy. Written in the aftermath of the L.A. riots and the Rodney King beating, this hulking ex-con becomes a contemporary inquisitor, asking difficult moral questions of a society that has retained a dogmatic grip on the letter of the law but has lost purchase on its fair and compassionate spirit.

"First you got to survive," Socrates says at one point. "Then you got to think; think and dream." And he does, recounting his dreams vividly as they inform his waking life: his boyhood self walks along a shore with his aunt Bellandra while she tells him about God:

> "He ain't black. If he was there wouldn't be all this mess down here wit' us. Naw. He's blue. Blue like the ocean. Blue. Sad and cold and far away like the sky is far and blue. You got to go a long way to get to God. And even if you get there he might not say a thing. Not a damn thing."

Or when asked to undertake what he sees as an impossible task, he tells of another dream:

> "It was like I was a child seein' lightnin' for the first time. The light show made me all giddy but the thunder scared me down to my boots."

After the dream he resolves to do something, the best thing he can possibly do to make things better: try.

I may have given the impression that this novel is a sentimental slushfest. Nothing could be farther from the truth. The prose is staccato, as hard as the life Socrates is leading, but not without passages of beauty and lyricism, especially in the roughest and most unexpected of places. Just like life, really.

Socrates Fortlow appeared in a couple more novels. They were good but, I think, not as good as this one. There was even a movie made of it, directed by Michael Apted and starring Laurence Fishburne. I didn't see it. Deliberately, I might add, because I didn't want anyone else's vision of the book to get in the way of mine.

This novel, for me, is a direct line to the heart of what I love about crime fiction and good writing. No one is born bad or born evil. No one is born good. We're all made and shaped by heredity and environment. And in turn, we then go on to shape the heredity and environment of others. Our stories are ours alone to tell. We sometimes get the endings we deserve. We always get the endings we create.

That was the message I tried to impart to the guys I worked with in prison. Hopefully they listened to it.

Hopefully, so did I.

Martyn Waites is the Newcastle-born author of the critically acclaimed Joe Donovan mystery series. More recently, he and his wife, Linda, have collaborated, under the pseudonym of Tania Carver, on a hugely successful series of novels featuring Phil Brennan of the Major Incident Squad and psychologist Marina Esposito, the most recent of which is Choked. *Visit him online at www.martynwaites.com.*

Black and Blue
by Ian Rankin (1997)

BRIAN MCGILLOWAY

Ian Rankin (b. 1960) is one of Britain's leading mystery writers, and a major figure in the "Tartan Noir" school of Scottish crime writing. He is the author of more than thirty books, the majority featuring the character of Detective Inspector John Rebus, set in and around the city of Edinburgh, Scotland, in which Rankin still lives. Knots and Crosses, *the first Rebus novel, was published in 1987; the seventeenth Rebus book,* Standing in Another Man's Grave, *will appear later this year. Rankin has also published two books featuring an internal affairs investigator, Inspector Malcolm Fox. He has won every major mystery award, including the 2004 Edgar for Best Novel for* Resurrection Men.

Ian Rankin's position as one of the great modern crime writers is beyond dispute. The recipient of various awards, honorary degrees, and an OBE, he was, famously, at one point the author of one in every ten crime novels sold in the U.K.

Also beyond dispute is the reputation of *Black and Blue,* the eighth of his Inspector Rebus mysteries. The novel encompasses the geography of most of Scotland, and merges four separate plot strands: the impaling of an oil rig worker on a set of railings; a case involving the 1960s killer Bible John and a modern copycat dubbed Johnny Bible; an investigation from Rebus's own past that may have resulted in the unfair imprisonment of a criminal called Lenny Spaven; and a drugs case involving a local thug called Uncle Joe.

It includes many of the features one would expect of a Rebus novel: musical references (not least of which is the Rolling Stones–inspired title); Big Ger Cafferty, and Rebus's ongoing dance with that particular devil; the image of the lonely detective, drinking to forget his troubles;

and the fears of his young protégée, afraid that she'll become too much like her mentor. And her fears are echoed in turn, much like the Johnny Bible case echoes the earlier investigation into Bible John, as Rebus reflects on his relationship with his own mentor, Lawson Geddes, even as he watches one of his junior officers crack under the pressure of being a cop.

Yet the book is also markedly different in tone, structure, and scope from the previous Rebus novels: indeed, *Black and Blue* is really where the series comes of age. Bleaker, darker, and intrinsically Scottish in theme and locale, this was the breakthrough novel for Rankin, and one that is still cited to all midlist authors as an example of how, sometimes, it takes a while for a series to catch its readership.

But my fondness for the book is not due simply to its considerable strengths. Shortly after I completed my degree at Queen's University in Belfast, a new bookstore called No Alibis opened nearby. I wandered in on one of its first days of trading and hunted around for something to buy. While I'd read classic crime, including Christie, Collins, and Conan Doyle, I had not read any modern crime fiction. The first book I bought that day was *Black and Blue*. Two days later I returned, buying all the previous Rebus novels, before moving on, in turn, to Dexter and Burke, Connolly and Connelly, Crais and Coben and beyond. My buying habits ballooned as I was introduced to series after series, great author after great author. But the starting point was *Black and Blue*.

What struck me most forcibly was that the book was so Scottish, so rooted in the region, stretching across Edinburgh, Glasgow, Aberdeen, and out to the oil rigs in the North Sea, and yet it was that which I found so refreshing. A state-of-the-union novel for a newly empowered Scotland, it was no massive surprise that it was part of the wider "Tartan Noir" movement in crime writing burgeoning alongside the devolution of political power, almost as if a group of authors were examining their own identity by appropriating the genre and making it very much of their place.

And, once again, *Black and Blue* is very much of its place. Referencing the actual Bible John killings of the 1960s as a starting point, Rankin weaves a fictional narrative through real streets, real bars, intertwined with real events, the verisimilitude provided by the latter allowing him to carry the reader along the fictional strands.

It is also a novel filled with guilt. The Lenny Spaven case weighs heavily on Rebus throughout, the same case that drives his old superior Lawson Geddes to suicide. Rebus himself is described by one of his friends as "the world's longest surviving suicide victim," and Rebus's colleague, Brian Holmes, suffers guilt for his beating of the criminal known as Mental Minto.

For guilt, in many forms, is intrinsic to crime fiction. It is often the driving force compelling the detective to seek truth, to bring about justice. In *Black and Blue*, Rebus is so sure of his role in this search for justice that he accuses others of being bent coppers; yet, ironically, he believes that his own lies to protect Geddes, and the bullying of Minto, are justifiable. But this is where Rankin most obviously reflects the real world, for there is no "right" in this book. The killer is punished at the end, but not in the traditional sense. The cops are as corrupt as the villains, and Rebus remains in purgatory throughout, though by the close of the book he finds himself "somewhere North of hell."

The novel also carries with it a sense of the frontier. Living near the border regions in the north of Ireland, that awareness of boundaries, even within a city, appealed to me. And, of course, the boundaries are internal as well as physical: many of the characters cross their own moral boundaries, often dragging others across with them.

Ultimately, though, my love of this book is because it, in part, inspired me to want to write. Coupled with the works of the other authors I've mentioned, and many more besides, it convinced me that the crime narrative was the perfect one for engaging with real social issues. All police procedurals are, at their most basic, an examination of past events in order to better understand a present situation. I had not before found a form and genre which better allowed an author to reflect the reality of life, and to engage with the kinds of social changes and issues that were impacting on the newly flourishing Northern Ireland, a place finding its feet and trying to come to terms with thirty years of mayhem. It is no exaggeration to say that I would not have started writing crime fiction had it not been for *Black and Blue*.

Brian McGilloway was born in Derry, Northern Ireland, in 1974. He is currently head of English in St. Columb's College in the city. His Inspector

Devlin novels have been short-listed for a CWA Dagger, the Ireland AM Irish Crime Fiction Book of the Year, and the Theakstons Old Peculier Crime Novel of the Year, while the first Lucy Black novel, Little Girl Lost, *was awarded the McCrea Literary Award by the University of Ulster in 2011. The fifth Devlin novel,* The Nameless Dead, *was published earlier this year. Brian lives near the Irish borderlands with his wife and their four children. Visit him online at www.brianmcgilloway.com.*

The Ax
by Donald E. Westlake (1997)

Donald E. Westlake (1933–2008) was a prolific writer of novels and short stories, most of them in the mystery genre, and operated under more pseudonyms than many convicted fraudsters. He was a committed writer from his youth, and began writing soft-porn novels under the pen name Alan Marshall at the end of the 1950s before finally publishing his first novel as Donald Westlake, The Mercenaries, *in 1960. He won Edgar Awards in three different categories, and many of his works were adapted for film, most famously his 1962 novel* The Hunter, *written under his Richard Stark pen name, which became the basis for John Boorman's 1967 film* Point Blank, *starring Lee Marvin, as well as Ringo Lam's* Full Contact *(1992) and the Mel Gibson vehicle* Payback *(1999).*

I came to Donald Westlake embarrassingly late, and I admit to lying on a few occasions when asked if I'd read him. It was my secret shame that I'd never picked up a Westlake or Richard Stark book. My early crime writing heroes were Jim Thompson and Patricia Highsmith. It never occurred to me that you could get much better than that. For years, one friend asked me repeatedly if I'd read *The Ax*. "You really should read *The Ax*," he'd say each time, alternating between pity and scorn. Finally, I read it just to shut him up.

When you think of Westlake, one of his two most famous criminals probably comes to mind—the hard-boiled Parker or the brilliant but luckless John Dortmunder. Each inspired a great, long series of books. Burke Devore, the antihero of *The Ax*, bears little resemblance to either character.

Likewise, the book has little in common with Westlake's other novels, or with conventional crime fiction in general. In a typical crime novel, a highly motivated character does something beyond the bounds of acceptable norms. Twists and complications ensue, all the way up to a surprising and thrilling conclusion.

While I love stacks of engrossing, action-packed, plot-driven crime novels populated with dynamic and ruthless characters as much as the next gal, the one that I call my favorite is not one of those, exactly. It skips most of the dependable pleasures of the genre in favor of something harder and more mundane. If it's extraordinary—and I think it is—that's because it's the most ordinary crime novel I've ever read.

The Ax is neither hard-boiled nor colorful, nor is it even suspenseful in the usual sense (though it does maintain a brand of cavalier tension that only Westlake could pull off). The protagonist wants something, so he kills a number of people to get it. That's a reasonable enough premise for a crime novel, and we could expect things to get complicated from there. But surprisingly, that's as complicated as the plot gets.

Burke Devore, an ordinary, responsible man, has been looking for work since his job as a project manager at a Connecticut paper mill was eliminated by corporate downsizing eleven months before. In a shriveling industry, Devore can count the number of potential new jobs on one hand. For every job that's available, there's always a better candidate. Eventually, he finds his dream job at a paper-processing plant in Arcadia, New York, except the position is already filled. With mounting debt and a family to take care of, Burke has only one idea left: eliminate the competition. Literally.

It's tough to think of another work, including any of Highsmith's, that treats a criminal transformation so matter-of-factly, without even an occasional wink or nudge to lighten the mood. It could be argued that a few recent TV series (hi, *Dexter*) have drawn inspiration from *The Ax*— but, if so, inspiration was all they drew from it. Burke Devore may have broken bad a decade before Walter White cooked his first batch of meth, but the similarities end there. The pleasure of *Breaking Bad* lies in the increasingly twisted consequences of its hero's decision to do wrong in order to do right by his family. By contrast, Burke Devore's path from milquetoast to murderer couldn't be straighter.

Devore manages his project just as you'd expect a project manager to do. He puts out an employment ad in a trade journal to identify other applicants and then whittles down the list of prospects to the seven most likely to beat him out of the job. And then he sets out to kill them, one by one.

What follows is not a series of surprises and increasingly intricate plot points, or entanglements with alluring women and compromised accomplices, but a straightforward account of Devore's steady progress toward his mundane goal of landing a secure job. Some of the killings go smoothly, some do not. He's questioned by the police, and lies to his wife about his missions. Through it all, despite the grisly acts, he remains steadfastly, disquietingly normal. He's just a guy who wants to work at the only thing he's qualified to do.

So where's the interest? What makes this story more than just a bunch of stuff that happens? Westlake hints at it in *The Ax*'s two epigraphs. The first is a relatively long section from Henry James's *The Art of Fiction*, concluding with, "The only reason for the existence of a novel is that it does attempt to represent life." The second is a chilling quote by Thomas G. Labrecque, former CEO of Chase Manhattan Bank: "If you're doing what you think is right for everyone involved, then you're fine. So I'm fine."

To me, *The Ax*, more than any other crime novel, attempts to represent the kind of life that real people live. For most of us, life is not about a big heist, or crimes of passion, or hunting down a clever serial killer in Iceland. For an increasing number of us, normal life is about managing to get by. Crime may not often enter our lives, but Westlake uses it to ask such vital questions as, "What are we willing to do to get what we want or need?" and, "What norms are we willing to transcend in an effort to remain normal?"

Devore's motivation isn't so open-ended. Unlike Parker or Dortmunder, he explains himself quite plainly. And this is where *The Ax*, in addition to being a hell of a great read, is even more pertinent now than when it was written:

> The end of what I'm doing, the purpose, the goal, is good, clearly good. I want to take care of my family; I want to be a productive part of society; I want to put my skills to use; I want to work and pay my own way and not be a burden to the taxpayers. The means to that end has been difficult, but I've kept my eye

on the goal, the purpose. The end justifies the means. Like the CEOs, I have nothing to feel sorry for.

Lisa Lutz is the author of the Spellman series of comedic crime novels (beginning with The Spellman Files *and* Heads You Lose *(with David Hayward). She lives in rural New York. Visit her online at www.lisalutz.com.*

Murder in the Marais
by Cara Black (1998)

YRSA SIGURDARDÓTTIR

American-born author Cara Black (b. 1951) sets her Aimée Leduc mystery novels, of which there have been twelve to date, in Paris. Her first novel, Murder in the Marais, *was published in 1998 and nominated for an Anthony Award for Best First Novel, while her third,* Murder in the Sentier, *received an Anthony nomination for Best Novel. Her most recent book,* Murder at the Lanterne Rouge, *arrived in 2011. Cara Black was included in Elizabeth Lindsay's* Great Women Mystery Writers *(2nd Edition).*

Few authors of any genre conduct such successful and meticulous research into the location and history surrounding their works as Cara Black. It probably helps that her mystery series about private investigator Aimée Leduc is based in Paris, so the site-work can't be very shabby or dismal. Each title in the series carries the name of a district, an arrondissement, or a particular location in the city, with events within the pages linked to that same location. To date Cara has written twelve novels about her half-French, half-American protagonist, two of which have been nominated for an Anthony Award and all of which are thoroughly entertaining.

As all readers know, the single most important factor in a series is the protagonist. If well developed, this character has the power to bring you back for more, the exact quality that Aimée Leduc has in spades. She is not your average private detective, specializing in corporate security and computer forensics instead of missing persons and cheating wives. Despite this, her cases focus on much more interesting things than bytes and processors as they invariably lead her down intriguing paths, paved by human ethical failings. Aimée is a hands-on type of girl: she will leave no stone unturned once engaged, and very often finds herself in precarious situations that call for all sorts of craftiness and quick thinking.

But despite the action often thrust upon her, Aimée is not one of those "female males" that one sometimes comes across in crime novels, the ones who just don't feel right. To the contrary, Aimée rings true. Despite being tough she is also vulnerable. She harbors strong convictions, and feels for those whom she seeks to assist. She has a mystery in her past involving the disappearance of her mother, and together with the horrific and untimely death of her father, one can easily imagine these two events sculpting her into the relentless yet softhearted truth-seeker the pages of the books convincingly make her out to be.

Aimée dresses well, managing to do so on her far from high-flying income by purchasing vintage. Her being fashionable is as refreshing as it is unique. Considering the setting of the books it would have been a total turnoff had she been frumpy; in Paris, you hardly expect a heroine to walk around in dungarees. To make her even more of a standout, her sidekick in the computing business is an odd accessory who adds charm to the mix; hacker René is a dwarf.

It is next to impossible not to give another *dame* the status of a main protagonist when dissecting Cara's series. This *dame* is no more a slouch than Aimée, if anything less so. I am referring here to the grand old *dame* that is Paris herself, so extremely well described by Cara that it is hard to imagine anyone doing it more effectively. There can be no questioning the author's familiarity with every nook and cranny of the area placed in the spotlight in each installment. In places one can almost smell fresh coffee being served in a tiny bistro on a charming street corner, or taste a flaky, buttery croissant upon one's tongue. Not to mention the feeling of being transported into high-ceilinged, Parisian abodes and buildings, or onto narrow streets lined with decorative lampposts. This knack for bringing to life the city's surroundings applies to descriptions of Paris both past and present, as the plots in the series often involve events from the past, old truths and secrets hiding behind the cobwebs of time.

The novel presently up for dissection is the first of the series, *Murder in the Marais*, originally published in 1998. Although the works need not be read in chronological order, it feels right to start at the beginning, at least for the purpose of this anthology. The author herself names *Murder in Rue de Paradis* as the one that remains closest to her heart and, having read it, I urge those not lucky enough to have done so to rectify this situation at the earliest convenience. But, for now, we will return to the point of origin, and *Murder in the Marais*.

As the book's title implies, most of the events described occur in the Marais district, which has, since the beginning of the nineteenth century, been host to Paris's Jewish community and thus home to more than its fair share of atrocities during the Second World War, following the occupation of the city by the Nazis. The reader is introduced to thirty-four-year-old private investigator Aimée Leduc, who has turned her back on fieldwork in the aftermath of a case that led to the death of her father, which was witnessed by her. Aimée now only takes on cases involving corporate security and so manages to get by, but only just. When an old rabbi asks her to accept an assignment involving the examination of a photograph, it is mostly due to the parlous state of her small agency's finances that she agrees. As soon as Aimée has worked out the puzzle of the picture, she visits the original owner, an old woman from the rabbi's synagogue. Intending to discuss her findings, Aimée instead discovers that the old woman has been murdered and her body mutilated, a swastika cut into her forehead. This strongly ties in to the result of Aimée's investigation, as the image turned out to be one of the SS officers in a Parisian café.

The promising intro delivers what the reader surely expects. The plot is as engaging as Aimée herself, reaching back to the atrocities of WWII and slowly bringing to light buried secrets involving one of the strongest drivers of human action: hate. But this ugly emotion is not the only one propelling the story, as its counterpart, love, also makes an absorbing showing. The unwinding of a tightly knotted past and present evils is very well done, touching various bases on the way, such as the problems of immigration and the need of some, unjustifiably, to see whole groups of people as being their inferiors. And last, but not least—the ending is a surprise.

Bravo, Cara Black, not only for this book, but for the series in its entirety.

Yrsa Sigurdardóttir is an international best-selling crime writer from Iceland. Yrsa has written six books in a series about her protagonist, the lawyer Thóra Gudmundsdóttir. The fourth novel in this series, The Day Is Dark, *was recently published in the U.K., and the fifth,* Someone to Watch Over Me, *is due for publication in 2013. Yrsa's recent stand-alone novel,* I Remember You, *has been nominated for the Scandinavian crime fiction prize the Glass Key, and is scheduled for publication in the U.K. in 2012. It is presently being adapted for the big screen.*

On Beulah Height
by Reginald Hill (1998)

VAL MCDERMID

Reginald Hill (1936–2012), known to his friends and fans simply as Reg, was an English mystery writer who gained gradual, well-deserved acclaim through his novels featuring the mismatched Yorkshire police detectives Andrew Dalziel and Peter Pascoe, the former earthy and instinctive, the latter urbane and reflective. They made their first appearance in 1970's A Clubbable Woman *and went on to feature in more than twenty further novels and a handful of short stories, although Hill, sometimes pseudonymously, wrote over thirty other novels, including five involving a black private detective named Joe Sixsmith. Hill delighted in wordplay and literary allusions, perhaps a consequence of his early career as a teacher. He appeared to have no qualms about his chosen literary direction, commenting in 2009: "When I get up in the morning, I ask my wife whether I should write a Booker Prize–winning novel or another best-selling crime book. We always come down on the side of the crime book."*

Picking a favorite crime novel is like choosing your favorite wine: so much depends on mood and situation. And once you've narrowed down the genre—Champagne or Shiraz, Muscatel or Riesling?—you still have to choose individual vineyards and vintages . . .

My martini crime novel—anytime, anyplace, anywhere—is Reginald Hill's *On Beulah Height*. It's beautifully written—elegiac, emotionally intelligent, evocative of the landscape and history that hold its characters in thrall—and its clever plotting delivers a genuine shock that does not cheat the reader. There's intellectual satisfaction in working out a plot whose counterpoint is Mahler's *Kindertotenlieder* song cycle.* There's darkness and light, fear and relief. And then there's the cross-grained pairing of Dalziel and Pascoe in their seventeenth outing. Spot on.

I chose Reginald Hill's *On Beulah Height* as my exemplar of the perfect crime novel with a light heart. But I sit down to write this appreciation with great heaviness of spirit because, in the interval, Reg Hill died, leaving his readers and his friends bereft.

There is a terrible irony in the choice of *On Beulah Height*. As we read, we are constantly reminded of the mutability and the impermanence of our human state; rereading it, I felt the presence of my old friend most poignantly.

When *On Beulah Height* was published in February 1998, I was the crime reviewer of the *Manchester Evening News*. I reviewed the book thus:

> When a long hot summer reveals the drowned village of Dendale, it resuscitates memories the former inhabitants would have preferred to remain dormant. The villagers were evacuated fifteen years before to make way for a new reservoir, all but four of them—three missing girls and the man suspected of abducting them, the strange and swift Benny Lightfoot.
>
> As the water level drops, old feelings start to emerge, exposed to fresh scrutiny by the graffiti that appears on the walls of the town where the Dendale villagers were rehoused. "Benny's back," it announces ominously. Then another girl goes missing.
>
> Every copper has a case that haunts and obsesses him, and for the eternally vulgar but acute Andy Dalziel, it's the missing girls of Dendale. Now he's faced with what appears to be a rerun of his old failure. This time, he's determined not to be defeated. As past and present intertwine like the complex musical composition that also has its place in the story, we share the elegiac sense of loss that threatens to engulf Hill's characters.
>
> With his customary wit and wisdom, Reginald Hill has given his readers a jewel of a book. He manages with enviable ease the difficult task of blending marvelously evocative writing with a

---

*Translated, variously, as *Children's Death Songs* or *Songs on the Death of Children*.

plot that turns as cleverly as anything in the genre, leaving the reader sighing, 'Of course!' in affectionate exasperation. This is a master-class in the art of writing fiction. I doubt I'll read a better book this year.

I see no reason to change a word of that review, or alter my later decision to garland it as my book of the year.

Although Hill's roots were firmly in the traditional English detective novel, he brought to it an ambivalence and ambiguity that allowed him display the complexities of contemporary life. Among the most literate of writers in the field, he brought to life a cast of characters who changed and developed in response to their experiences.

I urge you to read this with a glass of Andy Dalziel's favorite Highland Park and toast a great book and the memory of a great writer.

Val McDermid is best known for her novels featuring Tony Hill and Carol Jordan, the first of which, The Mermaids Singing, *appeared in 1995. In all there have been seven novels in the series, most recently* The Retribution *(2011). McDermid made her debut in 1987 with* Report for Murder, *the first in the six-book Lindsay Gordon series. Another six-book series features the private eye Kate Brannigan. McDermid has also written six stand-alone titles.* The Mermaids Singing *won the CWA's Gold Dagger in 1996.* The Torment of Others *(2004) won the Theakstons Old Peculier Crime Novel of the Year award in 2006. In 2010, Val McDermid was awarded the CWA's Cartier Diamond Dagger in recognition of her life's work. Visit her online at www.valmcdermid.com.*

Tomato Red
by Daniel Woodrell (1998)

REED FARREL COLEMAN

Daniel Woodrell (b. 1953) has published eight novels to date, most of them set in the Missouri Ozarks and characterized by a tone Woodrell describes as "country noir." He debuted with Under the Bright Lights *in 1986. His most recent publication is* The Outlaw Album *(2011), his first collection of short stories. Woodrell received the PEN Center USA Award for Fiction for his novel* Tomato Red *(1998); it was also long-listed for the IMPAC prize.* Winter's Bone *(2006) was adapted for film by director Debra Granik and released in 2010. It won the Grand Jury Prize at the Sundance Festival, and was nominated for the Best Picture Oscar.*

I recently did a piece for the *Huffington Post* in which I discussed those novels written by the current generation of crime fiction authors that would have the most influence on coming generations. Chief among my selections was Daniel Woodrell's compact bombshell of a book *Tomato Red*. Originally published in 1998 by Henry Holt, *Tomato Red* never quite lit the fire that it should have. Much to Mr. Woodrell's dismay, I'm sure, *Tomato Red* became the stuff of cult legend. As I would tour my own novels, traveling from independent bookstore to independent bookstore, I would hear the whispers. The words *"Tomato Red"* were spoken in hushed, reverential tones, almost as if they were passwords into a private club. What I discovered when I finally got my hands on a pink-and-black-covered uncorrected proof of the novel at the Poisoned Pen Bookstore circa 2006 was that *"Tomato Red"* were indeed passwords, but not into Skull and Bones or some other snootily exclusive club. They were passwords into another world; a world in which the tour guide, Daniel Woodrell, used a language that was something akin to the

American-English prose I wrote in, but had far more in common with distilled poetry and the serrated edge of a knife.

That was the thing, the language, that initially caught my eye, and I didn't have to get to the second paragraph before it did. I didn't even have to get to the second sentence. Wait, I'm getting ahead of myself. Let me back up a small step, one page back to be precise. Before I began reading the text itself, something else got my attention. As if I wasn't already curious enough, the dual epigraphs that open the novel fascinated me. The first, by renowned psychoanalyst Theodor Reik, is a philosophical observation about self-defeating behaviors. The second, an oddly prescient and related quote by Boston Red Sox pitcher Oil Can Boyd, is a statement about the disconnect between what a person should know and what he does know. Boyd says, "It's not all peaches and cream. But I haven't learned that yet."

Oh, about that first sentence: it's two hundred and seventy words long, give or take. Lest you fear Mr. Woodrell is a gassy writer prone to endless bouts of self-indulgence, the second paragraph is all of four words long: "That's how it happens." The third is eight words long: "Can't none of this be new to you." The thing about Woodrell's writing is that word count and page count—the novel is short by any standard—are completely irrelevant measures. No writer, not even Ken Bruen, packs so much into so little. To paraphrase the poet, if there were world enough and time, I might be tempted to reproduce that first sentence/paragraph in its entirety. But no, I wouldn't want to ruin it for you. Let me instead quote Edgar-winning author Megan Abbott from her foreword to the star-crossed Busted Flush Press reprint of *Tomato Red*.

> Woodrell does it with language . . . The thing Woodrell does to words is the stuff of dark alchemy. He breaks language apart, shatters it to glittery pieces, then stitches it together new. You don't even know what it is—are those words? Sentences? Or am I bewitched?

Although I am at a loss to explain it, there are some writers and readers out there who aren't floored by *Tomato Red*. Yet even those few people who have confessed to me that the book didn't do it for them cannot help but be dazzled by his otherworldly use of the English language. Or as Robbie Robertson put it in the lyrics to "Up on Cripple Creek," "I can't take the way he sings, but I love to hear him talk." It says something that even the book's detractors can't escape the gravitational pull of Mr. Woodrell's language.

The book itself is a self-contained masterpiece, a portal to a world that has some recognizable features, but is as alien to most readers as Rabat or Jupiter. I have heard the book referred to as "Ozark" or "hillbilly noir," but to say that is to miss the point. To try and categorize it somehow trivializes the gritty majesty of the work. Would you brush off *Crime and Punishment* by calling it "Russian noir"? In some ways, *Tomato Red*—a reference to the hair color of the novel's tragic femme fatale, Jamalee Merridew—is more like speculative or science fiction than most crime fiction. No, even that doesn't quite do it justice. It is such a singular accomplishment that the damned book, as much as I love it, just defies comparison. That elusiveness more than anything else probably accounts for the book flying under the radar for all these years.

One suspects that a person reading the book fifty years from now—and I assure you, people will be reading it fifty years from now—won't find it any more dated than it was in 1998. That world, the world of West Table, Missouri, and nearby Venus Holler, as created by Woodrell, is a timeless place, but it ain't the Ozark Shangri-la. That's for shit sure, as my old friends from Brooklyn might say. West Table is a place with a wrong side of town, a very wrong side, a place where crank supplies more energy than the public utility and where it's gray and rainy even when it isn't. If you want a job, there's always the dog food factory in town. Still, West Table's most abundant resource seems to be desperation. And it is on desperation that the story turns.

I am loath to give too much of the book away and spoil it for someone who comes to *Tomato Red* after reading this dark love letter to the novel. The funny thing is that after I've spent all this time telling you how singular the novel is, I must confess that the plot of *Tomato Red* relies, at least to get it rolling, on one of the great conceits of crime fiction: a drifter comes to town. This drifter is an ex-con loser named Sammy Barlach. And Sammy is true to his bad karma when, cranked up and in the company of some local losers, he breaks into a house on the good side of town only to find that he's late to the party: in the house already are the brother-and-sister team of Jason and Jamalee Merridew. But the pair aren't so much robbing the house as they are playing house, living out, at least for a little while, their fantasies of wealth and escape. Sammy, truly a drifter in temperament and soul, falls under the influence of the Merridews.

Although Jamalee has womanish charms and assets beyond her tomato-red hair—assets to which Sam Barlach is not immune—the looker in Woodrell's novel isn't whom you might expect. It's not Jamalee or her mom, Bev, a woman of questionable taste and morals, but Jason. Jason, blessed with drop-dead good looks, is the categorical object of local female desire. It is on this commodity that Jamalee plans to trade in order that they might escape the gray inertia of Venus Holler and West Table. Nice plan in a fantasy world, but not one with much chance of success. It's a child's scheme born of desperation and a desire for escape. Problem is, the plan, which even under the best of circumstances was unlikely to produce the desired result, has a fundamental flaw. Jason may well be desired by women, but he isn't desirous of them, not any of them. Talk about helping your fate along . . . For me, it is reminiscent of the utterly doomed and ridiculous scheme of the bank robbers in Sidney Lumet's *Dog Day Afternoon*. That film, by the way, was closely based on an actual robbery. I'm sure it seemed like a good idea to rob a bank in order to fund a sex-change operation. No doubt Jamalee Merridew would have agreed and Sammy Barlach would have gone along for the ride.

Beyond what I have already written, I won't reveal any more about the novel. I get the sense that the more I write, the farther away I get from capturing the essence of this incredible work of fiction. Please pick up a copy of this novel and let yourself be taken out of your life and transported to a place you have never been to before. In my classes and during my book talks, I often say that writers can be at a disadvantage vis-à-vis filmmakers. Filmmakers, I explain, have words, images, sound tracks, special effects—a whole host of tools in their toolbox. All a writer has in his toolbox are words. In the hands of Daniel Woodrell, words are more than enough. In *Tomato Red*, those words are magic.

Called "a hard-boiled poet" by NPR's Maureen Corrigan and "the noir poet laureate" in the Huffington Post, *Reed Farrel Coleman has published fifteen novels. He is a three-time recipient of the Shamus Award for Best P. I. Novel of the Year and is a two-time Edgar Award nominee. He has also won the Macavity, Barry, and Anthony awards. He is an adjunct professor of English at Hofstra University and a founding member of MWA University. He lives with his family on Long Island. Visit him online at www.reedcoleman.com.*

Disgrace
by J. M. Coetzee (1999)

MARGIE ORFORD

John Maxwell Coetzee (b. 1940) is a South African–born writer and academic. He was awarded the Nobel Prize in Literature in 2003, and has won the Man Booker Prize for two novels, Life & Times of Michael K *(1983) and* Disgrace *(1999). He now lives in Australia.*

I stand next to the corpse of a twelve-year-old. The girl is laid out on a steel tray. She has been raped. Before, during, or after, she has been stabbed one hundred and three times. It takes an intentional vigor to do that, a vigor that is born from power, from a clear-eyed hatred. It is a disgrace.

Standing in the chill air of that Cape Town mortuary five years ago, I thought of *Disgrace,* the novel by South Africa's most celebrated author, J. M. Coetzee. *Disgrace* is a violent book—its moments of great tenderness notwithstanding—that is shaped by Coetzee's bleakly ethical questing in a violent country. It was Coetzee, a literary writer reminiscent of Beckett, of Kafka, who addressed the issue of crime in the new South Africa in all its unadorned and incomprehensible brutality.

"What if after an attack like that, one is never oneself again?" the protagonist in *Disgrace* asks himself. "What if an attack like that turns one into a different and darker person altogether?" What if, indeed? It is a haunting question; it is the question that has informed my own writing, which is, on one level, an exploration of violence and survival.

Coetzee is an austere writer and *Disgrace* tells a simple story. David Lurie, the protagonist, is a fifty-two-year-old professor in Cape Town. He has an affair with a pretty young student and, after she makes a complaint against him, he loses his job. Shunned by colleagues and friends, he seeks refuge with his daughter, Lucy, on her remote smallholding in the Eastern Cape. This ambiguous sanctuary—Lurie has little talent for agrarian life—is shattered when three strangers, two men and a boy, arrive one afternoon. During a vicious attack, Lurie is doused with methylated spirits, set alight, then locked in the bathroom. His daughter is gang-raped. Before they leave, the Luries' assailants shoot Lucy's penned dogs, and take everything of value with them. They will never be arrested. Lucy is pregnant as a result of the rape. Lurie wants his daughter to fight, to go to the police, to maintain the fiction of justice and retribution, and to turn in the predatory boy when he returns to skulk about on Lucy's farm. She refuses. She is "like a dead person." Lurie, after returning briefly to Cape Town, moves back to the Eastern Cape where he volunteers at an animal welfare clinic whose main business it is to euthanize unwanted dogs.

While treating his burns in the immediate aftermath of the attack, Lurie muses on the theory that crime is nothing more than a Robin Hood–like redistribution of assets, a facile theory that posits that it is "not human evil, just a vast circulatory system to whose workings pity and terror are irrelevant." Pity and terror, which Coetzee evokes in equal measure in *Disgrace,* are grand, archaic emotions that one associates with Greek tragedy, with the hubris of its heroic figures, with the catharsis that results when they fall.

Pity and terror were what I felt when I first read *Disgrace*. Pity and terror were what I felt that morning as I stood beside the twelve-year-old girl's violated corpse. Pity for her, and terror at what is unleashed when a man, a society, capitulates to the lure of violence.

The edition of *Disgrace,* from which all the quotes in this essay are taken, is the original U.S. hardback edition. I bought it in 1999, the year I left South Africa to take up a two-year scholarship in New York City, the first time I had an opportunity to reflect away from my turbulent, beloved country. The jacket of that first edition is a virginal white apart from Coetzee's name in looped, blue cursive on the top, and "Disgrace" in small black type in the center.

I wondered about it at the time: that *Disgrace,* in its first public outing, was visually silent. It struck me then—it still does—as a graphic indication of the lacuna into which crime and its writing falls. That blank cover seemed to suggest that, even though the novel itself is a form of representation, there is a level at which violence is impossible—or too disturbing—to represent. At a point, it is impossible to bear witness to the horror of violation. Yet the people who do survive violence—"it happens every day, every hour, every minute, Lurie tells himself, in every quarter of the country"—must find a way to endure, to pick up what is left of themselves, to carry on living.

David Lurie, a man shunned for having taken advantage of his age, his position, his power and prestige in seducing a student and then refusing to hear her accusation, must endure his own helplessness when his daughter is violated. Later, too, he must endure the accusation— outrageous to him—that he does not, cannot, know what his daughter suffered.

> What more could he have witnessed than he is capable of imagining? Or do they think that, where rape is concerned, no man can be where the woman is? Whatever the answer, he is outraged at being treated like an outsider.

But Lurie is a man, and this fact makes him, in the eyes of the female characters in the book, an outsider. Vengeance, action, abandoning the farm, are the options he offers his daughter, who is catatonic with shock, stunned by the hatred that her assailants—men she has never met before—felt for her. Lucy, however, refuses all of her father's pleas. Obdurately, she refuses to leave her land; she refuses the option of aborting her hate-conceived fetus.

In Coetzee's writing of Lucy's story, Lurie has no access, beyond a certain point, to what Lucy endures, to the reasons behind her decision (a passive one, leading to a greatly reduced life), to her choice of survival strategy. This was the narrative lacuna in *Disgrace* that fascinated me. I wanted to write into that silence, that imaginative blind spot.

If violence does have a grammar, and therefore a meaning, then the crimes represented in *Disgrace* are, in essence, violent conversations between men about land, possession, revenge, and access to women. The bodies of women are, in a profound sense, incidental, the women themselves either silenced or inaudible. And yet, as Lurie insists, "There must be a niche in the system for women and what happens to them."

In my writing I have tried to locate that niche. I have tried to find ways to imagine Lucy's story, to find the truth of her experience. I did not accept the fiction created by Coetzee that Lucy would accept this forced-into-her child, the child of one of her three rapists. There was something in me that said no, that is not how it would happen. That child—that product of historical hate—would not atone for anything that Lucy's father, and what he represented, may have done. It would not atone for the past. It certainly would not release her to live on the land freely as she wished to live.

Lucy would, I imagined, or perhaps I only hoped, resist.

The questions that have framed my writing are simple. Why is contemporary South Africa so violent? Is violence a consequence of our history? Is violence what happens when law and morality are uncoupled from what is right, as happened under apartheid? Why do some men hate women so? Why do they rape? Why do they kill? Is it revenge? Is it for fun? Is it some ghastly combination of all these things? Why won't it stop? How do we carry on?

For Coetzee, the answers are complicated. "The real truth, he [Lurie] suspects, is something far more—he casts around for the word—anthropological, something it would take months to get to the bottom of, months of patient, unhurried conversation with dozens of people, and the offices of an interpreter."

The crime novel, if done well, is a way of interpreting the society on which it focuses its lens. Coetzee's notion (one that is never pursued by Lurie) of accessing the "real truth" (if there is such a thing) through a kind of anthropological investigation appealed to me. So did the idea of an interpreter, for the investigators that populate crime fiction can be very astute social interpreters.

The impulse of the crime novel may be described as anthropological. The genre attempts to understand what men do, and why they do it; the investigative crime novel asks questions of a range of people who might or might not know something about an act of violence. And I felt sure that I could put my shoulder to the genre and shift the questions sufficiently to make them work also for a woman.

Crime fiction, especially noir fiction, is a genre that, since its hard-boiled inception with writers like Raymond Chandler, has shown women their place in no uncertain terms. There is, in much noir fiction, a delight in the torture and murder of women. The demonization of the woman as the femme fatale can make it appear that any fate that befalls her is, in some fundamental sense, her just desserts. Misogyny is part of the grammar of crime fiction, as if the male hero, so central to the genre, is premised on a dead or silenced woman. Despite its roots—or perhaps because of them—crime fiction is a genre that is capable of revealing the workings of the psyche, and the masculine psyche in particular.

Crime fiction is, however, a flexible genre that can be bent enough out of shape to tell women's stories, too. It can even exact a woman's fictional revenge. Creating a female investigator has enabled me to explore that silence that lies at the heart of *Disgrace*, at the heart of South Africa, and to try to find some answers to my own questions.

Disgrace, a literary novel, opened my eyes to this possibility. Lurie is emasculated during the attack; unable to save his daughter, unable to avenge himself or her (as would happen in a typical crime novel). Crucially, he is unable to bend Lucy to his will and make her do what he thinks is best for her.

Adrift in the aftermath of the attack, he takes it upon himself to carry the carcasses of maltreated animals to the hospital incinerator so that he can ensure they are disposed of in a dignified way. He rents a room near this charnel house, comforting the very animals that he will shortly help to kill. The dogs are terrified when the allotted day comes. They know what is going to happen to them. They fear what Coetzee calls the "disgrace of dying."

I thought about what Lurie was doing with those dead dogs. Lurie's accompaniment of the dog carcasses mirrored what the plot of the crime novel does so compulsively with the corpse. The crime novel "accompanies" a corpse to its end, to its truth. It tries to find a way to decipher the grammar of the violence suffered in order to avenge the wrongs done to the once living person. The investigation, the forensic ferreting is, in a postreligious age, the only way we have of honoring and avenging the dead—indeed, of bearing witness—and of hiding from ourselves the disgrace of dying violently.

Coetzee's *Disgrace* offers pity and terror, but it is not a novel that offers either solace or comfort. The crime novel, on the other hand, with its cathartic rituals of resolution and serial repetition, acts like Perseus's mirror. It offers a way of looking at violence, at violation, at death, and surviving. That, at least, is some kind of solace.

Journalist and writer Margie Orford is at the forefront of a new generation of South African mystery writers. She has written four acclaimed novels featuring criminal profiler Dr. Clare Hart, the latest of which is Gallows Hill. *She is executive vice president of South African PEN and a patron of both the Rape Crisis Trust in Cape Town and Little Hands Trust, a children's book charity. She lives in Cape Town. Visit her online at www.margieorford.com.*

A Small Death in Lisbon
by Robert Wilson (1999)

SHANE MALONEY

Robert Wilson (b. 1957) is a British-born crime writer who has largely es-chewed his homeland as territory for his novels, choosing instead to write about Benin, West Africa, for his early Bruce Medway series, and Seville, Spain, the setting for his Javier Falcón books. He has won numerous awards, including the CWA Gold Dagger for the nonseries novel A Small Death in Lisbon.

Robert Wilson was once a shea nut broker, and his fiction covers a wide swath of territory, often venturing into places where few crime writers in English have ever set foot. His first four novels were Graham Greene–ish intrigues set in West Africa, and voiced by a booze-soaked expat fixer named Bruce Medway. Sweat-sticky stuff, they play out in a miasma of corruption punctuated with vivid flashes of casual brutality—a check-point made of stacked corpses, dope-crazed boys with AK-47s—that take noir deep into the heart of the Dark Continent. His African books were followed by two novels set in wartime Portugal, *A Small Death in Lisbon* and *The Company of Strangers*, an espionage story. Next came four police procedurals in which Javier Falcón, Inspector Jefe of the Seville Homicide squad, pits himself against financial corruption, the Russian mafia, Islamic terrorists, and a fair quantity of tapas.

For my money, *A Small Death in Lisbon* is the pick of the crop. It taught me everything I know about the politics of wolfram and the fi-nancial underpinnings of the *Estado Novo.* The pace is fast, the style eco-nomical, the politics sound, the heat palpable. Even the most shopworn minor characters have a real presence. Nobody is entirely blameless. If not for the Nazi gold and the bullets in the back of the head, you might almost call it literature.

A Small Death comes down the same ratline employed by Martin Cruz Smith, Manuel Vázquez Montalbán, Philip Kerr, and Robert Harris—novelists whose fictitious crimes come wrapped in layers of real history, where politics is a matter of life and death, and violence reverberates through the generations in often unpredictable ways. Part historical thriller, part police procedural, it posits a mystery that can only be unraveled by following a chain of causation that leads all the way back to the darkest core of the twentieth century.

We start in Berlin in 1941, in the certain knowledge that the Third Reich is riding for a fall. Klaus Felsen, a small-scale manufacturer, is making easy money supplying the German war machine with railway couplings. When the SS invites him in for a chat and makes him an offer he can't refuse, he finds himself undertaking a secret mission in Portugal. His orders are to ensure a steady supply of wolfram, the ore form of tungsten, a strategic material needed to produce armor-piercing shells for the tank divisions already warming their engines for the imminent invasion of the Soviet Union.

Although Felsen is a schmoozer, a profiteer, and a womanizer, he's not particularly likeable, even when he's beating the downright evil SS Gruppenführer Lehrer in a game of poker. But like him or not, we're stuck holding his tailored coattails when he arrives in Lisbon, the capital of a neutral country ruled by a Fascist dictator, a city swarming with spies.

Meanwhile, in a parallel plot, it's six decades later. Portugal is still in the process of emerging from the Salazar dictatorship. A teenage girl from a well-off family has been raped and murdered. The investigation falls to Inspector Zé Coelho, a homicide cop with a daughter the same age as the dead girl. In the time-honored manner of the cantankerous dick, Coelho carries his own historical baggage. He was both an opponent of the dictatorship and the son of an army officer who participated in an attempted coup d'état against the unruly democracy that succeeded it. A widower who spent part of his life in exile, he's a cop by default, not vocation. He works in an atmosphere of induced social amnesia, the let-sleeping-dogs-lie consensus that has replaced the euphoria of the 1974 Carnation Revolution, the military coup that ended the dictatorship. By contrast, his rookie sidekick has carried his own family's leftist politics across the generational divide. He thinks that consumerism sucks, and Coelho's father should have been shot.

The murdered girl's father is a wealthy lawyer with more than a whiff of the old regime. Her mother is a deeply unhappy individual, all the more so since she caught her boyfriend fucking her daughter, a discovery patently orchestrated by the girl. All in all it's a pretty sordid business, with the girl turning tricks between classes in a shitbag hotel operated by a washed-up sleaze who was once a torturer in the dungeons of the secret police. Pretty soon, psychosexual tentacles are slithering all over the page.

Back at the war, the wolfram business is hotting up. The tide is turning in Russia, and Felsen's superiors are getting nervous. Failure is not an option. The British control the most productive mines and Salazar is happy to keep taking their money, despite much arm twisting from his beleaguered fellow Fascists. Fortunately for Felsen, mining is not the only source of wolfram. Lumps of the jet-black mineral can be grubbed from the surface of the barren hills in the north of the country. Impoverished peasants are swarming into the area, *volframistas* intent on getting rich as fast as possible by selling sackloads of fossicked rocks to the highest bidder. Felsen strikes up an alliance with a brutish local thug, Joaquim Abrantes. When a young British agent shows up, Felsen tortures him to death as a warning to potential suppliers. Felsen and Abrantes corner the market, financed by shipments of Nazi gold. This is vivid geopolitical cloak-and-dagger, redolent of Eric Ambler but nastier.

The two plots switch back and forth. Coelho and his partner pursue their leads through the seedy side of late-'90s Lisbon, sweltering their way back in time to the period of the dictatorship. Felsen and his partner emerge from the war with enough of that Nazi gold to found a multinational banking corporation and bequeath it to their progeny. Sex and violence are the threads that stitch the stories together. It becomes pretty obvious where all this is leading and, in due course, it arrives there. But it's the wrong destination, of course. The deal with the devil has a twist in the tail.

The past is never dead. It's not even past. Somebody famous said that. Perhaps he was thinking of *A Small Death in Lisbon*.

Shane Maloney is the author of a series of six novels featuring Murray Whelan, a political fixer and accidental detective. They are written in Australian English. Like it or lump it. He is a winner of the Ned Kelly Award. In 2009, the Australian Crime Writers Association presented him with a Lifetime Achievement Award and a halfway decent bottle of red. Anybody knowing the whereabouts of the wine should contact the author. Some of the Murray Whelan books have been published in translation in French, Finnish, German, Japanese, and American. Two were filmed and directed by Sam Neill. Maloney lives in Melbourne, a city on the way to nowhere. Visit him online at www.shanemaloney.com.

Nineteen Seventy-Four
by David Peace (2000)

EOIN MCNAMEE

David Peace (b. 1967) is the British-born author of nine novels, among them the Red Riding Quartet, an intense saga of linked books detailing police corruption in the north of England, and the hunt for the real-life serial killer known as the Yorkshire Ripper. He is also the author of The Damned Utd, *based on Brian Clough's brief, ill-fated period in charge of Leeds United Football Club, which was adapted for the 2009 film of the same name.*

2010. Leeds station, 11:45 p.m. on a January night. Me and publicist Parul have been traveling from Scotland but the Edinburgh train's been stalled twice by suicides on the track and we're running late for the last train to Halifax. We've spent most of the frozen day sitting in the darkness on the borderlands somewhere around Carlisle waiting on the forensics, the scoop-up boys, to clear the line. Everybody's gloomy and it befits me for a darkness to come.

We're the last people on the platform in Leeds, which looks as if it hasn't changed for decades, and the atmosphere of the book comes seeping in around me like moor fog. The destination board reads like a charnel house tour of Peace destinations. Bradford. Huddersfield. Sheffield.

Nineteen Seventy-Four. The first book of the Red Riding Quartet. The most malign year in a malign decade. Fred West is cranking up, Peter Sutcliffe is settling into his groove. The genius of the book is in its portrayal of England, corrupted and degraded on every level, politically and spiritually. You could read (as people do) Ellroy into Peace's work, but I find Blake and Milton, more Marston Moor than Mulholland Drive.

I'd hitchhiked this country in the '70s. Up and down the M6 and the M1. Taken lifts with the misfits and the loners, not to mention the decent types who wouldn't see a youngster with a cut-price combat jacket and faux-defiant attitude stuck on the Bullring on-ramp for the rest of his life. I've done the squats and the ferry queues and the Special Branch men in badly fitting sports coats. Read the malice. Saw how you can slip up.

In *Nineteen Seventy-Four* a young journalist, Eddie Dunford, joins a Yorkshire newsroom. He starts to report on a child killing. As he delves into the crime, an occult weave of political and sexual corruption reveals itself. The writing is brilliant, staccato, an edge-of-reason whirr. There's a rawness to the prose, and it's all the better for it.

The central image of the book is that of swans' wings stitched into a child's back. Angels and devils. It's an image that Peace now regards as a cruelty too far. There's a point at which you have to turn your eyes away, where the unflinching have to flinch. As a father, it's hard not to concur. As a reader, it won't leave you alone.

2011. Me and Marc and Jon are sitting on a sunny rooftop in London discussing a TV project about the Birmingham Six* when it comes back, the jolt, the grimy fist in the kidneys, the doubled-over handcuffs slammed down on the back of your hand. It's the 1970s. *No way out.* A memory returns, it could be straight from Eddie Dunford's notebook . . .

1986. I'd been a journalist for eight weeks. I'm at a badly attended press conference for the Birmingham Six. It's nine in the morning and I'm hungover: still drunk, truth be told, didn't get home the night before and picked up the call to attend the conference. A kindly woman gives me a cup of tea and finds me a Silk Cut Red. Turns out the woman is Annie Maguire—*AUNT ANNIE'S BOMB FACTORY.* Her son, Patrick Maguire, gets up to speak. It's desolate. Scooped up at fourteen along with his mother and other innocents, and sent down at Her Majesty's Pleasure. He's lost his youth. Sent down as a child, released as a man. He presents it as plain fact. There's no getting it back. Convicted? December 7, 1974, and sentenced to four years.

The North of the 1970s keeps coming up in Peace's work. It's a malign outworking of the parapolitical swirl of British politics of the decade. What's going on is beyond rational. You reach for a word. *Occult.* Relating to the supernatural. Inscrutable. Concealed. Available only to the initiate.

---

* Six men, all of whom were born in Northern Ireland but lived in Birmingham, sentenced to life imprisonment for bomb offenses in the U.K. in 1975, and released after sixteen years when their convictions were declared unsound.

Nineteen Seventy-Four, Nineteen Seventy-Seven, Nineteen Eighty, Nineteen Eighty-Three. The Red Riding Quartet. The books are seen as difficult and I made it more difficult for myself by starting at the last and reading back toward the first. Just an accident: I wasn't keeping an eye on the book world, and the first three had passed me by. I read them as I found them in bookshops. So *Nineteen Seventy-Four* was a crescendo, an explosion of squalor and pity. I'm not sure if reading them in reverse order was a good thing or a bad thing. Sometimes it's good to be off-balance as a reader. But it meant that the work hadn't finished with me.

2006. It's the Kilkenny Arts Festival. I'm programming the literature strand and I'm at war with the organizers. They should be down on their fucking knees with gratitude as Gordon Burn and David Peace take to the stage. It's the time of the prostitute murders in Ipswich and I realize that no matter how much I thought that I'd got it with Peace, I still hadn't got it. When he starts to read you realize that the style isn't high literary grandstanding. It's demotic. Clear as a bell. How we speak. What we say. And in this case it's children missing their mothers and their mothers are murdered prostitutes. The refrain is *Without Mummy.* Going to the shops. *Without Mummy.* Waking up in the morning. *Without Mummy.* Going to sleep. *Going to sleep without Mummy.* Not mawkish. It reaches inside you.

Knowing how it works zones the humanity of the work but doesn't take the concentration out of reading it. You need to bring deep focus to what you're doing. You need to be on your game. Alert. *Initiate.*

Nineteen Seventy-Four . . . It acknowledged a psychic landscape that I'd been writing about for years. The occult cat was out of the bag. I'm grateful for it.

Irish author Eoin McNamee made his debut in 1994 with Resurrection Man, *a novel set in Belfast during the Troubles, and among the notorious Shankill Butchers, which set the tone for his fictionalized versions of recent Irish history. He has also published* The Ultras *(2004), and* 12:23 *(2007), and the first two parts of a proposed trilogy:* The Blue Tango *(2001), which was nominated for the Man Booker Prize, and* Orchid Blue *(2010). McNamee has also written a series of spy thrillers under the pseudonym John Creed, featuring the intelligence officer Jack Valentine.*

The Ice Harvest
by Scott Phillips (2000)

EOIN COLFER

Scott Phillips (b. 1961) worked as a photographer, translator, and screen-writer before publishing his first novel, The Ice Harvest, *in 2000. Set in his native Wichita, Kansas, the novel was short-listed for the Edgar Award, the Hammett Prize, and the Crime Writers' Association Gold Dagger, and was adapted for a film that starred John Cusack and Billy Bob Thornton. Phillips published a prequel,* The Walkaway, *in 2002, which was set in the 1940s. Phillips has subsequently explored other genres.* Cottonwood *(2003) is a Western set in California, while* Rut *(2010) is a dystopian tale set in the near future.* The Adjustment *(2011) is a post-WWII noir thriller.*

Every Christmas I get a dozen comedy-crime books as gifts. Perhaps because I try to write humorous novels, people think that I must spend my time reading them. The tagline on ten out of these twelve books will name-check Elmore Leonard or Carl Hiaasen, and guarantee the reader that this book will catapult the author into the big time alongside the aforementioned Elmore and Carl. As all readers have learned to their cost, these taglines often exaggerate quite a bit, so much so that, whenever I see Elmore Leonard's name on the cover of a book he didn't write, I tend to give it a wide berth.

The problem with writing comedy-crime is that crime is not inherently funny: when you try to force a comic structure on this genre, you are pulling the literary rug from under yourself. That's not to say that funny things do not happen to criminals or at crime scenes, but they are generally darkly comic, ironic, sardonic, or pathetic. The comedy lurks below the tragedy or bubbles through in the gallows humor of the homicide cops. Custard pies are rare.

So to find a book that is genuinely hilarious but also atmospheric and completely effective as a noir thriller is indeed a treat. Scott Phillips managed to achieve all of this in his debut novel, *The Ice Harvest*, and what's more, he made it look easy.

The Ice Harvest tells the story of one Christmas Eve in the life of Charlie Arglist, a shyster lawyer who has been operating on the far side of Wichita's ice-blue line for many years. Tired of his sordid existence as a failed father and a manager of strip clubs, Charlie decides to make a fresh start and skip town with the million bucks he has been gradually skimming from the owner of the clubs, mob boss Bill Gerard.

Fueled by seasonal sentimentality and a hip flask of strong liquor, Charlie decides to visit each of his clubs one last time before a late-night rendezvous with his partner in crime. Charlie is mere hours away from making a clean break. What could go wrong?

Everything, as it turns out.

A blizzard of epic proportions descends on the town, transforming his simple route into a hazardous maze where black ice and snowdrifts confound him at every intersection. The clubs are deserted, the girls are touchy, and the barmen are psychotic to a man. Relatives pop up to drunkenly sabotage his plans, and a simple act of kindness involving a photo of a local politician in a beyond-compromising position backfires with catastrophic results. Coccyxes are bruised, bones are broken, and the bodies pile up to block Charlie's way out of town. He ricochets between strip clubs, bars, and massage parlors like a drunken pinball. As his escape plan slowly and bloodily unravels, Phillips expertly layers the tension to almost unbearable levels.

All of which doesn't sound very funny. But it is. Totally hilarious in every way, from acerbic one-liners to unashamed slapstick—which, as I've said, should not work in a noir novel, but does here, and resoundingly so. Phillips's narrative is so authentically banal that we feel sorry for this poor schmuck who is just trying to get out of his sordid life with a few bucks in a bag, and we totally buy the increasingly ludicrous situations that mount up until the big showdown is inevitable.

Of course it doesn't hurt that there are strip joints and naked ladies to keep us distracted as we read. And even though the joints and ladies are in no way glamorized, we are still given an insight into the seedy attraction of this world that exists underneath, and parallel to, our own, frequented, perhaps, by guys that we actually know and salute every day. And so you have to envy Charlie his ability to limp into these establishments unhindered by any sense of morality or trepidation, and envy, too, how unflustered he is when surrounded by gyrating strippers clad in little more than attitude and tattoo ink.

Scott Phillips succeeds in peeling back the carpet of dirty snow and giving us a long look at Wichita's underbelly with such detail and authenticity as to convince us that this guy spent a lot of time wallowing in the underbelly at one time or another. Or perhaps he's just a good writer. Whichever one it is, there's not a false note in the entire book. As Charlie zigzags between the familiar, workaday world and the exotic underworld, we realize, with a not unpleasant frisson, that such a place might exist in our own tranquil town. Through Charlie's everyman character, albeit an everyman in the process of ripping off a mob boss, we get a glimpse of the sleazy side and maybe secretly relish the idea of one day paying a visit there ourselves. The far-off humps are greener and so on and so forth. Obviously this is other guys I'm talking about. Lowlifes. Not me.

But it's not just the sleaze that makes this book great. The characters are finely constructed and refreshingly unheroic. There is barely a spark of decency to be found in the entire novel, which increases the enjoyment quotient hugely. The blizzard is layered into the story so well that it almost becomes a character in its own right, foiling Charlie at every turn, knocking him on his ass and turning his automobile into a chariot of death. Scott Phillips is a wonderful storyteller who strings the reader along expertly, weaving in clues as to Charlie's intentions and his dodgy past, evidence that quickly mounts up, funneling us toward a bloody finale. And when the endgame does arrive it is handled with a mordant wit and an abrupt brutality that lives up to everything the reader could hope for.

When I found *The Ice Harvest* I knew nothing about it, and so was not expecting much more than a competent thriller. What I got was a modern classic that has become one of my favorite novels, and no small source of inspiration. Scott Phillips has, with this one book, made me a fan for life, someone who will buy whatever Phillips writes as soon as it hits the shelf. There are only five modern crime authors about whom I can make the same claim (I'm sure those not on the list are crapping themselves), but in my head, that claim means something. Of course, if I ever meet Scott I will play it cool and pretend that I haven't gotten round to *The Ice Harvest* just yet.

Writers' rule number one: never let them see you read.

Eoin Colfer is the author of the internationally best-selling Artemis Fowl, *which was recently named the public's favorite Puffin Classic of all time. Other titles include* The Wish List, The Supernaturalist, *and the Legends series for younger readers. Eoin's books have won numerous awards, including the British Children's Book of the Year, the Irish World Literature Award, and the Children's Book of the Year in Germany. The BBC made a hit series based on his book* Half Moon Investigations. *In 2009, Eoin was commissioned by Douglas Adams's estate to write* And Another Thing . . . , *the concluding episode of the Hitchhiker's Guide to the Galaxy series, which became a worldwide best seller. His first crime novel,* Plugged, *was released last year on an unsuspecting and largely innocent public. Visit him online at www.eoincolfer.com.*

Tell No One
by Harlan Coben (2001)

SEBASTIAN FITZEK
(translated from the German by Ellen Clair Lamb)

Harlan Coben (b. 1962) is the New Jersey–born author of more than twenty novels, including the Myron Bolitar series of mystery stories featuring a former-basketball-player-turned-sports-agent and occasional investigator, but it was Tell No One, *published in 2001, that catapulted him to a new level of fame. The novel was subsequently filmed by director Guillaume Canet and released as* Ne le dis à personne *in 2006.*

Of all the questions one gets asked as an author, the most difficult to answer—other than "Where do you get your ideas?"—is "Which of your colleagues' books can you recommend?"

On the one hand you want to make a unique recommendation, instead of citing yet another of the usual suspects on the best-seller list. On the other, I've learned that a writer's taste doesn't always match his readers', even when he writes popular books. What surprises a writer often seems far-fetched or absurd to a reader, and vice versa.

This may be because people who earn their living by writing often lose the ability to read with their hearts alone. I, for one, can never read a thriller without automatically turning on my analytical eye, and trying to figure out what's going on—or how the author has somehow managed to handcuff me to my chair.

The request for a recommendation is a classic dilemma. My preference would be to suggest something only a few people know about, but that has what it takes to become an international best seller. That's where Harlan Coben comes into play, at least if you live in Germany.

Although stacks of his editions proliferate in the rest of the world—a compelling reason for me *not* to recommend something—he has not (yet) sold in Germany in amounts comparable to the superstars of our literary world. As far as I know, his book *Tell No One* has only scratched the best-seller list, and I became aware of it only by accident, through a book club's special edition. Like many before me, however, I devoured it in a single day, even though Coben writes anything but "fast-food literature."

Like any good thriller, *Tell No One* even begins with a haunting "what if?" question, one that no ordinary mortal ever wants to confront but that will hold us in thrall for hundreds of pages. *Tell No One*'s question is as follows:

What if, one day, you receive an email from the love of your life, years after you saw her kidnapped and murdered by a serial killer?

This is exactly what happens to the pediatrician David Beck.

Every summer on the same day, David and his wife, Elizabeth, travel to the lakeside spot where they kissed for the first time at the age of twelve. And every year they leave an additional line in the bark of "their" tree, just below the heart carved with their initials (EP + DB).

On their twelfth anniversary, shortly after the stroke of 1:00 p.m., fate, in the form of a serial killer, intervenes. David is struck unconscious, and Elizabeth is kidnapped. Later, her mangled body is found.

Eight years after the tragedy, David gets an email. The subject is clear: "EP + DB," followed by thirteen strokes. And the content of the email consists of a single command: "TELL NO ONE!"

Harlan Coben is described, not inaccurately, as a master of multi-dimensional plotting, although this is faint praise, as we shall shortly see. But he is, in any case, *also* a gifted high-voltage architect who has constructed this novel perfectly from foundation to roof.

Many good thrillers start with exceptional "what if?" questions. The genius of *Tell No One*'s is that the story that follows from this question, while not obvious, is so well written that it can be understood by almost every reader. Michael Crichton could conjure up a futuristic thriller from it, and if Stephen King asked this question, his answer would probably spirit us away into unreal worlds of horror. But with Coben, the horror stays real and present. And herein lies the attraction of this journey, a psychological nightmare that pushes the hero, David Beck, to the limits of human endurance.

With this email from the dead, Coben has a brilliant premise. Great, but the idea on its own serves only as a blurb to encourage us to pick up the book. A single idea, even a brilliant one, is not a unique selling point, nor does it make the book a thriller worth reading. The best "what if?" question is wasted if the author doesn't understand his craft, or if he cannot create exceptional characters, brought to life with his own unique style.

In the summer of 2010, I had the pleasure of meeting Harlan Coben personally at ThrillerFest in New York. In the course of a panel discussion, he told the audience that each of his stories begins not with the plot, but with the characters. *Tell No One* offers proof of this, for it is not only the main characters that stand out: Coben strives to draw tangible, realistic portraits of even the apparently least important and most marginal of figures. This requires no thick brushstrokes, no pagelong explanations of design, history, social status, or the like. Sometimes a rough sketch is enough to enshrine the person forever in the reader's memory, as at the beginning of the book's second chapter, when Coben introduces us to the hero's grandfather.

Many authors would have been content to mention in an aside that the grandfather suffers from Alzheimer's disease. Instead, Coben gives us this:

> His mind is a bit like an old black-and-white TV with damaged rabbit-ear antennas. He goes in and out and some days are better than others and you have to hold the antennas a certain way and not move at all, and even then the picture does the intermittent vertical spin.

Two sentences, and the scourge of this disease is perfectly drawn for each reader to understand.

But good metaphors and vivid comparisons can be found in many works. So what, exactly, makes Coben's style so unique, so distinctive, and, ultimately, so successful? This question is answered most easily with a look at his acknowledgments. I had always skimmed these lists of (to me) meaningless names, which for male authors traditionally end with a mention of the understanding wife who so patiently and selflessly endured her partner's social incompetence during the writing period.

At the end of his thriller *Just One Look,* however, Coben ends his acknowledgments with this, after expressing his thanks for the advice of renowned experts: "As always, if there are errors, technical or otherwise, the fault is with these people. I'm tired of being the fall guy."

Nerve, at a level that I didn't expect, and an expression of thanks that makes me laugh. No, even better, a note of thanks that wasn't the usual Oscar acceptance speech blah-blah, but actually told me something about the experts behind the name on the cover. It also told me that the writer had a sense of humor, and his characters do as well.

It is this humor that runs through Coben's work and makes it so distinctive—that he can, for example, show us the embattled hero of *Tell No One* wrestling with his fate in this self-deprecating way:

> I know I flirt with being an alcoholic. I also know that flirting with alcoholism is about as safe as flirting with a mobster's underage daughter.

Humor and suspense—which in theory go together about as well as toothpaste and orange juice—work perfectly in Coben's fictional reality.

Without descending to the level of an action comedy, Coben's wordplay approaches stand-up quality ("The makeup artist gasped in horror when he saw Shauna. 'What are those bags under your eyes?' he cried. 'Are we doing a shoot for Samsonite luggage now?' "). Coben gets us to laugh without sacrificing momentum or turning the story into something grotesque, which would be very easy with a plot as complicated as that of *Tell No One*.

The problem faced by authors is almost always that of squaring the circle. We must invent realistic figures that are still quite exceptional. Frankly, most people in real life aren't suitable templates for heroes. And most heroes in fiction are so exaggerated that, in real life, they'd look like aliens.

Coben builds these figures (real but not boring, unusual but not far-fetched) primarily through everyday language, and particularly through dialogue. Injecting humor into a thriller is no simple feat. A wisecracking hero on the run can be funny, but he's more likely to be laughable. Not with Coben. In his books, if a shady ex-junkie offers the hero help, it sounds like this:

> "Something bad's happening with you, Doc." He spread his arms. "Bad is my world. I'm the best tour guide there is."

A wise man once said that every great story is a family story. *Tell No One* supports this theory, with its external action driven by the question of whether the impossible can be possible and David Beck's wife can still be alive. That this thriller has room for a deeper story, dealing with the effects of tragedy on the bereaved, is an impressive feat given Coben's breakneck pace. This pace makes it almost impossible to introduce a character over several pages, but Coben shows us that's not necessary. Do you need more than this to understand the character of lawyer Hester Crimstein?

> "Good. Look, Beck, you're a doctor, right?"
> "Right."
> "You good at bedside manner?"
> "I try to be."
> "I don't. Not even a little. You want coddling, go on a diet and hire Richard Simmons. So let's skip all the pardon-mes and excuse-mes and all that objectionable crap, okay? Just answer my questions."

Okay, I admit I'm a fan—you've probably guessed that already—and fans tend to idealize the works of their idols. For me it's even worse, I'm afraid. To categorize my remarks here accurately, I must confess that Coben's works have shaped my career as a writer—especially *Tell No One.*

Before I became a writer, I worked as program director of a Top 40 station in Berlin. Because I wasn't a host myself I didn't have to put my face in the window, but I could pull the strings, which was a very comfortable situation. Even as a drummer in my (not very successful) band, I was used to staying in the background while setting the beat. When I submitted my first thriller, *Therapy,* to an agent, I did so under the name "Paul Lucas." Standing in the back row was so deeply ingrained in me that I didn't want to put myself forward in my writing, either. The pseudonym was a cowardly shield.

My agent put his head in his hands and tried to persuade me to use my real name, as they tell us to do these days on Facebook. At that stage I didn't have a contract; I read Coben's books, including the acknowledgments, and was once again reminded that no one can become a good writer without 100 percent commitment, and no one can create lifelike characters if they're hiding from life themselves.

On those grounds, you won't find any somber biographical texts on my home page, and my acknowledgments are slightly different—as, for example, in my psychological thriller *The Eye Collector,* where I've printed photos next to the names, so that for once a reader can get a clear picture of all the people whose help goes into the creation of a book.

For writers like me, then, Coben provides inspiration in more ways than one. My first impulse is to lay one of his books down in the middle of a chapter and sit at my own desk in the hope of producing something of similar quality. (The author-as-reader, however, brooks no interruption before finishing the story, with all of its punch lines.)

That said, I'm often asked whether writers who read their colleagues' work don't run the risk of imitating it, if only subconsciously. The answer is a resounding yes—and no. To be perfectly honest, after I read *Tell No One* for the first time, at the very beginning of my career, I deliberately tried to give my work "the Coben touch." They were the two worst paragraphs I've ever written, and immediately went into the trash.

So Coben has not influenced my style, but he's saved me from writer's block in one way or another. When I stare at the cursor on my screen and have no ideas, I grab a good book. I don't get ideas that way. But it's better for my mood than sitting in frustration at the computer.

So often successful writers (read: writers who no longer need a second job to pay their rent) forget why we wanted to get to this point. Deadlines, readings, reviews, interviews, sales figures, and trillions of other distractions mean that we no longer see the differences between the best job of our lives and any regular job. We originally wanted (read: while we were being rejected by every publishing house) to tell a story that was important to us, one that would entertain people. I could be wrong, but when I read Coben I see this desire in every one of his books, and so I am reminded of my own goals when I first sat down at my desk, hell-bent on becoming a writer.

Thus, for me, Harlan Coben is not only an author, but a motivator. For thrill-seeking readers, he tells a great story. For authors, he gives this important writing tip: differentiate yourself. Do it differently.

If you're funny, write funny, even if the subject is tragic. If you want to change perspectives (*Tell No One* is written partly in the first person, and partly in the third) then do it, even if the so-called experts tell you that this doesn't work, as an editor in a large publishing house once tried to convince me. My reference to *Tell No One* did nothing to help, because the editor (in Germany, of course) had not read Coben. But—and this is crucial—differentiating oneself also means differentiating oneself from Coben.

To sum up, for its inconsistencies alone *Tell No One* is a "book to die for" for me. It starts with a question that sounds almost supernatural, but leads to a real story, which leads to a logical ending. It's about extraordinary people we have never met in real life, but take at face value. And it is funny, even in places where we resist any further stimulation.

With this book Coben has not invented a new genre, but he has pushed the boundaries toward new frontiers. It makes him one of the few popular authors whose style can be recognized without looking at the name on the cover.

And it makes him my favorite "inside tip" whenever readers ask whose books I would recommend. I fear that it's only a matter of time, however, before I can no longer play this trump card because soon most of the people in the room will have read his books.

You can't keep good books down forever, not even in Germany.

———

People who see Sebastian Fitzek for the first time say that he doesn't look anything like a psychothriller author, but that's definitely his passion. Sebastian Fitzek, born in 1971 in Berlin (where he still lives), is one of the most-read thriller authors in Germany, despite his harmless appearance. His books are now read in twenty-five countries, including the United States (with his first novel, Therapy), even though he originally wanted to be a drummer, a tennis player, or a veterinarian. In each of these cases he failed because he was all thumbs, as he admits himself. He is married to Sandra, and is the father of two little children. Visit him online at www.sebastian fitzek.de.

Mystic River
by Dennis Lehane (2001)

CHRIS MOONEY

Dennis Lehane (b. 1965) is one of the most highly regarded mystery writers of his generation, described by Michael Connelly as the "heir apparent" to Raymond Chandler and Ross Macdonald. Born in Boston, Massachusetts, to Irish immigrant parents, he has used the city as the setting for most of his novels, including his series of six books featuring the private detectives Patrick Kenzie and Angie Gennaro; The Given Day, *his historical novel centered on the Boston police strike of 1919; and the hugely acclaimed* Mystic River *(2001). Unusually, he has been well served by film, and* Mystic River, Shutter Island, *and* Gone Baby Gone *have all been the recipients of high-profile and careful adaptations.*

When I was around eleven or so, my grandfather got a part-time job delivering flowers. I accompanied him periodically, and the bulk of our deliveries were in Boston's blue-collar, and predominately Irish Catholic, neighborhoods. The people living in the apartment buildings and sagging, paint-chipped triple-deckers reminded me of the people from my neighborhood in Lynn, a city less than seventeen miles north of Boston: fathers covered in grease and plaster dust smoking and sharing beers with friends as the Red Sox game played from portable radios; mothers off to the corner grocery store or stopping to "shoot the shit" with neighbors while kids played street hockey or tossed a baseball or, on some blocks, cooled off in a spray of water from an opened hydrant.

The front doors opened to muggy air thick with cigarette smoke and stale cooking odors baked into the wallpaper, and the people who greeted me wore polite but forced smiles. What I remember most, even now, were the stares. Not hostile, necessarily, but guarded. They watched me from doorways and, sometimes, windows, but always on the street. I felt their collective glares the moment I stepped out of the van. I asked my grandfather about it.

"Lots of things happen around here," he told me. "Not necessarily good things, you know? People living here are wary of outsiders, and they've got good reason to be. They've got to keep their eyes and ears open."

"Because of Whitey Bulger?" I asked. Whitey, the head of the Irish mob, was at that time viewed as South Boston's version of Robin Hood—someone who kept the streets safe, and clean of drugs and crime. This was 1980. Another fifteen years would pass until the truth came out: that Whitey Bulger was not only Boston's most powerful and notorious mobster but also the city's most prolific serial killer, all while being the FBI's top-echelon informant.

My grandfather shrugged, the signal that my question may or may not have some validity, and with that the conversation was officially over, not to be discussed further or brought up at any point in the future. Those secretive Boston neighborhoods I visited that summer cast a powerful allure over me and made me want to know more about the people who lived there: their stories, what they had seen and endured, and the lengths they went to in order to protect themselves and their families.

Dennis Lehane, having grown up in Dorchester, explored these neighborhoods, to great success, with his excellent detective series featuring Patrick Kenzie and Angela Gennaro. After five books, he took a break from his popular characters and wrote *Mystic River*. Thank God he did. That book, a hybrid of pulp and literary fiction, lifted the veil of secrecy shrouding these tight-knit Irish clans and offered an insider's view of their "code of silence" street ethic. Not an easy task, but Lehane accomplished it with such incredible authenticity that *Mystic River* became Boston's definitive novel, and a gold standard by which all crime fiction can be judged.

Lehane shrewdly opens his masterpiece in 1975, focusing on three boys living in East Buckingham, a fictional city located along the shore of Boston's Mystic River. The city is as claustrophobic as the real Boston neighborhoods on which it's based: cramped corner stores and small playgrounds, Irish bars, and local butchers, a place where everyone knows your name and your personal business. Sean Devine, from the upper-class area known as the Point, is smart and destined for college. Jimmy Marcus, fearless, tough, and streetwise, seems destined for a life of crime. And Dave Boyle, a boy being raised by a single mother, seems destined for . . . well, nothing. Dave is that boy we can barely recall from our own childhoods, a nameless and faceless shadow whose sole trait is an aching, desperate need to be liked. When a pair of roving sexual predators posing as police officers pull up next to the boys, they target the weakest prey, Dave, who, although scared and crying, willingly climbs into the backseat of a car that "smells of apples."

The loss of innocence has been a constant theme in Lehane's work. What I've always admired about him is his unvarnished take on the subject. He holds nothing back. What Dave Boyle is forced to endure during his four-day ordeal is never discussed in any graphic detail, but the way he is psychologically tortured by the neighborhood's tribal mentality is brought up again and again. It starts the day Dave returns to school. In one of the book's most heartbreaking scenes, we see him confronted by the kind of garden-variety bully we remember from our own childhoods: "Yeah," the bully says to Dave, "you sucked it." Dave does what any one of us would do in this situation: he breaks down and starts crying.

> It was the range of emotions he could feel pouring from the boys in the bathroom that cut into him. Hate, disgust, anger, contempt. All directed at him. He didn't understand why. He'd never bothered anyone his whole life. And yet they hated him. And the hate made him feel orphaned. It made him feel putrid and guilty and tiny, and he wept because he didn't want to feel that way.

But this is merely the start of Dave's repeated victimization and eventual isolation. The neighborhood ostracizes anyone who is different, even if that person is an eleven-year-old boy who is the victim of a horrendous crime. In the ensuing days Dave is shunned by his "sort-of friends" and eventually ignored completely. "But in a way, that was worse," Dave reflects. "He felt marooned by their silence." Even Jimmy Marcus views him with an "odd mix of pity and embarrassment."

When the book resumes twenty-five years later, the loss of innocence revolves around another East Buckingham boy, a teenager in love: "Brendan Harris loved Katie Marcus like crazy, loved her like movie love, with an orchestra booming through his blood and flooding his ears. He loved her waking up, going to bed, loved her all day and every second between." Katie Marcus, unbeknownst to her father, Jimmy, is planning on leaving with Brendan. Katie goes out for a last night on the town with her girlfriends and, like Dave Boyle, climbs into a car and disappears. The next day she's a no-show at her younger sister's First Communion. Katie's bruised and badly beaten body is found shortly thereafter, dumped in a neighborhood park.

The murder and the mystery surrounding it make *Mystic River* a more than satisfying crime novel. Lehane, however, cleverly uses the event as a catalyst, a sort of black hole that by its sheer force of gravity pulls Sean Devine, Jimmy Marcus, and Dave Boyle back into each other's orbit. Each man has been scarred by the neighborhood. Sean, the only college graduate, is a homicide investigator for the state police. Despite the fact that his personal and professional lives are a mess, he's assigned the case since he grew up in East Buckingham and knows the neighborhood's primal mentality, its street loyalties, its generational family alliances. Jimmy and Dave have never left the neighborhood. Jimmy, a widower and reformed safecracker who did prison time, has remarried and now operates a convenience store. Dave Boyle, drifting through a series of dead-end jobs and sleepwalking through his roles as husband and father to his only child, a young boy, is more ghost than human.

East Buckingham looms large through the entire novel. The city is undergoing gentrification; properties are being snatched up and turned into condos and town houses, and the yuppies, with their Volvos and soy lattes, are appearing on street corners along with antique stores. The old neighborhoods and the families who lived there for generations are slowly vanishing. The tribal mentality, however, endures, making you wonder if it's some sort of incurable virus infecting the entire city rather than a primal survivalist mind-set ingrained from one generation to the next. "Once you got in that car, Dave, you should never have come back," an older Jimmy Marcus tells his childhood friend. "You didn't belong. Don't you get it? That's all a neighborhood is: a place where people who *belong together* live. All others need not fucking apply."

The solution to the crime is shocking, but it's nowhere near as unsettling as the brutal psychological terrain Lehane chronicles with a ruthless efficiency. Everything inside the city is laid bare. Every door is opened, every stone overturned, every motivation, secret, and sin exposed. *Mystic River* is haunting and epic in its scope, a Shakespearean tragedy played out on the cracked sidewalks, in apartment complexes and triple-deckers. And yet at the same time it's a Springsteen ballad to the old neighborhoods, a poignant and oftentimes grim reminder of the scars we carry on our hearts, a hymn to the ghosts that linger in our souls.

––––––––––––––––

Chris Mooney is the internationally best-selling author of the Darby McCormick series and the stand-alone Remembering Sarah, *which was nominated for the Edgar Award for Best Novel. Foreign rights in the Darby McCormick series have been sold in over twenty territories. The* Killing House, *his latest novel, is the first book featuring former profiler, and now the nation's most wanted fugitive, Malcolm Fletcher. Mooney lives in Boston, where he is at work on the next Darby McCormick thriller. Visit him online at www.chris mooneybooks.com.*

The Broken Shore
by Peter Temple (2005)

JOHN HARVEY

Peter Temple (b. 1946) was born in South Africa and moved to Australia in 1980, where he pursued a successful career as a journalist and editor. He became self-employed in 1995 in order to begin writing crime fiction, and published his first novel, Bad Debts, *in 1996. It featured the central character of Jack Irish, a part-time lawyer based in Melbourne, who featured in a number of Temple's subsequent novels. It was* The Broken Shore, *a stand-alone novel, that brought him to a wider international audience, and won him the CWA Gold Dagger award for best crime novel. His novel* Truth *received the Miles Franklin Literary Award in 2010.*

It begins calmly enough, on a cold morning in late autumn; a bloke out walking his dogs, routine. Time to notice the last leaves on the maples before the call from the station, an intruder, a woman living alone. *He felt the fear rising in him like nausea.* Cashin. Melbourne police, homicide, put out to grass. This, or something like it, has happened before. Darkness, danger, blood puddling on tarmac, in corners, life leaking away. Another phone call, fast after the first, fast as night follows day: a rich old man found facedown, his naked back lined with stripes of dried and drying blood. Nothing as simple as a robbery gone wrong: nothing simple here at all.

Conspiracy in Peter Temple's novel creeps up on you as conspiracy should: wealth, power, the power to corrupt, the sweet stench of it echoing back to Chandler's *The Big Sleep* and another rich old man, living out a living death in a hothouse of orchids, the cloying smell of their flesh too much like the flesh of men, ripe with decay.

> Cashin thought there was no firm ground in life. Just crusts of different thicknesses over the ooze.

A decent man, Cashin, not above mistakes, mistakes that have taken the lives of others, good and bad, foe and friend. Mistakes that, like the enduring pain from injuries incurred, he can never forget.

"A man going forward while looking back," said Cashin. "I know that feeling."

Going forward, looking back. Cashin's father died when he was twelve. His mother packed two suitcases and, for three years, took him with her on the road. Gone walkabout. Shacks, rented rooms, motels. Ever since, perhaps without recognizing it, he has been looking for a father, looking for a home. Desperate for the sight of his own unacknowledged son.

All he wanted was to see him, talk to him. He didn't know why. What he knew was that the thought of the boy ached in him like his broken bones.

Right now, Cashin is living in the lee of a memory he is trying, with the aid of a swagman he's befriended, literally, to reconstruct—the grand palace of a house his great-grandfather's brother built then dynamited to the ground. Something of a lesson there, you might think: a moral.

But if the family home Cashin is intent on rebuilding is one of the book's organizing metaphors, the other—more dynamic, more central—is the Broken Shore of the title and the Kettle at its violent heart, within which the water rips and tears.

They went to see it for the first time when he was six or seven, everyone had to see the Kettle and the Dangar Steps. Even standing well back from the crumbling edge of the keyhole, the scene scared him, the huge sea, the grey-green water skeined with foam, sliding, falling, surging, full of little peaks and breaks, hollows and rolls, the sense of unimaginable power beneath the surface, terrible forces that could lift you up and suck you down and spin you and you would breathe in icy salt water, swallow it, choke, the power of the surge would push you through the gap in the cliff and then it would slam you against the pocked walls

of the Kettle, slam you and slam you until your clothes were
threads and you were just tenderised meat.

It was called the Broken Shore, that piece of coast.

It is here that the body of one of the potential murder suspects is
found, here that the teenaged Cashin, *full of lust and full of wonder*, sat
close and in awe alongside the young Helen Castleman, too beautiful,
too rich, too far out of his class—Castleman, who is now a lawyer working for the Aboriginal Legal Service on behalf of another suspect and
the owner of a property neighboring Cashin's unbuilt dream. Here that
Cashin's father committed suicide.

And there is one further thing that, for this reader, anyway, resonates from the title: the echo of Robert Hughes's 1987 account of the
founding of Australia, *The Fatal Shore*. For this novel is not just expertly
set in a particular country—a particular area of country, a particular
place—permeated by generations of history: it shows both the shifts
and virtual disintegration of some communities, and the rabid racial
discrimination—shockingly outspoken in some instances here—that
demonizes the Aboriginal people as belonging to a feral underclass.

When it was published, I was happy to be quoted as saying: "Put simply,
Temple is a master, and *The Broken Shore* is a masterful book." Nothing,
in the four or five times that I have since read it, has given me cause to
change my mind.

What was it Raymond Chandler said about Dashiell Hammett?
Something about him taking murder out of the Venetian vase and dropping it into the alley. No longer the candlestick in the library, but the sap
to the back of the head going the wrong way up a dingy one-way street.

Real crimes committed by real people.

Chandler didn't do a bad job of that himself.

Neither, closer to hand, did Maj Sjöwall and Per Wahlöö with their
ten books featuring the Swedish policeman Martin Beck; nor William
McIlvanney in his brilliant and inspirational 1977 novel *Laidlaw*, set in
Glasgow.

Whether Temple has read McIlvanney or Sjöwall and Wahlöö, or
whether he's read George Pelecanos, say, or Walter Mosley, is neither
here nor there. What is relevant is that they all utilize the crime novel
in similar ways: telling a story, yes, and a story about people, some of

whom you come to care about, care deeply, but also—more importantly? as importantly—they use it as a tool, a tool with which to open up and expose a small area of society for us to examine and understand.

> I am drawn to the sparse and the dry and to the idea that if you concentrate you can do powerful things with a few sticks and bones.

Peter Temple's own words.
The Broken Shore is very powerful indeed.

Ever since he was awarded the CWA Cartier Diamond Dagger for Sustained Excellence in Crime Writing in 2007, John Harvey has been trying, unsuccessfully, to shrug off the implication that everything, henceforth, is downhill. No matter how many push-ups, how many twelve-mile yomps across the South Downs, the label "veteran crime writer" clings to him like a shroud. His latest effort to disprove the onset of senility is the novel Good Bait, *published in 2012 to the sound of muted applause and the disgust—well earned, one hopes—of the* Daily Mail. *Visit him online at www.mellotone.co.uk.*

The Outlander
by Gil Adamson (2007)

C. J. CARVER

---

*Gil Adamson (b. 1961) was first published as a poet, in 1991, with her col-
lection* Primitive. *She subsequently published a collection of short stories,*
Help Me, Jacques Cousteau *(1995), and another volume of poetry,* Ash-
land *(2003). Her debut novel,* The Outlander, *won the Hammett Prize in
2007. It remains her only novel to date.*

I read the first line of *The Outlander* in a newsagent's at Paddington station. I was in a rush, with only seconds to buy the right book for my
journey.

> It was night, and the dogs came through the trees, unleashed
> and howling.

Oh, boy, I thought. There's a problem ahead. Brilliant.

It may not go down in history as the best first line of a novel ever written, but style, content, and genre were all there, and I bought the book
without reading any further. By the time my train pulled in to my home
station two hours later, I knew that I was reading something truly special
and was trying to proceed as slowly as possible, savoring every word and
desperate to make the story last as long as I could. A gripping, compelling tale of a woman on the run, it had everything needed to sweep me
away: adventure, survival, murder, love, abandonment, betrayal, fear,
horror, humor, and happiness (not necessarily in that order).

What grabbed me in particular was not just the central character's predicament but the book's setting. Gil Adamson takes one of the harshest
and most forbidding environments on earth—the Canadian Rockies at
the beginning of the last century—and throws into it nineteen-year-old

Mary Boulton who is, we're told, "widowed by her own hand." Hot on Mary's heels are her husband's vengeful twin brothers who have been "deputized" to bring her to justice.

It is 1903. Mary has been raised for genteel society, not wilderness survival. She doesn't know which direction to take, or whether she can eat grasses or the centers of pinecones, and makes herself sick trying. She begins to starve, but is saved when she falls upon a wolf's kill. Adamson's description of what happens when you eat rotting, raw venison on a starving stomach had me reaching for the antacid. But the real tension is ratcheted by the creepy red-haired twins who have employed a native tracker and are following her every move.

This is no whodunit because we know right from the start that Mary is a murderess, but the question that burns through the book is, *Why?* And, furthermore, can she outwit the twins and find her true place in the world?

Mary is a rare, wild girl. Although she's obviously beautiful, she has an almost feral air about her. She is also in the thick of grief over the death of her baby son, and suffers from visions and hallucinations, but she doesn't submit to them. This dual conflict—fighting for survival externally as well as internally—is at the heart of the novel. Although Mary is independent and strong-willed, determined to live, the trials she faces are immense. Female characters rarely rise to heroic status in this kind of situation—there is a danger that they might become unbelievable to the reader—but Mary's character is completely credible, and with every step she takes you are willing her to win, to triumph over adversity and, perhaps, find happiness.

This is an archetypal story that creates settings and characters so rich that you feast on every detail. The frontier towns into which Mary stumbles are captivating and peculiar places with their toughened miners and outcasts, the odd cat-skinner and lunatic, all troubled souls scratching a living in a monstrously hostile landscape. You are with Mary as she meets guides and guardians, tricksters and rogues, but even when she has a tender romance with a gentle mountain man—a chronic thief with a warrant for his arrest—there is a continuous sensation of dread as the twins close in on her.

Adamson is an acclaimed poet and her writing is gratifyingly earthy, immersing you in a foreign world so absolutely that you swear you can smell the smoke from Mary's campfire, the damp of the earth seeping through her clothes. If you have ever wondered how it feels to take laudanum, to survive a landslide, or to be shot with an arrow, look no further. The descriptions are so convincing that you wonder if Adamson has personally experienced each and every sensation related in her story.

The Canadian wilderness comes alive beneath Adamson's pen, becoming almost like another character, brutal and unforgiving, frightening and beautiful. But a location is more than just a place. It is also the moral environment in which characters live, and challenge the values imposed there. The plot illuminates age-old conflicts that are true to all humankind no matter what culture they come from: love/hate, despair/hope, justice/injustice, good/evil. Although the story is set over a hundred years ago, it feels contemporary because the values and humanity are the same today.

In *The Outlander*, Mary struggles with her husband's infidelity, her dependence versus her desire for independence, her illiteracy; but it is Adamson's observation of Mary's freedom from the control, influence, and support of others that most fascinates. Because of her crime Mary cannot return to her previous existence, or prevail upon her parents for help. For the first time in her life she is alone, and she enters a foreign world peppered with strange and remarkable characters and rough towns, exotic and hostile places where the ordinary becomes extraordinary.

Immersed in Mary's world, in her conflicts and her fight for survival, we discover our own humanity as we at last come to understand what drove her to kill her husband. We witness her inner nature exposed when she faces her enemies. At the climax, we see that the choices she has made throughout the story have profoundly changed her. She stands before us glorious in her new identity: whole, healed, and triumphant.

The arc of character change is not just for Mary, but also for her pursuers, who are now "addled and alarmed, exhausted." The twin brothers have spent months chasing Mary through freezing nights, torrential rain, and snow. They are not the same men that they were at the beginning of the story.

I loved every bit of this book. Dramatic, richly atmospheric, and full of unexpected twists, *The Outlander* is a gripping page-turner, and a classic thriller. But, best of all, this story has been extremely well crafted. Craft is rarely mentioned when people rave about a book, but without craft even the most profound material can appear shallow.

The Outlander's structure, setting, character, and genre are perfectly blended to give you that rare delight: a fabulous story, beautifully told.

Caroline (C. J.) Carver was born and brought up in the U.K. before moving to Australia, where she lived for ten years. She has been a travel writer and long-distance rally driver, heading an all-female crew driving from London to Saigon and London to Cape Town. Her first novel, Blood Junction, *won the CWA Debut Dagger. Since then she has written six more novels, published in the U.K., the United States, and translated into over twenty languages. She lives with her husband—a fighter pilot—near Bath, England. Visit her online at www.carolinecarver.com.*

The Tin Roof Blowdown
by James Lee Burke (2007)

KATHERINE HOWELL

James Lee Burke (b. 1936) is one of America's greatest living novelists. His first novel, Half of Paradise, *was published in 1965; it was followed by* To the Bright and Shining Sun *(1970) and* Lay Down My Sword and Shield *(1971). The first offering in the Dave Robicheaux series,* The Neon Rain, *appeared in 1987; Burke has published nineteen Robicheaux titles in total, the most recent being* Creole Belle *(2012). The author of thirty-one novels in total, Burke has also published two collections of short stories,* The Convict *(1985) and* Jesus Out to Sea *(2007). James Lee Burke has twice received the Edgar for Best Novel from the Mystery Writers of America, first for* Black Cherry Blues *in 1990, and again in 1998 for* Cimarron Rose. *In 2009, James Lee Burke received the MWA's Grand Master Award.*

James Lee Burke is a North American crime writer, Pulitzer nominee, winner of two Edgar Awards, and, to date, the author of thirty-one novels. These include stand-alones, a series set in Texas and Montana about former cop and Texas Ranger–turned–lawyer Billy Bob Holland, and another about Billy Bob's cousin Hackberry Holland, ex-ACLU attorney and now sheriff of a tiny Tex-Mex border town. While both series have topped best-seller lists and won wide critical and popular acclaim, there is no doubt that Burke is best known for his long-running and equally successful series about recovering alcoholic, ex-cop, Vietnam vet, and sometime bait-shop owner Dave Robicheaux.

The first book in the series, *The Neon Rain,* was published in 1987 and has Robicheaux working as a homicide investigator in New Orleans. In later novels he is a detective in the sheriff's department in the town of

New Iberia, two hours' drive west of the city. With this region featuring in so much of Burke's work, and with him being a resident himself, it's natural that he would have written about the effect of Hurricane Katrina, which so devastated the area in August 2005. In the sixteenth novel in the series, *The Tin Roof Blowdown*, Burke presents us with characteristically masterful descriptions of these events combined with a trademark well-plotted, and well-peopled, crime story.

The book opens with Robicheaux dreaming about a time in Vietnam when he lay wounded and waiting for medevac, knowing the North Vietnamese army could be coming through the waving elephant grass at any moment, and seeing a medical chopper loaded with his wounded comrades blown up by an RPG. He wakes to tell himself that he will "never again have to witness the wide-scale suffering of innocent citizens, nor the betrayal and abandonment of our countrymen when they need us most," but then tells us "that was before Katrina."

Turn the page and we meet priest and addict Jude LeBlanc on a rainy New Orleans morning. It is August 26, three days before Hurricane Katrina hits. With his distinctive and lyrical prose Burke describes the water pouring down the buildings into the gardens, and the way LeBlanc's prostate cancer causes him intractable pain. LeBlanc doesn't talk about the misdiagnosis that put him in this state because he "doesn't wish to rob others of their faith in the exactitude of medical science. To do so is, in a way, the same as robbing them of the only belief system they have." Faith and belief systems, and the loss thereof, are powerful themes in many of Burke's novels, and in this one more than most. LeBlanc's awareness of their importance is matched by the conviction of the next character we encounter, insurance salesman Otis Baylor, that proper preparation is all it takes to get through the worst of calamities. The hope and determination of these characters in the face of despair and trouble—another common theme in Burke's work—are made more poignant by the reader's preexisting knowledge of the destruction Katrina is destined to wreak, and intensify the usual feelings of unease and anxiety aroused by a potential threat to Burke's characters.

Burke's use of multiple points of view, and the insight and empathy with which he builds his characters, help develop strong connections between them and the reader. Whether criminals, police, or ordinary people, his characters are often portrayed as lost and looking for redemption: here we see bail-skip, looter, and rapist Bertrand Melancon try to make amends for his past sins, and despite all that he's done we can't help but cheer him on in his struggle. The theme of redemption is also played out through the characters of Robicheaux and his friend and fellow ex-cop Clete Purcel. Robicheaux believes that Purcel is working hard to recapture Melancon and his brother because doing so might somehow undo the damage caused by Katrina and restore the devastated New Orleans. The impossibility of this, and the fact that Purcel keeps trying, as does Robicheaux himself, in this book and others, to fight against an unending tide of crime, emphasizes their courage in the face of failure: they can never win, but they struggle on regardless.

The best writing makes you feel as if you're right there with the characters, and for me Burke never fails. The descriptions by Robicheaux and Purcel of experiencing apprehension comparable to the last days of the Vietnam War as Katrina descends, that they are "witness to a holocaust in the making," caused this reader at least to feel a similar dread. Burke describes the changes in air and sea as the hurricane approaches, the damage Robicheaux sees when he and his boss drive into New Orleans, the bodies floating in the flood, and the plight of so many people stranded by rising water on the roofs of houses and cars with a detail and intensity that made me shiver. Even the things he leaves out strike right at the heart: referring to the people who drowned when trapped in their attics, he writes, "If by chance you hear a tape of the 911 cell phone calls from those attics, walk away from it as quickly as possible, unless you are willing to live with voices that will come aborning in your sleep for the rest of your life."

The Tin Roof Blowdown is, at times, a difficult and heartbreaking book to read. Like all Burke's novels, it is full of truth about people and their relationships: we see that everyone is doing the best they can, trying to understand themselves and each other better, and seeking a connection with their fellow human beings. Great writing not only puts us right in the story but shows us something of ourselves: again, for me, in this Burke never fails.

Katherine Howell is a former paramedic and the best-selling author of five crime novels featuring paramedics alongside Sydney police detective Ella Marconi. Her critically acclaimed and award-winning work is pub-

lished in multiple countries and languages, in print, ebook, and audio form. She holds two degrees in writing, is studying female doctor investigators in crime fiction for her PhD at the University of Queensland, and teaches writing and editing. She lives in Queensland with her partner, who owns a bookshop. Her latest book is Silent Fear. *Visit her online at www.katherine howell.com.*

What the Dead Know
by Laura Lippman (2007)

BILL LOEHFELM

Laura Lippman (b. 1959) was born in Atlanta, Georgia, but raised in Baltimore, the city that has become the setting for much of her work, including the series of mysteries featuring Tess Monaghan, a journalist (as was Lippman)-turned-PI, with which Lippman began her career in 1997. She had already won every major mystery award before the publication of the stand-alone novel What the Dead Know *in 2007. It brought her even greater levels of critical acclaim, and confirmed her as one of the leading mystery novelists of her generation.*

Laura Lippman's 2007 stand-alone stunner, *What the Dead Know,* begins with a collision. Two cars crash on a highway outside suburban Baltimore. One of the drivers, a middle-aged woman, leaves the scene, only to be picked up by police not far away. She offers no coherent reason for fleeing. She has no ID. She tells police that she's Heather Bethany, one of two sisters who disappeared from a popular Baltimore mall thirty years previously, never to be seen or heard from again. Questions ignite: Where has she been? Where is her sister? Is this woman really who she claims to be? There are reasons to believe her, and reasons not to. Can any of the questions be answered? Can the answers be proven? Police, lawyers, and social workers compete for Heather's capricious attention, and for scraps of truth about the present and the past.

As the accident happens on the highway, Heather catches a glimpse of a child, a young girl, riding in the other car. She later learns, in an almost throwaway scene, that the young girl she swore that she saw is in fact a young boy—a boy who is not only not a girl, but whose appearance differs in other significant ways from what Heather recollects. She learns that something that she could have sworn was true is, in fact, false.

The traffic accident, its depiction of lives colliding and sent careening out of control, functions as a simple but brilliant metaphor with which to launch the story. The accident forces the mystery woman into contact with curious law enforcement officials, setting the plot in motion, but the idea of what we think we see and know smashing to pieces against cold hard reality is the collision that truly drives the book.

The boy in the other car suffers minor injuries and we're left believing that he makes a full recovery. We never learn his name and, at least in terms of plot, he turns out to be of negligible importance. We never see him except for that single unreliable glimpse through Heather's eyes. His importance lies in the fact that he was never who we thought he was. He introduces another crucial concept that lies at the heart of *What the Dead Know*.

Don't believe what you see.

Deception energizes the novel, and not only the typical deceptions of a crime novel but the realistic everyday human deceptions that children practice on adults, that siblings practice on one another and their parents, that couples use to manipulate and protect each other, that law enforcement practices on the guilty and the innocent alike, and ultimately, and perhaps most importantly, the deceptions we practice on ourselves in the mirror and the tricks our own memories play on us. These deceptions have a thousand stimuli in the book, both mundane and profound, including the greatest motivator of them all: the need not to get caught, the need to protect lies already told in order to keep the whole house of cards standing.

What happens to us, the novel asks, when we're confronted with realities that contradict what we recall, that undermine what, to us, are essential, inarguable truths? Are we liars whether we like it or not? Are we inherently false and dishonest? Are we sometimes better off with lies than we are with the truth? Who are we really when what we think makes us ourselves is revealed to be untrue? Maybe that's the knowledge that the titular dead possess: the debatable value of the truth, because the truth is usually very bad news. In Lippman's suburban Baltimore, the truth is not revealed in a seductive act of peeling away, like the dropping of Salome's veils. Instead, the truth needs to be dug out with sharp instruments like a rotten tooth rooted deep in an aching jaw. In this book, as in Lippman's others, she probes and pokes at deep psychological and emotional infections. By the end, we know more, and we feel better, but we're left with an open wound and an extended recovery.

One of my favorite aspects of *What the Dead Know* is that it does all kinds of things that novelists in training (especially "genre" novelists) are told not to do. The novel shifts points of view, climbing inside the heads of over half a dozen characters. It moves in time from 2005 to 1975, and various points in between. Names are stolen, borrowed, turned around, and abandoned, as are entire identities. Histories delivered through one set of eyes morph into something else entirely when seen through another set of eyes, and usually something sadder. Family members miles and years apart enact similar responses to tragedy, offering questions about human nature. The narrative spends extended time with the eventual victims of the central crime, and even more with those left behind. One person's set of defensive lies is another person's self-reinvention. Reader empathy is strained. Judgments are difficult to make. We linger in the brutal emotional aftermath of a crime, not just the legal ramifications of it. We get more broken hearts than we do pools of blood.

While one answer to the central crime story strikes with a wallop, in a late-arriving twist worthy of Hitchcock or *The Twilight Zone*, another critical answer lands with a pathetic and mundane thud, and is all the more heartbreaking for its banality.

Yet, for all its acts of misdirection, the book is never unwieldy, never confusing. The story never stumbles, which makes it impressive not just as a thriller, but also as a technical achievement of complex architecture. The reader never feels duped or lied to, the victim of parlor tricks, even as the characters deceive and manipulate one another in every area from marriage to murder. Instead of low-rent cleverness, Lippman roots her convolutions in human frailties like fear, denial, and faulty memory, which is what makes them believable. Things change from true to false and back again, facts go from there to gone because of what the characters hope and fear and believe and desire, and we never see Lippman's hand in the process. We're so busy watching the moving cups to see which one hides the little red ball that we not only never see the magician's hands, we forget she's even there.

The events that comprise the plot of *What the Dead Know* are not the essential puzzle. The people who comprise the story are the real mystery.

Bill Loehfelm is the author of three novels, most recently The Devil She Knows, *as well as* Fresh Kills *(2008) and* Bloodroot *(2009). All three novels are set in Bill's hometown of Staten Island, NYC. Bill moved to New Orleans in 1997. He currently lives in New Orleans with his wife, A.C. Lambeth, who is a writer and yoga instructor, and their two dogs. When not writing, Bill practices yoga, plays the drums, cheers the Saints, eats oysters, and gets tattoos, all with varying frequency and success. Visit him online at www .billloehfelm.tumblr.com.*

Escape
by Perihan Mağden (2007)

MEHMET MURAT SOMER
(essay translated from the Turkish by Amy Marie Spangler)

Perihan Mağden (b. 1960) has written novels, poetry, and columns in Turkey's national daily newspapers, first in Radikal *and later in* Taraf. *She is the author of four novels currently available in English:* The Messenger Boy Murders, 2 Girls, Ali and Ramazan, *and* Escape, *as well as one title not yet translated,* The Companion. *Her novels have been translated into eighteen languages. She is an honorary member of British PEN and winner of the Grand Award for Freedom of Speech by the Turkish Publishers Association.*

"So simple, however it hurts so deep and is hard to digest."
—Perihan Mağden, *Escape*

Some crime novels drive me mad with curiosity; they leave me breathless as I tear through the pages in a frenzied rush to get to the end. If I'm deriving genuine pleasure from what I'm reading, though, I rein in my desire; I resist the temptation to race to the conclusion and instead proceed slowly, savoring the details. That way, both my curiosity and my pleasure last longer. How delightful!

But then the time comes when the number of pages remaining grows fewer and fewer, dwindling down to zero. When books by authors with whose works I'm well acquainted, or of whom I'm especially fond, come to an end, it's not shock or surprise that I feel, regardless of the increasing number of twists as the finale draws closer. Rather, I'm enveloped by warm, fuzzy feelings: the relaxation that comes with release, the afterglow in the wake of satisfaction. I feel good.

Only rarely does the opposite occur. In those cases, when I finish the book, I feel completely out of whack, utterly incapable of describing my thoughts and my feelings. Sometimes it's anxiety that overwhelms me, and sometimes it's anger. In the latter case, my disappointment is not connected to the conclusion, for I will have forgotten the book somewhere at home before I've even made it a third of the way through.

Perihan Mağden's novel *Escape* is the most recent book to have thoroughly rocked my sensibilities and thrown me for a complete loop. (Note to the curious: others include Patricia Highsmith's Ripley series and *Those Who Walk Away*, the Marquis de Sade's *Justine*, Balzac's *The Splendors and Miseries of Courtesans* . . . The list goes on and on, but I think you get the picture.)

Escape or, by its Turkish title, *Biz Kimden Kaçıyorduk, Anne?* (*Who Were We Running From, Mother?*), is a slim volume of less than two hundred pages. You think you'll be able to coast right through it and then move on to the next book on your list, but no, that is a misconception. It's not what happens, because the book is not easy to digest. It's a very challenging read, *Escape*.

I believe that its strength lies in its vicious simplicity and supramodern minimalism. The language is plain or, in places, even simple, almost like the spoken language of the child narrator. The story is without frills or playthings, flowing along smoothly without getting caught up in unnecessary details. And in each new chapter it successfully injects the reader—in this case, me—with another dose of rage.

If I were to very briefly summarize the story, it would go something like this. A mother and daughter are trying to live their lives while disguising their identities. In the book, they don't have names. One is called simply "Mother," and the other "my Bambi," in reference to the book they often read together. The majority of the book is narrated by the little girl, who naturally blossoms a bit over the course of the novel. She's in complete awe of her mother, and really, truly loves her. Her mother is virtually the only person in her life. She is everything to the girl. Here is the very first sentence of the novel: "Nothing about Mother is like anyone else. But then again, I can't say I've known anyone else."

Then as we read, we learn that the mother is a killer. They're on the run, constantly. The span of time between each murder grows shorter and shorter. They continue to run until . . .

It sounds simple, doesn't it, especially considering how Perihan

Mağden makes such obvious reference to "Bambi" from the very beginning of the novel. This is from the first chapter:

> In the double bed of a hotel room, propped up against the pillows, the covers pulled up. The two of us illuminated by the bedside lamp, you reading *Bambi* to me. And *Bambi* isn't just any book. It's important for us.
>
> "It's full of signs," Mother says of *Bambi*. "Rocket flares."
>
> There are two important people in *Bambi*. Two creatures, that is: Bambi and his mother.
>
> My mother's so annoyed at Bambi's mother. I mean, if we met Bambi's mother, came across her in one of the hotels, Mother might beat her up. Teach her a good lesson. That's how mad she is at Bambi's mother.
>
> "If Bambi's mother hadn't been such a fool, hadn't been so careless, Bambi would never have been left alone in the forest. If you're Bambi's mother, you have to stay alive. You must never leave Bambi alone."
>
> I know what Mother means.
>
> Mother will never be foolish or careless, will never leave me motherless. Never.

But no, that's not how it is. That's not how it is at all!

At this point, a few words about the author would seem to be in order. You see, in our country, Turkey, Perihan Mağden is known primarily as a newspaper columnist rather than as a novelist. Her writing reflects her quick wit and sharp tongue; it's mischievous, and she never censors her progressive thoughts, nor does she try to disguise her anger. She writes not only about politics, but about daily life and popular entertainment as well. Due to her antimilitarist articles, the Turkish Armed Forces have taken her to court, having charged her with the bizarre crime of "alienating the people from the military service." A wide array of people, ranging from the current prime minister, Recep Tayyip Erdoğan, to a folk singer who has voiced Fascist, ultranationalist views, have pressed charges against Mağden in libel suits. And in turn she, to put it in her own words, has doled out their compensation without batting an eyelash.

No columnist can top her when it comes to questioning commonly held norms and breaking the mold. And, because she approaches issues analytically and interprets them precisely as they should be interpreted, her target is left with little recourse but to take her to court. There are so many issues and people to which she's opposed that, other than her devoted readership, the majority of which I imagine must belong to that category of "youth who stubbornly hold on to their passion," it is hard for her to remain in the good graces of, well, pretty much anyone. But then, frankly, I doubt that she could care less.

I agree wholeheartedly with Orhan Pamuk's description: "Perihan Mağden is one of the most inventive and outspoken writers of our time."

Now to turn our attention back to *Escape* (which, indeed, we should), things progress slowly during the first few chapters. In fact, you understand only quite late in the book that you're actually dealing with a crime novel, and, once you do, everything you've read thus far starts to make sense. As the story moves forward, and the noose tightens around the mother and daughter, the novel picks up speed, sprinting toward a breathtaking finale. At this point, as you read, you start asking yourself, Good Lord, what kind of a traumatic mother-daughter relationship is this? and, What kind of a traumatic world is this?

How far will a mother go to protect her child? Since even the gentlest of animals grows wild and vicious when its young are in peril and its maternal instinct to protect is triggered, one must wonder: Under the same circumstances, how long can a human being possibly remain tame? Though this appears to be the fundamental question, we come upon another chain of questions when we dig deeper. From what, or whom, is the mother in *Escape* trying to protect her daughter? From how much of the outside world can she possibly insulate her? What is the "purified world" that she desires, the one in which she strives to live and in which she wishes her daughter to live as well? Is it even a possibility, or is it merely a utopian dream? Will those ranged against mother and daughter ever allow such a thing to be?

No, they won't, of course. And in order not to allow it, everyone—sometimes consciously and spitefully, like the land registry office manager and the hotel receptionist in New York, and sometimes unconsciously, such as the police at the end—takes the opportunity to withhold the very chance of such a life from them.

Mağden's strength as a writer lies in her ability to make the reader take sides. As is the case with Patricia Highsmith's Ripley quintet, Mağden gets the reader to side with the criminal, to empathize. The reader starts to see reason in the crime, which, in Highsmith's hands, even becomes justifiable to a degree. That is to say, no matter how intelligent, educated, or "civilized" we may fancy ourselves to be, Highsmith is able to arouse our deep-seated potential for savagery. At times she makes us think, Come on, get it over with already. Kill the guy, why don't you! Sometimes, when the desired murder occurs, whether between the lines, or in all of its naked savagery, she makes us think, If I were him, I would have done the exact same thing! This is actually a very provocative, very anarchist sentiment; believe me, I know. Once you begin to think like that, to deem murder justifiable, you might find yourself caught up by a different wind, whisked away in a whole new direction. Before you know it, you're delving into your own past, devising vicious schemes. For my own part, I have most certainly gotten caught up in such a wind. Any regrets? No, sir, Your Honor!

As with Highsmith, so, too, with Mağden: by the time we reach the finale of *Escape*, that empathy for the perpetrator of the novel's crimes becomes painful to the point of being almost unbearable. The book draws inexorably to its conclusion; it has no choice. The ending is undesired, if not unexpected. And there we are, left to our own devices, alone with that sense of justification, with that potential for justified savagery (in this case, murder) having welled up inside of us, a giant swollen tangle of knots about to burst.

It is precisely that potential for savagery—which is so difficult to accept, to digest—that made me feel like I'd taken a hard punch in the gut. In order to be certain of the power of that punch, I reread the book after some time had gone by, and then later I had another look at it as I was getting ready to write this essay. Indeed, each time it had the same effect.

Of course, this is not the first, nor the last, time that Perihan Mağden has done this. Her novel before *Escape*, *2 Girls*, had a similar power, although it was, in my opinion, a bit gentler, balancing the harshness with a dash of humor here and there. Clearly it was preparing readers for *Escape*, the novel that would succeed it.

Ali and Ramazan, however, which was published three years after *Escape*, is a devastating true-crime novel that cuts to the quick. Its veracity, and the poignancy of the topics upon which it touches, result in a work that is a cut above your typical crime novel. Yet again it doesn't pull any punches, no, sir!

In all three of these novels, each of which deals with different emotions and tackles a very different subject matter, Perihan Mağden's writing style is at once divergent yet clearly shares a common source, and is without exception distinctively minimalist. While in *2 Girls* she makes relatively frequent use of plays on language, repetition, and abbreviation, in *Escape* she employs, for the most part, the simple, plain language of the narrating child. As I mentioned above, this apparent simplicity has a similar effect on the reader to a bright fluorescent light. It is glaringly naked and, for that precise reason, painful to look upon.

The language of much of *Ali and Ramazan*, meanwhile, is more like that of a news report, laying the soul of the novel bare. It contrasts with the language of the young men who people it, young men who have grown up in orphanages, are starved for love, and therefore grow madly attached to the first welcoming embrace that offers refuge. Their language naturally belongs to a lower class and, where necessary, is tinged with the slang, tone, and litanies of swear words that belong to the slums.

I view these three novels as a trilogy of books that complete one another, each adding depth to the reading experience of the others, with each subsequent title multiplying the overall violence and bitter effect. And that's how I would recommend these books as well, as a trilogy. Perihan Mağden presents her reader with a different world. You may hate it, you may feel a wrenching pain inside, and the potential for savagery she invokes may give you a cramp in the stomach. But one thing that you will not feel is indifferent.

Literature and music are two branches of art that I have always thought of as being analogous to each other. I come up with the most outrageous analogies for the two. Such analogies may be repulsive to some, beneficial to others, and in some cases meaningful to me, and to me alone. Nevertheless, I deign to repeat one here. My more attentive readers will know that I have a penchant for baroque, bel cantos, and the early romantics of classical music and, for the most part, have no taste at all for twenty-first-century contemporary music. However, perhaps because I find it somewhat analogous to baroque, I do like minimalism, and particularly admire Philip Glass. His unembellished music, with its extensive repetitions meandering among just a few notes, has a complex, profound structure that seems simple on the first take, and, when I lose myself in it, makes me feel purified. And sometimes it serves to smooth my ruffled nerves.

Escape, too, in many ways, is precisely just such a minimalist jewel.

Mehmet Murat Somer was born in Ankara, Turkey, and is the author of the acclaimed Hop-Çiki-Yaya crime novels set in Istanbul. The series, which consists of six novels so far, features an unnamed amateur sleuth who also happens to be a transvestite. The latest to be published in English is The Serenity Murders.

The Perk
by Mark Gimenez (2008)

ANNE PERRY

Mark Gimenez grew up in Galveston County, Texas. He graduated magna cum laude from Notre Dame Law School in 1980, was hired by a Dallas law firm, and eventually became a partner, but after ten years he walked away in order to start his own practice, and write fiction. His first novel to be published was The Color of Law *in 2005, although he had already written two books that remain unpublished. Of one of those books, he remarked to New Zealand website Crime Watch that "once it got to 1,600 pages I stopped, you know because I didn't know what I wanted to do with it. And a big part of that was not outlining it first, just starting writing . . . from then on I've outlined." He has since written four more books, the latest of which is* Accused.

Why would I recommend a book to someone? Firstly, because I enjoyed reading it myself. It drew me in and made me care about its characters. It had emotion, tension, vivid scenes, sometimes humor, and above all compassion. I could not recommend one that I had read and then forgotten.

Secondly, I would not choose one in which I did not admire the quality of the writing. Above all, the issues must be ones that have a depth and immediacy, and yet also hold some element that is universal.

Is that asking a lot? Of course it is. And even that is not all. If I am going to place it higher on my list than others, then it must make me see something in a way I had not done before, waken new thoughts in me, change my judgments and my understanding. I should be a little different after I close its covers. I should have been added to.

Now I'm really asking a lot!

The Perk, by Mark Gimenez, did all of these things for me.

It begins rather slowly, with the main character, Beck Hardin, a lawyer and ex–star football player, returning to his childhood home in the Texas Hill Country. He is newly a widower, with two small children. That area of America is highly individual and one I had not known even existed. The sense of utter bereavement in the hero is devastating. It doesn't sound very inviting yet, does it?

But immediately I cared, especially for the little girl, Meggie, who refuses to believe that her mother isn't going to come back someday soon. She carries her doll with her everywhere, and confides in it as if it were a direct contact with the mother she needs so much. How desperately human! Is that not the child in all of us whom we long to comfort, but don't know how?

How many of us have come home again, wounded at heart, needing the familiar to heal us, and found not much of it is really as we remembered? There are old relationships to be mended, and that can be so much more difficult and painful than we thought it would. People are complicated, and they have wounds, too.

Before the end of the first chapter I was totally involved. I even felt the unique nature of the land and its history of settlement, its harsh economic difficulties, and my mind's eye saw some of its beauty. I felt its heat, tasted the dust, the pride, and the poverty. I was soaked when it rained and I smelled the wet earth's fragrance. And I knew why to win the big football championship was everyone's dream. It was the way to be on top again.

And then, so naturally, the crime was upon me, there with its grief and the burning injustice that it remained unresolved. Time was desperately urgent. The statute of limitations on rape was about to run out, after which the wound might never even begin to heal. The young girl dies. Her father's life was wrecked by it. He is Beck's old friend and he asks for help, before it is too late.

I didn't want to get to the end because I was enjoying the journey too much. I identified with the people, I liked their company, but I had to find out what happened. I had to see justice done, the innocent illegal immigrant boy freed from the weight and ruin of suspicion. Perhaps it is not a pleasant part of my nature, but I also wanted to see the violent and arrogant local bully punished, in spite of the fact that he was the football star who could guarantee their victory, which made him all but immune. So I raced on, page after page.

But if it is no more than an emotional satisfaction that I gain from the reading experience then I would simply say that the book in question is good, and one should go ahead and enjoy it. For me to recommend it to others, though, there must be unusual and lasting qualities. I like surprises, elements I did not see coming. I think we all appreciate those. But far more than a twist in events, I truly savor a twist of emotions. I love to learn something of human nature that I had seen but not understood. What greater gift could a book give you than to leave you wiser at the end, with a deeper compassion toward people to whom you previously had been too impatient even to listen? It is so easy to judge without thought.

Yes, the hero of *The Perk* is good, very human, and in the end he is also genuinely heroic. The mystery is laid bare in all its compelling tragedy. The old relationships are mended, deepened, but there is no sugar-sweet answer. There is laughter, a little romance, but this is reality. Some griefs do not end.

What makes it remarkable is that Fredericksburg is in so many ways a mirror of all small towns. In its characters I see people I have known, and reflections of other tragedies I did not understand at the time because I thought the players too different from myself. Now I see their lives with acute empathy. Their dreams, their hungers, and their desperation are so much more like mine than I had imagined. In their shoes, I would have felt as they did! I might even have done as they did.

I have never willingly watched a football match in my life (although I have done so on occasion to please friends) and yet now I understand the passion and the heartache of a hyped-up teenaged football player in Texas. I know why he feels as he does, and I care. I have to be wiser and richer for that.

Something that can give me a new gentleness and make me rethink old conclusions—and enjoy doing so—has to be a good book.

Today mysteries are much more than "who did it—why—how— and we must see them get caught." They are about reality, about complicated lives where something went wrong and people struggled to understand it, and then, as much as was possible, to put it right.

It sounds such a pompous phrase, but I can't think of a better one: they address "the human condition," but they do it with a darn good story.

The Perk is one you should try.

Anne Perry (b. 1938) has published an astonishing number of mystery novels, in addition to young-adult fiction, fantasy writing, and assorted short stories. Her two principal series, both historical, revolve around couples: the Monk novels are set in the earlier Victorian era, and concern the amnesiac investigator William Monk and the woman who eventually becomes his wife, the nurse Hester Latterly; the Pitt novels, meanwhile, feature the London police inspector Thomas Pitt, a man of humble origins, and his upper-class wife, Charlotte, and are set at the end of the nineteenth century. Morality and justice, sin and repentance, redemption and the possibility of forgiveness, are all recurring themes in her work. Visit her online at www .anneperry.net.

ACKNOWLEDGMENTS

The editors would like to thank all those writers, publishers, editors, agents, and assistants who helped to bring this anthology together. Your time, patience, knowledge, and generosity are very much appreciated. Special thanks, too, to Ellen Clair Lamb, for whom the title "editorial assistant" doesn't seem quite sufficient, given that she collated, translated, advised, edited, and copyedited for this volume. Thanks, too, to Jennie Ridyard, who fact-checked and saved some of our blushes. Any errors that remain do so despite all of our best efforts, and we apologize for them.

We are grateful to David Brown and Caroline Porter at Simon & Schuster, Kerry Hood at Hodder & Stoughton, and Clare Wallace at the Darley Anderson Literary Agency, all of whom helped us to reach out to those authors whom we didn't personally know. Similar aid came from Delia Louzán at Tusquets in Spain; Sophie Thiébaut at Place des éditeurs in France; Anne Michel and Solène Chabanais at Albin Michel; Misa Morikawa at the Tuttle-Mori Agency in Japan; Antonio Lozano in Spain; and Stefano Bortolussi in Italy.

Finally, thanks to Sue Fletcher, Swati Gamble, and all at Hodder & Stoughton; Emily Bestler, Judith Curr, and all at Atria Books; and Darley Anderson and his staff at the Darley Anderson Literary Agency who, in these straitened times for books and publishing, agreed to support this labor of love.

CREDITS

In a Lonely Place by Dorothy B. Hughes © Megan Abbott, 2012
Act of Passion by Georges Simenon © John Banville, 2012
The Goodbye Look by Ross Macdonald © Linwood Barclay, 2012
The Adventures of Sherlock Holmes by Sir Arthur Conan Doyle © Linda Barnes, 2012
Early Autumn by Robert B. Parker © Colin Bateman, 2012
The Light of Day by Eric Ambler © M.C. Beaton, 2012.
The Maltese Falcon by Dashiell Hammett © Mark Billingham, 2012
120, Rue de la Gare by Léo Malet © Cara Black, 2012
Dirk Gently's Holistic Detective Agency by Douglas Adams © Christopher Brookmyre, 2012
A Tale of Two Cities by Charles Dickens © Rita Mae Brown, 2012
Daddy Cool by Donald Goines © Ken Bruen, 2012
The Pledge by Friedrich Dürrenmatt © Elisabetta Bucciarelli, 2012
The Assassin by Liam O'Flaherty © Declan Burke, 2012
The Big Blowdown by George Pelecanos © Declan Burke, 2012
The Outlander by Gil Adamson © Caroline Carver, 2012
Have His Carcase by Dorothy L. Sayers © Rebecca Chance, 2012
Last Bus to Woodstock by Colin Dexter © Paul Charles, 2012
The Damned and the Destroyed by Kenneth Orvis © Lee Child, 2012
Different Seasons by Stephen King © Paul Cleave, 2012
The Man Who Smiled by Henning Mankell © Ann Cleeves, 2012
Tomato Red by Daniel Woodrell © Reed Farrel Coleman, 2012
The Ice Harvest by Scott Phillips © Eoin Colfer, 2012
I, the Jury by Mickey Spillane © Max Allan Collins, 2012
The Little Sister by Raymond Chandler © Michael Connelly, 2012
The Chill by Ross Macdonald © John Connolly, 2012
The Black Echo by Michael Connelly © John Connolly, 2012
A Crime in the Neighborhood by Suzanne Berne © Thomas H. Cook, 2012
Toxic Shock (Blood Shot) by Sara Paretsky © Natasha Cooper, 2012
The Wrong Case by James Crumley © David Corbett, 2012
A Night for Screaming by Harry Whittington © Bill Crider, 2012
Cover Her Face by P. D. James © Deborah Crombie, 2012
The Executioners by John D. MacDonald © Jeffery Deaver, 2012
The Holy Terror by Leslie Charteris © David Downing, 2012
The Moving Toyshop by Edmund Crispin © Ruth Dudley Edwards, 2012
Prótesis by Andreu Martín © Cristina Fallarás, 2012

INDEX OF CONTRIBUTING AND SUBJECT AUTHORS